urban myths, and with illuminating detail presents the tangled stories, especially, of French traditionalism, papal policy, and the SSPX."

—**JOSEPH SHAW**, editor of *The Case for Liturgical Restoration: Una Voce Position Papers on the Extraordinary Form* and chairman of the Latin Mass Society

"At long last we have a major history of Catholic Traditionalism! Thanks are due to Yves Chiron, distinguished author of a vast number of works on modern Catholic history. Chiron's book, focused primarily on France, is by far the most thorough work on the history of Traditionalism available today. Relying heavily on primary sources, Chiron chronicles (from its earliest beginnings before World War I) a diffuse movement involving many different directions, objectives, leaders, and organizations—yet sharing the same spirit. *Between Rome and Rebellion* is essential reading for anyone wanting to understand the historical roots and current state of this movement, once fringe, that has acquired fundamental significance for the Church."

—**STUART CHESSMAN**, author of *Faith of Our Fathers: A Brief History of Catholic Traditionalism in the United States*

BETWEEN ROME & REBELLION

Between Rome & Rebellion

A History of
Catholic Traditionalism

WITH SPECIAL ATTENTION TO FRANCE

YVES CHIRON

Translated by John Pepino

Angelico Press

For information, address:
Angelico Press, Ltd.
169 Monitor St.
Brooklyn, NY 11222
www.angelicopress.com

ppr 979-8-89280-026-6
cloth 979-8-89280-027-3
ebook 979-8-89280-028-0

Book and cover design
by Michael Schrauzer

CONTENTS

TRANSLATOR'S NOTE

READERS WHO HAVE DERIVED BENEFIT FROM THE recent translations of Yves Chiron's work into English—*Annibale Bugnini: Reformer of the Liturgy* (2018); *Paul VI: The Divided Pope* (2022)—know this French historian's thoroughness and rigor. They will find that he has remained true to these qualities in the pages to follow. In fact, chief among his critics' complaints is that he is insufficiently partisan (scil. to their own cause).

This version of *Between Rome & Rebellion* incorporates the few minor corrections that the original required, as the author requested.

Our translation does not include the latter part of the French original, "Dictionnaire biographique des catholiques de Tradition" (pp. 443-614). The "Dictionnaire" is a prosopography of traditionalist figures; such reference works, as specialists' tools, are customarily left in their original language. We shall only point out that it does not claim to be exhaustive (Michael Davies, for example, is absent) and that it is supplemented by a biannual *Bulletin d'histoire du traditionalisme*. Subscriptions are free (contributions are appreciated) and may be directed to this address:

Yves Chiron, 16 rue du Berry, 36250 Niherne (FRANCE).

Regarding actual translation, we should also add that different languages use different ways of describing Church realities. In French, clergymen from tonsure onwards are traditionally termed *Abbés*; monsignors, bishops, and archbishops are all *Monseigneur*; *Père* is reserved for priests in religious orders (while *Révérend Père* is for Jesuits, simply *Monsieur* for Sulpicians, etc.). Our translation reflects the modern English custom (Deacon, Father, Monsignor, Bishop, Archbishop).

The term *intégrisme* is difficult to render into English, as it denotes both a religious and a political outlook, of which the latter is foreign to the Anglo-Saxon world. We have opted simply for "integrism." The author addresses the meaning of the term and contrasts it with "traditionalism" in the pages to follow—one of the many rich contributions of this work.

A final note: this *History* focuses (though not exclusively) on France, a country that in many respects can claim to be the birthplace of Traditionalism. Two more recent works complement this volume in presenting more of the English and continental history and its American counterpart: Joseph Shaw, ed., *The Latin Mass and the Intellectuals:*

Petitions to Save the Ancient Mass from 1966 to 2007 (Waterloo, ON: Arouca Press, 2023) and Stuart Chessman, *Faith of Our Fathers: A Brief History of Catholic Traditionalism in the United States, from* Triumph *to* Traditionis Custodes (Brooklyn, NY: Angelico Press, 2022).

INTRODUCTION

IN 1978, A YEAR AFTER MGR DUCAUD-BOURGET, FATHER
Coache, other priests, and some laymen occupied Saint Nicolas du
Chardonnet, the Renseignements Généraux [equivalent to the FBI or
MI5–*Translator*] drew up a report on the "traditionalist movement" in
Paris. This report, which we shall discuss later, attempted to present
an overview of organizations, movements, and personalities. Even
within the limited scope of the capital, it was far from complete. But
concerning the people it listed, the data (name, date of birth, address),
based on police investigations, were accurate. The *Renseignements
Généraux* qualified some as "integrists," others as "traditionalists,"
though without clearly defining this distinction.

Are the two terms equivalent? A few years earlier, in 1974, Cardinal
Daniélou had described in his Memoirs a "formidable" tendency: "In
seeking to save and preserve what is essential, [it] preserves at the
same time that which is not essential and which leads us to fall into
bad traditionalism, into integrism."[1] There would seem to be, therefore, a "good traditionalism," but it could degenerate into "integrism,"
a tendency or attitude that could be defined as a sort of fixism. The
Dominican theologian Yves Congar, in the 1950s, considered that integrism is not "primarily a doctrinal position," but is first of all linked
to a "right-wing mentality."[2]

Throughout the twentieth century and up to the present day, the
term "integrist" has been used almost constantly in a pejorative sense.
Since the 1980s, it has also been used to designate extremists within
Islam or Judaism.

Within Catholicism, the label "integrist" was rejected by most of
those to whom it was applied, but some – for example, Louis Salleron,
who was not an extremist – claimed it. Father Dulac, who was a much
consulted canonist during the decades-long crisis in the Church, published a "Praise of Integrism"[3] in 1952; twenty years later he justified
the label "traditionalist priests": "Since certain innovators have sought
to distinguish themselves by sticking this label on others as a mark
of contempt, why shouldn't the latter accept the title as an honor?"[4]

---

1 Jean Daniélou, *Et qui est mon prochain?* (Paris: Stock, 1974), 234.
2 Yves Congar, "Mentalité 'de droite' et intégrisme," *La Vie spirituelle* (June 1950), 644-66.
3 Raymond Dulac, "Éloge de l'intégrisme," *La Pensée catholique* 21 (1952): 7-25.
4 Dulac, "Un Congrès international de prêtres traditionalistes," *Itinéraires* 142 (April
1970): 54.

The term "traditionalist," understood as a defense of Catholic tradition against the attacks of innovators, did not appear after the Second Vatican Council, as is often stated. It dates from the beginning of the twentieth century. It has a less polemical connotation than "integrist" and has been taken up more often. In the United States, for example, there is a Catholic Traditionalist Movement (CTM) founded in 1964 by the theologian Gommar De Pauw.

Nevertheless, the label "traditionalist" has been challenged by other Catholics attached to Tradition. For example, Father Barbara, who became a leading figure of sedevacantism (which does not recognize the authority of contemporary popes), preferred to speak of "traditional Catholics." After Jean Madiran's death, the daily newspaper *Le Monde* referred to him as the "theoretician of traditionalism" and "one of the leading figures of national-Catholicism" (another polemical qualification which dates from the end of the 1950s). He too rejected these terms, including that of integrist, and preferred the term "traditional Catholic." Today, many religious communities in communion with the Holy See, while remaining committed to the preconciliar liturgy and to the ancient traditions and observances of religious life, also refuse to be called traditionalists and especially do not want to be assimilated to what some call "Lefebvrism."

Archbishop Lefebvre is the best known figure of traditionalism in the history of the contemporary Church. The Priestly Society of St. Pius X he founded is numerically the largest of the traditional institutes. In the dramatic conversation he had with Paul VI on September 11, 1976, Archbishop Lefebvre defended himself: "I am not the leader of the traditionalists." But he did not object to the term: "Do not let yourself be taken in, dear reader, by the term 'traditionalist' which they would have people understand in a bad sense. In a way, it is a pleonasm because I cannot see who can be a Catholic without being a traditionalist."[5]

It is therefore in a generic way that we shall here use the word "traditionalist" or "traditional" to designate religious congregations, communities, priestly fraternities, bishops, priests, movements, organizations, writers, and periodicals that have been and are attached to the defense and transmission of Catholic tradition. In 1994 Christophe Geffroy, director of *La Nef*, a monthly magazine that claims to be "faithful to the Church and to Tradition," published a special issue

---

5 Archbishop Marcel Lefebvre, *An Open Letter to Confused Catholics* (Dickinson, Texas: Angelus Press), 206.

devoted to traditional Catholic communities recognized by Rome. He made the following remark on this question:

> The term "traditional" is not a very satisfactory qualifier, for is not every Catholic worthy of the name necessarily attached to Tradition? We therefore are yielding to the easy way out by using a practical term which has the advantage of being fairly well understood, although it remains too reductive for our taste.[6]

But this Tradition needs to be defined. In Catholic theology, Tradition and Sacred Scripture are distinct but closely related. Through Tradition, according to the definition of the conciliar constitution *Dei Verbum*, "the Church, in her teaching, life and worship, perpetuates and hands on to all generations all that she herself is, all that she believes." Tradition is therefore both the act of transmitting and the content of what is transmitted. "In the Church, Tradition is the integral treasure of divine truth transmitted to us by the Apostles," but, as Dom Éric de Lesquen, who was one of the founders of the Abbey of Randol and its first Abbot, points out: "To reduce this Tradition to such and such a particular custom or category of faithful would be to do the greatest harm to Tradition in the Church; Tradition has never existed without a visible authority established by God."[7]

Catholics who are called traditionalists, therefore, are attached to an integral and faithful transmission of "doctrine," and want to defend it against widespread errors and dubious teachings. For some, this defense of traditional doctrine goes so far as to question the teachings of the Second Vatican Council; for others, it is an effort to interpret them in the light of Tradition.

Catholics who are called traditionalists are also attached to the traditional liturgy. This is not a sentimental attachment, but a conviction that this traditional liturgy fully expresses the Catholic faith (*lex orandi, lex credendi*). Some Catholics attached to the traditional liturgy do not reject the liturgical reform undertaken after the Vatican Council. Since 1984, and even more so since 2007, it is possible for a priest to be bi-ritualist, that is, to celebrate with the 1962 missal or with the 1970 missal. On the other hand, other Catholics attached to the traditional liturgy reject the "new Mass" as "equivocal"; some even consider it "invalid." The range of Catholics attached to Tradition is therefore very broad.

---

6 Christophe Geffroy, foreword, *Les Communautés catholiques "traditionnelles" en France*, *La Nef*, special issue 2 (October 1994): 5.
7 Dom Éric de Lesquen, "Contre la tentation dialectique," in Éric Vatré, *La Droite du Père. Enquête sur la Tradition catholique aujourd'hui* (Paris: Guy Trédaniel, 1994), 185.

For a long time, Catholic traditionalism appeared to many, including the ecclesiastical hierarchy and historians, as a marginal phenomenon, even as an aberration that would be swept away by the wind of history and the evolution of attitudes. Far from being an epiphenomenon, traditionalism has become a durable and ever-growing trend, even if it amounts only to a minority among priests worldwide.

Pope John Paul II had described the episcopal consecrations Archbishop Lefebvre carried out in 1988 without a papal mandate as a "schismatic act." He considered that "at the root of this schismatic act is an incomplete and contradictory notion of Tradition." In the same apostolic letter, the Pope expressed his concern for "the Catholic faithful who feel attached to certain earlier liturgical and disciplinary forms of the Latin tradition." He asked the bishops to give them a place in the Church. Since 1988, then, Catholic traditionalism has been divided into two groups: those who approved the episcopal consecrations without a papal mandate and are not in communion with the Holy See, and those who have remained in or regained communion with the Holy See. But these two camps are not always irreconcilable or impermeable to each other.

The aim of this history of Traditionalists will first be to present a rigorous and, if possible, indisputable panorama of names, dates and facts. It will also be attentive to the canonical situation of the personalities or founders mentioned.

This history also seeks to situate traditionalists, or, more simply, Catholics attached to Tradition, within the more general history of the Church. Bishop Tissier de Mallerais, one of the bishops consecrated by Archbishop Lefebvre in 1988, said "[w]e are *Syllabus* Catholics,"[8] meaning that the *Syllabus of Errors*, in which Pius IX condemned many errors in 1864, remains a doctrinal norm to which Catholics must refer. Catholic traditionalism did not begin with the Second Vatican Council. The word "integrism," as well as the words "traditionalism" and "progressivism," predate it by several decades.

Nor can Catholic traditionalism be reduced to a kind of far right-wing current. While among the great figures of French traditionalism there have been royalists, Pétainists, partisans of French Algeria, and supporters of the National Front, there have also been authentic Resistance fighters and Gaullists. On the other hand, a common characteristic of French Catholic traditionalists and those of other

---

8 Bp Tissier de Mallerais, "Nous sommes des 'Catholiques du *Syllabus*,'" *Fideliter* 161 (September-October 2004): 19-24.

countries is certainly that they are part of the heritage of what Émile Poulat called the "Catholic counter-revolution," as distinct from political counter-revolution.

In the course of this history, however, we shall be careful not to have too extensive a conception of traditionalism, or to include in it personalities, movements, or publications that are too far away from it – even though the traditionalist world is vast, diverse, and anything but monolithic. It is crisscrossed with diverse tendencies and positions. It has known and still knows a fragmentation that seems to defy description. Evolutions and divisions are multiple, leading to oppositions that are often, but not always, irreconcible. We will mention here only one emblematic case. Four of the ten children of a "traditionalist" family in the North of France have consecrated their lives to God: one has become the abbess of a traditional abbey recognized by the Holy See; another is a monk in another traditional abbey faithful to Rome; a third is a priest of the Society of St. Pius X; and the fourth is a priest of the Priestly Fraternity of St. Peter.

This book is the fruit of research begun some thirty years ago and of publicly accessible documentation accumulated over the decades. It was completed through the exploration of numerous archives and questions posed to many actors and witnesses. Yet it is worth remembering that a single memory, testimony, or document is not enough completely to shed light on the subject.

CHAPTER 1
From "Integrism" to Romanity

I N ESTABLISHING THE INTELLECTUAL GENEALOGY of twentieth-century traditionalism, one finds that it is the direct descendant of intransigent Catholicism. It was born in opposition to the French Revolution. This is what Émile Poulat calls the "Catholic Counter-Revolution." He distinguishes it from the "political Counter-Revolution" because it is opposed to the Revolution and its ideology "for reasons and on bases that are above all religious."[1] This counter-revolutionary Catholicism can be summarized as consisting of a critique of the philosophy of the Enlightenment, a rejection of "human rights without God," and the rejection of a system in which laws no longer have a religious foundation. This religious opposition to the Revolution, or the Catholic Counter-Revolution, began with Pope Pius VI, who condemned the Declaration of the Rights of Man and the Civil Constitution of the Clergy in 1791.

Throughout the nineteenth century, so-called "liberal" Catholics accepted, though with some nuance, the ideas and values of the French Revolution. They took them as givens, or thought they could use "modern liberties" to build a new Christianity.[2] Conversely, "intransigent" Catholics condemned these ideas and values and refused any accommodation with them. The condemnations pronounced by Pius VI in 1791, that of modern liberties by Gregory XVI in the encyclicals *Mirari vos* (1832) and *Singulari nos* (1834), that of the "errors of our time" – notably liberalism, religious liberty, and indifferentism – by Pius IX in the encyclical *Quanta cura* and in the *Syllabus* (1864) are the major magisterial teachings to which this intransigence looks. It was also exemplified by eminent anti-liberal authors such as Donoso Cortès, Louis Veuillot, Auguste Roussel, and others.

In the nineteenth century, the word "traditionalism" meant something quite different. In France, it was a philosophical school (Louis de Bonald, Abbé Bautain, Augustin Bonnetty) which, in the face of rationalism, asserted that moral and religious truths could only be known

---

1 Émile Poulat, *Aux carrefours stratégiques de l'Église de France. XXe siècle* (Paris: Berg international, 2009), 148.
2 Jean-Marie Mayeur, "Catholicisme intransigeant, catholicisme social, démocratie chrétienne," *Annales E. C. S.* 27.2: 483-99.

by a "tradition stemming from a primitive supernatural revelation" and not by reason. This traditionalism, bordering on fideism, questioned the priority of reason over faith, and the idea that the existence of God can be demonstrated by the light of reason alone. It was condemned by the Church.

The word "integrism," on the other hand, at first had a political meaning. In 1888, the Spaniard Ramón Nocedal seceded from the Carlist movement[3] and founded the Partido Integrista or Partido Católico Nacional. The integrist Party advocated "Catholic unity with its consequences," considered "freedom of conscience, freedom of thought, freedom of worship, and all freedoms of perdition" to be "abominable," and meant to "fight against liberalism, progress and modern civilization."[4] The party intended to support only "integrally Catholic" candidates. Independently of the party, Father Sardá y Salvany's book, *Liberalism Is a Sin*, published in 1884, was widely distributed in Spain and abroad.[5] The Spanish Integrist Party was twice reprimanded by Pius X,[6] not because of its opposition to liberalism, but because of its polemics against the Spanish bishops and Jesuits, who were in favor of voting for the "least bad" candidates, especially those of the Liberal-Conservative Party.

But by the end of the nineteenth century, fideist traditionalism had disappeared, and Spanish political integrism was in decline.

"TRADITIONALIST" AND "INTEGRAL CATHOLICS"

In the last years of the nineteenth century, the term "traditionalist" began to be used in France for Catholics committed to defending the doctrine of the Church, which was then under threat from innovators. Without making an exhaustive list, one notes one of its first uses in 1898: in an article devoted to the Parliament of Religions which had met five years earlier in Chicago, Auguste Sabatier, dean of the Protestant theology faculty of Paris, deplored the attitude of "traditionalist Catholics of the old world" who had condemned this

---

3 A Spanish legitimist movement that defended the dynastic rights of the elder branch of the Bourbons of Spain.

4 *Credo político-religioso* (1902).

5 Felix Sardá y Salvany, *El liberalismo es pecado*, published in 1884 to great controversy, received the approval of the Sacred Congregation of the Index on January 10, 1887. This work went through at least twenty editions up to the end of the twentieth century, and was translated into several languages. It was translated into French twice (1887 and 1890) and has been reedited by French traditionalists in 1975 and 2003. [Condé Bernoist Pallen produced an English translation, *What Is Liberalism?*, in 1899; it was republished in 1979 and 1989 – *Translator.*]

6 Pius X, Letter *Inter Catholicos Hispaniae*, February 20, 1906, and Declaration of the S. Congregation for Extraordinary Ecclesiastical Affairs, *Acta Apostolicae Sedis* 4 (1912): 707-8.

first initiative of interreligious dialogue.[7] A few years later, during the modernist crisis, in an article against "destructive neo-criticism" and the "new biblical-critical-progressive school," Father Prévost-Badino, professor of Sacred Scripture, deplored the fact that the defenders of "ecclesiastical and apostolic tradition" were qualified as "retrogrades, hyperconservatives, old traditionalists."[8] The epithet was used again by the modernist Fogazzaro to disqualify Pope Pius X, who "knows nothing" about biblical and theological questions: "He is not informed about them, for lack of modern culture; his intellectual milieu has always been rigorously traditionalist."[9]

Pius X himself used the term in a positive sense once. In 1910, in condemning Le Sillon – the movement that the Catholic Marc Sangnier had founded to promote democracy – the Pope recalled the principles that ought to guide the Christian organization of society and affirmed: "The true friends of the people are neither revolutionaries nor innovators but traditionalists."[10] Nevertheless, the epithet was not in common use until the last decades of the twentieth century, even though it is found occasionally; thus, in the 1920s, Abbé Emmanuel Barbier, one of the principal representatives of Catholic anti-liberalism, designated the Vendée as one of the "most traditionalist regions in both religion and politics."[11]

The term "integrist," in the religious sense (and not in the political sense as in Spain), was much more widespread in the first decades of the twentieth century. It was born in the context of the struggle against Modernism.

Alfred Loisy (1857-1940), the principal representative of modernism, deemed necessary an "adaptation of the Gospel to the changing condition of humanity," and sought "the agreement of dogma and science, of reason and faith, of the Church and society."[12] In his view "adaptation" and "agreement" necessarily led to challenging certain dogmas and interpreting Holy Scripture in novel ways. While modernism claimed to be a "critical method," Pope Pius X considered modernism to be, in a formula that remains famous, not a heresy but "the synthesis of all heresies." He fought it in different ways: through doctrinal documents (the decree *Lamentabili* and the encyclical *Pascendi Dominici gregis* in

---

7 *Courrier de Genève*, October 20, 1898.

8 *La Vérité française*, August 2, 1906.

9 Antonio Fogazzaro to Paul Sabatier, November 13, 1903, quoted in Émile Poulat, *Histoire, dogme et critique dans la crise moderniste* (Paris: Casterman, 1979), 249.

10 Pius X, *Lettre sur le Sillon*, 25 August 1910, in *Acta Apostolicae Sedis* 2 (1910): 631.

11 Emmanuel Barbier, *Histoire du catholicisme libéral et du catholicisme social en France* (Bordeaux: Y. Cadoret, 1923), 488.

12 Alfred Loisy, *L'Évangile et l'Église* (Paris: Alphonse Picard and Sons, 1902), 234.

1907); by placing dozens of books and magazines on the *Index librorum prohibitorum* (the "Index of forbidden books"); disciplining modernist priests with sanctions that could go as far as excommunication; founding the Pontifical Biblical Institute (1909) to promote the study of Sacred Scripture "according to the spirit of the Catholic Church"; instituting a "committee of vigilance" in each diocese, and requiring priests to take an anti-modernist oath (1910).

To defend the Catholic faith from such threats, various publications and organizations were created, often with the Pope's blessing. In Italy, the principal figure of doctrinal and social anti-modernism was Msgr Umberto Benigni (1862-1934), under-secretary of the Congregation for Extraordinary Ecclesiastical Affairs from 1906 to 1911, founder in 1907 of the bulletin *Corrispondenza romana* and, in 1909, of the *Sodalitium Pianum* ("Sodality of St. Pius V"), a "friendly association of various groups" all devoted to "the integral Catholic Cause."[13] This organization, colloquially called *La Sapinière* in France ("The Pinetree Forest"), had lay and clerical correspondents in various countries who contributed to its diverse publications and bulletins. It functioned as an intelligence and information-gathering network–as a "secret society" and a "denunciation outfit," as its opponents called it. La Sapinière worked, in the words of Bishop Benigni, for "the defense of religion against its enemies, especially those from within (modernism, etc.)." It received encouragement and subsidies from Pius X on several occasions. The Sodalitium was placed "under the control" of the Consistorial Congregation in 1911, and was officially recognized by the same Congregation in 1913.

In France, the anti-modernist and anti-liberal struggle was embodied in particular by *La Foi catholique* (an anti-Kantian critical review, published from 1908 by Canon Gaudeau, a former Jesuit), as well as by *La Critique du libéralisme religieux, politique et social*, also published from 1908 (by Father Emmanuel Barbier, also a former Jesuit), and by the weekly *La Vigie*, published from 1912 by Henri Merlier and Father Paul Boulin. While Gaudeau and Barbier did not belong to the network founded by Bishop Benigni, Merlier and Boulin were members. Henri Merlier had made a long career as a journalist in Picardy, in the Catholic and royalist press; Abbé Boulin, a priest of the diocese of Troyes, had come to Paris to indulge his passion for writing, multiplying articles, novels, and history books (often under the pseudonym of Roger

---

13 Msgr Benigni to Cardinal de Lai, Letter, December 28, 1912, published in Émile Poulat, *Intégrisme et catholicisme intégral. Un réseau secret international antimoderniste: La "Sapinière" (1909-1921)* (Paris: Casterman, 1969), 104.

Duguet). If the adventure of *La Vigie* was short-lived (less than two years of publication), it is because the war interrupted its publication.

None of these anti-modernists and anti-liberals wished to "be confused" with the Spanish integrists, and they distinguished themselves from them on several occasions. Some defined themselves as "integral Catholics": "We are integral Roman Catholics," reads the statement of purpose of *La Vigie*,

> that is to say, we place above everything and everyone not only the traditional teaching of the Church in the order of absolute truths, but also the directions of the pope in the order of practical contingencies. The Church and the Pope are one and the same. *Ubi Petrus ibi ecclesia* [Where Peter is, there is the Church].[14]

On the other hand, Canon Gaudeau, one of the most ardent anti-modernists, challenged the term "integral Catholics":

> We must be and we must call ourselves "Catholics." We must be sincerely, fully, entirely Catholic; in the field of faith (and that is where we are), if one is not Catholic in this way, one is not Catholic at all.... To call ourselves integral Catholics is to allow the modernists, whom we oppose, to call themselves moderate or conciliatory Catholics; it is almost to invite them to do so. Now, this is precisely the lie on which error feeds. To be a modernist, in the real and theological sense of the word, is no longer to be a Catholic: that is the name, the mask that needs to be torn off them.... Let us not play into the hands of our enemies. *Christianus mihi nomen, catholicus cognomen* [Christian is my name and Catholic my surname]. This is our baptismal certificate; as long as the Church has not changed it, we have no right to add one iota.[15]

The campaign of Pope Pius X and the Roman congregations against "the modernist peril" found its most zealous supporters among these Catholics, whether or not they claimed the label of integral for themselves. The program of the *Sodalitium Pianum* stated:

> The integral Roman Catholic is "papalist," "clerical," anti-modernist, anti-liberal, anti-sectarian [i.e., opposed to Freemasonry]. Thus he is integrally counter-revolutionary, because he is the opponent not only of the Jacobin revolution and of sectarian radicalism, but also of religious and social liberalism.[16]

Their opponents found it more convenient to call them "integrists,"

14 *La Vigie* 1 (December 5, 1912).

15 Bernard Gaudeau, *Le Péril intérieur de l'Église. Études d'histoire théologique contemporaine* (Paris: Aux bureaux de la "Foi catholique," 1914), 286-87.

16 Program of the *Sodalitium Pianum* published by É. Poulat, *Intégrisme et catholicisme intégral*, 119-26.

and many historians and commentators have taken up this term. In an erudite lexicographical study,[17] the historian Francesco Siccardo notes that the first to use the word in a negative sense was the modernist Father Albert Houtin, who in 1902 spoke of "the intransigents who, for the sake of 'integrism,' have declared scientific discoveries to be invalid." From that date on, the term "integrist" has been constantly used, always in a pejorative sense.

The Italian modernist Antonio Fogazzaro presented modernism as a "renovation of the old formulas of the Catholic faith," and contrasted it with "blind traditionalism."[18] The opposition between modernism and integrism or traditionalism dates back to the beginning of the twentieth century; after the Second World War, it was replaced with the opposition between progressivism and integrism or traditionalism, which continued during and after the Second Vatican Council, further oppositions being added along the way.

Some historians believe that integrism was "one of the factors of the modernist crisis," with "agents of suspicion" maintaining a climate of denunciation that, in turn, prompted modernists and more daring Catholic thinkers to "dissimulation" or silence.[19] This is a false symmetry. While modernism is not a single doctrine, it is, in the words of Pius X, a "system," that is, a method that leads to challenges to Catholic doctrine. On the other hand, not only has integrism never been condemned as such by the popes, but the words "integrism" or "integrist" have never been used in an act of the Papal Magisterium. As one of its apologists notes: "'Integrism' has never been defined or condemned by the Pope or the Holy Office."[20]

"TO APPEASE DISSENSION AND STRIFE"

It is sometimes said that Benedict XV, the successor of Pius X, condemned integrism in the first encyclical he published, in 1914. In fact, in this programmatic encyclical there is a renewed condemnation of "modernism," which is explicitly named, but there is no condemnation of "integrism," and the word is never used.[21]

---

17 Francesco Siccardo, *"Intégriste" e "Intégrisme." Stratigrafia di due vocaboli francesi* (Genoa: Il Melangelo Edizioni, 1979).

18 Antonio Fogazzaro to Paul Sabatier, November 13, 1903, quoted in É. Poulat, *Histoire, dogme et critique dans la crise moderniste*, 249.

19 Pierre Colin, *L'Audace et le soupçon. La crise du modernisme dans le catholicisme français (1893-1914)* (Paris: Desclée de Brouwer, 1997), 56, 475.

20 René Bertrand-Serret, *L'"Intégrisme," cet inconnu* (Lausanne: Les Éditions du Cèdre, 1956), 7.

21 *Ad Beatissimi*, November 1, 1914. English version at vatican.va.

Far from calling into question what Pius X had done in defense of doctrine, Benedict XV counted it among the "blessings" of the recently ended pontificate. The new pope praised his predecessor for having fought and condemned "the monstrous errors of modernism." He added: "We hereby renew that condemnation in all its fulness.... Nor do We merely desire that Catholics should shrink from the errors of Modernism, but also from the tendencies or what is called the spirit of Modernism."

Benedict XV defined the modernist "spirit" as a search for "novelties" at all costs "in the way in which they carry out religious functions, in the ruling of Catholic institutions, and even in private exercises of piety." He urged that "the law of our forefathers should still be held sacred: *'Nihil innovetur, nisi quod traditum est* (Let there be no innovation; keep to what has been handed down).'" In other matters he urged a second rule: "*Non nova, sed noviter* (Old things, but in a new way)."

The new pope, as defender of "Tradition," nevertheless wanted to put an end to "dissension and strife ... amongst Catholics." He asked that "no private individual, whether in books or in the press, or in public speeches, take upon himself the position of an authoritative teacher in the Church." In questions

> in which without harm to faith or discipline – in the absence of any authoritative intervention of the Apostolic See – there is room for divergent opinions, it is clearly the right of everyone to express and defend his own opinion. But in such discussions no expressions should be used which might constitute serious breaches of charity; let each one freely defend his own opinion, but let it be done with due moderation, so that no one should consider himself entitled to affix on those who merely do not agree with his ideas the stigma of disloyalty to faith or to discipline.

The *Sodalitium Pianum* of Archbishop Benigni, and the publications described as integrist by their opponents, were clearly, though anonymously, targeted in this text; they are those who were too quick to judge and condemn.

In another passage, Benedict XV also asked that:

> Catholics should abstain from certain appellations which have recently been brought into use to distinguish one group of Catholics from another.... Such is the nature of Catholicism that it does not admit of more or less, but must be held as a whole or as a whole rejected.... There is no need of adding any qualifying terms to the profession of Catholicism: it is quite enough for each one to proclaim "*Christianus mihi nomen, catholicus cognomen*" [Christian is my name and Catholic my surname].

This time, the very expression "integral Catholics" was proscribed, though not explicitly. In this passage there are certain similarities with the text of Canon Gaudeau quoted above. The latter did not boast of this, but he did consider that his position had been confirmed:

> This way, all the parasitic and dangerous labels that made certain groups look like so many sects are swept away for good. From now on, there will no longer be liberal Catholics, social Catholics, or integral Catholics in the Church. [22]

At the dawn of a new pontificate, modernism was thus condemned once again, while integral Catholics were called upon to fall in line, and not to use a superfluous label.

THE END OF THE *SAPINIÈRE*

Bishop Benigni's organization was not immediately suppressed. The long denunciation of the Sapinière that Archbishop Mignot of Albi, a friend of Loisy's, wrote in a memorandum sent to the Secretariat of State in October 1914 had no immediate effect. [23] In 1915, the new statutes of the *Sodalitium Pianum* were even approved by Cardinal De Lai, Secretary of the Consistorial Congregation. Its object remained the same: to defend the Church and the Pope "against the [modernist] sect in all its manifestations and all its accomplices." But its activity no longer had the scope and influence it had had under the pontificate of Pius X; it did not enjoy the support of the new pope.

In the last months of Benedict XV's pontificate, an anonymous publication caused a sensation. Starting in May 1921, Father Fernand Mourret, a professor of Church history at the seminary of Saint-Sulpice, began to circulate, anonymously and in typewritten copies, a thoroughly documented memorandum against the *Sodalitium Pianum*. Known as "The Anonymous Memorandum [Mémoire anonyme]," this document bore the title "A Secret Society." [24] It had been written on the basis of some archives discovered in Belgium during the war. It described the organization as a "Federation of Secret Societies," "a vast enterprise of denunciation, with Bishop Benigni at its center." Among other things, the document listed the "auxiliaries of Bishop Benigni," in Rome and

---

22 B. Gaudeau, "L'encyclique de S. S. Benoît XV et la doctrine anti-moderniste," *La Foi catholique* 14 (1922): 302.

23 Memorandum first published after the death of Archbishop Mignot in the review *Le Mouvement* (January–May 1924); annotated excerpts in É. Poulat, *Intégrisme et catholicisme intégral*, 515-23.

24 Émile Poulat has provided an annotated edition in *Intégrisme et catholicisme intégral*, 548-63.

in different countries, and also a much longer list of "the principal persons denounced" by the *Sapinière*.

This memorandum was sent to many French bishops, to the Apostolic Nuncio in Paris, as well as to Cardinal Gasparri, the Secretary of State. It revealed a highly organized system of vigilance that had been operating for years, without the high authorities who had encouraged the *Sodalitium Pianum* being aware of precisely what means it employed. The Congregation of the Council opened an investigation. In November of 1921, Benedict XV and Cardinal Sbarretti, prefect of the Congregation of the Council, judged it opportune "to dissolve the *Sodalitium Pianum*, given the changed circumstances."[25]

Yet Bishop Benigni did not give up his activities and publications. Between the wars, and until his death in 1934, he founded and led other information networks, now dedicated to political and social issues, notably the "Roman Entente of Social Defense."[26] Nina Valbousquet described Bishop Benigni's new struggle as "anti-Semitic, counter-revolutionary, and anti-communist." Émile Poulat considered that the anti-Semitism of Bishop Benigni and of the "integral Catholics" in his entourage was rather a new form of Christian anti-Judaism. In this view, the Jews are no longer just the heirs of those who refused Christ and crucified him, but also have a harmful influence on society, politics, and culture. This "modern Christian anti-Judaism owes nothing to the Aryan myth," as Émile Poulat pointed out. Bishop Benigni did not like the term "anti-Semite" and never professed any racial theory. Nina Valbousquet, however, believes that by essentializing the Jew, Bishop Benigni and his friends were moving towards a "racial anti-Semitism."

AGAINST "JUDEO-MASONRY"

In reality, anti-Semitism was not central to the actions and publications of Bishop Benigni in the 1920s and 1930s. The anti-liberal prelate was in contact not with groups and publications that advocated the superiority of the white race, but with organizations and magazines which, in various countries, denounced the action and influence of Freemasonry, and, more specifically, a "Judeo-Masonic plot."

This thesis goes back to the early nineteenth century, and to the letter a certain Jean-Baptiste Simonini wrote to Father Augustin Barruel. The Jesuit Barruel was the author of the famous *Mémoires pour*

25 Cardinal Sbarretti to Msgr Benigni, November 25, 1921, ibid., 599.
26 Émile Poulat, *Catholicisme, démocratie et socialisme* (Paris: Casterman, 1977); Nina Valbousquet, *Catholique et antisémite. Le réseau de Mgr Benigni, 1918-1934* (Paris: CNRS Éditions, 2020).

servir à l'histoire du jacobinisme, which sought to demonstrate that the French Revolution was the result of a plot hatched by a Masonic sect: the Illuminati of Bavaria.[27] With Simonini's letter, dated 1806 but published much later,[28] the focus shifted from a Masonic plot to a Judeo-Masonic plot. In ten points, Simonini sought to establish that the "Judaic sect" worked, with "its gold and money," to "support and multiply the modern Sophists, the Freemasons, the Jacobins, the Illuminati." He also claimed that "the Jews, along with members of all the other sects, form but a single party dedicated to annihilating, if possible, the very name of Christian" and that they "are dead-set on becoming the masters of the world within a century."

This document is actually apocryphal. As Pierre-André Taguieff has pointed out, Simonini's letter already includes most of the themes of the "Judeo-Masonic conspiracy" as it was to develop in the last two decades of the 19th century:

> The central idea is the following: far from being just the aggregate of believers in Judaism, the Jews in reality form an "anti-Christian sect" or an international secret society motivated by a design of world domination, and Freemasonry is one of their satanic creations.[29]

In the early part of the twentieth century, Msgr Henri Delassus and Msgr Ernest Jouin were the principal promoters of this "Judeo-Masonic plot" thesis in France. These were not marginal figures in the Church in France. Msgr Delassus was the director of the *Semaine religieuse* weekly of the diocese of Cambrai. In 1904, Pius X named him Prelate of the Papal Household. In 1910, he published *La Conjuration anti-chrétienne* ["The Anti-Christian Conspiracy"] in three volumes, with a brief of approval from Cardinal Merry del Val, Secretary of State. The following year, Pius X named him apostolic prothonotary. Msgr Jouin was the highly esteemed pastor of the parish of Saint-Augustin in Paris. In 1912 he founded the *Revue internationale des sociétés secrètes* (RISS)

---

27 This five-volume work was first published in London in 1797-1798; it has undergone many editions since, most recently in a two-volume revised edition by the Éditions de Chiré (2005).

28 This letter, dated 1806, was not published until decades later in the Catholic review *Le Contemporain* 16 (1878): 58-61.

29 Pierre-André Taguieff, "L'invention du 'complot judéo-maçonnique.' Avatars d'un mythe apocalyptique moderne," *Revue d'histoire de la Shoah* 198 (2013), 23-97. For a deconstruction of the "Judeo-Masonic conspiracy" myth that does not deny the influence of Jewish intellectuals and militants, see Julia David, *Ni réaction ni révolution. Les intellectuels juifs, la critique du progrès et le scrupule de l'histoire* (Paris: L'Harmattan, 2013) and "Tous réactionnaires? Des intellectuels juifs et le progrès," *Hypothèses*, October 2, 2014, https://hdja1945.hypotheses.org/1220 [accessed 4/4/2024].

and, in 1913, the *Ligue franc-catholique*. He was appointed Prelate of His Holiness by Benedict XV in 1918. He and Bishop Benigni were in communication with each other. In 1920, he began to publish *Le Péril judéo-maçonnique*, a series of volumes in which he published the first French translation of the *Protocols of the Elders of Zion*, another apocryphal document. But none of this prevented Pius XI from appointing him apostolic prothonotary in 1924. In 1932, his funeral was celebrated by Cardinal Verdier, Archbishop of Paris. Émile Poulat remarks:

> Today one can no longer imagine what place the great international conspiracy of Judaism, Protestantism, and Masonry, all satanically united to destroy Catholicism, held in the mentality of the "Church under siege." A forgotten, repressed history, of which the anti-Masonic associations are all that is left. . . . [30]

The denunciation of Freemasonic influence in contemporary societies remains a constant of the traditionalist current to this day, though with very diverse tonalities. The Holy See has maintained its condemnation of Freemasonry to the present, and in recent years several French bishops (Bp Brincard in Puy-en-Velay, Bp Rey in Toulon, Archbp Barsi in Monaco) have, through declarations or in books, denounced the influence of Freemasonry and reminded the public of the incompatibility between membership in the Church and membership in Freemasonry.

ACTION FRANÇAISE AND INTEGRISM

The "Mémoire anonyme" [Anonymous Memorandum] that Father Mourret distributed in samizdat form from 1921 onwards, and that was published in 1923 by the review *Le Mouvement social*, contributed a great deal to giving credence to the existence of an integrist current within the Church, a current that was characterized by intellectual obtuseness and a taste for denunciation.

The condemnation of *Action française*, which started in 1926, was to revive this phobia. This condemnation has sometimes been presented as a "second Ralliement," with Pius XI condemning the monarchist movement in order to encourage Catholic support for the Republic [as Leo XIII had done in the first "Ralliement" – *Translator*]. *Action française* considered its condemnation as a political decision prompted by its Christian Democrat opponents.

Without retracing the whole history of this condemnation and its many twists and turns,[31] let us note the principal stages and its diverse

---

30 É. Poulat, *Intégrisme et catholicisme intégral*, 282.

31 Jacques Prévotat's dissertation, *Les Catholiques et l'Action française. Histoire d'une condamnation 1899-1939* (Paris: Fayard, 2001), is the most complete presentation of the

and important consequences. The starting point was a letter published by Cardinal Andrieu, Archbishop of Bordeaux, in his diocese's *Semaine religieuse*, on August 25, 1926. It was a strict warning against Action française and its leaders: "They reject all the dogmas that the Church teaches. She teaches the existence of God, and they deny it." This warning, which contained various factual errors, was clumsy and exaggerated. The Action française had no trouble responding that while its president, Charles Maurras, was still agnostic, it counted among its leaders and thousands of members "practicing and devout Catholics." This warning, as was not learned until later, had been issued at the request of Pius XI. The Pope therefore hastened to support Cardinal Andrieu in a letter dated September 5, 1926. In it he deplored the inadequacies of a "new religious, moral and social system." On December 20, 1926, in a consistorial address, he took a further step by issuing multiple prohibitions:

> Catholics are in no way permitted to adhere to the enterprises and, so to speak, interests of parties that are above religion and make the latter serve the former. They are never permitted to expose themselves or others, especially young people, to influences or doctrines that are dangerous for faith and morals as well as for the Catholic formation of youth.... Catholics are not permitted to support, encourage, or read newspapers published by men whose writings, in departing from our dogma and morals, cannot escape reprobation.

Pius XI, who in three encyclicals condemned certain aspects of Fascism as well as Communist and Nazi doctrines, did not publish an encyclical or doctrinal statement on *Action française*, even though he had plans to do so. His condemnation was primarily based on religious grounds: in its doctrine as in its practice, the *AF* practiced a naturalism or a "political modernism" that disregarded the traditional teaching of the Church on the subject. This teaching, which Pius XI had recalled in his first encyclical, *Ubi arcano Dei* (1922), asserts that in all areas "true peace can come only from Christ and his Church. It is necessary to re-establish 'the Reign of Christ' in the family, in school, in society." The *Action française* was composed mostly of believers. In the past – during the time of the Inventories – it had been in a position to defend the Church [In 1905, consequent to the law on separation of Church and State, the government had drawn up inventories of Church property, which led to troubles throughout France – *Translator*]. During the war, it had been one of the most sincere supporters of the positions and teachings of Benedict XV.

---

subject, but some of its arguments suffer from partiality. The cause of this condemnation is principally religious rather than directly political; cf. Yves Chiron and Émile Poulat, *Pourquoi Pie XI a-t-il condamné l'Action française?* (Paris: Éditions BCM, 2009).

But its doctrine, according to Pius XI, did not recognize the "necessary relationship" between Catholic dogma and morality, and politics.

Action française responded to the December 20 papal address with an article published by the Catholic leaders of the movement under the title "Non possumus." They made a distinction between "the religious field," where "the Church will never have more submissive or devoted sons than ourselves," and "the political field," where "we have the duty to preserve our rightful freedom." They judged that "the act of killing *Action française* is not a purely or primarily religious act. It is principally a political act." Consequently, these Catholic leaders felt it was impossible for them to obey the pope's injunctions: "In obeying we should cease to be good Frenchmen. We shall not betray our country: *Non possumus.*" This insubordination scandalized Pius XI. Nine days later, in a decree dated December 29, seven works by Maurras, the review *L'Action française*, and the newspaper of the same name were placed on the Index of Prohibited Books. In a new official letter to Cardinal Andrieu on January 5, 1927, the Pope justified the condemnation of *Action française* as that of a "particular species of political, doctrinal, and practical modernism."

One can think, with Émile Poulat, that "the leaders of *Action française* misunderstood what the pope expected of them": they believed that he was asking them to renounce their monarchism and especially their nationalism. At the same time, "Pius XI misunderstood the Catholics of *Action française*"; he did not see that the agnosticism of Maurras was no obstacle to the solid Catholic faith of many of its leaders and militants.[32] And by encouraging the movements of *Catholic Action* and the National Catholic Federation (the FNC) of General de Castelnau, he seemed to condemn the *Action française* for political reasons.

This "multiple trigger condemnation," as Émile Poulat puts it, provoked a lasting crisis, including among the clergy and some intellectuals sympathetic to the *AF*. From submission to refusal to obey the injunctions of Pius XI, all attitudes were found among the sympathizers or adherents of this monarchist movement. The episcopate itself was divided at first. The image of an entire episcopate committed to the cause of *Action française* "is the stuff of myth," as Jacques Prévotat insists, even if it is true that the assembly of cardinals and archbishops included a dozen or so defenders of the *AF*, to which were added several dozen bishops who were at least sympathetic to the movement and grateful for the services it had rendered to the Church. It took all the authority of Pius XI and his repeated interventions to ensure that

---

32 Y. Chiron and É. Poulat, *Pourquoi Pie XI a-t-il condamné l'Action française?*, 43-44.

his decisions were respected. From the first months of 1927, canonical
sanctions were taken against the insubordinate. The faithful who continued to read *L'Action française* or to be active in the movement were
deprived of the sacraments and excluded from Catholic organizations.
Between autumn 1927 and 1940, at least 121 funerals took place without a funeral Mass because the deceased was denied the last rites.[33]
Many also were the weddings celebrated in the sacristy for militants or
readers of *L'Action française*, as was done at the time for the marriage
between a Catholic and a non-baptized person.…

Seminarians who did not submit were also subject to various penalties, and were considered "unfit for the ecclesiastical estate." For
priests, there was a gradation in the sanctions. The ultimate point was
that those who continued to absolve the unsubmissive faithful were
guilty of a "mortal sin," from which they could be absolved only by
the pope himself.[34] In Rome, alleged supporters of *Action française*
were punished: the superior of the French Seminary, Father Le Floch,
had to resign and a French cardinal, the Jesuit Louis Billot, an eminent
theologian, had to renounce his cardinalate. The sanctions against
Action française Catholics were not lifted until 1939, under Pius XII.

Based on this years-long *Action française* controversy, Louis Canet
attempted to substantiate the thesis that there had long been a collusion between integrism and *Action française*, and that resistance to the
latter's condemnation was encouraged by prelates and priests whom
he called "integral Catholics" or "integrists" interchangeably. This Louis
Canet, a high-ranking professor ["professeur agrégé"] of grammar and
former student of the French School of Rome, was a technical advisor
for ecclesiastical affairs at the Ministry of Foreign Affairs. Since he was
bound by professional discretion, he published his study under the
pseudonym of Nicolas Fontaine. This well-informed friend of Loisy and
Laberthonnière, two authors condemned under Pius X, first published
his text in *L'Année politique française et étrangère* (January 1928). He then
published it as an offprint, augmented with various documents including
a new edition of Father Mourret's memorandum.[35] Louis Canet wanted
to show that "Maurrassism and integrism have been closely associated
since the reign of Pius X" and that "they have fought for each other
and shared each other's victories." He also considered that ever since

---

33 This list was drawn up from various sources by J. Prévotat, *Les Catholiques et l'Action
française*, 500-2.
34 *Documentation Catholique* [henceforth *DC*] 22 (22 December 1928): 1184.
35 Nicolas Fontaine, *Saint-Siège, "Action française" et "Catholiques intégraux"* (Paris:
Librairie Universitaire J. Gamber, 1928).

the *Action française* was condemned, "integrism is asserting itself more audaciously than ever." By identifying integral Catholicism or integrism with *Action française*, Louis Canet initiated an approach to the issue that was to be repeated to this day in a multitude of books and articles without ever being questioned. It is a political interpretation of integrism, of which Maurrasism is understood to be the matrix. The explanation was to be taken up by the theologian Yves Congar in 1950, by the historian René Rémond in 1958, and by many others, as we shall see.

When the traditionalist challenge enjoyed renewed publicity and a whole new scope with Archbishop Lefebvre from the early 1970s on, most commentators and analysts equated Lefebvrism with integrism and also Lefebvrism with Maurrasism. In the aftermath of Archbishop Lefebvre's famous Mass in Lille in August 1976 – one month after he was suspended from office by Pope Paul VI – *Le Monde* considered that the founder of Écône had "thrown off the mask" and that he "bases his entire action on integrism and Maurrassian principles."[36] Yet neither at that time nor later can it be said that Archbishop Lefebvre had followed "Maurrassian principles" – he had not been trained in that thought – but it is undeniable that Maurrassians and Action française militants were enthusiastic about this Mass in Lille, just as they were among the first supporters of the occupation of Saint-Nicolas-du-Chardonnet the following year.

More recently, the historian Florian Michel has extended this symmetry by comparing the refusal of Maurras, along with most of the leaders and many of the adherents of *Action française*, to submit to the Roman condemnations of 1926-1927 with Archbishop Lefebvre's refusal to submit to the Roman sanctions that struck him in 1976 and 1988. In both cases, he says, we have "an example of an ecclesial 'Ultraromanity' which ultimately and paradoxically leads to a doctrinal 'anti-Romanism.'"[37] Florian Michel explains this through the "doctrinal, familial, human, and intellectual" filiation "between Maurrasism and Lefebvrism," particularly in the formation the future Archbishop Lefebvre received at the French Seminary in the 1920s, which at the time – if one is to believe what has been said time and again – was thoroughly given over to *Action française*. This assertion is factually questionable and ignores the importance of a completely different influence: the French Seminary formed several generations of priests and future bishops attached to Rome, to the Holy See, and to the Catholic tradition. It was a breeding ground, but not the only one, for French traditionalism.

---

36 Alain Woodrow, "Le Masque est jeté," *Le Monde* (31 August 1976).
37 Florian Michel and Bernard Sesboüé, *De Mgr Lefebvre à Mgr Williamson. Anatomie d'un schisme* (Paris: Lethielleux/Desclée de Brouwer, 2009), 14.

ROMANITY

After the French Revolution and after the Concordat [between Napoleon and the Holy See in 1801 – *Translator*] with its "Organic Articles" limiting her field of action, the Catholic Church in France increasingly turned towards Rome. Bishop Antoine de Salinis of Amiens reckoned in 1853 that "the characteristic feature of our time is the movement towards Rome." Before his clergy gathered in synod, he defined it as a desire to be attached to the Catholic tradition: "There is in Rome an institution to which nothing can be compared . . . it is unchanging; the traditions of the Vatican are those of the catacombs." The attachment to the Pope, "Vicar of God," must be unwavering: "let us swear to him that he can count on us."[38]

In another address to his clergy, he explained that the current situation "imposes upon the churches of France the duty to strengthen the bonds linking them to Rome. . . . Barbarity, through revolution, is threatening modern civilization; we are living in a time when Catholicism alone can regenerate the world. Before us lie death, or life through Catholicism. Rome, therefore, is the center for our hopes of catholicity; from Rome therefore the regenerating movement of human societies must originate."[39]

This "movement towards Rome" is a tendency which, historically speaking, shows up early in the first half of the nineteenth century, gaining steam throughout the second Empire [1852-1870] and later on. It had different manifestations. The restoration of the great religious orders after their disappearance during the revolution went through Rome. "It is in Rome that Dom Guéranger pronounced his vows (1837); in Rome that Lacordaire took the Dominican habit (1839). These religious orders became 'Roman' and depended on the pope, who supported their exemptions in whatever disputes they may have had with the bishops."[40] The "movement toward Rome" can also be observed in the liturgy. With an impetus given from the priory of Solesmes as restored by Dom Guéranger, the Roman rite progressively replaced local liturgies in the dioceses of France, despite some resistance on the part of bishops and priests attached to their particular rite (Parisian, Lyonnese, Viennois, etc.). *Ad limina* visits (meaning visits to Rome), which bishops are supposed to undertake every five years, had long since fallen out of use; they pick up again regularly from the 1840s onwards.

---

38 "Discours prononcé par Mgr de Salinis," *L'Université catholique* 16.91 (1853): 83, 87.
39 Quoted in Casimir de Ladoue, *Vie de Monseigneur Antoine de Salinis, évêque d'Amiens, archevêque d'Auch* (Paris: Tolra, 1873), 246-50.
40 Paul Christophe, *Le Concile Vatican I* (Paris: Cerf, 2000), 26.

In general, the "movement towards Rome" characterizes an impulse that led French Catholics – but the tendency is also seen in other European countries – to turn towards the Pope, to await his directives, to submit to his teaching, and, if necessary, to come to his aid.[41] Trips and pilgrimages to Rome were on the increase; volunteers (the Papal Zouaves) came to the assistance of the Papal States, which were gradually being invaded by the Kingdom of Italy. The centripetal attraction of French Catholicism to Rome is illustrated, for example, by Louis Veuillot's famous book, *Le Parfum de Rome*. Recounting his stays in the Eternal City, he concluded that nowhere better than in Rome could French Catholics feel they were "children of the Holy Church," "know her, love her, share her sorrows, live on her hopes." He added: "I believe that since the world cannot live without authority, it will come to seek authority at its source here below, which is the Holy See.... [t]o establish order, it will be necessary to begin with a solemn affirmation of the rights of the Papacy, which are the rights of God."[42]

This "movement towards Rome" was further reflected in the second half of the nineteenth century and at the beginning of the twentieth century by the foundation of numerous institutions of ecclesiastical formation in the eternal city, on the initiative of a number of nations' bishops and religious orders. These included the establishment of the Belgian Pontifical College in 1844, the Pontifical North American College in 1859, and the Pontifical Athenaeum of St. Anselm for the Benedictines in 1867.

The creation of a French Seminary that was open to all French dioceses was a fruit of the "movement towards Rome" as much as of the concern for a good intellectual and spiritual formation of the French clerical leadership.[43] Founded in 1853 at the request of several ultramontane bishops, among them the future Cardinal Pie, and entrusted to the Congregation of the Holy Ghost (the Holy Ghost Fathers), the French Seminary was established in 1855 in Via Santa Chiara, where it is still located. It was canonically approved by Pope Pius IX in 1859, and elevated to the rank of Pontifical Seminary in 1902. At the end of the 19th century, it had some eighty students, and 140 by 1914. The

---

41 Philippe Boutry, "Le Mouvement vers Rome et le renouveau missionnaire" in *Histoire de la France religieuse* (Paris: Seuil, 1991) 3: 423-52. See also Bruno Horaist, *La Dévotion au pape et les catholiques français sous le pontificat de Pie IX (1846-1878)* (Rome: École française de Rome, 1995).

42 Louis Veuillot, *Le Parfum de Rome* (Paris: Gaume frères et J. Duprey, 1862), 2: 332-33.

43 Paul Airiau, "Le Séminaire français de Rome," *Histoire et Missions chrétiennes* 10 (June 2009): 35. See also Alphonse Eschbach, seminary rector from 1875 to 1904, *Le Séminaire pontifical français de Rome* (Rome: Desclée/Lefebvre and Co., 1903).

French Seminary was, first of all, a place of spiritual formation and
the acquisition of ecclesiastical discipline. According to the formulas
of the time, it was a matter of "forming conscience and acquiring
habits," "repeating frequently, consciously, and as perfectly as possible
the acts of priestly virtue: piety, work, silence, charity, modesty."[44] Its
students took courses in philosophy, theology and Sacred Scripture at
the great Roman institutions (the Gregorian or the Athenaeum Saint
Apollinare), but also received an intellectual formation within the
seminary through series of lectures. Father Le Floch was rector of
the French Seminary from 1904 to 1927. His solid, traditional Breton
Catholicism became romanized. His long stay in Rome, for almost a
quarter of a century, had made him familiar with the staff of the Curia,
with the professors of the pontifical universities, and with the Roman
congregations. At the height of his career, he was a consultor to four
Roman congregations: the Holy Office, the Consistorial, Propaganda
Fide, and Seminaries. At the French Seminary, he saw to it that his
students acquired the "priestly virtues" mentioned above. As an anti-
liberal, anti-naturalist, and anti-modernist, he also formed them in this
spirit and in "Romanity." Romanity is not a doctrine but a spirit, and
it is not unique to Father Le Floch. The historian Paul Airiau says that
it was an "official quality": "Romanity is a quality, and, no doubt from
the modernist crisis until Vatican II, the supreme quality of Catholicism,
or at least of the Catholic priest."[45] Theologians could show how this
explicitly claimed and accepted "Romanity" is the application of one
of the "notes" of the Church as defined in the Creed: "I believe in the
one, holy, catholic, apostolic and Roman Church."

In his June 19, 1913 Declaration mentioned above, Archbishop Benigni
established the equivalence between "integral Catholicism" and "Romanity." He affirmed that "integral Catholics" are "Catholics who want
to be entirely, integrally Roman, faithful to the Holy See and to its
directions in individual and social life." He specified: "In the face of
the minimization of Roman Catholicism attempted by liberal Catholics,
modernizers, etc., they affirm the integrity of their Romanism. That
is all."[46] When the appellation "integral Catholics" was prohibited by
Benedict XV, "Romanity" remained more than ever a characteristic

---

44 Lecture delivered by Father Dujardin in 1910, quoted in P. Airiau, "Le Séminaire
français de Rome," 54.
45 Paul Airiau, "La Pensée catholique, 1946-1956. Romanité à la française ou intégrisme?"
Advanced Studies Diploma thesis (IEP Paris, 1995), 65.
46 Déclaration de l'A. I. R., 19 juin 1913, fully reproduced in Émile Poulat, Intégrisme et
catholicisme intégral, 132.

claimed by anti-liberals and anti-modernists. In doing so, they were in full agreement with the popes. Every year, Pius XI received in audience the students of the French Seminary and their teachers. On two occasions he spoke of "Romanity" as a quality to be acquired and preserved, because it is "the perfection of Catholicity," "the very soul of the Catholic faith."[47]

At the French Seminary, Father Le Floch trained two or three generations of priests in this anti-liberal, Roman spirit. It is remarkable how many of the leading figures of traditionalism in the 1950s-1980s had been trained by him, even if some would have refused the traditionalist label. One might mention Luc Lefèvre, Alphonse Roul and Robert Prévost, who entered in 1919, as did Georges Frénaud, who joined the Benedictine abbey of Solesmes; Raymond Dulac, who entered in 1920, Victor Berto in 1921, Marcel Lefebvre and Augustin Rivière in 1923, Pierre-Martin Ngô Dinh Thuc in 1926. One might add many more names of lesser-known priests. These traditional Catholics represent only a minority of the students trained by Father Le Floch. Many others, in the same period, such as future bishops Gabriel-Marie Garrone (entered in 1918) or Alfred Ancel (entered in 1921), did not follow the same itinerary and, at a time of crisis for the Church, made different choices. But they all acknowledged their debt to the French Seminary.

Father Le Floch to this day has the reputation of having been an inveterate Maurrassian. After the condemnation of *Action française*, some in Rome and in France accused him not only of having been a supporter of the monarchist movement and of having become the propagator of the journal, but also of having kept documents from the Holy Office (of which he was a consultor) in an attempt to prevent the 1926 condemnation, and of having become an opponent of Pius XI after the papal condemnations. This fourfold accusation led him to resign. The work done by Paul Airiau, to which can be added the archives of Father Berto, a disciple of Father Le Floch, allows us to sift the validity of this fourfold accusation. It is undeniable that the rector of the French Seminary, a monarchist by conviction, considered *Action française* to be a useful ally of the Church, and admired its struggle against the republican form of government and against liberalism (economic and social). He also hailed Maurras as a man who, although an unbeliever, not an atheist, claimed to be "Roman." But it is a matter of fact that he did not steal and retain any document from the Holy Office and did not

---

47 Allocution of April 19 and of December 3, 1927 published in Jean-Baptiste Frey, *Le Saint-Siège et le Séminaire français de Rome. Lettres et allocutions pontificales* (Rome: Libreria Vaticana, 1935).

incite his students to revolt against the pontifical condemnations, even if he considered them to be lacking in doctrinal justification.

His reputation as a Maurrassian has attached itself to those of his former students who became "traditionalists"; it is even, in the eyes of certain historians and commentators, one of the keys to explain the choices they made. Thus, a recent history of contemporary Catholicism presents Archbishop Lefebvre as "coming from a bourgeois and Maurrassian family." This is an unfounded assertion. Neither his parents nor the young Marcel Lefebvre were adherents of *Action française*; he was later to say that he had never read a book by Maurras and one of his confreres at the French Seminary would relate: "Among friends, we talked about *Action française*, but I never heard Marcel [Lefebvre] talk about that. One of his mottoes was: 'Rome has spoken, the case is at an end.'"[48]

That *L'Action française* was read at the French Seminary before the condemnation is undeniable, as were other French newspapers, Catholic and otherwise. That some seminarians had read works by Maurras is also undeniable. But after the condemnation, the students and alumni of the French Seminary reacted in different ways.

After Father Le Floch's departure, the French Seminary did not break with its anti-liberal and Roman spirit. For all the seminarians and priests in formation in Rome, of whatever nationality, Romanity remained a kind of priestly virtue one had to acquire. In the last days of his pontificate, Pius XII mentioned it once again. In an address to the young priests of the Spanish Pontifical College, he distinguished the "three characteristics of Romanity, characteristics that should distinguish you for the rest of your life." The perfection of Roman formation: "A priest trained in Rome should be more than any other a perpetual example of profound and sure doctrine, a flexible and cultured mind; he should be, above all, a perfect example of all the priestly virtues"; universality, "as if Romanity were synonymous with Catholicity": to rise above national particularisms in order to make hearts and minds beat in unison with Rome, "the center of the Church"; fidelity to the Holy See and to the pope: to be "faithful echoes of every word that comes from Rome."[49]

Until the Second Vatican Council, traditional or traditionalist Catholics would not only refer to the Pope and the Holy See to fight their battles and defend their positions, but even ask for their support.

---

48 Quoted in Bernard Tissier de Mallerais, *Marcel Lefebvre: The Biography* (Kansas City, MO: Angelus Press, 2004), 50.

49 *Allocution to Young Spanish Priests*, March 21, 1957, in *DC* (April 28, 1957): coll. 523-25.

VÉRITÉS VERSUS SEPT AND TEMPS PRÉSENT

Following the condemnation of *Action française*, Pius XI sought to give a new direction to the Catholic Church in France. There has been exaggerated talk of a "second *Ralliement*": according to this view, Pius XI wanted to force French Catholics to submit to the republican regime, just as Leo XIII had done before him. In fact, his primary objective, like that of Leo XIII, was to unite Catholics beyond their particular political choices into a union against secularism, against immoral laws, for freedom of education, for the Christian reconquest of society, and so forth. It is in this perspective that one must consider the support given by the Pope to both the National Catholic Federation ("Fédération Nationale Catholique," or FNC) and to the Catholic Action movements, as well as his appointment of bishops who shared this outlook. Pius XI, who was attentive to intellectual life and to the press, also wanted new publications to be launched to defend his "Catholic first" policy. Father Bernadot, a Dominican of the convent at Saint-Maximin, was one of the pope's men in this regard. In 1919 he founded *La Vie spirituelle*, which aimed to show the links between asceticism and mysticism and to consider them in the light of St. Thomas Aquinas. This review soon became a journal of record.

At Pius XI's request Father Bernadot undertook another mission. According to Father Boisselot, who was his second in command and his successor, "like many priests, he had been attracted to the doctrines of the AF, and had made friendships and connections in that milieu." After the Pope's condemnation of the AF, he felt he had to "obey his conscience and the Holy Father's call to fight against what he had once supported."[50] Pius XI received him in Rome in May 1927, and encouraged him to create a monthly review that would be the equivalent of *La Vie spirituelle*, but in the realm of ideas. It was also at the suggestion of the Pope that Father Bernadot was associated with the collective work against *Action française* published under the authority of Jacques Maritain: *Pourquoi Rome a parlé* (December 1927) and it was at his request that he published with Fathers Georges Desbuquois and Michel Riquet, a Jesuit, a "response to the theologians of *Action française*," *Le Joug du Christ* (April 1928). It took the intervention of Pius XI to allow Father Bernadot to leave the convent of Saint-Maximin and settle in Juvisy, near Paris, to launch the new review that the pope desired. The first issue of *La Vie intellectuelle* appeared in October 1928. Through

---

50 Quoted in André Laudouze, *Dominicains français et Action française. Maurras au couvent* (Paris: Les Éditions ouvrières, 1989), 132.

some of its columns (culture, philosophy, sciences, social questions), it clearly wanted to counterbalance the *Revue universelle,* which had ties to *Action française.* But its particularity was its firm will to "be a *Catholic* review, in the simplest, frankest, and also broadest sense." Its original spirit, in fact, can only be considered that of intransigent Catholicism. By way of introduction, Father Bernadot wrote:

> To teach, to criticize, to praise: these require clear-sightedness: we claim to have the clearsightedness that the Christian faith gives. We do not represent any party; we are neither of the right nor of the left, but simply Catholics. Our light comes from the teaching of the Church, from traditional doctrine, and from the directives of the Roman Pontiff.

This editorial stance was not maintained. In June 1930, a serious health issue forced Father Bernadot to withdraw from the magazine and indeed from the Éditions du Cerf, which he had founded the previous year. "His forced eclipse lasted two years, during which his assistants departed from the prescribed stance in favor of an intellectual eclecticism that roused Maritain's wrath and raised concerns at the Nunciature."[51] Once he had returned to his review in September 1932, Father Bernadot had two trusted assistants, Fathers Pierre Boisselot and Augustin Maydieu; both of them later gravitated towards what would by then be called progressivism.

Received in private audience once again by the Pope in December 1930, Father Bernadot was given a new mission: "To create a weekly that would do for the masses what *La Vie intellectuelle* was already doing for the elites."[52] The project only came to fruition in March 1934 with the publication of *Sept,* "the weekly of the present time," according to its subtitle. Directed by Father Bernadot and Father Boisselot, it sought to give a Christian view of current events in all fields. "We remain above the fray. Neither of the right nor of the left, independent of politics in order to better serve the City," stated the headline of the second issue (March 10, 1934).

At this time a young woman entered the scene who was to play a central role in the wing of the Catholic press that would later be called "progressive": Ella Sauvageot. Historians of the Christian Left, except for Yvon Tranvouez, have often been insufficiently aware of her role. Almost half a century after her death, the biography that her daughter wrote, and the excerpts of her correspondence that she published, have

---

51 Étienne Fouilloux, "Bernadot, Marie-Vincent," *Dictionnaire biographique des Frères prêcheurs,* https://journals.openedition.org/dominicains/1200 [accessed 4/4/2024].
52 *Pourquoi le journal Sept a été supprimé,* undated anonymous pamphlet [1938].

revealed an extraordinary personality: a woman at once of the left and very wealthy, a mystical Christian who was also tormented in the moral sphere.[53] Born to a non-Catholic family in 1900, Ella Sauvageot lost her father, a wealthy entrepreneur, the following year. He left her a solid inheritance, which she was able to make prosper. She was married with three children, divorced in 1932, converted the following year under the influence of Father Boisselot, and received baptism in 1934. Father Boisselot became her spiritual director and confessor. Through him she also became familiar with the world of the Catholic press, and then devoted her life and fortune to it. She assiduously frequented the Maison Saint-Dominique in Juvisy, the headquarters of *La Vie intellectuelle*, of *Sept*, and of the Éditions du Cerf; the "Juvisy Soviet," as their opponents soon called it. Ella Sauvageot endeavored to give *Sept* a wide distribution, canvassing parish priests in Paris to subscribe and to permit hawking the paper outside their churches after Mass on Sundays. She also organized fundraisers and subscription campaigns. Soon "Les Amis de *Sept* [the Friends of *Sept*]" was created to support and publicize the weekly, with Ella Sauvageot as treasurer. She multiplied meetings in the provinces to recruit new subscribers, mobilize readers, and turn them into distributors. When Fathers Bernadot and Boisselot left Juvisy and set up the headquarters of their publications and the Éditions du Cerf in Paris, at 29 boulevard de Latour-Maubourg, Ella Sauvageot, according to her daughter, "not content with bringing in the money from the great support campaigns, fed the newspaper's coffers directly,"[54] bought shares of stock in the Éditions du Cerf, and sat on their board of directors. She was to become a key financier of the most politically committed wing of the Christian press.

Sept ceased to appear in 1937, after three years of publication, by order of the Master General of the Dominicans, Father Gillet, officially "for budgetary reasons." In reality, the finances of the weekly, with its list of 25,000 subscribers, were quite healthy. It was the evolution of the paper and certain of its positions that had concerned the authorities of the Dominican Order as well as the Holy Office. The "Farewell to readers" in the last issue (August 27, 1937) mentions "campaigns, whether public or covert, that manifest a rather contemptible conception of Christian life and which, to a great extent, are responsible for our present difficulties by hindering our growth." No publication was named. Historians have mentioned a small "integrist" magazine,

---

53 Jacqueline Sauvageot, *Ella Sauvageot. L'audace d'une femme de presse. 1900-1962* (Paris: Les éditions de l'Atelier, 2006), 194-200.
54 Ibid., 106.

Vérités, and referred to one or another of its articles hostile to *Sept*. A quick look at *Vérités* is enough to conclude that its denunciations cannot have been enough to condemn the weekly.

Vérités was not sold by subscription but in individual fascicles, which probably explains why no major library today (neither the Bibliothèque Nationale nor the library of Le Saulchoir [where the Dominican House of Studies is situated – *Translator*]) has a complete collection. I found one, quite by chance, at a flea market in provincial France. *Vérités* produced 62 issues, published between 1927 and 1940, in the form of brochures of varying thickness (between two and 64 pages). Most of the pamphlets, on different themes each time, were signed "Luc-Verus." This was the pseudonym shared by Abbé Boulin and Henri Merlier, who had already collaborated, as we have seen, in the publication of *La Vigie* before the First World War. After Abbé Boulin's death in 1933, Henri Merlier continued the publication alone.

Vérités was characterized by its hostility to the Jesuits (one of Abbé Boulin's hobby horses) and to Christian democracy, and by its critical tone toward Pius XI, accused, among other things, of having "sacrificed doctrinal integrity to politics" (issue 44). Also recurrent was the denunciation of ecclesiastical careerism. Issue 26 was entirely devoted to mocking "the race for the mitre" of Bishop Fontenelle, a young French prelate in the Roman Curia, and issue 40 insolently lampooned "A candidate for the tiara: His Impudence [sic] Cardinal Pacelli, Secretary of State." This pamphleteering tone spared no one. Issue 14 challenged Pius XI: "Most Holy Father, have you read your own encyclicals?"

While Father Bernadot was twice taken to task during the first years of *Vérités*, it was always incidentally and in connection with *La Vie intellectuelle*. It was only in November 1936 that a campaign was launched against *Sept*. Issue 50 contained a long open letter to Pius XI, which was more than a little disrespectful in some passages ("age, the emotions of a pontificate that has been particularly fertile in ruins, exhaustion . . . we fear that all of this has ended up somewhat blurring in you an intelligence that used to be called so lucid. . . ."). A large part of this letter was dedicated to *Sept*, described as "the organ of the left-wing Dominicans." It denounced the weekly's complacent attitude towards the communists and the praises it lavished on the champions of secularism, Émile Combes, Ferdinand Buisson, and Jean Jaurès, whom *Sept* had qualified as "honorable men." The following issue (51) was entirely devoted to denouncing the way in which *Sept* transgressed "the Church's traditional rules in moral issues." These two issues of *Vérités* were certainly read in Rome, but it is doubtful that they were enough to condemn the weekly, especially since the all-out campaigns of *Vérités* and its outrageous tone against the highest authorities of the Church discredited it.

The reasons that prompted the authorities to put an end to the publication of *Sept* were politico-religious.[55] On the Italian war of annexation in Ethiopia as well as on the Spanish Civil War, *Sept* had taken positions that contradicted those of the Holy See and of most of the French episcopate. Rome and certain bishops also judged that in its interpretation of the social doctrine of the Church, the weekly was too favorable to trade unions. Yet it also received encouragement and support from other bishops, notably Cardinal Verdier, Archbishop of Paris. The most heated controversy arose from the so-called "interview" with Léon Blum, head of the Popular Front government, published in *Sept* on February 19, 1937. In fact, it was a short written response that the socialist leader had made in response to an inquiry sent him by the weekly. He had expressed the judgment that a collaboration between French Catholics and the Popular Front government was "possible" and even "desirable." The weekly's lengthy commentary recalled Pius XI's condemnation of socialism in *Quadragesimo Anno* ("socialism . . . cannot be reconciled with the teachings of the Catholic Church"), but asserted that Catholics could "loyally give their support" to "certain initiatives of the Popular Front."

Léon Blum's remarks, and especially the commentary of *Sept*, caused a controversy in the press and increased the profile of the weekly (which reached a circulation of 100,000 for this issue). The leaders of *Sept*, Fathers Bernadot and Boisselot, and the ever-active president of the "Friends of *Sept*," Ella Sauvageot, prepared a new title, which appeared on July 2, and a congress, to be held in October as an "exceptional gathering" to give the weekly new life in a different direction. But in August 1937 the order to stop the publication came down. A last issue was published on August 27, with the "Farewell to the readers" mentioned above.

Since it was published under the responsibility of the Dominicans, *Sept* had "seemed to commit the Church"; the decision was therefore made to "continue the adventure by launching a new title under a purely lay direction."[56] The new weekly was called *Temps présent*, in explicit reference to *Sept*, whose subtitle had been *l'hebdomadaire du*

---

55 Magali della Sudda, "La Suppression de l'hebdomadaire dominicain *Sept*. Immixtion du Vatican dans les affaires françaises (1936-1937)?" *Vingtième siècle. Revue d'histoire* 104 (2009): 29-44.

56 Yvon Tranvouez, *Catholiques et communistes. La crise du progressisme chrétien, 1950-1955* (Paris: Éditions du Cerf, 2000), 53.

temps présent ["the weekly for the present time"]. It took up its motto: "Neither of the right, nor of the left." The Éditions du Temps Présent were set up as an incorporated company, of which Ella Sauvageot was the largest shareholder. This company, which is still in existence, was to be the structure that enabled the foundation of many Christian Left publications after the Second World War.

Stanislas Fumet, a man close to Maritain who had not participated in the adventure of *Sept* and had, on several occasions, distanced himself from the conservative right, was appointed director; Joseph Folliet, who came from social Catholicism, was made editorial secretary. Ella Sauvageot, the weekly's administrator, kept a close eye on the editorial staff, since the editorial committee meetings were held every Thursday in her apartment, located a stone's throw from the weekly's headquarters. As her daughter writes, "far more than her fortune, it was her organizational skills, and perhaps also the strength of her convictions, that made her 'the Boss,'" a nickname that would remain hers until her death. Proclaiming itself "outside and above the parties," in addition to the collaboration of some great writers (François Mauriac, Jacques Maritain), the editorial staff of *Temps présent* reflected various tendencies: the first secretary of the editorial staff was Joseph Folliet, who came from social Catholicism; the second secretary of the editorial staff was Georges Hourdin, who came from *La Vie catholique*. "Though I was still clinging to the Christian Democrat current," Hourdin said, "I very soon discovered that the position of these new friends was stronger and juster than mine," and he moved to the left.[57] A weekly of the Catholic left, *Temps présent* nevertheless relied on the great encyclicals of Pius XI against Nazism and communism and wanted to be a newspaper of practicing Christians. As in the days of *Sept*, the meetings of the "Friends of Temps présent" in the provinces were always preceded by a "dialogue Mass."

The intransigent *Vérités* did not let up. In February 1939, the magazine launched an attack against *Temps présent*, devoting 24 pages of issue 60 to denouncing the weekly as the "glorious heir of *Sept*" (the formula is that of Bishop Dutoit of Arras). But this denunciation did not hit its mark: both *Temps présent* and *Vérités* ceased to appear in June 1940, following the entry of German troops into Paris.

---

57 Georges Hourdin, "De l'incarnation retrouvée à la lutte contre le fascisme," *Lettre* 231 (November 1977): 6-8, quoted in Y. Tranvouez, *Catholiques et communistes*, 61.

CHAPTER 2
The Crises of French Catholicism (1944-1958)

T HE CRISIS IN THE CHURCH DID NOT BEGIN WITH the Second Vatican Council. In France, it began at the Liberation [from German occupation], in an unprecedented historical context in which the end of the war marked in all areas (political, international, economic, cultural, including religious) the end of one world and the advent of another. "A transitional age," Cardinal Suhard, Archbishop of Paris, would soon say, in *Essor ou déclin de l'Église*. In this famous pastoral letter, which we will discuss again, he diagnosed the existence of a "crisis" of Catholicism in France, echoing the more general crisis. There is, he wrote, a "Church divided" between a "progressive mysticism" that pleads for "adaptation" and an "intransigence" that refuses "accommodations" and "compromises" and wants "an integral return to traditional forms."[1]

Historian Denis Pelletier, who also believes that "the crisis of contemporary French Catholicism began at the Liberation," considers that political and ideological causes partly explain this crisis. The bishops were taken to task by Christian militants and by certain priests over their majority support for the Vichy regime or over their wait-and-see attitude. From that time on, "between the Christian resistance fighters and the bishops, there was long-lasting and mutual resentment. This weighed on the crises that followed in the course of the next two decades."[2] The attitude of the French bishops during the Occupation was attacked by the victors. Later on, a persistent rumor would spread that the traditionalist current was one of the components of the Vichy regime: "A traditionalist Catholic right wing that had never accepted the Revolution and did not find itself in the Republic, believed that it had taken its revenge with Vichy and ultimately fell with it."[3] According to an analyst of contemporary integrism, the traditionalist current was "joined by a whole series of figures who had gone through

---

1 Cardinal Suhard, *Essor ou déclin de l'Église* (1st ed. in 1947; Perpignan: Artège, 2018), 32-35.
2 Denis Pelletier, *Les Catholiques en France de 1789 à nos jours* (Paris: Albin Michel, 2019), 206.
3 Cédric Perrin, "Pierre Loyer, itinéraire d'un technocrate réactionnaire de Vichy," *Revue historique* (2017): 73-92.

Pétainism"[4] and remains, to this day, among the defenders of Marshal Petain and the Vichy French State.

Before examining the relevance of these assertions – one might just as easily say that the traditionalist current was "joined by a whole series of figures who had gone through the Resistance" – one must briefly recall the place and role of the Catholic Church during these dramatic years.

During the Second World War and the Occupation, Catholics, like the rest of society, were deeply divided. The vast majority of the episcopate practiced what has been called "loyalty without subservience [*loyauté sans inféodation*]." Its leaders were happy to obtain financial support for Catholic education and the return of religious instruction in schools from the new regime – but this was not sustainable. They were also in agreement with the motto of the French state, *Travail – Famille – Patrie* ("Work – Family – Country"). They welcomed the new economic and social policy represented by the Charter of Labor and the revival of corporatism. But several bishops – Cardinal Suhard as spokesman for the cardinals and archbishops in July 1942, Cardinal Saliège in Toulouse, and others – were aware enough to protest against the round-up and the deportation of Jews.[5] The "loyalty" of many bishops prevented them from explicitly supporting armed resistance, which some equated with terrorism, while a certain number of Catholics and some priests joined the Resistance, created networks and clandestine newspapers, or joined de Gaulle in London or the maquis.

These divergent choices were, all in all, in keeping with those of the entire population. At the time of the Liberation, Pétainist bishops, clergy, and laity, whether mere Pétain supporters or actual collaborators with the Germans, were all considered by the new authorities, but also by Resistance Catholics, if not as guilty, then at least as having made the wrong choice. The severest indictment was written in 1944 under the title "The Matter of the Bishops under the Occupation." The document – seventeen typed pages long – was discreetly distributed in 1944 and 1945, in several copies. It blamed the bishops of France for their lack of courage during the Occupation and for having failed to enlighten "the conscience of Catholics." Without accusing them all – there were "many exceptions" – the text attacked the "Petainolatry" of many bishops and reckoned, in a more general judgment, that "the entire episcopal body suffers today from a serious deficiency from the point of view of doctrine." This very severe memorandum against the French

4 Nicolas Senèze, *La Crise intégriste* (Paris: Bayard, 2008), 57.
5 Jean-Louis Clément, *Les Évêques au temps de Vichy. Loyalisme sans inféodation* (Paris: Beauchesne, 1999) and Michèle Cointet, *L'Église sous Vichy, 1940-1945* (Paris: Perrin, 1998).

episcopate reached the Provisional Government, and was handed to Jacques Maritain in December 1944, before his departure for Rome as French ambassador to the Holy See. The document, which was discovered in the Maritain archives, was not published until 1992, and it was attributed to Father Henri de Lubac, a Jesuit and professor at the Faculty of Theology in Lyon, one of the few theologians who had been active during the Occupation in denouncing the anti-Jewish policy being applied in France.[6] A controversy arose not over the authenticity of the document, but over its attribution to Father de Lubac. The historian Émile Poulat, through internal criticism, considered that "Father de Lubac is not the author of this 'text,'" while André Mandouze, who was Father Chaillet's collaborator at *Témoignage chrétien* in 1944 and 1945, considered that "this text is a mixture of Chaillet and de Lubac."[7] Henri de Lubac, for his part, when presented with this document in 1988, declared to those close to him that he "did not recognize himself in this text"[8] and refused to allow it to be included in his *Complete Works*.

Whatever the authorship of this text, it was representative of the questioning of the attitude of the French bishops under the Occupation on the part of some Catholics and the new political authorities. When the authorities of Free France were based in Algiers in 1943, they had already drawn up an initial list of bishops and clergymen accused of having been too complacent towards the Vichy regime or the occupants: their resignation had to be obtained. Other lists were drawn up later, based on information provided by leaders of Catholic resistance movements. In all, the names of three cardinals (Suhard, Gerlier and Liénart) and some thirty archbishops and bishops appeared at one time or another on these lists. At the Liberation, the new nuncio in Paris, Archbishop Roncalli (the future John XXIII) and the Holy See negotiated with the Provisional Government, and succeeded in limiting to seven the number of bishops forced to abandon their functions.[9]

The clergy was also a victim of the post-liberation purge, although no precise national assessment has yet been established. The situation was very different from one diocese to the next. In the diocese of Luçon, in the Vendée, where a large part of the clergy, like its bishop, Mgr Cazaux, had been pro-Pétain but hostile to the Germans, "there

---

6 Henri de Lubac, "La Question des évêques durant l'Occupation," *Revue des Deux Mondes* (February 1992): 67-82.

7 Interviews with Émile Poulat and André Mandouze, *Golias* 29 (Spring 1992): 138.

8 Émile Poulat, *Aux carrefours stratégiques de l'Église de France. XXe siècle*, 122.

9 André Latreille, *De Gaulle, la Libération et l'Église catholique* (Paris: Cerf, 1978) and Yves Chiron, *Jean XXIII* (Paris: Tallandier, 2017), 194-97.

was no purge of the clergy,"[10] and two priests were called to be part of the Departmental Liberation Committee. On the other hand, in the diocese of Annecy, five priests were assassinated by the Resistance, before or after the liberation of the territory, and several others were forced to leave their parishes and go into hiding; most of them were accused of having supported the paramilitary Militia.[11]

During the Second World War, the clergy (bishops and priests) were not unanimously Pétainists, Resistance fighters, or collaborators. There were very different positions, and if there was a majority attitude, it was loyalty to the established authorities and a wait-and-see stance.

THE FUTURE "TRADITIONALISTS" UNDER THE OCCUPATION

When considering the personalities who would go on to become the leading figures of traditionalism, one finds very different situations and commitments during the same period.

The future Archbishop Lefebvre, who was thirty-five years old in 1940, was a missionary in Gabon. He was mobilized for some time and sent to Oubangui-Chari, where he did not have to fight. After Gabon joined Free France, the missionaries did not get involved in politics. Father Lefebvre maintained "the best relations" with the famous Doctor Schweitzer, a Protestant. In France, his father, a genuine Resistance fighter, was arrested by the Gestapo in April 1941, sentenced to death in Berlin, and ultimately sent to the Sonnenburg concentration camp, where he died in February 1944.[12]

Jean Arfel, who later used the pseudonym Jean Madiran and was the founder of the review *Itinéraires* and the co-founder of the daily newspaper *Présent*, was then a student in Bordeaux, and was beginning to work in journalism. He contributed to the Bordeaux Catholic daily *La Liberté du Sud-Ouest* and to *La Nouvelle Guyenne*, the periodical of Action française in the Gironde *département*.[13] In November 1940, with Jean-Maurice Bugat, Jacques Bentegeat, who had just defended his dissertation in medicine, and the future historian Henri Amouroux, who was a journalist in training at *La Petite Gironde*, he was one of

---

10 Daniel Billaud, "Église et société en Vendée sous l'Occupation," Master's Thesis (University of Rennes II, 2010): 74-75.

11 Esther Deloche, "Le Diocèse d'Annecy de la séparation à Vatican II (1905-1962)," PhD dissertation (University of Lyon II, 2009): 486-87.

12 Tissier de Mallerais, *Marcel Lefebvre*, 130.

13 Some of his polemical articles from this time would be taken to task for antisemitism by Jean-Marie Domenach in *Esprit* (1956), and then by Olivier Biffaud in *Le Monde* (1990). Jean Madiran issued a response to the latter in *"Le Monde" et ses faux* (Paris: Difralivre, 1997), 98-103.

the founders of the Légion d'Aquitaine-Jeunesse de France, a Pétainist organization.[14] The German Kommandantur of Bordeaux did not give its approval to the organization, which had to cease its activities in April 1942, and joined the national movement *Les Amis du Maréchal*.[15] Arfel was later awarded the Francisque [a Vichy-France medal]. In July 1941, he was one of the founders of *France: Revue littéraire et artistique*. From 1942, he also collaborated with the daily *L'Action française*, which had retreated to Lyon, and in 1943, in Pau, he met Charles Maurras, who would soon say that he saw in him one of the possible continuators of his work.[16] At the beginning of the school year in 1944, he joined the *École des Roches* as a philosophy teacher, in Maslacq, in Béarn. Its director was André Charlier, who had a decisive influence on him.

Gérard Calvet was a student at this school since 1940, where he had Jean Arfel as a philosophy teacher.[17] His older brother, Jean, suspected of wanting to carry out clandestine activities, was arrested by the Germans and spent a month in prison, while their father, a wine merchant in Bordeaux, a convinced Pétainist, refused any economic collaboration with the occupying forces. Gérard Calvet later joined the Benedictine Order, and then in 1970 founded a priory in Bédoin to maintain the observances of religious life and the traditional liturgy.

Father Georges Lapouge, born in 1914, had had to interrupt his studies at the Saint-Joseph des Carmes seminary in Paris because of the war. He joined the Resistance, became head of mission, and created an intelligence network of over five hundred agents. Twice a prisoner, twice an escapee, he was made an officer of the Legion of Honor, decorated with the Croix de Guerre, and awarded the Resistance medal. Ordained a priest in 1947, he acted as an intermediary in the post-war period between theologians known to be integrists and theologians known to be progressives. After the liturgical reform of 1969, he obeyed the official directives and celebrated according to the new rite, but, discreetly, he also continued to celebrate according to the traditional rite when he could.

Father Ducaud-Bourget, vicar at Saint-Louis-d'Antin during the war, was active in the Parisian Resistance as early as October 1940, and was a member of the Lapouge network, for which he was awarded

---

14 Interview with Jean Madiran, April 15, 2009.
15 Thanks are due to historian Michel Bergès, who provided this information on April 4, 2021.
16 Charles Maurras to Maurice Pujo, unpublished letter, July 2, 1943, Pierre Pujo archives.
17 See Yves Chiron, *Dom Gérard. Tourné vers le Seigneur* (Le Barroux: Éditions Sainte-Madeleine, 2018).

the Resistance medal and the Croix de Guerre.[18] In 1977, he was one of the organizers of the occupation of the church of Saint-Nicolas-du-Chardonnet to restore the traditional liturgy.

The future Mother Marie-Dominique, later one of the co-founders of the Dominican Sisters of the Holy Spirit with Father Berto, became involved in the resistance network *Confrérie Notre-Dame*, founded by her brother Gilbert Renault (alias Colonel Rémy). Arrested by the Gestapo in 1942, she remained in prison until 1944.

A young Michel de Saint-Pierre also joined the Resistance in Normandy, and created an intelligence network.[19] He was awarded the Croix de Guerre, the Resistance medal with rosette, the Volunteer Fighter's Cross, and the Military Medal. He was to become a great novelist and in 1975 founded the traditionalist movement *Credo*.

Louis Salleron, who had no qualms in calling himself an integrist in the positive sense of the term (one who keeps the faith in its integrity), had been a professor of political economy at the Catholic Institute of Paris since 1937. He also collaborated in various agricultural unionist associations. Under the French State, he was the theorist of agricultural corporatism and the principal writer of the law of December 2, 1940 that created the Peasants' Corporation, all the while collaborating with the Catholic weekly *Demain*. This weekly appeared in Lyon from July 1942, directed by Jean de Fabrègues, one of the figures of what was called before the war the Young Catholic Right – hostile both to parliamentary democracy and to totalitarian regimes, in favor of a new Christian and social order. *Demain* sought to bring together "rebuilders of the City," to lead "a spiritual revolution," to be "a journal of doctrine, a sower of ideas, and a defender of the values of Christianity that have made France great." It answered to the desire, often expressed since the defeat, to see the union of Catholics and French people realized.[20] Jean de Fabrègues, director of the weekly, succeeded in bringing together in the editorial staff Catholics of various sensibilities: Maurrassian Catholics, such as Robert Havard de La Montagne, as well as Christians from the *Esprit* movement (Jacques Madaule, François Perroux) and traditional Catholics such as Jean Le Cour Grandmaison, Marcel De Corte, and Jean Daujat, the founder, before the war, of the *Centre d'études religieuses*, which was committed to providing lay people with a philosophical and theological

18 Yvonne Desmurs-Moscet, *Monseigneur Ducaud-Bourget. Le Squatteur de Dieu* (Paris: Nouvelles Éditions latines, 1990), 76-77.
19 Sixte de Guitaut, "La Résistance," in *Michel de Saint-Pierre. Témoin de son temps* (Luneray: Éditions Bertout, 1997), 38-40.
20 Véronique Auzépy-Chavagnac, *Jean de Fabrègues et la Jeune Droite catholique* (Villeneuve-d'Ascq: Presses Universitaires du Septentrion, 2020).

education that was faithful to the Church, and the philosopher Gustave Thibon, who contributed to numerous reviews and was then publishing his first books, *Diagnostics* and *Destin de l'homme*. After the occupation of the free zone, in November 1942, when the main Catholic newspaper, *La Croix*, chose to cease publication, Jean de Fabrègues continued to publish *Demain* at the request of Cardinal Gerlier, Archbishop of Lyon, and of Mgr Chollet, Archbishop of Cambrai, who had taken refuge near Lyon. The Catholic weekly appeared until the Liberation, having been loyal to Marshal Pétain and at the same time critical of the regime, to the extent that censorship allowed. After the war, Jean de Fabrègues pursued a career in the press, notably as director of *France catholique*.

Jean Ousset, another future figure of traditionalism, was mobilized as a non-commissioned infantry officer in 1939, and was awarded the Croix de Guerre. He was taken prisoner and was interned in a stalag in Germany. When he returned to France, he became the director of *Jeune Légion*, a youth movement of the French Legion of Combatants and Volunteers of the National Revolution ["Légion française des combattants et des volontaires de la Révolution nationale," a Pétainist movement – *Translator*], at the end of 1942. He was the principal editor of the movement's magazine, *Jeune Légion*, which became *Bastions* in 1943, a publication that was more doctrinal than political. After the war, he and Jean Masson founded *La Cité catholique*, the principal traditional Catholic movement before the Council.[21]

These few examples show that the traditionalist-Maurassian-Pétainist equivalence is not valid for all the personalities of traditionalism. In no case did their traditionalism, or their traditional Catholicism, originate in a political commitment. Their reaction was primarily religious, in the face of successive crises in the Church.

THE "EFFERVESCENCE" OF FRENCH CATHOLICISM

As soon as the country was liberated, French Catholicism entered into "effervescence." It was Cardinal Gerlier, Archbishop of Lyon, who used the word a few years later, describing "a kind of intellectual effervescence" which, "for some time now, has been troubling some souls" and "certain audacities of thought [that] were flying thick and fast."[22] This "effervescence" manifested itself in various fields at the Liberation, but there had already been warning signs during the Occupation.

In theology, there was the rediscovery of patristics, with the

---

21 *Permanences* 312-13 (June-July 1994), special issue devoted to Jean Ousset.
22 *Note* published in *La Semaine religieuse de Lyon*, quoted in *La Croix* (September 10-11, 1950).

foundation of the "Sources chrétiennes" collection at the Éditions du Cerf in late 1942. The aim was to present readers with critical editions of the Greek and Latin Fathers of the Church and first-time translations into French. The Jesuits of Lyon-Fourvière (Fontoynont, de Lubac, and Mondésert) initiated it, along with Father Daniélou, a Jesuit from Paris. They also founded the collection "Theologie," published by Aubier, which broke with Thomistic demonstrations; this current would be called *la nouvelle théologie* ("new theology"). We shall meet it again later on. A third collection, "Unam Sanctam," launched before the war by the Dominican Yves Congar, was also to undergo great development, proposing a renewed ecclesiology and new ecumenical perspectives.

The effervescence was not limited to theology; it was also liturgical. The Liturgical Movement, born in 1909 in Belgian and German Benedictine abbeys, had spread to France in the 1920s and 1930s. At the same time, certain liturgical innovations began to spread. The practice of the "dialogue Mass" was approved under specific circumstances by the Congregation for Rites in 1935: when the priest celebrated a low Mass, the faithful might say the servers' responses as well as the *Gloria, Credo, Sanctus*, and *Agnus Dei*. Other innovations spread at the end of the 1930s and during the war. At the *Cité des Jeunes*, a large sponsorship center he had founded in Jouy-en-Morin for children and adolescents from Parisian parishes, the Marist Father Fillère instituted "living" Masses: the priest celebrated facing the congregation arranged in a semicircle, the hymns were in French, and the kiss of peace was exchanged among the participants.[23] What were then called "paraliturgies," that is, services outside of Mass, also multiplied. In the parish of Sacré-Coeur in Colombes, Father Michonneau had, since the early 1940s, been organizing "missionary and popular celebrations." A specialist in liturgy, Fr Martimort, described them at the time:

> There are spoken choirs, sketches, songs, acclamations, processions . . . an unusual spectacle, before which even the most biased person cannot avoid a deep emotion.[24]

Among other initiatives, one might also cite the offertory rite that Bishop Chevrot introduced into the Mass, between the Creed and the Preface, in his parish of Saint-François-Xavier in Paris.[25]

---

23 Based on participants' recollections quoted in Yves Chiron, *Le Père Fillère ou la passion de l'Unité* (Paris: Éditions de L'Homme nouveau, 2011), 72-74.

24 Aimé-Georges Martimort, "Une expérience des paraliturgies: 'Fêtes missionnaires et populaires' du Sacré-Cœur de Coulombes," *La Maison-Dieu* 3 (1945): 164.

25 Father Bugnini, who had attended one of these Masses in 1946, drew his inspiration from it in his reform of the Offertory after Vatican II. Annibale Bugnini, "La comunità e il rinnovamento liturgico attuale," *Annali della Missione* 69.6 (1962): 351.

In addition to these innovations and experiments in France, there were those of the four thousand or so priests, religious, and seminarians who were prisoners or deportees to Germany. In the camps, where religious celebrations were never forbidden, various "pastoral liturgical experiments," as one stalag chaplain put it, were put into practice and lived.[26] They transgressed certain liturgical norms in force at the time, and introduced new practices. When they returned from the camps, these thousands of priests, religious, and seminarians did not forget what they had experienced and practiced, and some of them wanted to introduce these new practices in their parishes or convents.

It was both to disseminate the research and work of the Liturgical Movement and to encourage, accompany, but also supervise the experiments that were multiplying in France that Dominican Fathers Pie Duployé and Aymon-Marie Roguet founded in turn the *Centre de pastorale liturgique* (CPL) in 1943, the collection "Lex orandi" at the Éditions du Cerf in 1944, and the review *La Maison-Dieu* in 1945. The CPL, through its sessions, conferences, and publications, carried out "activities of research, information, experience, and liturgical propaganda," to use the formula of Father Dubarle, then director of *Éditions du Cerf*. It was a "great laboratory of new ideas."[27] The CPL encouraged, guided, and inspired the liturgical innovations and experiments that multiplied in certain parishes and communities up until the Council, all the while trying to temper the impatience and imprudence of the most daring.

Finally, in the pastoral field, initiatives born during the war were to undergo a significant expansion. On July 24, 1941, on the initiative of Cardinal Suhard, Archbishop of Paris, the twenty-sixth Assembly of the Cardinals and Archbishops of France decided to found the *Mission de France* to train priests who would devote themselves to the evangelization of the dioceses of France that were poor in priestly vocations. The seminary of the *Mission de France* opened in Lisieux the following year, with Father Augros as its superior. Another initiative that had unexpected consequences was the following: in December 1941, with the agreement of his superiors, the Dominican Jacques Loew signed up as a docker in the port of Marseille. He recounted his experience in a book that was to meet with great success: *En mission prolétarienne*. In 1943, Fathers Henri Godin and Yvan Daniel, chaplains of the JOC (*Jeunesse Ouvrière Chrétienne,* "Young Christian Workers"), published *La France, pays de*

---

26 P. P., "Les Leçons d'un Stalag," *La Maison-Dieu* 1 (January 1945): 64-73. See also, among other sources, Anon., "Organisation de la vie religieuse dans un Oflag," *La Vie spirituelle* 68 (1942): 301-9.

27 See *Deux anniversaires: 1943-1963*, special issue of *La Maison-Dieu* 275 (2013): 27-28, 38.

mission? ("France, A Mission Territory?"). They felt that in the face of growing de-Christianization, especially in working-class areas, the traditional parish and specialized Catholic Action movements were not enough. A specialized clergy needed to be formed. The same year, Cardinal Suhard founded the Paris Mission, which was made up of priests who devoted themselves exclusively to an apostolate among working class communities whose lives they shared. The first worker priest, Christian du Mont, was hired at the Panhard motor factories in 1944.

In parallel to this innovative or progressive effervescence, a fair look at this period must also point to more traditional spiritual initiatives that had great popular success. First of all, there was the "Great Return" of Notre-Dame de Boulogne throughout France, begun in 1943 and continued until 1948, a manifestation of piety and penance that attracted crowds of faithful throughout the country.[28] There was also the consecration of France to the Sacred Heart, which took place in June 1945 at the Basilica of Montmartre, organized by the Apostleship of Prayer, a movement founded by a Jesuit in the previous century. The initiative – a national consecration by fathers from all the dioceses of the country – was born during the war, and could not take place until after the liberation of the country. Almost all the French bishops had taken up the initiative, and many of them had published pastoral letters on the subject. Many parish priests encouraged the faithful to perform this consecration in their homes if they were unable to go to Montmartre. The ceremony was finally set for June 17, 1945, the anniversary of the apparition of Jesus to St. Margaret Mary on June 17, 1689. Some 250 fathers had been officially delegated by their dioceses (two or three per diocese) and officially mandated by their bishops. The ceremony was presided over by the Apostolic Nuncio, Archbishop Roncalli, in the presence of Cardinals Suhard, Liénart, and Gerlier, and many archbishops and bishops of France. Pius XII delivered a radio message. Some 120,000 to 150,000 of the faithful were present at this "Consecration of France to the Sacred Heart by the French Family," a penitential act for France's past faults and an act of commitment to establish a "new order" based on the law of God.[29]

---

28 Louis Pérouas, "Le grand retour de Notre-Dame de Boulogne à travers la France (1943-1949). Essai de reconstitution," *Annales de Bretagne et des Pays de l'Ouest* 2 (1983): 171-83; and Pérouas, "Le grand retour de Notre-Dame de Boulogne à travers la France (1943-1949). Essai d'interprétation," *Archives des sciences sociales des religions* 56 (July-September 1983): 37-57.

29 The report of this ceremony and of the three-day congress leading up to it was published under the title *Le Sacré-Cœur de Jésus et la doctrine du Corps Mystique* (Toulouse: Apostolat de la Prière, August 1946).

The foundation of the Knights of Our Lady [*Chevaliers de Notre-Dame*] two months later was more discreet. This *Militia Sanctae Mariae* was founded on August 6, 1945 by a young man just under twenty years of age, Gérard Lafond, under the patronage of Dom Gabriel Gontard, the Abbot of the Benedictine monastery of Saint-Wandrille. The aims of this organization were to serve the faith, defend the Church, and promote Christianity and peace. It was a lay fraternity, governed by a rule, whose members went through a ceremony of dubbing to knighthood in the chivalric tradition and made three vows (private, since they were not religious): to live in all circumstances according to the laws of chivalry and the rule of the order; fidelity to the Militia and fraternal mutual aid towards all its members; to love and make others love the Church, her teaching, her discipline, and her hierarchy. On October 26, 1947, the feast of Christ the King, Gérard Lafond and three of his friends were knighted by Dom Gontard, and took their vows. Gérard Lafond entered Saint-Wandrille Abbey the following year, and was ordained a priest in 1955. Jehan de Penfentenyo succeeded him as Grand Master of the *Militia Sanctae Mariae*, which had several hundred members. But Dom Lafond remained until his death the leader of this organization which, through various satellite associations, played a discreet but important role at various times in the history of traditionalism.

A PROGRESSIVE PRESS

As soon as France was liberated, a Catholic press whose origins were in the Resistance flourished, accompanied innovative pastoral initiatives, and engaged in a more or less radical progressivism, depending on the publication. Many of these publications were heirs to pre-war publications or to those born in the Resistance. Ella Sauvageot, whom we have already met, played a central role in this press.

On August 26, 1944, the day after Paris was liberated, Georges Hourdin and Ella Sauvageot brought back the weekly *Temps présent*. Stanislas Fumet, who had been its editor before the war, returned to his position. Hubert Beuve-Méry, who, before the war, had published a few articles in *Temps présent*, and who had contributed to the daily *Le Temps*, became editor-in-chief. The weekly brought together various political tendencies: Stanislas Fumet was an enthusiastic Gaullist; Hubert Beuve-Méry had been one of the leaders of the *École des cadres d'Uriage* [a school intended to produce technocratic elites – *Translator*] before joining the Resistance; Georges Hourdin came from Christian Democracy and was to become a member of the MRP (*Mouvement républicain populaire). Temps présent* was not intended to be a Catholic newspaper. It rather saw itself as a newspaper produced by Catholics, to which certain politically committed theologians would contribute, notably Father Chenu, who, starting in the third issue, pleaded for "the necessary revolution": one that would put labor above capital.

The Tuesday luncheons at the "Petit Riche," a high-end restaurant on the boulevards of Paris near the *Temps présent* printing presses, date from this period. Every week the principal people in charge of the paper would gather around the "Boss," Ella Sauvageot: Georges Hourdin, Stanislas Fumet, Hubert Beuve-Méry, and also Father Boisselot, who had no function at the weekly, but was one of its inspirations and gave it a sort of moral endorsement. Often, other religious and journalistic personalities were invited to these luncheons at the "Petit Riche." They outlived *Temps présent* and continued for decades. They soon became famous thanks to a book by Jean Madiran, as we shall see.

Late in 1944, Hubert Beuve-Méry, at the request of General de Gaulle, founded a newspaper, *Le Monde*, all the while continuing to contribute to *Temps présent* with a foreign policy editorial that he published under the alias "Sirius."[30] The new daily was intended to take over from *Le Temps*, which before the war had been considered the newspaper of record. It began publication on December 18, 1944. Ella Sauvageot remained very close to Hubert Beuve-Méry, whom she considered her best friend, and he remained closely involved in the adventures of post-war Christian progressivism.

Soon Ella Sauvageot and Georges Hourdin founded a new weekly, *La Vie catholique illustrée*; it succeeded the pre-war *La Vie catholique*, but in a very different format and spirit. It began publication on July 8, 1945, under the direction of Georges Hourdin and Joseph Folliet, with Ella Sauvageot as administrator. These three personalities had quite different opinions: while Ella Sauvageot frequently blamed Georges Hourdin for being too moderate, the Lyonnais Joseph Folliet, who was secretary general of the *Semaines Sociales de France* and directed *La Chronique Sociale* in Lyon, once waxed ironical, though without naming her, about Madame Sauvageot's "bourgeois progressivism." The Dominicans Boisselot and Gourbillon, who were members of the editorial board, had a great influence on the weekly, though they did not direct it. Geneviève Laplagne, who was a collaborator of Georges Hourdin's from 1945, described the originality of the new weekly:

---

30 Laurent Greilsamer, *Hubert Beuve-Méry (1902-1989)* (Paris: Fayard, 1990).

> While the main concern of *La Vie catholique illustrée* was to see the Church transformed and incarnated in the modern world, it was at the same time a general-interest magazine.[31]

It was the first rotogravure magazine in France. From the very first issues, the photographs took up as much space as the text. It featured an advice column to mothers, "without moralizing" (Georges Hourdin), a page of games, and a letters to the editor section. Sold by subscription and in front of churches after Mass on Sundays, *La Vie catholique* was a considerable success: 100,000 copies in 1945, 500,000 in 1955, 600,000 in 1958. In this respect, it changed the mentality of hundreds of thousands of Catholics. Georges Hourdin said: "This trimmed-down faith, this insertion of Christians into the modern world as it was, prefigured the decisions of the Second Vatican Council; we were laying the groundwork for it in a completely disinterested way, since we did not even imagine that it could ever take place."[32]

Another Catholic weekly, *Témoignage chrétien*, which came from a clandestine Resistance publication, experienced a crisis in 1945. It was a manifestation of "communist temptations," to use the formula of its founder and director, Father Chaillet, a Jesuit; these temptations ran through several sectors of post-war Catholicism.[33] The editor-in-chief, André Mandouze, was in favor of "accepting the extended hand of the Communist Party," as were some other editors, such as the young Pierre Debray,[34] who would later become one of the most resolute opponents of progressivism in the Church. But Father Chaillet and other collaborators of *Témoignage chrétien* considered communism to be just as dangerous as Nazism. The first *Cahier Clandestin du Témoignage chrétien* had been (1941): *France, prends garde de perdre ton âme!* ["France! Take care not to lose your soul!"] by Jesuit Father Gaston Fessard. In it, he emphasized "the fundamentally anti-Christian character of the mysticism that inspires Nazism" and warned against "the underhanded methods of penetration and persecution employed by the Hitlerian spirit." In October 1945, the Éditions du Témoignage chrétien published another work by Father Gaston Fessard: *France, prends garde*

---

31 Geneviève Laplagne, *L'Histoire de* La Vie. *Un Journal et ses lecteurs* (Paris: Cerf, 1999), 32.

32 Georges Houdin, *Dieu en liberté* (Paris: Stock, 1973), 238-39.

33 This expression is Father Chaillet's in a letter to Father de Lubac, December 9, 1945, quoted in H. de Lubac, *At the Service of the Church. Henri de Lubac Reflects on the Circumstances That Occasioned His Writings*, trans. A. E. Englund (San Francisco: Ignatius Press, 1993), 276.

34 Pierre Debray would later publish *Un Catholique retour de l'URSS* (Paris: Éditions du Pavillon, 1950), an apologia for the USSR, where he had taken a trip.

de perdre ta liberté! ["France, take care not to lose your freedom!"]. In
it he defined communism as an "anti-Christian, anti-national, and anti-
human doctrine" and analyzed the "process of communist penetration:
1. seduce, 2. compromise, 3. pervert or destroy." He characterized the
Christian communist as one who allows himself to be seduced by the
"false historical dialectic" of the Marxists.

The work caused a great stir. It had been published by the *Éditions
du Témoignage chrétien* without the editor-in-chief, André Mandouze,
having been informed. He was furious that the name of the weekly
was associated with the work of "a knee-jerk anticommunist."[35] Jacqueline Sauvageot revealed in her mother's biography that Mandouze
succeeded in stopping the distribution of the book and even succeeded in having the remaining copies destroyed. The internal conflict
lasted for a few weeks until an editorial staff vote put Mandouze in
a minority; this precipitated his departure from the editorial staff. A
new, expanded edition of *France, prends garde de perdre ta liberté!* was
published sometime later, while Mandouze joined the editorial staff of
Temps présent. Ella Sauvageot tried to reconcile the three tendencies
that existed within the editorial staff: the Gaullism of Stanislas Fumet,
editorial staff director; the progressive communist tendency embodied
by Mandouze; the Christian Democrat tendency–not to mention the
politically indefinable Father Boisselot.

Elsewhere, other Dominicans also illustrated, to varying degrees,
Christian progressivism: the movement and the review *Économie et
Humanisme,* founded by Father Louis-Joseph Lebret; the group and
the review *Jeunesse de l'Église,* founded by Father Maurice Montuclard;
Masses ouvrières, the monthly review of the Workers' Mission, directed
by Father Albert Bouche. While aspiring to a renewal of the Church,
they proposed a radical critique of liberal society and developed a
communitarian utopia that in many ways was close to the communist
ideal.[36] For these three publications, political motivations remained
secondary to the missionary objective. They all shared "the same conviction that to give in to anti-communism would be to cut oneself off
from the working class, the masses, in a word the people."[37]

On the other hand, the *Union des Chrétiens progressistes* (UCP, "Union
of Progressive Christians"), created in 1947 by Marcel Moiroud and

---

35 Quoted in Cécile Hamsy, *Georges Montaron. Le roman d'une vie* (Paris: Ramsay,
1996), 69.
36 Denis Pelletier, "Utopie communautaire et sociabilités d'intellectuels en milieu
caholique dans les années 1940," *Les Cahiers de l'IHTP* 20 (March 1992): 172–87.
37 Y. Tranvouez, *Catholiques et communistes,* 155.

André Mandouze, had a political aim ("to prepare the way to a Patriotic Front" with the Communist Party) and a religious one (to transform the Church) in equal proportions. After initially recommending that its members join the Communist Party, the UCP's 1948 manifesto simply called for "unity of action among all progressives, the only ones capable of defeating imperialism." This earned the movement the approval of Emmanuel Mounier in *Esprit*: "It cannot be said that being Christian necessarily excludes any defined, lucid collaboration with the communists." He also felt that progressive Christians "may have a politically debatable position, but not a religiously debatable one."[38] The UCP and its bulletin, *Position*, remained the publication of a tiny minority and survived only on regular subsidies from Ella Sauvageot.[39]

LA CITÉ CATHOLIQUE (JULY 1946)

In the face of this progressivism, movements and publications were born that illustrated the permanence and vitality of an intransigent sort of Catholicism. They found some support in the episcopate and in Rome. It was also at this time that the terms "integrist" and "traditionalist" reemerged.

The *Cité catholique*, which was the principal lay organization of traditional Catholics until the mid-1960s, originated before the war. It was the fruit of a long intellectual and spiritual maturation that brought together two childhood friends: Jean Ousset and Jean Masson. They had met in middle school in the 1930s, at the Collège Saint Elme, run by the Dominicans in Arcachon. There they acquired "a passion for learning" and a taste for "beauty worth promoting." Afterwards, Jean Ousset studied in a disorganized manner, began training as a hatmaker, entered a painting and sculpture studio in Bordeaux, and then, during his military service, experienced a "period of absolute dereliction and confusion which led him to abandon all religious practice."[40] In 1935, on the advice of Jean Masson, who had remained a fervent Catholic, Jean Ousset visited Father Jean Choulot, the pastor of Montalzat, an eccentric and truculent personality of "strict orthodoxy." He listened

---

38 Quoted by Gaston Fessard, "Le christianisme des chrétiens progressistes," *Études* (January 1949): 65-93. This article was in pointed opposition to the positions of the UCP, André Mandouze, and Emmanuel Mounier.
39 J. Sauvageot, *Ella Sauvageot*, 180.
40 Raphaëlle de Neuville, *Jean Masson et la Cité catholique* (Poitiers: Dominique Martin Morin, 1998), 31. See also *Permanences* 312-13 (June-July-August 1994), special issue devoted to Jean Ousset after his death, and Cyril Duchâteau, *La Cité catholique et l'Office en France (1949-1982)*, Advanced Studies Diploma thesis in the history of religions (Paris IV-Sorbonne: June 1997).

to the young man, heard his confession, and opened up his library to him. "I left him some books," he later explained: "Pierre Lasserre, Blanc de Saint-Bonnet, *L'Homme, cet inconnu* by Alexis Carrel, *Les Trois Réformateurs* by Jacques Maritain, capital! And above all, Mgr Prunel: the five volumes of his *La Doctrine chrétienne*."[41] The young Jean Ousset discovered a solid presentation of the faith (Prunel), the apologetics of early Maritain against Luther, Descartes, and Rousseau, as well as counter-revolutionary thought. He and his friends, notably Jean Masson, met regularly with Father Choulot for discussions and debates. The "Montalzat group" remained informal for several years, and very diverse in its composition. In 1939, Jean Ousset met Maurras, for whom he retained a great admiration, even if he was never a Maurrassian, deploring the insufficiency of the doctrinal training of the members of *Action française*. Jean Masson, for his part, was at that time a reader of *Temps présent*. On August 15, 1939, the members of the small group in Montalzat—about ten people—vowed, in front of the parish statue of the Virgin, to devote their lives to "serving France and the Church through a work of doctrinal formation and education for action aimed at effective political and social leaders." The war interrupted the project. We have seen above what Ousset's commitments were during this period.

After the war, Ousset met up with Jean Masson, who encouraged him to make a retreat with the *Coopérateurs paroissiaux du Christ-Roi* (CPCR, "Parish Cooperators of Christ the King"). This congregation had been founded by a Spanish former Jesuit, Father Vallet (1884-1947). It was dedicated exclusively to preaching retreats for men according to the Spiritual Exercises of St. Ignatius of Loyola, in light of the doctrine of Christ the King who must reign over souls, but also in society and over nations. The congregation was established in Chabeuil, in the Drôme *département*, with the agreement of the local ordinary, Bishop Pic. Between 1934 and 1945, 235 retreats were preached there, all to men (seven thousand retreatants in that time-frame). The first five-day retreat that Ousset attended enlightened him on the purpose of the work he had in mind: to work for the re-Christianization of France by training active Catholic leaders for the temporal domain. Thereafter, he made some twenty-five retreats with the "Fathers of Chabeuil,"

---

41 Father Choulot quoted by Pierre Marchand, "Les débuts de la Cité catholique," *Permanences* 347: 18. The work by Msgr Prunel, vice rector of the *Institute catholique de Paris*, had been published in 1919-1929 with the title *Cours supérieur de religion*, in five volumes. It underwent several editions. The first volume is called *Les Fondements de la Doctrine catholique*, hence Father Choulot's shortcut.

who also welcomed, until the 1960s, a great number of militants of *La Cité catholique.*

From its very beginnings, *La Cité catholique* was neither an apostolate nor a political party; rather it was a school to form the laity: "Our work seeks to place itself at the intersection of Catholic action and political action, and thereby more effectively to infuse the doctrine of the Church into the various social bodies of the City in order to restore it by making it Catholic again."[42] The intuition of Jean Ousset and Jean Masson was in line with the desires of the episcopate, which, in a solemn declaration in favor of "national reconciliation" (February 1945), had asked

> that, in an area distinct from the apostolic domain of Catholic Action, numerous lay Catholics acting as citizens should boldly take on their personal responsibilities in temporal action: that they be present to the modern world and that they should loyally seek the specific good of the City! Let all Catholics understand their obligations of social justice and social charity towards the common good, and let them be most ardent in developing in France a public spirit, a love of the national community, a concern to make the general interest prevail over private interests.[43]

The movement was officially born on July 29, 1946. On that day in Paris, Jean Ousset, Jean Masson, and one of their friends, Denis Demarque, a young doctor who would become a great specialist in homeopathy, founded the Center for Critical Studies and Synthesis (*Centre d'études critiques et de synthèse*, CECS) and from the outset placed it on a supernatural plane by dedicating it to the Sacred Heart of Jesus in the Basilica of Montmartre, and, on the same day, to the Virgin Mary and to St. Joseph in the chapel of the Miraculous Medal, in the rue du Bac. The going was hard at first. At the time, Jean Ousset lived in Salon-de-Provence with Jean Masson, who had taken over the family printing business. A modest bulletin was published, entitled *Verbe* ("Word") from the third issue on, with the subtitle "Organ of Civic Formation for the Counter-Revolution." Study groups began to form. Jean Ousset published two books under the pseudonym "Jean Marial": *Au commencement* ("In the Beginning," 1946), which was a "reminder of some principles and notions" of Christian philosophy, and *D'où vient la France?* ("Whence France?" 1947), a return to "our origins."

---

42 *Pour qu'il règne sur nous...* (Paris: La Cité catholique, 1957).
43 Declaration of the Assembly of Cardinals and Archbishops of France, February 28, 1945, published in *DC* (March 18, 1945): 227-28.

LA PENSÉE CATHOLIQUE (NOVEMBER 1946)

A few months after the birth of *Verbe*, which at the time was only a humble newsletter, another publication was born, *La Pensée catholique*, which was to defend the "integrity of the faith" for half a century. The four founders were Father Luc Lefèvre, professor of philosophy in Paris, who directed the journal until his death in 1987; Canon Lusseau, professor of Sacred Scripture at the Catholic University of Angers; Father Roul, chaplain of the high school in Nantes; and Father Berto, chaplain of an orphanage in Brittany, founder of a teaching and educational congregation, the Dominican Sisters of the Holy Ghost. All four of them had been students of the French Seminary in Rome in the 1920s and all had obtained one or more doctorates (philosophy, theology, canon law) in pontifical universities. It was at this time that they conceived the project of a journal on doctrine with another student of the French Seminary, Father Raymond Dulac. After the war, the project was finally realized following a request from the Holy See: "Rome desired that a review should be launched whose aim would be to defend and promote sound doctrines."[44] Archbishop Roncalli, nuncio in Paris, shared the Holy See's desire with Bishop Beaussart, one of the auxiliary bishops of Paris, who had become his confessor. He contacted various theologians.[45] The review was from then on "regularly subsidized by the Holy See," as the Fr Lefèvre himself admits.

This Thomistic and Roman review – *Cum Petro, in Christo* was the motto on the cover – wanted to defend and illustrate an "honest" [*intègre*, a cognate of "integrity" – *Translator*] Catholicism. The editorial committee claimed that the term was used to forestall the accusation of integrism:

> Otherwise, we might be given the epithet used in such circumstances to discourage temperaments that do not want to bend to universal conformism. "Integrity" we like. Excess alone repels us.[46]

Confronting a "new faith" and the "abdication of intelligence," the review chose the cedar as its symbol, and soon the Éditions du Cèdre were created. The editorial board explained in the first issue:

> Our Cedar – the evergreen tree, a biblical symbol of renewing youth – will be for us the image of the eternal Life of that divine Truth, whose virtue the centuries will never exhaust.

---

44 Martin LeCerf, "Notice biographique," in *Notre-Dame de Joie. Correspondance de l'abbé V. A. Berto, prêtre (1900-1968)* (Paris: Nouvelles Éditions latines, 1989), 31.
45 Martin LeCerf, "L'abbé Raymond Dulac," *La Pensée catholique* 228 (1987): 39; LeCerf, "Notice biographique," 41, and P. Airiau, *La Pensée catholique, 1946-1956*, 20-28.
46 "Présentation au lecteur," *La Pensée catholique* 1 (November 1946): 5.

The choice of this symbol might be understood as a reference to the early-twentieth-century *Sapinière*, whether it was intended to be provocative or a mere nod.

The review's subtitle, *Cahiers de synthèse doctrinale* ("Notes on Doctrinal Synthesis") indicated its broad ambition to tackle "all the problems which solicit the attention of Catholics": philosophy, theology, exegesis, morals, along with "the noble concern to hold high authentic Christian Humanism" in the field of literature, history, and art; with the will to keep to the hierarchy of the disciplines, according to which theology, "the summit of human knowledge," is the only science able to judge the achievements of the other sciences or disciplines. Its readership was to include not only priests, but also "religious and lay professors," "leaders and militants of Catholic Action Movements," and the educated faithful.

The bi-monthly review sought to work at an intellectual and doctrinal "recovery" in reaction to the prevailing "decomposition" in all fields, including theology. Three of the articles in the first issue reflect this struggle against the tide. Father Lefèvre, who had just published an essay entitled "Is the Existentialist a Philosopher? [*L'existentialiste est-il un philosophe?*]" entered into the fray with a long article, "Aspects of Existentialism [*Quelques aspects de l'existentialisme*]." He tried to show that the current of ideas then in vogue was neither "a wisdom, nor a philosophy," but a "new religion," marked by immanence and individualism. Canon Lusseau deconstructed a work by Teilhard de Chardin, *Quelques réflexions sur la conversion au monde*, dating to 1936, which had been barred from publication and was then circulating anonymously and clandestinely in typewritten form. Criticism of Teilhard de Chardin's theses was constant in this review: some forty articles between 1946 and 1982.

Father Berto, in an article entitled "The Church as Theologian [*L'Église théologienne*]," began a long study spreading over three further issues that was an indictment of what was beginning to be called the "new theology [*nouvelle théologie*]." A good number of the contributors advertised in the flagship issue did not end up publishing articles, for example Father Joseph de Tonquédec, an eminent Jesuit theologian, known for his criticism of Bergsonism and modernism, a specialist in mysticism and religious psychology, and an exorcist in the diocese of Paris from 1925 to 1962. It may have been his superiors who forbade him to contribute to this journal, which was reputed to be integrist.[47] Similarly, the

---

47 So hinted the philosopher Louis Jugnet in the tribute he gave him after his passing: "Traditionel et moderne: le R. P. J. de Tonquédec (1869-1962)," *La Pensée catholique* 84 (1963): 42.

announced collaboration of two monks from the abbey of La Pierre-qui-Vire, Dom Irénée Gros and Dom Thomas Dassange, did not materialize, although another young monk from the same abbey, Dom Claude Jean-Nesmy, did contribute to the review articles devoted to authors, before becoming the director of his monastery's review. The two monks of the Benedictine abbey of Solesmes who had been presented as contributors, Dom Paul Nau and Dom Georges Frénaud, ultimately published only two articles each; they were active in other publications, however.

On the other hand, Father Raymond Dulac, a fellow student of the four founders at the French Seminary in Rome who was closely involved in the project, did not contribute significantly; he did so in fits and starts and only from the fifteenth issue on. We owe him in particular a subtle "eulogy of integrism," which he defines as a "fulness," a "perfection," a "chastity of the intelligence."[48] As the years go by one detects a great number of contributions from lay authors, notably including: Louis Jugnet, a professor in classics preparing for the *Grandes Écoles* entrance examinations and at the Institute of Political Studies of Toulouse, who defined himself as a "realist philosopher," a "disciple of Aristotle and Saint Thomas," a "counter-revolutionary Catholic and of scholastic formation"; Jules Artur, retired naval officer, who published about sixty articles between 1950 and 1979; Jacques Vier, a professor of literature at the University of Rennes, who also contributed to the journal for decades with articles on literary history that were later published as a stand-alone volume.

L'HOMME NOUVEAU (DECEMBER 1946)

One month after the publication of *La Pensée catholique*, Father Marcellin Fillère, a Marist priest whom we have already encountered, and Father Richard began the publication of a bi-monthly publication, *L'Homme nouveau*, which still exists. Unlike *La Pensée catholique* – a journal of ideas – the bi-monthly was devoted principally to current affairs; its principle was recalled in each issue: "To defend the cause of God alone." These two priests, who had also been trained at the French Seminary and at pontifical universities in the early 1920s, had founded the *Pour l'Unité* movement in 1935 to fight against "invading paganism" and to "make the masses Christian again by remaking a Christian mass." Unlike Catholic Action and its specialized movements, the *Pour l'Unité* movement sought to be open to all social levels, and made use of political propaganda methods of the time (tracts, posters, debates,

---

48 Raymond Dulac, "Éloge de l'intégrisme," *La Pensée catholique* 21 (1952): 5-25.

meetings). *L'Homme nouveau* wanted to distinguish itself from the new postwar news weeklies (*La Vie catholique illustrée*, *Témoignage chrétien*). It reported on pontifical teachings, giving, in each issue, extracts from the speeches or messages of Pius XII. It was clearly "Roman" and faithful to the Magisterium. The journal also gave a lot of information about the Church in France and in the world. From the very first issue, under the title "Blood of Martyrs: Seed of Christians," the paper published a long article devoted to the "Red Terror in Yugoslavia" (after the condemnation of Cardinal Stepinac) as well as information on the persecution of the Church in Hungary, Poland, and Soviet-occupied Germany. *L'Homme nouveau* would always be attentive to providing information on the "Silent Church" [i.e., the Church behind the Iron Curtain – *Translator*]. The bi-monthly also devoted a lot of space to culture (books, films, theater, arts) and soon entrusted a liturgical column to Dom Jean-Marie Beaurin of the Benedictine abbey of Sainte-Marie de Paris.

In his consideration of Father Fillère's various enterprises (the *Cité des Jeunes*, the *Pour l'Unité* movement, *L'Homme nouveau*), Émile Poulat noted that he could not be called an integrist or a traditionalist, not to mention a modernist or a progressive. He remains "enigmatic in terms of the categories we are familiar with" and "in a sense unclassifiable, or rather he explodes [our categories] and brings out their limitations."[49] Father Fillère nevertheless has a place here, because his opponents sometimes called him an integrist. Archbishop Roncalli received him several times at the Nunciature and he more accurately associated him with integrism, while approving of his action. After a long conversation, he noted in his Diary: "He follows the system of the integralists to some extent. He may be a little excessive, but *in multis* he is quite right."[50]

Seven months into the publication of *L'Homme nouveau* a first assessment was made.[51] The bi-monthly, which prided itself on being "the only journal fighting for Catholicism today," had received encouragement from Bishop Chappoulie, director of the secretariat of the Episcopate ("The bishops are following your efforts with great interest"), and from Bishop Courbe, secretary general of Catholic Action and auxiliary bishop of Paris ("You have the wind in your sails. If you did not exist, you would have to be invented"). But *L'Homme nouveau* had also been attacked by *Témoignage chrétien*, which reproached it for its lack of charity and its systematic anti-communism, and by *Esprit*, Emmanuel Mounier's journal.

49 Émile Poulat, Preface to Y. Chiron, *Le Père Fillère*, 10.
50 Angelo Roncalli, *Journal de France*, vol. 1, *1945-1948* (Paris: Cerf, 2006), 175.
51 *Rapport sur L'Homme nouveau*, no date (June 1947), five type-written pages kept in the Archives of the Éditions de la Propagande pour l'Unité.

INTEGRISM: "AN OPTION TO BE EXCLUDED"

The long pastoral letter *Essor ou déclin de l'Église* that Cardinal
Suhard published on February 11, 1947 is a milestone in the history
of integrism and the history of progressivism, because it was the first
time that these two terms had appeared in an official Church document.
Its magisterial authority was minor, since it was only a pastoral letter
addressed to the priests and faithful of a diocese, and not a formal
canonical condemnation that could be imposed on all. But, in fact,
to this day, it is a reference point in all controversies about integrism.
The striking formulas throughout the document would have long and
successful careers. One of Cardinal Suhard's biographers notes:

> What is new is the tone; the style is modern, dense, energetic.
> Every word signifies. It is a far cry from the usual ecclesiastical
> language of most episcopal and pontifical texts.[52]

It is matter of common knowledge that Cardinal Suhard's private secretary, Father Bernard Lalande, took an important part in writing the
pastoral letters of the archbishop of Paris.

In these post-war years, the Cardinal wrote, the Church in France
was confronted with a "common civilization" that was being built
without her, and with a "planetary humanism for which we were
not prepared." It is going through "growing pains." Unbelievers are
convinced of the inexorable "decline" of the Church, and even reject
her: "To build the new world, modern man expects nothing from
the Church." Faced with this rejection, Catholics are divided into two
"essential attitudes."[53] Some, writes the Cardinal, advocate "Rupture":

> Against aggressively militant atheism they oppose a defensive
> dogmatism. . . . The Church [in this view] is not behind the times.
> It is man who is sinning and losing his reason.

They call for "an integral return to traditional forms" and refuse all
"accommodation." On the other hand, a "progressive mysticism" is developing: "innovators" and "partisans of adaptation . . . do not spare their
criticism of the Church and the hierarchy," and wish for a "reform" in
all areas. Cardinal Suhard noted the three principal areas in which this
desire for change was manifested: preaching and catechism ("they want
a concrete and adapted religious teaching to replace a preaching and catechesis that are too cut off from the Gospel"), theology (they expect "an
effort of synthesis and realism, putting the major dogmas of Christianity

---

52 Jean-Pierre Guérend, *Cardinal Emmanuel Suhard. Archevêque de Paris (1940-1949)*
(Paris: Cerf, 2011), 295.
53 É. Suhard, *Essor ou déclin de l'Église*, 8-10.

at the center and within the reach of the spirituality of this century"), and the liturgy ("they point out that worship and liturgy are often incomprehensible"). Cardinal Suhard dismissed both these attitudes, "outrageous conservatism and progressivism," and sought to respond to the anguish of some and the impatience of others by recalling the true nature of the Church. Without denying the existence of "de-Christianized masses" and of "anti-Christian elites" whose activities were becoming more and more widespread, he preferred to point out the signs of a "renewal" in various fields, of an "efflorescence of life in the Church of this time."

It is the third part of the pastoral letter that has attracted the most attention. Examining "the conditions for growth" of the Church, Cardinal Suhard began by pointing out "two options to be excluded": modernism and integrism. The use of the word "option," which will be recurrent in the Church in France, seemed to imply a choice, but the cardinal specified that they are "contradictory solutions" which both constitute a "set of errors." The pages he devoted to them thus appeared to be condemnations. But the double condemnation was disproportionate: less than two pages were devoted to modernism, five and a half to integrism. One might think that this difference in treatment was because modernism had already been defined and condemned in the past by the Magisterium, while integrism had never been defined or condemned until then. Cardinal Suhard did not recall past condemnations of modernism, not even in a note, but simply referred to it as "Naturalism" and "outrageous Progressivism."

The long pages on integrism, however, were not a formal condemnation; they amounted to a series of warnings and criticisms against an "error of perspective." The cardinal denounced in turn "doctrinal integrism," "tactical integrism," and "moral integrism." No names or publications were mentioned, but the targets were clear. Concerning doctrinal integrism, the cardinal, while reaffirming that Thomism is the "official teaching" of the Church, ironically asked: "Should we conclude that St. Thomas has said everything and that his thought has exhausted and equaled the deposit of revelation? Should we, after him, give up thinking?" He was aiming, without naming them, both at certain Dominican theologians and at *La Pensée catholique*, who were warring against the "new theology" of the Jesuits at Fourvière. The denunciation of "tactical integrism" seemed to be aimed principally at Father Fillère's *Pour l'Unité* movement. When the cardinal affirmed that "the Church is not a party, and Christians are not partisans. She will not win the world by opposing it, as bloc vs. bloc" and when he denounced "the processes of enlistment and psychological 'shock' borrowed from the support of the 'secular arm' or from merely human propaganda," he is explicitly referring to the themes of Father Fillère and his methods of apostolate (to remake a "Christian mass," to implement a "Propaganda for Unity," etc.).

Finally, Cardinal Suhard warned against "moral integrism." This, he wrote, was that of Christians "whom one might – depending on whether they emphasize the uselessness of the world or its harmfulness – call Quietists and Jansenists." The term was rather clumsy if one considers that in both cases these were historical spiritual currents that had no descendants in this post-war period. On the other hand, the other name that the cardinal gave them, "Christians of the Apocalypse and Parousia," better designates an eschatological fundamentalist current that has always been present in the Church since the French Revolution and to which Paul Airiau gave the following good summary:

> He awaits and hopes for the Parousia in the face of tribulations, and he interprets history spiritually as the struggle between God and Satan. The world has an ambiguous status: given over to sin and Satan, it symbolizes everything that is opposed to God, while at the same time it is the object of God's love, Who hands over his Son for it.[54]

The apocalyptic current within traditionalism is based on the prophecies of certain mystics, private revelations, and Marian apparitions. In the immediate post-war period, this current was illustrated in particular by *La Mission divine de la France* by the Marquis de La Franquerie (a disputed title claimed by André Lesage), a work published in 1926 and regularly republished thereafter; *Malédictions et bénédictions*, published in 1947 by J. Gonthier (a pseudonym for Jean Vaquié, who had an abundant output from the 1970s on). One might see a link here, without making it his unique characteristic, to Father Fillère, who frequently referred to the Parousia but based himself only on the Holy Scriptures.

In general, in the pastoral letter of the Archbishop of Paris, integrism was described as "excessive traditionalism." Does this mean that there is a traditionalism that is not "excessive" and therefore acceptable? In any case, Cardinal Suhard evoked Tradition several times, multiplying distinctions:

> Tradition is quite different from the mechanical transmission of an inert "thing." It is the living communication and progressive manifestation – under the infallible control of the Magisterium – of a global truth of which each age discovers a new aspect.

---

54 Paul Airiau, *L'Église et l'Apocalypse, du XIXe siècle à nos jours* (Paris: Berg International, 2000), 86.

He also wrote a more nuanced sentence:

> Is one to identify Tradition, which is life, with routine, which is death? The "Law," which is "completed," with its applications, which are not? To safeguard life, Modernism sacrificed forms; to safeguard forms, Integrism sacrificed life.

The definitions of integrism and "excessive traditionalism" given by Cardinal Suhard in 1947 had a considerable impact. Father Jean Daniélou, a Jesuit in sympathy with the "new theology" of Fourvière at the time and who would later be made a cardinal himself, immediately agreed with the cardinal:

> While modernism consists in abandoning the essential deposit of the Church along with certain outdated structures, integrism is the opposite error that seeks to maintain at all costs obsolete forms along with what is essential, and hence comes to oppose a total refusal to the modern world, considered as intrinsically perverse.[55]

François Mauriac, for his part, was delighted that integrism, a "formidable evil," was defined for the first time "in an official act of the Church."[56] In the weekly magazine *Carrefour*, at the time still in the Christian Democrat movement but soon to go over to Gaullism, Louis Salleron – who was to be one of the principal pens of traditionalism in the 1970s and 1980s – vented his irony on this "new 'ism' born in the firmament of intellectual quarrels" and concluded: "Integrism is, when all is said and done, the harmful aspect of conservatism and traditionalism." He shrewdly pointed out that now that the archbishop of Paris had condemned two opposed attitudes, "the path to structural reforms is wide open," since Cardinal Suhard drew his intellectual inspiration from the thought of Fathers Henri de Lubac and Teilhard de Chardin and from that of Jacques Maritain.

Essor ou déclin de l'Église would be republished several times (last edition in 2018) and translated into twenty-four languages. This February 1947 condemnation became a reference, but for the time being it had no public consequences for the anonymously targeted authors and publications. One can only assume that this first episcopal intervention against "integrism" and "excessive traditionalism" reinforced the prejudices of those who were already hostile to, or suspicious of, this current.

---

55 *Témoignage chrétien*, April 11, 1947. He tackled the same theme in "Christianisme et histoire," *Études* (September 1947): 178.
56 *Le Figaro*, April 27, 1947.

DEFENSE OF SCHOOL AND FAMILY

Less than a year later, Pierre Lemaire launched a new magazine, *Paternité*, which was soon considered integrist by its opponents, although it did have the support of some bishops. Pierre Lemaire, an engineer by training and a pre-war activist in the *Pour l'Unité* movement, had also been in captivity until April 1941, before being put in charge of the Artisans' Service Administration for the Finistère *département*. He resigned in October 1942 to avoid collaborating with the Germans.[57] He then led an almost self-sufficient life in Morbihan with his large family, and homeschooled his children. In 1946, he founded the *Comité de parents pour la réforme de l'enseignement* (CoPaRE, "Parents' Committee for Educational Reform") and the *Société d'études et d'éditions pour l'éducation* (SEEE, "Society for Educational Studies and Publications"), with "the will to put Christ back at the center of education" through good textbooks and by encouraging all initiatives to preserve and develop Catholic education.

Pierre Lemaire had close ties with Canon Etienne Catta, a history professor at the Catholic University of Angers. He was on the leadership team of the *Revue des cercles d'études d'Angers,* which was to have great influence in Rome, and also a collaborator of *La Pensée catholique.* Canon Catta remained a precious adviser to Pierre Lemaire in the decades to come, and introduced him to the Benedictine abbey of Solesmes, in the Sarthe *départment*. Pierre Lemaire often stayed there and made retreats; two of his sons would later enter as monks. From Solesmes and from Dom Guéranger's great work, *The Liturgical Year*, republished at that time, Pierre Lemaire received "the love of the liturgy, the sense of doctrinal orthodoxy, the love of the Church, and the Christian sense of history."[58] He was also in contact with the Parish Cooperators of Christ the King, especially with Father Barrielle, the superior of the Nazareth house in Chabeuil, where he made several retreats.

From January 1948, he published *Paternité-Maternité*, presented as a "family magazine at the service of parents and educators."[59] From the second issue of the magazine onwards, a stylized image of St. Michael slaying the dragon appeared on the back cover, with the motto *Quis ut Deus?* The image would remain attached to all of Pierre Lemaire's

---

57 Yves Chiron, *Pierre Lemaire. Précurseur dans le combat pour la famille* (Saint-Cénéré: Téqui, 2015), 84-85.

58 Interview with Dom Jean-Philippe Lemaire by the author, December 27, 2010.

59 On the front cover, the title *Paternité* was in the foreground in white lettering, while *Maternité* was in the background in black. The magazine usually went by the title *Paternité* alone, however.

editorial initiatives (magazines and then publishing houses), as a symbol of the fight for the Good and the True against Evil. *Paternité* was first published at an unusual frequency (two issues per school term plus one issue during the summer vacations, that is to say seven issues per year), then, starting in the third year, it came out as a monthly. This change in rhythm reflected the success of the magazine – five thousand subscribers in the early 1950s – but also a diversification of its content, even if questions relating to education and teaching still held an important place.

Pierre Lemaire's activity in favor of "educational reform" was of a piece with the vast movement in defense of private schools that shook all of Western France between 1945 and 1951. He participated in several of the large gatherings that were organized in different cities in those years. Through CoPaRE, and then in *Paternité*, he supported the movement by publishing many documents and leaders' speeches. He was in regular contact with Bishop Cazaux of Luçon, the spiritual leader of what he called a "sacred cause." Without retracing the history of this great Catholic mobilization of all of Western France,[60] we will note its two high points: first, the gathering of the *Amicales de l'enseignement libre* ("Associations in Favor of Private Education") of all the departments of Western France in Poitiers in October 1949, featuring a long speech "On the freedom of education" delivered by Bishop Cazaux in the cathedral, the bishops of Poitiers, Nantes and La Rochelle attending; a few months later, on April 23, 1950, a second great gathering organized in Saint-Laurent-sur-Sèvre, where Bishop Cazaux again protested against the "blatant injustice" done to the parents of Catholic students who paid their taxes without the schools chosen for their children receiving the slightest public aid, and, "in full agreement" with the bishops of Nantes, Angoulême, Poitiers and Angers, he called for a tax strike.

But some bishops, notably Cardinal Roques, Archbishop of Rennes, and Bishop Chappoulie, the new Bishop of Angers, and the nuncio, Archbishop Roncalli, did not wish to enter into conflict with the government, of which the Popular Republican Movement, the Christian Democrat party, was a part. By August 1950, the tax strike had to end. As the legislative elections of the following year approached, discreet conversations and negotiations began between religious authorities and political leaders. These led to the passage of the Marie and Barangé laws in 1951, which opened up public aid for independent schools.

---

60 See especially Frédérick le Moigne, "1945-1950: les manifestations du militantisme scolaire catholique de l'Ouest," in Brigitte Waché ed., *Militants catholiques de l'Ouest* (Rennes: Presses universitaires de Rennes, 2004), 119-211; and Yves Chiron, "Mgr Cazaux évêque de combat et pasteur (1941-1967)," *Recherches vendéennes* 23 (2017-2018): 327-51.

Pierre Lemaire continued to fight for private education and educational reform in *Paternité*, but from the very first issues of the magazine, other subjects were tackled too: the transmission of the faith (catechesis), morality (sex education in schools and the immorality of certain publications for young people), liturgy (sacred art), and religious questions. In this last area, the magazine did not claim to make doctrinal statements, but was committed, without fear of controversy, to defending the Catholic faith and the Church against those who were attacking them from the outside and also against those who abused or even betrayed them from within. The nuncio Roncalli, who received Pierre Lemaire and one of his collaborators on two occasions, described them as "good people, but difficult to control."[61]

From the very beginning of his activities, Pierre Lemaire had sought the support of Rome and of the bishops. He led two pilgrimages of family men to Rome in 1950 and 1951. During the September 1951 pilgrimage, he and the 250 or so Catholic men with him were received by the Pope at the Papal Palace of Castel Gandolfo. Pius XII gave an important speech on the family and education; it is worth noting that he did so in French. Soon Bishop Villot, secretary general of the Episcopate, declared that this speech had been "inspired by Monsieur Lemaire."[62] This may be an exaggeration. The Pope had already spoken on the family and education often in his speeches and messages. At least, it is clear that Pius XII in this speech addressed themes that he knew were dear to Pierre Lemaire and the pilgrims he was leading. When they become available, the archives of his pontificate will certainly show that the pope and those who prepared the speech of September 18 were aware of various writings of Pierre Lemaire on these subjects and that, without being "inspired" by them, they at least wanted to develop, clarify, and reinforce some of his positions on the family and education.

The day after the papal audience, Pierre Lemaire was received at length by Msgr Ottaviani, at the time assessor at the Congregation of the Holy Office. He was accompanied by three other family men; among them was Pierre Virion, who contributed articles on subversion and secret societies to *Paternité*, and would remain one of Lemaire's close friends. Msgr Ottaviani was very supportive, and encouraged Pierre Lemaire to continue his activity: "Now you have to act. To act, there is no need to have anyone overseeing you in Catholic Action organizations. 'The Word of God is not bound' (St. Paul), so you can

---

61 A. G. Roncalli, *Journal de France*, 2: 471.
62 Quoted in Congar, *Journal d'un théologien. 1946-1956* (Paris: Cerf, 2000), 256.

act without having to belong to any movement.... If you encounter any difficulty with your bishops, let us know, keep us informed."[63]

Thereafter, Pierre Lemaire regularly sent reports and documents to the Holy Office. In Rome, he was in frequent contact, by mail or by personal visits, with Msgr Ottaviani, who was created a cardinal in 1953, with Archbishop Parente, professor of theology at the Pontifical Lateran University, consultor to the Holy Office and to various other Roman congregations, and later with Father Paul Philippe, a Dominican, commissioner at the Congregation of the Holy Office, and with Father Gagnebet, another Dominican, consultor at the same Congregation.

THE TRIPLE ALLIANCE

Up until the late 1960s, other French traditionalists (Jean Ousset, Jean Madiran, etc.) were well received by these authorities at the Holy Office, which in 1965 became the Congregation for the Doctrine of the Faith. They were given encouragement and advice. It can be said that in the 1940s and until the early 1960s there was a kind of tacit triple alliance between the Holy Office, certain professors of the pontifical universities, and various French Catholic publications with a view to denounce what appeared to them as theological deviations, and to defend the faith against threats. Archbishop Parente, receiving Father Congar one day and speaking of the French situation very freely, told him: "They say that Mr. Lemaire is an integrist. But what does 'integrist' mean? They also say of me that I am an integrist."[64] This alliance emerged as early as the end of the 1940s during the controversy over the "new theology" *à la française*. This "new theology" was characterized first of all by a refusal: "Our intention," declared Fr Congar about himself and Fr Chenu, "was to combat what in our own jargon we called 'baroque theology,' which consists rather in an exercise in logic based on propositions held to be true."[65] This "new theology" did not rely primarily on the Magisterium and scholasticism, but was intended to be more hermeneutical than dogmatic, open to the great contemporary currents and to ecumenism.

The expression "new theology" (*nouvelle théologie*) was used for the first time in 1942, when Archbishop Parente, a consultor at the Congregation of the Holy Office, commented and justified in *L'Osservatore Romano* the placing on the Index of two works: *Une école de théologie:*

---

63 Pierre Lemaire, "Report on the audience with the Holy Office, September 19, 1951" (two typewritten pages), Pierre Lemaire Archives.

64 Quoted in Congar, *Journal d'un théologie*, 340.

65 *Jean Puyo interroge le Père Congar* (Paris: Éditions du Centurion, 1975), 45, 47.

Le Saulchoir, by Father Chenu, and *Essai sur le problème théologique*, by Father Charlier.[66] He reproached the two Dominican theologians for "tracing the lines of a reform in the theological field . . . that is imbued with perilous principles lending themselves, in relation to orthodox doctrine, to real deviations." With a touch of irony, he opined:

> In short, this new theology, whose paladins our two excellent Fathers aim to be, while roughly demolishing the now classic system of our schools, presents no safe building blocks or healthy criteria.

The expression was taken up again in 1946. First Pope Pius XII on September 17, when receiving in audience the participants of the twenty-ninth General Congregation of the Jesuits, warned, without naming names, against the "new theology" which risked endangering the "immutable dogmas of the Catholic Church" and "the unity and stability of the faith." Shortly thereafter, referring to this papal discourse, the Dominican Réginald-Marie Garrigou-Lagrange, a professor at the Angelicum, a qualifier at the Congregation of the Holy Office, and a member, like Archbishop Parente, of the Roman Academy of St Thomas Aquinas, specifically challenged the works of three Jesuits: *Conversion et grâce chez S. Thomas d'Aquin* (1944) by Father Henri Bouillard, *Surnaturel* (1946) by Father Henri de Lubac, and various writings by Father Teilhard de Chardin.[67] The conclusion of his long study was without appeal:

> Where is the new theology going? It comes back to modernism, because it has accepted the proposal that had been made to it: that of substituting for the traditional definition of truth: *adaequatio rei et intellectus*, as if it were chimerical, the subjective definition: *adaequatio realis mentis et vitae*.

Archbishop Parente received the support of several theologians of *La Pensée catholique* from the moment the magazine appeared in late 1946. After four articles by Father Berto on "The Church as Theologian" published in the first issues, there were two more articles in 1948 by Dom Frénaud, a Benedictine from Solesmes, on "the gratuity of supernatural gifts," and another by Father Louis-Marie Simon, a missionary of the Oblates of Mary Immaculate (OMI).

The controversy around the "new theology" continued with critical studies by the Dominican Fathers Labourdette and Nicolas in the *Revue*

---

66 *L'Osservatore Romano* (February 9-10, 1942), with an unabridged French translation in *La Croix* (February 26, 1942).

67 Réginald-Marie Garrigou-Lagrange, "La Nouvelle théologie où va-t-elle?" *Angelicum* 23.3-4 (July-December 1946): 126-45.

thomiste, and by the Jesuit Charles Boyer, a professor at the Gregorian. Henri de Lubac escaped being put on the Index, thanks in particular to a "Theological Examination of Conscience" (*Examen de conscience théologique*) he wrote on March 6, 1947 at the request of his superiors, in which he expounded at length his attachment to Saint Thomas Aquinas and to Tradition:

> Those who really read me, even more so those who know me from my teaching or my conversations, know that my tendencies are very traditional. I never cease to react against the biases of modernity, against the drive of intellectual fashions, against excessive concerns for adaptation or overly triumphant theories on the progress of dogma. I always try to bring, sometimes quite brusquely, those who seem to me to be in love with "modern" thought back to traditional sources and classical data. I love the Tradition of the Church, in its varied unity. I love it in all its forms.[68]

Yet in June 1950, along with three other Jesuits from Lyon, he was dismissed from teaching, and soon some of his books were withdrawn from sale and from religious libraries.

On August 12 of the same year, Pius XII published the encyclical *Humani generis*, devoted to "certain false opinions which threaten to ruin the foundations of Catholic doctrine." Without naming any author or title, it targeted relativism in the exposition of dogmas, immanentism, idealism and existentialism in philosophy, and irenicism in relations with non-Catholics.

Another interaction between intransigent theologians and the Holy Office emerges at this time in connection with a work by Jean Guitton. In 1949, this Catholic philosopher had published a work on the Virgin Mary dedicated to "our Protestant, Anglican, and Orthodox brothers." The work was favorably received by the Catholic press; it was called "one of the most beautiful books of spirituality of our time, one of the most intelligent also" by Father Rouquette, in *Études*. Even the young Father de Nantes (who would later bring to Rome thunderous indictments against Paul VI and then John Paul II, accusing them of "heresy, schism, and scandal") considered it to be "the most beautiful book I know on the Virgin Mary."[69] Yet, a discordant voice was heard: Dom Frénaud, who had contributed to *La Pensée catholique*, and who regularly contributed to the *Revue des cercles d'études d'Angers*, published two long articles to "warn all the readers who might be seduced by the

---

68 Henri de Lubac, "Examen de conscience théologique," in *Mémoires sur l'occasion de mes écrits* (Paris: Cerf, 2006), 271.
69 In an article published under the pseudonym "Amicus" in *Aspects de la France* (June 19, 1951).

real qualities to be found in the author and his book."[70] He pointed
out in detail inadequate or erroneous expressions and rash hypotheses.
A few months later, Archbishop Parente intervened in *L'Osservatore
Romano* to warn against the book and to point out its "temeritous or
at least inaccurate assertions." He deplored the fact that Jean Guitton,
by "depreciating Scholasticism," had believed that he, "a layman, could
construct a humanism-inspired theology better adapted to the times."[71]

Jean Guitton was later to say, on several occasions, that it was Msgr
Montini, the future Paul VI–at that time working in the Secretariat of
State–who saved his book from being put on the Index. Did he know
that it was Dom Frénaud's article that had alerted Rome? In any case,
he had to correct his book, and published a revised edition in 1951.

From 1950 until 1965, two other French theologians, Canon Catta and
Bishop Lusseau, both professors at the Catholic University of Angers and
contributors to *La Pensée catholique*, sought to alert the Holy See to the
doctrinal deviations and dangerous tendencies of French Catholicism.
They did so by means of letters and notes addressed to Father Ernest
Mura, who was in charge of the Sacred Apostolic Penitentiary and in
contact with various officials of the Holy Office.[72]

THE FIRST SALVOS

Two months before the publication of *Humani generis*, Father Congar published an important article in *La Vie intellectuelle* devoted to
integrism in France. It was in fact the anticipated publication of a
study meant as an appendix to a large book that was to appear a few
months later, *Vraie et fausse réforme de l'Église*.[73] "I do not believe,"
wrote Father Congar, "that integrism is primarily a doctrinal position."
He even refused to make it an error opposed to modernism:

> Modernism as it existed in the years 1895-1910 is a heresy or even,
> as Pius X said at the time, a reunion of all heresies. Integrism
> is by no means a heresy, and for my part, I do not like to see
> it presented as the opposite error of modernism, because this
> implicitly groups within the same category of error two things
> that do not belong together.

70 *Revue des cercles d'Angers* (July and December 1950)–both anonymous articles, as
were most articles published in that review.
71 Pietro Parente, "Saggio teologico d'un credente laico," *L'Osservatore Romano* (June
25-26, 1951).
72 For an analysis of their letters, see Jean de Viguerie, "La Crise de l'Église en France
dans les années 1950 et 1951," *Bulletin de la Société française d'histoire des idées et d'histoire religieuse* 13 (2003): 5-41.
73 Yves Congar, "Mentalité de 'droite' et intégrisme en France," *La Vie intellectuelle* (June
1950): 644-66; *Vraie et fausse réforme dans l'Église* (Paris: Cerf, 1950), appendix III, 604-22.

He did, however, consider that integrism is "above all a certain way of feeling and affirming Catholicism, it is first of all a mentality or an attitude." It is an "extremism" which goes back, according to him, to Louis Veuillot; it rejects "*in toto* the 'conquests of the modern world.'" Two features characterize integrism according to Father Congar. On the one hand, a political option for the right – "integrism has almost always been linked, among us, to a political attitude 'of the right'" – marked by an attachment to order, to authority, a "fundamental disposition for what is determined from the outside and from above" and "a certain mistrust of the subject, of man." It is also a siege mentality:

> Integrist Catholics are in constant dread that if the drawbridges are lowered the enemy will pour into the keep; they are afraid that others within will fraternize with error; they sniff the whiff of heresy everywhere.

There is among integrists "an inclination to judge and condemn everything related to openness, research, or questioning of received ideas."

Father Congar's study, published twice in the space of a few months, had a considerable influence thanks to its argumentation – integrism is not a doctrine opposed to modernism, but a mentality – and to the stature of its author, a renowned theologian.

But he was soon disciplined. Some of the analyses in *Vraie et fausse réforme de l'Église* (1950) were judged dangerous or erroneous. The book was not put on the Index, but in February 1952 the Holy Office took several measures against Father Congar: he was forbidden to republish the book or to have it translated, and he had to submit all his writings to the censorship of the Master General of the Dominicans, Father Suarez. Father Congar was hurt by these sanctions. In his diary from that time he is pessimistic, and compares the Holy Office to the "Gestapo"![74] His diary also shows that he was able to count on some support and some intercessors who tried to soften the sanctions, notably Father Villot, secretary of the French Episcopate at the time, and, in Rome, Wladimir d'Ormesson, French ambassador to the Holy See, Msgr Baron, rector of San Luigi dei Francesi, and Msgr Montini, substitute at the Secretariat of State.

A long interview in *Le Monde* (March 30, 1952) caused a stir at the time. "A leading ecclesiastical figure," who had "judged it preferable to remain anonymous" – historians have not succeeded in discovering his identity to this day – deplored the fact that "analyses, research, or initiatives attempted in France to bridge the widening gap between the

---

74 Y. Congar, *Journal d'un théologien*, 196 (March 28, 1952).

Church and the modern world are sometimes accused of modernism
(whether doctrinal, juridical, or social) and ultimately discredited, if
not condemned." This "leading ecclesiastical figure" considered that
"the situation of Christian intellectuals is thus becoming more uncom-
fortable every day" and blamed it on the denunciations leveled by
a recently reborn integrism: those "who have only condemnations,
decrees, warnings and other arguments of authority in their mouths,
are earning themselves a reputation for orthodoxy and fidelity on the
cheap. Their method is denunciation and slander. They spread out in
the antechambers of the Vatican, 'work the lobby' as at the Chamber of
Deputies, and cover their political ulterior motives with doctrinal purity."

In the weeks following the sanctions against him, Father Congar collected the information and rumors that reached him about the integrists
in his Diary. According to him, by their denunciations or their articles,
they maintained a climate of suspicion, and, for some, they were at the
origin of the measures of which he, like the Jesuits of Lyon, had been
the victim. Over the course of the days, he noted the names of Bishop
Lusseau, Pierre Lemaire, Paul Lesourd, Father Dulac, Amicus,[75] Louis
Salleron, and Father François Ducaud-Bourget, who had just published
a very critical work about *Témoignage chrétien*, as we shall see.

Soon a whole volley of articles against integrism appeared in Dominican magazines. In August, *La Vie intellectuelle*, the journal in which
Father Congar had published his study on integrism, published another
article on the same subject. This long, unsigned text presented itself as a
"Document."[76] In fact, it was, for the most part, a history of integrism
in the time of St. Pius X and an evocation of *La Sapinière*, presented
once again as a "secret society." This was followed by a "definition of
integrism" which took up that of Father Congar, but without referring
to his study: "Integrism is not a doctrine, but a tendency, a state of
mind, and a method of action," whose characteristics are "a horror of
all novelty," "a constant one-upmanship in doctrinal integrity and purity,"
"a systematic preference for authoritative solutions," "suspicion of all
those who do not share one's views," "an easy rash judgment," and
"harshness in judging." The article ended—which Father Congar had
refrained from doing in his study—with a direct indictment of several
publications: *Verbe* (described as "a review that is both Maurrassian and
integrist"), *Aspects de la France*, the *Bulletin d'études et d'informations
de politique internationale* (BEIPI), *Rivarol*, *Paternité*, and *La Pensée*

---

75 Father Congar was unable to discover who this author was. It was in fact Father
de Nantes, who used this alias for the articles he contributed to *Aspects de la France*.
76 "Qu'est-ce que l'intégrisme?" *La Vie intellectuelle* (August-September 1952): 136-52.

catholique, and by denouncing "verbal campaigns conducted by certain retreat masters." The retreats given by the *Coopérateurs paroissiaux du Christ-Roi* (CPCR), which we have already mentioned, were here anonymously targeted.[77] This second article in *La Vie intellectuelle* on integrism was probably a collective work. What part did Father Congar play in it? We do not know. At least the editors were visibly inspired by his pages and were able to benefit from his information.

A month later, in *La Vie spirituelle. Supplément,* another Dominican review, Father Marc Oraison gave a psychoanalytical interpretation of integrism: he had studied medicine before entering the seminary. A doctor of medicine in 1942, and ordained as a priest in 1948, he had defended a doctoral thesis in theology in 1951, published in 1952: *Vie chrétienne et problèmes de la sexualité.*[78] In *La Vie spirituelle,* his long study was devoted to "fear in religious psychology." After distinguishing between fear of God, fright, and anxiety, and after examining how they function in religious psychology, he set out to present progressivism and integrism as "two types of neurotic reaction related to infantile anxieties."[79] As for integrism, Father Oraison defined it first of all in a general way, simply repeating verbatim, but without quoting him, entire paragraphs of Father Congar! Then, using the categories of psychoanalysis, he described the behavior of integrists:

> It is not essentially a principled and free thought; it is first and foremost an affective reaction that presents as neurotic. And the idea that immediately comes to mind is that of a morbid fear of freedom, linked to a tyrannical superego and a guilt complex.
>
> Whenever it is confronted with an original thought, it immediately resorts to the Supreme Pontiff as to a martinet, either as a threat, or – an even more infantile and fearful attitude – through a sly sort of tattling.

Father Oraison ultimately judged that:

> [t]here enters into the integrist reflex an undeniable anal-sadistic component. The conflict of aggressiveness is manifest with its acute balancing between self-punishment and aggressiveness against others.

He did not name any author or publication, but in a note he called

---

77 These retreats had been the subject of a highly critical article a few months earlier, in a Dominican-run review: Fr J.-H. Nicolas, "L'Œuvre de coopération paroissiale du Christ-Roi," *La Vie spirituelle* (December 1951): 465-97.

78 It was put on the *Index* through a decree of the Holy Office dated March 18, 1953, but its condemnation was not made public until 1955.

79 Marc Oraison, "Essai sur la peur en psychologie religieuse," *La Vie spirituelle. Supplément* 22 (September 15, 1952): 277-301.

into question "certain so-called 'parish' retreats that are darkly ascetical in appearance and dubiously claim St. Ignatius of Loyola as their inspiration." The Fathers of Chabeuil were once again targeted, but without being named.

A month later, *La Vie intellectuelle* published a third article on integrism, signed by the editorial board.[80] It expressed their satisfaction that the document on integrism they had published had "caused a stir: some applause, but also anger." The review went on to denounce "the reorganization of a kind of neo-integrism" and those who "today think that they, though lacking any mandate from the Church, are authorized to judge the orthodoxy of their brothers as if they had an infallible discernment."

This fourfold offensive of the two Dominican reviews against integrism was perhaps not the fruit of an orchestrated plan, even if the succession of articles shows a determined will to fight against a current that was more and more active and that benefited from help in high places. It was soon picked up by the Catholic philosopher Jean Lacroix, who before the war had co-founded *Esprit* with Emmanuel Mounier. In a long article in that review, he defined integrism as an "erroneous state of mind" and contrasted it with the Christian conception of freedom.[81] Following Father Congar's footsteps, he denounced "a mentality made up of an unyielding narrowness, constantly opposing the eternal to the temporal and desirous of achieving the 'thesis' here below without taking into account the 'hypothesis,' that is to say, history." He described integrism as "a mental block . . . an excess, a hypertrophy of dogmatism" and he illustrated his point by referring to various publications: *Paternité*, *Verbe*, *La Pensée catholique* and others. He particularly lambasted Pierre Lemaire's review, which, he wrote, "exceeds them all in mixing the ridiculous with the odious." Jean Lacroix also accused two other Catholic publications of being tempted, according to him, to dabble in integrism. One of them was *L'Homme nouveau*:

> It has often refused to be labelled integrist, and it must be acknowledged that it belongs rather to that Christian totalitarianism we have been talking about, to what one might call a Catholic integralism. But why is it that it so often provides the best examples of an integrist mentality?

The other was *France catholique*, "which suffers from integrist contaminations, but which one does not have the objective right to classify among integrist newspapers."

---

80 "Le Maquis intégriste," *La Vie intellectuelle* (October 1952): 1-4.
81 Jean Lacroix, "Intégrisme et liberté," *Esprit* (February 1953): 293-306.

"INTEGRISM" *VERSUS* "CHRISTIAN PROGRESSIVISM"

Father Fillère, the ardent leader of the *Pour l'Unité* movement and director of *L'Homme nouveau*, multiplied conferences and meetings. Starting in January 1948, in a series of lectures given in the Latin Quarter, he dealt in succession with "Karl Marx, theoretician of the Revolution," "Georges Sorel, psychologist of revolutions," and "Vladimir Illich Lenin, strategist of the Revolution." These weighty lectures, which were intended mainly for students, alternated with public meetings for a wider public, which he held in Paris or in the provinces.

Father Fillère was fond of debates and did not hesitate to give them a provocative title to attract attention. Hence the theme announced for a large public meeting held at the Mutualité on November 30, 1948: "God exists, therefore you cannot be a communist." Anti-communism remained one of the recurring themes of the *Pour l'Unité* movement, especially since while in France some Catholics and theologians were seduced by communism, in Eastern Europe communist regimes were persecuting the Church. At the end of 1948, Cardinal Mindszenty, Primate of Hungary, was arrested and charged with treason, conspiracy, and failure to respect the laws of the regime. After interrogations, torture, and an odious trial, he was sentenced to life imprisonment in January 1949.

That same month, Father Fillère published a work with a provocative title: *Le Parti communiste démasqué* ("Communist Party Unmasked"). Its subtitle, "Doctrine–Strategy–Tactics," was a better description of the systematic character of his study.[82] The book appeared at the same time as the ecclesiastical authorities in Rome and Paris were issuing warnings against Communist-leaning Catholics. In January 1949, the Holy See personally interdicted Franco Rodano, the leader of the Unitary Movement of Progressive Christians (the Italian equivalent of the UCP), and reminded Catholics that "allying with groups of atheistic materialism" was not permitted to them.[83]

A few days later, Cardinal Suhard, Archbishop of Paris, issued a lengthy warning that said in part:

> Some Catholics mean to carry out their political and Christian action within the Communist Party, others in close and habitual collaboration with this party. The movement of progressive Christians has adopted the latter attitude. It claims to be able to dissociate atheism, which communism professes but it rejects, from the political and social action of the party whose practical

---

82 M. Fillère, *Le Parti communiste démasqué* (Paris: Éditions de l'Homme nouveau, 1949).
83 *L'Osservatore Romano* (January 17 and 30, 1949).

objectives it adopts. We warn the faithful against the dangers
such an attitude entails.[84]

These interventions from Rome and Paris encouraged traditional
Catholics to continue their struggle. Father Garrigou-Lagrange, who had
received *Le Parti communiste démasqué*, wrote from Rome to Father
Fillère:

> The lucidity of your argumentation, its strength and your cour-
> age are captivating.... What you say about the alliance with the
> peasants, p. 73, sheds light on what is happening in Italy.... What
> you say about freedom of conscience as understood by the
> communists, p. 78, should dispel many illusions among those
> who still more or less believe in the "outstretched hand," like
> the progressive Christians who are currently a matter of concern
> to Cardinal Suhard.[85]

Father Garrigou-Lagrange also suggested sending a copy of the book
to his confrere, Father Cordovani, a consultor at the Holy Office and
the master of the Sacred Palace, and another to Archbishop Ottaviani,
so that he could send it to the Pope. At the end of the day, it was
through another intermediary that Father Fillère was able to send an
autographed copy of the book to Pius XII. He was well in tune with the
concerns of the Holy See, since a few months later the famous July 1,
1949 decree of the Holy Office appeared, forbidding Catholics to join
the Communist party or "to favor it in any way," because "Communism
is materialistic and anti-Christian." The decree excommunicated "the
faithful who profess the materialistic and anti-Christian doctrine of
the Communists and especially those who defend or propagate it."[86]

L'Homme nouveau published the complete text of the decree and
a translation of an article from *L'Osservatore Romano* on the subject.
Father Fillère, under the alias Paul Morin, also published an "Appeal"
to Communist Catholics or sympathizers. This was his last article; he
died in an accident the following month.

For all that, some Catholics did not stop collaborating with the Communist Party or writing to promote its propaganda. Father Desroches,
who directed the Catholic Center for the Study of Marxism-Leninism
(a part of *Économie et humanisme*), published "Signification du marxisme" in July 1947. It sought to show that dialectical materialism offers
a "coherent explanation of the world" in the social field. According to

---

84 Communiqué dated January 31, 1949, published in the *Semaine religieuse de Paris*
(February 5, 1949).
85 Garrigou-Lagrange to Fillère, letter dated February 6, 1949, Archives of *Mouvement
Pour l'Unité*.
86 *Acta Apostolicae Sedis* 41 (July 2, 1949): 334.

him, the "confrontation" of Marxism and Christianity led to the conclusion that there is, in the Marxist doctrine, in spite of its declared
atheism, an "availability to the religious truth." Father Fessard gave a
close reading of the work which could be summarized, according to
him, in a few words: "Communism goes in the direction of history."
He reproached the Dominican friar for having allowed himself to be
misled by a "false eschatology, the very one that communism dangles
before the eyes of everyday Christians."[87]

Some Dominicans continued as fellow-travelers of the communist
movement, in order to "bridge the schism between the proletariat
and the people of God," according to an expression of which Father
Desroches was fond. In certain circumstances, they found support
among various personalities of the progressive movement, as in the
case of the Stockholm Appeal. In the context of the Cold War, at the
instigation of the Soviet authorities, a World Peace Council (WPC) was
founded, with the French physicist Frédéric Joliot-Curie, a member of
the French Communist Party, as its president. Among other initiatives,
the WPC launched an international petition on March 15, 1950, calling
for an "absolute ban on nuclear weapons." This petition, known as the
Stockholm Appeal, gathered millions of signatures throughout the world,
including those of numerous personalities from different countries
(Pablo Picasso, Louis Aragon, Thomas Mann, etc.). French Catholics,
led by Father Desroches, decided to endorse the Stockholm Appeal
explicitly by publishing a manifesto entitled "Christians Against the Atom
Bomb." The manifesto was signed by several Dominican theologians
(Chenu, Desroches), by Father Hollande, the superior of the Mission
of Paris, and by several worker-priests, by leaders of *Action catholique
ouvrière* (ACO, "Catholic Worker Action"), by Father Montuclard of the
Jeunesse de l'Église ("Youth of the Church"), by André Mandouze of the
UCP, by Ella Sauvageot, by Georges Montaron, manager of *Témoignage
chrétien* (although the newspaper took a different collective stand: "Why
we do not sign the Stockholm Appeal"), by Jean Lacroix, co-founder of
Esprit (while Emmanuel Mounier publicly refused to join in).

A few months later, in November 1950, Fathers Desroches, Boisselot,
and Robert launched a fortnightly, *Quinzaine*, thanks, once again, to the
financial support of Ella Sauvageot. A progressive paper that refused
to be anti-communist and was hostile to what Father Desroches called
"integrist confessionality,"[88] *Quinzaine* sought to be a place for research
aimed at reconciling temporal commitments with the "missionary

87 Gaston Fessard, "Signification du marxisme," *Études* (January 1950): 86-102.
88 Quoted in Yves Tranvouez, *Catholiques et communistes*, 95.

project." After four issues, the Dominicans were forced to give up directing the publication, and entrusted it to lay people, while the title was changed to La Quinzaine. Ella Sauvageot, who was a Dominican Tertiary, also had officially to leave the administration, but she continued to be closely involved with the fortnightly, whose headquarters were located almost opposite her home. She soon became involved in a long homosexual relationship with "a young, committed poetess of Protestant origins," which morally tormented the devout Catholic that she was and affected her health and activities.[89]

For its part, the Jeunesse de l'Église group increasingly became more radical and political. It wanted "to participate in the construction of the new world of which the proletariat (and principally the atheist proletariat) is the instrument" while giving "a permanent witness of faith and of the Church within atheism. In this way, J. E. joins the worker priests."[90]

At that time, there were about a hundred worker priests, either incardinated in the Mission de Paris or the Mission de France, or belonging to certain religious orders (Dominicans, Jesuits, Capuchins, Assumptionists). Although none of them was a member of the Communist Party in those days, many had joined the Confédération Générale du Travail (CGT, "General Confederation of Labor" [the communist trade union – Translator]), which was preferred to the French Confederation of Christian Workers (Confédération française des travailleurs chrétiens, "CFTC"), which was considered to be too closely linked to the institutional Church. Many of them also participated in the great strikes of 1947 and signed the Stockholm Appeal. Their union and political commitments, and their desire to be fully immersed in the working class (a "presence," not a ministry) placed them "more than ever in contradiction with the spirit of the priesthood," the nuncio of the time, Archbishop Roncalli, noted in his Diary.[91]

Georges Montaron, a former leader of the Young Christian Workers (Jeunesse Ouvrière Chrétienne, "JOC"), joined Témoignage chrétien in 1948, managed the paper from 1949, was a member of the board of directors from June 1951, and signed the Stockholm Appeal, as we have seen. He moved the weekly towards an ever more assertive left-wing stance, giving it the motto "Truth and Justice at any cost." While France

---

89 J. Sauvageot, Ella Sauvageot, 194-200.
90 Minutes of the General Assembly, December 28, 1952, published in Thierry Keck, Aux sources de la crise progressiste en France: le mouvement "Jeunesse de l'Église" (1936-1955), thesis at Lumière-Lyon-2 University (2002).
91 A. G. Roncalli, Journal de France, 2: 463 (June 28, 1951).

was confronted with demands for independence from her colonies and was engaged in the war of Indochina, the newspaper supported the "emancipation" movements, considered that it was necessary to put "colonization on trial," and denounced military repression. The articles and positions taken by the weekly were the subject of several questions in the National Assembly and the Council of the Republic, and in January 1950 René Pleven, Minister of National Defense, banned *Témoignage chrétien* from military installations.[92]

The political commitments of the progressive press were denounced by those who continued to be called integrists. In March 1952, Father François Ducaud-Bourget, who had already caused controversy the previous year with his work on "Catholics in literature" (notably Claudel and Mauriac), published a well-documented yet ironic essay calling into question *Témoignage chrétien*.[93] For this study, he had read, pen in hand, every one of the periodical's issues. At the end of his demonstrations, supported by numerous direct quotations from the weekly, he concluded with an indictment in fourteen points: "indifferentism in dogma," "sympathies" with "Christian progressivism" and communism, etc. He concluded: *"Témoignage chrétien* presents a serious danger for the faith and morals of its readers" and he considered that it was up to "Rome to decide."

A few months later, in September 1952, Pierre Lemaire devoted a special issue of *Paternité* to the infiltration of Catholic circles by communist ideas. It contained an alarming account of how communist ideology was being imposed in the seminaries that remained open in China, and an article devoted to the "Marxist impregnation in France." Pierre Lemaire, following his usual practice of addressing the bishops directly, sent them this issue. A number of them contented themselves with thanking him, with a simple acknowledgment of receipt. Others were more receptive, indicating once again that the French episcopate was, at that time, divided into various tendencies. Bishop Touzé, one of the auxiliary bishops of Paris, wrote: *"Paternité-Maternité* has observed an interesting connection and provides very useful documentation."[94] Bishop Sembel of Dijon was thankful for "this document [which] is fortunately likely to enlighten many families."[95] Bishop Guerry, without denying the interest of this special dossier, gave a piece of advice:

---

92 *Journal Officiel* (January 27, 1950): 611 (intervention by Édouard Frédéric-Dupont).
93 François Ducaud-Bourget, *Faux Témoignage "Chrétien"* (Éditions du XXe siècle, 1952).
94 Bp Paul Touzé to Pierre Lemaire, Letter, September 18, 1952, Pierre Lemaire Archives.
95 Bp Sembel to Pierre Lemaire, Letter (undated), September 1952, ibid.

> Anything done to enlighten opinion about the dangers of commu-
> nist doctrine and techniques is highly praiseworthy and urgent.
> However, it must never be forgotten that Communism will only
> be effectively combated if, at the same time and in a positive
> manner, the social doctrine of the Church with all its demands
> is presented to the popular masses. This is what the Supreme
> Pontiff always does. We must all imitate him on this point as
> on all others.[96]

A month after the publication of this issue of *Paternité*–but the
timing was merely coincidental, as the document had been in preparation for some time–the Assembly of Cardinals and Archbishops
condemned *La Quinzaine* and the *Jeunesse de l'Église* group in a brief
but clear statement:

> The Assembly of Cardinals and Archbishops confirms the warn-
> ings it has already given to the activists of *Action catholique* con-
> cerning the bulletin *La Quinzaine*: that is not where they should
> take their directives. The Assembly also warns them against the
> doctrinal deviations of *Jeunesse de l'Église*, especially concerning
> the mission of the Church, the faith and current events, the con-
> ditions of evangelization, and, in a general way, [it warns them]
> against the Marxist impregnation of this movement of ideas.[97]

Roman condemnations followed: *Les Événements et la foi* (the twelfth
and last booklet of the *Jeunesse de l'Église* group) was put on the Index
by a decree of the Holy Office on January 7, 1953, and *La Quinzaine*
met the same fate on January 26, 1955.

In the meantime, on March 1, 1954, the worker-priests had been
condemned, as the established expression goes.[98] Various attempts to
"bring the men and their methods back in line"[99] and several warnings had preceded this decision. In February 1951, Msgr Ottaviani, the
Assessor at the Holy Office, asked Bishop Ancel, the Superior General
of the Prado Institute and responsible for the mission to the working
class, to draw up a Directory for working-class priests. The draft text
disappointed many of them, as it did Father Chenu, who was one of
their principal advisors. In June 1951, the Holy See asked for an end to

96 Bp Guerry to Pierre Lemaire, Letter, September 16, 1952, ibid.
97 This "Avertissement et mise en garde" by the Assembly of Cardinals and Archbishops was published in many local editions of *Semaine religieuse* and in *DC* (November
30, 1952): col. 1497.
98 Besides the "White Book" the insubordinate worker-priests had published (*Les Prêtres-
Ouvriers* [Paris: Les éditions de Minuit, 1954]), the authoritative account remains Émile
Poulat, *Naissance des prêtres-ouvriers* (Paris: Casterman, 1965); second and enlarged
edition, *Les Prêtres-ouvriers. Naissance et fin* (Paris, Cerf, 1999).
99 Guillaume Cuchet, "Nouvelles perspectives historiographiques sur les prêtres-ouvriers
(1943-1954)," *Vingtième siècle. Revue d'histoire* 87 (July-September 2005): 185.

recruitment; it went unheeded. Successive measures followed through-out 1953, notably the prohibition on sending seminarians to work in factories, and the closing of the seminary of the Mission of France. In September, Father Congar published an article on the future of priest-workers in which he used a formula that was to become famous: "You can condemn a solution if it is faulty; you cannot condemn a prob-lem."[100] In November, three cardinals (Liénart, Feltin, and Gerlier) went to Rome to plead the cause of the worker-priests, the other two French cardinals (Saliège and Grente) being hostile to the continuation of the "experiment." Pope Pius XII decided that, as of March 1, 1954, the priest-workers had to agree to work only three hours a day, to cease all membership in "workers' councils, unions, and other orga-nizations specific to the world of labor, and any efforts at extension" and to "devote themselves in a new form to the evangelization of the workers."[101] The prohibition was not absolute, contrary to what has been often been said – the actual total prohibition did not take place until 1959, during the pontificate of John XXIII – but it was refused by the majority of them. Seventy-three worker-priests wrote a manifesto that the communist newspaper *L'Humanité* was the first to publish, on February 3, 1954. They protested against the decision, which they said was an "abandonment of the working class" and expressed their determination to stay at work. Those who submitted to the papal decision did so, in many cases, merely as a formality:

> Most promptly went back to work, though for smaller, non-unionized companies, with the discreet blessing or tacit agree-ment of their bishops. Strictly speaking, therefore, one cannot speak of a "condemnation" in 1954, since Rome did allow some leeway and especially since things happened in such a way that there ended up being more priests at work between 1954 and 1965, the date of the official resumption, than before 1954.[102]

At the same time, in early February 1954, Father Suarez, the Mas-ter General of the Dominicans, came to France to carry out what Father Congar would call the "great purge": the three superiors of the Dominican provinces (Paris, Lyon, and Toulouse) were removed

---

100 Y. Congar, "L'avenir des prêtres-ouvriers," *Témoignage chrétien* (September 25, 1953). Fr Congar is sometimes erroneously presented as a worker-priest theologian. He soon wrote to his superiors "I have no contact with the worker-priests, and never have," quoted in É. Fouilloux, *Yves Congar* (Paris: Salvator, 2020), 170n1.

101 Letter sent by the bishops to each of the worker-priests in their diocese; excerpts published in *Le Monde* (February 2, 1954) and picked up in *DC* (February 7, 1954): cols. 131-32.

102 G. Cuchet, "Nouvelles perspectives historiographiques sur les prêtres-ouvriers," 187.

from their posts and replaced with appointed men (i.e., not elected by the provincial chapters) and four of the most famous theologians of the province of Paris (Fathers Chenu, Congar, Boisselot, and Féret) were deprived of their offices and assigned to provincial convents or sent abroad.

These different disciplinary measures on the part of the Holy See or of the Dominican Order were not enough to extinguish the progressive current. A few years later, Father Fessard, who was always a lucid and profound analyst, noted its persistence and explained it: "Poverty, justice, and the direction of history: so many ambiguous words through which the Marxist poison has crept in."[103]

FOUR STRIKES OF THE CROZIER

It was at this time that the first measures taken by three cardinals and a bishop against Pierre Lemaire and Jean Ousset were made public. It would be wrong to see this as a kind of retaliation for the disciplinary actions taken against certain progressives. The measures taken had been preceded, in the case of Pierre Lemaire, by oral and written warnings. At most, one can consider that the bishops in question judged that the condemnations against one tendency legitimized or called for condemnations against the opposite side.

Pierre Lemaire, who multiplied mailings and visits to the bishops in defense of the family and private schools, did not hesitate to impugn other Catholic publications and organizations in his review *Paternité*. In 1950, he launched a campaign against the magazine *Éducateurs*, published by the *Service central de recherche et d'action pour l'enfance* ("Central Service for Research and Action for Childhood"), which depended on the Union of Catholic Works (*Union des Œuvres catholiques*) and had published a special issue devoted to sex education; it was reprinted several times. In October 1953, Lemaire challenged the National Federation of Catholic Action (*Fédération nationale d'Action catholique*, "FNAC"), which had just published a "School Work Plan." Among the instructions given by the FNAC to the parish unions was that of "Catholics bringing aid to public schools" when necessary. Pierre Lemaire considered that such an instruction was a real surrender in the fight for free education, a betrayal even. That same month, he took on the Christian Teachers' movement. He reproached some of its leaders and members for "looking to the errors of naturalism and Marxism for

---

103 Gaston Fessard, *De l'actualité historique*, vol. 2, *Progressisme chrétien et apostolat ouvrier* (Paris: Desclée de Brouwer, 1960), 147.

their ways of thinking and acting." These public criticisms of Catholic organizations that were duly "mandated" by the hierarchy, according to the expression of the time, prompted the cardinals of three of the principal dioceses of France to issue warnings against Pierre Lemaire and *Paternité* within a few weeks of each other.

First, Cardinal Liénart published in the diocesan review of Lille a severe "Warning" which explicitly referred to the two quoted articles; it stated:

> These accusations are false and slanderous. What makes them even worse is that they are spread in the diocese through tracts published without any authorization from us and against our will.
>
> We therefore warn our clergy and faithful against the systematic denigration that the review *Paternité*, in defiance of the most elementary justice and charity, ceaselessly employs to divert Catholics from adhering to movements in perfectly good standing with the Church and recommended by the Bishops.
>
> We recall once again, on this occasion, that members of our diocese have no instructions to receive, whether from Mr Lemaire or from anyone other than the Pope and the Bishops, with respect to their faith and their Catholic Action apostolate.[104]

A few days later, Cardinal Gerlier, Archbishop of Lyon, reproduced the entire warning from Lille verbatim in his own diocesan paper. He also added a long personal commentary that matched the severity of Cardinal Liénart's condemnation.[105] A short time later, a third cardinal, Archbishop Roques of Rennes, intervened publicly against Pierre Lemaire. He reproduced Cardinal Liénart's warning and added a long note to condemn Pierre Lemaire's campaign:

> Moreover, one may well wonder in virtue of what authority or mandate the author of the article in *Paternité* believes he is authorized to lecture those who do not share his ideas. . . . What has been forgotten here is that systematic denigration never serves the cause one seeks to defend and that malicious insinuation is not a valid argument.[106]

These cardinals' warnings, which first appeared in their respective diocesan papers, were published with commentary in *La Croix*. They were also reproduced in *Le Courrier de l'Ouest* – the most widely read regional daily in Angers, where Pierre Lemaire lived – preceded by a caption in which he was described as "the McCarthy of integrism."

---

104 *Semaine religieuse du diocèse de Lille* (November 29, 1953): 510.
105 *Semaine religieuse du diocèse de Lyon* (December 4, 1953): 21.
106 *Semaine religieuse du diocèse de Rennes* (December 1953); unabridged quotation in *La Croix* (December 11, 1953).

The regional Catholic press, which was still widespread at the time, often echoed these warnings, sometimes with irony. Thus the principal Catholic weekly of Dijon wrote:

> Mr Pierre Lemaire is the father of a large family, which is good. But he also claims to be a Father of the Church, which is too much. In the name of doctrinal integrity, of which he believes himself to be the qualified representative, Mr Lemaire accuses, judges, and condemns. He everywhere sniffs the awful stench of modern errors.[107]

The three cardinals had blamed Pierre Lemaire for acting and intervening "without any authorization" (Liénart), for "encroaching on the mission of the Hierarchy" (Gerlier), and for being "without a mandate" (Roques). The same reproach was taken up a few weeks later by the bishop of Strasbourg against *La Cité catholique*. This enterprise, created in 1946 under the name of *Centre d'études critiques et de synthèse*, as we have seen, had had humble beginnings. It had enjoyed the support and advice of Dom Frénaud, a monk from the abbey of Solesmes, since its foundation. It was another monk of that abbey, Dom d'Aboville, who had provided a list of some two hundred names of friends and acquaintances of the monastery who might be interested in the nascent work.[108] Abbé Lefèvre had put an office at Jean Ousset's disposal on the premises of the Éditions du Cèdre, on rue Mazarine. But the study groups took time to be organized; it was done after lectures and meetings that Jean Ousset and Jean Masson organized throughout France. The movement's newsletter, which was presented as a "Working File," was austere, doctrinal, did not deal with current events, and had to stop its publication after three issues, as the finances of the Center reached their lowest point. In 1948, it took the financial help of the Marquis Amédée d'Andigné, of an old legitimist family, a doctor of law and a graduate of the *École libre des sciences politiques*, to save the enterprise, which was able to acquire a new review, *Verbe*. Thanks to Pierre Marchand, Jean Ousset, an estate attorney and a militant from the beginning, was received that very year by Archbishop Marmottin of Reims. Ousset was able to explain to Marmottin at length the goals of the enterprise he had founded two years earlier ("to promote a Catholic renaissance in the temporal order"), and the doctrine on which it was based (the teaching of the Church). As Bishop Marmottin would recall a few years later:

---

107 *La Côte-d'Or catholique* (December 11, 1953).
108 P. Marchand, "Les Débuts de la Cité catholique," *Permanences* 347 (December 1997): 21.

> You won me over as soon as I met you: your outlook, your
> doctrine corresponded so well to my own views that I was imme-
> diately drawn to you and told you as much.[109]

The archbishop of Reims gave his public support from then on,
on several occasions. The *Centre d'études critiques et de synthèse* held
its first congress in 1949 in Saint-Étienne. It was a modest congress
that brought together only seventeen participants, joined by a dozen
friends at the last minute. There were four lectures, given by the three
founders (Ousset, Masson, and Demarque) and by Michel Creuzet, a
teacher, and the founder of the Saint-Etienne group, who would later
play an important role nationally. It was during this first conference
that the *Centre d'études critiques et de synthèse* (a "sibylline, ridiculous,
and priggish" name, according to Jean Ousset) took the much more
explicit name of *Cité catholique*, in reference to the injunction of Saint
Pius X in the *Letter on Sillon*:

> No, there is no need to reinvent civilization, or to build a new
> city in the clouds. It has been, it is yet; it is Christian civilization,
> it is the Catholic city.

In 1950, on the advice of Dom Frénaud, and thanks to a letter from
auxiliary Bishop Beaussart of Paris, Jean Ousset was able to meet with
Msgr Ottaviani in Rome. This assessor at the Holy Office encouraged
him to continue his work and assured him of his support. The national
congress in July 1950 in Bordeaux brought together about sixty delegates.
A year later, the national congress was held in Marseilles and brought
together some 150 participants. It was honored by three messages of
support from bishops (Marmottin of Reims; Chappoulie of Angers;
Robin of Blois). In July 1953, the congress was held in Dijon, with the
theme: "The Social Kingship of Our Lord Jesus Christ, or Religion
as the Foundation of the Social Order." Several bishops, including
the Bishop of Dijon, once again came to lend their support through
messages read at the congress, and for the first time Pius XII, via a
telegram sent by the Secretariat of State, sent his apostolic blessing to
"all the members of the *Cité catholique* Association" and assured them
of his "paternal encouragement in the study of the social doctrine of
the Church and of papal teaching."[110] The reports of Jean Ousset on
naturalism and Michel Creuzet on secularism were intended to show
that these two ideologies lead to revolution in morals as well as in the

---

109 Archbishop Marmottin, Letter dated July 20, 1956, published in *Verbe*, supplement
10 (September-October 1956): 10.
110 Telegram published in the proceedings of the *Congrès national 1953*, 5.

political order. After the congress, the participants met at the Abbey
of Auberive, in the Haute-Marne, which was then dependent on the
Abbey of Sainte-Marie de Paris. Dom Édouard Guillou, a monk of this
monastery, who published articles in *Verbe* under the pseudonym
"Funditor," welcomed them and gave a long speech which, according
to Jean Ousset, was "like the recapitulation, if not the spiritual grand
finale of the whole congress."

Yet, a few months after the first papal blessing sent to *La Cité
catholique*, a first warning appeared, which took the not insignificant
form of a ban. On January 1, 1954, Bishop Weber of Strasbourg issued
a declaration about the "*Cité catholique* Movement." He did not deny
that the organizers had "good intentions," and he did not express any
reservations or doctrinal condemnation:

> We assume no lack of good will in the work of maintaining
> and increasing the faith in our diocese, or in the reconquest
> of the groups of people that have all too often left the orbit of
> the Church.

But he criticized *La Cité catholique* for being "without a mandate":

> This movement of ideas has not obtained any official recognition
> from the Assembly of Cardinals and Archbishops of France, or
> any authorization from the Bishop of Strasbourg. It therefore
> has no mandate to present itself, less even to impose itself, in
> the name of the hierarchy, at least amongst us.

He also criticized it for competing with Catholic Action movements:

> Organized as it is in our dioceses, it runs the risk of harming
> Catholic Action and causing confusion among the people.[111]

This double reproach, of being "without a mandate" and of competing with the institutional movements of Catholic Action, had already
been formulated before the war by Cardinal Liénart against Father
Fillère's *Pour l'Unité* movement and taken up again, in 1953, as we have
seen, against Pierre Lemaire. It would be repeated thereafter against
the same people or against other organizations and other publications.
This double reproach testifies to a globalizing conception of Catholic
Action in which the different specialized movements must act under
the authority of the bishops and according to an express "mandate"
received from them. It was only in 1975 that the French episcopate
officially abandoned this notion of a "mandate," thus granting more
recognition to the autonomy of the laity in temporal actions.

---

111 Declaration of Bishop Weber, "Le Mouvement de la Cité Catholique," *Bulletin
ecclésiastique du diocèse de Strasbourg* 73.1 (January 1, 1954): 9-10.

Pope Pius XII did not share this specifically French understanding of the mandate. In an important speech to the first World Congress of the Lay Apostolate, the Pope had admitted that there were "degrees" in the dependence of apostolic movements on the hierarchy:

> The dependence of the lay apostolate on the hierarchy admits of degrees. This dependence is closest for Catholic Action, which is the official lay apostolate; it is an instrument in the hands of the hierarchy, it must be like an extension of its arm; it is, therefore, subject by nature to the direction of the ecclesiastical superior. Other works of the lay apostolate, whether organized or not, have greater scope for free initiative, with the latitude required by the goals to be achieved. It goes without saying that, in any case, the initiative of the laity in the exercise of the apostolate must always be within the limits of orthodoxy, and not in opposition to the legitimate prescriptions of the competent ecclesiastical authorities.[112]

In the cases of both Pierre Lemaire and Jean Ousset, these first episcopal warnings or prohibitions occurred while other bishops, in private and in public, had given them support and encouragement. This support continued, which shows a division in the episcopate or, at least, attests to the freedom of the bishops at a time when Episcopal Conferences and their unwieldy structures did not yet exist.

JEAN MADIRAN MAKES A SPLASH

The young Jean Arfel, who in the immediate post-war period was a professor of philosophy at the École des Roches (which had moved to Maslacq during the war), left it in 1950 to devote himself to journalism and writing in Paris. Under the alias Jean-Louis Lagor (from the name of a village near Maslacq), he had already contributed in 1946 to *L'Indépendance française*, a monarchist weekly published by Marcel Justinien. Two years later, he had published *La Philosophie politique de saint Thomas d'Aquin* (a book he had written in 1944; its preface was by Charles Maurras) in which he sought to "draw out the main lines of a political philosophy that integrates Maurrassian physics with Thomistic thought."[113] Then he slowly "left the Maurrassian system," as he wrote to a correspondent.[114] He arrived in Paris in the summer of 1950, and contributed to the *Centre d'archives et de documentation*

---

112 Pius XII, Speech to the First World Congress of the Lay Apostolate on October 14, 1951, in *DC* (December 2, 1951): coll. 1501-2.

113 Jean-Louis Lagor, *La Philosophie politique de saint Thomas d'Aquin* (Paris: Nouvelles éditions latines, 1948), 76.

114 Jean Madiran to Joseph Folliet, Letter, June 20, 1957, copy kept in the Jean Madiran Archives.

politique et sociale founded by Georges Albertini. Albertini had come from the secularist and socialist left, passed through Marcel Déat's *Rassemblement National Populaire* (RNP, "National People's Movement"), and was, under the Fourth and Fifth Republics, a man of influence with various governments.[115] The Albertini Center, financially supported by the CIA and by the *Groupe des industries métalliques* (GIM) of the Paris region, collected information, drew up analyses, and sent them out to the press and to political, economic and social circles. There was the *Bulletin d'études et d'informations de politique internationale* (BEIPI) and the *Informations politiques et sociales* (IPS). The IPS came in various colored sheets. Jean Arfel was in charge of the weekly "red sheet" dedicated to the French Communist Party and communism generally. Then from 1952 on, he collaborated with the weekly *Rivarol* founded the year before by René Malliavin. *Rivarol* presented itself as the "national opposition weekly." Its editors included a number of journalists and authors who had published in the Vichy and collaborationist press, for which the rest of the press attacked them. It was "anti-system," at the same time anti-Gaullist, anti-communist, pro-European, and it constantly denounced the injustices of the purge [of pro-German collaborators— *Translator*]. When he began his collaboration with *Rivarol*, Jean Arfel took the pseudonym "Jean Madiran," in reference to the name of a village in the Hautes-Pyrénées where there was a monastery that had been important in his life. This alias remained his *nom de plume* until his death. In *Rivarol*, he wrote a political column that was not limited to political questions but also dealt with other subjects, especially religious ones. He ended up dealing with the question of worker-priests and of Christian progressivism on several occasions.

In November 1954, the insubordinate worker-priests published a white paper, a collective work in which one of them, the future historian Émile Poulat, played a very important role—one can already recognize in it his methodical and dispassionate approach. This book, "by no means a manifesto," sought to open "a true dialogue which so far has not succeeded in establishing itself with either the Hierarchy or public opinion."[116] Cardinal Feltin, Archbishop of Paris, published a communiqué regretting its "fragmentary" and "biased" documentation and expressing a harsh judgment of the worker-priests: they "seem to have exclusively become militants of temporal action" and "have allowed the faith in the priesthood as they received it from the Holy Spirit and the Church to be altered."[117] The Archbishop of Paris "one last time" urged those priests who were still working to accept the decisions taken by the hierarchy.

In a long article he published in *Rivarol*, Jean Madiran considered that "these worker-priests are victims, and we hope that, to the fullest extent that ecclesiastical authority deems possible, patience with them will not grow weary."[118] The expression "victims" may come as a surprise from an author who was fighting "their political errors" and "their theories on the priesthood, the apostolate, and the mission of the Church." He explained that the worker-priests are "morally prisoners of the diabolical communist phantasmagoria. Therein lies the essence of this horrible drama: they are in the state of men who have gone through a long hallucination and who are unable to shake it off." Besides the worker-priests seduced by communist analyses to the point of losing their priestly identity, he blamed Catholics who were insufficiently conscious of "the misleading mythologies of communist propaganda." He quoted *La Quinzaine*, *Esprit*, and *Témoignage chrétien,* as well as Father Bigo, the Jesuit director of the *Revue de l'Action populaire*.

Even as he published this article, Jean Madiran was finishing writing a book-length essay, *Ils ne savent pas ce qu'ils font* ("They do not know what they are doing"), which appeared in March 1955. It was an indictment of the collusion between the "left-wing" Catholic press (*La Vie catholique*, *L'Actualité religieuse dans le monde*, *Témoignage chrétien*, *La Vie intellectuelle*, *La Quinzaine*, *Esprit*) and the newspaper *Le Monde*, founded and directed by Hubert Beuve-Méry. Jean Madiran tried to show that all these press organs, by their complacency, their silences, and their biases, came to "discourage or suppress the spirit of resistance to communism." He gave numerous examples, such as the supposed "report" on agrarian reform in Communist China that appeared in *La Vie catholique illustrée*, which was merely a rehash of an official propaganda document that had already done the rounds in other complacent organs of the world press; he also pointed to the support given by some to the Stockholm Appeal. He likewise reproached the progressive press for having spoken about the worker-priests before their "condemnation" without explaining that "the major difficulties encountered by the worker-priests' enterprise were due to the cunning and cynicism of the traps that were daily set for them by the communist organization."[119] The worker-priests had been seduced, in varying degrees of thoroughness, by communist rhetoric

---

117 *Semaine religieuse de Paris* (November 27, 1954): 1083-84.
118 Jean Madiran, "Le Choix des prêtres-ouvriers: Rome ou Moscou?" *Rivarol* (December 2, 1954).
119 Madiran, *Ils ne savent pas ce qu'ils font* (Paris: Nouvelles éditions latines, 1955): 79.

and Marxist dialectics; Jean Madiran explained that communism was not only a doctrine, but also, since Lenin, a praxis. On the very first page of his book, he gave as proof of the collusion between the leaders of the progressive Catholic press and the director of *Le Monde* the lunch that brought them together every Tuesday at the restaurant "Au Petit Riche," on a boulevard not far from *Le Monde*. Hubert Beuve-Méry and Madame Sauvageot, the great boss of the progressive Catholic press, met there every week with their guests: "Editors, money men, political journalists, doctors in their white or black robes" (this last expression designated Dominicans or Jesuits, often doctors of theology). The director of *Le Monde*, who was a member of the board of directors of certain publications of this Catholic press and of the board of directors of *Actualité religieuse dans le monde*, was presented by Madiran as the "political spiritual director" of the progressive Catholic press.

The book, which called into question these publications and their directors (Georges Hourdin and Ella Sauvageot), Hubert Beuve-Méry, other journalists and writers (Albert Béguin, François Mauriac, Georges Suffert) and also theologians, notably Fathers Chenu and Boisselot, caused a great deal of controversy in the press. Jean Madiran, who had sent his book to many personalities, including Father Chenu (who sent him an ironic reply), and to many parishes, received an abundance of mail. *La Vie catholique* published a "Note on the Attacks Concerning *La Vie catholique illustrée*," a four-page text which pointed out the "serious errors" contained in the book: these were either "false affirmations" or "omissions."

A few days after the publication of the book, the director of *Le Monde* invited Jean Madiran to attend a lunch at the "Petit Riche." He accepted, but on the condition that he pay for his lunch and be accompanied by André Frossard as a witness. He recounted his immediate impressions of the episode in a letter to his father:

> They're frightfully bothered by the book. Yesterday I took lunch . . . at the Petit Riche with Beuve-Méry, Hourdin, Madame Sauvageot, Father Boisselot, Stanislas Fumet. I was accompanied by André Frossard. It was good sport and plenty of fun. . . . They wanted to convince me of their innocence, and everything I saw and heard convinced me even more of the opposite. But the fact that they made this attempt and wanted to meet with me to "seduce" me shows that I touched them on a sore spot.[120]

Forty years later, Hubert Beuve-Méry's biographer would, in his own way, recount this improbable lunch, indicating that Father Boisselot

---

120 Jean Madiran (Arfel) to Georges Arfel, Letter, March 23, 1955, private archive.

and Ella Sauvageot, both exasperated, left the table before the end of the meal, while Beuve-Méry spent a long time "talking with the pamphleteer one on one."[121]

The book had another consequence. Joseph Folliet and Jean Madiran began an assiduous correspondence that lasted several years. It would be an exaggeration to say that the two authors became friends; in spite of their different analyses, however, they did at least exchange arguments calmly, which led them both to change their positions on certain points.[122]

Eight months after the publication of his book, Jean Madiran gave it a sequel: *Ils ne savent pas ce qu'ils disent* ("They Do Not Know What They Are Saying"). It was both a reaction to the criticism that had greeted the first book and a broader extension of his analyses. Jean Madiran believed that "all of us together are temporally engaged in a process of decadence. This kind of process is not irreversible in theory; it often is in fact." He judged that "the only hope is revolutionary," but not through a political or social revolution, which is always a "trivial vanity." "The true, the only revolution is interior, spiritual, permanent." Christian journalists can contribute to it, "very modestly," not without failures, "until the day when one realizes, but long after the fact, that the spirit has changed, and that all things have long been imperceptibly but profoundly modified by it."[123] The success of these two books (the first was published twice in four months) prompted Jean Madiran to launch a review he had been thinking about for some time and which Louis Salleron, his elder by fifteen years, urged him to create. The monthly *Itinéraires* began to appear in March 1956. Four authors had promised Jean Madiran "regular contributions." The diversity of their profile and concerns shows the intellectual openness Madiran sought: Louis Salleron, professor of political economy at the *Institut catholique de Paris*, one of the founders of the *Centre d'études politiques et civiques* (CEPEC, "Center for Political and Civic Studies") and collaborator on the weekly *Carrefour*; Henri Charlier, a sculptor and painter, an acquaintance since the Maslacq years, who gave his full measure as a writer in his chronicles for *Itinéraires*; Marcel Clément, then a professor of social economics, who had made Jean Madiran discover the importance of the teaching of Pius XII, and who stopped writing in the magazine when he began

121 Laurent Greilsamer, *Hubert Beuve-Méry*, 408-10.
122 Correspondence between Joseph Folliet and Jean Madiran, kept in the Jean Madiran archive.
123 Jean Madiran, *Ils ne savent pas ce qu'ils disent* (Paris: Nouvelles Éditions latines, 1955), 182-83.

to contribute to *L'Homme nouveau* in 1962; the Auvergne writer Henri Pourrat, who published in the magazine until his death. The anaphoric "Opening Statement" ("We agree") in the first issue of *Itinéraires* opens with a confession of faith: "Christ is the way, the truth, the life. We agree on submission to the doctrine taught by the Catholic Church. We receive this doctrine as it is defined by the Church herself. We find in it the supreme rule of our thoughts and actions." While anti-communism does appear to be one of the characteristics of the magazine, it was above all a Catholic publication that found the "solution" to all questions "in the prayer of the Church, in interior life, in permanent conversion, in the works of Faith, Hope, and Charity." Its subtitle, "Chronicles and Documents," described more than mere content. In general, the "chronicles" took up more space than the "documents," the former being the personal expression of authors who did not reflect the viewpoint of the magazine as a whole, the essential point being "respect among Catholics for freedom of opinion in all matters on which the Church has not pronounced herself" and "the understanding charity with which the generous efforts of loyal Christians of good will must be considered or even challenged."

Itinéraires was to have a forty-year-long run, attracting, depending on the period, a wide variety of contributors. By its longevity, by the variety of subjects it treated, and by the important documents it published, it would establish itself until 1996 as the principal review of "traditional Catholics," to use the expression that Jean Madiran favored.

THE FIRST BATTLE OF THE CATECHISM (1956-1957)

The Roman condemnation of the "Progressive Catechism" in 1957 was seen by many as the catechetical equivalent of the condemnation of the worker-priests three years earlier: an unjust condemnation that reflected the fussy rigidities of Pius XII and of the Holy Office.[124] The process that led to this situation shows that "integrists" – as their opponents called them – played a decisive role.[125]

---

124 Such is the outlook of Gilbert Adler and Gérard Vogeleisen, *Un siècle de catéchèse en France, 1893-1980. Déplacements. Enjeux* (Paris: Beauchesne, 1981) and Joël Molinario, *Joseph Colomb et l'affaire du catéchisme progressif. Un tournant pour la catéchèse* (Paris: Desclée de Brouwer, 2010).

125 Jean-Dominique Durand has consulted the archives of Archbp de Provenchères and of Joseph Colomb to describe and explain "La Crise du catéchisme français de 1957," in *Enseigner le catéchisme: autorité et institutions, XVIe-XXe siècles* (Québec: Les Presses de l'université Laval/Paris: Cerf, 1997): 361-77. Cf. also the abundant Pierre Lemaire archives on this episode: Y. Chiron, *Précurseur dans le combat pour la Famille. Pierre Lemaire* (Paris: Pierre Téqui éditeur, 2015).

Since the 1930s, a "catechistic movement" (it was not yet called "catechetical") had developed in France. According to one of its promoters, Canon Boyer of the Diocese of Dijon, it was a matter of applying "the principles of pedagogy based on child psychology, avoiding theoretical presentations, and aiming above all at praxis."[126] In 1941 a National Commission for Catechetics was created, presided over by Archbishop Petit de Julleville and directed by Canon Boyer. Its purpose was to conduct a survey and do research for a completely revised edition of the 1937 Catechism for use in the dioceses of France. The new edition of the Catechism, called the "National Catechism," was published in 1947. Although it had 492 questions instead of 617, its structure was identical, in three parts: what to believe (dogma), the sacraments, what to do (morals). However, others were already working on other catechisms, and sought to apply different methods.

On May 14, 1946, under the authority of the Assembly of Cardinals and Archbishops (ACA), a National Catechetical Center ("Centre national du catéchisme," CNC) was created to serve as a link between the National Commission for Catechetics and the diocesan religious education departments. In particular, the CNC enforced, through circulars, the orientations and decisions of the Commission.

This CNC, which was the driving force, was directed at first by Canon Boyer. In 1950, a Higher Institute of Catechetical Pastoral Care ("Institut supérieur de pastorale catéchétique," ISPC) was founded, attached to the Catholic Institute of Paris and directed by Father Coudreau, a Sulpician. Finally, in 1951, an Episcopal Commission for Religious Education was created, presided over by Archbishop de Provenchères of Aix-en-Provence, who also presided over the National Commission for Catechetics. This superposition of various structures involved in the renewal of catechesis – Episcopal Commission, National Commission, National Center, Higher Institute – did not favor clarity in the project.

The central figure of the catechetical movement at that time was Canon Joseph Colomb, a Sulpician, who was first assistant director of religious education in the diocese of Lyon. In 1945 he published his first "teacher's book": *Aux sources du catéchisme*. The following year, he founded the first school for catechists in Lyon. That same year, in *La Grande Pitié de l'enseignement chrétien* ("The Great Pity of Christian Teaching"), he issued a severe judgment on the traditional catechism: "The catechism has fallen into a profound disaffection: its teaching is

---

126 André Boyer, *Un demi-siècle au sein du mouvement catéchétique français. Témoignages et documents* (Paris: Éditions de l'École, 1966), 83.

discredited in the eyes of many." Based on this observation, he considered that the catechism as used in the dioceses posed a "problem
in terms of the textbook and of the curriculum," it "is really not made
for our children," it is "shot through with an individualistic mentality...with a *negative* and *minimalist* or *juridical* mentality...with a
conceptualist mentality...with a *polemical* mentality."[127] In his view,
it was necessary to move from an "inductive method" (explaining definitions) to a "deductive method: starting from concrete experiences,
taken from the life and environment of the child." And there was a
need to develop "progressive programs." The term "progressive" was
to be the keystone of the catechetical revolution that Joseph Colomb
and others were to try to implement.

In a later work, he advocated a new "organization" of the catechism.[128] Catechism, he felt, must undergo "structural changes." It must
return to its sources, Sacred Scripture and the liturgy. It must abandon
the "dryness" of formulas to tell a "story," because the Christian message is "in its original state a concrete story." There was also, in Canon
Colomb, the conviction that religious teaching must take into account
the principles and methods brought to light by advances in psychology
and by the new pedagogy. In particular, the idea of progressiveness
which, applied to the catechism, should allow one to go "from the
implicit to the explicit, from the concrete to the abstract." In 1950, he
published a progressive Catechism in three volumes corresponding to
three age groups: 7-9 years, 9-11 years, 11-12 years.

Father Elchinger shared similar concerns. In 1945 in Strasbourg, he
had been tasked with creating the "Diocesan Direction of Christian
Education in Alsace." He who would later become bishop of Strasbourg
wanted, he said, to change the "climate" and the "content" of religious
teaching.[129] Believing that the catechism in force at that time was "a
collection of abstractions, notions with little meaning for a child" and
had "no contact with the Word of God," in 1948 he created a review,
Vérité et Vie, which published "religion pedagogy cards." The magazine,
published quarterly, had up to 13,000 subscribers.

In 1954 Canon Colomb was named director of the National Catechet-
ical Center and secretary of the National Commission for Religious
Education. He gave new orientations to catechesis in France. The
National Catechetical Center became the National Center for Religious

---

127 Joseph Colomb, *La Grande Pitié de l'enseignement chrétien* (Petit-Clamart: Centre
Jeunesse de l'Église, 1946), 24-32, emphasis in the original.
128 J. Colomb, *Pour un catéchisme efficace*, 2 vols (Lyon: E. Vitte, 1949).
129 Léon-Arthur Elchinger, *La Liberté d'un évêque* (Paris: Éditions du Centurion, 1976), 142.

Education (*Centre national de l'enseignement religieux*, CNER). It had a determining influence on many movements and publications dedicated to catechism, especially on two catechists, Françoise Derkenne and Jeanne-Marie Dingeon, who would each publish textbooks and have responsibilities in catechetical teaching in France. The FCTP (*Formation chrétienne des tout-petits* ["Christian formation of the little ones"]), a private association, but national in scope, was now judged to be too traditional in its methods and was transformed into an organization depending on the CNER. New textbooks were imposed on it (*Méthode progressive d'enseignement religieux*, in three volumes).

Pierre Lemaire was the first to question the new catechetical manuals, in *Paternité*, and he remained the most active even as other publications entered the fray, notably Pierre Virion in *Écrits de Paris*. There was also support from theologians. In January 1956, Pierre Lemaire published a first article in *Paternité*. He questioned the first volume of Canon Colomb's *Catéchisme progressif* and two issues of Father Elchinger's *Vérité et Vie*[130] which "in fact skirt around fundamental dogmas." He noted the ambiguity of the term "progressive": "It indicates a pedagogical intention, but in fact it cuts through the dogma. Is a catechism that minimizes the fundamental truths of the Faith still Catholic?" The pedagogical and psychological argument seemed to him to be flawed.[131] There followed a rather lively exchange of letters with Archbishop de Provenchères, the president of the Episcopal Commission for Religious Education and president of the National Commission for Religious Education. In May 1956, Pierre Lemaire also sent a long report on the catechism to Cardinal Roques to be examined by the Assembly of Cardinals and Archbishops. In this matter, he did not have to face a French episcopate that was entirely committed to the new pedagogical methods. Among the bishops, too, some were also concerned about the weaknesses and dangers of this "progressive catechism." Bishop Villot, then secretary general of the Episcopate and one of the auxiliary bishops of Paris, alerted Archbishop de Provenchères:

> One member of the Commission expressed a few misgivings about the progressive method. Several thought care should be taken not to over-apply psychological and pedagogical methods that could lead to a certain forgetfulness of supernatural forces.[132]

---

130 Issue 183, *Découverte progressive de Dieu* and issue 224, *L'Éveil des petits au sens de Dieu*.

131 Pierre Lemaire, "Sur l'enseignement du catéchisme. Lettre à une Mère de famille," *Paternité* 65 (January-February 1956): 33-37.

132 Bishop Villot to Archbishop de Provenchères, Letter dated June 28, 1956, quoted in J. Molinario, *J. Colomb et l'affaire du Catéchisme progressif*, 99.

Pierre Lemaire wrote many letters to the authorities, as well as circulars to parents. Through Canon Catta, who was his spiritual advisor, he was able to benefit from the "suggestions" and advice of Father Ernest Mura, Procurator General of the Congregation of the Religious of Saint Vincent de Paul in Rome and official at the Sacred Apostolic Penitentiary. On October 13, 1956, he wrote to Cardinal Ottaviani to ask for an intervention from the Holy See: "We fully understand the difficulty that there could be in publicly condemning works as widespread (and officially imposed) as those of Canon Colomb, under the title 'Progressive Catechism,' because of the disturbance that would result," but at least precise directives should be issued that "would ultimately compel, without condemnation, the new catechisms to reform themselves."[133] At the end of 1956, Lemaire went to Rome to visit and alert various authorities. He was received at the Holy Office and at the Congregation of the Council. He handed over various documents, including Jeanne Dingeon's *Méthode progressive d'enseignement religieux*, and again asked the Holy See to intervene. He probably did not know that the Holy Office had already taken up the matter. In November, Archbishop de Provenchères had been received in Rome by Cardinal Ottaviani, who had asked him "for explanations on the *Catéchisme progressif*" and to "make a report."[134]

In December, Pierre Lemaire published a second article in *Paternité* to show how the progressive catechism was being applied at the parish level.[135] He soon found strong support in Bishop Lusseau, the dean of the faculty of theology at the Catholic Institute of Angers, with whom he had been acquainted for several years. But it was not Pierre Lemaire who suggested to Bishop Lusseau that he make a critical study of the "progressive catechism." He had done so, he says in the first lines of his study, "on high authority." We are doubtless here to understand a request from Rome, from Cardinal Ottaviani. Bishop Lusseau's long study, with its rather anodyne title – "Catechetical Literature" – appeared in early 1957 in three issues of the *Revue des cercles d'études d'Angers*.[136] It was then published in a separate issue, which increased its circulation.

While Bishop Lusseau quoted the writings of Canon Colomb and Father Elchinger abundantly and with precise citations, he did not name them, contenting himself with evoking "the authors of the catechetistic

---

133 Pierre Lemaire to Ottaviani, Letter dated October 13, 1956, copy preserved in the Pierre Lemaire archives.

134 Archbishop de Provenchères, "Une simple chronologie. La crise du catéchisme," unpublished four-page document quoted in J. Molinario, *J. Colomb et l'affaire du Catéchisme progressif*, 90-91.

135 Pierre Lemaire, "Une séance de 'catéchisme,'" *Paternité* 63 (December 1956): 595-98.

136 *Revue des cercles d'études d'Angers* 4 (January 1957): 92-96.

method." He did not stray from an irenic tone, as he sought to proceed "with only one concern: to say charitably what I think is true." He did not question the good intentions of the propagators of the new catechetical methods, but he pointed out a number of silences or insufficiencies on original sin, the mystery of the Trinity, the Incarnation of God, the Real Presence in the Eucharist, etc. He concluded his long presentation, which was illustrated with numerous extracts from the incriminated texts, with the judgment that the procedures of this new catechesis could only "accelerate the movement" of dechristianization:

> Indeed, it is not possible for intelligences whose initiation from a young age to the truths of the revealed Faith is incomplete not to find themselves forever deprived of the deep convictions that make up the Christian life.

These criticisms from a theologian who was also a faculty dean were not without effect. According to an unpublished note by Archbishop de Provenchères, they caused "a great shock," and during the *ad limina* visit of the French bishops from March to April 1957, "more than thirty bishops seemed to have disclosed their concerns in Rome."[137]

At the same time, other theologians intervened in the debate, without mentioning the names of the authors in question either, but disputing the new pedagogical principles of the progressive catechism: Father Lefèvre, in *La Pensée catholique*, and Father Rimaud, a Jesuit and professor at the Catholic Institute of Paris, in *Études*.[138] In March 1957, Pierre Lemaire devoted two new articles to the progressive catechism.[139]

On the following April 19, Father Paul Philippe, OP, then commissioner of the Holy Office, came to France. He met with Archbishop de Provenchères and informed him, *sub secreto*, of "seventy-five clarifications, criticisms, omissions, and errors"[140] that had been discerned in the works of Canon Colomb; he was asking for them to be corrected. A few days later, the Second National Congress on Religious Education was held in Paris, under the presidency of Cardinal Feltin, Archbishop of Paris, and Archbishop de Provenchères, who was doubly responsible for religious education. Twelve other bishops attended this congress, which brought together some five thousand participants, including

137 Quoted by J. D. Durand, "La Crise du catéchisme," 365.
138 Fr Luc Lefèvre, "Pédagogie et catéchèse de Notre-Seigneur," *La Pensée catholique* 47 (January-February 1957) and Fr André Rimaud, "Pseudo-chronique d'éducation pour le temps de Noël et de l'Épiphanie," *Études* (January 1957).
139 Pierre Lemaire, "À propos de catéchisme... Où est l'Église?" and "L'ancienne Formation Chrétienne des tout-petits et la nouvelle," *Paternité* 76 (March 1957): 146-50 and 151-56.
140 J. Molinario, *J. Colomb et l'affaire du catéchisme progressif*, 133.

a thousand lay people. Canon Colomb gave a talk titled "Enfant des hommes et enfant de Dieu" ("Child of men and child of God"). The Assembly of Cardinals and Archbishops issued a communiqué "renewing its full confidence in Mr Colomb and the members of the Commission on Religious Education" and asking them "not to be moved by criticism."[141]

For his part, Pierre Lemaire again wrote to several bishops to point out the dangerous statements contained in the new catechetical manuals and "pedagogical cards." Some bishops expressed their annoyance. Thus the bishop of Tulle:

> If your documents were communicated only to the Bishops, the matter might yet be understandable. But I have every reason to believe that you give them a completely different kind of publicity; your review and the *Paternité* documentation are addressed to a wide audience. I've come to wonder whether the direction or orientation of religious teaching in France is in the hands of the Hierarchy or in the hands of Mr Lemaire![142]

"You are engaged in a nasty business," wrote the bishop of Carcassonne.[143] Archbishop de Provenchères too regretted the "methods" of Pierre Lemaire, the "campaign of tracts, articles, and petitions carried out over several months." But, for the first time, he made the following acknowledgment: "I am the first to realize that there are things that are not going well, and I am trying to remedy them."[144]

On the other hand, Archbishop Marmottin of Reims was much warmer, and encouraged Pierre Lemaire to continue his fight:

> I admire your courage and your ever ardent zeal, as well as your holy wrath against so many errors and deviations. You know that I share your ideas; but I cannot go to war as you do.[145]

Then, on July 24, Cardinal Pizzardo communicated the Holy Office's decisions to Archbishop de Provenchères.[146] In the first place, the errors found in the various manuals and texts in question were listed. As a result, the method of the progressive catechism was to be abandoned, the incriminated works and texts withdrawn from sales and the national structures (National Commission, CNER and ISCP) reorganized under a

---

141 Published in *Documentation catéchistique* 36 (July 1957): 1, and quoted in G. Adler and G. Vogeleisen, *Un siècle de catéchèse en France*, 213.

142 Bishop Chassaigne to Pierre Lemaire, Letter dated April 20, 1957, Pierre Lemaire archives.

143 Bishop Puech to Pierre Lemaire, Letter dated April 24, 1957, Pierre Lemaire archives.

144 Archbishop de Provenchères to Pierre Lemaire, Letter dated April 21, 1957, Pierre Lemaire archives.

145 Archbishop Marmottin to Pierre Lemaire, Letter dated June 15, 1957, Pierre Lemaire archives.

146 Unpublished document quoted in J.-D. Durand, "La Crise du catéchisme," 369.

new leadership. This was a hard blow for the leaders of the catechetical institutions and for Archbishop de Provenchères, the "double president" of the episcopal and national commissions. But there is no doubt that other bishops were satisfied with this Roman intervention. Bishop Villot, secretary general of the Episcopate and auxiliary bishop of Paris, said:

> I have no doubts regarding the substance of the matter. It would be a waste of time and of one's credibility to defend the unfortunate criteria of the progressive catechism. The bishops trusted Archbishop de Provenchères, who trusted Fr Colomb, who went down the wrong path.[147]

On the other hand, Archbishop de Provenchères and Cardinal Gerlier tried to mitigate the Roman sanctions. Cardinal Gerlier had close ties to Canon Colomb, who had directed religious education in his diocese, and went to Rome from August 21 to 26. He successfully asked that the incriminated books not be withdrawn from sales and that the restructuring of the catechetical institutions be gradual.

Nevertheless, there was an almost complete turnover in the leadership of French catechetics: Françoise Derkenne, head of practical work at the ISPC, had been asked to resign as early as August 9; in the following October, François Coudreau, director of the ISPC, was replaced; in April 1958, Canon Colomb was sent "in penance" to Nice but was not officially replaced as head of the National Commission until the following June. In the meantime, Archbishop de Provenchères, "forever wounded by this painful affair,"[148] had resigned as president of the Episcopal Commission for Religious Education and of the National Commission for Religious Education. Jeanne-Marie Dingeon, on the other hand, was able to stay in her functions because, by August 1957, she had gone to Rome to plead her case.[149] After his departure from the CNER, Canon Colomb was welcomed in the diocese of Strasbourg where, as we have seen, Father Elchinger directed the Diocesan Direction of Christian Education and the review *Vérité et Vie*. Father Elchinger himself had to correct some of his texts. He was to acknowledge:

> I had to withdraw a certain number of issues of our review from the market. There were also two or three articles that I had written which were reproved by the Holy Office.[150]

147 Bishop Villot to Cardinal Gerlier, Letter dated August 14, 1957, quoted in Durand, "La crise," 369-70.
148 Bernard Delpal, "Provenchères (Charles de)," *Dictionnaire des évêques de France au XXe siècle* (Paris: Cerf, 2010), 547.
149 Interview with J.-M. Dingeon.
150 Léon-Arthur Elchinger, *La Liberté d'un évêque* (Paris: Éditions du Centurion, 1976), 27-28.

The "crisis of 1957," as protagonists and historians call it, did not really resolve the question of the catechism and the teaching of the faith. It would re-emerge twice in the decades to come.

PIERRE LEMAIRE CONDEMNED BY HIS BISHOP

The condemnation of the "progressive catechism," which was made public in September 1957, provoked a backlash: one month later, Pierre Lemaire, who had been the most deeply involved in the battle, was condemned by his own bishop. One might see in this condemnation a petty revenge on the part of certain leaders among the bishops. The least one can say is that this public intervention against Lemaire counterbalanced, in Catholic opinion, the negative effect of the Roman intervention.

It was through the press (*La Croix* of October 31, 1957, *Le Monde*, and *Le Figaro* of November 1) that Pierre Lemaire learned of the "severe condemnation" (*Le Figaro*'s expression) that Bishop Chappoulie of Angers, where he lived, was bringing against him. The communiqué was dated October 27. It stated in particular:

> The leaders of the magazine *Paternité-Maternité* and of *Documents-Paternité* are engaged in a nasty business, because it is not enough to practice one-upmanship in obedience and orthodoxy to render a true service to the Church. In reality, they are working to divide the Catholics of our country by constantly casting suspicion on their brothers in the faith. They sow discord, keep spirits in turmoil, and inflame controversies every chance they get.

He was asking "the faithful of the diocese of Angers not to lend any assistance to the undertakings of Mr. Lemaire, from whom they should receive neither advice nor instructions."[151]

The blow was hard, and risked causing great damage to all of Pierre Lemaire's activities. He became what, in the old canonical language, was called a *vitandus*, i.e., a person to avoid because of his pernicious influence.

Pierre Lemaire respectfully approached his bishop to express his "complete submission" and to ask him what "practical consequences" he should draw from this episcopal warning.[152] Was he supposed to put an end to the associations for the support of families that he had created over several years (CoPaRe, SEEE, *Débuts Rapides*) and to interrupt the three publications that he directed (*Paternité-Maternité*, *Documents-Paternité* and *Discours du pape et Chronique romaine*)? Archbishop Chappoulie did not dare forbid the latter review, which contained

---

151 Published in *La Semaine religieuse d'Angers*, November 3, 1957.
152 Pierre Lemaire to Bishop Chappoulie, Letter dated November 1, 1957 (copy kept in the Lemaire family archives).

only texts from the Magisterium, without commentary. On the other hand, he clearly specified the scope of his warning:

> You must cease publishing on the territory of the diocese of Angers the two incriminated publications: the review *Paternité-Maternité, Documents-Paternité*, and their supplement.[153]

No. 81 of *Paternité*, which was already at the printer's, was the last to be published.

Pierre Lemaire considered leaving Angers at that time, where he was now *persona non grata* with the bishop. He did not leave the city until two years later, when he had found a suitable place to continue his activities: it was Saint-Céneré, in Mayenne, where he set up a printing house and published books, brochures, and reviews. For the time being, he did not decide to retire from all lay apostolate – he was not yet fifty-five years old – and he did not give up publishing, distributing, and fighting. In March 1958, still in Angers, he launched a new "monthly magazine at the service of families" entitled *Défense du foyer*. In continuity with *Paternité*, this new publication was nevertheless different from it by adding other concerns. The cover defined the magazine as an "Organe d'action et de documentation familiales et civiques" ("Publication of family and civic action and documentation") and displayed as its motto: *FOI FAMILLE PATRIE* ("Faith, Family, Country").[154] The order of the words indicated an order of priorities. Pierre Lemaire specified in the editorial of the first issue that the new journal would endeavor to "defend what is essential, that is, our faith, our family, our country." "It appears," he also said,

> at a serious moment: because we have denied the Author of all good, all authority is disappearing. The evil is so great that our overseas empire is collapsing.... Our sons are fighting in Algeria, but it is in France that the real problems arise. The impotent State no longer defends essential values. It is sinking into anarchy and corruption. We, fathers, have the obligation – it is a matter of life and death – to restore order, first at home, and then in the city.

This pessimistic analysis of the situation was rather premonitory, since two months later, on the occasion of the umpteenth political crisis linked to the Algerian war, the regime of the Fourth Republic did in fact collapse. Pierre Lemaire had asked General Weygand to contribute the opening article of the first issue. In a letter, the general stated:

---

153 Bishop Chappoulie to Pierre Lemaire, Letter dated November 4, 1957 (Lemaire family archives).
154 In continuity with *Paternité*, *Défense du foyer* also had an image of the Archangel Saint Michael defeating the dragon on its back cover.

> What is at stake is the independence, the dignity, the freedom of all Frenchmen, of all the families of France; it is the patrimony that we have received, it is the future of our children, it is our faith as Catholics. All of this is under threat.
> Our duty seems clear to me: to fight to defend our values which, on the natural level, engage every man worthy of the name, and, on the supernatural level, engage every Christian.

At a time when the Fourth Republic, undermined by chronic governmental instability, had to face a war in Algeria that dared not speak its name, the ninety-year-old general did not appear as a possible recourse to raise the country back up, but rather as a moral authority. He was honorary president of the CEPEC, a think tank for "restoring the civic spirit and political culture," and he presided over the *Alliance Jeanne d'Arc*, created the previous year to "devote all its energy to the defense of French honor, which is precisely proportional to the faithfulness of men and institutions to God."

GOD IN THE CONSTITUTION

On April 15, 1958, the fall of the government led by Félix Gaillard began a political crisis that lasted several weeks. The prospect of a new government favorable to negotiations with the FLN independence rebels led to a reaction from supporters of French Algeria, both civilian and military. A large patriotic demonstration was organized in Algiers on May 13, 1958 by Pierre Lagaillarde, a lawyer and president of the *Association générale des étudiants d'Algérie* (AGEA, "General Association of Algerian Students"), and by Robert Martel, a wine grower in the Mitidja plain and the founder of the *Union française nord-africaine* (UFNA, French North African Union). The demonstration, which brought together more than 100,000 people, led to the seizure of the French government in Algeria and the creation of a Public Safety Committee ("Comité de Salut Public," CSP) led by General Massu. Robert Martel, who was a member of this CSP, was a convert. He was nicknamed the "Chouan ["Vendean" – *Translator*] of Mitidja." He hoped that this revolt movement in Algiers would mark the beginning of a Catholic counter-revolution throughout France, under the emblem of the Sacred Heart. He was able to address the crowd once, on May 13, from the balcony of the General Government,[155] but he was isolated within the CSP, in which there were a number of different currents. On May 15, General Salan, commander-in-chief in Algeria, expressed solidarity with the

---

155 Robert Martel, *La Contrerévolution en Algérie* (Paris: Diffusion de la Pensée française, 1972), 288.

CSP, while other public safety committees were being formed in France. In metropolitan France, the left-wing parties and much of the press denounced a military coup and feared a takeover in Paris. On the other hand, some Catholics were enthusiastic about the reaction in Algiers, which occurred on May 13, the feast of the first apparition of the Virgin Mary at Fatima. It seemed to them that regime change was possible.

After two weeks of crisis, on May 29, the President of the Republic, René Coty, called upon "the most illustrious among the French," General de Gaulle, to form a new government. On June 1, the National Assembly voted to swear in the General by 329 votes out of 553. The next day, the representatives granted him the power to govern by executive order for a period of six months and authorized him to carry out a constitutional reform of the country. Some Catholic movements and various personalities then undertook a fight to have God acknowledged in the future Constitution.

In his inaugural speech, General de Gaulle had reaffirmed, against those who suspected him of wanting to establish a military dictatorship, that "universal suffrage is the source of all power." During the debates that took place in the following days in the Chamber of Deputies, a deputy from the independent group, Guy Jarrosson, with links to Jean Ousset's *Cité catholique*, challenged this statement: "It should be acknowledged," he declared,

> that the only source of power is God. Indeed, what does our republican motto mean without this guarantee? What becomes of liberty, equality, and fraternity if their foundation is only in the law, the fleeting expression of majorities, a law that can be constantly called into question?[156]

Pierre Lemaire attached great importance to this declaration. He saw it as so important an indication of a possible reaction by Catholics that he quoted it entire in the editorial of *Défense du foyer*. Even the diocesan paper of Paris seemed, in June, to move in this direction. In a four-page text, the *Semaine religieuse de Paris* examined the republican motto and sought to draw out "the Christian and true notion of liberty, equality, and fraternity." Multiplying quotations from the teachings of Leo XIII and St. Pius X, the text concluded that in a political constitution "abstract notions, enchanting and flattering as they may be, are more prone to equivocation and error than are concrete realities such as God, family, country, and work on which any balanced society rests."[157] This unsigned text appeared in the "unofficial part" of the

---

156 *Journal officiel. Débats de l'Assemblée nationale*, session of June 2, 1958, 2648.
157 "Liberté–Égalité–Fraternité," *Semaine religieuse de Paris* (June 21, 1958): 702-5.

Parisian diocesan review; it did not commit the Archbishop of Paris.

In August, a draft constitution was presented by the government to the Constitutional Advisory Committee. Article 1 of the draft proclaimed: "France is an indivisible, secular, democratic and social Republic," thus repeating the first article of the 1946 Constitution that had established the Fourth Republic. The episcopate, as a whole, regretted that God as the origin of all power did not appear in the Constitution. But few bishops made comments of a doctrinal nature. One of the few was Bishop Morilleau of La Rochelle, a fellow student of Archbishop Lefebvre's at the French Seminary in Rome who had stayed in touch with him. He published a communiqué to deplore the fact that, in the draft constitution, the reference to the Declaration of the Rights of Man of 1789 covers "a serious error, which can be called naturalism or political atheism, or practical atheism. Catholics cannot accept this transfer of the primacy of God to human nature." He was concerned that France would be defined as a "secular republic."[158]

Various Catholic organizations, both separately and together, sought to have this article modified so that the future constitution would at least make reference to God. Pierre Lemaire had a four-page, two-color (black and red) tract published denouncing "the secularism of the state, the rejection of God and his law" and making a demand: "We want God in our families, in our schools, and in our institutions." He distributed it in packets of one hundred copies. This tract was known in Algiers, and convinced Robert Martel, who urged General Massu and the CSP to reject the constitution that was being prepared and to vote "no" in the referendum that would be organized. Not being able to do so, he resigned from the CSP after reading out a statement in which he said:

> From now on I refuse to support this regime of the godless, source of the perversion that is destroying us, and it is my honor to give you my resignation from the May 13 Public Safety Committee.... [B]y saying "No" to the referendum, we will be saying "Yes" to the vocation of France, "Yes" to her empire, and "Yes" to her glorious Army.[159]

On August 18, Admiral de Penfentenyo, who was on the board of *Cité catholique*, addressed an open letter to General de Gaulle, President of the Council [equivalent to President of France – *Translator*], to protest the definition of France as a "secular Republic." He asked de Gaulle

---

158 *Bulletin religieux de La Rochelle et Saintes* (September 11, 1958), quoted in *DC* (September 28, 1958), col. 1271.

159 Quoted in Henry Coston, *Partis, journaux et hommes politiques d'hier et d'aujourd'hui* (Paris: La Librairie française, 1967), 1: 218-19.

to "earnestly set aside all equivocation, either by explicitly recognizing the divine origin of all rights . . . or, at least, by avoiding in the new Constitution any ambiguous term and any affirmation of principle likely to aggravate the division among Frenchmen." This letter was featured in *Défense du foyer* and in *La Pensée catholique*. During this same period, Deputy [comparable to a US Congressman – *Translator*] Jarrosson tried to obtain a meeting with Pius XII. On August 18, he was not granted a private audience, as he had hoped, but a "special audience" (i.e., as part of a group). The Pope could only say a few kind words to him and told him to present the matter to Monsignor Veuillot at the Secretariat of State. From his meeting with Veuillot, the deputy from Lyon understood that an intervention of the Holy See with the French government was "out of the question," as the Holy See usually refrained from "interfering in the internal affairs of states." [160]

In early September, as the referendum on the Constitution was scheduled for the 28th, Pierre Lemaire devoted the entire issue of *Documents-Paternité* to the subject: *Dans la confusion du référendum: une France à l'envers?* ["Amid the confusion of the referendum: An upside-down France?"]. He also published a fifteen-page brochure that summarized the argument: *Oui ou non? On ne se moque pas de Dieu*] ["Yes or No? God will not be mocked"]. Moreover, he wrote with Joseph Dévé an open letter to the President of the Council. In this "ultimate supplication" to de Gaulle, dated September 3, they asked that the text of the Constitution be revised, and that the qualification of "secular" be removed.

On September 13, General Chassin and Robert Martel put together the founding congress of the *Mouvement populaire du 13-Mai* (MP-13) in Paris. Robert Martel made a virulent declaration against the draft constitution: "The spirit of May 13 has been stolen from us in order to subject fifty-five million French people to the diktats of a million Freemasons and atheists. . . ." [161] Also on September 17, thirteen Catholic organizations and publications (notably the *Alliance Jeanne d'Arc*, *La Pensée catholique*, *Défense du foyer*, and Georges Sauge's *Centre d'études supérieures de psychologie sociale*) published a "Declaration" that demanded that the draft constitution presented to the French people should include the following statement in its preamble:

> The Constitution of France is founded upon the natural law which, having God as its author, is prior to and superior to any law of human origin and guarantees, by maintaining them within fair limits, individual and collective liberties.

160 Guy Jarrosson, *Note confidentielle* (undated), five typewritten pages, Pierre Lemaire archives.
161 *Le Monde*, September 26, 1958.

On the very same day, however, the five French cardinals (Liénart, Gerlier, Roques, Feltin, and Grente) signed a declaration disapproving of "the inappropriate propaganda that incites Catholics to abstain or to reject the draft Constitution by invoking only the demands of their faith." They reminded Catholics of "the duty to vote" and reckoned that "neither the absence of any reference to God . . . nor the use of the term 'secular' . . . can prevent Catholics from freely expressing their opinion on the proposed text." The five Cardinals' declaration nevertheless ended with a "fervent wish" that one day it would be "possible, with the agreement of all citizens, to include the name of God in the text of the institutions of France."[162]

On September 28, 1958, the new Constitution was adopted by referendum, with over 79% of ayes. It was promulgated on October 4. A debate of a similar nature resurfaced in 2004 when reference was made to the "Christian roots" of Europe in the draft preamble to the European Constitution.

THE "RELIGIOUS IMPACT" OF THE WAR IN ALGERIA

Catholics were divided on the policy to follow in Algeria both before and after the change in Constitutions. The "Integrists" were blamed for their support of French Algeria and of the OAS [*Organisation Armée Secrète*, an armed group in favor of keeping Algeria French – *Translator*].

Émile Poulat believes that the "religious impact" of the Algerian War on French Catholicism before the Second Vatican Council has been underestimated. It "strongly contributed to developing the feeling of mutual incompatibility between the extremes of French Catholicism: 'progressives' and 'integrists,'"[163] at least in their vision of history and civilization. Between the two, he claims there was an "intermediate level," that of the French bishops and *La Croix*, who sought a middle way: not support for the insurrection, but encouragement to move beyond frozen colonial situations. In fact, one can observe that the episcopate took divergent positions over the years.

A month after the November 1954 insurrection, the three bishops of Algeria (Duval, Lacaste and Pinier) called for "the establishment of a solid friendship between Christians, Muslims, and Israelites" and considered that the rebellion of the FLN (which was left unnamed) was first of all a demand for "social justice."[164] Then, as early as October 1956,

---

162 *DC*, 28 September 1958, cols. 1267-68.
163 Émile Poulat, *Une Église ébranlée. Changement, conflit et continuité de Pie XII à Jean-Paul II* (Paris: Casterman, 1980), 114.
164 "Déclaration de l'épiscopat algérien," *Semaine religieuse d'Alger*, December 2, 1954 and *DC*, January 23, 1955, cols. 85-87.

Archbishop Duval of Algiers evoked "the need to progressively satisfy the desire for self-determination of the populations of Algeria,"[165] a position the French government would not take until three years later, in General de Gaulle's famous September 16, 1959 speech.

Conversely, Cardinal Saliège, Archbishop of Toulouse, had joined the Union for the Safeguard and Renewal of French Algeria (*Union pour la sauvegarde et le renouveau de l'Algérie française*, USRAF) at its foundation by Georges Bidault and Jacques Soustelle in 1956. In 1959, Cardinal Feltin, Archbishop of Paris, during a visit to the troops in Algeria as Chaplain General of the Armed Forces, did not mention either self-determination or independence for Algeria and praised "the army's work of construction, education and true pacification."[166]

The differences within the episcopate were nevertheless less marked than the differences within the Catholic press and Catholics generally. The range of positions was considerable. The "Janson network" of aid to Algerian independence fighters had been organized in metropolitan France since 1957: it harbored FLN leaders, helped in getting them into or out of France, and routed funds "collected" by them. It included in its ranks a number of Catholics and several priests, such as Father Robert Davezies. While *Témoignage chrétien* supported the legitimacy of the demand for independence in Algeria from the outset – as it had done for Indochina, Tunisia, and Morocco – the weekly did not approve of the "mules" because "to participate really and directly in the military action of the GPRA is to break willingly with the French nation."[167] At the other end of the spectrum, Catholics in Algeria and in France joined the Secret Armed Organization (*Organisation Armée Secrète*, OAS), a clandestine political-military organization created in February 1961 to defend the French presence in Algeria through armed attacks, including against de Gaulle.

Certain priests, while they did not provide direct support to the OAS, did legitimize France's struggle to hang on to the territory of Algeria. Such is the case of Father Georges de Nantes, who was soon to become one of the first opponents of the Second Vatican Council. A brilliant young priest (with three degrees: philosophy, theology, social and economic sciences) and a teacher in various educational institutions, he had been contributing since September 1956 to *L'Ordre français*,

165 Confidential letter to the priests of Algiers dated October 7, 1956, quoted in Pierre Boz, *Une fin des temps. Fragments d'histoire des chrétiens en Algérie* (Paris: Desclée de Brouwer, 2009), 91.

166 *DC*, December 20, 1959, col. 1598.

167 *Témoignage chrétien* (March 18, 1960), quoted by Valentine Gauchotte, *Les Catholiques en Lorraine et la guerre d'Algérie* (Paris: L'Harmattan, 1999), 62.

a nationalist monthly created a few months earlier. He immediately published numerous articles on the war in Algeria in which he tackled the question in all its dimensions: the progressive theologians who refused to defend Christianity in Algeria (no. 5, 1956); French Algeria, "A historical community to be defended" (no. 6, 1956); the question of torture ("Morality and torture," nos. 14 and 15, 1957), and also a series of articles on the origins of Islam.[168] Father de Nantes claimed that military commitment to defend French Algeria was a struggle against "revolutionary and Islamo-Marxist Algerian nationalism," but he saw further, to the necessity of evangelizing Algeria. He had felt the call of a missionary monastic vocation since his youth, and in the spirit of Father Charles de Foucauld he wrote a *Provisional Rule for the Little Brothers of the Sacred Heart* in the summer of 1957.[169] In September of 1958, Bishop Le Couëdic welcomed him *ad experimentum* into the diocese of Troyes, and entrusted him with the parishes of Villemaur, Palis, and Planty. He settled down with his first three disciples, among whom were Gérard Cousin and Bruno Bonnet-Eymard, who had been his students at the college in Pontoise, and who would remain faithful to him until his death. On August 6, 1961, Bishop Le Couëdic, without yet giving the small community a canonical form, agreed to give its members the monastic choir habit. Father de Nantes continued to publish his *Lettre à mes amis*, which he had begun to publish on October 1, 1956. Originally it was a simple mimeographed sheet addressed to his spiritual sons and daughters, with a print run of about fifty copies, but over the years it became a publication that dealt more and more frequently with religious and political questions, and its circulation kept growing.[170]

Beginning in the autumn of 1961, the positions taken by Father de Nantes on French Algeria and against General de Gaulle, in his letters and also from the pulpit, caused divisions in the parish. Some boys from the church youth club, "without giving me too much notice," wrote Father de Nantes, "had made and distributed pamphlets, and organized night expeditions to paint pro-OAS graffiti; in short, they had caused a stir among the local police."[171] The communist weekly *L'Humanité*

---

168 This was an analysis of, and commentary on, the first two volumes of "Hanna Zakarias" (Gustave Théry, OP), *De Moïse à Mohammed* (1955, 1956), who sought to prove that Islam had originally been a Jewish heresy.

169 L. Perrin, "De l'appel du silence à Saint-Parres-lès-Vaudes. Un foucauldien malentendu," *Revue des sciences religieuses* 82 (2008): 483-96.

170 1,000 copies in the autumn of 1961; 6,000 by the end of 1963; 12,000 in July 1966; 16,000 in 1967.

171 Letter of Father de Nantes to the brothers in his community, March 16, 1962, published in Fr Michel de la Sainte Trinité, *Pour l'Église. Quarante ans de Contre-Réforme catholique*, vol. 1 (1988), 174-75.

Dimanche, no doubt alerted by some local militant, denounced "his reputation as an activist" and the "outrageous content of his sermons" and called on "the republican antifascist population of Villemaur" to "be vigilant and [to] take steps to neutralize this propagandist" (February 24, 1962). A month later, on March 14, the police searched the Villemaur rectory and Father de Nantes was taken into custody. Pending the outcome of the investigation (several of the youth-club boys were arrested and questioned), the priest was placed under arrest at the major seminary in Troyes. He remained there for fifteen days. During this time, the signing of the Evian agreements on March 18 and the coming into force of the cease-fire on March 19 put an end to the Algerian war, though not to massacres and bombings. Father de Nantes was still under house arrest at the seminary in Troyes when he heard on the radio, "with unspeakable emotion," the broadcast of the shootings in the Rue d'Isly on March 26, which left eighty dead and two hundred wounded.

Back in his parish of Villemaur on April 1, Father de Nantes was met with the city council's hostility. Bishop Le Couëdic asked him to submit his *Letters* to diocesan censorship before publication, as provided for by canon law. He refused, on the grounds that it was private correspondence (three hundred copies were printed at that time!). Finally, in a letter dated May 10, 1963, Bishop Le Couëdic withdrew the three parishes from him and asked him to leave the diocese. Father de Nantes appealed this decision to the Congregation of the Council, which was in charge of the clergy; it confirmed the bishop's decision. On September 16, 1963, he left Villemaur with the brothers of his community, and moved to a large house in Saint-Parres-lès-Vaudes, in the same diocese. A few years later, Father de Nantes would be the first priest to reject the Council as a whole.

"NATIONAL CATHOLICISM"

During the Algerian war, especially from the battle of Algiers (January-October 1957) onwards, the use of torture–to obtain information that would make it possible to avoid attacks–divided public and Catholic opinion. The books, articles, and manifestos published by Catholics who condemned the use of torture as immoral and degrading are well known: notably the posthumous writings of Jean Muller, a scout leader killed in Algeria in 1956; *Contre la torture* ("Against Torture") by Pierre-Henri Simon; and the articles by François Mauriac. On the other hand, some priests and Catholic laymen defended the legitimacy of seeking to obtain intelligence through exceptional means, while also reproving "abuses" and "odious acts of counter-terrorism." Both expressions are used by Father de Nantes, in the conclusion of his two 1957 articles on "Morality and Torture" mentioned above. At the same time, Father Louis Delarue, chaplain of the 10th paratroopers' division commanded by General Massu, wrote, at the request of certain officers of the division, "Réflexions d'un prêtre sur le terrorisme" ("A Priest's Thoughts on Terrorism"). He legitimized the use of "effective, even if unusual, means" to combat and prevent FLN terrorist attacks. Interrogations intended to avoid the death of innocent people were justified by the doctrine of the lesser evil: between "making a bandit suffer temporarily" and "letting innocent people be massacred . . . one should not hesitate to choose the lesser of the two: not a sadistic interrogation, but an effective one." [172] His text, intended only for the officers of the 10th DP, was nevertheless revealed by the press in June 1957. It provoked indignation among certain Catholic publications and personalities. Cardinal Feltin, General Chaplain of the Armed Forces, reproached him for having written and distributed his note without having referred it to his superiors at the chaplaincy, although he gave this assessment of it: "It's a good paper. It is! It is! Serious, well studied." [173] Father Delarue remained in office until 1960. After 1961, he encouraged officers and former officers to join the OAS.

A year after the controversy surrounding Father Delarue's text, the debate on torture recommenced with a study in *La Cité catholique*. But this time the controversy extended to attacks against *La Cité catholique* and its influence in the army, and ultimately led to the denunciation of "National Catholicism." A study signed "Cornélius," and entitled "Morality, Law and Revolutionary War" (*Morale, droit et guerre révolutionnaire*) was published in 1958 in three successive issues of *Verbe*, the monthly review of *La Cité catholique*. [174] This pseudonym, which refers to the centurion Cornelius in the Acts of the Apostles, actually covered a collective that certainly included Jean Ousset, other contributors to the journal, one or more theologians, and military officers. The study sought to demonstrate the legitimacy of the war waged in Algeria, its particular nature (a "revolutionary war"), and above all addressed the specific means to be used. The need to use "adapted means and methods of defense" and also to frame them with a new "legislation" was evoked.

---

172 Quoted in Xavier Boniface, "L'aumônerie militaire française en guerre d'Algérie," *Vingtième siècle. Revue d'histoire* 77 (January-March 2003): 50-51. See also Sylvie Thénault, *Algérie: des "événements" à la guerre. Idées reçues sur la guerre d'indépendance algérienne* (Paris: Le Cavalier bleu, 2012), 73-79.

173 Louis Delarue, *Avec le paras du 1er REP et du 2e RPIMa* (Paris: Nouvelles Éditions latine, 1961), 51.

174 Cornélius, "Morale, droit et guerre révolutionnaire," *Verbe* 90 (February 1958): 75-89; 91 (March 1958): 56-71; 92 (April 1958): 55-75.

It went on to consider the understanding of the law and morality:

> Law is not above morality: it is only a part of it. . . . It is not the
> dignity of the person which, in the final analysis, is the basis
> of the moral value of acts. Man finds his dignity only in his
> submission to the moral order.

This lengthy and highly doctrinal study concluded with an examination of "the lawfulness of corporal punishment, of the death penalty, and of non-lethal punishment." According to the constant teaching of the Church, the review recalled, "the use of corporal punishment" to induce a man to confess is not permissible; but it is morally justifiable that penalties, under certain conditions, be inflicted on a guilty person to induce him to say things he has not yet said:

> A guilty party may be sentenced to a punishment, that is, to
> suffering, and this, not only as a just punishment – i.e., vindic-
> tive punishment – but also for the immediate common utility –
> i.e., medicinal punishment – which is to provide information
> indispensable to the protection of the common good, when
> it is practically impossible otherwise to thwart projects that
> threaten this common good: a very frequent instance in times
> of revolutionary war.

The articles that appeared in *Verbe* were simultaneously reproduced in *Contact*, the publication of the tenth military region published in Algiers in conjunction with the Army's Psychological Action Service. This Service was directed until recently by Colonel Lacheroy, the theorist of "psychological warfare" and of the "psychological weapon."[175] The press campaign that was to develop denounced not only the legitimization of torture by *La Cité catholique*, but also its influence in the army, particularly in the *Cinquième Bureau* [the French military intelligence service – *Translator*] in charge of psychological action.

After *Témoignage chrétien*, which denounced the articles in *Verbe*, Father Jean-Marie Le Blond, in a long article published in the Jesuit review *Études*, protested against a "rudimentary theology" and a "solution" that are "neither Christian nor reasonable."[176] He summarized the position of *La Cité catholique* as follows:

> In short, while one cannot torture suspects, one may, one even
> must torture the guilty. . . . The conclusion is inescapable: all

---

175 See Paul Villatoux, "Le colonel Lacheroy théoricien de l'action psychologique," in *Des hommes et des femmes en guerre d'Algérie* (Paris: Autrement, 2003), 494-508; Paul and Marie-Catherine Villatoux, *La République et son armée face au péril subversif: guerre et action psychologique en France, 1945-1960* (Paris: les Indes savantes, 2005).
176 Jean-Marie Le Blond, "Les dangers religieux de la politique," *Études* (December 1958): 385-96.

revolutionaries, all rebels, and especially all intellectuals who
are in collusion with them, may be tortured.

Jean Ousset was indignant at this caricature. He responded to Father
Le Blond in January 1959 in a supplement of *Verbe* in which he published
the entire article of the Jesuit on the left page, answering it, point by
point, on the facing page. He also obtained, the following month, an
agreement that this long reply should be published in *Études*. Then he
was able to meet Father Le Blond. If we are to believe the biography of
the founder of *La Cité catholique*, the Jesuit theologian, "after having met
Jean Ousset, found himself in agreement with him on many points."[177]

But this controversy with the Jesuit magazine was only the prelude
to a campaign that began at the same time – and lasted for several
years – against *La Cité catholique* and its supposed allies, grouping them
all under the name "National Catholicism." It lasted several years and
was launched by *L'Express*, which was the first to coin the neologism,
on February 19, 1959. Obviously, it was coined by analogy with the term
"National Socialism," in order to stigmatize a current of ideas that had
never been defined by that term. The historian René Rémond, famous
for his typology of the right, to which several generations of students
and political commentators have referred, used the neologism himself
to designate "the close conjunction between the most intransigent
interpretation of dogma, the fussiest of nationalisms, and the counter-
revolutionary version of the right."[178]

At the time when it coined the term in February 1959, *L'Express* did
not bother to characterize it. The two-page anonymous article simply
identified this supposed National Catholicism with the "French integrist movement," and, curiously, devoted most of the article to Georges
Sauge, presented as "one of the principal animators of the movement."
The article multiplied errors and confusions. Two errors among others:
Sauge was presented as having separated in 1952 from Father Fillère, the
founder of the *Pour l'Unité* movement and of *L'Homme nouveau* – when
in fact the priest had died in 1949 – and as being one of the leaders of *La
Cité catholique*, whereas he had never belonged to the organization and
had never collaborated with the review *Verbe*. Georges Sauge, a former
communist and a convert of Father Fillère's, had founded in November
1956 the *Centre d'études supérieures de psychologie sociale* (CESPS), with
Jean Damblans, another convert of Father Fillère's. The main program
of the CESPS was to "show communism as it is," to oppose "Christian

---

177 R. de Neuville, *Jean Ousset et la Cité catholique*, 243.
178 René Rémond, *Les Droites en France*, 4th ed. (Paris: Aubier-Montaigne, 1982), 253.

mysticism" to it, and to disabuse the "hope of the communists" with the "hope of the Christians."[179] In addition to lectures and debates organized throughout France, the CESPS had tried to set up a "Psychological Force" made up of local "bases" for training and propaganda (towns, neighborhoods, businesses, etc.). From December 1959 onwards, they were succeeded by the Civic Committees for the Christian Social Order (*Comités civiques pour l'ordre social chrétien*) launched by Georges Sauge and Pierre Debray. But these two initiatives were mere flashes in the pan.

A few months after the article in *L'Express*, and other articles in the same vein (*France-Observateur*, May 21, 1959, and *L'Humanité*, October 12, 1959), Madeleine Garrigou-Lagrange published a much more developed and better informed study in *Esprit*.[180] She had met a certain number of the personalities she mentioned, had read their publications, and had attended some of their meetings. She sought to give credence to the idea that "integrism," as it was active in the late 1950s, was a kind of "National Catholicism." There was a "united front" of integrism, despite the differences in style among its leaders: she spoke of Jean Ousset's "abstruse syllogisms," of Pierre Lemaire's "invectives," of Paul Scortesco's "pseudo-prophetic symbolism," of Georges Sauge's "demonstrations," of the "veritable inquisition of the Catholic press" conducted by Jean Madiran. Referring to the analyses of Father Congar mentioned above, she defined the Integrists as "soldiers of order" who share a desire "to defend certain institutions, certain traditions considered as constitutive of 'Christian civilization.'"

Madeleine Garrigou-Lagrange also condemned *La Cité catholique* study groups that had been organized among officers serving in Algeria as well as the influence of *La Cité catholique* in the *Cinquième Bureau*. That influence was undeniable, as shown by Cornélius's study reprinted in *Contacts*, or by the participation of officials of the *Cinquième Bureau* (Colonel Goussault, Colonel Feaugas, Major Cogniet) in meetings organized around Jean Ousset in Paris. Ousset also kept up regular communications with other officers, notably Colonel Gardes and Colonel Château-Jobert, who went on to participate in the Algiers putsch in April 1961 or in the OAS. But Jean Ousset did not encourage them to take rash actions or to rebel; he insisted on the necessity of a good doctrinal training.[181]

The campaign against "National Catholicism," or, specifically, against *La Cité catholique*, continued in 1960 and 1961. Not that it was

179 Georges Sauge, *Échec au communisme* (Paris: Les Iles d'Or, 1958).
180 Madeleine Garrigou-Lagrange, "Intégrisme et national catholicisme," *Esprit* (November 1959): 515-43.
181 R. de Neuville, *Jean Ousset et la Cité catholique*, 241-42.

orchestrated by anyone, but whether through a ripple effect or through imitation, many publications, Catholic or not, published articles or dossiers. Without dwelling on it, we shall note the publication at the beginning of 1960 of a dossier of GETES (*Groupe d'études économiques et sociales*, "Group of Economic and Social Studies") devoted to the "National-Catholic Lobby." The various movements and journals considered to be part of this current (*La Cité catholique*, the CESPS and the *Comités civiques de sauge, Itinéraires, La Pensée catholique*, etc.) were presented in a rather summary manner. An organizational chart showed the supposed links between them. This organizational chart was reproduced by many newspapers and magazines and spread the idea that "National Catholicism" was an organized movement. A sociologist attached to the CNRS, Jacques Maître, a specialist in religious questions with links to Émile Poulat, at that time took a more thorough and better documented interest, in what he called not "National Catholicism" but "extreme right-wing Catholicism." He saw it as "a phenomenon of counter-acculturation in the face of certain aspects of secularization" and explained the links between the different organizations, movements, and reviews by common "orientations" which "favor collaboration between groups by convergence or complementary needs."[182]

Paradoxically, the articles critical or hostile to *La Cité catholique* were multiplying just as the organization took on international dimensions. There were already study groups in several countries. The year 1961 saw the establishment of autonomous organizations in Spain (first Congress of *Ciudad catolica*) and Argentina. In each of these countries a journal with the same title, *Verbo*, was published. It contained translations of articles that had appeared in the French magazine, information on the activities of the movement in the country, and articles written by authors who were to become the most notable representatives of Spanish traditionalism, Juan Vallet de Goytisolo and Eugenio Vegas Latapie. Jean Ousset's two principal works, *Pour qu'Il règne* and *Le Marxisme-Léninisme*, were also translated into Spanish during this period. Starting from issue 124 of *Verbe* (September–October 1961), in order to draw out the international dimensions of the movement and also to clarify the purpose of *La Cité catholique*, the magazine presented itself as the organ of the "International Center for Civic Formation and Doctrinal Action according to the Teachings of the Church" (*Centre international de formation civique et d'Action doctrinale selon les enseignements de l'Église*).

---

182 Jacques Maître, "Le catholicisme d'extrême droite et la croisade anti-subversive," *Revue française de sociologie* 2.2 (1960): 106-17.

In January 1962, Father de Soras, a Jesuit specialist in social questions and Catholic Action, devoted a study to *La Cité catholique* under a
cryptic title.[183] The booklet was widely read. "For the first time, there
was an in-depth study of *La Cité catholique*; it is a critical study, a highly
critical one even, but at last an argument," said Jean Madiran. The
first part presented in a rather factual way (not without underscoring
contradictions) the "broad outlines" of *La Cité catholique*; the second
part, which was far more critical, examined the "somewhat inopportune
use of pontifical documents." Father de Soras concluded his study with
the judgment that Jean Ousset and *La Cité catholique* often betrayed
"documents of the pastoral magisterium in political, economic and
social matters" by presenting them as definitive and univocal when
they should be the object of "exegesis" and historical contextualization.
Jean Ousset in a special issue of *Verbe* and Jean Madiran in a series of
articles in *Itinéraires*, Abbé Lefèvre in *La Pensée catholique*, and the
Revue des cercles d'études d'Angers responded to Father de Soras' analyses.
Jean Madiran invented a neologism, "Sorassism," to designate Fr de
Soras's position, which Madiran claimed both minimized or relativized
the teaching of the Church in political, economic and social matters
and reserved its application and explanation to theologians.

At this point various personalities gave their support to *La Cité
catholique*. On March 4, Marcel Lefebvre, who had just been named
bishop of Tulle, sent a long letter to Jean Ousset. In it he deplored
"the press campaign that is persistently being waged," but also, without
naming it, he blamed the daily newspaper *La Croix*: "The newspaper,
considered, rightly or wrongly, as the mouthpiece of the Church of
France, opens its columns wide to this odious campaign." He blamed,
again without naming him, Father de Soras ("the priest who wrote the
brochure that concerns you"): "One could not do better to remove
all moral authority from pontifical documents."[184] Sometime later,
a group of nine personalities (among them Marshal Juin, General
Weygand, Michel de Saint-Pierre, and Gustave Thibon) published a
declaration to deplore "the denigrations and moral aggressions" of
which *La Cité catholique* was a victim and to offer it "our sympathy
and our encouragements."[185]

In spite of its development abroad and the rare public support it

---

183 Alfred de Soras, *Documents d'Église et options politiques. Points de vue sur "Verbe"
et sur la "Cité catholique"* (Paris: Éditions du Centurion, 1962).
184 *Lettre de S. Ex. Monseigneur Lefebvre, Archevêque, Évêque nommé de Tulle à M. Jean
Ousset, Directeur de la "Cité catholique,"* supplement to *Verbe* 30.
185 Declaration published in *Verbe* 132 (June-July 1962): 59-60.

received, there was no end to hostile articles,[186] and Jean Ousset decided
to go to Rome to seek the advice of Cardinal Ottaviani, secretary of the
Congregation of the Holy Office, who had several times given his public
support to *La Cité catholique*. The cardinal "recommended that he leave
France and establish the international headquarters of *La Cité catholique*
in another country."[187] In the spring of 1962 the installation of the
"international managing offices" of *La Cité catholique* in Québec City was
made official. Jean Ousset would divide his time for some years to come
between France and the American continent (Canada and Argentina).

BRAZILIAN TRADITIONALISM

At the time *La Cité catholique* did not have any formal groups in
Brazil, although it had some support there. There was another influential and well-organized traditionalist movement that had developed
there since before the war.

The name of Plinio Corrêa de Oliveira stands out among the pre-
cursors of Brazilian traditionalism. The son of a former Prime Minister
who had remained faithful to the Brazilian imperial dynasty despite the
proclamation of the republic, as a student Oliveira created the Catholic
University Action (*Ação Universitária Católica*, AUC) to bring together
the Catholic students of the University of São Paulo Law School. In 1932,
together with two young Catholic activists, he founded the Catholic
Electoral League (*Liga Electoral Católica*, LEC). He was elected deputy
to the Constituent Assembly in 1933, and served there until 1936. During
this period, he invited two professors at the major seminary of São
Paulo, Fr Antonio de Castro Mayer and Fr Geraldo de Proença Sigaud,
to contribute to the magazine he had founded, *O Legionario*. In 1936,
the magazine became a weekly distributed throughout the country. In
1943, Plinio Corrêa de Oliveira, who was then president of the Arch-
diocesan Office of Catholic Action in São Paulo, published *Em Defesa
da Ação Católica*. In it, he denounced the progressive errors that were
spreading within Catholic Action and Brazilian society: the neglect of
the interior life, religious indifferentism, the equality between clergy
and laity, the attraction to profane and immodest leisure activities
(dancing, the beach, Mardi Gras). Because of their links with Corrêa
de Oliveira and their support for his book, Fathers Proença Sigaud and

---

186 The *France-Observateur* of July 20, 1962 accused *Verbe* of forging the "ideology"
that inspires the "terrorists" of the OAS; *L'Express* of September 27, 1962 denounced
the close links between Colonel Bastien-Thiry, who had organized the Petit-Clamart
assassination attempt against de Gaulle, and *La Cité catholique*.
187 R. de Neuville, *Jean Ousset et la Cité catholique*, 216.

Castro Mayer lost their professorships at the major seminary in 1946. Proença Sigaud was sent to Spain, but his exile was short-lived. Thanks to the intervention of Cardinal Benedetto Aloisi Masella, who had been Apostolic Nuncio to Brazil until February 1946, he was able to return to Brazil in the summer of 1946. On October 29 he was appointed Bishop of Jacarezinho and the following year Bishop de Castro Mayer was appointed Coadjutor Bishop of Campos. In 1951 he founded a monthly magazine, *Catolicismo*, which was to become the principal periodical of Brazilian traditionalism. The very long opening article of the first issue, unsigned but written by Corrêa de Oliveira, was entitled "The Crusade of the 20th Century" and outlined a political-religious ideal very close to that of the French *Cité catholique*: to establish the Reign of Christ in souls but also in society. Life on earth is a "novitiate" that must "prepare for the contemplation of God face to face," a "path" that will lead to Heaven through the fulfillment of the Christian virtues and of the evangelical counsels. Corrêa de Oliveira also presented a "Christian ideal of social perfection": "civilization will be Catholic" if "the spirit of the Church becomes the normative and vital principle of its morals, institutions, and literary and artistic achievements." Did Plinio Corrêa de Oliveira, Bishop de Proença Sigaud, and Bishop de Castro Mayer already know about *La Cité catholique* and *Verbe* at this time? In any case, a few years later, the two bishops became familiar with it and found in it the same ideal and the same struggle as their own. For the congress of *La Cité catholique* held in Angers in September 1954, which was devoted to the Social Kingship of Christ, Bishop de Proença Sigaud sent an enthusiastic message praising the effort to give "a temporal physiognomy to the message of Christ."[188] Two years later, Bishop de Castro Mayer informed *La Cité catholique* that "*Verbe* has spread among us and is doing us considerable good."[189] In imitation of what *La Cité catholique* was doing in France, groups for the dissemination and study of the magazine *Catolicismo* were created throughout Brazil.

In 1959, *La Cité catholique* printed a translation of the important pastoral letter published by Bishop de Castro Mayer in 1953, "On the Problems of the Modern Apostolate," which included a *Catechism of Opportune Truths that Oppose Modern Errors.*[190] This *Catechism* responded to eighty erroneous statements with eighty Catholic statements, followed each

---

188 *Verbe* 64 (August–September 1954).

189 Letter dated July 14, 1956, quoted in R. Neuville, *Jean Ousset*, 201.

190 This 116-page booklet, published as a supplement to *Verbe* 103 (July 1959), would be published again as an offprint in 1962, once *La Cité catholique* was headquartered in Québec.

time by a lengthy "Explanation." It should be noted that the first errors denounced by Bishop de Castro Mayer concerned liturgical practices which, in some cases, would become widespread in the Church following the liturgical reform after Vatican II: the Mass *versus populum*, the altar in the form of a table, etc. This *Catechism* fought against errors in all areas: "balls, dances, and swimming pools" are "proximate and voluntary occasions of sin, from which one must abstain" (no. 11), as are "carnival entertainments" (no. 56); the State cannot declare itself neutral and "must place all its resources at the service of the preservation and expansion of the faith" (no. 66); in economic matters "Catholics must accept neither liberalism nor socialism" (no. 80).

That same year, 1959, Plinio Corrêa de Oliveira published what is considered to be his masterpiece, *Revolução e contra-revolução*. The book describes "Revolution" as a gnostic and egalitarian ideology that originated in humanism and the Renaissance, and later took different forms in the French Revolution and the Russian Revolution of 1917. The book also describes the counter-revolutionary action to be taken. It was to have a great diffusion, with 26 editions and translations in many languages (in French from 1960 by *Catolicismo* Editions, under the title *Révolution et contre-révolution* [first English edition: *Revolution and Counter Revolution*, Fullerton, California: Educator Publications, 1972]).

On July 26, 1960, Plinio Corrêa de Oliveira founded the *Sociedade Brasileira de defesa da Tradiçao, Familia e Propriedade*, better known by the initials TFP (Tradition, Family, Property), in São Paulo. This organization, whose president, Plinio Corrêa de Oliveira, and vice-president, Fernando Purquim de Almeida, were appointed for life, had branches in more than twenty countries. It multiplied campaigns on various subjects, and was, as we shall see, controversial in itself, as well as for its methods of recruitment and propaganda, and for the cult of personality that developed around the *Fundador* and his mother.

At the time there was complete agreement between Bishop de Proença Sigaud, Bishop de Castro Mayer, and Plinio Corrêa de Oliveira. The *Vota* that the two Brazilian bishops wrote in 1959, in preparation for the coming Council, exhibit analyses close to those of *Revolução e contra-revolução*. In 1960, Plinio Corrêa de Oliveira prepared a book to oppose the government's agrarian reform. He had the two bishops review the theological part of his text. The book, published in November 1960, *Reforma Agrária. Questão de Consciência*, caused a great deal of controversy, even among some traditional Catholics, such as the writer Gustavo Corção. This book, as well as the pastoral letter of Bishop de

Castro Mayer "against the artifices of the communist sect" (1961), the anti-communist Catechism published by Bishop de Proença Sigaud in 1962, and the pastoral letter he published against "the communist sect" in 1963, contributed to the fall of President João Goulart, who was accused of collusion with the Brazilian Communist Party (PCB) and the Brazilian Socialist Party (PSB).

At the Second Vatican Council, which opened in 1962, the two Brazilian traditionalist bishops, along with Archbishop Lefebvre, were among the most active members of the "minority" who opposed the doctrinal changes in preparation.

CHAPTER 3

The "Minority" at Vatican II

O F THE ROUGHLY TWO THOUSAND BISHOPS WHO participated in the Second Vatican Council (1962-1965), very few are still alive. The texts that were promulgated—four constitutions, two of which are described as "dogmatic," nine decrees, and three declarations—are part of the Church's Magisterium. This twenty-first Ecumenical Council is now part of the history of the Church, and has been the subject of countless historical and theological studies.[1] But almost sixty years after its inauguration, the texts it promulgated are still the subject of discussion, and give rise to divergent interpretations. Several of the reforms it initiated—notably that of the liturgy and the aggiornamento of religious orders and congregations—were, from the outset, the object of criticism and contestation, which sometimes went as far as outright rejection.

Without giving a complete outline of the history of the Council, we will mention the way in which traditionalists experienced it, and tried to intervene in its development and the drafting of its texts. At the first Vatican Council (1869-1870), there was a "liberal minority" in the face of a very large majority of bishops in favor of the Pope's project. The Council was able to pass only two constitutions, one on revelation and faith, the other on papal primacy, which defined the dogma of papal infallibility. It had to leave off its work on September 1, 1870, following the invasion of the Papal States by the Kingdom of Italy. Pius XI in the 1920s, and then Pius XII after the Second World War and until 1951, gave some thought to resuming this interrupted council. They set up study commissions, but both then abandoned the project, each for different reasons.[2]

---

1 The most complete chronicle of the council is that published from 1959 onwards by Fr Giovanni Caprile, SJ, in *La Civiltà cattolica*, and then printed as a monograph: *Il concilio Vaticano II*, 6 vols. (Rome: Edizioni La Civiltà Cattolica, 1966-1969). The largest history of the council is that edited by Giuseppe Alberigo and an international team of researchers: *History of Vatican II*, 5 vols. (Maryknoll, NY: Orbis, 1995-2005). In counterpoint to this history, which exists in several languages, cf. Msgr Agostino Marchetto, *The Second Vatican Ecumenical Council: A Counterpoint for the History of the Council* (Eugene, Oregon: Wipf and Stock, 2010) and *Il Concilio Vaticano II. Per la sua corretta ermeneutica* (Vatican City: Libreria Editrice Vaticana, 2012).

2 Giovanni Caprile, "Pio XI e la ripresa del concilio Vaticano," in *Il Concilio Vaticano II*, I, 3-14; "Un nuovo progetto di concilio al tempo di Pio XII," ibid., 15-35 and "Alcune osservazioni su 'Pio XII e il Concilio,'" ibid., 687-89.

John XXIII, the successor of Pius XII, said that the idea of convening an ecumenical council came to him on January 20, 1959, while he was examining the situation of the Church and the world with his Secretary of State, Cardinal Tardini:

> Our interlocutor listened in an attitude of respectful expectation. Suddenly, a great idea arose in Us and illuminated Our soul. We accepted it with an unspeakable confidence in the divine Master, and a solemn, imperative utterance rose to Our lips, Our voice expressed it for the first time: a Council![3]

The reality is rather different. In fact, as soon as John XXIII was elected on October 28, 1958, as the conclave was about to end, Cardinals Ruffini and Ottaviani, who instigated the project for a council that was discussed under Pius XII's pontificate, suggested it to the new Pope. A few days later, Cardinal Ruffini was received in audience by John XXIII and brought it up again. Soon, John XXIII spoke about it again with his secretary, Monsignor Capovilla. The idea therefore predates the conversation of January 20, 1959 with Cardinal Tardini. On the other hand, it is true that it was only after this conversation that John XXIII asked about the projects prepared under his predecessors. Then, on January 25, before the cardinals gathered in consistory, he announced the convocation of "an ecumenical council for the universal Church."

In the first encyclical of his pontificate, *Ad Petri Cathedram*, dated the following June 29, he specified the guiding ideas he wished to give to this future council: "Truth, unity, and peace under the inspiration of charity," with "the hope of leading minds to a wider and deeper knowledge of the truth, a salutary reform of Christian morals and the restoration of unity, concord, and peace." This agenda exhibits a balance between a traditional, classical aim – knowledge of the truth and moral reform – and the generosity of the other, more vague ambition: to restore "unity, harmony, and peace." But more than the agenda itself, it was the historical context that was radically different from that of previous councils.

The Second Vatican Council was to take place in a world where there was no longer a Catholic empire, and in which few states had a concordat with the Church. Half of Europe, Russia, China, and other Asian countries were under communist rule, with officially atheistic states. In at least two dozen countries in Europe and Asia, the clergy – up to the highest ranking members of the hierarchy – were persecuted or at least severely hampered in their apostolate. It cannot be denied that this prospect distressed the Pope's heart, but he thought it necessary

---

3 Allocution during the audience of May 8, 1962, *DC* (June 3, 1962): 711. See also Y. Chiron, *Jean XXIII*, 275.

to use different methods and language from those of his predecessors to address the communist world. Hence the controversies that would arise during the Council.

In 1959, there was also the anxiety of war. The Second World War had ended less than fifteen years earlier, and peace had not ensued. The atomic threat and the "Cold War" between the two great powers were real. The Korean War (1950-1953) was a recent event and had raised fears of a third worldwide conflict. At the end of the 1950s, the Pope's thought, and that of many bishops following him, was to do everything possible to avert the danger of a new war. The preparatory period of the Council and its first session coincided with the end of the "Cold War" and the beginning of "détente" between the two great powers: the Khrushchev-Kennedy meeting in Vienna in 1961, and the installation of the "red telephone" between the Kremlin and the White House after the Cuban missile crisis in October 1962, the last of the great crises of the Cold War. A certain optimism now prevailed.

Mentalities, too, were undergoing significant changes, especially in the West. The Western world was embarking on what Canadian sociologist Louis Rade has called "Sixties-ism." He defines it as "an ideology of modernity that reached its peak in the 1960s and continued until the mid-1970s. It is characterized by individualism, a more or less radical rejection of authority, the refusal of duty, the demand for rights, youthism, consumerism and, at the same time, the contestation of this consumerism."[4] This "1960s" state of mind had become widespread before the Council met, and the bishops gathered in Council could not ignore it. It can be said that many of them, without approving it, did not want to contradict it head-on.

Finally, from a strictly religious point of view, in the still predominantly Catholic countries of Europe and in North America, secularization of society and education, as well as other factors, had led to an ever-decreasing number of regular Massgoers. In 1962, the year the Council opened, in Austria only one-third of Catholics attended Mass regularly; in France, the proportion was between 27 and 28%.[5] The de-Christianization of the Church goes back before the Council. John XXIII and a majority of the Council Fathers wanted to confront it with a new method and a new language. This was the intention proclaimed by the Pope in his famous opening address to the Council:

---

4 Louis Rade, *Église conciliaire et années soixante* (Paris: L'Harmattan, 2011).
5 Erich Bodzenta, *Die Katholiken in Österreich. Ein Religionssoziologischen Überblick* (Vienna: Herder, 1962); Yvon Lambert, "L'Évolution religieuse de la France au long de cinquante années," in *HAL. Archives-ouvertes*, 2000 [online].

This same sure and unchangeable doctrine, to which faithful
reverence must be shown, is to be deepened and presented in
the manner that our times demand. For the deposit of Faith,
that is, the truths contained in our venerable teaching, is one
thing, while the manner in which these are uttered is another,
albeit with the same meaning and sense. Much attention will
need to be paid to this manner and, if necessary, much work
will have to be patiently devoted to it. Methods of presentation
will need to be introduced that better suit a pedagogy whose
characteristic is above all pastoral.[6]

THE CONSULTATION OF BISHOPS

More than three years passed between the announcement of the
Council (January 1959) and its opening (October 1962). These three
and a half years of official preparation by various commissions created
by the Pope were also three years of growing excitement, debate, and
suggestions. Cardinals, bishops, theologians, priests, lay people, and the
Catholic press in every country spoke out about what they expected from
the Council, the questions they hoped to see addressed, and the reforms
they wished to see. This is what I have called the "peri-Council."[7] It
began before the Council, during the preparatory period, and continued
throughout the Council, though outside St. Peter's Basilica (*extra aula*),
in the innumerable meetings and lectures that took place in Rome after
the General Congregations, and also in the writings of the chroniclers
and commentators of the press around the world. In addition, there
were the debates, books, articles, and lectures that increased and multiplied between the sessions of the Council. It has been said that the
"Church was in a state of council." The image is historically accurate,
even if it is theologically and canonically questionable.

On May 17, 1959, John XXIII set up a pre-preparatory commission,
which he entrusted to the Secretary of State, Cardinal Tardini. Its
first task was to consult all the cardinals, archbishops, and bishops of
the world, as well as the superiors general of religious congregations.
Sometime later, in an audience with the philosopher Jean Guitton, he
explained his project in simple terms:

> I'm going to do a council. Not to condemn, though. We'll put
> aside the past and its misery. We won't start arguing about all
> that again. Naturally, I don't want to create a parliament. No, I

---

6 John XXIII, "Allocutio . . . in Sollemni SS. Concilii Inauguratione 'Gaudet Mater Ecclesia,'" *Acta Apostolicae Sedis* 54 (1962): 792, our translation.

7 Yves Chiron, "Paul VI et le péri-concile," in *La Papauté contemporaine (XIXe-XXe
siècles)*, eds. J.-P. Delville and M. Jacov (Louvain: BRHE/Vatican City: Archivio Segreto
Vaticano, 2009), 585-603.

will not invite the Protestants to have discussions with us. But I
will tell you the idea that came to me. It is not by arguing that
we will give them the idea to unite. The real way is to clean up
the face of the Church in all areas; let us give up what is not
essential, to purify ourselves, to rejuvenate ourselves.[8]

Jean Guitton adds:

I understood that he didn't want to rush anything, and above
all that he didn't have a clear idea of the methods and means,
or of the people involved. And he probably never would. But
he wanted to give lift, a momentum, an impulse, a movement
driven by love.

The responses of the bishops of the whole world and of the superiors general of religious orders arrived in Rome in July 1959. They had
been invited to express "in all freedom and sincerity, their remarks,
consilia and *vota* . . . on matters and subjects that might be discussed at
the next Council" as well as the reforms they would like to see introduced in the Church (even though the word reform was not used in
the letter addressed to the bishops). The antepreparatory commission
received some 2,150 responses. These were later published in full by
the Vatican in eight volumes, plus two volumes of thematic analysis.
Historians have studied many of these votes by country. A complete
and systematic study of the responses received in Rome is still lacking,
but Etienne Fouilloux has already drawn up a very significant panorama.[9] He points out that the three most frequent requests are "better
definition of the role of the bishop, speeding up liturgical reform, and
restoration of the permanent diaconate, which had been proposed by
Pius XII to compensate for the growing dearth of priestly vocations."

For our purposes, it is interesting to know the responses of those
who would soon become the principal representatives of what will
be called the "conciliar minority," as opposed to the majority current. Their opponents would call them traditionalists, even integrists.
They organized themselves in the *Cœtus Internationalis Patrum* (CIP)
whose five leaders were: Archbishop Lefebvre, the Brazilian bishops
de Proença Sigaud and de Castro Mayer, mentioned above, Dom Jean
Prou, elected Abbot of the Abbey of Saint-Pierre de Solesmes in July
1959, and as such President of the Confederation of Solesmes, which
encompassed eight abbeys, and Bishop Carli of Segni.

8 Words reported by Jean Guitton during his deposition for the beatification process,
quoted in Enrico Galavotti, *Processo a Papa Giovanni. La causa di canonizzazione di
Angelo Giuseppe Roncalli (1965-2000)* (Bologna: Il Mulino, 2005), 336.
9 Étienne Fouilloux, "The Antepreparatory Phase. The Slow Emergence from Inertia
(January, 1959-October, 1962), IV: The Responses," in *History of Vatican II*, 1: 109.

Philippe Roy-Lysencourt, who wrote his dissertation and numerous other works about the CIP, has analyzed the *vota* of its future leaders. The two Brazilian bishops were able to consult each other on the response to be made to Rome, but the other three were not: in 1959, they did not yet know each other. Nevertheless, there were common doctrinal concerns, notably the wish that the future Council condemn certain errors.[10] Bishop de Proença Sigaud was the most radical, judging that the Church had been facing a single enemy for several centuries: the Revolution. It had many faces—Freemasonry, communism, international Judaism—and used the "Trojan horse strategy." It was necessary to oppose it with a planned "counter-revolutionary struggle." Bishop de Castro Mayer denounced an "anti-Christian conspiracy" and hoped that the future Council would renew the condemnations made by Pius IX in the *Syllabus*, "in a highly solemn way, making the adaptations and numerous additions that our times demand." But several of these prelates also had pastoral concerns, and made proposals for reform. Dom Prou, the abbot of Solesmes, wanted an extension of the concelebration of the Eucharist; Archbishop Carli wanted, among other things, a reform of the liturgical calendar, the reduction of the days of fasting and abstinence, and the suppression of sponsors for baptism and confirmation; Archbishop Lefebvre advocated an increase in the number of bishops so that dioceses would not have more than 200,000 faithful, "accelerating the annulment process, simplifying the rules for Church benefices, extending the power to hear confessions, and granting wider permission for the celebration of evening Masses."[11] Traditionalists, therefore, were not obtuse conservatives concerned only with condemnation.

In the summer of 1960, John XXIII began the actual preparation of the Council. The ante-preparatory commission was dissolved, and ten preparatory commissions were set up to study the topics to be dealt with at the Council: Theology Commission, Bishops' Commission, Commission for Religious, Liturgy Commission, Commission for the Missions, and others. Their role was to prepare *schemas*, that is, draft constitutions or decrees that would then be submitted to the Council for discussion, amendment, and vote. Three secretariats were also set up, including the Secretariat for Christian Unity, presided over by Cardinal Bea, which was to have a decisive influence on the ecumenical perspective that Pope John XXIII intended to give to the Council. A

---

10 Philippe Roy-Lysencourt, *Les Vota préconciliaires des dirigeants du Cœtus Internationalis Patrum* (Strasbourg: Institut d'études du christianisme, 2015).

11 Tissier de Mallerais, *Marcel Lefebvre*, 273.

Central Preparatory Commission, composed of 120 members, presided over by the pope and with Archbishop Felici as secretary, would meet regularly to examine the plans drawn up by the preparatory commissions. Archbishop Lefebvre was a member of this commission.

Each commission was presided over by a cardinal and was composed of dozens of members chosen from among the bishops, priests, or religious competent in the matter assigned to them. They also included "consultors," that is, theologians whose opinions on particular points could be consulted. Several hundred theologians from all over the world were appointed as consultors. The Theological Commission included among its consultors two theologians who had been sanctioned under the pontificate of Pius XII, the Dominican Yves Congar and the Jesuit Henri de Lubac. The two had experienced their appointment as a rehabilitation. At the first meeting of the Central Commission in June 1961, Archbishop Lefebvre respectfully protested:

> We were very surprised, in my humble opinion, to read in the list of preparatory commissions the names of certain theologians whose doctrine does not seem to be endowed with the required qualities.... [12]

But among the members or consultants of the Theology Commission, there were also several theologians who would go on to collaborate with the CIP: the Dominicans Gagnebet and Labourdette, the Franciscan Ermenegildo Lio and Monsignor Lattanzi, dean of the Faculty of Theology at the Lateran.

In all, the commissions drew up seventy-five schemas on a multitude of topics. These schemas were examined as they were drafted by the Central Preparatory Commission during its seven sessions from June 1961 to June 1962. Archbishop Lefebvre would later say that, on the whole, these pre-conciliar texts contained "a solemn profession of sure doctrine in the face of modern problems." [13] But some members considered them insufficient, excessively stamped with Roman theology, and not sufficiently reflecting the direction that Pope John XXIII wanted to give to the Council. The discussions were lively. The two tendencies that would come to a head during the Council began to emerge in this preparatory period: "Among those most critical of the prepared texts were Alfrink, Döpfner, Frings, Hurley, König, Léger, Liénart, Maximos IV, Montini, and Suenens. Among the defenders

---

12 Ibid., 296.
13 M. Lefebvre, "Réponse au cardinal Ottaviani," December 20, 1966, published in *J'accuse le concile!* (Martigny: Éditions Saint-Gabriel, 1976), 109.

of the texts, Browne, Lefebvre, Ottaviani, Ruffini, and Siri were the most vocal." [14]

Without mentioning all of Archbishop Lefebvre's interventions during the sessions of the Central Commission, we will highlight three that point to his future struggle.

During the examination of the schema "On the deposit of faith to be preserved in its purity" presented by Cardinal Ottaviani, president of the Theological Commission, Archbishop Lefebvre asked that doctrinal errors be condemned by "canons" (formulas) redacted "precisely and almost scientifically" and that they be accompanied by a more positive and affirmative statement. [15]

During the examination of the schema on the liturgy presented by Cardinal Larraona, but which had been drafted under the direction of the secretary of the commission, Father Annibale Bugnini, Archbishop Lefebvre warned against too brutal and artificial a reform of the liturgy:

> We know from experience that the bishops are not asking for changes; it is certain priests of the liturgical pastoral commissions who have no other activity than to change things in the liturgy! . . . We must never forget that we are to "keep the traditions"; therefore, changes must be accepted with great caution. What is Tradition, if not the work of the Church throughout the ages? And this work generally brings with it the fruit of elaboration over many generations. [16]

Lastly, on the penultimate day of the seventh and final session of the Central Commission, two competing views of the relationship between Church and State were examined. One, presented by Cardinal Ottaviani, defended the traditional doctrine of "religious tolerance" for non-Catholic groups, while the other, presented by Cardinal Bea, argued for the affirmation of a right to "religious liberty" and for the "civil equality of cults." Archbishop Lefebvre supported Cardinal Ottaviani's scheme, regretting, however, that "it does not sufficiently show the goal of this doctrine, which is none other than the reign of Christ," and he voted against Cardinal Bea's scheme, which "is based on false principles" condemned by Pius IX in the encyclical *Quanta cura* (1864). [17] The question would be among those most argued about during and after the Council.

---

14 Joseph A. Komonchak, "The Struggle for the Council During the Preparation of Vatican II (1960-1962)," *History of Vatican II*, 1: 304.

15 Quoted in Tissier de Mallerais, *Marcel Lefebvre*, 276.

16 De Mallerais, *Lefebvre*, 296.

17 Ibid., 303-4.

THE "OCTOBER REVOLUTION"

Father Congar, who played an important role as *peritus* in the drafting of some of the texts promulgated by the council, had a famous expression: "The Church has carried out its October revolution peacefully." [18] He was not applying the comparison to the entire council but specifically to the doctrine of collegiality.

Nevertheless, from the very first days, the "Liénart incident" showed that some cardinals and bishops would not hesitate to upset the rules of the Council. The plan was that the schemas discussed in the general congregation would be corrected and completed by specialized commissions—there would be ten of them—before being examined again in the plenary session. The election of the members of these commissions was to take place during the first general congregation, on October 13, 1962. On that day, the secretary of the Council, Archbishop Felici, caused the list of the members of the pre-conciliar commissions that had drafted the schemas to be distributed, along with ten sheets of paper on which to write in the names of the members of the conciliar commissions. Did this not all but encourage the Council Fathers to copy over the names of the old commissions?

Cardinal Liénart, bishop of Lille, a member of the Council of Presidency, intervened to ask for an adjournment of the vote so that the Council Fathers could get to know each other, consult each other in episcopal conferences, and propose names themselves. The proposal was applauded. It challenged the rules, but it was not a personal initiative. In fact, the text read by Cardinal Liénart had been given to him, just before the session, by Cardinal Joseph Lefebvre and had been drafted by Archbishop Garrone, coadjutor of Toulouse. And another member of the Council of Presidency, Cardinal Frings, immediately intervened to approve the French cardinal, declaring that he was also speaking in the name of Cardinals Döpfner and König. This was the first public manifestation of a kind of coalition of certain European episcopates (France, Germany, Belgium, and the Netherlands) that would have a great deal of influence, and that would be summed up by an American chronicler of the council under the title *The Rhine Flows into the Tiber*.

Cardinal Tisserant was only able to postpone the vote scheduled for October 13 and to adjourn the session. The incident was widely reported in the press. *Paris-Soir* ran the headline: "French Bishops in Revolt at the Council!" Historian Philippe Levillain more accurately stated: "The intervention of Cardinal Liénart constitutes a very fine example of the

---

18 Yves Congar, *Le Concile au jour le jour, 2e session* (Paris: Éditions du Cerf, 1964), 115.

happy outcome of 'lobbying' activity by which the course of history is inflected."[19] The day after the "Liénart incident," John XXIII decided to give the bishops three days to consult each other before proceeding to the election of the members of the conciliar commissions.

The remainder of this first session at the Council, which lasted until December 1962, was marked by the rejection of the important schema *De Fontibus* ("On Revelation"), which a majority of the Council Fathers considered needed to be completely rewritten from a new perspective, and by passionate debates about the schemas on the liturgy and on ecumenism. The clashes of tendencies and opinions multiplied; they began to reveal a "majority" willing to incorporate new theological and pastoral orientations into the texts and a "minority" that was traditional in orientation. Archbishop Lefebvre, who was to be one of the major voices of this minority and who was then Superior General of the Holy Ghost Fathers, soon wrote to the religious of his congregation:

> One cannot conceive a council that does not express dogmatic clarifications against the modern errors that tend to distort dogma or even deny it. Hence the need to reaffirm traditional truths in such a way that these errors are formally eliminated.[20]

On the very day that the first session of the Council ended, December 8, 1962, Father de Nantes stated abruptly: "We can already be sure that the great confrontation between traditionalism and reformism will take place." And he noted that the only text adopted at the end of this first period of the Council was a *Message to All Men* that was "all the more disturbing in that the content and the form of this message bring us back to the preoccupations, conceptions, and hackneyed formulas of our very own French progressives."[21]

More radical yet was the campaign that Father Boyer and his group *Action-Fatima* launched at the time. Father Jean Boyer was an atypical personality within French Catholicism.[22] Ordained a priest in 1947, he joined the *Mission de Paris* two years later and became a worker-priest.

---

19 Philippe Levillain, *La Mécanique politique de Vatican II. La majorité et l'unanimité dans un concile* (Paris: Beauchesne, 1975), 188.

20 *Letter of Archbishop Lefebvre to the members of his congregation regarding the first session of the Council*, March 25, 1962, published in Philippe Roy-Lysencourt, *Recueil de documents du Cœtus Internationalis Patrum pour servir à l'histoire du concile Vatican II* (Strasburg: Institut d'étude du christianisme, 2019), 42.

21 Father George de Nantes, *Lettre à mes amis* 125 (December 8, 1962).

22 Besides his biography on the website of the *Communauté Notre-Dame de Fatima* he founded (www.fatima-la-salette-landes.fr), there is a sizable file on him at the historical archives of the archdiocese of Paris (*Archives historiques de l'Archevêché de Paris*, henceforth AHAP), 5 C 4.

In 1952, with the agreement of the Archbishop of Paris, he was "put on leave" (still incardinated in the diocese of Paris, but without an official assignment) and founded, with lay people, "The Community." It brought together, around him, young men and women who pooled their salaries and possessions and devoted themselves to the workers' mission after their day jobs. After the end of the priest-worker experience, Father Boyer gave in and moved with "The Community" to an abandoned house in Seignosse, in the Landes forest, to lead a life of prayer and work. In 1959, he discovered the message of the apparitions of the Virgin Mary at La Salette (1846) and at Fatima (1917). Considering that these messages concerned the present day, Father Boyer and his community decided to dedicate themselves to spreading them. "The Community" became the Community of the Hermits of Our Lady of Fatima and was approved as a "pious union" by Bishop Mathieu of Dax. The community prepared for the "events" that were to purify the world and allow "the Gospel to be proclaimed to the whole world before the Antichrist and the end of the world." An association, Action-Fatima, was created to publish and distribute–free of charge, it should be noted–brochures and books written by Father Boyer and the members of his community. It had branches in Paris, Bordeaux, and other cities. A first work against Father Teilhard de Chardin was published and distributed in 1962. And at the end of the first session of the Council, Father Boyer denounced the progressive drift of the Council and of the Church of France in leaflets and in an interview given to the magazine *Le Monde et la Vie*. This earned him a very severe public warning from Cardinal Feltin, Archbishop of Paris:

> The author of these lines has no credibility. What he writes about the Council is totally unfounded, and the reprobation in which he indiscriminately lumps together Freemasons, Teilhard de Chardin, the *Institut catholique*, seminaries, the Jesuits, and pastoral ministry as a whole shows a pitifully low level of information. Priests and the faithful should refrain from such harmful reading.[23]

This communiqué was reprinted in many diocesan newspapers in France. In February 1963, Cardinal Richaud, Archbishop of Bordeaux, published a "Severe Warning" against *Action-Fatima*, "formally forbidding, on the territory of his diocese, any action or diffusion of this work of propaganda" and placing "a serious obligation on all the faithful and priests of his diocese not to participate in any

---

23 *Semaine religieuse de Paris*, December 22, 1962.

way in '*Action-Fatima*.'"[24] Father Boyer did not heed these warnings. At the beginning of 1963, he published a new brochure entitled
S. O. S.... Council (eighty pages long) once again to denounce the
conciliar assembly's drift towards progressivism, while announcing
an impending war by the end of the year. The members of *Action-
Fatima* distributed leaflets and brochures in several cities, outside
the churches. In a communiqué, Cardinal Feltin warned against them
again: "[They] show up in public Catholic meetings, or distribute
leaflets at the door of churches. Young people are also being asked
to join these groups." The Archbishop of Paris warned that "such
publications and initiatives do not have the approval of ecclesiastical
authority."[25] Finally, on June 15, 1963, the Cardinal declared Father
Boyer suspended *a divinis* (i.e., forbidden to exercise priestly functions)
and struck him down as irregular. Father Boyer filed an appeal against
this decision in Rome and continued his action.

THE *OPUS SACERDOTALE*

At about the same time, though having nothing to do with the Boyer
case, an association of priests attached to tradition and to priestly holiness began to be formed. The founder was Canon Catta, a professor at
the Catholic University of Angers, mentioned above as a collaborator
of *La Pensée catholique* and of the *Revue des cercles d'études d'Angers*.
Every summer he would gather a few priests from the surrounding
area in his family home in Chiché, a village in the Poitou region. On
August 5, 1963, Father Jean Chessé, the pastor of Chiché, and three
other priests from the surrounding area met around Canon Catta.[26]
The principal topic of conversation was the Council, whose first session
had ended a few months earlier. All were worried about the turn the
Council debates had taken and the repercussions they had already
had in the life of certain dioceses and parishes. On three occasions
in the preceding months, the Assembly of Cardinals and Archbishops
of France had had to recall that "lay dress is absolutely forbidden to
clerics."[27] In the same period, Archbishop Lefebvre, in a long letter

---

24 *L'Aquitaine*, February 1, 1963.
25 *Semaine religieuse de Paris*, March 2, 1963.
26 Albert Jacquemin, *L'Opus sacerdotale: fondements historiques et canoniques d'une
association sacerdotale (1964-1974)*, Canon Law licentiate thesis, Institut catholique de
Paris (2007) and id., "*L'Opus sacerdotale*. Naissance, développement, apport et héritage
d'une société sacerdotale en France au XXe siècle (1964-1974)," *Revue d'histoire de l'Église
de France* 93 (2007): 175-89.
27 *DC*, August 19, 1962, 1079-1080; February 3, 1963, 213; May 5, 1963, 616-17.

to the members of his congregation, recalled the obligation to wear the cassock, the meaning and value of the ecclesiastical habit, and its abandonment as "cowardice" and a missed opportunity for "living preaching."[28]

Concurrently, the lively debates on the liturgy during the first session – especially on the use of the vernacular at Mass – and the prospects opened up for a reform of the Mass had encouraged and, in a certain number of parishes, legitimized liturgical changes and experiments. The Assembly of Cardinals and Archbishops of France, a few months after the end of the first session, had to publish a note to disapprove of these "liturgical anticipations":

> Nothing in the current rules and disciplines is to be changed before the final adoption and official promulgation of the new texts. Any anticipation would be unwise and unwarranted. In the present state of affairs, it would constitute an offence that would harm those who commit it and compromise rather than serve the cause of the liturgy.[29]

On top of this there was a general spirit of rebellion which claimed to be in the "spirit of the Council." The death of John XXIII on June 3, 1963, and the election of Paul VI on June 21, 1963, did not suspend the preparatory work for the second session. The new Pope confirmed the continuation of the Council, from which he expected a renewal of the life of the Church and a rapprochement with the "separated brethren."

The five priests gathered in Chiché on August 5, 1963 were concerned about the new debates that were going to roil the Council in the second session, to open the following month. That day, without yet founding an association, Canon Catta and the four priests who surrounded him, invoking the protection of the Virgin Mary at the foot of a statue of Our Lady of Lourdes, committed themselves to thinking about what initiative could be taken.

Each of them got other confreres interested in the concerns of the group and on April 1-2, 1964, the five of them met at the abbey of Notre-Dame de Fontgombault (of which Canon Catta was an oblate). They represented about twenty priests, belonging to six different dioceses. After two days of study with Dom Jean Roy, Abbot of Fontgombault, they decided to create a "priestly association" which would be called

---

28 Archbishop Lefebvre, *Lettre à tous les membres de la Congrégation du Saint-Esprit sur le port de la soutane*, February 11, 1963, republished in *Un évêque parle* (Poitiers: Dominique Martin Morin, 1974), 6-14.
29 Note of the Assembly of Cardinals and Archbishops, March 15, 1963, in *DC*, May 5, 1963, 617-18.

Opus Sacerdotale. It was not a new religious congregation, or even a brotherhood of priests, but an association for spiritual support and mutual doctrinal assistance among priests.

> We simply are priests who propose to support and strengthen each other, both from the point of view of our personal position and for the benefit of our apostolate, as we go through circumstances that are difficult, even serious, for the Church.[30]

The *Opus Sacerdotale* maintained close ties with the Abbey of Fontgombault and *La Pensée catholique* of Father Lefèvre, who joined the organization. The number of members continued to grow, reaching 810 in September 1974, the date of its founder's death. To these were added hundreds of religious who, although they could not join this type of priestly association, shared its views and concerns, and were able to receive the Circulars that *Opus Sacerdotale* regularly distributed. These circulars, written by Canon Catta, gave news of the association and contained doctrinal studies devoted mainly to priestly identity, the life of the priest, and the theology of the priesthood. Appendices or supplements were soon added to the circulars to disseminate "doctrinal formation courses" of about ten pages on current topics: ecumenism, collegiality, etc. The other means of action of *Opus Sacerdotale* was the regular regional meetings that allowed members of nearby dioceses to meet, pray, and study together certain topics discussed at the Council.

THE *CŒTUS INTERNATIONALIS PATRUM* AT THE COUNCIL

The second session of the Council, from September 29 to December 4, 1963, gave rise to even more debates and saw the "minority" organize itself to make its arguments better heard and to respond to the majority's various initiatives.

From the very first days of the Council, a "small committee" had been formed around Archbishop Lefebvre so that the "traditionally oriented" Council Fathers could consult each other on certain subjects. But it was still only an informal grouping, without a "clearly defined strategy."[31] This decision to form an organized group was taken during the first intersessional period, in the course of working days which brought together around Abbot Dom Prou, at the Abbey of Solesmes: Archbishop Lefebvre; Archbishop de Proença Sigaud; Dom Frénaud, who was the *peritus* chosen by Dom Prou for the Council; and Father Berto, who later became the *peritus* of Archbishop Lefebvre from the

---

30 *Circulaire* 1 (April 19, 1964), quoted in A. Jacquemin, *L'Opus sacerdotale*, 28.
31 P. Roy-Lysencourt, *Recueil de documents du CIP*, 15.

second session of the Council.[32]

The unofficial birth of the *Cœtus Internationalis Patrum* (CIP)–it did not yet have a name–took place on Wednesday, October 2, 1963, that is, three days after the opening of the second session. About fifteen Council Fathers met, set up a steering committee, and entrusted its presidency to Archbishop Lefebvre. The group's activities would be twofold: meetings every Tuesday evening for a conference on a theme debated at the Council, and the writing of notes, draft interventions, and amendments concerning the conciliar texts under debate.

Philippe Roy-Lysencourt, who has pored over the archives of the CIP, distinguishes a steering committee of five members (Archbishop Lefebvre, Dom Prou, Bishop de Proença Sigaud, Bishop de Castro Mayer and Bishop Carli), a group of nine "sympathetic cardinals" (Browne, Ferretto, Cerejeira, Larraona, Ottaviani, Rossi, Ruffini, Santos and Siri), sixty or so "fellow travelers" more or less involved in the initiatives of the CIP, and 22 theologians who contributed regularly (notably Fathers Berto, Dulac and Lusseau and Dom Frénaud) or occasionally (the Dominicans Gagnebet and Labourdette, the Jesuits Pozo Sanchez and Molinari, Bishop Lattanzi, and others).[33] Without tracing the whole history of the CIP in the last three sessions of the Council, it is worth noting that on all the most debated subjects–the liturgy, the Church (particularly the question of collegiality), ecumenism, and religious liberty–it had multiple activities: the organization of lectures open to all, interventions in the aula by one or other of its members, proposals for schemas or amendments, notes and supplications addressed to the pope, petitions.

It was only at the end of the second session that the Constitution on the Liturgy, *Sacrosanctum Concilium*, was voted on and promulgated December 4, 1963. This constitution called for a complete revision of the rites in order to promote "active participation by the faithful" – "due care being taken to preserve their substance; elements which, with the passage of time, came to be duplicated, or were added with but little advantage, are now to be discarded; other elements which have suffered injury through accidents of history are now to be restored to the vigor which they had in the days of the holy Fathers, as may seem useful or necessary" (*SC* 50).

But the conciliar constitution did not draw up a complete list of

---

32 Roy-Lysencourt, "Le Concile de l'abbé Victor-Alain Berto, théologien de Mgr Marcel Lefebvre et du 'Cœtus Internationalis Patrum,'" in P. Chenaux and K. P. Kartaloff eds., *Il Concilio Vaticano II e i suoi protagonasti alla luce degli archivi* (Vatican City: Libreria Editrice Vaticana, 2017), 425-43.
33 P. Roy-Lysencourt, *Les Membres du CIP*.

reforms to implement. It usually kept to wishes and recommendations, without going into the details of their application, while at other times giving quite precise indications: whether it was a question of a greater variety of biblical readings (*SC* 51), of the restoration of the universal prayer or general intercessions (*SC* 52), of communion under both species (*SC* 55), or of concelebration (*SC* 57). On the use of the vernacular in the liturgy, the Council text did not envisage it for the whole of the Mass, but for certain parts only, and wished Latin to remain the liturgical language: "Particular law remaining in force, the use of the Latin language is to be preserved in the Latin rites" (*SC* 36). Similarly, it considered that Gregorian chant was "specially suited to the Roman liturgy" and that it "should be given chief place [*principem locum*] in liturgical services" (*SC* 116).

The final text of the Constitution on the Liturgy was voted on by the Council Fathers almost unanimously: 2,147 *placets* and 4 *non placets*. Even Archbishop Lefebvre, who was to become a determined opponent of the Second Vatican Council and the great defender of the "Mass of all time," voted for the text. At the time he recognized that a reform of the Mass was necessary:

> Something needed to be reformed and recovered. It is clear that the first part of the Mass, which is intended to teach the faithful and make them express their faith, needed to achieve these ends in a clearer and, in a sense, more intelligible way. In my humble opinion, two reforms in this sense seemed useful: first the rites of this first part and some translations into the vernacular. To have the priest approach the faithful, communicate with them, pray and sing with them, stand at the ambo, say the orations, the readings from the Epistle and the Gospel in their language; that the priest sing in the divine traditional melodies the Kyrie, the Gloria and the Credo with the faithful. These are all good reforms which restore to this part of the Mass its true purpose.[34]

He could not imagine at that time that the reform as executed would go far beyond the desires of the Council and lead to considerable upheaval. He hoped that Rome would be able to put an end to the untimely and anarchic innovations that were multiplying. Noting that "there are many churches where the liturgical rules are violated with impunity," he still hoped that a return to order would occur: "Soon the official instructions of the Holy See will be made public. It is to be hoped that the first result of their publication will be the cessation

---

34 Archbp Marcel Lefebvre, "Perspectives conciliaires entre la 3e et la 4e session," 6 June 1965, *Itinéraires* 95 (July-August 1965): 78-79.

of private initiatives."[35]

VATICAN II AND COMMUNISM

The CIP also tried to cause the Council to condemn communism, twice.

At the time of the Council, half of Europe and huge countries such as the USSR and China were dominated by communist regimes, all of which, without exception, persecuted the Church. Communism was on the rise in Asia, Africa, and Latin America. During the preparatory period, many bishops, in their *vota* addressed to Rome, had asked that communism, as a doctrine, be condemned again and that the question of the situation of the Church in communist countries be raised. But a willingness to dialogue with all sides was developing. The interventions of Cardinal Montini (the future Paul VI) in the Central Preparatory Commission bear witness to this. On the question of communism, he wanted "our polemic to be rational, not offensive." He considered it necessary to adopt a new attitude towards the communists; they "have had the experience of our severity," he said, "but not of our charity. . . . Patience is necessary for us. Our faith will win if it is patient."

At the opening of the Council, the absence of many bishops was a matter of comment. No bishops from the USSR, China, Romania, or North Vietnam were able to come to Rome (many of them were in prison or living in hiding). In the other communist countries, permission to attend the Second Vatican Council was granted in very small numbers. The Russian Orthodox Church, on the other hand, was allowed to send two "observers." It is known that the Soviet authorities had given their consent with conditions. A meeting in Metz, in August 1962, between Cardinal Tisserant and Bishop Nicodemus (Nikodim), the man in charge of foreign affairs of the Russian Orthodox Church, made it possible to find an agreement. According to the testimony of Bishop Schmitt of Metz:

> As a result of this meeting, Bishop Nicodemus agreed to someone bringing an invitation to Moscow, provided that guarantees were given regarding the apolitical attitude of the Council.[36]

This guarantee given to the Soviet and Orthodox authorities was translated into a strict command given by Pope John XXIII. Father Wenger, correspondent for *La Croix* in Rome during the Council, later

---

35 Archbp Lefebvre, "Après la IIe session du Concile. Faisons le point sous la conduite du successeur de Pierre," January 21, 1964, *Itinéraires* 81 (March 1964): 21.

36 Interview given to the daily *Le Lorrain* (February 9, 1963). See also Jean Madiran, *L'Accord de Metz* (Versailles: Via Romana, 2006).

reported that during one of the first meetings of the French episcopate at San Luigi dei Francesi on October 23, 1962, "Cardinal Feltin made a confidential intervention. The Pope asked him to tell the bishops that he did not want any political allusions in their interventions.... Now even communism must not be brought up."[37]

Yet on several occasions, some bishops floated petitions asking that the question of socialism and communism be placed on the agenda. During the second session, in November 1963, on the initiative of Bishop de Proença Sigaud and Bishop de Castro Mayer, a first petition gathered 295 signatures of bishops from all over the world, and was handed over to the Pope through Cardinal Cicognani, Secretary of State.

The debate did not stop there. Bishops from communist countries considered it necessary for the Council not to remain silent about communism. Thus, on October 23, 1964, in his intervention in the aula, the exiled Archbishop Yu-Pin of Nanking was indignant:

> The schema on the Church and the modern world has an inex-
> plicable omission: it says nothing about communism. But even
> if one wants to ignore the political-economic aspects of the
> system, it is not possible to ignore its ideology, which has the
> most serious consequences for the whole of life in the world.
> Communism dominates almost half of humanity and threatens
> the other half. It is the gravest danger in the modern world.

The question resurfaced when Schema XIII on "The Church in the Modern World" was discussed. In September 1965, a new text was circulated requesting that the future constitution should include, in the passage devoted to atheism, a paragraph that "deals openly with the problem of communism." The petition, written at length by Archbishop Carli of the CIP, was signed by twenty-five Council Fathers who urged their confreres to add their signatures, but the names of Archbishop Lefebvre and Archbishop de Proença Sigaud did not appear among the signatories "because there was great antagonism toward them, both in the liberal camp and in the press."[38] The petition received 472 signatures, which shows that it went far beyond the CIP and its supporters. The petition, submitted to the Council's Presidential Council, was "forgotten" among other papers and was not examined in time. Archbishop Carli filed an appeal with the Council of the Presidency, the Council of Moderators, the General Secretariat, and the Administrative

---

37 Antoine Wenger, *Les Trois Rome. L'Église des années soixante* (Paris: Desclée de Brouwer, 1991), 98, 105.
38 R. M. Wiltgen, *The Rhine Flows into the Tiber: The Unkown Council* (New York: Hawthorn Books, 1967), 274.

Tribunal of the Council.[39]

The Pope could not ignore this petition, which exceeded the scope of the "minority" alone, but he stood by the position taken by his predecessor. In a meeting with Cardinal Garrone, the *relator* of Schema XIII, he manifested his "express wish" that the Council should not make an explicit condemnation of communism.[40] Then on November 26, during a final meeting, the Pope took Cardinal Tisserant's position: it was preferable not to use the word "communism" and simply to recall past condemnations in a footnote.[41]

In the event, the Constitution *Gaudium et Spes*, promulgated on December 7, 1965, merely alludes to communist regimes without using the word, though it condemns the persecutions they commit:

> Not to be overlooked among the forms of modern atheism is that which anticipates the liberation of man especially through his economic and social emancipation.... [W]hen the proponents of this doctrine gain governmental power they vigorously fight against religion, and promote atheism by using, especially in the education of youth, those means of pressure which public power has at its disposal. In her loyal devotion to God and men, the Church has already repudiated and cannot cease repudiating, sorrowfully but as firmly as possible, those poisonous doctrines and actions which contradict reason and the common experience of humanity, and dethrone man from his native excellence. (GS 20-21)

The conciliar text merely gave, in a note, references to four condemnations of communism issued by Popes Pius XI, Pius XII, John XXIII and Paul VI.

MICHEL DE SAINT-PIERRE ENTERS THE FRAY

A few weeks before the opening of the third session of the Council, the writer Michel de Saint-Pierre entered the anti-progressive fight with a splash. A novelist who was appreciated among literary critics, he had enjoyed great success in bookstores with *La Mer à boire* and *The Aristocrats*, for which he was awarded the Grand Prix du roman by the Académie française. In the religious field, he was known for his biographies of Bernadette Soubirous and the Curé d'Ars. More recently, he had published two sociological investigations: one on youth (*La

---

39 Latin text dated November 13, 1965; French translation in P. Roy-Lysencourt, *Recueil de documents du CIP*, 1025-28.
40 Jan Grootaers, "Le Crayon rouge de Paul VI. Les interventions du pape dans le travail des commissions conciliaires," in M. Lamberigts, C. Soetens, and J. Grootaers, eds., *Les Commissions conciliaires à Vatican II* (Louvain, 1996), 330-31.
41 Vincenzo Carbone, "Schemi e discussioni sull'ateismo e sul marxismo nel Concilio vaticano II," *Rivista di storia della Chiesa in Italia* 44 (1990): 330-31.

Nouvelle Race, 1961), the other on juvenile delinquency (*L'École de la violence*, 1962).

The New Priests, which he published in August 1964, caused considerable controversy. The book is presented as a novel, and the author uses characters and stories that he has invented, but it is the result of a long investigation. Michel de Saint-Pierre soon explained:

> It took several years – and during certain months of 1964, it was daily. I had definitely chosen the great urban areas of Paris as my setting, the so aptly named "red" (i.e., communist-leaning) neighborhoods. And I lived there from morning to night. There I engaged in "dialogue" with dozens of priests, with more than a hundred lay people from all walks of life and all professions. I even had the opportunity of attending priests' meetings.[42]

The novel features a classically-minded priest, Father Delance, appointed to a large parish in the urban area around Paris, where the pastor is struggling with other vicars who are progressive and Marxist-leaning, "presumptuous and panicky at once." The book is also sometimes a *roman à clef*: one recognizes François Mauriac under the name of Leroy-Maubourg, *Témoignage chrétien* under the title *Messager chrétien* ("divided between partisan hatred and social bitterness," writes Michel de Saint-Pierre), *Les Informations catholiques internationales* under the title *Catholicisme international illustré*. Without directly mentioning the ongoing Council, the book questioned the conciliar spirit:

> Under pretext of *aggiornamento* in the Church and the new pastorate we have tolerated our priests' serving men instead of God. . . . We live in difficult times, because there are too many reformers in the Church and not enough children of God.[43]

The book scandalized some and was applauded by others. Father Georges Michonneau, pastor of Saint-Jean-Baptiste in Belleville, published a vehement protest in *Témoignage chrétien* under this title: "In the name of my confreres I accuse Michel de Saint-Pierre of defamation." He ended by accusing the author of "throwing our most authentic priestly entrails to the dogs who will buy your book, and they will feast on them."[44] That is how concerned or critical Catholics like Michel de Saint-Pierre came to be called "dogs." . . . Jean Madiran defended them in a strongly-worded polemical brochure.[45]

Father Xavier de Chalendar, in the *Semaine religieuse de Paris*, saw in

---

42 Michel de Saint-Pierre, *Sainte colère* (Paris: La Table Ronde, 1965), 91.

43 De Saint-Pierre, *The New Priests* (St. Louis: Herder, 1966), 156-57.

44 *Témoignage chrétien* (October 22, 1964).

45 Jean Madiran, *Les Chiens*, supplement to *Itinéraires* 89 (1964), 61 pages.

The New Priests nothing but a "pamphlet [that] will probably no longer be read in two years' time"; Gilbert Cesbron, an old friend of Michel de Saint-Pierre, expressed his disagreement in *Le Figaro*; Pierre-Henri Simon, another Christian novelist, accused Michel de Saint-Pierre in *Le Monde* of "collectively defaming" all the priests who exercised their ministry in working-class areas and described his novel as "a nasty book that is a worthless book"; Pierre Veuillot, coadjutor archbishop of Paris, published a communiqué to "defend the honor of so many admirable priests who are poor among the poor, authentic servants of the Gospel, loving sons of the Church." Conversely, Jacques Vier, in *L'Homme nouveau*, saluted "the courage" of Michel de Saint-Pierre, even if he had some reservations, and the *Revue des cercles d'études d'Angers* noted that in this novel, which does not lapse into "caricature," "it is indeed the understanding of the priesthood, of its character, and of its mission that is in question."

The press, from which we have only quoted a few extracts, discussed the book for several weeks. It had a considerable success – 200,000 copies were sold in six months – and Michel de Saint-Pierre received a great deal of mail ("thousands of letters," he would say). He gave many lectures throughout France to present his book and to evoke the situation of the clergy in France. In the following months, with Jean Madiran's support, he launched an "Appeal to the Bishops of France."

THE FIRST "INTEGRIST COMMANDOS"

In one scene of his novel, Michel de Saint-Pierre refers to a Polish Christian who is spreading propaganda for a pacifist movement, *Pax Hominum*. Many of his readers recognized the Pax movement, which had divided French Catholics for several years.

The Pax Association, also known as the "Movement of Progressive Catholics in Poland," was founded in 1947. Influential through its press – a daily newspaper and several periodicals – and its publishing house, Pax was close to the Polish Communist Party. Under the pontificate of Pius XII, Bolesław Piasecki, its leader, had seen one of his books, *Essential Problems*, and the weekly magazine of the movement, *Dzis i jutro*, condemned by the Holy Office (June 8, 1955). Then priests were forbidden to contribute to the movement's publications and editions (June 7, 1957). Abroad, however, the image of this Catholic movement was not always negative. On November 1, 1961, the *Informations catholiques internationales* (ICI) published a dossier on the Church in Poland signed by José de Broucker; it contained an article favorable to Pax. A Polish writer who had taken refuge in France, Maria

Winowska, replied to this dossier with a series of unsigned articles in *La Croix* in February 1962.[46] At the beginning of 1963, Cardinal Wyszyński, Primate of Poland, addressed a very critical report on Pax to the Secretariat of State. He described it as an "organ of the police apparatus" charged with "infiltrating and subjugating the Church."[47] In a part of this report devoted to France, Cardinal Wyszyński questioned the ICI and the trips to Poland of French priests and laity, trips organized by Pax, whose beneficiaries returned "with a partial and one-sided, even erroneous, vision of Polish reality." In June 1963, the Wyszyński report was transmitted, through the intermediary of the Apostolic Nuncio in Paris, to the secretariat of the Episcopate, which distributed it, on a confidential basis, to all the bishops and superiors general of France.

This report came to be known to the press. While ICI protested its independence from Pax, other Catholic publications warned against Pax and campaigned against ICI. For over a year, talks that were supposed to be given by Georges Hourdin, Jean-Pierre Dubois-Dumée, and José de Broucker, respectively director, deputy director and editor-in-chief of the ICI, were disrupted by groups that the press and the Episcopate conveniently termed "integrists."[48] On closer inspection, it is clear that these actions were carried out by movements operating independently.

On February 26, 1964, Georges Hourdin, who was to give a talk on the laity and the Council in the crypt of the church of Notre-Dame-de-Grâce in Passy, "was prevented from doing so by a group of people made up in part of Polish émigrés."[49] The police had to intervene, and the talk was cancelled. Responsibility for the action was later claimed by a previously unknown movement, "Promotion of the Laity." A few months later, on May 19, a similar action was carried out at the sanctuary of Notre-Dame de Liesse, near Laon, where Jean-Pierre Dubois-Dumée was to speak on the theme "The world awaits the Church." *Le Monde* implicated the group Promotion of the Laity, and also Father Boyer and his group Action-Fatima. Other actions of the same kind followed, always targeting the same leaders of ICI.

Then, at the end of the year, it was a lecture by Father Congar that

46 These articles were gathered together as a volume under the pseudonym Pierre Lenert, *L'Église catholique en Pologne* (Paris: Éditions du Centurion, 1962).

47 Report published unabridged in *France catholique* (June 5, 1964) and in *DC* (June 21, 1964): 843-53.

48 Christian Sorrel, "Offensive intégriste: l'affaire *Pax*," in *Le Catholicisme français de la Séparation à Vatican II* (Paris: Éditions Karthala, 2020), 361-75.

49 *Le Monde* (February 28, 1964).

was disrupted for the first time by what he called in his Diary "an integrist commando."[50] It happened on December 14, 1964, during a lecture organized at the Mutualité by the *Centre français des intellectuels catholiques* and devoted to an "assessment of the third session [of the Council]." According to Henri Fesquet, who reported on the conference in *Le Monde*, the lecturer "was hindered several times by agitators" shouting "Go back to Moscow!," "Marxist priest!" and the police had to intervene to expel a demonstrator. Commenting on the incident, Henri Fesquet added:

> The Catholic Church now manifestly has, so to speak, its very own "OAS." Lacking any mandate, they claim to speak in the name of the Church and to defend it against its legitimate leaders.[51]

The comparison between anti-progressive Catholic militants and the armed actions of the OAS was more than exaggerated. Yet Father Congar took it up again when, a few weeks later, he noted another one of his lectures that had been disturbed. This time it was in Nîmes, on January 24, 1965:

> Lots of commotion from the crazies, a kind of OAS. About fifteen were armed with whistles or chanted: "Congar back to Moscow!," "Unity, yes; Pax, no!," etc. It was impossible to give the lecture unless they were removed. This was done after thirty-five minutes of commotion, half from the police, half from men in the audience.[52]

Again, in March 1966, José de Broucker, who was supposed to give a lecture and to participate in a debate in Alençon, was prevented from doing so by a group of young demonstrators, three of whom were arrested and charged with "infringement of the freedom of assembly, violence, and possession of prohibited weapons." One of them, Philippe Vaur, later declared to the police that he was a member of the *Jeune Alliance* movement and that he was "the person in charge of the commando group responsible for disrupting the meetings organized by *Informations catholiques internationales*."[53]

One can therefore identify three groups at work in the anti-Pax campaign that developed from 1964 onwards: *Action-Fatima, Promotion of the Laity* and *Jeune Alliance*. Action-Fatima was the oldest organization, directed by the turbulent Father Boyer mentioned above. But while members of this organization, and Father Boyer himself, may have

---

50 Y. Congar, *Mon journal du Concile*, 2: 293.
51 *Le Monde* (December 16, 1964).
52 Y. Congar, *Mon journal du Concile*, 2: 305-6.
53 *Le Monde* (March 24, 1966).

participated in some of the events, they had not organized them. It was a new movement, *Promotion du laïcat*, which was the most active. Little is known about this movement. The diocesan archives of Paris preserve the communiqués and typed letters that the organization sent to the bishops of the dioceses where it intervened.[54] On June 4, 1964, *Promotion du laïcat* sent an open letter to all the bishops of France, in which it gave the following warning:

> Our action will continue to grow; it is not for us to reveal our plans; we will act
> – when necessary
> – where necessary
> – for as long as necessary.
>
> Such is the price of protecting our homes.
>
> *Promotion of the Laity* will not disarm until the progressives and crypto-communists who are ensconced at the head of Catholic organizations and media outlets have been kicked out by our Higher Clergy.

No names of leaders or members appear on the communiqués and letters distributed by *Promotion du laïcat*. It is only through an article in *Le Monde* (May 20, 1964) that the names of some of those detained during the incidents at Notre-Dame de Liesse are known: Étienne Péricard and Christian Bailly, journalists; Father Vincent Serralda; retired Lieutenant-Colonel de Belleval; and Augier de Crémiers, a retired General Commissioner for the Navy. Father Serralda, a priest repatriated from Algeria, would be, a decade later, one of the priests who occupied the church of Saint-Nicolas-du-Chardonnet to restore the traditional liturgy. And in 1969, Lieutenant-Colonel de Bonneval was one of the founders of the *Alliance Saint-Michel*, which practiced a kind of activism very close to that of *Promotion du laïcat*.

As for *Jeune Alliance*, it was originally a youth movement created in 1964 in connection with the *Comités TV*, founded to support Jean-Louis Tixier-Vignancour's candidacy in the presidential election. *Jeune Alliance* stayed on after the presidential election and was the youth branch of the new party created by Tixier-Vignancour, the "Republican Alliance for Freedoms and Progress" (*Alliance républicaine pour les libertés et le progrès*, ARLP). Throughout the year, Jeune Alliance organized training sessions whose speakers were often personalities of the Catholic right (Jean Madiran and others) and also a summer camp (in 1965, 1966, 1967) with a chaplain among the leadership. It thus participated in

---

54 *Archives Historiques de l'Archidiocèse de Paris*, 1 S1 1.

certain anti-Pax actions, but disappeared fairly quickly, swept away
by the break-up of the Tixier-Vignancour party. The bridges between
right-wing political organizations and religious reaction movements
would be rebuilt again.

The anti-Pax activism of 1964-1966 was the prelude to a Catholic
activism that would have many other objectives in the years to come.
It is also one of the aspects of the militant ferment that accompanied
the last years of the Council, both on the traditionalist side and on
the progressive side.

THE PASTOR OF MONTJAVOULT

On November 21, 1964, the third session of the Council ended with
the promulgation of three texts: the Dogmatic Constitution on the
Church, the Decree on the Eastern Catholic Churches, and the Decree
on Ecumenism. Paul VI had to intervene to impose a "Preliminary
Explanatory Note" (the *Nota explicativa praevia*) to clarify the authentic
meaning of collegiality, to mark the limits of the episcopal "functions"
(which are not a "power"), and to reaffirm the "fulness of the power
of the Roman Pontiff." Archbishop Lefebvre praised this "Explanatory
Note" as a "message truly come down from Heaven," a "divine light
cast anew on the immutable constitution of the Church."[55]

At the same time, Father Coache, a simple country priest who until
then had been unknown, began to make his voice heard and soon
attracted the media's attention. Ordained a priest in 1943 and pastor
of various rural parishes in the Oise region, he had been concerned
since the beginning of the 1950s about a growing independence among
certain priests and religious "with regard to discipline, morality, and
liturgy." He noted at that time a "degradation of the Faith" which, he
said, "always happened under the pretext of clarification or better
expression, of adaptation or charity."[56] In 1958, he was appointed pastor
of Montjavoult, a position he would hold for eleven years. After the
end of the third session of the Council he was concerned about what
he was observing in many churches and what the press was reporting,
and at Christmas 1964 he published at his own expense the *Lettre d'un
curé de campagne à ses confrères* ("Letter from a country priest to his
confreres," 32 pages). He wanted to alert them to the

---

55 Archbp Lefebvre, "Perspectives conciliaires entre la 3e et la 4e session," *Itinéraires*
95 (July-August 1965): 71.
56 Louis Coache, *Les Batailles du Combat de la Foi* (Poitiers: Éditions de Chiré, 1993), 18.

real tidal wave that is breaking on the various beaches of our Roman Church. In a great number of religious and ecclesiastical circles, there is a desire to shake the authority of the Church, to make a world religion for a world that must be pleased at all costs.... The authority and principles of the Church are being undermined under the silly pretext of abolishing triumphalism or clericalism ... disobedience is taking hold, evil is no longer denounced; attitudes, virtues, and prayers that correspond to the most authentic Christian principles are condemned as rigorism, pharisaism or narrowness.

But at the time, both Father Coache and Archbishop Lefebvre (whom he had known since 1961, but with whom he was not yet in regular contact) did not question the Council as a whole. Father Coache still praised Pope Paul VI and his interventions as "the supreme guardian of doctrine."

In September 1965, a few days before the beginning of the fourth session of the Council, he published a *Nouvelle Lettre d'un curé de campagne* ("New Letter from a Country Priest," 36 pages). In it he denounced the "errors or half errors, deviations, and massive omissions that are eating away at the Church like a cancer." He saw in it the appearance of a "new religion [which] takes the opposite view of the true one." Nevertheless, he rejoiced in the encyclical on the Eucharist, *Mysterium Fidei*, which Paul VI had just published, and which reaffirmed the doctrine of the Real Presence and transubstantiation. "Let us thank the Pope for having restated dogma on this sacrament of love," wrote Father Coache, who called for fidelity, including to the Council: "We cry out for obedience to the Pope, to the Council, to the Bishops, for total fidelity to the faith and to the papal and conciliar texts."

A few weeks later, but this time under the pseudonym of Jean-Marie Reusson, Fr Coache finally published the work he had been preparing since 1955. As a good canonist and as a priest respectful of the authority of his bishop, he had previously submitted his manuscript to the ecclesiastical censor. This was in 1963. He had obtained the *nihil obstat*, an attestation that it contained nothing contrary to faith and morals, but the auxiliary bishop of Beauvais had refused the *imprimatur*, considering that the text was too much against the current of the renewal that the Council was pursuing. Father Coache then used a subterfuge to obtain the imprimatur elsewhere. He also had difficulty finding a publisher. Michel de Saint-Pierre, whom the priest had met during the publication of *The New Priests*, succeeded in convincing his publisher, Roland Laudenbach, director of the *Éditions de la Table ronde*, to publish the priest's book. Laudenbach imposed a new, catchier title, *La Foi au goût du jour* ("A Fashionable Faith"), and ensured that the book would receive an unhoped-for distribution.[57] This also earned Father Coache a first public warning from his bishop. Bishop Desmazières, recently appointed bishop of Beauvais, had been enthroned on October 17. Less than three weeks later he published a communiqué to "warn" against a book that was "one-sided, without nuance" and that "tends to discredit the conciliar renewal and, in particular, the Church of France."[58] He also reproached Father Coache for his "disobedience": not only for having obtained an imprimatur elsewhere than from the diocese of Beauvais, but also for "making people believe that his Superiors agree with him." In this communiqué published in the diocesan weekly, he stated that Father Coache "has acknowledged his fault and promised to make reparation" and insisted that "I hold him in high esteem and affection, for he deserves it." These good intentions were not to last on either side.

Father de Nantes, for his part, in his *Letter to My Friends*, whose readership continued to grow, developed a much more radical critique of the Council and the Pope. The encyclical *Ecclesiam Suam* that Paul VI had published in August 1964 – an encyclical dedicated to the dialogues that the Church must undertake – had seemed to him to reveal the "messianic" agenda of Paul VI and the "conciliar revolution" that consisted in wanting to "reconcile" with the world and the various religions. He interpreted all the debates of the third session of the Council in the light of this supposed danger. In January 1965, Bishop Le Couëdic of Troyes published a *Note* to warn against the *Letters to My Friends* and to ask the faithful "to abstain from collaborating, in any form whatsoever, in the reading and propagation of these writings, which are more and more injurious to the Church considered in the person of her august Head, to the episcopate, and to the Council."[59] Father de Nantes did not stop his virulent criticism of the pontificate there. He invented an acronym, MASDU (*Mouvement d'Animation Spirituelle de la Démocratie Universelle*, "Movement for the Spiritual Animation of Universal Democracy"), to denounce "the apostasy and idolatry under the mask of universal religion" advocated, according to him, by Paul VI. The name, which Fr de Nantes introduced to the

---

57 Fr Coache would publish it again under his own name under the title *Vers l'apostasie générale* ("Towards General Apostasy") (Paris: La Table Ronde, 1969). It is an abbreviated version of *La Foi au goût du jour*, augmented with the three *Lettres d'un curé* and a hitherto unpublished text.

58 Bishop S. Desmazières, "Communiqué aux prêtres," *Bulletin religieux du diocèse de Beauvais* (November 6, 1965).

59 *Revue catholique du diocèse de Troyes* (February 11, 1965), quoted in *DC* (March 21, 1965), 565-66.

public on February 22, 1965, was taken up in a series of articles and further popularized by two long articles that the writer Jacques Perret devoted to him in *Monde et Vie*.

THE COUNCIL OF THE MEDIA

Each session of the Council lasted two to three months. During the long periods in between – the intersessions – the work of the council was carried on by commissions, consultors, *periti*, and more or less informal groups of bishops scattered around the world. Notes, proposals, and draft amendments on the schemas still under discussion were written and sent to the general secretariat of the council or to the pope himself.

Benedict XVI, in a famous speech, criticized the "hermeneutics of discontinuity and rupture" that some have implemented since the time of the Council.[60] On another occasion, he pointed to the media as the primary disseminators of this distorted hermeneutic of the Council. He spoke of a "Council of the media":

> It was almost a Council apart, and the world perceived the Council through the latter, through the media. Thus, the Council that reached the people with immediate effect was that of the media, not that of the Fathers.... [T]he Council of the journalists, naturally, was not conducted within the faith, but within the categories of today's media, namely apart from faith, with a different hermeneutic. It was a political hermeneutic: for the media, the Council was a political struggle, a power struggle between different trends in the Church. It was obvious that the media would take the side of those who seemed to them more closely allied with their world.... Therefore, this was the dominant one, the more effective one, and it created so many disasters, so many problems, so much suffering: seminaries closed, convents closed, banal liturgy... and the real Council had difficulty establishing itself and taking shape; the virtual Council was stronger than the real Council.[61]

Jean Madiran, at the end of the second session of the Council, made an identical observation in *Itinéraires*, using different language and from a less theological perspective: "Since October 1962, the 'normal play of public opinion' has in fact been translated into a one-sided pressure."[62] On the one hand,

---

60 Benedict XVI, *Address to the Roman Curia* (December 22, 2005), vatican.va.
61 Benedict XVI, *Meeting With the Parish Priests and Clergy of Rome* (February 22, 2013), vatican.va.
62 Jean Madiran, "Le Concile et le jeu normal de l'opinion publique," *Itinéraires* 77 (November 1963): 9-18.

divergent voices have not been admitted into the concert, or
the 'play,' of public opinion. They have been insulted, discredited, quarantined – disqualified as 'integrist.' From the
very opening of the Council in October 1962, lists of names
of cardinals and bishops were publicly drawn up, each noted
with infamy once and for all; in advance, they were suspect,
in advance, crushed: in advance, not to heeded: and besides,
the 'news' did not report their words, except in truncated and
distorted form, and to make fun of them or to hand them over
to public indignation.

On the other hand,

all sorts of newspapers, even Catholic ones, have put forward
all sorts of ideas and judgments that objectively harm the faith
and the Church. They have smeared the memory and the doctrine of several popes, they have slandered previous councils,
openly attacked dogmas defined by the Church (especially the
"Marian dogmas"), discredited speculative theology, caricatured
religious orders dedicated to contemplation, proposed reforms
and changes concerning not only the laws, but even Christian
doctrine itself.

Archbishop Lefebvre, between the third and fourth sessions, made
an identical observation and deplored the fact that "the Church in some
of its highest members" had been "influenced by the magisterium of
the modern age: public opinion."[63] But he still thought that salutary
reactions were possible.

DOES ERROR HAVE RIGHTS?

The fourth session of the Council, which took place from September 14 to December 8, 1965, was that in which the greatest number of
texts were discussed, voted on, and promulgated: eleven constitutions,
decrees, and declarations out of sixteen. The examination of some of
the texts had already begun in the previous sessions. This session was
also the one in which the discussions were among the most intense,
especially those of the schema concerning Judaism and the schema
concerning religious freedom.

Without going into the details of all the debates, it should be noted
that Archbishop Lefebvre, who had already intervened several times on
religious liberty during the previous sessions, spoke twice on this theme
during the fourth session: on September 9 and 15, 1965.[64] According to

---

63 *Itinéraires* 95 (July-August 1965): 68.
64 See the synoptic chart of Archbishop Lefebvre's fourteen written and oral interventions drawn up by B. Tissier de Mallerais: *Marcel Lefebvre*, 318-19.

him, and to many of the Fathers of the CIP or allied to them, the schema on religious liberty was based on an erroneous definition of liberty as immunity; in reality, "liberty is good and true insofar as it is regulated by the truth." Without the will to do good, there is no dignity of the person, and under the pretext of respecting consciences, one must not give rights to error. At most, error can be tolerated if its repression would cause a greater evil.

This question divided the conciliar assembly quite widely, since in the first days of the fourth session an official request was made for the "other [i.e., traditional] way of conceiving and declaring this doctrine [on religious liberty]" to be the object of a "general proposal" which would be read in the general congregation before the new examination of the official schema. This request was signed by "almost three hundred fathers."[65] The CIP intervened in diverse ways to obtain corrections to the text; its arguments won over a significant number of Fathers. During the vote on the sixth version of the text, on November 19, 1965, there were still 249 *non placet* votes against 1,954 *placet* votes. But during the final vote, on December 7, in the presence of Paul VI, there were only 70 *non placet* votes (among them Archbishop Lefebvre), as the rest no longer dared to oppose a text that the Pope had approved. That same day, after Mass, Paul VI promulgated the declaration on religious freedom and the last three texts voted on that day: the Decree on Missions, the Decree on Priests, and the Pastoral Constitution on "the Church in the Modern World." Then each Council Father added his signature to the promulgated texts. Only twenty-two Fathers refused to give their written assent to the promulgation made by the pope, while Archbishop Lefebvre approved all the texts with his signature. Subsequently, despite the publication of Vatican archive documents,[66] he always denied having given his assent to the declaration on religious liberty.[67] His official biographer acknowledged that on this point Archbishop Lefebvre had been misled by "an error or a memory slip."[68]

At the end of the Council, the Church had been enriched with a new doctrinal and pastoral corpus: sixteen constitutions, decrees, and declarations, not all of which had the same authority. They had all been discussed at length and could be voted in only at the cost of

---

65 The Latin text of the request, with a French translation and the list of signatories, is in P. Roy-Lysencourt, *Recueil de documents du C. I. P.*, 945-54.
66 *Sedes Sapientiae* 31, 41-44 and 35, 32-45.
67 E.g., in *Fideliter* 79 (1991): 7.
68 B. Tissier de Mallerais, *Marcel Lefebvre*, 313.

compromises that combined traditional formulations with new ones.

In the closing address of the Council on December 7, 1965, the Pope used a formula that was a nice surprise for some and a scandal to others. Describing the "new humanism" that the Council wanted to promote, he said:

> [W]e, too, in fact, we more than any others, honor mankind [*hominis sumus cultores*]. . . . this council, which exposed itself to human judgment, insisted very much more upon this pleasant side of man, rather than on his unpleasant one. Its attitude was very much and deliberately optimistic.

Jean Madiran, without explicit reference to this text, but bearing it in mind, would later write that the Church had made a "Copernican revolution": it had passed "from theocentrism to anthropocentrism," specifying that this was due to the forgetfulness or neglect of the natural law and to giving action primacy over contemplation.[69] Father de Nantes, for his part, would seize directly on the expression "we more than any others, honor mankind [*hominis sumus cultores*]," take it literally, and conclude, once again, that Paul VI had committed an act of apostasy.[70]

---

69 Jean Madiran, *La Révolution copernicienne dans l'Église* (Paris: Consep, 2002), 10.
70 Fr de Lubac sought to respond to this accusation in a text he would publish later: "Le 'culte de l'homme.' En réparation à Paul VI," in *Petite Catéchèse sur Nature et Grâce* (Paris: Fayard, 1980), 181-200. [The most common French translation of this address renders *sumus hominis cultores* by "nous avons le culte de l'homme," meaning, if translated literally, "we have the worship of Man" – *Translator*].

CHAPTER 4
1966: A Year of Condemnations

I N JUNE 1966, FATHER COACHE PUBLISHED A LONG
article in the magazine *Le Monde et la Vie*.[1] The article was
announced on the front cover, illustrated with a photograph of
an anguished Paul VI. The headline introduced the author of the article
as follows: "A priest, Father Louis Coache, a country pastor, explains
the anguish of the Church and the anxiety of the Pope." He again
denounced the "New Religion" that was being established: "The religion
of the world and the cult of Man." He protested against the "abomination of the catechetical sheets" in use before the expected publication
of a new catechism, and the arbitrary liturgical innovations by which
"an entire clergy is causing us to slide into heresy and abomination."
More generally, he criticized the "dialectic" and the "brainwashing" by
which certain clerics and a certain press were changing the "mentality"
of the faithful: truth and error were put on the same footing and "the
religious spirit is fading." This four-page call to arms, published in a
magazine with a circulation of 200,000, irritated the episcopate. Coadjutor Archbishop Pierre Veuillot of Paris wrote to Archbishop Marty of
Rheims (at the time): "Once again I ask myself the same question: can
we remain mute in the face of a generalized and passionate attack on
all the efforts at renewal in the Church?"[2] Nevertheless, he recognized
that this article, "however outrageous and slanderous" it was, "does
point to real difficulties." And, setting traditionalism and radical progressivism back to back, he added: "It is indeed obvious that we have
to fight on two fronts, against the excesses of each."

The reaction happened in two stages. On June 18, in his diocesan
bulletin, Bishop Desmazières published a new communiqué, deploring
the fact that Father Coache was "renewing the same errors: under
the pretext of denouncing certain abuses, he casts suspicion on the
conciliar renewal and the bishops of France. He can only spread trouble and confusion in people's minds."[3] A first disciplinary action was

---

1 Fr Louis Coache, "La 'Nouvelle Religion,'" *Le Monde et la Vie* 157 (June 1966): 13-16.
2 Archbishop Veuillot to Archbishop Marty, Letter dated June 14, 1966, *Archives Historiques de l'Archidiocèse de Paris* 1 S, 3, 1 (copy).
3 Bishop Desmazières, "Communiqué," *Bulletin religieux du diocèse de Beavais* (June
19, 1966).

taken against Father Coache; it was announced curtly at the end of the communiqué: "He used to come to hear confessions every Friday at the cathedral: I am withdrawing this power from him." Five days later, an official communiqué from the Permanent Council of the French Episcopate disapproved, not of Father Coache specifically, but of "a campaign," "a trial by allegation." The rather lengthy communiqué, dated June 23, 1966, emphasized that the "body of authorized teachings and decisions" given by the recent Council had been adopted "with remarkable unanimity."[4] Consequently, "the duty of Catholics is clear. They must filially receive and implement these teachings and decisions. "However," the communiqué continued, "a minority, with ever more assertive boldness, is challenging, in the name of fidelity to the past, the principles of the renewal now under way." It denounced the "trial by allegation" that was being brought against "the episcopate and priests of France."

This communiqué was a fairly comprehensive summary of traditionalist critiques:

> Religious education is in crisis; Christian schooling is in peril; the personal authority of each individual bishop is undermined by bishops' collective bodies; the primacy of the Holy Father is compromised by collegiality; the social doctrine of the Church is distorted by progressivism; the faith of many clerics is perverted by grave doctrinal and moral errors. These people question the application of the Liturgical Constitution. They criticize apostolic movements and their methods.

The Permanent Council of the Episcopate urged Catholics "not to allow themselves to be led astray by this campaign, which goes far beyond what is permitted by the free divergence of opinions on freely debated issues." And it concluded by warning "against articles that have appeared in magazines such as *Le Monde et La Vie*, in reviews such as *Itinéraires* and *Défense du foyer*, and in bulletins such as *Lumière*."

The fact that several titles of the Catholic press were involved was surprising. It was a "thunderclap in the Church in France," according to *Paris Match*, which devoted a full page to the event. Robert Serrou noted:

> The bishops have gone on the counter-attack. They have even gone further. For the first time, they name their adversaries — there are Catholics, even among those who are not integrists, who regret this. It is no longer only certain tendencies that they are attacking, but the publications in which those tendencies are expressed.[5]

---

4 "Mise en garde des cardinaux et du Conseil permanent de l'épiscopat français contre une campagne de presse," *DC* (July 17, 1966), 1285-88.
5 *Paris Match* (June 25, 1966).

The list was not exhaustive, but it is surprising that *Lumière*, a modest bulletin published for only two years in Boulogne-sur-Mer by lay people without any particular competence, and characterized by its virulence, was put on the same footing as *Itinéraires*, a review of ideas, which had been in existence for ten years and had been able to attract contributors of repute.

The Permanent Council of the Episcopate expressed the fond hope "that this warning would bring light to those responsible for these articles, and bring peace to the many Catholics who are deeply attached to the Church's doctrine and who are today troubled in their faith and in their docility towards the hierarchy."

The word "condemnation" was used at the time, both by those who were delighted at it and by those who were targeted by it. In fact, if it was a condemnation at all, it was a moral one, not a canonical or doctrinal one. It was a "warning."

But the response was considerable. Twenty-two diocesan bulletins reprinted the communiqué of the Permanent Council of the Episcopate in their official sections. André Giovanni for *Le Monde et la Vie*, Pierre Lemaire for *Défense du foyer*, and Jean Madiran for *Itinéraires* joined forces and decided to lodge a protest with each of the official bodies concerned by sending legally drawn-up appeals. Their briefs were rejected by the diocesan ecclesiastical courts on the grounds that the reprinting of the communiqué of the Permanent Council was an "administrative act." At the instigation of Jean Madiran, a procedure was initiated at the Tribunal of the Apostolic Signatura in Rome. It lasted several years, with many appeals, until it was finally rejected in 1972.[6] Later, Jean Madiran would acknowledge:

> What I have called the "condemnation" of *Itinéraires* was an exaggeration on my part; it was in fact a simple episcopal communiqué of disapproval.... It blamed the magazine for criticizing "the spirit of the renewal underway" and did not include or accompany any disciplinary action.[7]

A little over a month after this warning, a condemnation, this time in a properly canonical form, struck Father de Nantes.

SUSPENSION *A DIVINIS*

The *Lettre à mes amis* that Father de Nantes published every month had a growing audience (12,000 copies in the summer of 1966). His

---

6 This drawn-out procedure contains several volumes of items, kept in the Jean Madiran archives.

7 Jean Madiran to the author, Letter, April 6, 2009.

publication was not included in the above-mentioned communiqué, because he had already initiated a procedure himself to have his writings judged by the former Holy Office.

Father de Nantes's criticism of the Council had become more radical after the encyclical *Ecclesiam Suam* (1964), which seemed to him to reveal the intention of Paul VI and the Council to seek to "reconcile" with the world and the various religions. Between the third and fourth sessions of the Council, in several issues of his bulletin— from No. 197 (February 22, 1965) to No. 208 (July 14, 1965)—he had explained that the Council and the Pope were aiming at making the Catholic Church abandon "its former title" and "replace it with the far more evocative acronym: MASDU (Movement of Spiritual Animation of Universal Democracy). A decatholicized Christianity, the friend of men!" The Pope's visit to the UN headquarters in New York, and the speech he gave there in October 1965, seemed to him to be an apostasy: "The speech of G. B. Montini illustrates and exalts the theses of Freemasonry," "the messianic times of Judaism are proclaimed open by Paul VI."[8] Then the closing speech of the Second Vatican Council on December 7, 1965, with its famous formula: "We too, more than anyone else, have the cult of man" [as it was rendered in the French version—*Translator*], seemed to him to confirm the "heresy" of the Pope. On December 10, 1965, Bishop Le Couëdic of Troyes sent Father de Nantes a letter asking him once again to leave the diocese and to stop publishing the *Lettre à mes amis*. He had until Christmas to comply, on pain of being struck with a suspension *a divinis* (i.e., a ban on administering the sacraments). Father de Nantes refused to obey this double injunction and asked to be judged on the merits of the case by Rome. Finally, on December 29, 1965, Bishop Le Couëdic agreed that the Abbé de Nantes and his community could continue to reside in his diocese until Rome had judged his writings, and he authorized him to continue the publication of the *Lettre à mes amis* on the condition that he "submit in the future the complete text" to diocesan authority before publication.[9] After an attempt at conciliation by Cardinal Lefebvre, Archbishop of Bourges, on April 20, 1966, Father de Nantes wrote a long "personal request" to Cardinal Ottaviani, proprefect of the Congregation for the Doctrine of the Faith. It is dated July 16, 1966 and extends to eleven printed pages.

In the copious style that was always his characteristic, he introduced himself at length, explained the evolution of his publication, explained

---

8 *Lettre à mes amis*, 218 (December 8, 1965).
9 Communiqué of Bishop Le Couëdec, *La Revue catholique de Troyes* (December 29, 1965).

his growing opposition to the Council, and once again denounced "the doctrine and practice of the new Church [which] are the negation of centuries of tradition." He then solemnly asked the Congregation for the Doctrine of the Faith to judge his writings, sending Cardinal Ottaviani the complete collection of his *Lettre à mes amis*. He claimed, pridefully as his opponents and some of his friends were later to say, that through his person and his writings "the time has come for the Church of Rome, Mother and Teacher of all the Churches, to carry out with power and decision an indispensable work of discernment of spirits."

Two days later, he had this "request" handed to the bishop of Troyes for him to send it to Cardinal Ottaviani. Bishop Le Couëdic, upon reading it, refused to send it to Rome, judging it "unacceptable" and "outrageous in tone." [10] Father de Nantes then sent his "request" to Cardinal Ottaviani and decided to publish it in his monthly bulletin [11] even before its recipient had had a chance to reply, which was a first breach of basic politeness. Moreover, he violated the injunction of Bishop Le Couëdic not to publish anything without his authorization.

The judgment of the Congregation for the Doctrine of the Faith did not come until 1969, as we shall see later. In the meantime, Archbishop Le Couëdic suspended Father de Nantes for disobedience and, under canon 2344, for having published a text "gravely injurious to the Council, to the Bishops, and to the Holy Father himself." [12]

The sanction was never lifted and Father de Nantes was later struck with further canonical sanctions, for other reasons, as we shall see.

THE OTTAVIANI LETTER

This "request" to Rome by Father de Nantes, dated July 16, had little immediate echo, especially because a Roman initiative took the lead in religious affairs. A few months after the end of the Council, Paul VI began to worry about a crisis of faith that was affecting the Church itself and the identity crisis that was affecting some of the clergy in certain countries. In this regard, the philosopher Jacques Maritain, a friend of the Pope, was able to alert him successfully to an increasingly disturbing situation. In 1966, he published a book entitled *The Peasant of the Garonne* in which he was alarmed by a "neo-modernism" that was spreading, including among theologians, and by the "horizontalism"

10 *Lettre à mes amis*, 235 (September 23, 1966), 8, and Br. François de Marie des Anges, *Pour l'Église. Quarante ans de contre-réforme catholique*, vol. 2 (Poitiers: Chiré, 1993), 264.
11 *Lettre à mes amis*, 231 (July 1966).
12 Communiqué of Archbishop Le Couëdec, *La Revue catholique de Troyes* (August 25, 1966).

that was becoming more and more characteristic of the clergy. Father Congar criticized what he considered a pessimistic view of the situation in a major article in *Le Monde*.[13] On the other hand, Father de Lubac wrote to Maritain approvingly: "There is a groundswell which, if it were given in to, would lead us to collective apostasy in short order."[14] The word "apostasy" will be found again in Father Coache and other traditionalist authors.

Also in 1966, Cardinal Ottaviani, pro-prefect of the Congregation for the Doctrine of the Faith, sent a long letter in Latin to all the presidents of the Episcopal Conferences about "doctrinal errors" and "dangers to the faith" that were spreading in the Church.[15] He was concerned that "on various sides" there were reports of "growing abuses in the interpretation of the Council's doctrine" and that "strange and daring opinions" were spreading which "greatly disturbed the minds of many of the faithful." He pointed out ten of them: the recourse "to Sacred Scripture, deliberately leaving tradition aside"; the relativization of "dogmatic formulas"; the minimization of the ordinary magisterium of the Church "which is almost relegated to the realm of free opinions"; the denial "that there is an absolute, firm, and unchanging objective truth"; "a certain Christological humanism . . . which reduces Christ to the simple condition of a man who, little by little, became aware of his divine sonship"; an "exaggerated symbolism" in the conception of the Eucharist, and the Mass reduced to the idea of a meal "to the detriment of the idea of sacrifice"; the abandonment of "the personal confession of sins"; the disfiguring of "the doctrine of the Council of Trent on original sin"; the rejection of "the objective reason of morality" and the refusal to consider that there is a natural law; "ecumenical activity that offends the truth about the unity of the faith and of the Church, promoting a dangerous irenicism and indifferentism, which is entirely foreign to the spirit of the Council."

Cardinal Ottaviani asked the presidents of the Bishops' Conferences to forward this letter on "doctrinal errors" to all the bishops of their country, "so that each one, according to his function and office, may strive to eradicate or prevent them." He also asked that each Episcopal Conference send a report to the Holy See on the situation of the faith in their country.

---

13 Yves Congar, "Une certaine peine," *Le Monde* (December 28, 1966).
14 Fr de Lubac to Jacques Maritain, Letter, March 13, 1967, quoted in Georges Chantraine and Marie-Gabrielle Lemaire, *Henri de Lubac* (Paris: Cerf, 2013), 4: 421.
15 Letter "Cum œcumenicum Concilium," *AAS* 58 (1966): 659–61.

This letter of July 24, 1966, was supposed to remain secret, as also were the replies sent to Rome. But in several countries indiscretions leaked it to the press. *Le Monde* published it thanks to "a prelate" who had given him a copy of the document. Some commentators minimized this document of the Congregation for the Doctrine of the Faith. Father Rouquette, in his monthly column in *Études*, considered that "it is simply a matter of investigation."[16] However, it was not an investigation, but an act of the Holy See which first urged the bishops to be vigilant, urged them to "repress" and "prevent" errors and dangers, and to send a report to the Holy See "by Christmas 1966."

Still, the expression "Ottaviani investigation" was to prevail and remain in use among historians. The responses from the different Episcopal Conferences are known. In hindsight, the historian can see that difficulties "were rather systematically minimized" and that "most responses recommended prudence to the Magisterium: condemnations are useless."[17]

We will limit ourselves here to the French responses and reactions. At its plenary meeting in Lourdes, October 17-22, the French Episcopal Conference examined the response to the letter of the Congregation for the Doctrine of the Faith. Coadjutor Archbishop of Paris Pierre Veuillot was asked to prepare a preliminary report, which was discussed. In an interview with the press, he tried to minimize the problem:

> There are no grounds for alarm or pessimism at the present time, and the attitude of the bishops is very constructive. A certain effervescence of thought in the secular sector naturally has an impact on the theological field. If there are manifestations here and there of some petulance, they are rather a continual invitation to theological work.[18]

Note the expression "petulance" to designate possible theological errors...

In the following weeks, after reception of written observations sent by some fifty bishops, a definitive report was drafted, dated December 17, 1966, and sent to the Holy See.[19] This document gave a rather lucid

---

16 Fr Robert Rouquette, "La Lettre du cardinal Ottaviani à l'épiscopat universel," *Études* (November 1966): 577.
17 Denis Pelletier, "Le Catholicisme entre deux mondes," in Charles Sorrel ed., *Renouveau conciliaire et crise doctrinale. Rome et les églises nationales (1966-1968)* (Paris: LARHA, 2017), 395-96.
18 *La Croix* (October 21, 1966).
19 It was printed in its entirety in *DC* (February 19, 1967): 327-38. Christian Sorrel has studied the drafting of this response: "La Conférence épiscopale française et l'enquête Ottaviani. Fonctionnement institutionnel et positions doctrinales," in *Renouveau conciliaire et crise nationale*, 143-217.

assessment of the situation, presenting at length "the principal points of concern." Among other things, it noted "pastoral or liturgical imprudences which could compromise faith in the Real Presence," "priests insist more readily on the Eucharistic meal than on the sacrifice," "the authority of the Magisterium is not always recognized," "the meaning of original sin suffers as if it were eclipsed in the personal consciousness of a great number of people," "original sin, as well as the Last Things and the [final] judgment" cause "difficulty for many of the priests responsible for teaching them. They remain silent because they do not know how to speak." But the conclusion of the report was optimistic: "It is less a matter of denouncing the evil than of seeking the remedy." The bishops, the document said, have undertaken "a double effort: for the doctrinal formation of future priests and for the doctrinal support of priests engaged in ministry" and the "shadows must not make us forget the light projected by the Council on the life of our dioceses. The symptoms of vitality are many and comforting, both among the clergy and among the laity."

When he learned of this report, Paul VI was distressed by the doctrinal difficulties it raised, but he was also dismayed by the optimism of the French bishops. Receiving in audience Father Antoine Wenger, editor of *La Croix*, on February 7, 1967, he expressed his concern. He felt that the report of the French episcopate constituted "an indictment of the French clergy.... The letter reveals a more serious situation than what the investigation of the Holy Office had led one to suspect. Poor clergy of France, otherwise so deserving!"[20]

Archbishop Lefebvre, as Superior General of the Congregation of the Holy Ghost, also had to respond to Cardinal Ottaviani's inquiry. He made a general statement which, he wrote, "emerges from my conversations with many bishops, priests, and lay people in Europe and Africa, and from my readings in English and French countries."[21] He considered that "[t]he present evil seems to me much more serious than the denial or questioning of a [single] truth of our faith" and that it was "only the logical continuation of the heresies and errors which have undermined the Church for the last few centuries, especially since the liberalism of the last century which tried at all costs to reconcile the Church with the ideas which led to the revolution." And, for the first time in detail and with explicitness, he blamed the Second Vatican Council, which he described as "the greatest tragedy the Church has

---

20 Quoted by Antoine Wenger, "Paul VI et la croix," in *Paul VI et la modernité* (Rome: École française de Rome, 1984), 758.
21 He would publish his response to the investigation in *J'accuse le Concile*, 106-11.

ever suffered. We have witnessed the marriage of the Church with liberal ideas." The Superior General of the Holy Ghost fathers listed the various points where the Council "undermined the certainty of the truths taught by the authentic Magisterium of the Church . . . whether it be the transmission of the jurisdiction of bishops, the two sources of Revelation, scriptural inspiration, the necessity of grace for justification, the necessity of baptism, the life of grace in heretics, schismatics and pagans, the ends of marriage, religious liberty, the Last Things, etc." He then listed the "consequences" of the doubts introduced by the Council: "the disappearance of priestly vocations," "the disappearance of religious vocations, the ruin of traditional spirituality in the novitiates, the uselessness of the missions," "the disregard for baptism which is now postponed, the abandonment of the sacrament of penance." "The Council has favored in an inconceivable way the spread of liberal errors. Faith, morals, and ecclesiastical discipline are shaken to their foundations. . . . The destruction of the Church is advancing apace." However, Archbishop Lefebvre still believed that "the successor of Peter and he alone can save the Church." He made suggestions:

> Let the Holy Father surround himself with vigorous defenders of the faith, let him appoint them in the important dioceses. Let him deign to proclaim the truth and to pursue error by means of important documents, without fearing he might be contradicted, without fearing schisms, without fearing to call into question the pastoral provisions of the Council.

Several traditionalist reviews, *Défense du foyer*, *La Pensée catholique*, and *Itinéraires* mentioned the investigation to rejoice at the Roman initiative, which was in line with their concerns about the doctrinal crisis.[22]

THREE NEW REVIEWS

The episcopal warning of 1966 against certain traditionalist publications did not prevent the appearance of new titles which, each in its own style, would have a large readership and would disseminate analyses or slogans (as the case may be) that would meet with a large echo among Catholics attached to Tradition.

In January 1967, on the initiative of two laymen, General Lecomte, who had had a brilliant career in the army – he had commanded the *École d'état-major* and the *École supérieure de guerre* – and Paul de Méritens, a pressman known as Paul Dehême, and Father Mottier, the vicar of the parish of Saint Dominic, the *Courrier de Rome* was founded. This

---

22 See Philippe Roy-Lysencourt, "Les Catholiques traditionalistes et la première réception de Vatican II," in *Renouveau conciliaire et crise doctrinale*, 99-118.

monthly magazine, whose subtitle was "Religious Information–Documents–Commentary–Questions and Answers," at first had as its almost sole and often anonymous editor Father Dulac. In the first issue of the magazine, he said that he wanted to distinguish "the true Council from the Paracouncil, which had sought to infiltrate it and to divert it from its purpose"[23] and he said that he was determined to "collaborate in the work of doctrinal purification and elucidation begun in Rome."

In November 1967, a priest from Algeria, Father Noël Barbara, who lived near Tours, published a new magazine called *Forts dans la Foi*. It presented itself as a "bi-monthly review of Catholic catechesis." At a time when Paul VI had just proclaimed a Year of Faith, Father Barbara wanted to respond to this exhortation by publishing "fundamental articles" (the first two were devoted to Faith and Revelation) and by answering readers' questions in a section entitled "Let's Dialogue." Very quickly, the new magazine would increasingly address topics related to current religious events and would engage in the controversy over the "new catechisms."

Father Coache, for his part, published in 1967 a *Last Letter from a Country Priest* ("Dernière lettre d'un curé de campagne," 24 pp.), significantly subtitled: "Heresy is declared." Then, beginning on February 11, 1968, he published a bulletin, *Le Combat de la Foi*. For several years it was one of the most aggressive publications in the crisis of the Church, announcing and commenting on the many initiatives of its founder. The Eucharistic procession that Fr Coache organized in his parish of Montjavoult for the Feast of Corpus Christi in 1968, in spite of the prohibition of the bishop of the diocese, Mgr Desmazières, together with the continuation of his publications, would earn him, on June 12, 1969, a suspension *ab officio*, and, the following July 4, dismissal from his office as pastor of Montjavoult. This was to give rise to a drawn-out procedure before the Roman authorities, as we shall see.

In the period immediately following the Council, 1966-1967, there was not yet a unanimous rejection of the Second Vatican Council among traditionalists. They were alarmed by the changes in religious practices, by the first liturgical upheavals–to which we shall return–and by the innovative speeches of certain priests and bishops, but there was no questioning of all the texts of the Council. Only Father de Nantes and Archbishop Lefebvre, with different arguments, engaged in an ever-increasing criticism of the Council.

---

23 The future Cardinal de Lubac, while probably unaware of this article by Fr Dulac, repeated this distinction in his *Petite catéchèse*, 165-80.

CHAPTER 5

The Second Battle over the Catechism (1967-1969)

A SECOND BATTLE OVER THE CATECHISM WAS TO begin in 1967. The catechetical movement had not been broken after the crisis of 1957 and the condemnation of the "progressive catechism." Without going into the eventful history of the National Center for Religious Education (*Centre national de l'enseignement religieux*, CNER) from the end of the 1950s, it should be noted that a new Directory for Catechetical Pastoral Care was approved, with difficulty, in 1963, and preceded the writing, in stages, of new catechisms. An important step was the drafting of a first Compulsory Fund–there were to be three–which was approved by the Plenary Assembly of the Episcopate in October 1966, and which was to be used for the drafting of "catechetical manuals" for the fourth and fifth grades. This Compulsory Fund was drafted by a six-member editorial committee (five priests responsible for diocesan catechesis and one lay person, a "specialist in religious pedagogy") appointed by the Episcopal Commission for Religious Education.

"THE DEATH OF GRANDPA'S CATECHISM"

Even before this Compulsory Fund was known and published, the magazine *Paris Match* announced with sensational flair: "The episcopate has condemned Grandpa's catechism to death," and predicted that the new catechism "will even be revolutionary."[1] Two months later, having been able to obtain the text of the Compulsory Fund ("a 127-page mimeographed booklet"), *Le Monde* presented its contents in a long article published on December 8, 1966: "So that's the end of a single, all-purpose national catechism, whose relatively mediocre assimilation depended on volunteer catechists who were sometimes unaware of the most basic principles of sound pedagogy."[2]

With some satisfaction the newspaper noted "significant changes":

---

1 Robert Serrou, "Au petit concile de Lourdes, l'épiscopat français au complet met en route l'Église du XXIe siècle," *Paris Match* (October 29, 1966).
2 "Les Nouveux catéchismes présentent des changements significatifs," *Le Monde* (December 8, 1966).

The Precepts of the Church have purely and simply vanished. Mortal sin too, which so traumatized young children, has vanished.... Venial sin goes unmentioned. There is no definition of Original Sin. The very names of the devil, or demon, and evil spirits are not even mentioned.

The famous "guardian angels" of so many generations' lullabies no longer figure in this "obligatory fund." All mention of hell has vanished, as well as its definition as a place of torment, of suffering, and of fire. All that is specified is that "those who refuse to love God to the end would not be able to live with God."

This long and anonymous article aroused the concerns of Father de Nantes in his *Lettre à mes amis* as well as of Jean Madiran in *Itinéraires*. The latter, in an article entitled "The Massacre of the Catechism," warned that if the information in *Le Monde* was accurate, "it would not be possible in conscience to accept" this future catechism.[3] A few months later, Jean Madiran republished the catechism of Saint Pius X in a special issue of *Itinéraires*. This large volume of nearly four hundred pages included the different manuals promulgated under the pontificate of Saint Pius X: *First Notions*, for young children, the *Small Catechism*, the *Large Catechism*, the *Instruction on Feasts*, and the *Little History of Religion*. He explained: "Lay people must, today, vicariously provide the faithful with the Roman catechism that no one provides any more."[4]

This volume was published in September 1967. The following month, the Compulsory Fund was finally published. This publication was done discreetly, as a supplement to the specialized review *Catéchèse*. The text was not intended for families, nor even for catechists, but was "for the use of the authors of adaptations," that is to say, it was intended for those who would be in charge of writing the future catechisms which would not come into effect until a year later, in October 1968.

The Compulsory Fund was intended to be a new presentation of the Christian faith, where "each lesson is rooted in the human experience of children." It did indeed contain what *Le Monde* had revealed a few months earlier. Paradoxically, it was also in *Le Monde* that the article that really launched the battle against the freshly announced new catechism appeared. It was a long "free opinion" published by Louis Salleron in February 1968.[5] He noted that the "Compulsory Fund" was already normative, since it gave the "formulations" and the "questions" which "will have to be integrated, as they stand, into the textbooks."

---

3 *Itinéraires* 100 (February 1967): 297-300.
4 In the same spirit he republished the *Catechism of the Council of Trent*, as *Itinéraires* 136 (September-October 1969), 582 pages.
5 Louis Salleron, "Le Nouveau catéchisme," *Le Monde* (February 20, 1968).

He noted: "What is immediately striking in the new catechism is its revolutionary character," particularly "the number of omissions": "The new catechism makes no mention of angels, nor of the Ascension, nor of the Assumption, nor of the sacraments of order, marriage, and extreme unction, etc." He also noted, and deplored, the fact that:

> The new catechism, referring as it does mainly to the Bible and Vatican II, completely ignores the great dogmatic formulations of the early Councils.

He concluded:

> All in all, if one refers to the meaning of modernism as defined by Pius X, we can say that the climate of the new catechism is typically modernist.

This opinion piece, which appeared in the newspaper of reference at the time, set the tone for the criticisms that were to multiply. Father de Nantes, who a few months earlier had transformed his modest *Lettre à mes amis* into a monthly review entitled *La Contre-Réforme catholique au XXe siècle*, began in April 1968 a lengthy critique of what he called "the catechism of the MASDU." Pierre Lemaire, who had been at the forefront of the fight against the "progressive catechism" in 1957, also launched a battle against the "new catechisms." In *Défense du foyer*, and in widely distributed tracts, he criticized the content of this Compulsory Fund, believing that it no longer allowed for the teaching of the faith to children. Soon he summarized its deficiencies:

> The Compulsory Fund for the new catechisms does not say that Jesus is true God and true man. It does not say that the Blessed Virgin is the Mother of God. It does not speak of original sin. Four sacraments are "forgotten": Confirmation, Extreme Unction, Holy Orders and Marriage. Many of the Scripture texts quoted are altered, truncated. Many important texts are omitted, in particular all that concerns the sacrifice and the priesthood, and Pentecost. The miracles performed by Jesus are de-emphasized. Only two are mentioned. The Passion is reduced to the Crucifixion, and the presence of the Virgin Mary is eliminated. There is no mention of the precepts of the Church.[6]

Father Coache in *Le Combat pour la foi*, Father Barbara in *Forts dans la foi*, Father Calmel in *Itinéraires*, and Pierre Debray in his *Courrier hebdomadaire* also undertook, each in his own way, to criticize the Compulsory Fund. Cardinal Lefebvre, archbishop of Bourges and president of the Episcopal Conference, published a communiqué in defense

---

6 Pierre Lemaire, *Vers l'apostasie de la foi catholique? Les Nouveaux catéchismes* (Chavagne: Éditions Saint-Michel, 1968).

of the Fund. Without citing the publications in question, he deplored "articles that have appeared in the press," a "campaign [that] distorts the meaning and scope" of the Compulsory Fund. He considered that "such an attack" was based "on quotations taken out of context, isolating this or that expression from other complementary expressions." He also affirmed that the Compulsory Fund "does not represent the totality of the teaching given to the children of France, but only a step which will be followed by the Catechism for the later classes."[7]

The following month, Jean Madiran published a long study dissecting what he called the "French National Catechism" and showing the "terrible moral dilemma" that it would pose to the faithful, to priests, and to catechists if it came into force.[8] The same month, March 1968, a new organization was born, called "Renewal of Christian Order" (*Renouveau de l'Ordre Chrétien*, ROC). The founders were former senior officers who had had brilliant careers in the French armed forces: Admiral Hervé de Penfentenyo and General Jean Lecomte. The stated purpose of the ROC was "to revive, renew, promote, strengthen, and defend the traditions, principles, morals, and honor of Christian order."[9] The association had some financial means at its disposal from the start, which were then fed by high membership fees (distinguishing between sympathizing members, active members, and benefactor members). The leaflet introducing the ROC ran to 50,000 printed copies. One of the first initiatives of the new organization was to publish a press release to "demand from the religious authorities the re-establishment of the four obligatory points of the catechism: the Creed, the *Paternoster*, the Decalogue, the seven sacraments."

From this same period dates the birth of the movement of the "Silent Ones of the Church" (*Silencieux de l'Église*). Pierre Debray, who for several years had been publishing a weekly *Courrier* that had a growing readership, was the founder, along with another lay person, Françoise Lucrot.[10] The "events" of May '68, which were at first a subversion of the established order, had accelerated in the Church a movement of contestation or questioning that had been going on for

---

7 *La Croix* (March 1, 1968); *DC* (March 17, 1968).

8 Jean Madiran, "Le Nouveau catéchisme" and "Précisions complémentaires," *Itinéraires* 121 (March 1968): 65–119.

9 The Association was formally founded by registration at the Prefecture on March 26, 1968: *Journal officiel* (April 26, 1968): 4279.

10 Jean-François Galinier-Pallerola, "Le Rassemblement des Silencieux de l'Église, Pierre Debray et le combat liturgique," in J.-F. Galinier-Pallerola, Ph. Foro, and A. Laffay, eds, *Les laïcs prennent la parole. Débats et controverses dans le catholicisme après Vatican II* (Paris: Parole et Silence, 2014), 203–40.

some time. In Paris and in other cities, many parishes and chaplaincies, won over by this climate of contestation, organized many meetings and general assemblies, especially from the spring of 1968 onward. During this period, Pierre Debray published *À bas la calotte rouge!* ("Down with the Red Clergy!," printed May 25, 1968), a pamphlet against the revolutionary Dominican Jean Cardonnel. Then he and Françoise Lucrot began to attend parish meetings to give some push-back. Françoise Lucrot recalls: "We'd hear these fiery speeches advocating all sorts of upheavals, often made by naïve people who imagined they had solutions to all the problems of the Church and brilliant ideas for adapting it to the modern world"; others who were more radical, wanted "to destroy the traditional structures of the Church."[11] The push-back that Pierre Debray, Françoise Lucrot, and others – Charles de Langalerie, the journalist Georges Daix – gave was not a dialectical opposition; rather, they would refer to the texts of the Second Vatican Council. The principle of their argumentation at that time was simple: "Apply the Council, the whole Council, nothing but the Council." The movement grew and no longer limited itself to challenging the protesters, but also attacked the liturgical experiments that were spreading, as well as illegitimate pastoral innovations. The movement became structured, and officially took the name of *Rassemblement des Silencieux de l'Église* ("Assembly of the Silent Ones of the Church") in October 1969.

THE *DUTCH CATECHISM*

The controversy over the Compulsory Fund in France ran in parallel with the so-called "Dutch Catechism Crisis," which was only one facet of the more general crisis that the Catholic Church in the Netherlands had been experiencing for several years.

Even before the opening of the Council, Dutch Catholicism had entered a bold effervescence, according to optimists, and a disturbing maelstrom, according to others. From the beginning of the 1960s, "grassroots groups" and "critical parishes" had developed throughout the country. They wanted to initiate the transformation of Dutch Catholicism:

> Modernization of the liturgy, but also criticism of society and contestation of the functioning of the church – especially clerical celibacy and the obstacles placed in the way of intercommunion between Protestants and Catholics.[12]

11 Françoise Lucrot, "Les Silencieux prennent la parole," interview in *La Nouvelle revue universelle* 56 (2019): 123.
12 Lodewijk Winkeler, "Au-delà du concile. Le Catholicime néerlandais, un laboratoire du renouveau ecclésial (1960-1975)," in *Histoire@Politique* 30 (2016): 7-24; https://www.cairn.info/revue-histoire-politique-2016-3-page-7.htm [accessed 4/4/2024].

This mutation had multiple causes.[13] The Dutch bishops accompanied it, and tried to limit its disastrous effects, but also, through some of their initiatives, encouraged it. A month before the end of the Second Vatican Council, they announced in Rome itself that a "provincial council" would be organized in the Netherlands "to implement Vatican II."[14] It was eventually called a "pastoral council." It was a broad consultation that was not limited to bishops and theologians and was not organized in any single place. It took place all over the country, beginning on November 27, 1966, and lasted several years. It was the work of some 12,000 work groups in which bishops, priests, religious, and laity were involved. During the meetings, which often took place in the presence of the press and under the watchful eye of the cameras, all subjects concerning the Church and the life of Christians were discussed: the expression of the faith, authority in the Church, the ministries, priestly celibacy, the reform of religious life, relations with non-Catholics, conjugal morality, etc.

As this pastoral council was about to begin, on October 9, 1966, *De Nieuwe Katechismus, geloofsverkondiging voor volwassenen* ("The New Catechism, a proclamation of faith for adults") was published. This work, commissioned by the bishops of the Netherlands and later known as the Dutch Catechism, was a large book of six hundred pages that sought to "announce the eternal faith in the language and style of our time" and also "express the desire for renewal that was manifested during the Council." It was published with the imprimatur of Cardinal Alfrink, Archbishop of Utrecht.

The very next month, on November 22, 1966, a group of Dutch Catholics, both priests and lay people, who since 1964 had been publishing *Confrontatie*, a magazine to defend the faith and the Church, published an open letter to Paul VI in the principal Dutch daily newspaper, *De Tijd*. They deplored the crisis that the Church in Holland was going through:

> For many years now, several Dutch Catholic writers and orators, lay people and priests, regular and secular, have been propagating in our country opinions which not only do not agree with Catholic doctrine, but even contradict it. This behavior causes a great scandal which not only continues, but increases day by day, and causes suffering and sadness to a great number of the faithful.[15]

---

13 See Jan Bots, SJ, *Le Catholicism hollandais hier et aujourd'hui* (Saint-Cénéré: Téqui, 1979): 33-48.
14 Declaration of Bp De Vet of Breda, November 16, 1965.
15 Letter translated into French in Aldo Chiaruttini, *Le Dossier du catéchisme hollandais* (Paris: Fayard, 1969), 65-66.

The signatories denounced the errors and inadequacies of the *Dutch Catechism* in particular. "This book," they wrote, "develops a number of themes that are partly or totally contrary to the faith, or interpret the truths of the faith in an ambiguous way." They noted, "among others," seven erroneous or deficient presentations: on the virginity of Mary, original sin, the Eucharist, the way Protestantism is introduced, birth control, the origin of man and the creation of the soul, and the existence of angels. "The explanation of various dogmas," the letter to Paul VI said, "generally deviates from the way in which the Church has understood them and continues to understand them." The *Confrontatie* group therefore asked the pope to "intervene so that the faith does not run into even greater perils in our country and through our fault."

Subsequently, other complaints and critical observations from theologians reached the Holy See. By the end of January 1967 – and not the following spring as many have written – Paul VI set up a commission of cardinals to examine the work and to advise on the necessary corrections. There were six of them: Frings, Archbishop of Cologne; Jaeger, Archbishop of Paderborn; Florit, Archbishop of Florence; Lefebvre, Archbishop of Bourges; Browne, Master General of the Dominicans; Journet, still a professor of theology at Fribourg.[16] In addition, three theologians belonging to various congregations, Fathers Edouard Dhanis, a Jesuit, Benedict Lemeer, a Dominican, and Jan Visser, a Redemptorist, were charged with discussing the controversial passages with a delegation of three theologians named by the bishops of Holland: Fathers Guillaume Bless, a Jesuit; Piet Schoonenberg, a Jesuit, a professor of theology at the Catholic University of Nijmegen and one of the principal editors of the Catechism; and Edward Schillebeeckx, a Dominican, also a professor of theology at Nijmegen. The two groups of theologians met in Gazzada, near Milan, April 8-10, 1967. The participants were unable to come to an agreement regarding the passages to be corrected.

The Cardinals' Commission met for the first time on June 27-28, 1967. It suggested drawing up a "typical Catechism of the Universal Church" of the kind that had been drawn up after the Council of Trent – a suggestion that would not come to fruition until the pontificate of John Paul II. It also considered it necessary for the *Dutch Catechism* to be revised before the publication of any new edition or of any of the translations already being prepared. To this end, a new commission of theologians was appointed. It included, beyond Dhanis and Leemer,

---

16 See Georges Cottier and Michel Cagin, "Sur le Catéchisme hollandais," in Charles Journet and Jacques Maritain, *Correspondance*, vol. 6: *1965-1973* (Paris: Éditions Saint-Augustin, 2008), 1029-41.

five theologians from different countries: the Italian Carlo Colombo, the pope's private theologian; the Frenchman de Lubac; the German Ratzinger; the Irishman Doolan; and the Spaniard Alfaro. They met twice, from September 13-17, and again from October 30-November 3, 1967, and produced a report–known as the Dhanis report–which contained 31 pages of observations and requests for corrections.

The Cardinals' Commission then met for a second time in Rome from December 12-14, 1967, and began to work out the corrections that would be required in the *Dutch Catechism*. Although Rome had expressly asked that all translations be suspended, it began to be published in various languages in late 1967 and the first months of 1968: in English, German, and French.[17]

TWO "GLIMMERS OF HOPE"

The political and social crisis that shook France in May 1968 pushed the controversy over the catechism into the background. Conversely, the *Credo of the People of God* proclaimed by Paul VI in June 1968 gave comfort to those in France, the Netherlands, and elsewhere who were alarmed about the Church's ability to transmit the Catholic faith in its integrity.

The idea of a solemn profession of faith on the part of the Pope came from the philosopher Jacques Maritain, who had been on friendly terms with Paul VI for a long time. In January 1967, he wrote to his friend Cardinal Journet:

> A thought came to me several days ago with such an intensity and clarity that I don't think I can overlook it. It was like a flash of light as I prayed for the Pope and thought about the dreadful crisis through which the Church is passing. On the one hand, the seriousness of this crisis, which threatens the foundations of the Faith and is linked to the immense crisis that is shaking the world and civilization, cannot be exaggerated. On the other hand, one cannot be under any illusions about the weakness of the means available to the Magisterium and to all those who, along with it, strive with all their heart to defend the Truth in the face of such a crisis.... Only one thing, in such circumstances, is capable of striking minds universally, and of maintaining the absolutely essential good, which is the integrity of the Faith: it is a decisive and striking act of the only force that remains intact, a sovereign act of the supreme authority which is that of the Vicar of Jesus Christ; not a disciplinary act, nor exhortations, nor directives, but a dogmatic act, at the level of the Faith itself.[18]

---

17 *A New Catechism: Catholic Faith for Adults* (London: Burns & Oates; New York: Herder and Herder, 1967).

18 Jacques Maritain to Charles Journet, Letter dated January 14, 1967, in Journet-Maritain, *Correspondance*, 6: 328-29.

The idea met with the pope's approval. Maritain was asked to prepare a draft of the profession of faith, which was revised by Father Duroux, a Dominican and consultant to the Congregation for the Doctrine of the Faith. On June 30, 1968, Paul VI proclaimed a solemn profession of faith. It has sometimes been presented, in order to minimize its scope, as a "personal profession of faith" engaging only the Pope. In fact, he was speaking as the head of the Church. Ten years later, when assessing his pontificate, he said that he wanted to pronounce this profession of faith "in the name of the whole Church and by publishing it as the 'Creed of the People of God' in order to recall, reaffirm, and confirm the capital points of the Church's faith."

The pope took as his starting point the ancient formulation of the faith as defined at the Council of Nicaea in 325, the first ecumenical council in the history of the Church, but developed it further. Each article of the Nicene Creed was taken up and explained. The proclamation of the *Creed of the People of God*, "without being a dogmatic definition in the strict sense of the word," the Pope said, was the fulfilment of his "mandate" as Pontiff to "confirm the faith." He hoped that his profession of faith would be well received and would provoke an awakening.

The Catholic press, generally speaking, stressed the importance of the event. In *La Croix*, Father Daniélou hailed this proclamation of faith as "an exceptional doctrinal event [which] dispels some of the false prejudices of a certain modern intelligentsia." He called for it to be considered from then on as "a test of authentic faith, which makes it possible to judge the value of the opinions spread in certain books or articles.... It is in the light of this text that the Christian people have the right and the duty to challenge opinions which are not in conformity with it."[19]

The encyclical *Humanae Vitae* appeared the following month. In it Pope Paul VI maintained the traditional teaching on the ends of marriage and reaffirmed the Church's condemnation of contraception and abortion. It also appeared to be an act of courage in the face of the irreversible current of liberalization of morals (the law authorizing contraception had been passed in France the previous year). In an article published in *Le Monde*, Louis Salleron greeted "the challenge of Paul VI" whose "voice resounded like thunder."[20] Jean Madiran, in *Itinéraires*, considered that the encyclical had "struck the collective conscience of humanity" in its then prevailing state of blindness and

---

19 Article reprinted in Jean Daniélou, *Tests* (Paris: Beauchesne, 1968), 35-39.
20 *Le Monde* (6 August 1968).

smugness. In the same issue, Archbishop Lefebvre considered that the Pope, through his profession of faith and through the encyclical, had given "reasons for hope" which "can only come from the Holy Spirit."[21]

This solemn confirmation of the Catholic faith by the pope encouraged the defenders of the traditional catechism to continue their struggle. More discreetly, during this same period, Dom Jean Roy, Abbot of Fontgombault, had the theologian monks of his abbey study the Compulsory Fund paragraph by paragraph. The result was a critical study some twenty pages long that was sent to Paul VI and other Holy See authorities.[22]

Pierre Lemaire reprinted the *Grand catéchisme en images* [a large-format illustrated catechism for children] that Father Bailly, founder of the Maison de la Bonne Presse, had published in 1909, and which had been reprinted many times until the 1950s. He also reprinted 10,000 copies of the catechism that was in use in the diocese of Paris in 1930, under the title *Catéchisme de nos enfants* ("Our Children's Catechism").

In October 1968, Bishop Gand of Lille, the president of the Episcopal Commission for Religious Education, and Father Saudreau, the director of the CNER, went to Rome to present the five catechisms that had finally been published under various titles (*Chrétiens partout, En suivant Jésus-Christ*, etc.) from the Common Compulsory Fund.

In that same month, Pierre Lemaire published a critical study of the Compulsory Fund under the title *Que faut-il penser du Nouveau Catéchisme?* ("What Is One to Think of the New Catechism?"). It had been written by theologians, priests, and family men. The booklet opened with a letter from Archbishop Lefebvre, who was soon to resign as Superior General of the Fathers of the Holy Ghost. He wrote:

> You are to be heartily congratulated for the campaign you are on to enlighten families about the harmfulness of the new catechisms. Children will not only retain nothing of religious teaching, but will have a false idea of it, contrary to the whole tradition of the Church. The Church of France is bringing the curses of God upon herself. "The children asked for bread and were given scorpions." May the Good Lord help you and bless your efforts to save the faith of the families of France.[23]

This critical study was sent to all the bishops gathered, as every year, in a plenary assembly in Lourdes. The few lines of Archbishop

---

21 Archbp Marcel Lefebvre, "Lueurs d'espérance," *Itinéraires* 127 (November 1968): 226-31.
22 Dom Jean-Louis Robien, *Dom Jean Roy. Abbé de Notre-Dame de Fontgombault, 1921-1977* (unpublished, 2002), 131. Archives of the Notre Dame de Fontgombault Abbey.
23 Archbp Lefebvre to Pierre Lemaire, Letter dated September 18, 1968, published in *Que faut-il penser du Nouveau Catéchisme?*, *Documents-Paternité* 135 (October 1968): 2.

Lefebvre scandalized many. Cardinal Lefebvre, Archbishop of Bourges, wrote as much to Archbishop Lefebvre (they were cousins) in a long letter. He told him of his "saddened amazement" at the sentence: "The Church of France is drawing the curses of God upon herself." Cardinal Lefebvre, speaking in the name of the French episcopate, felt:

> Certainly, we know that we are fallible and are absolutely ready to bow, not only with docility, but with joy to any direction given by the Supreme Pontiff. But that one of our brothers in the episcopate should claim to be our judge and publicly accuse us was deeply painful for us. I have felt this particularly keenly and believe it my duty to tell you in all simplicity.

He also added:

> I cannot understand how, based on a "Common Fund," one can condemn in advance a catechism that does not yet exist.... I am fully aware of the many dangers that the purity of the faith is currently facing. However, I do not believe that suspecting heresy everywhere, and condemning in advance those who have no desire to fall into it, is an effective way to remedy the evil.[24]

This indictment of the "Church of France" as a whole by Archbishop Lefebvre offended many bishops and added to the dispute that would grow until his exclusion in 1972.

The battle against the "Catechisms" continued. In February 1969, Father Barbara organized a large public meeting at the *Palais de la Mutualité* in Paris. He invited Pierre Lemaire, "an educator," "a country priest," and Father de Nantes to speak at his side. When he learned of this conference, Mgr Marty, who had been archbishop of Paris for a few months, tried to discourage Pierre Lemaire from participating. He wrote to him, as if to intimidate him:

> I want you to know that under the circumstances you have no mission to talk to the Catholics of Paris on this subject. I cannot approve an initiative that does not respect the norms of the Church of which you are a member.

THE HERESY OF THE TWENTIETH CENTURY

Before this battle over the catechism was over, two books, very different in form, appeared at the end of 1968: a large book of philosophical and theological reflection, *L'Hérésie du XXe siècle* ("The Heresy of the 20th Century"), written by Jean Madiran, and a small pamphlet a few pages long, both synthetic and polemical, published by Father

---

24 Cardinal Joseph Lefebvre to Archbp Marcel Lefebvre, Letter dated November 14, 1969, Lefebvre archives (Écône).

Coache: *Vademecum du catholique fidèle* ("Vademecum of the faithful
Catholic"). The booklet had a considerable circulation, while Jean
Madiran's book had to wait twenty years before being republished.
But both of them were united in being a refusal. Not a refusal of the
Second Vatican Council as such, but a refusal of the rupture initiated
by the Council, according to them.

After the "condemnation" of *Itinéraires* by the episcopate in June
1966 – although we have seen that he ultimately withdrew the term
"condemnation" himself – Jean Madiran had asked three times (October 15, 1966, June 12, 1967, and January 12, 1968) to be heard by the
Plenary Assembly of the French Episcopal Conference. He wanted to
be able to explain himself. He exchanged letters with various bishops
and had a meeting with two of them, but was not received by the
Plenary Assembly as he had requested. He then decided to publish a
book. This was *L'Hérésie du XXe siècle*,[25] which he considered to be
his most important book. Twenty years later, in the afterword written
for the new edition, he would say:

> If I had to leave only one book behind, it would be this one.... In
> *L'Hérésie* I have expressed all the reasons for my refusals and
> also all the ideas for which I am fighting. All the fights to which
> I have, in a way, dedicated my life.

The book opened with a sentence for which Jean Madiran was much
reproached: "The heresy of the twentieth century is that of the bishops."
Such a statement, in itself, was not unheard of. Throughout the history
of the Church, erroneous assertions or denials of doctrine became
heresies only because they were relayed by bishops. The theological
conceptions of the priest Arius in the fourth century became the Arian
heresy because they were taken up and developed by a significant
number of bishops and theologians. Jean Madiran did not say that all
the bishops of France after the council had become heretics, but that
the heresy "is taught by bishops and is not contested by other bishops."
He defined this heresy as a denial of the natural law, which was even
more widely observed outside the Church.

Summarizing his argument, he wrote:

> The heresy of the twentieth century is first and foremost the
> disregard, contempt, and refusal of the natural order....Cer-
> tainly the refusal of this objective truth does not constitute,
> strictly speaking, a formal heresy; but rather an infirmity, the

---

25 First edition in 1968 at the Nouvelles Éditions Latines; second edition in 1988 at the
same press with a new afterword; third edition in 2018 at Via Romana with a preface
by Michel de Jaeghere and an historical appendix by Philippe Maxence.

consequences of which in the religious order lead to what can
be called a heresy: that is to say, the corruption of dogmas.

Jean Madiran sought to characterize this heresy in seven propositions. With the first–"The transformation of the world teaches and
imposes a change in the very conception of salvation"–he pointed to
an inversion: in the post-conciliar conception it is no longer the world
that must listen to the teaching of the Church, it is "the faith [that]
listens to the world." A few years later, the philosopher Maurice Clavel,
who had moved from the far left to Catholicism, would inveigh against
the proponents of modernity in the Church in the same way: "You
have not gone *out* to the world, you have gone *over* to the world. The
spirit of the age has taken hold of you, intimidated you . . . it got you."[26]

Father Coache too warned against what he called "the Great Heresy,"
but the word did not mean the same thing as it did for Jean Madiran.
For Father Coache, it was more simply a question of "the doctrinal and
moral confusion" that was spreading ever more widely in the Church
and meant that "many of the faithful are, in our day, troubled by the
audacities and extravagances attacking their Faith."[27] The *Vademecum of
the Faithful Catholic* which he published at the end of 1968, and which
he developed with Father Barbara, was not a demonstration. It was
made up of reminders and warnings. The booklet was thus subtitled
in its first edition: "Facing the concerted destruction of the Church,
150 priests recall the essential principles of Christian life." The titles of
the very short chapters usually gave advice: pray much, confess regularly, receive Communion often with the proper dispositions, remain
firm in the faith, keep the true morals, spread God's love around you.

The extraordinary distribution of this booklet–four editions, for a
total print run of 360,000 copies–is explained by the simplicity of its
content, the practicality of its presentation (28 small-format pages), the
fact that it was distributed free of charge, and also by the fact that it
undoubtedly corresponded to the expectations of many of the faithful
who were disoriented by the maelstrom that the Church was going
through. Before its publication the *Vademecum* was sent to a certain
number of priests and religious who had subscribed to *Combat de la
Foi* or *Forts dans la Foi*. They were invited to endorse the text and to
have it signed by priests or religious of their acquaintance who shared
their conviction. The first edition published at the end of November
1968 listed the names of 150 priests who had signed the *Vademecum*.

---

26 Maurice Clavel, *"Dieu est Dieu, nom de Dieu!"* (Paris: Grasset, 1976).
27 *Vademecum du catholique fidèle* (1968), 2.

As more editions came out, more priests set their names to it: a total of 263 names were published. With the third edition, in the second quarter of 1969, the number of signatures exceeded 400 priests (but the names of the new signatories were not published), to whom were added a cardinal and two bishops: Cardinal Bacci; Archbishop Lefebvre; and Bishop Messmer, a Capuchin missionary. The *Vademecum* was also published in Italian, Spanish and Portuguese.

An examination of the 263 names published both reveals a landscape of traditionalism at the time and constitutes a sort of prehistory of the commitments and initiatives to come. One finds, among others, the Capuchins who were already trying to maintain the traditions of their order, and of whom we will speak again; the Dominicans who were contributors or friends of the review *Itinéraires* (Fathers Calmel, de Chivré, Guérard des Lauriers); Father Bénéfice, pastor of Malaucène, who would be one of the supporters of Dom Gérard when he founded the Benedictine monastery at Bédoin; Father Lecareux, who would soon found the Fraternity of the Transfiguration at Mérigny; certain priests and religious who would be among the first teachers at Écône (Abbé Gottlieb, for example) and also, of course, many of the priests who would soon refuse the new Mass.

The great lecture on the crisis of the Church that Father Coache gave at the Mutualité in Paris on October 24, 1969, was published under the title "Évêques, restez catholiques" ("Bishops, stay Catholic") and ran to 120,000 copies.[28] In 1970, Father Coache, along with Élisabeth Gerstner, the leader of a traditionalist movement in Austria and a friend of Jean Madiran, initiated a "March on Rome," an international pilgrimage which was repeated, with the support of other organizers, in 1971 and 1973.

---

28 First edition, *Le Combat de la foi* (1969); second, revised edition in 2021 (Chiré-en-Montreuil: Éditions de Chiré, 2016).

CHAPTER 6
Against the "New Mass"

T HE CONCILIAR CONSTITUTION ON THE LITURGY, *Sacrosanctum Concilium*, promulgated on December 4, 1963, while giving rise to debate and concern, had ultimately been welcomed by those who would soon reject liturgical reforms. In January 1964, Paul VI founded a Consilium to implement the conciliar constitution on the liturgy. It was first presided over by Cardinal Lercaro, Archbishop of Bologna, who quickly obtained an agreement that the Consilium should be autonomous from the Congregation of Rites, traditionally responsible for liturgical matters. But the principal architect of this reform—not the inspirer, but the conductor—was, from the beginning, Father Annibale Bugnini, secretary of the Consilium.[1] He played a central role until 1975.

But even before the conciliar constitution was voted on and promulgated, changes in the liturgy had taken place in many parishes. They had been introduced by certain priests on their own initiative. Thus, from 1964 onwards, there was a legal reform, enacted by Rome in stages, by successive instructions, and at the same time–in some countries and in many parishes–there were upheavals beyond the scope of any oversight, upheavals anticipating changes that Rome had not yet authorized, or taking the new spirit opened up by the Council as a pretext to change things *hic et nunc*.

As early as January 1964, just as the Consilium was created, Archbishop Lefebvre deplored "so many improbable initiatives of which thousands of the faithful are helpless and deeply distressed witnesses. There are many churches where liturgical rules are violated with impunity."[2]

AN ARMY OF EXPERTS

The Consilium answered only to the pope. This was its strength. As Piero Marini, who was Archbishop Bugnini's secretary from 1965 to 1975, pointed out: "The *Consilium*, in the end, unlike the dicasteries of the Roman Curia, was not bound by procedural habits or by any particular

---

1 See Yves Chiron, *Annibale Bugnini* (Brooklyn, OH: Angelico Press, 2018).
2 Archbp Marcel Lefebvre, *Lettre à tous les membres de la congrégation du Saint Esprit* (January 21, 1964) in *Un évêque parle* (Poitiers: Dominique Martin Morin, 1974), 34.

regulations."[3] It had 42 members, most of whom were diocesan bishops from different continents, "bishops on the ground," not Vatican prelates. The disadvantage of this internationalization was that the members rarely all met in Rome. Like all Roman congregations, the Consilium also relied on a number of consultors, experts in liturgy. Their number would grow, far more than in any other organ of the Curia. In his book, Bugnini lists 149 names. To these he adds a list, which he specifies is not exhaustive, of "advisors" who were consulted directly by the Consilium, without official appointment. This second list contains 74 names.[4] It was therefore an army of more than 200 consultants and advisers scattered throughout the world who would work on the projects launched by the Consilium.

From March 1964 to July 1975, this body elaborated 439 schemas that led to the drafting and promulgation of new rites and new liturgical books. In the years leading up to the promulgation of the new missal (1969), instructions and decrees were issued between 1964 and 1968, which brought about very important changes, such as the practice of concelebration, Communion under both species, the introduction of the vernacular, celebration facing the people, new Eucharistic prefaces, and Communion in the hand, not to mention modifications to the Order of Mass.

The two new rites promulgated were those of concelebration and Communion under both species. They were the result of various schemas worked out by the Consilium and also of numerous "experiments" that had been previously authorized. On May 17, 1964, by special permission of Paul VI, Cardinal Lercaro, on the occasion of the celebration of his priestly jubilee in Bologna, was able to celebrate Mass with other priests. This was the first experimental concelebration. A month later, the Pope authorized other experimental celebrations in six Benedictine abbeys (St. Anselmo in Rome, Montserrat in Spain, En-Calcat in France, Maredsous in Belgium, Maria Laach in Germany, and Collegeville in the United States) and in the Dominican convent of Le Saulchoir in Paris. A month later, he authorized the Consilium to issue indults for concelebration and Communion under both species "in particular cases." This was no longer a question of experimentation, but of conceding new practices while the rites in question had not yet been fixed. Between July 1964 and March 1965, the Pope granted more than 900 concelebration indults to bishops, diocesan priests, and religious

---

3 Piero Marini, "Elenco degli 'schemata' del 'Consilium' e della Congregazione per il Culto divino," *Notitiae* 195-196 (October-November 1982): 459.

4 Annibale Bugnini, *The Reform of the Liturgy (1948-1975)*, trans. Matthew J. O'Connell (Collegeville, MN: The Liturgical Press, 1990), 950-52.

congregations. It can be said that concelebration had become familiar to many of the faithful and communities before the rite was fixed. On February 25, 1965, Paul VI concelebrated with 24 newly created cardinals, a huge square altar having been built for the occasion. The new rite of concelebration was finally promulgated on March 7, 1965.

On the same day the rite of Communion under both species was promulgated. It considerably widened the possibility of communion with the chalice for the faithful: eleven cases in all. While concelebration had been the subject of much debate for several decades, the same could not be said for communion under both species. A specialist in the question, the Sulpician Charles Michel-Jean, acknowledged at the time: "The restoration of this rite, it must be admitted, was not really asked for by the faithful or by the clergy." This restoration, he believed, had a symbolic scope and an ecumenical aim: to get closer to the Orthodox and Protestants who practiced communion from the chalice.[5]

Considering it now with the hindsight of history, one realizes that while concelebration has become widespread well beyond what was foreseen in the texts cited—which has given rise to doctrinal debates on the equivalence between a Mass concelebrated by five or ten priests and five or ten Masses celebrated individually—communion from the chalice has remained, to this day, an "exceptional practice" [outside the USA—*Translator*].

FACING THE CONGREGATION AND IN THE VERNACULAR

On that very March 7, 1965, the first Instruction on liturgical reform came into effect.[6] It was very long—99 articles—and it set the framework and conditions for its application and, without constituting a complete upheaval of the Mass, it did list the authorized changes, notably:

> —the use of "the vernacular" for the readings (Epistle and Gospel), for the chants of the Common, "as well as the introit, offertory, and communion antiphons";
> —the "use of the vernacular in those parts of the Mass that the celebrant sings or recites alone" with permission from the Holy See;
> —the celebration of the Mass "facing the people";
> —the introduction before the offertory of a "universal prayer or prayer of the faithful";

5 Charles Michel-Jean, "La Communion au calice," *La Maison-Dieu* 85 (1966): 168-78.
6 Consilium, Instruction *Inter Oecumenici* on the orderly carrying out of the Constitution on the Liturgy, in International Commission on English in the Liturgy, *Documents on the Liturgy 1963-1979: Conciliar, Papal, and Curial Texts* (Collegeville: The Liturgical Press, 1982), #23 (henceforth *DOL*).

-the recitation of the Lord's Prayer by the priest and congregation "in the vernacular";
-two unexplained suppressions at the end of the Mass: "the last gospel is omitted; the Leonine Prayers are suppressed."

It was almost surreptitiously–one article among 99–that a true spatial revolution in the liturgy took place. For centuries, the Mass had been celebrated *ad orientem*, with the priest facing God, turning towards the faithful only for the homily, and then to distribute communion. The celebration of the Mass *versus populum* was more in keeping with the communal sense of the Mass, but it diminished the mystical aspect of worship. This possibility of a Mass "facing the people" was not included in the Council's Constitution on the Liturgy. This new concession would soon become the norm, with the Pope himself setting the example.

On March 7, 1965, in All Saints' Church in Rome, Paul VI celebrated Mass in Italian for the first time–only the Canon remained in Latin–and facing the people, on an altar set up in the church choir for the occasion. In the address he gave a few hours later, during the Angelus, he justified "the sacrifice of an age-old tradition" that had just taken place:[7]

> Today is a memorable Sunday in the spiritual history of the Church: the vernacular, as you have perceived this morning, has officially taken its place within liturgical worship.... The Church has sacrificed its native tongue, Latin, a language that is sacred, measured, beautiful, richly expressive, and graceful. The Church has made the sacrifice of an age-old tradition and above all of unity in language among diverse peoples to bow to a higher universality, an outreach to all peoples.

Paul VI was convinced that the faithful would "pass over from being simply spectators to becoming active participants."

While this massive irruption of the vernacular language and the altar facing the people were disrupting the Mass, lively controversies were developing in France over the official translations of the Creed and the *Paternoster*. These translations had been produced by the experts of the CNPL (*Centre National de Pastorale Liturgique*) and promulgated by the Episcopal Liturgical Commission.[8] With regard to the translation of the Creed, published in December 1964, the controversy concerned mainly the *consubstantialem Patri*, translated as "of the same nature

---

7 Paul VI, "Remarks at the Angelus to the People in St. Peter's Square on the Beginning of the Vernacular in the Liturgy," March 7, 1965, *DOL* #26.

8 Regarding the composition of these translations and those that followed as well as of the controversies they occasioned, see Florian Michel, *Traduire la liturgie. Essai d'histoire* (Paris: Éditions CLD, 2013).

as the Father" ("de même nature que le Père"), under the pretext that the notion of substance was incomprehensible for the faithful. The controversy was launched by Étienne Gilson in a resounding article published in *La France catholique* on July 2, 1965. He protested against the disappearance of the term "consubstantial" which had been adopted at the Council of Nicea in 325 to define the mystery of the Trinity against the Arian heresy. The article attracted all the more attention because of the fact that Étienne Gilson, a famous philosopher, former professor at the Collège de France, and member of the Académie française, affirmed his attachment to the liturgical reform, which he judged "opportune, beneficial, necessary." He was supported by Jacques Maritain, another Catholic philosopher and friend of the Pope, and by other personalities.

As for the translation of the *Paternoster*, the controversy was even more intense because a classic French formula, dating back to Bossuet, "had become almost universally accepted by all French Catholics."[9] In January 1966, the French bishops decided to adopt an "ecumenical translation" that had been produced by a commission composed of Catholics, Protestants, and Orthodox. The controversy concerned the use of the informal French pronoun "tu" [to address God – *Translator*] ("que *ton* nom soit sanctifié," etc.) and various formulas, in particular the sixth request: *ne nos inducas in tentationem* translated as "submit us not to temptation" ("ne nous soumets pas à la tentation") instead of the traditional "let us not succumb to temptation" ("ne lous laissez pas succomber à la tentation"). This classic translation was not itself completely satisfactory. According to scholars of the New Testament – it was originally written in Greek, based on a Hebrew or Aramaic text – the more authentic meaning would be "Make it so that we do not enter into temptation" or "Do not allow us to enter into temptation."[10]

Once again, it was Étienne Gilson who was the first to protest, in an article published in *La France catholique* on February 18, 1966. Alexis Curvers published a major study in *Itinéraires*.[11] An exegete, Father Jean Carmignac, had already alerted the translators during the preparation of the text. As a former student of the École Biblique de Jérusalem and as founder and director of the *Revue de Qumrân*, he was an internationally recognized specialist. He would later testify:

---

9 Fr Dominique-Marie de Saint-Laumer, "Les traductions du *Notre Père*," *Sedes Sapientiae* 68 (Summer 1999): 44-63.

10 Ibid., 59.

11 Alexis Curvers, "Le Nouveau 'Pater,'" *Itinéraires* 103 (May 1966): 52-70 and *Itinéraires* 104 (June 1966): 132-66.

> When I learned that a new French translation of the Lord's Prayer
> was going to contain the formula "submit us not to temptation,"
> I was indignant, first of all, because this translation is false, and
> above all because it constitutes an insult to God, who has never
> subjected anyone to temptation. I therefore protested to the
> authorities responsible for this error, but I did not succeed in
> getting them to change this regrettable translation.[12]

Father Carmignac then prepared a doctoral dissertation to demonstrate the deficiencies of the official translation.[13]

It was not until 2017, for the *Paternoster*, and 2019, for the Creed, that corrected translations came into effect: "Submit us not to temptation " was replaced by "Do not let us enter into temptation" and "of the same nature as the Father" was replaced by "consubstantial with the Father."

UNA VOCE

Even before the September 1964 Instruction went into effect, one of its provisions had caused great concern. Article 57 stipulated that the chants of the Mass could be sung in the vernacular, including those of the Ordinary of the Mass: the *Kyrie*, the *Gloria*, the *Credo*, the *Sanctus* and the *Agnus Dei*. This new provision contradicted the conciliar constitution on the liturgy, which had stated: "Particular law remaining in force, the use of the Latin language is to be preserved in the Latin rites" (*SC* § 36).[14]

Some laymen, priests, bishops, and cardinals were alarmed at the possibility of giving up centuries-old chants that were familiar to the faithful. The possible disappearance of Latin and of Gregorian chant in the churches seemed to many, even to non-practicing Catholics and non-Christians, to be the loss of an immemorial patrimony.

In May 1964, Bernadette Lécureux, an archivist-paleographer and research engineer at the CNRS (*Centre National de Recherche Scientifique*), published *Le Latin, langue de l'Église*. She defended the pre-eminence of Latin as a liturgical language with four arguments: it is a language "fixed," "sacred," and "universal," and it is the "traditional language of the Church." At the suggestion of Father Caillon, who had just returned from Norway, where a group of the faithful had already been formed,

---

12 *Les Nouvelles de l'Association Jean Carmignac* 2 (April 1999): 3.

13 Dissertation defended at the Institute catholique de Paris in January 1969 and published the same year with the title *Recherches sur le Notre Père*.

14 [For a detailed account of how the Council Fathers had been solemnly assured that the Mass would remain at least partly in Latin, see Shaw, *The Latin Mass and the Intellectuals: Petitions to Save the Ancient Mass from 1966 to 2007*, ed. Joseph Shaw (Waterloo, ON: Arouca Press, 2023), esp. 114-18. – *Translator.*]

Bernadette Lécureux and her husband, the historian and journalist Georges Cerbelaud-Salagnac, took the initiative of bringing together the faithful attached to Latin and Gregorian chant.[15] A first circular sent out in October 1964 received an enthusiastic welcome. The constitutive meeting took place the following Saturday, December 19, in the crypt of the church of Saint-Charles in Monceau; it was called to order by the first vicar of the parish, Canon Bernard Calle. Some 500 people were present, among them several priests and religious. It was decided to create an association "to safeguard the Latin language and Gregorian chant in the Roman Catholic liturgy." It was Father Réginald Omez, OP, who proposed the name *Una Voce*, in reference to the preface of Trinity Sunday *(una voce dicentes...)*.[16]

The idea was to approach priests, bishops, and Roman authorities to defend the legitimacy and usefulness of Latin and Gregorian chant, as well as to support the choir schools and choirs at the parish level. Sections were to be created in the parishes, with delegates in the dioceses. A central office, a steering committee, and a board of directors were constituted. Georges Cerbelaud-Salagnac, who remained the linchpin of the association for several years, was named delegate general, leaving the presidency to a personality better known in the world of Church music and chant, Amédée de Vallombrosa, composer, the choirmaster at Saint-Eustache [a musically renowned parish in Paris – *Translator*] and a professor of religious music. The writer Stanislas Fumet and, surprisingly, the attorney Alec Mellor, best known for his books aiming at "reconciling" the Church and "regular" Freemasonry, were appointed vice-presidents. A modest two-page mimeographed newsletter began to appear in December 1964; it soon became a bi-monthly journal.

Una Voce was a movement created by lay people and directed by lay people, which the first issue of the bulletin noted, with a touch of irony, with reference to Vatican Council II:

> The adult laymen that we have become (according to a rather spectacular proclamation of the Council) have the right to expect the conciliar Constitution to be applied in its entirety: no one can deny us this. Even if we are only a minority in each parish. We could not accept the application of majority rule, which has no place here. Every soul must be able to find the spiritual comfort it seeks.

---

15 "Il y a cinq ans...," *Una Voce* 30 (January-February 1970): 1-3; and private interview of the author with Georges Cerbelaud-Salagnac on March 16, 1992.
16 Georges Cerbelaud-Salagnac, "Le Père Omez," *Una Voce* 51 (July-August 1973): 115.

This first issue also indicated the attitude of the association in its demands: "Our general attitude must, of course, be one of perfect courtesy, marked by the most authentic Christian charity, which in no way excludes firmness." Respect for the Pope and refusal to participate in acts of rebellion – such as the occupation of churches or the disruption of religious services – and, at the same time, constant pleas to the Holy See and complaints to the ecclesiastical authorities, would remain the hallmark of *Una Voce* to this day.

The association grew very rapidly (8,000 members by August 1966), numerous sections were created in France, and similar associations were created in the following months in England (the Latin Mass Society in April 1965), Germany, Scotland, Switzerland, Austria, Belgium, Australia and Norway. On April 12, 1966 the International Federation Una Voce was founded in Rome. Eric de Saventhem was its first president and remained so for nearly forty years; he was very active in defending the use of the traditional Mass before the Holy See.[17]

THE *CATHOLIC TRADITIONALIST MOVEMENT*

Contemporary with *Una Voce*, the Catholic Traditionalist Movement (CTM) was born in the United States as a reaction to liturgical innovations which, there too, had begun long before the end of the Council. The two movements, although born at the same time, are completely independent of each other, and they differ in their mode of action as also in their objectives.[18] From the very start the CTM, and especially its initiator Father De Pauw, showed themselves to be resolute, pragmatic, and very well organized, in typical American fashion.

In December 1964, lay people and priests from different parts of the United States met for several days to examine the state of the liturgy in their churches, to share their experiences, and to consider what could be done. After several meetings, it was decided to draft a *Catholic Manifesto*, to release it to the press, and to create an organization that would explicitly affirm the desire to preserve the traditional liturgy: the "Catholic Traditionalist Movement." Gommar De Pauw,

---

17 Leo Darroch, *Una Voce. The History of the Foederatio Internationalis Una Voce* (Leominster: Gracewing, 2017).

18 Louis Salleron introduced CTM to France, in a major article published in *La Nation française* on March 24, 1965. For an historical approach to the American religious context, see Michael W. Cuneo, *The Smoke of Satan. Conservative and Traditionalist Dissent in Contemporary American Catholicism* (Baltimore: Johns Hopkins University Press, 1999), 90-91. [See also Stuart Chessman, *Faith of Our Fathers: A Brief History of Catholic Traditionalism in the United States, from* Triumph *to* Traditionis Custodes (Brooklyn, NY: Angelico Press, 2022) – *Translator.*]

who was a professor of moral theology and canon law at Mount Saint Mary Seminary in Maryland, suggested that such a manifesto should not be rushed, that it should be circulated to the US bishops, and that one should await their reactions before making it public. The text was extensively revised by Father De Pauw and was sent to all the US bishops on December 31, 1964, along with a letter of introduction to the CTM. The *Manifesto* was also sent to Paul VI, to all the Cardinals of the Curia, and to the Cardinals of the Council Presidency.

It has a clear structure in ten items ("whereas") followed by twelve suggestions. The tone of the items is aggressive. It speaks of "the 'progressive' agitation in the liturgy," the liturgical "progressivism" that is "increasingly and alarmingly appearing to many as only the first phase of a broader scheme intent to 'protestantize' the entire Catholic Church." The *Manifesto* also asserts that "these liturgical changes were not called for by 'public opinion,' but were rather subtly extorted from our Bishops by a small but well-organized minority of self-appointed so-called liturgical experts." This statement has a polemical edge, but a sociological analysis of the process of liturgical reform in the United States has shown that it did not happen in response to an expectation of the faithful, but that it was initiated by "liturgical professionals," a "new knowledge class" which had been able to convince the ecclesiastical hierarchy in the name of its "expertise" and to impose an "agenda of reforms." [19]

The twelve suggestions in the *Manifesto* were in fact requests for "urgent consideration." They were often very concrete, for example, on the compulsory wearing of the religious habit, on the manner of receiving communion, or on the teaching of Latin in the seminary. The principal request was the fourth: "That the centuries-sanctioned liturgical Latin form of the Mass not be banned," that it be possible for all the faithful to participate in it and for all priests to celebrate it "on Sundays as well as weekdays."

Many of the bishops who had received the *Manifesto* answered Father De Pauw with comments. In a press conference a few months later, he stated that he had received the support of 30 US bishops and the explicit approval of more than 50,000 of the faithful. [20] The *Manifesto* was eventually released on March 15, 1965. De Pauw was opposed by his bishop, Cardinal Shehan, and had to be incardinated into the Diocese of Tivoli. But he continued to work for maintaining the traditional Mass. With the support of Cardinal Spellman, Archbishop of New York, who died

---

19 William D. Dinges, "Ritual Conflict as Social Conflict: Liturgical Reform in the Roman Catholic Church," *Sociological Analysis* 48.2 (Summer 1987): 138-57.
20 Report of the press conference in *Time* (April 9, 1965).

in December 1967, Father De Pauw was able to open Ave Maria Chapel on Long Island the following year. He celebrated the traditional Mass there until his death in 2005, established a worldwide radio broadcast of the traditional Mass every Sunday, and published magazines, books, and videotapes. The CTM was a pioneer in defending and perpetuating the traditional Mass in the United States, even before the promulgation of the Novus Ordo, while remaining aloof from the Vatican II protest movements and the canonically marginal organizations that would develop a few years later: the Orthodox Roman Catholic Movement (ORCM) and the Tridentine Latin Rite Church (TLRC).[21]

FOR LATIN AND GREGORIAN CHANT

Among the unauthorized liturgical innovations, there were also new formulas introduced arbitrarily in some Masses to replace the traditional formulas. Some theologians also developed new ideas about the Mass and the Eucharist in books and articles.

Paul VI then sought to intervene in a solemn way with an encyclical on the Eucharist, published on September 3, 1965.[22] The Pope expressed his "concern and anxiety" about certain opinions "that are disturbing the minds of the faithful and causing them no small measure of confusion about matters of faith." He vigorously condemned the theory that the "community" Mass is better than the improperly called private Mass, "[f]or each and every Mass is not something private, even if a priest celebrates it privately; instead, it is an act of Christ and of the Church." The Pope also challenged the replacement of the doctrine of "transubstantiation" with the notions of "transsignification" or "transfinalization." He also protested against the opinion that "Christ Our Lord is no longer present in the consecrated Hosts that remain after the celebration of the sacrifice of the Mass has been completed." On all these points, the Pope reaffirmed the traditional doctrine, relying on the definitions of previous councils and quoting extensively from the Fathers of the Church. He insisted on the importance of doctrinal formulas and theological concepts related to the mystery of the Eucharist:

> Who would ever tolerate that the dogmatic formulas used by the ecumenical councils for the mysteries of the Holy Trinity and the Incarnation be judged as no longer appropriate for men of our times, and let others be rashly substituted for them?

21 Mary Jo Weaver and R. Scott Appleby, eds., *Being Right. Conservative Catholics in America* (Bloomington: Indiana University Press, 1995), 247-49.
22 Encyclical *Mysterium Fidei*, AAS 57 (1965): 753-74; DOL #176.

Paul VI also intervened to try to stop another trend. Without waiting for the reform of their constitutions initiated by their order or religious congregation, many convents and monasteries had abandoned their traditional office, and had begun to sing it entirely or partially in the vernacular.

In February 1966, the Italian writer Cristina Campo, who had converted a little over a year earlier, and who was distressed to see Latin and Gregorian chant disappearing from the churches of Rome, wrote a letter-manifesto to the Pope asking that the Latin and Gregorian liturgy at least be preserved in convents and monasteries.[23] The letter, dated February 5, 1966, was signed by 37 artists and writers from different countries, including Jorge Luis Borges, Robert Bresson, Giorgio De Chirico, Augusto Del Noce, Julien Green, François Mauriac, Evelyn Waugh. This appeal came after others from various horizons. A few days later, on February 26, a group of Portuguese intellectuals – university professors, writers, musicians, journalists – addressed a four-page memorandum to Father Bugnini and the Pope in favor of Latin and Gregorian chant.[24] The following August, Paul VI published an apostolic letter solemnly exhorting the superiors of religious orders to keep Latin and Gregorian chant in the choral office.[25] Two months later, he issued a warning to the body responsible for preparing the liturgical reform. For the seventh plenary session of the Consilium, on October 13, 1966, he received all the participants (members and consultors) and gave a lengthy address.[26] While expressing his "great satisfaction" for the work already accomplished, he made recommendations for the general reform in progress. He asked those working on it to have "certain qualities of spirit," including "a reverence for the sacred" and "respect for tradition, which has passed on a priceless heritage." These insistent recommendations ("[t]he search must be for what is best rather than for what is new ") were accompanied by a request that could appear as a reproach. Indeed, Paul VI wanted the *Consilium* to exercise its "guidance" and supervision with greater "vigilance" and "prudence":

> You must check misguided attempts that may here and there appear and constrain those who follow their own preferences at the risk of disturbing the right order of public prayer and of occasioning doctrinal errors.

---

23 Cristina De Stefano, *Belinda et le monstre. Vie secrète de Cristina Campo* (Paris: Éditions du Rocher, 2006), 145.

24 *Una Voce* 9 (May-June-July 1966): 3.

25 Paul VI, Epistle "*Sacrificium laudis* to Superiors General of the Clerical Religious Institutes Bound to Choir, on the Celebration of the Divine Office," August 15, 1966, *DOL* #421.

26 Paul VI, "Address to the Members and *Periti* of the Consilium," October 13, 1966, *DOL* #84.

Soon the Consilium was taken to task in a book that was quickly translated into several languages: *La Tunica stracciata. Lettera di un cattolico sulla "Riforma liturgica."*[27] The author, Tito Casini, was a well-known Italian writer and one of the founders of *Una Voce* in Italy. His book, published in the spring of 1967, was presented as an open letter to an unnamed cardinal, whom everyone identified as Cardinal Lercaro, president of the Consilium; it called him a "Luther redivivus." The book caused a fracas that was magnified by its being prefaced by another Cardinal, Cardinal Bacci, a former secretary of Briefs to Princes and an eminent Latinist. This was no courtesy preface; it was a four-page-long text. Cardinal Bacci protested against "rabid and outrageous innovators" and felt that the unlimited use of the vernacular at Mass betrayed the conciliar constitution on the liturgy, which had stated, "[p]articular law remaining in force, the use of the Latin language is to be preserved in the Latin rites." Specifically, he asked

> in cathedral churches, sanctuaries and tourist centers, and everywhere that enough priests are to be found, for a certain number of Latin Masses to be celebrated, at fixed times, to meet the just desires of all, whatever their nationality, who prefer Latin to the vernacular, and Gregorian chant to the mean and trivial type of popular ditty.

The Italian press took hold of the polemic and published a great many articles quoting Casini's criticisms and the support Cardinal Bacci had lent him.

The pope made a public defense of the Consilium and Cardinal Lercaro in which he denounced an "unjust and irreverent attack" and protested against Casini's accusations:

> Obviously, we do not agree with this publication, which surely in no one inspires piety nor helps the cause it pretends to advance, namely, that of preserving the Latin language in the liturgy.[28]

Yet in the same address Paul VI voiced his indignation at forms "deliberately patterned on the personal preference of certain individuals and often . . . wholly at odds with the precepts now in force in the Church" and a "widening movement toward a liturgy . . . rashly described as 'desacralized.'" He hoped that bishops would "keep a close watch

---

27 Published in Florence in April 1967. English translation: *The Torn Tunic. Letter of a Catholic on the "Liturgical Reform"* (Rome: Fidelity Books, 1967; reprinted Angelico Press, 2020). It was translated into German the same year by Élisabeth Gerstner, who was very active in German-speaking traditionalism, and into French in 1968 by Father Dulac, under the title *La Tunique déchirée. Lettre d'un catholique sur la réforme liturgique.*

28 Paul VI, Address to the members and *periti* of the Consilium, April 19, 1967; English translation, *DOL* #86.

on such episodes and that they will safeguard the balance proper to Catholic worship" and that priests and the faithful would not "allow themselves to burn with the inane desire for experiments inspired by personal preference."

On May 4, 1967 the second instruction on the reform was published.[29] Once again, it introduced significant modifications to the celebration of Mass. On the one hand, it continued to simplify the rite of the Mass, by reducing the number of the priest's genuflections and the number of kisses given to the altar, and by retaining only one sign of the cross over the offerings. On the other hand, the instruction completed the introduction of the vernacular into the Mass by authorizing the Canon to be said aloud and in the vernacular.

Fr Bugnini presented these changes and commented on them in long article published in *l'Osservatore Romano* on the very day of the instruction's publication.[30] He justified the simplifications by minimizing their importance; he did not consider that they might contribute any further desacralization of the Mass: "These are not major changes." Fr Bugnini was also somewhat nonchalant when speaking of the genuflections and signs of the cross:

> The celebration in the language of the people is often done facing the assembly; this makes certain gestures seem anachronistic or superfluous ... which, especially in certain circles, causes incomprehension and weariness.

He also announced that a new "ordering of the Mass" would be presented at the next Synod.

These new changes caused further concern among those who were attached to the traditional form of the liturgy. The International Federation *Una Voce*, headed by Eric de Saventhem, addressed a long supplication to Paul VI on May 25 to express his "consternation and stupefaction." The Federation *Una Voce* was afraid that the new reforms might contribute to fostering the "weakening of the faith" and drive some of the faithful away from church. Like Cardinal Bacci a month earlier, it asked

> that the ancient Roman liturgy, that is, the religious rite in Latin with its own chant, Gregorian chant, should continue to be celebrated side by side with that in the vernacular in all the Catholic churches of the world.[31]

---

29 Instruction *Tres abhinc annos*, dated May 4, 1967; *DOL* #39.
30 *L'Osservatore Romano*, May 7, 1967.
31 Saventhem to Paul VI, May 25, 1967, published in *Una Voce* 14 (May-June-July 1967): 2-4.

From this period also dates what Jean Madiran now called the "book of the resistance":[32] *Le Chant grégorien,* by André and Henri Charlier. Far from being a polemical book, it was a didactic work in two parts: "Why Gregorian Chant" by André Charlier, and "Origin and Practice of Gregorian Chant" by Henri Charlier. But it was also a book of "meditated experience, of faith" as Jean Madiran put it. André Charlier issued a warning:

> This is a serious matter. We are not defending Gregorian chant out of a taste for archaism or a kind of ridiculous aestheticism, but because Gregorian chant is the highest expression in the musical art of Catholic spirituality.

Gregorian chant "is not like the voices of nature: it says what the human voice no longer dares to express: nostalgia for our lost homeland, a taste for a never-reached perfection, the desire to see God.... [I]t opens up the soul to eternal realities."[33]

THE *MISSA NORMATIVA*: A MASS REJECTED

In October 1967, the first synod to be called since the council took place in Rome. It brought together some 180 cardinals and bishops and treated of a number of subjects: the revision of Canon Law; doctrinal questions; liturgical reform. At the pope's request, the "new ordering of the Mass" was introduced to the synod fathers by Cardinal Lercaro and then, on October 24, Father Bugnini celebrated an "experimental" or "normative" Mass in their presence. Besides the changes that had already been introduced with the 1964 and 1967 instructions (Mass facing the people and in Italian, including for the Canon; reduced number of genuflections and signs of the Cross, etc.), the *Missa normativa* that Father Bugnini celebrated that day added new elements: a more developed Liturgy of the Word (three readings in total); a completely transformed Offertory text; a new Eucharistic Prayer instead of the ancient Roman Canon; and a multiplication of hymns.

During the synod's four general congregations devoted to the liturgy (October 21-25), there were many interventions on the part of the cardinal and bishops. There was a broad spectrum of opinion among them. According to the official report that Father Caprile made, "out of sixty-three orators, thirty-six explicitly expressed, in the warmest, most enthusiastic, and unreserved terms" their agreement with the reform

---

32 Jean Madiran, "Le livre de la résistance," *Itinéraires* 118 (December 1967): 1-5.
33 André and Henri Charlier, *Le Chant grégorien* (Poitiers: Dominique Martin Morin, 1967), 152-53.

underway and its results.[34] Some bishops even wanted further changes, such as the possibility of receiving Communion in the hand, that of using ordinary bread for Communion, the preparation of a specific Mass for young people, etc. Yet the general tone was more prudent, with even some sharp criticism. The English-speaking bishops met at the English College to define a common position on the "normative" Mass. On October 25, at the Synod, Cardinal Heenan, Archbishop of Westminster and president of the Conference of Catholic Bishops of England and Wales, took the floor in the name of English-speaking bishops and accused the *Consilium* of technicism and intellectualism, and blamed it for lacking pastoral sense. More significant yet, in the sense that they came from the highest authority in the Church after the pope, were the words of Cardinal Cicognani, Secretary of State, who on the very same day asked for an end to liturgical changes "lest the faithful be troubled."

Twice during the debates on the liturgy the participants were invited to express their opinion through a vote. Leaving aside a detailed analysis of these twelve votes, it is noteworthy that for half of them, the required two-thirds majority was not reached.[35] The vote on the general structure of the *Missa normativa* amounted to a refusal: 71 *placet*; 43 *non placet*; 62 *placet juxta modum*; 4 abstentions.

Father Dulac, in *Le Courrier de Rome* – which was increasingly read by priests and faithful attached to tradition – was kept well-informed by his Roman friends and marshalled his theological verve against this "normative Mass" which

> is allegedly destined to replace the one that Gregory the Great, Thomas Aquinas, Philip Neri, Bossuet, the Curé of Ars celebrated without ever suspecting that they were celebrating a passive, unconscious, individualistic, and complicated Mass. The *normativa* suppresses *Kyrie*, *Gloria*, and Offertory; it pulverizes the *Confiteor*; it glosses over the intercession of the saints, over the commemoration of the souls in purgatory, over anything that expresses the personal offering of the human priest; it proposes two spare Canons; it corrects the words of the consecration; and, of course, it replaces Latin with the national idiom.[36]

The Synod's public disavowal of the "normative" or "experimental" Mass resulted in a restructuring of the bodies in charge of the liturgy. Cardinal Lercaro had to resign as president of the *Consilium* and as

---

34 Giovanni Caprile, "Il Sinodo dei vescovi," *Civiltà cattolica* (December 16, 1967): 595-603.
35 According to the anonymous report in *Notitiae* 3 (1967): 353-70.
36 Raymond Dulac, "Une 'première' à la chapelle Sixtine," *Le Courrier de Rome* 19 (November 1, 1967).

archbishop of Bologna, Cardinal Larraona had to resign from the Congregation of Rites, and Cardinal Gut, a Benedictine who was already a member of the *Consilium*, became its president at the same time as he was named prefect of the Congregation of Rites. This double appointment preceded a merger of the two bodies that would take place the following year. But Father Bugnini remained the irremovable secretary of the *Consilium*, and continued to work on the elaboration of what was soon to be called the "new Mass."

On January 4, 1968 the pope asked Fr Bugnini to organize three new "experimental" celebrations to take place in his presence in the Matilda chapel, on the second floor of the Apostolic Palace.[37] These three "normative" Masses were all celebrated in the following few days in the presence of the pope and of about thirty people (the cardinal Secretary of State, various members of the Curia, several members of the *Consilium*, two religious women, and four lay people). These three "experimental" Masses presented a structure identical to that of the "normative" Mass celebrated a few months earlier before the synod, but with some innovations, particularly the use of a different Eucharistic Prayer in each instance and the introduction of a "sign of peace" that all those present exchanged after the instruction "give each other the sign of peace."

After each of the Masses the pope welcomed some of the participants along with Fr Bugnini in his private library to share his impressions and comments on the celebration. On the following January 22, Paul VI provided his own written observations. The pope made seven suggestions, asking in particular that the Offertory should be further developed, that the expression *Mysterium fidei* should be maintained at the end of the formula of consecration "as a concluding acclamation of the celebrant, to be repeated by the faithful," and that the triple *Agnus Dei* invocation should be retained. Paul VI also echoed some "pressing requests" that the last Gospel at the end of Mass (the prologue of the Gospel according to St. John) should be restored. Lastly he asked that "the words of consecration . . . not be recited simply as a narrative but with the special, conscious emphasis given them by a celebrant who knows he is speaking and acting 'in the person of Christ.'" His suggestions and requests were not all followed.

On May 23, 1968, a decree authorized the use of the three new Eucharistic prayers and eight new prefaces.[38] Once again, the tradi-

---

37 Ibid., 359-64.
38 Decree *Prece eucharistica* of May 23, 1968, *DOL* #241.

tional rite of the Mass was being corrected or modified in important points even before the new rite was ever completed and promulgated.

On June 2, 1968 the revised draft of the new *Ordo Missae* was sent, as Paul VI had wanted, to fourteen Curia cardinals (Congregation prefects and secretariat presidents). Fr Bugnini was to report that "[o]f the fourteen cardinals involved, two did not reply, seven sent observations, and five said simply that they had no remarks to make or were 'very pleased' with the schema."[39]

Paul VI had the revised draft and the cardinals' responses examined by two of his close collaborators: Mgr. Carlo Colombo, his private theologian; and Bishop Manziana of Crema. Then he read and reread the draft himself, inserting marginal notes and underscoring the text in red and blue pencil, though without seeking to impose his views.[40]

THE "NEW MASS" AND COMMUNION IN THE HAND

On November 6, 1968 Paul VI, after rereading its text one more time, gave his written "approbation" to the *Novus Ordo Missae* (NOM). The apostolic constitution *Missale Romanum* of April 3, 1969 was presented to the press on May 2, the very day on which was published in a single volume what was soon called the "new Mass," even though that has never been its official name.[41] After an interval of four centuries a new missal, soon commonly termed the "Paul VI Missal," had succeeded the Roman Missal codified by Saint Pius V in 1570. It was to take effect on November 30, 1969 in its original Latin version, while each country prepared translations that would take effect later.

This "new Mass" was actually not an absolute innovation; rather, it was the end result of a continuous reform whose steps have been outlined above. It synthesized changes that had already been taking place since 1964 and introduced new ones, notably the replacement of the traditional Offertory by a "preparation of the gifts." The very words of Consecration received a new formulation.

A lengthy *Institutio generalis Missalis romani* ("General Introduction of the Roman Missal," GIRM) accompanied the new *Ordo Missae*. In its eight chapters this long document had not been submitted to the Congregation for the Doctrine of the Faith before publication. It contained innovations in some of its definitions and formulations.[42] Paragraph

---

39 Bugnini, *Reform*, 372.
40 Ibid., 377. Bugnini further specifies whether, and how, the pope's observations and proposals were adopted.
41 *Ordo Missae* (Vatican City: Typis Polyglottis Vaticanis, 1969), 174 pages.
42 The best edition of this controverted text and of its successively emended versions is that by Maurizio Barba, *Institutio generalis Missalis romani. Textus, Synopsis. Variationes*

7 defined the Mass as "the sacred assembly or congregation of the people of God gathering together, with a priest presiding, in order to celebrate the memorial of the Lord." This definition – which was not the traditional definition of the Mass as the unbloody renewal of the sacrifice of the Cross – and the new *Ordo Missae* itself were immediately to cause ever-increasing controversies, as we shall see.

A few weeks after the "new Mass" was promulgated, a major change occurred in the rite of Communion. Back in 1965, Cardinal Lercaro, president of the *Consilium* at the time, still considered the fact of "depositing the Host in the open hands of the faithful" a "deplorable and fanciful initiative."[43] Yet in several countries the practice kept spreading, sometimes with a transformation of the Mass that looked more like a concelebration with laymen. Such, for example, was the Mass celebrated on May 25, 1969 for Pentecost in Notre-Dame-des-Champs parish in Paris. A member of *Una Voce*, who was present at this Mass (a Dutch choir provided the music), provided a precise and also rather ironic report:

> The choir, with its beatnik-type boys and mini-skirted girls, was crammed into the Saint Joseph chapel, which was too small to house the singers and their jazz drum-set. This choir, naturally, sang in Dutch. . . . But the main point of interest was elsewhere, at the altar, facing the people as per regulations. That's where the five celebrants were. On the Epistle side, a young man in mufti, well-dressed enough, who might have been mistaken for an altar server. To his right, the parish vicar, an activist priest, a member of the "Exchange and Dialog" group (Notre-Dame-des-Champs parish has the distinct privilege of numbering four of its priests among this group). Then, the principal celebrant, a Dutch priest. And lastly, to his right, two girls of about eighteen, in a truly scandalous get-up: extremely clinging dresses with low-cut necklines, entirely uncovered arms, and oh-so-miniskirts.
>
> The two girls stayed at the altar throughout the entire service, shimmying and sashaying to the rhythm of the music. At the Consecration, they stretched their hand over the altar. At Communion, the Dutch celebrant broke the big Host into five and presented the paten to them first: ladies first, evidently. . . . They each took a piece of the Host in their fingers and that is how they stayed, hands in the air, facing the people, just like the concelebrating priests. Once the three other characters got their share of the Host, all self-communicated. Then it was the chalice's turn: the celebrant offered it to one of the girls, she grabbed it with both hands, drank from it, handed it on to her neighbor who did the same.

(Vatican: Libreria Editrice Vaticana, 2006). [The English version of the GIRM in *DOL* #208 is based on the 1975 edition, but footnotes give the original 1969 text where it differs – *Translator*.]
43 Lercaro, *l'Avennire d'Italia*, March 2, 1965.

> In a word, these two girls were acting as concelebrating priests. Naturally, Communion was given in the hand....The same applied to the choir members, who came to Communion laughing, jostling each other, as if in line to get a lottery ticket.[44]

In other parishes of France and elsewhere, Communion in the hand was probably distributed more reverently than this, but the Vatican had not yet authorized the practice. Four days after this extreme example of the abuse at Notre-Dame-des-Champs, the Congregation for Divine Worship published a long instruction on Communion in the hand.[45] It had been prepared over a long time and had been preceded by a consultation of the entire episcopacy.

This May 29, 1969 instruction looks like a composite document, as Jean Madiran soon pointed out.[46] It starts out with a long defense of the traditional manner of receiving Communion on the tongue, based on a variety of arguments (theological, spiritual, and practical), and states that it must remain the norm, since "[n]ot only is it based on a practice handed down over many centuries, but above all it signifies the faithful's reverence for the Eucharist." In support of maintaining this tradition the same document published the results of a survey conducted among all Latin-rite bishops. Without getting into the detail of the answers given to the three questions, we furnish here only those given to the first question: "Do you think that a positive response should be given to the request to allow the rite of receiving communion in the hand?":

In favor:	567
Opposed:	1,253
In favor with reservations:	315
Invalid votes:	20.

On the basis of the survey's results, the Instruction prescribed the following:

> [Pope Paul VI's] judgment is not to change the long-accepted manner of administering communion to the faithful. The Apostolic See earnestly urges bishops, priests, and faithful, therefore, to obey conscientiously the prevailing law, now reconfirmed....

Yet in the second part, which is shorter and looks tacked on, the same text granted episcopal conferences the possibility of authorizing Communion in the hand:

---

44 Testimony signed "M. D." published in *Una Voce* 28 (September-October 1969): 32.
45 Instruction *Memoriale Domini* published May 29, 1969; *DOL* 260.
46 Jean Madiran, "Le processus de la communion dans la main," *Itinéraires* 163 (May 1972): 213-21.

> Wherever the contrary practice, that is, of communion in the
> hand, has already come into use, the Apostolic See . . . entrusts
> to the same conferences of bishops the duty and task of evalu-
> ating any possible special circumstances. This, however, is with
> the proviso both that they prevent any possible lack of reverence
> or false ideas about the Eucharist from being engendered in
> the attitudes of the people and that they carefully eliminate
> anything else unacceptable.

Cardinal Larraona, former prefect of the Congregation for Rites, confided to Dom Jean Roy, Abbot of Fontgombault, that he had begged the
Pope on his knees not to change the traditional mode of Communion.
But, in this matter as in others, Paul VI was torn between different
sentiments. Cardinal Oddi reported that, from a concern not to restrict
the freedom of episcopal Conferences and to respect the diversity of
opinions, Paul VI refused to impose a single law in the matter, although
he was personally opposed to Communion in the hand.[47]

In the event, what had been a mere concession in 1969 has become
the norm in a great many countries and parishes. Communion rails
would soon be moved out or left unused, even though no diocese
would ever officially proscribe Communion on the tongue.

THE "OTTAVIANI INTERVENTION"

As soon as the "new Mass" was promulgated, doctrinal critiques
proliferated, some with the support of eminent authorities. They aimed
both at the *Ordo Missae* and at the *Institutio Generalis* prefacing it.

In France, the first full critique of the new Mass was that published
by Father Dulac, who, as we have seen, had reacted against the liturgical reforms in the very first issues of *Le Courrier de Rome*, in 1967.
On June 27, 1969, in a long article that was to set the tone for a good
many other commentators after him, he attacked an "ecumenical Mass"
that could well suit Protestants, a "polyvalent Mass," since some of its
"rites [were] left to the celebrant's choice" and it contained "equivocal"
words; it "annihilated the Offertory"; it was a "Mass that hides its
face." The article ended with a clear and definite rejection: "We refuse
to follow the *Novus Ordo Missae*."[48] At about the same time in Italy,
Msgr Celada, who was a professor of music and Gregorian chant at the
Pontifical Lateran University, deplored the "progressive destruction of
the liturgy": "In less than five years, the thousand-year-old structures
of this divine worship, which was called the *opus Dei* for centuries,

---

47 Cardinal Oddi, Letter to the author, 18 August 1992.
48 Raymond Dulac, "Vers une messe œcuménique," *Le Courrier de Rome* 49 (June
25, 1969).

have been dismantled."[49] He also mentioned the judgment of another Lateran professor, Msgr Spadafora, who had written to him: "In the new *Ordo Missae*, dogma itself is compromised." Such also would be the judgment of two eminent cardinals, as we shall see.

Even a review as attached to *romanità* as *La Pensée catholique* published as collective articles–by "a group of theologians" and "a group of canonists"–two lengthy critiques of the new *Ordo Missae*.[50] They particularly deplored that the new Mass should "entirely pass over in silence the doctrine of the Council of Trent regarding the Mass: *incruens sacrificium*."

One bishop, Bishop de Castro Meyer of Campos, Brazil, turned to the Pope before the new *Ordo* had even come into effect to express his "anxiousness" to him. He had wept when he first saw the text of the new Mass and the GIRM.[51] On September 12, 1969, he published a pastoral letter, *On the Holy Sacrifice of the Mass*, to recall the teaching of the Council of Trent on the Mass and on the ministerial priesthood. At the same time, though without making it public, he sent a supplication to Paul VI. In it he divulged his "anxiousness of conscience": the new Mass, "through its omissions and changes" as well as "a great number of its general norms" not only "failed to inspire fervor" but also weakened the faith in "the Real Presence of Jesus in the Most Holy Sacrament, the reality of propitiatory sacrifice, the hierarchical priesthood." In view of these considerations, he asked the pope to authorize his diocese to "continue using the 'Ordo Missae' of St. Pius V."

The most striking opposition came from a *Short Critical Examination of the Novus Ordo Missae*, dated June 5, 1969, but not published until several months later. This document was unsigned. It was written by "a select group of theologians, liturgists, and pastors of souls." It was later revealed that Dominican theologian Michel Guérard des Lauriers, then teaching at the Pontifical Lateran University, and a laywoman, Cristina Campo, mentioned above, played a decisive role in drafting it. The original text was written in Italian by Cristina Campo, and the French translation was the work of Father Guérard des Lauriers.

The *Short Critical Examination* began by questioning the definition of the Mass given in the GIRM 7, quoted above, and lamented that this vocabulary "implies neither the Real Presence, nor the reality of the Sacrifice, nor the sacramental character of the consecrating priest,

49 *Lo Specchio* (June 29, 1969), article translated in *La Contre-Réforme catholique au XXe siècle* 23 (August 1969).
50 *La Pensée catholique* 122 (September–October 1969): 5-47.
51 David Allen White, *The Mouth of the Lion. Bishop Antonio de Castro Mayer and the Last Catholic Diocese* (Kansas City: Angelus Press, 1993), 93.

nor the intrinsic value of the Eucharistic Sacrifice independently of
the presence of the assembly." It also questioned the formulas of the
consecration and the position of the priest in the new rite, a role that
it considered to have been "minimized, altered, distorted." This impla-
cable critique ended with a total rejection of the "new Mass" which
"can only be a cause of division through the innumerable licenses it
implicitly authorizes, by the insinuations it encourages, and by its
manifest attacks on the purity of the faith."

Two cardinals, Bacci and Ottaviani, neither of whom held any official
function at the Curia any more, agreed to present this brief to the pope
[hence the more usual English title, *The Ottaviani Intervention* – *Translator*]. Others too had agreed, notably Cardinal Larraona,[52] prefect of
the Congregation of Rites until January 1969, but they had demurred.
Bacci and Ottaviani presented the text in a letter that accompanied it.
In this letter, dated September 3, 1969, the two cardinals judged that
"if one considers the innovations implied or taken for granted which
may of course be evaluated in different ways, the new *Ordo* represents,
both as a whole and in its details, a striking departure from the Catholic
theology of the Mass." As a result, they called for the "abrogation" of
the new rite of Mass. Although other cardinals and bishops had been
approached to sign the petition, none decided to take that step. Cardinal Siri, Archbishop of Genoa, felt that the Brief was "more Bacci's
initiative than Ottaviani's" and that Ottaviani had given his signature
after the text had already been printed.[53] He added that he himself
"would not have given his signature if he had been asked."

This *Ottaviani Intervention*, along with the letter of the two cardinals, began making the rounds in October 1969. At the initiative of *Una
Voce*, representatives of several Catholic associations from Europe and
America were in Rome October 10-15 "to examine the doctrinal and
pastoral implications of the *Novus Ordo Missae*." Priests from various
countries also participated in the meeting, including Father Coache
and Father Michel André, a Holy Ghost missionary from Argentina.
Louis Salleron was also present. Father Guérard des Lauriers distributed the *Ottaviani Intervention* among the participants, which naturally
influenced the long communiqué issued at the end of the meeting.
The "new ordering of the Mass presents itself as an amalgam of the
Lutheran Lord's Supper and the Catholic Mass," said the communiqué,
which also judged "the whole 'post-conciliar' liturgical reform to be

52 Archbishop Marcel Lefebvre to Dom Jean Roy, Letter dated August 5, 1969, Archives
of the Abbey of Our Lady of Fontgombault.
53 E. Cavaterra, *Il Prefetto del Sant'Offizio. Le opere e i giorni del cardinale Ottaviani*
(Milan: Mursia, 1990), 188.

intolerable" and considered that as a whole, the reforms undertaken since the Council threatened "the institution of the Church visible and hierarchical" and "at the same time, Catholic dogma, ethics and spirituality." Consequently, these Catholic associations demanded that the *Novus Ordo* be "abrogated" or "at least radically reformed, so that all ambiguities of a dogmatic nature be removed," that the doctrine of the sacrifice of the Mass, of the Real Presence, and of the priesthood be solemnly reaffirmed, and "that the priests and faithful who use the Ordo of St. Pius V not be disturbed in the age-old possession of that use."[54]

After this meeting in Rome, the *Ottaviani Intervention* and the letter of Cardinals Bacci and Ottaviani spread throughout the world. Father de Nantes was the first in France to publish the two Cardinals' letter. This was on October 15, 1969, in an off-print sheet, printed entirely in red ink, of issue 25 of *La Contre-Réforme catholique au XXe siècle*. It was then Jean Madiran's turn; he published it in December in *Itinéraires*[55] and was the first to publish the French translation of the *Intervention* under the title *Bref examen critique de la nouvelle messe*.[56] Father André, on his return to Argentina, translated the document into Spanish, had 10,000 copies printed, and distributed it himself by taking packages of brochures to most of the capitals of Latin America where he had connections.[57] When Bishop de Castro Mayer learned of the document, he translated it into Portuguese and sent it to all the priests of his diocese and to all the bishops of Brazil.

The Italian press got wind of the *Ottaviani Intervention* and of the two Cardinals' letter at the end of October 1969. It made the headlines. The major Italian daily *Il Messagero* announced on its front page on October 30: "For Cardinals Ottaviani and Bacci, the new Mass is 'heretical' and 'profane.'"

The media storm alarmed Paul VI. He submitted the *Ottaviani Intervention* to the Congregation for the Doctrine of the Faith. Cardinal Šeper, prefect of the Congregation, replied on November 12 that the document "contains many superficial, exaggerated, inaccurate, biased, and false statements."[58] Nevertheless, the Pope caused certain passages of the Missal and of the *General Instruction* to be corrected, as we shall see.

---

54 Communiqué published in *La Pensée catholique* 122: 48-49.
55 The letter of Cardinals Bacci and Ottaviani would not be published in the official French *DC* until March 1, 1970, 215-16.
56 *Itinéraires* 141 (March 1970): 219-51.
57 Claude Mouton-Raimbault, *Un prêtre vrai. Le père André* (Chiré-en-Montreuil: Éditions de Chiré, 2001), 352-53.
58 Quoted in A. Bugnini, *The Reform of the Liturgy, 1948-1975*, trans. Matthew J. O'Connell (Collegeville, MN: The Liturgical Press, 1990), 287.

"DEVOTION TO THE POPE"

There was a danger that the growing opposition to the "new Mass" might challenge the Pope himself. At the suggestion of Father de Chivré, theological advisor to *Itinéraires*, a meeting of several publication directors and Catholic personalities was discreetly organized in Versailles around Dom Jean Roy, Abbot of Fontgombault. In addition to Father de Chivré, those who came included Jean Madiran for *Itinéraires*, Pierre Lemaire for *Défense du foyer*, Louis Salleron for *Carrefour*, Marcel Clément for *L'Homme nouveau*, Admiral Auphan, and other press men. Dom Roy had been in contact with each of them for several years, even though he had no formal authority over them. The meeting took place on November 26, 1969, in a private apartment in Versailles (Jean Barbier's). This was four days before the "new Mass" officially came into effect in France.

After a dinner where all could exchange and compare opinions, Dom Jean Roy took the floor to give everyone advice and recommendations. In his well-prepared speech he started out by recommending that the men who were fighting and working for the Church should keep a "supernatural" view of the situation and nourish it through the practice of virtues, prayer, and the sacraments.[59] He asked them to maintain "love and cultivation of the truth," "doctrinal correctness," and "historical correctness." He also suggested that "before publication, every doctrinal writing of any importance should be submitted to a competent and reliable ecclesiastical censor, a man of complete confidence." The abbot of Fontgombault also invited them to collaborate with each other:

> It is good to work, to some extent at least, as a fraternal team. *Vae soli*, says Scripture. Giving each other advice with good will yet remaining demanding, guarding against going overboard or doing too little, is perhaps one of the best services you can render each other.

Dom Roy's long address also dealt with the attitude that Christian journalists should have towards the Pope. The recommendations he made were based on a sound theology of the Church and inspired by a supernatural view of the present situation:

> Of course, even when it comes to the Pope, we have no right to call evil good, or error truth. If the pope were to tell us to do something intrinsically evil, there would be no need to obey him, because authority exists only for the good. It is sometimes legitimate, sometimes obligatory to inform authority, even sovereign authority, of one's doubts, of one's difficulties, and to approach it to counterbalance dishonorable pressures by just means.

---

59 Unabridged text in Dom J.-L. Robien, *Dom Jean Roy*, MS, Archives of the Abbaye of Fontgombault.

That said, one must acknowledge that very often we do not have sufficient information to form an adequate judgment—not of the pope's intentions and heart, of which God alone is the judge, but even of his external conduct, because he sees things from a higher vantage point than we do.

And then, if we have the practical certainty that he is wrong, we must nevertheless exercise faith in the Pope's office and obedience to his orders, filial veneration for his person.... There may be days when it takes a great deal of humility and charity, a great deal of courage and greatness of spirit, to be what one should be in relation to the Holy Father. Let us then remember the example of the saints, and let us remember that among the gifts of the Holy Spirit is the gift of piety, by the use of which God will make us heroic, if necessary, in the exercise of the virtues of veneration.

The various participants in this meeting reacted in differing ways to this long speech/exhortation, which was then mimeographed in booklet form with a limited number of copies. Pierre Lemaire and Marcel Clément were strengthened in their unwavering attachment to the Pope. In the quarrel over the Mass, which was to grow in intensity, they took a moderate attitude, defending the orthodoxy of the "new Mass." Father de Chivré, at first in agreement with the views of Dom Jean Roy, was soon convinced by the contrary arguments of Jean Madiran. The latter judged that the exhortation of Dom Jean Roy had been too irenic and "monastic," and that supernatural considerations were not sufficient in view of the gravity of the situation. He felt that he had to continue the "great struggle" for the defense of the faith that he had been engaged in since 1967, by calling out the bishops and by addressing the Pope directly. He stopped attending the subsequent meetings, which were always held at Jean Barbier's house and soon came to an end.

THE NOVEMBER 1969 ADDRESSES

Pope Paul VI did not remain insensitive to the growing criticisms of the New Mass and of the General Instruction. He intervened in several ways to rectify and correct texts that he had at first approved and promulgated.

First there were the addresses given at the general audiences of 19 and 26 November 1969, two Wednesdays in a row. They were entirely devoted to the "new Mass." On November 19, Paul VI insisted on the definitive character of the reform introduced ("it is not a transitory or optional experiment"), but he also wanted to reassure those who were worried and scandalized: "keep this clearly in mind: Nothing has been changed of the substance of our traditional Mass.... The Mass of the

new rite is and remains the same Mass we have always had": a sacrifice
offered by the priest; "[o]nly the manner of offering is different, namely,
an unbloody and sacramental manner; and it is offered in perennial
memory of Himself, until His final return."[60] The Pope also affirmed,
"So do not let us talk about 'the new Mass.' Let us rather speak of the
'new epoch' in the Church's life." On the following Wednesday, November
26, he explained the two reasons for the change that was about to take
place.[61] The first was "obedience to the Council. That obedience now
implies obedience to the Bishops, who interpret the Council's prescriptions and put them into practice." Through them, "[i]t is Christ's will,
it is the breath of the Holy Spirit which calls the Church to make this
change." The second reason for the reform was "associating the assembly
of the faithful more closely and more effectively with the official rite,
that of the Word and that of the Eucharistic Sacrifice."

The Pope recognized that abandoning Latin was a "great sacrifice," and
that giving up Gregorian chant represented a sacrifice of a "stupendous
and incomparable artistic and spiritual thing"; it was "reason indeed for
regret, reason almost for bewilderment." But he felt that the "[u]nder-
standing of prayer is worth more than the silken garments in which it is
royally dressed." In concluding this second address, Paul VI reaffirmed
the sacrificial character of the Mass and the reality of transubstantiation:

> Christ, the victim and the priest, renews and offers up his
> redeeming sacrifice through the ministry of the Church in the
> symbolic rite of his last supper. He leaves us his body and blood
> under the appearances of bread and wine, for our personal
> and spiritual nourishment, for our fusion in the unity of his
> redeeming love and his immortal life.

Cardinal Journet, on the eve of celebrating the new Mass for the first
time, said that he would do so "with great obedience," and that Paul VI's
address had reassured him. "Of course," he agreed, "we are losing great
riches...[t]here is no doubt about it," but he hoped that the monasteries would remain "islets" that would know how to "preserve the Latin
tradition, as a witness to the catholicity of the Church through time."[62]

A few weeks later, Pierre Lemaire created a controversy by publishing
a "Doctrinal Note on the New Ordo Missae."[63] This 44-page booklet was

---

60 General Audience of November 19, 1969 in *L'Osservatore Romano* (November 20,
1969); English translation in the Weekly Edition in English (November 27, 1969).
61 General Audience of November 26, 1969 in *L'Osservatore Romano* (November 27,
1969); English translation in the Weekly Edition in English (December 4, 1969).
62 Cardinal Journet, Address given on Saturday, November 29, 1969, *DC* (May 1, 1977):
444-45.
63 "Note doctrinale sur le Nouvel Ordre Missae," *Défense du foyer* 111 (February 1970),
supplement.

presented as having been written "by the Order of the Knights of Our Lady" to which he belonged. In fact, the principal author of this Note was Dom Gérard Lafond, chaplain of the Order and monk of the abbey of Saint-Wandrille where he taught Sacred Scripture. Before its publication the study had been submitted to various authorities. Excerpts from the responses it received were published: Cardinal Journet praised these "solid, luminous, balanced pages"; Father Louis Bouyer–a close friend of Dom Lafond–found the work "quite good"; Bishop Agustoni, Cardinal Ottaviani's secretary, praised a "serious, profound, serene work, accomplished in the midst of the storm." The "Doctrinal Note," while critical of the translations of the new Ordo Missae then circulating in France, defended the orthodoxy of the new Mass. It was also stated that "Cardinal [Ottaviani] could not have approved the *Short Examination*; in all likelihood it was deliberately not read to him."[64]

Then, the next month, Pierre Lemaire published a letter from Cardinal Ottaviani which created even more controversy.[65] This letter, addressed to Dom Lafond to thank him for the Doctrinal Note, was in almost complete counterpoint to the *Ottaviani Intervention* published a few months earlier. In this letter, dated February 17, 1970, Cardinal Ottaviani described the Doctrinal Note as "remarkable for its objectivity and the dignity of its expression." He also deplored the publicity given to the letter that he and Cardinal Bacci had addressed to Paul VI: "I regret that my name has been abused in a way I did not wish, by the publication of a letter addressed to the Holy Father without authorizing anyone to publish it." He also expressed his satisfaction with the addresses given by Paul VI during the general audiences of November 19 and 26, and judged that from now on "no one can be scandalized," even if "it will be necessary to undertake a prudent and intelligent work of catechesis in order to remove some of the legitimate perplexities that the text [of the new Mass] may raise."

Jean Madiran thought that Cardinal Ottaviani's letter to Dom Lafond was an attack on truth. A lively polemic ensued. Madiran published a pamphlet to contradict the Doctrinal Note, its author, and Pierre Lemaire for publishing it. He also questioned the authenticity of Cardinal Ottaviani's letter to Dom Lafond.[66] He did so in very polemical terms, believing that Dom Lafond and Pierre Lemaire had been "manipulated and duped" in this whole business.

---

64 Cardinal Ottaviani had been blind for some years by this time.

65 Cardinal Ottaviani to Dom Lafond, Letter, February 17, 1970, also published in *Défense du foyer* (March 1970) and abundantly quoted in the press (*Le Monde*, *La Croix*, *Le Figaro*). It was published in full in *DC* (April 5, 1970): 342-43.

66 Jean Madiran, "Sur la lettre du cardinal Ottaviani à Paul VI," *Itinéraires* 142 (April 1970), supplement.

In fact, both sides were right. It appears from a visit Jean Madiran made to him in March 1970,[67] that Cardinal Ottaviani had at first approved the *Short Examination,* of which he was not the author. Then, a few months later, he approved the *Doctrinal Note* of Dom Lafond. His position on the "new Mass" (which he would later celebrate) had changed because, in the meantime, Paul VI had made corrections and rectifications that he considered significant.

ARTICLE 7 AND THE *PROEMIUM,* CORRECTED

Besides the two addresses mentioned above, Paul VI had the *General Instruction on the Roman Missal* significantly corrected and completed.[68] These additions and corrections are easily observed if one compares, in a synoptic way, the two editions of the document (1969 and 1970).[69] On the one hand, a very long *Proemium* ("Preamble") in fifteen paragraphs was added. It recalls the traditional Catholic doctrine of the Mass as a propitiatory sacrifice, citing in particular the definitions of the Council of Trent on several occasions. On the other hand, the chapters of the *Institutio* have been corrected at many points, either by additions or by new wording. The famous § 7, which in the 1969 edition gave a more than incomplete definition of the Mass, was corrected to a more complete and theologically accurate definition. After having again presented it as a "gathering" and "memorial," the new text also defines it as a sacrifice and insists on transubstantiation and the Real Presence:

> . . . at the celebration of the Mass, which perpetuates the sacrifice of the cross, Christ is really present to the assembly gathered in his name; he is present in the person of the minister, in his own word, and indeed substantially and permanently under the Eucharistic elements.

The *editio typica* of the Roman Missal published in Rome in 1970 also included significant corrections, while its structure remained unchanged.

In fact, within a few months, the text of the new Ordo Missae as well as that of the General Instruction had undergone revisions that were more than merely marginal. These revisions did not satisfy many of those who for several months had been making many criticisms of both its form and its content. Jean Madiran observed that the text of

---

67 "Maundy Thursday 26 March 1970. Cardinal Ottaviani," handwritten note, Jean Madiran archives.

68 "Variationes in 'Institutionem generalem missalis romani' inductae," *Notitiae* 54 (May 1970): 177-90.

69 See the synoptic tables by Maurizio Barba, *Institutio generalis Missalis romani,* 389-667 [and the English version with the variations in footnotes, *DOL* #208 – *Translator*].

the Mass remained "uncertain, variable, ever-changing, because the options offered to the celebrant and the liberties he may take mean that there is no longer *the* new Mass, but new *Masses*."[70]

On the other hand, some were convinced and changed their minds. Thus, Father Luc Lefèvre reversed his initial critical position and stated in an editorial of *La Pensée catholique*: "The ambiguities are thus definitively and officially set aside. *Bene. Recte. Optime*."[71] He did continue to celebrate the traditional Mass, however.

Still others, though attached to tradition, had from the start a "position of obedience," such as Cardinal Siri:

> The Council did not ask for such a revolution. The liturgical reform was done, the Pope approved it, and that's enough: I adopt a position of obedience that one must always have with regard to the Pope. If he had asked me, I think I would have made some observations, several. But once a law is approved, there is only one thing to do: obey.[72]

THE NEW MASS: OBLIGATORY – WITH EXCEPTIONS

This is not the place to give an exhaustive account of the way in which the new Mass was made obligatory in the Church universal, except to point out that in some countries, including France, bishops made decisions ahead of the Roman prescriptions, and that the Holy See granted a few derogations.

The new *Ordo Missae* was published in April 1969 and was to be implemented in its Latin version on November 30, 1969, the first Sunday of Advent. Translations had been undertaken, with some haste, in every country. In France, by October 4, 1969, Bishop Boudon of Mende, the president of the International Translation Commission for French-speaking countries, had approved an *ad interim* (i.e., temporary) translation of the ordinary of the Mass. The translation of the prefaces, readings, and of the proper of Saints had yet to be done.

The bishops of France, in their Plenary Assembly at Lourdes, decided to authorize the existing partial translation in a decree adopted on November 12.[73] As requested by the Holy See, the new *Ordo Missae* was authorized on the first Sunday of Advent, November 30. But the bishops added that it would be "obligatory" from January 1 in its Latin text, and "obligatory" from the first Sunday of Advent 1970 (i.e., November 29, 1970) in the vernacular translation, which, in both

---

70 Jean Madiran, *La Messe, état de la question* (1st ed. 1972; 5th revised edition June 1976).
71 *La Pense catholique* 128 (1970): 6.
72 Testimony of Cardinal Siri in E. Cavaterra, *Il Prefetto del Sant'Offizio*, 117.
73 *DC* 1552 (December 7, 1970): 1078-79.

cases, went beyond the Roman directives. The decree envisaged only
two exceptions, termed "special cases": "Older priests who celebrate
'without the people' and have too much trouble getting used to the new
Ordo Missae, as well as to the new texts of the Roman Missal and of the
Ordo lectionum missae, may, with their Ordinary's consent, follow the
current rites and texts"; as for "other particular cases, concerning for
example sick or infirm priests, they should be referred to the Ordinary."

The *editio typica* of the new Ordo had yet to be promulgated by
Rome, however. This did not occur until March 26, 1970, by a decree
of the Congregation for Divine Worship.[74] Between the publication of
the "new Mass" by Paul VI on April 3, 1969, and the obligatory entry
into force of its French translation, more than a year and a half passed.
During this period, some priests continued to celebrate the traditional
Mass in its revised 1965 version; others immediately adopted the authorized partial translation of the new Ordo, voluntarily or because they
were compelled to do so by their bishop; in other parishes yet, in the
absence of definitive texts, priests engaged in "liturgical experiments."

Depending on the country and the parish, the "new Mass" came
into effect more or less quickly. On June 14, 1971, the Congregation for
Divine Worship issued an imperative notification:

> The conferences of bishops . . . should . . . settle on a definite date
> when translations, having their own approval and the Apostolic
> See's confirmations, may or must be put into use in whole or
> in part.
>
> From the date on which the translated texts become obliga-
> tory for celebrations in the vernacular only the revised form of
> the Mass and the liturgy of the hours will be allowed, even for
> those who continue to use Latin.[75]

This obligatory character was emphasized by the only derogation the
notification granted: "[T]hose who because of their advanced years
or illness find serious difficulties in using the new Order of the Mass"
might continue using the former *Ordo*. But this concession involved two
conditions: that the celebrants who maintained the old rite should do
so "with the consent of the Ordinary and only in celebrations without
a congregation."

Many took this notification, which was published in the *Osservatore
Romano* on June 16, 1971, as a prohibition on celebrating according to the
ancient rite of the Mass from then on. Three weeks later, on July 6, 1971,

---

74 Decree *Celebrationis eucharisticae* dated March 26, 1970, *Acta Apostolicae Sedis* 62
(1970): 554; *DOL* #213.
75 SC Divine Worship, Notification *Instructione de Constitutione*, June 14, 1971, *AAS* 63
(1971): 712-15; *DOL* #216.

the *Times* of London published a petition from many British and overseas personalities who, in the name of culture and civilization, wished

> to call to the attention of the Holy See, the appalling responsibility it would incur in the history of the human spirit were it to refuse to allow the Traditional Mass to survive, even though this survival took place side by side with other liturgical forms.

The petition had an international impact.[76] Not all the signatories were Catholic; some were not even Christian. Among them were, notably, Agatha Christie, Graham Greene, Yehudi Menuhin, Jorge Luis Borges, Roger Caillois, Julien Green, Henry de Montherlant, Augusto del Noce, and many other personalities. The list was prestigious and, it is said, impressed Paul VI.

Shortly thereafter, in an audience granted by Paul VI on October, 29, 1971, Cardinal Heenan, archbishop of Westminster and president of the Catholic Bishops' Conference of England and Wales, asked in the name of the British episcopate for the possibility of the older liturgy being used by certain groups. For the first time, the pope gave in.

In an official letter to Cardinal Heenan dated the following November 5, Archbishop Bugnini informed him that the pope was authorizing, for England and Wales, the celebration of Mass in the older rite for the "groups" who made "the request for reasons of genuine devotion, and provided that the permission does not disturb or damage the general communion of the faithful."[77] This indult for England and Wales, commonly termed the Heenan indult or "Agatha Christie indult" because of the petition that led to it, was "criticized," as Archbishop Bugnini later acknowledged, "by part of the French episcopate and by liturgical experts."[78] On the other hand, other groups attached to the traditional liturgy, particularly in France and in the United States, hoped that a similar indult might be granted to other countries. "But the pope was inflexible and unwilling to grant the indult to any other conference," observed Archbishop Bugnini, adding:

> The reason for this, I think, is to be found in personal considerations, in a subjective relationship between the pope and Cardinal Heenan, rather than in any rational causes of the matter.[79]

Only one diocese was able to maintain the regular celebration of the traditional liturgy: the diocese of Campos in Brazil, as we have

---

76 *The Times* (London), July 6, 1971. [For a detailed study of this petition and its complex history, see Shaw, *The Latin Mass and the Intellectuals. – Translator.*]

77 Letter to Cardinal Heenan from the Sacred Congregation for Divine Worship, signed A. Bugnini, November 5, 1971, Protocol number 1897/71.

78 Bugnini, *Memorie*, 85.

79 Ibid., 86.

seen. In most communities, convents and monasteries, the transition from the traditional liturgy to the new liturgy was gradual, beginning in 1965. In many places, the 1970 missal was seen as the completion of a transformation of the liturgy rather than a break with it. Perhaps the most emblematic case is the Benedictine abbey of Solesmes, a bench-mark for decades for Gregorian chant, which immediately adopted the new Latin missal. On the other hand, at the abbey of Fontgombault, daughter of Solesmes, the abbot, Dom Roy, obtained permission to keep, for a time, the traditional Mass. He went to Rome in November 1969:

> As I saw the date approach for us to adopt the new *Ordo*, I resolved to go and ask Cardinal Gut [prefect of the Congregation for Divine Worship] for permission for the monastery of Font-gombault to keep all the liturgy that was ours at that time for two more years, with the understanding that during this time we would prepare a monastic liturgy of the Mass to submit to the Congregation for Divine Worship. I saw the Cardinal and Father Bugnini, and I obtained all that I wanted.[80]

Ultimately, the Abbey of Fontgombault was unable to complete the monastic Missal that had been considered, and had to adopt the new Mass, as we shall see.

Generally speaking, the situation in convents and monasteries was variable, depending on the will of the superiors, external influences or pressures, and how much autonomy the diocesan Bishop granted them. By way of illustration, we will note two contrasting cases. The Dominican Sisters of the Holy Spirit, a small teaching congregation founded by Father Berto, as we have seen, have been able to preserve the traditional liturgy without interruption to this day.[81] Conversely, two communities formed around the mystic Mother Marie de la Croix, the Little Sisters of Mary Mother of the Redeemer, in Saint-Aignan, and the community of the Little Brothers of La Cotellerie, under the influence of Father Régamey, a Dominican, who was their spiritual advisor and helped them to write their constitutions, had to adopt the liturgical reform from 1975 onwards.[82]

"RESISTANCE" FROM LAYMEN AND PASTORS

Starting in 1969, the doctrinal fight against the new Mass was led by theologians and religious – Father Dulac and Father Guérard des

---

80 Dom Jean Roy to Archbishop Lefebvre, Letter, January 20, 1970, Archives of the Abbey of Our Lady of Fontgombault (copy).
81 [Sadly, this community has suffered tremendous upheaval in recent years and it would appear that the Novus Ordo is now being forced upon it. – *Translator*.]
82 Régamey archives, V 842 400, Archives of the Dominican Province of France.

Lauriers among the first – with the support of laymen: Louis Salleron and Jean Madiran in France, Cristina Campo in Italy, Michael Davies in the United Kingdom. Madiran, in *Itinéraires*, published, throughout the year 1970, the firm and well-argued "Declarations" by theologians, priests, and religious who stated their refusal to celebrate the new Mass. These were, in turn, the declarations of Father Calmel, Father Guérard des Lauriers, Father Avril, and Father Dulac.[83] Father de Chivré, whose superiors had forbidden him to write in *Itinéraires*, gave many lectures on the Mass to small groups in Paris and Versailles in the years 1968-1970. In these lectures he did not engage in a controversy about liturgical transformations, but emphasized the theological depth of the traditional Mass and its spiritual benefits for the priest and the faithful. These lectures were collected as a volume after his death, under the title *La Messe de saint Pie V*.

Louis Salleron, for his part, devoted numerous articles to the Mass of Paul VI in the weekly magazine *Carrefour*, in which he pointed out its weaknesses and already called for its reform. He gathered his articles in a 1970 monograph: *La Nouvelle Messe*. He concluded his work by writing rather prophetically: "We are not witnessing the birth of a new Mass or the end of an old Mass. We are witnessing the eclipse of the eternal Mass."[84]

In the event, it was grassroots "resistance" that allowed the traditional Mass to continue despite the prohibitions from Rome, from the Episcopal Conferences, and from the chanceries. It was a double reaction. There was that of the laity, of the run-of-the-mill faithful, and then there was that of the simple priests, parish priests, in both city and country. In some cases, the laity organized themselves to support their parish priest who was attached to the traditional liturgy or, conversely, they left a parish that had gone over to the new liturgy to organize a place of worship and to find a priest who would come to celebrate, at least on Sundays, the "Mass of ages" [*la Messe de toujours*].

A systematic exploration of the *Official Journal* [France's official gazette] of the 1970s makes it possible to identify, for each *département*, the creation of 1901-law [i.e., non-profit] associations committed to safeguarding the traditional liturgy. One of the first, if not the first, was the "Association Saint-Pie V," registered at the Pyrénées-Orientales *département* prefecture on June 16, 1970.[85] Dozens were created in

---

83 Published in *Itinéraires* between January 1970 and January 1971, these were republished as a booklet with the title *Déclarations sur la messe*, March 1971.

84 Louis Salleron, *La Nouvelle Messe* (Paris: Nouvelles Éditions Latines, 1970), 184. An expanded second edition came out in 1981.

85 *Journal officiel de la République française* (July 4, 1970): 6294.

the following months and years in many *départements,* under this same name or under other names: "Oratoire Saint-Pie V" (Marseille); "Association Sainte-Athanase" (Calvados); "Communauté catholique romaine de rite latin" (Nancy), etc. On October 8, 1972, on the initiative of Gérard Saclier de La Bâtie – the founder, a few months earlier, of the "Association Saint-Pie V du Centre" – a coordinating committee was created with the task of linking the various existing associations and helping to found new groups and places of worship.[86]

Sometimes local municipalities, which, in France, own most of the churches, fostered the maintenance of traditional worship. Such is the case in Saint-Martin-de-Bréthencourt, in the south of the Yvelines *département.* The town council had undertaken major restoration work in the early 1970s, even though the church no longer had a permanent priest (it was part of the parish of Ablis). Once the work was completed, the mayor was saddened to see his church go unused, as the clergy of Ablis had refused even to come and celebrate funerals there. A local Catholic family, Jean-Marie and Monique Berger (the granddaughter of Admiral Hervé de Penfentenyo), who traveled dozens of kilometers to attend the traditional Mass every Sunday, became aware of the situation. They contacted the mayor: "We asked him for permission to use this church to celebrate the traditional Mass regularly; he responded favorably."[87] An association, "Églises et Culture," was created on March 26, 1974, and the mayor issued a municipal decree: in exchange for the maintenance of the church and the completion of the work, the association could use the building for traditional Catholic worship. The first Mass was celebrated by Father Bayot, then chaplain at Stanislas College; later on, priests of the SSPX came to serve the church on Sundays and holidays: Father Jean-Yves Cottard, then Father Denis Coiffet.

Furthermore, a not inconsiderable number of parish priests were able to remain faithful to the traditional Mass. Without being able to give a complete history and geography of this "resistance," I will mention a few significant figures, showing the great diversity of situations depending on the local diocese.

In the diocese of Nancy, two priests symbolized the resistance to the new Mass: Father Emmanuel Son and Father Henri Mouraux. Both had signed the *Vademecum* of Father Coache in 1968. Father Emmanuel Son had been the parish priest of a small village in Lorraine, Gripport, since 1954, and served the church of the neighboring

---

86 *Monde et Vie* (April 27, 1973).
87 Jean-Marie and Monique Berger, *Souvenirs et repères* (2007), 198-202.

town, Bainville-aux-Miroirs. A good Latinist and a great connoisseur of traditional hymns, when the new Mass was imposed in the diocese, starting January 1, 1970, he refused to change rites, with the support of the vast majority of his parishioners. Soon, laypeople came from Nancy and the surrounding areas to attend the traditional Mass in his church. For a long time, Father Son was protected from episcopal measures by the mayor of the town, whose wife played the harmonium in the church. Then, when under Bishop Bernard's tenure (1971-) a written order to leave his parish was sent to him, Father Son ignored it, and continued to celebrate the traditional Mass until his death in 1986, without any canonical sanction.[88] In 1972 he was one of the founders of the Noël Pinot Association, whose aim was to gather priests faithful to the traditional Mass.

Father Mouraux, ordained to the priesthood in 1937, was pastor of Croismare until 1961, at which date he was placed, because of his difficult temperament, it seems, "on temporary leave," that is to say, without any parochial duties. The Sisters of the Holy Childhood of Mary, in Nancy, asked him to serve the chapel of the clinic they were running. In 1970, when the parishes of Nancy adopted the new rite of Mass one after the other, the faithful attached to the traditional liturgy found refuge in the chapel of the Holy Childhood. In May 1970, Bishop Pirolley of Nancy tried to impose the new Mass there, too. On Sunday, May 10, the vicar general of the diocese, Mgr Breton, came to the chapel to announce and explain that the Mass would be celebrated from the following Sunday according to the new rite. As soon as he took the floor, he was interrupted "by a chorus of a dozen voices chanting a woman's name: his concubine's."[89] He promptly left. The next day, in a communiqué, Bishop Pirolley forbade the celebration of Mass in that chapel.[90] Abbé Mouraux obtained from Cardinal Gut, prefect of the Congregation for Divine Worship, an authorization to celebrate Mass at his home on rue du Maréchal-Oudinot, in Nancy. There he established an oratory, dedicated to St. Pius V, which could accommodate a few dozen faithful. From 1973 on, he published a bi-monthly bulletin, *Bonum certamen*, which had more than 3,000 subscribers throughout France and abroad. On August 15, 1975, the feast of the Assumption, the "Communauté catholique romaine de rite latin," established on the rue du Maréchal-Oudinot, was registered at the prefecture with three

---

88 As Jean-Marie Cuny told the author, December 11, 2020.
89 As Philippe Schickling told the author, December 2020.
90 *Le Républicain lorrain* (May 12-13, 1970) and *Notre Église. Bulletin diocésain de Nancy et Toul* (May 31, 1970): 231.

goals: "Maintenance, defense, and development of the Catholic faith; celebration of the Mass according to the rite of St. Pius V; practice of the rosary according to the traditional rules of the Roman Catholic Church."[91] In June 1978, Father Mouraux bought from a Protestant pastor a small church near his home and set up a chapel dedicated to the Sacred Heart, which Msgr Ducaud-Bourget came to bless the following December 17.

In the diocese of Besançon, it was a dispute of a canonical, not primarily of a liturgical, nature that produced a traditional place of worship. Father Patingre, appointed pastor of Saint-Joseph in 1943 at the age of forty-two, proved to be, with the help of his parishioners, a brick-and-mortar priest: he built in turn a new church, a parish building, a cinema, and a rectory.[92] As a reward for his zeal, he was named honorary canon in 1958. At the beginning of 1968, the new bishop of Besançon, Mgr Lallier, wanted to appoint him to a small parish in the territory of Belfort. Canon Patingre refused this transfer, arguing that the rectory where he resided had been built with his own money. In May 1968, he was asked to resign. When he refused, Bishop Lallier issued a suspension *a divinis* (a ban on celebrating the sacraments) in October 1968 and appointed an administrator to the parish. The canon retired to his presbytery, which was his property, leaving the church to the administrator. He also appealed the sanction to the Congregation for the Clergy, and then to the Supreme Tribunal of the Apostolic Signatura, while the Bishop of Besançon sought his expulsion through the courts. He had an altar moved to a room in his rectory where he celebrated Mass for those faithful of the parish who supported him. On July 14, 1970, the Supreme Tribunal of the Apostolic Signatura asked the bishop of Besançon to lift the suspension *a divinis* and to provide for the canon's subsistence by giving him a benefice or an office. At the same time, the canon was asked to "make arrangements for the rectory to be vacated as soon as possible."[93] This sentence, which did not rule on the ownership of the rectory, did not settle the dispute. Canon Patingre continued to reside in his rectory and to celebrate Mass there. When the new Mass was imposed in the diocese, as in all of France, he continued to celebrate the traditional Mass, which attracted lay people from other parishes in Besançon and the surrounding area. The canon died in December 1978, and the Mass of St. Pius V that he

---

91 *Journal officiel* (September 13, 1975): 9468.
92 Manuel Tramaux, "Patingre, Joseph," in *Dictionnaire du monde religieux dans la France contemporaine*, vol. 12, *Franche-Comté* (Paris: Beauchesne, 2016), 566-67.
93 *Le Monde* (August 15, 1970) and *Église de Besançon* (August 23, 1970).

had requested for his funeral was denied.[94] After his death, the traditional Mass was celebrated "in various rented halls" by priests from outside the diocese, and then from 1989 by the Society of St. Pius X.[95]

In the diocese of Amiens, the most notable figure of traditionalism was, for almost forty years, Father Philippe Sulmont. He was the second of fourteen children in a family where piety was combined with charity (his father was for decades a discreet prison visitor). Ordained a priest in 1944, he was appointed in 1970 the pastor of Domqueur and "minister" to six neighboring parishes (1,200 inhabitants). He remained in this position for thirty-seven years. When the diocese switched to the new Mass, he remained attached to the traditional Mass and the cassock. Beginning in January 1972, he published a monthly parish bulletin which quickly became known beyond his parish and then beyond the diocese of Amiens, with up to 4,200 subscribers. The successive bishops of Amiens took no action against this priest who remained faithful to the traditional Mass and who did not hesitate to defend Archbishop Lefebvre. He was undoubtedly protected by his popularity and the high level of religious practice that he was able to maintain in a largely dechristianized or non-practicing diocese.

Sometimes, the supernatural seems to confirm a pastor's resistance, as in the case of Castelnau-de-Guers, in the diocese of Montpellier. The pastor in office since 1951, Father Caucanas, was also a signatory of Father Coache's *Vademecum* in 1968. After 1970, he remained attached to the traditional liturgy. A journalist (from the left) who came to investigate on the spot wrote:

> He is reputed to be a formidable integrist. He says Mass in Latin. For years he has been in constant opposition to Cyprien Tourel, bishop of Montpellier, an old seminary chum. The bishop reproaches him for not applying the liturgical reforms of Vatican II? Each time, he retorts: "Get lost." Castelnau comes off as an integrist island in the Socialist-leaning, secular, Masonic South of France.[96]

During the Mass of the Presanctified, on Good Friday, April 12, 1974, Father Caucanas saw the face of the crucified Christ on the ciborium veil. The thirty or so faithful who attended the service were also able to see, for several minutes, the face of the *Ecce Homo*, which disappeared when the priest removed the veil from the ciborium to distribute

---

94 *L'Est Républicain* (December 18-20, 1978).
95 "District de France. Expansion et structure," *Cor unum* 93 (June 2009): 32.
96 Yvon Le Vaillant, "Le Christ s'est-il arrêté à Castelnau?" *Le Nouvel Observateur* (April 29, 1974): 58-59.

Communion. Another journalist who came to investigate the event wrote: "Father Caucanas, who is extremely attached to the classical forms of the liturgy, considers this event to be calling us back to respect for traditions, so often neglected nowadays."[97] The local and national press got hold of the affair, and the diocesan bishop issued a skeptical statement: "The Lord does not build his Church on the extraordinary." Father Caucanas, while remaining very discreet about the 1974 event, would remain faithful to the traditional Mass until his death.

TWO PRIESTLY ASSOCIATIONS

At that time, two priestly associations were created, one in Spain, the other in France, to gather the priests attached to the defense of the integrity of the faith.

The *Hermandad sacerdotal* (Priestly Fraternity) was founded in 1969. It was first an initiative of Catalan priests who formed the *Asociación de Sacerdotes y Religioses de S.-Antonio Maria Claret*. Meeting in Vic on May 12, 1969, they published a long "Declaration of Principles" to "reaffirm the great ideals, duties, principles, and criteria of our priesthood." They also affirmed: "We revere and love the tradition of the Church as manifested in the example and life of the great teachers of priestly formation." They called on other priests in Spain to form similar priestly associations. Two months later, on July 9, 1969, seven hundred priests from all over Spain gathered around Cardinal de Arriba y Castro, Archbishop of Tarragona, and Bishop Castán Lacoma, Bishop of Sigüenza-Guadalajara, and formed the Priestly Brotherhood.[98] It soon brought together several thousand priests in Spain and Latin America, organized in local sections. This Anthony Mary Claret Association remained the most numerous. It was also the most determined to defend the traditional Mass. On November 5, 1969, its two leaders, Father José Bachs, president, and Father Mariné, secretary, sent a letter to Paul VI, "in the name of the 6,000 priests" of the association, asking him to allow "the universal Church to preserve the Mass of St. Pius V alongside the new Ordo." They repeated their request in a letter dated December 11, 1969, while on the same day they addressed an almost identical letter to Msgr Bugnini.[99] In both letters they expressed

---

97 *Ouest-France* (April 18, 1970). See also *Le Monde* (April 23, 1974).

98 Juan Manuel González Sáez, *La hermandad sacerdotal española. La resistencia del clero conservador al cambio eclesial y político (1969-1978)*, PhD diss. (University of Navarra, 2011) and id., "El catolicismo tradicional español ante el 'caso Lefebvre' (1976-1978)," *Hispania Sacra* (July-December 2014): 489-513.

99 Both of these December 11, 1969 letters were published in *Itinéraires* 140 (February 1970): 31-33, under the title "Six mille prêtres espagnols refusent la nouvelle messe."

their indignation at a declaration from Max Thurian, theologian and co-founder of the ecumenical community of Taizé, on the new Mass: "Non-Catholic communities will be able to celebrate the Lord's Supper with the same prayers as the Catholic Church: theologically, it is possible."[100] They concluded: "If, then, this celebration by a Protestant is theologically possible, it is because the new Ordo no longer expresses any dogma with which Protestants disagree."

The *Hermandad sacerdotal* published a monthly bulletin, *Dios lo quiere* ("God wills it"), from January 1970 onwards, and in February it organized a congress at the Benedictine monastery of Valle de Los Caídos to which priests from different countries were invited. There were seventy participants from eight countries. Among the French were Father Dulac, who gave a talk on the crisis of the Church, "the gravest in its history,"[101] Father Coache, Father Barbara, Father André from Argentina, and Canon Catta, founder of *Opus Sacerdotale*. The English were present with Reverend Flanagan's *Cephas* association, and the Mexicans with Father Joaquin Saénz y Arriaga, the president of the *Hermandad* section in Mexico City, who would soon be the first to support the idea of the vacancy of the Holy See. Archbishop Lefebvre had strongly encouraged this meeting, the purpose of which was to constitute an international federation of priestly associations sharing the same convictions. He was unable to attend, but a paper he had prepared, "The Church in the World: A Bird's Eye View Today," was read. As we shall see, he was himself at that time in the process of founding the Priestly Society of St. Pius X and the seminary of Écône.

At the end of the meeting an organization was formed under the name of *Fraternitas sacerdotalis* to represent the various priestly associations already created or yet to be created and to coordinate their actions. But this agreement did not last, as the existing priestly associations, including the *Hermandad*, were divided, especially on the question of the Mass and on the authority of the Second Vatican Council. Archbishop Lefebvre, however, supported the Association of Saint Anthony Mary Claret for some years; he came to give spiritual conferences during priestly retreats twice, in March 1971 and in April 1972.

He also encouraged a priestly association created in France by Father Michel André, a Holy Ghost missionary stationed in Argentina. He had translated and distributed the *Ottaviani Intervention* throughout South America. When he returned to France, he hoped that Opus Sacerdotale

---

100 Words reported in *La Croix* (May 30, 1969).
101 "Rapport de l'abbé Raymond Dulac au Congrès," *Itinéraires* 142 (April 1970): 58-65.

would become involved in the defense of the traditional Mass. Taking stock of Canon Catta's cautious choice of sticking to the defense of doctrine, Father André decided to create "a priestly association charged especially with the defense of the Holy Mass."[102] The decision was made on June 13, 1972, during a meeting at the rectory of Thal, in the Vosges, with Father André, Father Siegel, Father Son, and a few others. The association was registered at the prefecture under the name *Association sacerdotale Noël Pinot* (ANP), named after the priest from Anjou who was executed during the Revolution and who went to the scaffold wearing priestly vestments while saying the first words of the Mass: *Introïbo ad altare Dei* ("I will go to the altar of God"). The ANP soon gathered several hundred priests attached to the traditional Mass (about four hundred in 1975) and published a newsletter, *Introïbo*, which was modest in appearance but well-informed, and which fully supported Archbishop Lefebvre.

At this point in the story, it is worth pondering the reasons for which Paul VI was so determined and inflexible in imposing a new rite of Mass. He himself, by temperament, was inclined to beautiful liturgies in Latin and Gregorian chant, as he had discovered them in his childhood among the Benedictines of Chiari, near Brescia.[103] But since at least the 1950s he was convinced that the faithful wanted greater participation in the liturgy and/or were incapable of relating to a more intellectual worship (as he saw it). He soon felt that it was legitimate to sacrifice Latin, Gregorian chant, *ad orientem* celebration, and certain other practices, in order to make the Mass more accessible to the greatest number. There was also a more subjective reason: Paul VI had entrusted the preparation of the liturgical reform to a new organism, the *Consilium*, which answered directly to him, and had left a great deal of freedom to the person actually in charge of it, Father Bugnini, whom he made a prelate and then an archbishop. Paul VI, an intellectual pope, put all his trust, for several years, in the army of liturgical specialists who had been at work in this *Consilium*.

The clergy and faithful attached to the traditional Mass, however, were not defending it solely on grounds of sentiment (for being the Mass of their youth or ordination) or aesthetics, but for primarily doctrinal reasons: the Mass as "propitiatory sacrifice" and "pure oblation" (to quote the Council of Trent), offered through the ministry of the priest whose primary function this is. Within this attachment to the traditional Mass, there is also a traditional notion of the priesthood.

---

102 C. Mouton-Raimbault, *Un prêtre vrai. Le père André*, 426-29.
103 Yves Chiron, *Paul VI: The Divided Pope*, trans. James Walther (Brooklyn, NY: Angelico Press, 2022), 9-10.

CHAPTER 7
Archbishop Lefebvre,
a Gentle Yet Unyielding Soul

URING THE COUNCIL, ARCHBISHOP LEFEBVRE'S interventions in the conciliar *aula* against the most innovative *schemas*, the articles he published in *Itinéraires* and *Rivarol*, and the few lectures he gave made him better known to Catholics attached to tradition. When he became Superior General of the Spiritans in 1962 and moved to the Motherhouse of the Congregation on rue Lhomond, "priests, families, and candidates for the priesthood who were looking for solid training" came to consult him regularly.[1] For several years, he had sent vocations to the French Seminary in Rome, on the via Santa Chiara, which was run by his congregation and of which he had appointed Father Roland Barq, one of his former students, as director.

THE CONSERVATIVES OF SANTA CHIARA

Father Paul Aulagnier, who was later to be one of the first priests ordained by Archbishop Lefebvre for the Society of St. Pius X, entered the French Seminary in Rome in September 1964, not on the advice of Archbishop Lefebvre, whom he did not yet know, but sent by his ordinary, Bishop de La Chanonie of Clermont-Ferrand. In the first year, he said, there were twelve seminarians, all "conservative":

> If we were there, it was because a more traditionalist priest had sent us there to avoid the diocesan seminaries that had already been won over to progressivism. This phenomenon, of course, was relatively recent and, at the beginning, the seminary authorities did not take notice of it: in a short time, the house of Via Santa Chiara had become the refuge of young traditionalists; this is why their number swelled from year to year.[2]

For the year 1965-1966, the "conservative traditionalist tendency," to use Father Aulagnier's expression, represented "over thirty" seminarians (out of 108 students). Among them, Father Maurice Gottlieb, from the diocese of Bourges, future professor at the seminary of Écône; Father Bruno Salleron, son of Louis Salleron, one of the main contributors

1 B. Tissier de Mallerais, *Marcel Lefebvre*, 405.
2 Fr Paul Aulagnier, *La Tradition sans peur*, conversations with Fr Guillaume de Tanoüarn (Paris: Éditions servire, 2000), 32.

to *Itinéraires*; Father Bernard Dumont, who was to be expelled from
the seminary for "ultra-integrism" and would later found a politico-
religious organization, the Institute of Cardinal Pie (ICP); Father Roger
Péquigney, who, three years later, founded a community that became
the Canons Regular of the Mother of God (CRMD); Father Eric Aumonier,
who became Auxiliary Bishop of Paris, then Bishop of Versailles. Some
had been sent there by their bishop, others had come on the advice
of Archbishop Lefebvre.

It was then the middle of the Council. During the four sessions (from
1962 to 1965), many French bishops were housed at the seminary. The
conciliar debates penetrated the seminary through the press and the
numerous talks given by bishops and theologians. Father Aulagnier
reports:

> Our way of life, too, was changing considerably. After four years,
> the rules of the seminary had practically disappeared. There
> was no more silence since everyone had a radio in his cell, no
> more liturgy since every morning saw a new improvisation. The
> Council had celebrated "openness to the world," and the world
> had entered into minds and hearts.[3]

FRIBOURG

At the beginning of the 1967 academic year, several of these seminarians, judged too "traditionalist" and reluctant to accept the Second
Vatican Council, were refused tonsure and minor orders. When they
turned to Archbishop Lefebvre, he first urged them to attend the Pontifical University of the Lateran, which he considered safe. They were
welcomed by the Fraternity of the Most Holy Virgin Mary which a convert from Orthodoxy, Father Théodossios, had just founded under the
patronage of Cardinal Siri, Archbishop of Genoa. But the orientalizing
liturgy and Father Théodossios's emphasis on doctrine over spirituality
was not to the taste of all the seminarians.

Archbishop Lefebvre, for his part, had long been pursuing a "dream"
that God had "made him glimpse one day in the cathedral of Dakar":
"Faced with the progressive degradation of the priestly ideal, to transmit, in all its doctrinal purity, in all its missionary charity, the Catholic
priesthood of Our Lord Jesus Christ,"[4] and to do so by founding an
international seminary. During a visit to her in Easter week 1964, the
reputed mystic Marthe Robin had told him without hesitation: "You

---

3 Ibid., 33.
4 Archbishop Marcel Lefebvre, *Itinéraire spirituel* (Bulle, Switzerland: Tradiffusion,
1991), 5.

must found this seminary and God will bless you."[5] Three years later, the project seemed to become a reality when a house was offered to him in the diocese of Aire and Dax. To Dom Jean Roy, abbot of Fontgombault, he confided: "I have a tiny hope of being able to make it happen in the Landes, with Bishop Bézac. I will talk to him. Who can say?"[6]

But he was still superior of the Congregation of the Holy Ghost Fathers and the project did not succeed. He then directed some of the seminarians to Fribourg, where they lived in a Spiritan house on Botzet Street, while attending classes in the schools of philosophy and theology run by Dominicans. After leaving his position as Superior General of the Holy Ghost Fathers in October 1968, he was able to devote himself to his seminary project. To the mystic Claire Ferchaud, he wrote on May 13, 1969:

> I believe that at this moment in time, my most urgent duty is to train priests. This is my constant concern and it fills all my time.... I am also convinced that it is the holiness of the priesthood that will save us. This is why I'm devoting all my energy and prayers to that end.[7]

This project came to fruition only gradually and after the consideration of various solutions. A decisive meeting took place on the following June 4, in Fribourg, at the home of Professor Bernard Faÿ, who at the liberation of France had been condemned to forced labor for life for his collaboration in Vichy's anti-Masonic policies, and had managed to flee to Switzerland in 1951. Around Archbishop Lefebvre there were Father Marie-Dominique Philippe, OP, professor at the Catholic University of Fribourg, Dom Bernard Kaul, abbot of the abbey of Hauterive, and a layman, Jean-François Braillard, head of the Department of Education of the State of Fribourg. The young Aulagnier, who was doing his military service at the time and was passing through Fribourg, attended the meeting. He testified: "All spoke of the priestly crisis, all encouraged the Archbishop to 'do something.'"[8] Among the most ardent was Father Philippe. It was decided to ask for an audience with Bishop Charriere of Fribourg, because Archbishop Lefebvre did not want to found anything without the agreement of the diocesan bishop. On June 6, he was received by Bishop Charriere, who was very favorable to the project, and authorized the former Superior General

---

5 Quoted in B. Tissier de Mallerais, *Marcel Lefebvre*, 409.
6 Archbishop Lefebvre to Dom Jean Roy, Letter, May 24, 1969, Archives of the Abbey of Notre-Dame de Fontgombault.
7 Quoted in B. Tissier de Mallerais, *Marcel Lefebvre*, 430.
8 P. Aulagnier, *La Tradition sans peur*, 60.

of the Spiritans to open a "coenobium" for seminarians from different countries. An "Association Saint-Pie X pour la formation sacerdotale" was created to support the project. Twelve rooms were reserved for the 1969-1970 school year at the Foyer Jean-Bosco, on the route de Marly, which belonged to the Salesians.

At the same time, Archbishop Lefebvre had the idea that there should be a preparatory year before entering the seminary. The young men who aspired to become priests in the years 1968-1970 came from diverse backgrounds, had very different levels of education, and had been immersed in a largely dechristianized society. It seemed necessary to him to "propose to all those who expressed their desire to be priests, a year of preparation, of spirituality, of a special study of the ecclesiastical sciences with a view to the priesthood."[9] This innovative idea was later taken up by many French dioceses. By this time, Archbishop Lefebvre had already found the ideal place for this "preparatory year": a former house of the Canons Regular of the Great St. Bernard (CRB) located in Écône, in the Valais, which had been purchased a year earlier by five faithful Catholics, members of the Knights of Notre-Dame and retreatants of the Parish Cooperators of Christ the King.

Cassocks were not taken at Écône until November 1, 1970. In the meantime, the "boarding school" in Fribourg had received its first nine seminarians. Unable to find a suitable priest to direct this house, which was not yet formally and canonically a seminary, Archbishop Lefebvre wrote to his friend Dom Roy:

> I am committed to taking the little group in hand myself. I shall leave Rome and devote myself entirely to this work. That is undoubtedly what Providence desires.[10]

On October 13, 1969, nine seminarians entered the "coenobium." The retreat was preached by Father Théodossios, and Archbishop Lefebvre commented on the Directory [i.e., rule of life and work] he had written for the new seminary. The young clerics attended classes at the University of Fribourg. There were seven Frenchmen, one Argentine and one Swiss. At the end of that first year, there were only two: Aulagnier, mentioned above, who was finishing his first year of theology, and Bernard Tissier de Mallerais, who was finishing his first year of philosophy and who would be, in 1988, one of the four bishops consecrated by Archbishop Lefebvre.

---

9 Archbishop Lefebvre to Dom Jean Roy, Letter, July 1, 1969, Archives of the Abbey of Notre-Dame de Fontgombault.
10 Archbishop Lefebvre to Dom Jean Roy, Letter, September 19, 1969, Archives of the Abbey of Notre-Dame de Fontgombault.

BIRTH OF THE SOCIETY OF SAINT PIUS X

Yet despite the disappointments, and the temptation to give up, Archbishop Lefebvre persevered. On May 19, 1970, he obtained from Bishop Adam of Sion the authorization to inaugurate a year of spirituality in Écône at the beginning of the next school year; on June 26, a house was purchased in Fribourg, on the route de la Vignettaz, where the seminarians who were studying at the university would be housed; on July 1, he submitted to Bishop Charrière of Fribourg a "Draft of the Statutes of the Society of the Apostles of Jesus and Mary." The idea was to create not a new congregation of religious, but "a society of priests, without vows, of apostles, centered on the priesthood." Finally, under the name of Priestly Fraternity of Saint Pius X (SSPX), it was canonically approved *ad experimentum* for six years, on November 1, 1970. On that same day, eleven seminarians took the cassock in Écône, while their elders continued their studies in Fribourg.

Archbishop Lefebvre had recruited three diocesan priests to supervise the first "preparatory year" at Écône. Father Jacques Masson, who had come from the diocese of Meaux where he had directed the minor seminary, was the first director of Écône. Father Maurice Gottlieb, who had studied at the French Seminary in Rome, and who had signed the *Vademecum* of Father Coache, was in charge of teaching spirituality. Father Claude Michel, the spiritual son of Father Berto, was in charge of the bursar's office. The program for this year of spirituality was developed during the summer at Fontgombault Abbey, with the advice of Dom Dominique Marc, the abbey's novice master. In addition to the spirituality course, Father Gottlieb taught Latin and an introduction to Sacred Scripture, Father Michel gave a course in liturgy based on Dom Guéranger's *Liturgical Institutions*, and Canon René Berthod, of the Congregation of Canons Regular of the Great St. Bernard, gave a course on modern errors, which would later be called the "course on the Acts of the Magisterium."[11] All these priests and religious came to teach at Écône with the agreement of their bishop or superior.

During that first academic year, 1970-1971, after having consulted various authorities – notably Cardinal Journet, who told him: "The university is not suitable for the majority of seminarians and does not foster seminary discipline"[12] – Archbishop Lefebvre decided that the further formation of seminarians would continue not in Fribourg, but in Écône. For this reason, he asked Archbishop Adam's permission to

---

11 B. Tissier de Mallerais, *Marcel Lefebvre*, 428.
12 Interview, January 14, 1971, quoted in Tissier de Mallerais, *Lefebvre*, 464.

have a complete seminary in Écône. He obtained this authorization, orally, on December 26, 1970,[13] and he decided to put up new buildings.

It was also during this first year at Écône that Archbishop Lefebvre rejected the "new Mass." Until then, as his biographer explains, "he kept the 'old Mass' because it was still permitted" and he did not found the seminary of Écône and the SSPX "against the new Mass, but for the priesthood."[14] But on June 9, 1971, in a clear and definitive manner, he affirmed his firm and irrevocable choice to preserve the traditional Mass and to refuse the new *Ordo Missae*. On that day, in Écône, he gathered professors and seminarians. According to the testimony of Aulagnier, still a student of theology at the time:

> In fact, the most decisive event in the entire history of the Society as in the life of Archbishop Lefebvre is certainly the moment when he made the decision to reject the new *Ordo Missae*.... On this rare occasion he had made a little summary of his talk and handed it out to us. That day, theology students that we were, we had the distinct feeling that we were living a moment that was capital, historic, for the Church.[15]

The Mass, Archbishop Lefebvre explained, rests on "three truths of defined Catholic faith–*de fide divina catholica*": the priest, "alone capable of consecrating the Eucharist"; "the sacrificial nature of the Mass and its propitiatory role"; and "the real and substantial presence" of Christ. Now, the liturgical reform, Archbishop Lefebvre affirmed, "directly or indirectly undermines these three essential truths."[16]

This absolute rejection of the "new Mass" was only gradually presented to the faithful. It was implicit, since the SSPX priests celebrated only the traditional Mass, but for the time being Archbishop Lefebvre still allowed the faithful to attend the "new Mass" if they could not do otherwise. Fathers Coache, Barbara, and Sáenz, on the pilgrimages they organized each year in Rome, asked the faithful to take an "oath of fidelity to the Mass of St. Pius V." Archbishop Lefebvre, on the other hand, felt that "one cannot affirm in a general way that the new Mass is invalid and heretical" but "it leads slowly to heresy" and "the number of invalid Masses is on the rise."[17] Gradually, however, he would proscribe all participation in

---

13 There never was a written authorization, hence the controversy that arose some years later when Rome ordered the seminary to be closed (cf. B. Tissier de Mallerais, *Marcel Lefebvre*, 439).

14 B. Tissier de Mallerais, *Marcel Lefebvre*, 462.

15 Testimony published in *Fideliter* 59 (September-October 1987): 118.

16 Spiritual conference of June 9, 1971, quoted in B. Tissier de Mallerais, *Marcel Lefebvre*, 461.

17 Tissier de Mallerais, *Marcel Lefebvre*, 463.

the Mass according to the new rite. The doctrine of the SSPX, to this day, is that it is better – during vacations, for example – to break the Sunday precept than to attend an "equivocal" or "questionable" Mass.

On June 28, 1971, Archbishop Lefebvre ordained a first priest for the SSPX, Father Peter Morgan, who soon established the first house of the young Society in London. Then, on October 17, he ordained Father Aulagnier. In both cases, these priestly ordinations were made with the consent of the bishop of their diocese of origin, who had issued dimissorial letters for the purpose.

At the autumn semester retreat in Écône, in October 1971, there were 38 seminarians, five of whom were still to attend class in Fribourg. It was preached by two CPCR priests, Fathers Riviere and Barrielle. Father Barrielle joined the seminary the following year to give regular spiritual conferences. Until his death in 1983, he was an esteemed spiritual director.

The faculty at Écône was very diverse during these early years. Besides Father Gottlieb and Canon Berthod, already mentioned, there was Father Dubuis, a former married Protestant pastor, who taught history and patrology; Father Christian Dumoulin, from the diocese of Bourges, Church history; Father Dominique de La Presle, a Discalced Carmelite, apologetics; Father Thomas d'Aquin, a Benedictine of La Pierre-qui-Vire, philosophy; Father Ceslas Spicq, Dominican, professor at the University of Fribourg, exegesis of the New Testament (from 1972); Father Thomas Mehrle, another Dominican, theology (from 1973).

THE "WILDCAT SEMINARY"

Archbishop Lefebvre's relations with the French episcopate were never cordial, except for a few individuals who were friends of his, such as Bishop Morilleau of La Rochelle. As early as the last months of 1961, when Archbishop Lefebvre was to leave the archdiocese of Dakar, the Assembly of Cardinals and Archbishops had delegated Cardinal Richaud, Archbishop of Bordeaux, to Rome, so that the Holy Ghost prelate would not be appointed to the vacant archiepiscopal see of Albi. Then a request was made to the government "that Archbishop Lefebvre be given a small diocese and that he not be a member of the Assembly of Cardinals and Archbishops." Jean-Marie Soutou, director of European Affairs at the Ministry of Foreign Affairs, summoned the nuncio and gave the reasons for these demands: "integrist tendencies and the protection he provided to *Verbe*."[18]

---

18 Minutes of the January 17, 1961 audience, quoted in Tissier de Mallerais, *Marcel Lefebvre*, 271.

That is how Archbishop Lefebvre came to be named to the modest diocese of Tulle. His election as superior of the Holy Ghost Fathers a few months later and his participation at the Council brought him back into the limelight and confirmed the distrust of a large majority of French bishops, who saw in him one of the leaders of the conservative "minority."

When Archbishop Lefebvre undertook the training of future priests, he did not encounter immediate hostility from the French bishops. As we have seen, several bishops allowed young men or seminarians to enter Fribourg or Écône, accepted that priests from their dioceses would serve as professors at the seminary, and issued the dimissorial letters that allowed Archbishop Lefebvre to proceed with ordinations. But the first alarm came in 1970. Pierre Piqué, who had begun his studies at the French Seminary in Rome and who had joined the "coenobium" of Fribourg with Aulagnier, had received the subdiaconate from Archbishop Lefebvre's hands in February 1970, with a dimissorial letter from his ordinary, Bishop Bézac of Dax. But two months later, perhaps alerted by other bishops, he asked Piqué to leave the seminary.[19]

In the early 1970s, the bishops of France could not help but notice the growing number of entries to the seminary of Écône, whereas their own seminaries were receiving fewer and fewer candidates. An exemplary case is that of the diocese of Meaux. At that time it still had a minor seminary, the Sainte-Marie school, which Father Masson had directed before joining Écône at the beginning of the 1970 school year, as we have seen. At the beginning of the 1971 school year, three students from Sainte-Marie school had entered the seminary of Écône, and five young men from the same diocese were preparing to do the same at the beginning of the 1972 school year. "There is a serious hemorrhage from the diocese," wrote Bishop Ménager of Meaux in a confidential report and a "Canonical Note" addressed to the priests of his diocese and to his fellow bishops.[20] He protested that the seminary of Écône had been opened without the bishops of France having been consulted, and concluded:

> I cannot accept seeing a seminarian for the diocese of Meaux attend the seminary at Écône.... I will not ordain any one for the *département* of Seine-et-Marne who has spent all of his seminary years over there.

The "hemorrhage" of which Bishop Ménager complained was observable in other dioceses too. The decrease in the number of entrants to French seminaries in those years is certainly explained

---

19 *Marcel Lefebvre*, 456.
20 Bishop Jacques Ménager, *Comment se préparer à être prêtre en Seine-et-Marne*, June 9, 1972, and *Note canonique*, June 29, 1972, AHAP, 1 S 2, 1.

by the continuous drop in vocations for several years, but also by priestly vocations going to Écône or to other houses of formation for the priesthood. In 1963, French seminaries had received 917 candidates for the priesthood; in 1971, 354, a decrease of 61%. On the other hand, the number of those who left the seminary after one or more years increased: 333 departures in 1963, 439 in 1971.[21]

At Écône, there had been 33 entries in 1971, 35 in 1972 (three quarters of which were French). At that time, Archbishop Lefebvre was considering opening a seminary in the Val d'Aosta, for Italian vocations.[22]

Other independent houses of formation were attracting vocations. Dom Meugniot, secretary to the abbot of Solesmes, directed candidates for the priesthood who were looking for a solid formation to the University of Fribourg. They were welcomed at the Salesian "coenobium" and were more or less supervised by Father Marie-Dominique Philippe. At the beginning of the 1970 school year, there were about thirty of them. When he learned of the existence of this group "without proper oversight and without a solution for the future," Archbishop Lefebvre became worried.[23]

There was also, without any link with Écône, the "pre-seminary" opened at Paray-le-Monial in September 1970 by Father Jean Ladame, superior of the basilica chaplains. Its aim was to offer a traditional formation as an alternative to the diocesan seminaries.

"There are young men who wish to serve God and the Church," wrote Father Ladame.

> But they ask, in order to commit themselves, to be offered something both serious and stable: not a Christianity reduced to social action tinged with politics, nor a priesthood in perpetual search of its identity and usefulness! The day, on the contrary, when these young people discover that the priesthood is first and foremost a loving response to a loving call from Jesus, Son of God – "Come and follow me!" – they decide to walk in the footsteps of the Master, in joyful renunciation of all that is not Christ, in complete availability to the tasks that the Church will one day entrust to them in the name of the Lord.[24]

---

21 Figures quoted by Bishop François Frétellière in the report, *Préparation au ministère presbytéral*, that he presented to the plenary assembly of the French episcopate at Lourdes in October 1972 and published under the same title at Éditions du Centurion in 1972.
22 Bishop Ménager, in a hand-written postscript to his *Note canonique* quoted above, wrote: "I have it on good authority that a similar seminary for Italian speakers is going to open in the Val d'Aoste."
23 Archbishop Lefebvre to Dom Jean Roy, Letter, July 22, 1969, Archives of Notre-Dame de Fontgombault Abbey.
24 Jean Ladame, *À Paray-le-Monial, des jeunes s'orientent vers le sacerdoce*, June 1972, two printed pages, AHAP.

This "pre-seminary" ("a sort of 'propaedeutic' of a supernatural order" or "a kind of 'novitiate' for a possible entry into a major seminary," wrote Father Ladame) had opened with the agreement of the bishop of Autun. At the beginning of the 1970 school year, it welcomed a dozen young people from different dioceses who, the following year, joined the French Seminary in Rome. At the beginning of the 1971 school year, twelve others entered Paray-le-Monial. Father Ladame wanted this "pre-seminary" to become a full-fledged seminary, and the bishop of Autun was not hostile. A house was bought for this purpose about twenty kilometers from Chalon-sur-Saône. The project was discussed at the Plenary Assembly of the French Bishops in Lourdes in the fall of 1972 but was not approved. The pre-seminary of Paray-le-Monial could only continue, for the time being, as a propaedeutic year.

It was therefore in a context of acute crisis among French seminaries that Écône was first condemned and Archbishop Lefebvre was first ostracized in the autumn of 1972. This condemnation and ostracism were done *mezza voce*, without any official communiqué, but they did emanate from the French episcopate, and were reported as such by the media.

The term "wildcat seminary" (*séminaire sauvage*), as applied to Écône, spread in the French press in the fall of 1972, without anyone indicating where the term came from. It had circulated widely in ecclesiastical circles. Its original source was Father Marcus, a Sulpician, the superior of the seminary of Issy-les-Moulineaux.[25] During a retreat of priests from the diocese of Paris around Cardinal Marty, he had been invited to give a talk on "the formation of the priests of tomorrow." He mentioned "wildcat enterprises of priestly formation." He used the plural because he was denouncing both the seminary of Écône (without naming it explicitly) and, on the other hand, small Christian communities where "young men are fed the idea that they will be ordained without any specific spiritual, intellectual, and pastoral formation." Écône was indeed targeted when the superior of Issy-les-Moulineaux described "the attempt of an ultraconservative seminary, in which candidates are enrolled without the agreement of their bishop," and which "claims to give the Church safe priests." But, warned Father Marcus, "she will not be able to acknowledge them as her own. Who today can venture into this calling without being actually 'taken from among men,' that is, marked by the common demands of contemporary life?"[26]

25 He later was auxiliary bishop of Paris, bishop of Nantes, and archbishop of Toulouse.
26 Émile Marcus, "Comment s'oriente la formation des prêtres de demain?" Lecture published in *La Quinzaine diocésaine de Cambrai* (December 1971): 527-30.

During this same period, Bishop Frétellière, Auxiliary Bishop of Bordeaux, was asked to prepare a report on "preparation for the priestly ministry" which was to be presented and discussed at the Plenary Assembly of the French Episcopate in Lourdes from October 23-30, 1972. In order to write his report, in which he would evoke the different types of priestly formation existing in France – seminaries, and also GFU, GFO, GFI and GFR [27] – Bishop Frétellière had asked Archbishop Lefebvre for information about his seminary. Lefebvre responded by proposing to Cardinal Marty, President of the French Episcopal Conference, that he come to Lourdes "to dialogue and correct false information." Cardinal Marty replied with a letter that was a flat refusal: "I must tell you, in consultation with the Bureau of the Permanent Council, that your coming to Lourdes seems neither opportune nor possible. Only bishops who are members of the Episcopal Conference or who are officially invited are admitted to the Assembly." [28]

The argument put forward for not allowing Archbishop Lefebvre to come and explain himself at Lourdes was fallacious. While it is true that the prelate of Écône was not on any board at the French Episcopal Conference, he did remain a member of the French episcopate: the *Annuario pontificio* designated him as Archbishop-Emeritus of Tulle, and he was also listed as a consultor to the Congregation for the Evangelization of Peoples. At the Lourdes Assembly in October 1972, there were 136 French bishops, some of whom were emeritus, five "non-Catholic observers" (three Protestants, one Orthodox, and one Anglican) and, for the first time, five delegates from Episcopal Conferences of other countries. Yet the presence of Archbishop Lefebvre was judged "neither opportune nor possible."

On October 16, Archbishop Lefebvre sent a letter to all the bishops of France expressing regret at his exclusion and recalling the authorization he had received from Bishop Adam of Sion to open his seminary, the approval *ad experimentum* of the SSPX given by Bishop Charrière of Fribourg, and the encouragement he had received from Cardinal Wright, prefect of the Congregation for the Clergy. "Could these testimonies exist if my work were not regular and canonical? If, as has been falsely claimed, my seminary were a marginal and wildcat seminary?" [29]

---

27 GFU: "Groupes de formation en monde universitaire" (Groups of Formation within Universities"); GFO: "Groupes de formation en milieu ouvrier" (Groups of Formation in the World of Labor"); GFI: "Groupes de formation en milieur indépendant" ("Groups of Independant Formation"); GFR: "Groupes de formation en milieu rural" ("Groups of Formation in the World of Agriculture"). These were the various priestly formation tracks at the time.
28 Cardinal Marty to Archbishop Lefebvre, Letter, September 21, 1972, AHAP, 1 S 2.2 (copy).
29 Archbishop Lefebvre to the bishops of France, Letter, October 16, 1972, AHAP 1 S2.2.

The expression "wildcat seminary" was not used again by Bishop Frételliere in the report he presented to the Assembly of Bishops in Lourdes a few days later, although he did mention the seminary of Écône and Fribourg in veiled terms: "Others receive their priestly formation outside of France in institutions that have no connection with the French Episcopal Conference." But word got around and was picked up by the press, which, for the most part, identified Écône as a "wildcat seminary."[30] The Plenary Assembly of Lourdes adopted by almost unanimous votes six "new decisions called for by the present situation." Two of these were aimed specifically at the seminary of Écône, without naming it. The first: "We commit ourselves to call [to ordination] only young men or adults preparing for the priesthood in centers of priestly formation chosen in agreement with us"; and the third: "No center of formation preparing for the priestly ministry can be created or recognized without the agreement of the local ordinary and input from the episcopal commission for clergy and seminaries."[31]

At that time, Archbishop Lefebvre had not yet taken a public position against the "new Mass," nor against the Second Vatican Council as a whole. This plenary assembly in Lourdes was, however, a decisive moment in the deterioration of relations between the founder of the Society of Saint Pius X and the French episcopate.

This double rebuff against Archbishop Lefebvre – the refusal to allow him to come to Lourdes and the refusal to recognize his seminary – had no immediate effect on his work, which still had the approval of the Bishop of Sion and the Holy See. The number of entries to the seminary continued to increase. Even as the Plenary Assembly at Lourdes expressed hostility against Archbishop Lefebvre, 35 young men entered Écône in October 1972 for the year of spirituality. Their itineraries were not uniform. One of those who entered in 1972, the German Franz Schmidberger, would become in 1982 the first Superior General of the SSPX after Archbishop Lefebvre. Another, Denis Coiffet, disapproved of the episcopal consecrations in 1988, and was one of the founders of the Fraternity of Saint Peter. Yet another, Jean-Michel Faure, after having been one of those who implanted the Society of Saint Pius X in Latin America, contested the doctrinal discussions initiated by his superiors with Rome, was excluded from the Society of Saint Pius X in 2014, and was consecrated a bishop in 2015 without the agreement of the Holy See.

---

30 *La Croix*, October 27, 1972; *L'Est républicain*, October 30, 1972; *Ouest-France*, October 30, 1972; etc.

31 Decisions taken by the Plenary Assembly, published in *DC* (November 19, 1972): 1025.

CHAPTER 8
Religious in the Post-conciliar Upheaval

THE CONCILIAR DECREE *PERFECTAE CARITATIS*, promulgated on October 28, 1965, had fixed "general principles of the adaptation and renewal of the life and discipline of Religious orders." It left it to the authorities of each order or congregation to establish "the particular norms" of this expected renewal. Nevertheless, a few months later, a *motu proprio* set forth 43 general "norms" for the application of this decree.[1] All religious institutes were to convene a "special general chapter, ordinary or extraordinary... within two or at most three years." One norm, the sixth, granted great power to these future chapters since they had "the right to alter certain norms of the constitutions... as an experiment." It was even specified that "[e]xperiments contrary to the common law, provided they are to be undertaken prudently, will be willingly permitted by the Holy See as the occasions call for them." All the members of the congregations and institutes were to be associated with this process of renewal, which would not be decided by the authorities alone.

In certain religious institutes, self-questioning and reappraisal had begun well before the Council, as Yann Raison du Cleuziou has shown for the Dominicans in his enlightening historical survey.[2] Then, the conciliar and periconciliar debates had aroused among many religious desires for reform, expectations of change or, on the contrary, fears of upheaval and abandonment. The immediate post-conciliar period would see the meeting of a multitude of general chapters, at which each order and congregation would revise its constitutions, give its original rule a new interpretation, and engage in *aggiornamento*. It was "the continuation of the more or less complete, more or less radical, but now institutionalized liberation of the word, to prepare the chapters for revising the rules of life and

---

1 Motu proprio *Ecclesiae sanctae*, Latin text in *L'Osservatore Romano* (August 13, 1966); *AAS* 58 (1966) 757 -87; *DOL* #106 (excerpts); full English translation: https://www.vatican. va/content/paul-vi/en/motu_proprio/documents/hf_p-vi_motu-proprio_19660806_ecclesiae-sanctae.html [Accessed 4/4/2024].
2 Yann Raison du Cleuziou, *De la contemplation à la contestation: la politisation des dominicains de la province de France, années 1940-1970* (Paris: Belin, 2016).

government."[3] Father Louis Bouyer, an Oratorian and eminent theologian, noted in 1975 that the "crisis of Catholicism affected first of all the religious" and he denounced "the headlong rush to which religious superiors and prelates tried to give their blessing even as the fruits of their Council were massive defrockings and a generalized confusion of apostolate with apostasy."[4]

This is not the place to go into the history of the reforms undertaken and accomplished in all religious institutes after the Council. We will only call to mind the reactions and resistances of those who wanted to remain faithful to the Rule and traditions of their order or congregation, even to the point of leaving it in order to remain faithful to the spirit and letter of their order or congregation. We will also call to mind the new communities founded by laymen who referred to a religious tradition that they considered to have been betrayed by the existing convents or monasteries.

A text by Cardinal Daniélou was frequently quoted in traditionalist journals and newsletters in the 1970s:

> I think that the only and urgent solution is to stop the false orientations taken in a number of institutes. To do this, we have to stop all experiments and decisions contrary to Council directives; warn against books, magazines, sessions where these erroneous conceptions are spread; restore in their integrity the practice of the constitutions with the adaptations requested by the Council. Where this seems impossible, it seems to me that religious who want to be faithful to the constitutions of their order and to the directives of Vatican II cannot be refused the right to form distinct communities. Religious superiors are bound to respect this desire.
>
> These communities must be allowed to have houses of formation. Experience will show whether vocations are more numerous in houses of strict observance or in houses of mixed observance. In the event that superiors oppose these legitimate requests, recourse to the Supreme Pontiff is certainly allowable.

This text has often been presented as an intervention made by Cardinal Daniélou in 1972 "at the plenary assembly of the Congregation for Religious," of which he was indeed a member. In reality, we do not know the exact content of the interventions or presentations that he may have made there. On the other hand, this widely circulated text is

---

3 Christian Sorrel, "Perspectives pour une histoire de la vie religieuse autour du concile Vatican II," in C. Sorrel, ed., *Le Concile Vatican II et le monde des religieux (Europe occidentale et Amérique du nord, 1950-1980)* (Lyon: Laboratoire de Recherche Historique Rhône-Alpes, 2019), 15.

4 Louis Bouyer, *Religieux et clercs contre Dieu* (Paris: Aubier-Montaigne, 1975), 10, 22.

quite authentic and corresponds to an interview that the cardinal gave to Vatican Radio on October 23, 1972, at the end of a plenary meeting of the cardinals and bishops who were members of the Congregation for Religious.[5] It has often been quoted by the founders of traditional communities to justify their resistance to innovations they considered unacceptable.

THE BENEDICTINES

In the Benedictine Order, situations and reactions were very diverse, as the Order was then composed of thirteen independent monastic congregations, the congregations themselves being composed of monasteries enjoying great autonomy. Dom Gabriel Brasó, coadjutor abbot of Montserrat, a Spanish abbey of the Subiaco congregation, played a leading role in the reform of the Benedictine Order. The Council was not yet over when, in the summer of 1964, he invited all the Benedictine abbots of the world to meet in Montserrat to discuss the future Congress – the Congress of the Benedictine Confederation, which brought together the thirteen congregations of the Order – to be held in 1966. Only seven abbots responded to the invitation, including two Frenchmen, Dom Denis Huerre, the abbot of La Pierre-qui-Vire, who represented the Subiaco congregation, and Dom Jean Roy, abbot of Fontgombault, who represented the Solesmes congregation. The meeting, which took place from December 1-2, 1964, was marked by very free discussions and various proposals. Dom de Robien, Dom Roy's secretary, who accompanied him to Montserrat, reported the reaction of another participant, Dom Ghesquieres, abbot of St. Andrew's in Bruges: "You realize that we are in the process of making a revolution!"[6] The process continued in the following years, with the *Congresso* that met in 1966 and 1967 – without, however, having the power to adopt normative texts binding each congregation – and with the General Chapters that each congregation held separately from 1966 onwards.

Without going into the details of the changes that occurred in each Benedictine congregation – they were more or less numerous depending on the congregation – we will note various reactions and resistances to those evolutions and experiments that were considered unfaithful to the Benedictine Rule and to the constitutions.

In 1966, Dom Maur Le Cour Grandmaison and Dom François Roy left the abbey of Tournay, which belonged to the congregation of Subiaco,

5 Interview published in *DC* (November 19, 1972): 1029-31.
6 Dom Jean-Louis de Robien, *Dom Jean Roy, abbé de Notre-Dame de Fontgombault, 1921-1977*, unpubl. (2002), 77, Archives of the Abbey of Fongombault.

to join the abbey of Fontgombault of the congregation of Solesmes, where a traditional monastic life continued. In those years, Fontgombault welcomed a dozen monks from other abbeys. Another monk from Tournay, Dom Louis-Marie Buffet, joined the diocesan clergy in 1968. Another monk, Dom Gérard Calvet, after two stays in a Carthusian monastery and a year spent in a hermitage in the Hautes-Alpes, settled in July 1970 in a former Benedictine priory in Bédoin, in the Vaucluse. Dom Gérard wished to found there "a Benedictine monastery of a traditional spirit," faithful to the spiritual doctrine of the founders of the congregation (Father Muard and then Dom Romain Banquet) and to the traditional liturgy.[7] This foundation was at first established with the agreement of the abbot of Tournay. Soon vocations presented themselves, but when Dom Gérard asked his abbot for authorization to open a novitiate, the latter delayed granting it, while the bishop of Avignon, on whom the place depended canonically, refused to recognize the community of Bédoin as a monastery.

On two occasions, Dom Gérard made decisions that placed him afoul of canon law: on December 8, 1972, without the agreement of the Abbot of Tournay, on whom he still depended, he had the first brother of the community, Jehan de Belleville, who had joined him two years earlier, take religious vows; and on June 10, 1974, instead of appealing to the bishop of the diocese, he asked Archbishop Lefebvre to confer minor orders on the first brothers of the community. These two initiatives led to a rupture with the Archbishop of Avignon and with the Benedictine Order. Refusing to leave the nascent community to another superior, and refusing to adopt the new Mass, Dom Gérard was expelled from the Benedictine Order in 1975 and declared suspended *a divinis*. He remained closely linked to Archbishop Lefebvre until 1988, having his monks ordained by the Prelate of Écône. The growth of the community (eleven members at the beginning of 1977) necessitated the building of a new monastery, the site of which was Le Barroux, a dozen kilometers from Bédoin, in 1978.

Another traditional Benedictine foundation of the early 1970s is characterized by the atypical itinerary of its founder, Maurice Joly, who became a religious under the name of Augustin-Marie.[8] He was born in

---

7 See Yves Chiron, *Dom Gérard. Tourné vers le Seigneur* (Le Barroux: Éditions Saint-Madeleine, 2018).

8 There is no historical study devoted to Joly to date. Besides the various communications sent him by Church authorities starting in 1975, interviews held at the abbey of Saint-Joseph-de-Clairval with Fathers Antoine-Marie Beauchef, and Emmanuel and Jean-Bernard Bories, July 18-19, 2021, have allowed me to gather information on Father Augustin-Marie Joly's trajectory.

1917, admitted in 1936 to the military school of Saint-Cyr, and began a career as an officer in the infantry. Married in 1938, he had six children, one of whom became a Benedictine and another a Carmelite. During the Occupation, he joined the gendarmerie, where he continued his career up to the rank of commander. After the war, he practiced the Spiritual Exercises of Ignatius of Loyola every year with the priests of Chabeuil (Coopérateurs paroissiaux du Christ-Roi) and became a spiritual son of Father Barrielle. Widowed in 1952, he raised his children alone, with the desire of becoming a priest and devoting himself to preaching the Spiritual Exercises. So, while continuing his career in the gendarmerie, he engaged in studies that allowed him to obtain a doctorate in canon law and a bachelor's degree in theology. In August 1965, he left the gendarmerie and entered as a postulant at the Benedictine abbey of Maylis, in the Landes, which he knew was committed to the practice and preaching of the Spiritual Exercises. On August 28, he was admitted to the novitiate where he received the religious name of Augustin-Marie. In consideration of the ecclesiastical studies he had already completed before entering the monastery, he was ordained a priest on December 19. He made his religious profession in 1966, and took solemn vows in 1969. When his abbey gave up preaching the Spiritual Exercises, he and two other religious (Antoine-Marie Beauchef and Pierre Joly, his son, who had also become a monk) obtained, on February 22, 1972, permission from their abbot to leave their monastery to join Father Barrielle, who was planning to found a branch of strict observance of the Congregation of the Parish Cooperators of Christ the King. But the project did not succeed. That same year, on the advice of Archbishop Lefebvre and Father Barrielle, Dom Augustin-Marie founded the monastery of St. Joseph in Martigny, Switzerland, where Benedictine religious life would be combined with the practice and preaching of the Spiritual Exercises. At that time, as he had done at Maylis, Dom Augustin-Marie celebrated Mass according to the new Ordo in Latin. When Archbishop Lefebvre visited the fledgling community in the spring of 1972, he suggested that they return to the traditional Mass. He got Bishop Rudolf Graber of Regensburg to incardinate the monks in his diocese and to issue them the necessary dimissorial letters for ordination by Archbishop Lefebvre. In June 1975, the monastery had to leave Martigny, and moved to Finhaut, about thirty kilometers away, in a former sanatorium called "Clairval," hence the name Saint-Joseph de Clairval which has remained attached to the monastery. The parish of Finhaut was under the canonical jurisdiction of the abbey "nullius" of Saint-Maurice d'Agaune. The abbot Henri Salina published a communiqué to protest against this installation:

> None of the authorizations prescribed by the law of the Church
> has been requested of us; this installation has occurred against
> our express will as notified to the person in charge of that com-
> munity, by a letter that has remained unanswered.

The abbot also declared that "this community alone is responsible for itself and we acknowledge no mandate to exercise ministry for it."[9]

In 1976, the monastery of Saint-Joseph de Clairval moved to Flavigny-sur-Ozerain, in the Côte-d'Or, in the former diocesan minor seminary; Father Coache had sold it to him. At that time, the monastery numbered 23 monks. Bishop Decourtray, then bishop of the diocese, issued a statement warning that the monastery was "in a completely irregular situation," approved "neither by the Holy See, nor by any bishop, nor by any Benedictine monastery."[10] Nevertheless, he added: "It goes without saying that the day these religious agree to be reconciled with the Church, we will welcome them into the diocese with joy." This in fact would happen in 1984-1985, as we shall see in another chapter.

Other Benedictines who were attached to the traditional liturgy, and in disagreement with the evolution of religious life in their abbey, left it without for all that going on to found a new community. This was the case of Dom Guillou, of the Abbey of Sainte-Marie in Paris, whose links with *La Cité catholique* and collaboration with the *Nouvelles de Chrétienté* have already been mentioned. In November 1969, he obtained a "leave of absence for one year," but he did not ask for the renewal of this leave, which placed him in an irregular situation. From 1971, he assisted Father Avril in his educational work in Salérans, in the diocese of Gap. On July 5, 1974, he was offered exclaustration from his home abbey, but he did not accept this offer. In September 1974, he accepted Archbishop Lefebvre's offer to organize the seminary library in Écône. He was also a professor of liturgy. At the end of 1977, he settled in Tourrette-Levens, a village in the Alpes-Maritimes, living as a hermit faithful to the rule of Saint Benedict. Soon, at the request of the faithful of Nice and the surrounding area, he came down every Sunday and Holy Day to celebrate the traditional Mass, first in a rented hotel room, then in a chapel set up in a former cabinetmaker's workshop on rue Ségurane.[11] His situation in relation to the Benedictine Order was not clearly known to the faithful, or even to the priests of the Society

---

9 Abbot Henri Salina, Communiqué, June 29, 1975, published by the Kipa press agency on June 30, 1975.

10 Communiqué dated November 2, 1976, published in *Église en Côte-d'Or* (November 5, 1976).

11 Father Charles Moulin to the author, Letter, April 24, 2021.

of St. Pius X who were brought to Nice to collaborate with him. In fact, the Abbey of St. Mary ordered him to return to his monastery three times (on September 9 and November 13, 1977, and December 16, 1978). After his formal refusal on December 29, 1978, a procedure was initiated which resulted in his dismissal from the Benedictine Order in 1979.[12] This did not prevent Dom Guillou from remaining faithful to his Benedictine habit and to the monastic office until he died.

Another Benedictine was very closely linked to the Society of St. Pius X, even to the point of joining it: Father Le Boulch. He entered the Benedictine abbey of Kerbénéat, in the Finistère, where he took his vows in 1928 and was ordained a priest in 1934. The abbey moved to Landévennec in 1958. Dom Le Boulch had a very important preaching ministry: from 1937 to 1974, he preached numerous retreats to religious communities and parish missions. Faced with the changes in monastic life and out of fidelity to the traditional Mass, after two years of reflection, he left the Landévennec Abbey in 1972 and became chaplain to the Dominican teaching sisters of Sainte-Marthe in Grasse. From 1975 to 1977, he was chaplain to the Sisters of the Society of St. Pius X in Albano, near Rome. The canonical procedure initiated by his abbey of origin for breaking his vow of stability and obedience did not lead to his dismissal from the Benedictine Order until 1978.[13] Nevertheless, in October 13, 1976 he had joined the Society of Saint Pius X. In 1977 he became professor of Sacred Scripture and liturgy and spiritual director at the seminary of Écône, positions he held until the end of his life.

On the other hand, other Benedictine monks were able to remain faithful to the traditional Mass even though their abbey had adopted the new Mass. This was the case with Dom Vincent Artus, a monk of the Abbey of Saint André in Bruges. He made his religious profession in 1940 and was ordained a priest in 1944. From 1970 on, he obtained from his abbot the right "to live as a hermit in the community"[14] and to continue to celebrate the traditional Mass. This wish corresponded to a deep and ancient aspiration which led him to write statutes for the faithful (lay people, religious) who, in several countries, felt called to a hermit's life, and to send them letters of spiritual encouragement regularly. He also published several works of spirituality. He was able to remain faithful to the traditional Mass until his death in 2001.

One might also mention Dom Hugues Portes, from the abbey of En-Calcat. Initially a diocesan priest, he soon felt drawn to the most

---

12 Letter from the archivist of the abbey of Saint-Marie in Paris, April 19, 2021.
13 Letter from the archivist of the abbey of Saint-Guénolé of Landévennec.
14 Letter from the archivist of the abbey of Saint-André in Bruges, June 8, 2021.

rigorous version of Benedictine life. In 1941, he entered the novitiate
of the abbey of En-Calcat. For many years he was a master of ceremonies, as well as holding other positions. When the abbey adopted the
new Mass and a new monastic office, in French, Dom Hugues refused
to submit to it. According to one of his friends, the historian Hervé
Pinoteau, "his abbot wrote to him that he no longer had a place in
the community and he himself replied that it was the abbot who was
no longer there."[15] The abbey archives have not revealed any trace
of these two letters, but it is attested that until the end of his life, in
2009, Dom Hugues Portes was able to remain "faithful to the individual celebration of the Mass in the Tridentine rite, faithful also to the
celebration of the breviary, following St. Benedict."[16] He was not a
marginal figure in his monastery, however, and continued to participate
in the life of the community and to be the confessor of the nuns of
the neighboring abbey of Dourgne, a position he held for thirty years.

On the other hand, some traditionalist priests who had left their
dioceses tried to find in the Benedictine spirit and rule a substitute for
the deficiencies of the secular clergy. So it was with Father Pierre Verrier
(1922-2011) of the diocese of Besançon. In 1964, "following a dispute with
a Catholic Action group that had been disrespectful towards his jurisdiction,"[17] he left, at his own request, the parish of Aboncourt-Gésincourt
and was appointed pastor of Monjustin. The liturgical upheavals and
the introduction of the new Mass, which he rejected, put him at logger-
heads with certain Catholic movements and to one of the diocese vicars
general. On November 15, 1970, he was granted time off and retired to
his family home in Vesoul. From then on, until 1983, the diocesan ordos
would report him as "on temporary leave." He had been a Benedictine
Oblate at Solesmes Abbey since 1966, and made frequent visits to Notre
Dame de Fontgombault Abbey, where he met Canon Catta and joined
the *Opus Sacerdotale*, which Catta had founded. He also exercised various pastoral ministries in the villages near the abbey, then in 1974 he
joined the Fraternity of the Transfiguration founded in Mérigny (in the
département of Indre) by Father Lecareux. A few years later he returned
to the Haute-Saône, and in 1982 he acquired the former farm of Father
de Faverney and founded the priory of Our Lady of Bethlehem, in the
spirit of a Benedictine monastery, but without any recognition from
the diocese or the Benedictine Order. From then on he exercised his

---

15 Hervé Pinoteau, "Requiescat in pace," *Le Lien légitime* 32 (March–April 2010): 10.
16 Letter from the archivist of the abbey of En-Calcat to the author, March 8, 2021.
17 Vincent Mercier, "Verrier Pierre," *Dictionnaire du monde religieux de la France contemporaine*, vol. 12, *Franche-Comté*, 737-39.

ministry with the support of Archbishop Lefebvre and in connection with the SSPX. In 2002, he adhered to the "formal vacancy" of the Holy See, and entered into close relations with the Mater Boni Consilii Institute, where he sent several young men for training. After his death, he was succeeded by a priest trained at this institute's seminary.

BENEDICTINE NUNS

Dom Gérard Calvet, mentioned above, was to take a decisive part in the foundation of two traditional communities of Benedictine nuns.

The communities of Benedictine nuns also underwent an *aggiornamento* similar to that of the Benedictine monasteries in the 1960s and 1970s. Depending on the congregation and whether the community of nuns was a sister community with a Benedictine abbey or was independent, changes occurred more or less swiftly. The changes in religious life paralleled the changes in liturgical life.

A Benedictine nun, Mother Gertrude de Maissin (1914-2005), who had been prioress of the ancient abbey of Notre-Dame de Faremoutiers, in the diocese of Meaux, from 1956 to 1969, had left it in 1978 when the office in French was adopted. She wished to reconstitute a community faithful to the Benedictine Rule and the traditional liturgy. She had received the support of two Benedictine oblates, and hoped that a nun from her home monastery would join her. On the initiative of Father Aulagnier, at the time superior of the French district of the Society of St. Pius X, she contacted Dom Gérard. She visited him in Bédoin in April 1979 and he promised her his support and help for the foundation of a community of nuns. A facility near Bédoin had been envisaged, but no place had yet been found.

At the same time, another Benedictine nun, Mother Élisabeth de La Londe (1922-2015), came into contact with Dom Gérard. She entered the order of the Benedictine nuns of the Blessed Sacrament in 1945, and belonged to the priory of Notre-Dame-de-Bonsecours in Couvrechef, near Caen. From 1965 onwards, the monastery underwent many changes as a result of the *aggiornamento* of religious life and the application of the liturgical reform: introduction of the vernacular in the Divine Office from 1965, adoption of the new Ordo Missae from 1970, communion in the hand, and changes in the application of the Rule and Constitutions, notably the suppression of perpetual adoration of the Blessed Sacrament, a perpetual adoration which was one of the reasons for the congregation's existence. In the case of the community of Caen-Couvrechef, the developments and changes took place with the approval, and sometimes under the pressure, of the diocesan bishop, through the intermediary of "intercontemplative meetings" which brought together the superiors of the six contemplative communities of the diocese (three monasteries of Benedictine nuns, two Carmels, and one Visitandine monastery). The successive changes that took place at Notre-Dame de Bonsecours, most often without the community being consulted, caused Mother Élisabeth a great deal of sorrow.[18] They appeared to her not as natural developments, but as infidelities to the Rule and to the vows she had professed.

At the beginning of 1979, she discovered the preface that Dom Gérard had given to Dom Guéranger's republished *Liturgical Institutes*. Mother Élisabeth found herself completely in tune with the spirit of these pages. Then in June 1979, she met a priest attached to the traditional liturgy, Father Jehan de Bailliencourt (1929-1990), who told her about Dom Gérard and the priory of Bédoin, where he had been for the first time in March 1975. Mother Élisabeth welcomed the news with joy, happy to know that there was a community of monks in France attached to the Benedictine observance and the traditional liturgy. At the end of June, during ordinations at Écône, Father de Bailliencourt met Dom Gérard and told him of Mother Élisabeth's dismay, while Dom Gérard informed him of Mother Gertrude's project. Mother Élisabeth, having learned of it, was tempted to join.

In the Benedictine tradition, the vow to remain in one's monastery is added to the vow of obedience and the vow of conversion of life, which includes chastity and poverty. However, the possibility of changing monasteries does exist, under obedience, when there are serious reasons to do so. Mother Élisabeth thought that this change of stability would be refused by her superior. Father de Bailliencourt argued that fidelity to God and to her vocation allowed her to leave her monastery without the permission of her superiors, and to continue her religious life in another community. On July 24, 1979, without informing anyone in her community, and seizing the opportunity provided by having to receive medical care on the outside, Mother Élisabeth "fled"[19] her monastery and took refuge, at first, with her sister in Versailles. She was fifty-seven years old, and had been in consecrated life for almost

---

18 In August 1979 Mother Élisabeth wrote a six-part report listing the reasons that led her to leave her monastery. It is a fifteen-page typed manuscript, undated, which is kept at the archives of the abbey of Our Lady of the Annunciation. I have also been able to take down her testimony in person on August 18, 2009.

19 The causes and circumstances of this departure are mentioned in *De Fuga,* a 48-page manuscript, based on Mother Élisabeth's testimony, composed in 1985 and kept in the Archives of Notre-Dame-de-l'Annonciation.

thirty-four years. She stayed with her sister for almost a month. On August 1, in Paris, she met with Mother Gertrude de Maissin, and on August 21, she went to Bédoin to meet with Dom Gérard. She discovered a monastery faithful to the traditional observances, a young community, which at that time numbered sixteen monks. The next day, August 22, on the feast of the Immaculate Heart of Mary, she attended Mass for the first time in the priory chapel and, almost ten years after being deprived of it, rediscovered the traditional Mass.

Dom Gérard told her of a small group of young women who, for some time, had wanted to become nuns in the Benedictine tradition. He also showed her a property in Montfavet, about forty kilometers from Bédoin, where the monks came to celebrate Mass every Sunday in a chapel that had been put together there. A visit to the place – a house, an adjoining chapel, and a large park – convinced Mother Élisabeth that community life could take root there. Returning to Paris on August 23, she reported her visit and the possibility of settling in Montfavet to Mother Gertrude. Meanwhile, however, Mother Gertrude had found a place to settle, in Lamairé, in the Deux-Sèvres, in an old school that a secular Oblate had just bought. For each of them, a dilemma presented itself: to be independent in a house of their own, or to settle near a growing Benedictine priory. Mother Gertrude opted for a foundation in the Deux-Sèvres, Mother Élisabeth for a settlement in Montfavet. She had the assurance of being able to rely on the spiritual support of Dom Gérard, on his help in the formation of the postulants (who were already emerging), and on the material support of the community of Bédoin.

And so, in the autumn of 1979, two traditional Benedictine communities were born, one in Lamairé, on the initiative of Mother Gertrude de Maissin, the other in Montfavet, on the initiative of Mother Élisabeth de La Londe. In both cases, the foundations were irregular with regard to canon law, founded by nuns who had broken away from their communities, and the bishops of the dioceses concerned soon issued warnings. Both communities, however, were to prosper.

THE CAPUCHINS

The Capuchin Order also underwent significant transformations and evolutions in the post-conciliar period. These were initially scattered and experimental, and were ultimately formalized by the revision of the Constitutions, a process that lasted a quarter of a century: begun in 1964, this revision resulted in a text adopted at a special General Chapter held in 1968, but which was not officially completed until 1990. By the mid-1960s, in many convents, the austerity and mortification that had characterized the Capuchin Order – the chapter of faults, penances in the refectory on the eve of feasts, and the discipline – were effectively abolished. The monthly "assemblies" in each community, or the regular assemblies at the provincial level, acquired greater decision-making power than the traditional authorities (the Father Guardian, superior of the convent, and the provincial). Concelebration became the rule, prayer in the conventual church disappeared almost everywhere.

Eugène de Villeurbanne and other religious men of the Capuchin province of Lyon tried to resist what they saw as a catastrophic development. Eugène had been a missionary in Central Africa for many years, and had returned to France in the early 1960s. He was engaged in an extensive ministry of preaching parish missions, priestly retreats, and retreats in various religious houses. After the Minister General of the Capuchin Order, in May 1965, made known the direction the revision of the Constitutions would take, Father Eugène asked him in a letter:

> 1. Do you intend to create Capuchin communities where one might remain faithful to what was promised in the past: Rules, constitutions, ordinances? 2. If you do not foresee the creation of these communities, do you intend to facilitate, for religious who want to live until their death the form of life of their Religious Profession, a situation of men who are loaned out for chaplaincies, preachers at the service of one diocese or another... where they could pursue their fidelity to their observances, while making themselves useful to the Church, to the extent their strength allows?[20]

The dilatory response of the Capuchin Minister General did not reassure him, but over the years he persisted in his request to the various authorities of the order. Five religious of the province of Lyon, who resided in various convents, joined his request, notably Father Philibert de Saint-Didier who had been provincial three times, and who was one of the four definitors of the province. While waiting for the authorities of the Capuchin Order to decide on the possibility of establishing a convent where traditional Capuchin life could continue, Fr Eugène obtained permission to live *extra claustrum* ("outside the convent"). With the approval of the Archbishop of Bourges, he settled in 1966 in Poulaines, in the Cher region, leading a hermit's life while doing extensive preaching and teaching in various parts of France, and in 1970 he settled in Ronce, in the diocese of Le Puy. After the six religious had made numerous requests to their provincial, the Capuchin

---

20 Father Eugène de Villeurbanne to Father Clémentin de Vlissingen, Letter, August 19, 1965, Archives of the convent of François de Morgon (copy). See Yves Chiron, *Veilleur avant l'aube. Le père Eugène de Villeurbanne* (Paris: Clovis, 1997).

minister general, and the Congregation for Religious, the provincial chapter, meeting in May 1972, authorized them to regroup in the convent of Besançon, where Father Philibert already resided, and to lead the Capuchin life in its traditional observance, including the liturgy.

But they had to share common life with religious who accepted the reforms, and there would be no possibility of opening a novitiate to transmit the traditional Capuchin spirit. Four priests (Philibert de Saint-Didier, Gabriel de Villeurbanne, Jean-Damascene de La Javie and Jean-Louis des Estables) accepted this "mutilated solution," and settled in the convent of Besançon. Father Eugene de Villeurbanne and Father Elzéar des Estables refused to follow them. In August 1972, they settled in Verjon, in the Ain *département*, founding a "Capuchin Franciscan Community of Observance" without the explicit consent of the authorities of their order. Archbishop Lefebvre immediately encouraged Fr Eugène: "May God bless the true renovators. May they unite around the true liturgy of the Holy Mass and the religious habit, as well as the Divine Office!"[21] It was not until 1981, after a novitiate had been opened by Fr Eugène, that the authorities of the Capuchin Order initiated a canonical procedure against him, which resulted in a suspension *a divinis* sanction and his expulsion from the Order in 1983, just before the community moved to Morgon, in a former vineyard.

The Besançon four were able to continue to live according to traditional observances in a community that was not traditional, and were able to continue to celebrate traditional Mass in the conventual church open to the faithful. They were already elderly and passed away one after the other in the 1970s and 1980s, and the traditional Mass ceased to be celebrated in the conventual church after the death of the last of them.

In other countries, Capuchin men pursuing the same ideal as Father Eugène were able to continue to lead a traditional religious life without the Church considering them rebels and sanctioning them. In Brazil, Father Teodoro Ferronato and eleven other Capuchins, upset by the evolution of their order, had also sought to open a house of observance. The authorities of the Capuchin Order did not authorize it, so in 1972 they asked the Congregation of Religious for permission to leave their order, which was granted to them; nevertheless, by indult of the Holy See, they were able to keep their solemn vows.[22] On August 15, 1973,

---

21 Archbishop Lefebvre to Fr Eugène de Villeurbanne, Letter, August 26, 1972, Archives of the convent of Saint-François de Morgon.
22 D. Kalverkamp, "Frati Minori Missionari," *Dizionario degli Istituti di Perfezione*, vol. 4 (Rome: Edizione Paoline, 1977), 838.

Bishop Micheletto Pellanda of Ponta Grossa recognized them as the
Pious Union of the Fathers of St. Francis of Assisi. Later, other Capuchin religious and a Franciscan (OFM) joined them. In February 1975,
they received their first novices and on the following September 17,
Bishop Micheletto Pellanda approved their constitutions and erected
the Friars Minor Missionaries (FMM), their new name, as an institute
of consecrated life of diocesan right.

Italian Capuchins followed the same path. On June 5, 1968, anticipating the results of the Special General Chapter, three religious from
different provinces of the Capuchin Order, Frs. Crescenzio da Jesi,
Bonaventura da Gangi, a renowned canonist, and Mario d'Ostra, founded
a "Fraternity" in Fabriano, with the approval of their superiors and the
bishop of the diocese, in order to return to the "sources of their spirituality." Other Capuchins, both Italian and French, joined them. But
difficulties with their order forced them to leave it. They were welcomed
in the diocese of Monreale, Sicily, where Bishop Mingo constituted them
on December 24, 1972 as a Pious Union of diocesan right under the
name of Renewed Friars Minor (*Rinnovati*). On April 4, 1973, an indult
of the Holy See allowed them to keep the solemn vows they had taken
in their original order.[23] Other religious men of the Franciscan family
joined them. On June 11, 1983, Archbishop Cassisa, the new archbishop
of Monreale, approved their constitutions and erected the renewed
Friars Minor (FMR) as an institute of consecrated life of diocesan right.

Furthermore, as with the Benedictines, some Capuchins, without making a fuss and without seeking to found a community, found
individual solutions to remain faithful to the traditions of their order
without breaking with it. So Father Porphyre des Pennes, who had been
guardian of the convent of Bastia, "no longer able to bear the changes
in our religious life as it was led in our convents,"[24] successfully asked
his superiors for permission to withdraw in 1970 to a hermitage in Riez,
in the Alpes-de-Haute-Provence, where he died in 1976.

Still within the Capuchin family, there was the situation of the Little
Sisters of Saint Francis of Assisi. This congregation was founded in 1873
in Angers by Louise Renault and the Capuchin Louis de Saint-Etienne.
Recognized by the State in 1875 as a hospital congregation, it had been
aggregated to the Capuchin Order in 1934.[25] The congregation had also

---

23 G. Rocca, "Frati Minori Rinnovati," 839.
24 Fr Jean-Damascène de La Javie, "Nécrologie des capucins des diverses régions de
la Province actuelle de Lyon . . ." typed manuscript, Archives of the convent of Saint-
François de Morgon.
25 Fr Philibert de Saint-Didier, *Du cloître au service des âmes. Les Petites Sœurs de Saint-
François* (Lyon, 1960).

established itself in mission lands. In the years 1947-1968, four small Franciscan congregations had joined it. In 1966, the Little Sisters of St. Francis of Assisi had 42 houses and 416 sisters. This expansion took place at a time when the congregation was in the process of applying *aggiornamento* to its constitutions after the Council. At the end of 1969, when the new Mass began to take effect, the superior of the Merville community, Mother Thérèse-Marie Coache, sister of Father Coache, refused to have it celebrated in their chapel. She also refused, in 1971, to allow the abbreviated French office, *Prière du temps présent*, to replace the Latin office, and the possibility for the nuns to wear lay clothes.[26] That same year, with another religious, Mother Marie-Xavier, she left the Merville community. They found refuge in the Maison Lacordaire in Flavigny, which Father Coache had just acquired. In 1973, postulants presented themselves and Mother Thérèse-Marie decided to restore their original congregation under the name of Little Sisters of Saint Francis and to write new constitutions. The first taking of a habit took place on December 31, 1973. Father Eugène de Villeurbanne and other Capuchins from the province of Lyon (Fathers Philibert, Jean-Damascène, and Gabriel-Marie) came for several years, until 1988, to preach retreats or give them talks. The congregation, which moved to Trévoux (Finistère) in 1986, now has about forty nuns.

One traditional Franciscan community, born in 1970 from the Friars Minor Conventual, was to experience a great expansion, although it was not originally opposed either to the Council or to the new liturgy. Father Stefano Maria Manelli, born in 1933, entered the minor seminary of the Friars Minor Conventual of Copertino at the age of twelve, and took his vows in the same order in 1949. He was ordained a priest in 1955, and received a doctorate in theology with a thesis on the Immaculate Conception. For a long time he taught Mariology and Patrology in several institutions of his order and in several diocesan seminaries. In 1965, the conciliar decree *Perfectae Caritatis* on "the renewal and adaptation of religious life" encouraged religious orders and congregations to "renew" and "adapt." The Friars Minor Conventual, like many others, favored the path of adaptation. Father Manelli, on the other hand, was more attached to a recommendation of the same decree:

> Therefore let their founders' spirit and special aims they set before them as well as their sound traditions – all of which make up the patrimony of each institute – be faithfully held in honor. (2.b)

---

26 *Les Fioretti du monastère Saint-François d'Assise* 45 (March 2021): 7-8; and Mother Marie-Catherine de l'Eucharistie to the author, Letter, September 7, 2021.

He began a "long rediscovery and meditation" of the founding texts
of the Franciscans and the writings of Father Maximilian Kolbe, a Polish
Franciscan conventual, the founder of the Militia of the Immaculata,
who died in Auschwitz in 1941. The Friars Minor Conventual embarked
on a long and difficult *aggiornamento*: the revision of the constitutions,
begun in 1969, was not completed until 1985. In 1970, Fr Minelli and
another Franciscan conventual, Fr Gabriele Maria Pellettieri, obtained
permission from their superiors to try an "experiment" of renewed
Franciscan life based on a return to the traditional observances, "Franciscan community poverty" and the spirituality of Fr Maximilian Kolbe
(whose beatification process was nearing completion). On August 2, 1970,
they founded the *Casa Mariana*, near the shrine of Our Lady of Good
Counsel in Frigento. This *Casa Mariana* ("Marian House," the name that
the convents would bear) would become the mother house of the future
congregation of the Franciscan Friars of the Immaculate. A novitiate was
opened in 1971, the year of the beatification of Father Kolbe. The influx
of vocations allowed the rapid opening of other houses. In 1990, the
Franciscans of the Immaculate (FFI) were recognized as an institute of
diocesan right, and in 1998 as an institute of pontifical right. It is worth
noting that for a long time, in the houses of the congregation, Mass
was celebrated only according to the rite of Paul VI, in Italian or Latin.
It was only after the historic motu proprio of Benedict XVI (2007) that
Father Manelli, founder of the congregation, and some of his convents
returned to the traditional Mass. The interventions of the Holy See in this
congregation, from the end of that pontificate and during the following
pontificate, will be discussed in another chapter.

THE DOMINICANS

Yann Raison du Cleuziou, in his work dedicated to the politicization
of the Dominicans of the province of France or province of Paris – it
went from Le Havre to Strasbourg and from Lille to Dijon – in the years
1940-1970, has produced an exceptional sociological and historical
survey of the evolution and the crisis of the Dominican Order, even if
there is little mention of the liturgy. This study is limited to one of the
three French provinces of the Order, but it has several merits. On the
one hand, it brings to light the mechanisms of this evolution, which
led to an internal crisis with dramatic consequences: fifteen simple
professions in 1969, none in 1975, 1977 and 1979; eighty returns to the
lay state between 1967 and 1978. On the other hand, this study shows
that the crisis began decades before the Council, as it did among the
Capuchins and in many other congregations. Among Yann Raison du

Cleuziou's conclusions, it is worth noting "the extreme autonomy of the Province of France in relation to diocesan authorities" and also the authority and influence of the successive provincials who, at that time, took precedence over the exhortations and calls to order from the minister general whose "margin of maneuver was reduced."[27]

Yann Raizon de Cleuziou qualifies as "dissenting loyalties" the acts of resistance that occurred, at the beginning of the 1970s, in the convent of the Annunciation, in Paris, and in the convent of Nancy. These were Dominicans who, "in the name of their fidelity to the constitutions and to the tradition of the order," expressed their opposition to the positions and to certain decisions of the provincial and the provincial chapter. At the Annunciation convent, these were Fathers Auvray, Spitz, Lelong, and Lefevre; at Nancy, Fathers Maniere, Bonnet, and Chauvet. It would be erroneous to qualify them as "traditionalists," for they did not question the Council and the liturgical reform, although some of them, in articles or books, virulently questioned their implementation. For example, Father Serge Bonnet, in *À hue et à dia* (1974), strongly denounced "the avatars of clericalism under the Fifth Republic" and called into question "conciliar blackmail":

> Just yesterday, the Council of Trent was always to blame. Today, Vatican II sheds nothing but light. . . . Yesterday: "Rome has spoken," today: "The Council has decided."[28]

Father Maurice Lelong exercised his polemical verve in a *Lexicon de l'Église nouvelle* (1971) and wrote the religious column in *L'Aurore* in the early 1970s. In addition, several Dominicans from the Annunciation convent (Lelong, Auvray, Spitz) agreed to publish articles in *La Pensée catholique*, a review its opponents considered to be integrist from its very beginnings. The most assiduous collaborator was Father Spitz, who published in that review from 1974 until his death in 1982.

We will here mention, on the one hand, resistance on the part of individuals in the province of Paris and in the other provinces and, on the other hand, communities in the Dominican spirit founded by young men who did not wish to enter a Dominican Order that was, in their view, deviationist and decadent.

The most famous dissident in the Dominican Order was of course Father Bruckberger (1907-1998), who belonged to the province of Toulouse, but who lived a large part of his life outside the convent, in Paris and elsewhere. The man whom Georges Bernanos described

---

27 Yann Raison du Cleuziou, *De la contemplation à la contestation*, 314.
28 Serge Bonnet, *À hue et à dia. Les avatars du cléricalisme sous la Ve République* (Paris: Cerf, 1974), 176.

before the war as a "young predestined monk, with a soldier's will, the heart of a child and a poet," nicknamed "Bruck" in the Resistance, was a rebellious Dominican long before the Council, and was not short on flagrant contradictions:

> He upheld a demanding Christianity, yet was fascinated by worldly life; he venerated the Virgin and Mary Magdalene, yet succumbed to very carnal passions. With this, a good dose of pride, an extravagance considered as the expression of his freedom, an uncommon stubbornness, an inability to respect the duty of obedience connected with the monastic state. This led to numerous disputes with his hierarchy, to exile, disavowal, and quarantine.[29]

Traditionalists would forget his tumultuous past when, in his weekly columns in *L'Aurore*, in 1976 and 1977, he supported Archbishop Lefebvre and the occupation of Saint-Nicolas-du-Chardonnet, and spoke of his attachment to the Mass of Saint Pius V and his refusal of "the concealment of the Eucharistic mystery." In 1985, Dom Gérard invited him to deliver the sermon during the solemn Mass of Saint Madeleine, patron saint of the monastery of Le Barroux, and had it printed in a handsome edition.[30]

Of a completely different temperament and far more faithful to the rule of their order were three other Dominican figures, each of whom had a profound and lasting influence: Fathers Calmel, de Chivré and Guérard des Lauriers. In 1968, all three had signed the *Vademecum du catholique fidèle* written by Father Coache. All three had taken a position against the new Mass, as we have seen. But they did not maintain relations with each other and did not take concerted action. Father Calmel belonged to the Dominican province of Toulouse, and even though Father de Chivré and Father Guérard de Lauriers belonged to the same province of Paris, they had never resided in the same convent. In the early 1970s, Father Guérard de Lauriers had been living for several years in Etiolles in an independent house where his superiors allowed him to reside, and Father de Chivré lived at the house of Notre-Dame du Roc, in Normandy, which he had turned into an intellectual and spiritual center. The three Dominicans were all linked to Madiran and to *Itinéraires*. Calmel had begun contributing in 1958, and did so until his death in 1975. That same year, 1958, Jean Madiran had also asked Father de Chivré to write in the review, but the Minister General of the Dominicans had forbidden him to do so, though authorizing him to be the "theological advisor" of the review. Guérard des Lauriers did not begin to contribute to *Itinéraires*

---

29 Claude Jacquemart, "On l'appelait Bruck," *Valeurs actuelles* (September 22, 2011). See also Bernard and Bernadette Chovelon, *Bruckberger, l'enfant terrible* (Paris: Cerf, 2011).
30 Raymond-Léopold Bruckberger, *Sermon pour la Sainte-Madeleine* (Le Barroux: Éditions Sainte-Madeleine, 1986; 2nd ed., 2018).

until 1968, but only did so for a short time, his last article appearing in the December 1971 issue. Thereafter, his positions on the crisis of the Church distanced him from Jean Madiran and his review.

Beyond this there were two splits within the Dominican Order, each different in scope, in 1975 and 1977. Father Marie-Dominique Philippe, a professor of philosophy at the Catholic University of Fribourg (Switzerland), had ardently supported the foundations of Archbishop Lefebvre at their beginning, as we have seen. He soon distanced himself from them. In 1975, unable to obtain the Dominican Order's go-ahead to open a novitiate, he gathered his young disciples at the Cistercian abbey of Lérins, from which the Community of St. John was born in 1978, and which experienced a great expansion. But it cannot be considered a traditionalist community, since it called into question neither the teachings of the Second Vatican Council nor the new liturgy. The same is true of the monastic fraternity created by the Fathers Jean-Miguel Garrigues and Jean Legrez.[31] Dominicans of the province of Paris, they had first obtained their transfer to the province of Toulouse, where the rupture with the past was less flagrant. Then they left the Dominican Order in 1977 and founded, with other young religious, a monastic fraternity established in the parish of Saint-Jean-de-Malte in Aix-en-Provence. This fraternity, like the one they later established in Avignon and then in Lyon, cannot be qualified as traditionalist either, since neither the post-conciliar liturgy nor the teachings of Vatican II were called into question. Fathers Garrigues and Legrez returned to the Dominican Order in the 1990s.

There were also what might be called internal exiles: Father Tonneau of the province of Paris and Father Sineux of the province of Toulouse. Both had signed in 1968 the *Vademecum du catholique fidèle* written by Father Coache. Nevertheless, they did not leave their convent, all the while challenging their order's new orientations to the extent that they could. Father Sineux, a resident of the Bordeaux convent and a specialist in St. Thomas Aquinas, agreed to teach at the traditional Benedictine community of Dom Gérard in Bédoin, in the Vaucluse département. During his trips from Bordeaux to Bédoin, he would stop in Narbonne to celebrate the traditional Mass in a chapel set up at the initiative of François Cathala, a local vintner attached to Tradition. He was no longer able to have his books published, even by the Éditions du Cerf, a publishing house run by his Dominican confreres. He published his imposing *Sommaire théologique,* based on St. Thomas Aquinas (1969, in

---

31 Jean-Michel Garrigues, *Par des sentiers ressérrés. Itinéraire d'un religieux en des temps incertains* (Paris: Presses de la Renaissance, 2007), and, with Jean Legrez, *Moines dans l'assemblée des fidèles à l'époque des Pères. IVe-VIIIe siècles* (Paris: Beauchesne, 1997).

three volumes), at his own expense; it was with the neo-Dominicans of Avrillé that he had his last book published, *Les Lois du monde* (Éditions de la Nouvelle Aurore), in 1975, a few months before his death.

DOMINICAN TEACHING SISTERS

The congregation of the Sisters of the Holy Name of Jesus had been founded in Toulouse in 1800 to devote itself to the education of girls.[32] In 1886 it became affiliated with the Dominican Order. The congregation thoroughly revised its constitutions after the Second World War. Father Calmel, whom we have already met, was confessor and teacher at the congregation's novitiate and played an important part in drafting its new constitutions, together with Mother Hélène Jamet, the Prioress General. They revitalized the congregation in a Dominican spirit and in its teaching vocation. These new constitutions were approved by the Holy See in 1953. The congregation was now called the Congregation of the Dominican Teaching Sisters of the Holy Name of Jesus to emphasize its "special end": "A work of teaching and education according to the spirit of the Gospel." But in November 1954, following an apostolic visit, Father Calmel was dismissed from the congregation. This was not for moral failings, but because his influence was deemed harmful by the provincial authorities of the Dominican Order. Nevertheless, the two works he published in 1958, *École chrétienne renouvelée: L'Éducation des filles* and *École et sainteté*, extended his influence among the nuns and became reference works in the congregation.

In 1963, the new Prioress General, Mother Marie-Rose Tassy, who was imposed by Rome and by Archbishop Garrone of Toulouse rather than elected by the General Chapter, committed the Congregation to an *aggiornamento* corresponding to the spirit of the then ongoing Council. This led to divisions between what would later be called the "progressives" and the "traditionalists." The latter were in a large majority, as various consultations soon showed. In 1967, a new General Chapter elected Mother Anne-Marie Simoulin as Prioress General. She was not yet forty years old, and had to obtain a dispensation from the Holy See, which was granted. At that time, the Congregation had about twenty houses in the South of France, and about 180 nuns. As early as July 1967, Mother Simoulin "organized her government as a fight against what she would later call 'the deviations of the conciliar Church.'"[33] In 1969, through a request to the Congregation for Religious,

---

32 Sister Alice-Marie, *Histoire de la Congrégation du Saint-Nom-de-Jésus de Toulouse de 1800 à 1953* (Toulouse: Privat, 2006).
33 Sister Alice-Marie, *Rupture ou Fidélité. 1948-1975: une congrégation religieuse dans l'Église ébranlée* (Paris: Clovis, 2016), 176.

she obtained advice from Father Calmel for the nuns again, through correspondence and occasional visits. In December 1971, Mother Simoulin publicly expressed her rejection of the new Mass. The divisions within the congregation on this point, on educational practices, and on the *aggiornamento* of religious life, prompted her to appeal to Rome. An apostolic visitor was appointed in January 1972. The General Chapter scheduled for 1973 was postponed twice.

Mother Marie-François Dupouy, who had been prioress of the Saint Dominic school in Toulon, then mistress of the professed novices in Toulouse, suggested in January 1973 to the prioress general of the Congregation, Mother Anne-Marie Simoulin, that houses be established which would preserve the educational and liturgical traditions of the Dominican teaching sisters. She wrote: "I will specify that the first fidelity is to maintain the traditional liturgy and Ordo, the Latin Dominican Office, the traditional catechism, orthodox doctrinal teaching, and Christian education supported by pious sodalities."[34] At the end of 1973, Mother Simoulin agreed, and had the decision ratified by the congregational council. A property was found in Saint-Pré, not far from Brignoles. But in May 1974, following the apostolic visit, a decree of the Congregation for Religious dismissed Mother Simoulin and appointed a general administrator, Mother Marie-Rose Tassy, pending the general chapter and the election of a new prioress general. The General Administrator opposed the move to Saint-Pré. Mother Marie-François Dupouy and twenty other nuns overrode this ban, which seemed unjustified to them, and settled there in July 1974. Father Calmel, with his superiors' go-ahead, agreed to be their chaplain. Because of their disobedience, Mother Dupouy and all the professed nuns of the house of Saint-Pré were reduced to the lay state by a rescript from the Congregation of Religious dated May 24, 1975. A new congregation was formed, the Dominican Teaching Sisters of the Holy Name of Jesus and of the Immaculate Heart of Mary, which was to expand greatly. At the time of Mother Dupouy's death in 2014, the congregation numbered some 120 religious and 9 schools in France and Argentina.

For her part, Mother Simoulin and other Dominican teaching sisters tried to maintain the traditions of their congregation, both in the educational field and in liturgical and religious life. But in 1975, as they were about to be scattered in several houses, Mother Simoulin, eighteen other nuns, and two postulants regrouped in Fanjeaux on July 2, 1975, first residing at La Clarté-Dieu where a first school was opened. The

---

34 Marie-François Dupouy to Mother Anne-Marie Simoulin, Letter, January 1, 1973, quoted in Jean-Dominique Fabre, *Le Père Roger-Thomas Calmel* (Paris: Clovis, 2012), 562.

Congregation for Religious sanctioned them through a rescript dated June 7, 1976, which reduced them to the lay state.

Archbishop Lefebvre immediately lent them his support. On September 8, he received the religious vows of several novices and celebrated a Mass of thanksgiving for the twenty-five years of religious life of Mother Simoulin. It was then the "hot summer," when the Prelate of Écône had been suspended *a divinis* a few weeks earlier. The announcement of his coming to Fanjeaux had attracted the press and hundreds of onlookers, who had to stay outside the door. The local press reported that "a small aeroclub plane threw leaflets at the crowd, accusing Archbishop Lefebvre of supporting 'L'Action française,' but these leaflets, blown by the wind, fell into the surrounding countryside."[35] The Dominican province of Toulouse issued a communiqué to specify that the occupants of La Clarté-Dieu "are no longer Dominicans or religious sisters" and that since having been dispensed from their vows by the Holy See "they no longer have any link with the Dominican order and the term Dominican which is still abusively applied to them no longer corresponds to any reality."

The sisters ignored this and formed a new congregation, the Congregation of the Dominican Teaching Sisters of the Holy Name of Jesus of Fanjeaux. Beginning in August 1977, the new congregation received spiritual support from Father de Chivré. Until his death seven years later, while continuing to reside at Notre-Dame du Granit, he came to give spiritual conferences to the Dominican Teaching Sisters of Fanjeaux, to celebrate Mass and Confession, and to preside over the ceremonies of taking the veil and of profession. New houses and schools were opened as the congregation attracted a large number of vocations. By the time Mother Simoulin died, the congregation she had founded had fourteen houses in France, Germany and the United States and some two hundred sisters.

In a curious twist of history, the two foundresses, Mother Simoulin and Mother Dupouy, died within a day of each other, the first on June 16, 2014, the second on June 17. A month earlier, on May 26, the foundress of another Dominican teaching congregation died: Mother Marie-Dominique. After the war she had founded, with Father Berto, the Congregation of the Dominican Sisters of the Holy Spirit. She had not experienced the torments the two others had.

THE FRATERNITY OF SAINT DOMINIC

Father Guérard des Lauriers, who took an essential part in the drafting of the *Ottaviani Intervention*, as we have seen, also played a

---

35 *Sud*, September 8, 1976.

determining role in the birth of two Dominican-inspired communities, though without the consent of Dominican Order authorities.

This decision to bypass the authorities of the Order, to which he still belonged, came from the doctrinal position he had begun to develop in 1976. At that time, residing *extra conventum* at Étiolles with the agreement of his provincial superior, he regularly came to give theology courses at the seminary in Écône. Archbishop Lefebvre had proceeded to ordinations to major orders (diaconate and subdiaconate) without the necessary dimissorial letters for the first time in April 1976, as we shall see. In order to justify and support this decision, which was contrary to canon law, and to explain in a more general way the crisis of the Church, Father Guérard des Lauriers privately expounded the thesis that the Pope, although validly elected and therefore Pope *materialiter* ("materially"), was no longer Pope *formaliter* ("formally") because he no longer exercised his universal magisterium. This is what would later be called the "Cassiciacum thesis," named after the publication in which it was first presented to the public in 1979.

At the end of the 1970s, Father Guérard des Lauriers assisted at the birth of two *ex nihilo* communities of Dominican spirituality.

The first of these stemmed from a youth organization officially founded in 1970: the MJCF (*Mouvement de la jeunesse catholique de France*).[36] The founder and first president of the MJCF, Christian Marquant, dates the effective birth of the movement to September 29, 1967, but it was not officially registered until June 8, 1970.[37] The purpose of the movement was to welcome and "form in a spirit of faith in the light of the teachings of the Church the young men and women who so desired and to help them to live in this spirit." This foundation was a reaction to the Catholic Youth Action movements that existed at the time (JOC, JEC, JAC, etc.)[38] and which, according to Marquant and his friends, were unfaithful to their mission. The movement was organized in "teams" led by "animators" and the activities proposed were diverse: "courses," conferences, study sessions during the year, summer and winter camps, and retreats. These activities allowed the "four foundations" of the movement to be lived out: "Prayer, friendship, formation, and action." Formation also took place through the movement's magazine, *Savoir et servir*, which began to appear in June 1970 in the form of a modest bulletin. The motto

36 *MJCF: 50 ans d'aventure missionnaire*, special issue of the review *Savoir et servir* 81 (December 2020), 198 pages.
37 Interview in *Paix Liturgique*, September 2017.
38 JOC: "Jeunesse ouvrière chrétienne" ("Young Christian Workers"); JEC: "Jeunesse étudiante chrétienne" ("Young Christian Students"); JAC: "Jeunesse agricole chrétienne" ("Young Agricultural Christians").

of the movement – *Christus semper et ubique imperat* ("Christ reigns always and everywhere") – indicated a missionary orientation. The goal of the MJCF was to "form a Christian laity that is aware of its role, educated, and active." One of the first actions of the movement was against abortion, which, at the time, was not authorized in France, but which was widely practiced in a clandestine way, and which various movements, associations, and lobbies were working to have legalized. As early as 1970 there was a poster campaign and also support for movements opposed to abortion, in particular by providing security for the first congress of *Laissez-les-vivre* [an anti-abortion movement – *Translator*].

The first organization born from the MJCF was the Young Christians for the Respect of Life, which became Youth for Life ("Jeunes pour la vie," JPV). The MJCF was to have a diverse progeny. Former members of the MJCF were, in the 1990s, at the origin of other movements or associations active in various fields: *Domus Christiani* (for couples), *Renaissance catholique*, *Oremus* and then *Paix liturgique* (for the traditional Mass), CIEL (liturgical studies), and others. The MJCF was also a breeding ground for priestly and religious vocations: 147 male vocations and 209 female vocations, according to the census drawn up by the movement for its fiftieth anniversary.[39]

Of the two foundations in the Dominican spirit which will interest us here, nine religious of the Fraternity of Saint Dominic of Avrillé and two religious of the Fraternity of Saint Vincent Ferrer of Chémeré would come from the MJCF.

On August 22, 1974, the movement had purchased a former priory of the Grandmont order in La Haye-aux-Bonshommes, near Avrillé, in Anjou, to develop its activities there. A few months later, on November 11, 1974, some boys from the movement, who felt attracted to the Dominican religious life, decided, while remaining with their families and continuing their studies, "to follow a small rule of life: recitation of a part of the office each day, Mass as often as possible, quarterly retreats, etc."[40] They were already planning to make a life of their own, but they did not know what to do. Were they already planning to make the former priory of Avrillé their future convent? Probably not. The buildings were the property of the movement and required very substantial work. The young members of the movement enthusiastically undertook the work during their vacations, but without the necessary knowledge and authorizations (the priory is a registered historical

---

39 *MJCF: 50 ans*, 191-92.
40 *Dossier de présentation de la Fraternité Saint-Dominique* (Avrillé, photocopy, November 1987), personal archives.

monument). To help finance the work, the MJCF started publishing. Thus, in 1974, the Éditions de la Nouvelle Aurore was born, with its headquarters in Paris but its printing plant in Avrillé. Thus, in 1975, eight works were published: the work of Father Sineux, already mentioned; *Las Casas, Apostle of the Indians*, by another Dominican, Father André-Vincent; and reprints of classic works of traditional Catholic thought, notably *Liberalism Is a Sin*, by Félix Sarda y Salvany (with a preface by Archbishop Lefebvre) and two works by Louis Jugnet.

In October 1975, the small group of young men attracted to religious life – there were eight of them, including the founder and president of the MJCF, Christian Marquant – decided to move into a house in Clamart. Their ambition was to "lay down some markers with a view to resuming a completely Dominican life, that is to say, in a convent," "to found a Dominican community of exact observance, since to our knowledge there is no longer a convent that has kept the traditional liturgy."[41] They made this observation after having met Dominicans from different provinces and having gone as far as the convent of Bologna where it had been possible to maintain a traditional Dominican way of life, but where the "new Mass" was being celebrated.

The small group lived in a house that belonged to the Passionists. The Passionists, thinking they were hosting peaceful Catholic students, were unaware that they were hosting a nascent traditionalist community. Each member had a room on the second floor, and in the basement they had set up their kitchen, their refectory... and a clandestine chapel.

> Some priests came to celebrate Mass, in secret. So, for example, Father Emmanuel du Chalard [of the Society of St. Pius X] was already vested when the Passionists showed up. The father was rushed into a cupboard with chalice and paten, while the young people settled down around a glass. Greetings and chit-chat with the Passionists, who left without noticing anything out of the ordinary....[42]

While still laymen – some still students, others already engaged in professional life – they followed a simple rule of religious life. They were supported by Father Guérard des Lauriers, who came to give them classes, give lectures, celebrate Mass, and give them material assistance. They also received spiritual support from Father Reynaud, the chaplain of the MJCF, and from other religious, notably Father Eugène de Villeurbanne and Dom Gérard, who kept up a correspondence with some of them and occasionally visited the group.

41 Ibid., 5.
42 *MJCF: 50 ans*, 88.

The small community experienced its first crisis in the early months of 1976, when the leader of the group, who was also the president of the MJCF, had to leave, according to his successor, "because of serious failings affecting both his personal life and his work in the movement."[43] It was essentially his imprudent management of the MJCF that was at fault. He was replaced as president of the MJCF by Jean-François Chassagne, who was also a member of the Clamart group.

Father Eugène preached a long retreat to the group in January 1977 at the Maison Lacordaire. His thirteen preaching sessions dealt with the foundations of Christian life and of religious life. The following October, three of them, Guillaume Devillers, Jean-Marc Rulleau, and Philippe Roulon, decided to commit themselves further by founding a "Dominican community of exact observance." They settled in Camaret-sur-Aigues, about thirty kilometers from the priory of Bédoin, in order to benefit from the advice and spiritual and material assistance of Dom Gérard.

On October 7, 1977, on the feast of Our Lady of the Rosary, a feast dear to the Dominicans, the "Fraternité Saint-Dominique" was officially founded. On the following December 8, in the presence of Dom Gérard, Father Guérard des Lauriers clothed them in the Dominican habit. The ceremony took place in the private chapel of Saint-Ariès, in Bollène. Guillaume Devillers became Brother Marie-Réginald, Jean-Marc Rulleau became Brother Marie-Thomas and Philippe Roulon became Brother Marie-Dominique. Father Guérard des Lauriers had no authority to give the Dominican habit to aspirants to the religious life. It was therefore improper, and in contradiction with canon law, for these religious to have called themselves "Dominicans." Another Dominican attached to Tradition, Father de Chivré, had refused to give the Dominican habit without his superiors' authorization:

> The Father will never accept anyone's entering the Order as an intruder. Since he was unable to obtain the power to give the beautiful habit of St. Dominic to potential aspirants, he will never approve or accept anyone's putting on the habit without having received it from the Order itself, through the hands of its legally elected superiors.[44]

Father de Chivré's biographer also reports: "I believe I have the right to say that these pseudo-Dominican pretensions literally undermined the last years of the Father; he was bruised in his deepest attachments." At that time – December 1977 – Father Guérard des Lauriers was already defending his sedevacantist-leaning thesis (i.e., that Paul VI is

---

43 *Lettre aux amis du MJCF* 1 (1976): 1.
44 Michel Simoulin, *Le Chouan de Dieu, Carnets spirituels* 2 (November 2004): 43.

pope *materialiter* but not *formaliter*) and he refused to recognize his pontifical authority. The young men to whom he had given the religious habit shared this position. This is evidenced by an impromptu visit made to them by a Dominican from the Paris province, Father Philippe Dagonet. They were now established at Fonsalette, about ten kilometers from Camaret. Father Dagonet, who introduced himself to them as a "conciliar Dominican," was astonished to see "the Dominican coat of arms and an inscription, 'Prieuré Sainte-Catherine,' on the door of the house." He was able to have long conversations with them; he was invited to participate in a service and to have a meal with them. He gave an account of this visit and of their exchange in a long report to his superiors.[45] They presented themselves as religious who were very attached to the ancient customs of Dominican life. Conscious of having taken the habit and the name of Dominicans illegitimately, they justified themselves: "Faced with the deficiency of the Church and of the Dominican Order, we were led to make decisions of this kind following our conscience, with the approval of Father Guérard, of course." With summary formulas, if we are to believe Father Dagonet, they challenged both the Second Vatican Council and the Pope:

> You are no longer the Catholic Church. It is we who preserve her memory.... Since the Pope endorses this entire modernist wave, which was condemned by his predecessors, he is no longer the Pope. For us, the Holy See has been vacant since the appearance of John XXIII.

A month later, three other members of the Clamart group joined them and on October 14, Father Guérard des Lauriers conferred the Dominican habit on one of them, Jean-François Chassagne, second president of the MJCF, who became Brother Innocent-Marie. All of them left for Écône the next day, where they began their ecclesiastical studies. Two of them, Brother Marie-Réginald (Devillers) and Brother Marie-Thomas (Rulleau) left the Dominican habit to enter the Society of St. Pius X. In September 1979, the three religious of the community, who had not yet taken their vows and were pursuing their studies in Écône, came to La Haye-aux-Bonshommes. This was to showcase their future convent, still in the process of being restored, during an open house. The event, which had some eighty visitors, attracted the attention of the local press and the diocese of Angers (which discreetly sent a priest to report on the day's

---

45 Philippe Dagonet, *Compte rendu d'une visite au "séminaire" du Père Guérard des Lauriers*, September 4, 1978, nine type-written pages, Archives of the Dominican Province of France, Guérard des Lauriers collection (copy).

events).[46] The Dominican province of Lyon, on which Anjou depends, published a communiqué from Father Moreau, prior provincial, to specify that "these people are in no way Dominicans of the well-known Order. They have not made a vow to the Master of the Order nor to the friar provincial; they have not undergone any recognized novitiate. It is distressing that such serious ambiguities should be maintained in the name of a saint who devoted himself to the search for and the manifestation of the truth."[47] Since the New Dominican community had broken with Father Guérard des Lauriers in 1978, it was Archbishop Lefebvre who, by virtue of the "supplied jurisdiction" thesis, received the religious profession of the New Dominicans. And on June 29, 1982, he ordained Brothers Marie-Dominique and Innocent-Marie as priests. Two days later, the two new priests and six brothers moved to Avrillé where the restoration work was well underway but far from complete.

THE FRATERNITY OF SAINT VINCENT FERRER

At the end of the 1970s, another community in the mold of Dominican spirituality was born. The founder was a young priest, Father Olivier de Blignières. After "a period of rebellion and atheism"[48] (November 1965-March 1970), brilliant studies in mathematics, physics, and astrophysics at the University of Paris-X-Orsay (1969-1972) and a conversion during Holy Week in 1970 at the Benedictine Abbey of Maylis, where he had followed the Spiritual Exercises of St. Ignatius, he entered the Benedictine monastery of St. Joseph, which Dom Augustin Joly had just founded in Martigny, Switzerland, on August 26, 1972. He made his religious profession there on December 8, 1973. He collaborated in the writing of *Une fausse contre-révolution: L'Office*, a very critical study of Jean Ousset, and the successive editions of *Pour qu'Il règne*, which Dom Augustin Joly published in 1975. Brother Louis-Marie de Blignières left the monastery on September 29, 1975 to join the seminary of Écône, in his fourth year, and to enter the Society of Saint Pius X. At Écône, he discovered the thought of St. Thomas Aquinas, and the great Dominican figure, St. Vincent Ferrer; and he was strongly influenced by the personality and teaching of Father Guérard des Lauriers, still a professor of philosophy at the seminary. In December 1976, Father de Blignières,

---

46 "Porte ouverte à La Haye aux Bonhommes," September 9, 1979, four unsigned typewritten pages, Archives of the Dominican Province of France, Guérard des Lauriers collection (copy).

47 Communiqué published by Bishop Orchampt of Angers, who added that "these pseudo-Dominicans have nothing to do with the Order of Saint Dominic," *Semaine religieuse d'Angers* (September 9, 1979): 579.

48 Louis-Marie de Blignières, *Ma vocation* (unpubl., 2020).

by now a subdeacon, was expelled from the Society of Saint Pius X. On the recommendation of Jean Madiran,[49] whom he had been reading for a long time and of whom his brother was then the closest collaborator (under the pen name of Hugues Kéraly), he had contacted Dom Gérard, prior of the monastery of Bédoin mentioned above, in March 1977. The young Father de Blignières became an oblate regular of the Sainte-Madeleine priory. Archbishop Lefebvre agreed to ordain him as a deacon in 1977 in Carpentras, then as a priest, a few months later, in Chatelperron. Dom Gérard, without trying to attract Fr de Blignières to his monastery, and respectful of his vocation to theological studies and preaching, favored his installation in Fonsalette, near Lagarde-Paréol, the following September. A large house had been put at his disposal by a friend of the monastery. Bruno Schaeffer, who in 1975 had founded a scouting movement in Paris, the Scouts of Notre-Dame de France,[50] and who was preparing for the priesthood, joined him. Under the name of the priory of Notre-Dame de Fonsalette, independent of both the Society of St. Pius X and the monastery of Bédoin, a small group of young clerics was formed around Fathers de Blignières and Schaeffer who shared a radical vision of the crisis of the Church, under the influence of Father Guérard des Lauriers's theses on the "formal vacancy of the Apostolic See." Priests ordained by Archbishop Lefebvre in Écône, Fathers Guépin and Seuillot, ordained in 1977, and Fathers Lucien and Belmont, ordained in 1978, came for several years to the priory of Notre-Dame de Fonsalette to give retreats and to preach the Spiritual Exercises of Saint Ignatius. Each of them was to follow a different trajectory thereafter.

In 1978-1979, Father de Blignières served at the church of Saint-Nicolas-du-Chardonnet, gave a course in Thomistic spirituality from January 1979, and began to preach "Rosary Retreats." In June 1979, he founded the Society of Saint Thomas Aquinas in Paris; its purpose was "to restore Thomistic culture through the formation and education of young people and adults, especially in philosophical, theological, and historical matters."[51] In September 1979, with the support of Mgr Ducaud-Bourget and Dom Gérard, he founded the Saint-Thomas-d'Aquin priory of studies in Chémeré, in Mayenne, with some students attracted by religious life in the Dominican spirit. As one of the original members of the community later said:

---

49 Louis-Marie de Blignières in conversation with the author, November 27, 2011.
50 *Journal Officiel* (December 13, 1975): 12781. The movement settled in Fonsalette in May 1980, *Journal Officiel* (May 28, 1980): 4701.
51 Official registration at the Prefecture on June 5, 1979, *Journal Officiel* (June 20, 1979): 5155.

> We wanted to live the Dominican life with the classical means
> of tradition: conventual life (enclosure, silence, wearing the
> habit, monastic observances at the refectory and the chapter
> of faults, etc.); study based on St. Thomas Aquinas, not only
> historically, but as a teacher of truth; liturgy of the Dominican
> tradition for Mass and the Divine Office. But we were born in a
> context of crisis. None of the existing Dominican provinces could
> guarantee us this framework. So we made a new foundation of
> sons of Saint Dominic.[52]

The priory had a clearly doctrinal and apostolic purpose. Fr de
Blignières wrote that this foundation

> responds to an urgent necessity, in these times of great peril for
> the faith: to arm the intelligence in the service of God.... Souls
> troubled by the collapse of the teaching Church and the universal
> scuttling of the faith, do not, today, aspire only to the restoration
> of worship and the sacraments. They need to return to the tried
> and true principles of traditional spirituality and doctrine.[53]

The priory was to devote itself to study and offer formation sessions,
organize retreats, and also "assist in the ministry of traditional parishes."
For nearly two years, Father Guérard des Lauriers regularly came to
Chémeré to guide the young community's first steps in Dominican life
through courses, retreats, and advice.[54] All at the time held the thesis
of the formal vacancy of the Holy See. On December 22, 1979, Father
Guérard des Lauriers came to give Father de Blignières the Dominican
habit, as a regular tertiary. On January 17, 1981, he was still present when
the latter made his religious profession, but as he was aware of the non-
canonical status of his community, Father de Blignières pronounced only
private perpetual vows, awaiting a future confirmation by the Church.
On the following May 7, the other members of the small community,
Brothers Dominique-Marie de Saint-Laumer, Bernard-Marie Laisney,
and Thomas-Marie de Bazelaire, made their religious profession under
the same conditions. Unlike the religious of Avrillé, although they wore
the white habit received as tertiaries, they did not claim to belong to
the Order of Friars Preachers (OP), but to the Dominican tradition and
spirituality. We shall see in another chapter how they distanced themselves from the positions of Guérard des Lauriers, then the long road
that allowed them to enter into communion with the Holy See.

---

52 Fr Dominique-Marie de Saint-Laumer, interview in *L'Homme nouveau* (April 9, 2016).
53 "Pour la fondation d'un prieuré d'études," *Itinéraires* 234 (June 1979): 259-60.
54 L.-M. de Blignières, "*In memoriam*: le Père Guérard des Lauriers, o.p.," *Sedes Sapi-*
entiae 24 (Spring 1988): 23.

CHAPTER 9

Archbishop Lefebvre, from the "Declaration" to the Suspension *a divinis*

IN THE EARLY 1970S THE INTERNATIONAL SEMINARY of Écône was attracting more and more vocations (95 seminarians present at the beginning of the 1973 academic year). Criticism of the "wildcat seminary" was multiplying in the French episcopate, and found echoes in Rome and in the press. *Le Monde* noted that the seminary of Écône "is recruiting quite well, which is an achievement in the present situation. But the future priests who are educated there have received a formation such that very few dioceses are willing to take them on."[1] The Jesuit Louis de Vaucelles, in an article devoted to the vocations crisis, recalled that "the episcopate firmly excludes the return to a type of preparation for the priesthood that is considered outdated" and "rejected the solution advocated by Archbishop Marcel Lefebvre in his seminary at Écône."[2]

While he was rejected, on the whole, by the bishops of France by 1971-1972, Archbishop Lefebvre did receive the support of priests and theologians who were espousing positions far more radical than his own. This was the case of those who were soon to be called "sedevacantists." This thesis was first developed in Mexico by Father Sáenz y Arriaga.[3] He was a former Jesuit who had been incardinated into the Archdiocese of Mexico City in 1958 and who, during the Council, denounced the progressive and Jewish influences he thought were being exerted on the assembly: *El antisemitismo y el concilio ecumenico: que es el progresismo?* (1964). In 1969 and 1970, he published two books against the new "Protestantized" Mass. Then in 1971, in *La Nueva Iglesia Montiniana*, he accused Paul VI of schism, heresy, apostasy, and perjury, as well as of being simoniac and Judaizing. He concluded that the Roman Catholic Church was "acephalous." On December 20, 1971, Cardinal

---

1 *Le Monde*, December 6, 1973.
2 Louis de Vaucelles, "L'avenir des communautés et des ministères," *Les Études* (January 1974): 116.
3 See the bibliography of Fr Sáenz in the *Dictionnaire biographique* provided in Chiron, *Histoire des traditionalistes* (Paris: Tallandier, 2022), 552.

Miranda, the Archbishop of Mexico City, issued a decree suspending him *a divinis* and excommunicating him. Father Sáenz contested the penalties imposed on him, and in 1973 he developed his thesis on the vacancy of the Holy See in *Sede Vacante. Paulo VI no es legitimo papa* (1973). In France, he was in contact with Father Barbara and Élisabeth Gerstner, with whom he founded World Alliance PERC (*Pro Ecclesia Romana Catholica*), which organized pilgrimages to Rome in 1971 and 1973. From 1976 onwards, Father Barbara maintained his own brand of sedevacantism in lectures and magazines.[4]

Other priests who were in contact with Archbishop Lefebvre held sedevacantist opinions, but as long as they did not try to spread them in the SSPX or to convince him personally, he did not break with them. It was in 1979 that he had to take a public position on the subject, as we shall see.

A COMPLAINT IS SENT TO THE HOLY FATHER

Archbishop Lefebvre was soon fond of saying that he was not "the leader of the traditionalists." At that time, he wrote to Father André: "I do not want to be considered a leader anywhere, except in my seminary."[5] The Prelate of Écône encouraged or advised priests, communities or lay people who might ask his opinion on this or that initiative or project, but he did not try to impose his point of view. Jean Madiran directed his review *Itinéraires* with complete independence, even though he would soon give decisive support to the founder of the SSPX during his "condemnation." It was without consulting Archbishop Lefebvre that he addressed a public "complaint" to the Pope, which later gained the support of priests and lay personalities.

In 1970, as we have seen, Madiran became involved in the struggle to maintain the traditional Mass, by publishing several *Declarations* by theologians and a translation of the *Ottaviani Intervention* in *Itinéraires*. In the following years, he had continued to publish articles on the subject, convinced, with Louis Salleron, that "the crisis of the Mass is at the heart of the crisis of the Church." It should be noted that he allowed divergent practical positions to be expressed – what he called the "Salleron line," the "Una Voce line" and the

---

4 On the different sedevacantist theses, the reference is Cyrille Dounot, "Paul VI hérétique? La déposition du pape dans le discours traditionaliste," in C. Dounot, N. Warenbourg, B. Bernabé, eds, *La Déposition du pape hérétique. Lieux théologiques, historiques, modèles canoniques, enjeux institutionnels* (Sceaux: Mare & Martin, 2019), 131-65.
5 Archbishop Lefebvre to Fr Michel André, Letter, July 1, 1972, quoted in C. Mouton-Raimbault, *Un prêtre vrai. Le père André*, 422.

"Calmel line" – although they were united on the doctrinal essentials.[6]

The year 1972 was when Jean Madiran had a falling out with Jean Ousset over the Mass, although he never broke with him. He had participated in all the yearly international congresses organized by *L'Office* in Lausanne. These congresses, which lasted three days, gathered several thousand people from France and other countries. Each year Jean Madiran gave a talk on a subject related to the theme of the conference. After the new Mass was made obligatory, Jean Ousset refused to commit *L'Office* to the fight for maintaining the traditional Mass. If he "does not want to be drawn into the liturgical quarrel, it is because he believes that his work is and must remain civic."[7] This position divided the adherents and friends of the Office. The question arose about the celebration of Masses during the annual congress. At first, Jean Ousset thought he could solve it by saying that each priest who came to Lausanne would choose to celebrate Mass according to the rite dictated by his conscience. The 8th Congress of *L'Office*, scheduled for April 29 to May 1, 1972, was to have the theme "Strength and Violence." Jean Ousset had asked Jean Madiran, as he did every year, to give a talk on this theme. Madiran, during a meeting with Jean Ousset, had accepted, putting forward three conditions: that the Masses celebrated during the congress be celebrated only according to the traditional rite, that in his talk on violence he could give as an example the violence committed by the bishops "in liturgical, exegetical, and catechetical matters," and that Jean Ousset would preside over the session at which he would present his talk. After giving it some thought, the latter, "in spite of the desire of my friendship," he wrote, did not accept these three requirements and repeated his refusal "to engage *L'Office* in the present liturgical and exegetical combat."[8] Jean Madiran did not attend the 1972 Congress, and never returned, although he maintained his friendship with Jean Ousset, and expressed his esteem for the political and civic action of *L'Office*.

A few months later, it was regarding precisely this violence done to Catholics "in liturgical, exegetical, and catechetical matters" that Jean Madiran addressed a petition to the Pope. On October 27, 1972, he addressed a letter to Paul VI, which he would make public only several months later.[9] The first words were a threefold plea: "Holy Father, give

---

6 Jean Madiran, "La Messe, état de la question," *Itinéraires* 167 (November 1972): 10-37. This article was to go through several emended and enlarged offprint editions (fifth edition in 1976).

7 Cyril Duchateau, *La Cité catholique et l'Office (1979-1982)*, Master's thesis in religious history, Paris-IV-Sorbonne university, June 1997, 36.

8 Jean Ousset to Jean Madiran, Letter, July 9, 1971, Jean Madiran archives.

9 *Itinéraires* 169 (January 1973): 2-6.

us back the Scriptures, the catechism, and the Mass." Scripture is "now falsified by the mandatory versions that the new catechism and the new liturgy seek to impose," the new official catechisms "no longer teach the three things needful for salvation," while the new Mass has eclipsed the traditional Mass. He asked the pope to confirm "in their faith and in their just rights the priests and laity who, in spite of the foreign occupation of the Church by the party of apostasy, faithfully keep Holy Scripture, the Roman catechism, the Catholic Mass."

Rather than having this complaint signed by personalities simply adding their names to his, he published in *Itinéraires*, throughout 1973, a series of texts in which the authors gave their approval to the letter to Paul VI, and added their reasons. Thus, after Jean Madiran, twenty-five personalities joined his complaint, notably the philosophers Marcel De Corte and Thomas Molnar, Louis Salleron, Jacques Vier, professor at the University of Rennes and literary critic at *L'Homme nouveau*, Father Coache, Luce Quenette, founder of the school of La Péraudiere, Édith Delamare, the religious columnist of *Rivarol* and *Monde et Vie*, Éric de Saventhem of *Una Voce*, Hugues Kéraly, then the closest collaborator of Jean Madiran in *Itinéraires*, Gustave Corçao, and Jacques Trémolet de Villers, of *L'Office*.[10]

Jean Madiran maintained his threefold complaint to the end of Paul VI's pontificate, and was to repeat it under subsequent pontificates – not without seeing some of his "complaints" satisfied in part.

AN APOSTOLIC VISITATION

For his part, Archbishop Lefebvre publicly set out his criticism of the Second Vatican Council and of the "new Mass" in increasingly radical addresses that attracted large crowds: in November 1972, in Rennes; in March 1973 in Paris, at the Mutualité, on the initiative of the Union of Independent Intellectuals (*Union des intellectuels indépendants*) and the Club of French Culture (*Club de la culture française*). In January 1974, under the title *Un évêque parle* ("A Bishop Speaks"), he published his writings and speeches since 1963. At the initiative of his brother Michel, he presented the book at a large conference in his native town, Tourcoing, on January 30, in the presence of the town mayor.

He did not consider himself the "leader of the traditionalists" and rejected the term. In Tourcoing, he said:

---

10 Jean Madiran's Letter to Paul VI, enlarged with new explanations and considerations, as well as the responses of the twenty-five personalities, would ultimately be published under the title *Réclamation au Saint-Père* (Paris: Nouvelles éditions latines, 1974).

> Certainly, I can only encourage all those who work for the defense
> of the Faith, for Catholic conservation. That is why I sometimes
> encourage these movements, but I cannot for all that be linked
> to any of them; I insist on keeping total independence. [11]

The question arose because the ebullient Father Coache, [12] who
had already bought the Maison Lacordaire in Flavigny-sur-Ozerain, as
we have seen, had just acquired the former minor seminary of the
Diocese of Dijon in the same village, and proposed to open a minor
seminary and junior high school there, whose young students, if they
persisted in their vocation, were then to be sent to the seminary of
Écône. Archbishop Lefebvre had to clarify:

> I have nothing to do with the purchase of the minor seminary
> in Flavigny: it was Father Coache who took the initiative. He
> asked me if I encouraged him, and I told him that indeed, there
> was a lack of minor seminaries in France at the moment, and
> that if there was a good minor seminary, I could only rejoice.

Sometime before the opening of the seminary, Bishop Decourtray
of Dijon published a long communiqué in which he spoke of his past
dealings with Father Coache, and issued the following warning:

> The institution called "Petit Séminaire Saint-Curé-d'Ars de Flavi-
> gny" is not approved by the Holy See, nor by the French episco-
> pate, nor by the Bishop of Dijon. Its superior and its teachers have
> not been appointed by any qualified ecclesiastical authority. [13]

The seminary opened in October 1974, with thirteen students, but
was closed at the end of the first term by order of the academic district
supervisor for lack of qualified personnel.

In Écône, diocesan Bishop Nestor Adam was increasingly concerned,
and distanced himself from the seminary at Écône, to the point of
denying having authorized its opening. At the beginning of 1973, he
wrote to Cardinal Garrone, the prefect of the Congregation for Catholic
Education, on which seminaries depended: "Without my permission,
the pre-seminary became a seminary; I had to accept a *fait accompli*." [14]

---

11 *Un évêque parle*, 237.
12 On February 8, 1973, he had been given a suspended sentence of three years in
prison for "church purification" operations in two churches in Rennes, on June 8,
1972 and March 23, 1973. He had also been arrested, along with forty-five layman, as
Mass came to a close at the Church of Saint-Germain-l'Auxerrois in Paris, where those
arrested had come to protest the exhibition in that church of a work by the sculptor
Roger Bezombes depicting Christ crucified on a wheel.
13 Bishop Decourtray, Communiqué of August 15, 1974, published in *Église en Côte-d'Or*
(September 13, 1974) and *DC* (October 6, 1974): 847-48.
14 Bishop Nestor Adam to Cardinal Garrone, Letter, February 21, 1973, quoted by B.
Tissier de Mallerais, *Marcel Lefebvre*, 476.

He asked the Holy See for a "clarification." On the following March 17, he withdrew his support for Archbishop Lefebvre and his seminary. He wrote to him:

> The Mass of Paul VI is obligatory.... I cannot put up with the formation of a sect in the diocese.... All the history of the Church teaches us that true reformers... do not withdraw themselves from obedience.[15]

The foundation of a house in Albano, near Rome, in January 1974 (with the agreement of the diocesan bishop) and the project of founding a seminary in the United States, in Armada, caused as much concern as had Archbishop Lefebvre's opposition to the "new Mass." Bishop Adam, on whom Écône depended, and Bishop Pierre Mamie, on whom the Society of St. Pius X depended, were received in Rome on April 26 by the heads of the congregations concerned (Cardinal Garrone, prefect of the Congregation for Catholic Education, Cardinal Wright, prefect of the Congregation for the Clergy, and Archbishop Mayer, secretary of the Congregation for Religious). Archbishop Lefebvre was then summoned to Fribourg by Bishop Mamie on May 4. On June 23, the three dicastery heads involved (Cardinals Garrone, Wright, and Tabera) decided to subject the seminary at Écône to an apostolic visitation, a canonical visitation carried out by order of the Pope.

The visitation took place from November 11 to 13, 1974, and was conducted by two Belgian prelates, Msgr Albert Descamps, secretary of the Biblical Commission, and Msgr Guillaume Onclin, assistant secretary of the Commission for the revision of the Code of Canon Law. According to the testimonies of some seminarians and Archbishop Lefebvre himself, the two apostolic visitors scandalized the seminarians by making "theologically questionable remarks to them. They thought the ordination of married men was normal and inevitable, they did not admit that the truth was immutable, and they expressed doubts concerning the physical reality of Christ's Resurrection. They never went to chapel."[16] The report written by the two visitors is not available to historians, who must be satisfied with the testimonies from one side only.

Archbishop Lefebvre needed to travel to Rome in the following days for various visits. While in Albano, he wrote a "Declaration" dated November 21. He was subject to a strong backlash on account of it. He read it out to the professors and seminarians of Écône on the

---

15 Bp Nestor Adam to Archbishop Marcel Lefebvre, Letter, March 17, 1973, Tissier de Mallerais, *Marcel Lefebvre*, 476.
16 Ibid., 478-79 and minutes of the March 3, 1975 meeting in Yves Montagne, *"L'Évêque suspens." Mgr Lefebvre* (Rome: Catholic Laymen's League, 1977), 67.

following December 2, but it was soon known and spread abroad, first by Father Barbara who published it as a supplement to his review *Forts dans la Foi.*[17]

The "Declaration" started with a dichotomy:

> With our whole heart, with our whole soul do we adhere to Catholic Rome, guardian of the Catholic faith and of the traditions necessary to maintaining that faith, to Eternal Rome, mistress of wisdom and of truth.
>
> We refuse, however, and have always refused to follow the Rome of neo-modernist and neo-Protestant tendencies that clearly revealed itself in the Second Vatican Council and, after the Council, in all the reforms resulting from it.

The expression "all the reforms" shocked his Roman interlocutors.

The prelate of Écône was openly declaring his refusal of "the new Mass," just as he refused "the new Catechism, the new priesthood, the new seminaries, the new universities, the charismatic and pentecostal Church, all things that are opposed to orthodoxy as well as to the perennial Magisterium."

Even before any sanctions or decisions were taken against the seminary of Écône, Archbishop Lefebvre preemptively refused them, stating:

> Without any rebellion, bitterness, or resentment we continue our work of priestly formation under the lodestar of the perennial magisterium of all time, convinced that we cannot render a greater service to the Holy Catholic Church, to the Sovereign Pontiff, and to future generations.

Later, he would on several occasions grant that this "Declaration" had been "written in a mood of undoubtedly excessive indignation,"[18] but he would never redact or retract it. At Écône, the text aroused the enthusiasm of many seminarians on the spot, but it concerned the director, Father Gottlieb, and most of the professors. Christian Dumoulin, professor of Church history, felt that "Archbishop Lefebvre, by this declaration, has signed his own condemnation"; "Archbishop Lefebvre does not have the intelligence his work requires," judged Father Georges Salleron, one of Louis Salleron's sons.[19] Only Father Aulagnier, professor of Sacred Scripture and vice-rector of the seminary, was not

---

17 *Forts dans la foi* 37 (1975), supplement. Jean Madiran, with Archbishop Lefebvre's approval, published an "authentic and unabridged version" of it in *Itinéraires* 189 (January 1975): 5-8.

18 Archbishop Lefebvre, *Relation sur la manière dont la commission des trois cardinaux a procédé* (May 30, 1975), in *Itinéraires* 195 (July-August 1975): 138. See also the minutes of the March 3, 1975 meeting in which Archbishop Lefebvre twice acknowledged that he had written his manifesto "in a moment of indignation."

19 Fr Paul Aulagnier reports these reactions, *La Tradition sans peur*, 96-97.

shocked by the "Declaration." He testified that the faculty tried to get the founder of Écône to reconsider what they saw as a declaration of war:

> They imagined themselves on a rescue mission....They met on a Saturday to draft a new text. Archbishop Lefebvre did not want to attend this meeting. As a professor in the house, I was present. A text was drawn up and proposed to Archbishop Lefebvre. He took no account of it.[20]

Beyond the seminary, reactions were also varied. While Father Barbara and then Jean Madiran wasted no time in publishing the text, as we have seen, Dom Roy, Abbot of Fontgombault, considered that the "Declaration" was excessively radical in tone and that it went beyond Archbishop Lefebvre's actual thought. He wrote to him:

> One must admit that certain abrupt formulations can give the wrong impression to those who do not know you very well, and that they could easily be exploited by those who seek to use you.[21]

Eric de Saventhem, president of *Una Voce* International, and his wife, who were regulars at the morning Mass at Écône, also insisted that Archbishop Lefebvre reconsider his "Declaration," specifically deploring that he had called into question "all the reforms resulting from the Second Vatican Council."[22]

Archbishop Lefebvre never did alter his November 1974 "Declaration." He would often refer to it, and it has remained a major text in the SSPX to this day.

Yet the founder of the SSPX did not want to appear as a systematic opponent of the Pope. It is a little-known fact that he helped found the *Credo* association. Sometime after his historic declaration, he asked Michel de Saint-Pierre to "mobilize traditional Catholics for a pilgrimage to Rome that the founder of the seminary of Écône wanted to lead during the Holy Year 1975."[23] On December 9, 1974, Michel de Saint-Pierre and André Mignot founded the *Credo* association. Its purpose, according to its official administrative declaration, was "to propagate and defend the truths contained in the Nicene creed and to bear public witness to them; this action will be carried out in perfect communion with the Sovereign Pontiff, guardian and defender of the Catholic faith."

---

20 *La Tradition sans peur*, 97.

21 Dom Roy to Archbishop Lefebvre, Letter, April 10, 1975, Archives of the Abbey of Our Lady of Fontgombault.

22 P. Aulagnier, *La Tradition sans peur*, 98.

23 Jacques Plaçon to the author, Letter, September 7, 1998. Jacques Plaçon directed the review *Credo* and was among the successors of Michel de Saint-Pierre as director of the association.

The two-page *Manifesto* was more explicit. The association wanted to "make heard" the voice of "Catholics faithful to Tradition," "to tear down the rampart of contempt in which [the Hierarchy] has enclosed the traditionalist current" and "to enter into a real dialogue with it" in order to bring to fruition ten "legitimate demands." These concerned in particular the Catechism (that it "become once again a true religious teaching that will help children to remember the truths of the faith, which will accompany them throughout their lives") and the liturgy: that the Mass according to the traditional rite may be celebrated freely and "that the new ordo instituted by His Holiness Paul VI be celebrated only in its original formulation, not falsified by sacrilegious innovations, and that the translations into the vernacular be corrected in order to make them faithful to the Latin text." The association had chosen as its symbol St Peter's Basilica and its colonnade enclosing the word "Credo." It organized the pilgrimage to Rome, which was scheduled for May 23-26, 1975, and which Archbishop Lefebvre was to preside over. But neither the association nor the prelate could have imagined that this pilgrimage would take place the day after the first sanctions that were to strike Archbishop Lefebvre and his work.

Three months after his "Declaration," Archbishop Lefebvre was summoned to Rome to appear before the commission that had ordered the apostolic visitation. There were two meetings on February 13 and March 3, 1975. "I was invited for an interview," Archbishop Lefebvre wrote, "but in fact I had to deal with a tribunal that was determined to condemn me." Only the minutes of the second meeting are known.[24] The discussion was close and uncompromising. It was especially the "Declaration" of the previous November 21 that was at issue. Archbishop Lefebvre did not want to retract or qualify it. "You are against the Pope and the Council," accused Cardinal Garrone, who also reproached him for teaching his seminarians to "rely on their personal judgment, on tradition as they understand it. This is free thinking, the worst kind of liberalism!" He also hurled at him: "You are forming a sect. Archbishop Lefebvre will be the pope of a new Church!"

For his part, Father de Nantes, head of the *Ligue de Contre-Réforme catholique*, whose bulletin *La Contre-Réforme catholique au XXe siècle* had a circulation of 38,000, sought to draw Archbishop Lefebvre into his views. In April 1973, along with the brothers of his community and a group of fifty members of his league, he went to Rome to bring a 100-page *Liber accusationis* against Paul VI "for heresy, schism and

---

24 Published by Roland Gaucher, *Monseigneur Lefebvre. Combat pour l'Église* (Paris: Éditions Albatros, 1976), 215-61 and by Yves Montagne, *"L'Évêque suspens"*: 46-90.

scandal." It was necessary "that the pope change or be changed,"[25] that he convert and renounce the Second Vatican Council. The libel had been placed in the Pope's hands by surprise during a general audience, but was soon rejected without being read. The *Osservatore Romano* of April 13 denounced "an arrogant and fanatical gesture, which is in no way encouraged by any ecclesiastical authority, but which, on the contrary, is disqualified and regretted, as being devoid of any serious character or canonical foundation, and which gravely offends the person and the ministry of the Vicar of Christ." The "Declaration" made by Archbishop Lefebvre in November 1974 seemed to Father de Nantes to be the prelude to "an obligatory rupture of communion." In February 1975, he signed a thunderous editorial in his bulletin entitled "Strike at the head!" (*Frappe à la tête!*). Without naming Archbishop Lefebvre – but everyone understood that he was speaking to him – he exhorted him to break with Paul VI "who has knowingly and stubbornly inverted the meaning of his divine and apostolic mission." He claimed that

> a Bishop, who is also a successor of the Apostles, a member of the teaching Church, a colleague of the Bishop of Rome and, like him, ordained to the common good of the Church, should *break off his communion with him as long as he has not proved his faithfulness to the duties of his Supreme Pontificate.*[26]

Then he went to Écône to meet Archbishop Lefebvre, without succeeding in "speaking to him as he wished," while the latter "visibly saw him as a nuisance."[27] In March, in the issue of *La Contre-Réforme catholique au XXe siècle*, Father de Nantes reproduced the "Declaration" of November 1974 with a title that left some doubt: "In communion with Paul VI?" He also praised the "courageous bishop" who had dared to make a "declaration of justified insubordination."

Archbishop Lefebvre had to disassociate himself from the positions of Father de Nantes publicly. In a letter dated March 19, 1975, he wrote to him:

> Know that if a Bishop breaks with Rome it will not be me. My *Declaration* says as much quite explicitly and strongly. . . . Liberalism has been condemned by the Church for a century and a half. It entered the Church thanks to the Council. The Church is dying from the practical effects of this liberalism. We must therefore do everything possible to help the Church and those who govern her to free themselves from this satanic grip.

25 *Liber accusationis in Paulum sextum* (1973), 103.
26 *La Contre-Réforme catholique au XXe siècle* 89 (February 1975); underscored in the original.
27 Br. François de Marie des Anges, *Pour l'Église*, vol. 3, 399.

On May 6, 1975, Bishop Mamie of Fribourg withdrew the approval *ad experimentum* given to the Society of Saint Pius X; on the same day, the Cardinals' Commission, "with the full approval" of Pope Paul VI, confirmed that the Society no longer had canonical approval, that "its foundations, and in particular the seminary of Écône, have thereby lost the right to exist" and that "no support can be given to Archbishop Lefebvre as long as the ideas contained in the Manifesto of November 21, 1974, remain the basis for his actions."

As Louis Salleron was to point out in a long opinion piece published in *Le Monde*:

> The decisions of the cardinals' commission are solely based on [the] Declaration.... [n]o reference to the Mass, none to doctrine, none to the formation given to seminarians. The seminary of Écône is condemned for a few of its founder's words that betray an anti-conciliar spirit, which is today the real sin against the Spirit. [28]

There were diverse reactions to these sanctions, which brought out the divisions among the circles attached to Tradition. As soon as he learned of them, from his Benedictine priory in Bédoin, Dom Gérard telephoned Archbishop Lefebvre and then wrote to him to "reiterate our faithful attachment, our unceasing prayer, and our hope that the seminary will continue unperturbed on its way to holy orders.... We are more and more in solidarity with your work. The faithful rightly see in this latest setback a confirmation of the thesis of a Rome that is no longer in Rome." [29] He also told him that on the same day – it was Pentecost Sunday – during Mass (attended by "some eighty people"), he had made "a brief communication on the fact that canonical institution had been withdrawn [from the SSPX]" to explain "that the orders emanating from this jurisdiction [Rome] are null and void" because "they are exercised against the end for which it had been instituted."

This canonical and theological position, close to sedevacantism – the refusal to recognize the authority of the pope – was beginning to be disseminated by Father Guérard des Lauriers, who was still a professor at Écône, and who also sometimes gave courses at Bédoin. Sometime earlier he had written to Dom Gérard: the pope had made the decision "not to govern" – that is, not to accomplish what he had been elected pope to do – "under these conditions, we must not pay any attention to the decisions imputed to an authority which in reality does not

28 *Le Monde* (June 13, 1975).
29 Dom Gérard to Archbishop Lefebvre, Letter, May 18, 1975, SSPX archives.

exist as such."[30] On the other hand, six other professors at Écône, notably the Dominicans Mehrle and Spicq and Father Dumoulin, felt that it was no longer possible for them to teach in a seminary that was no longer authorized by the Roman authorities.

On May 21, Archbishop Lefebvre wrote to Cardinal Staffa, prefect of the Tribunal of the Apostolic Signatura, to tell him of his intention to appeal the sanctions taken against him (the appeal was made on June 5).

It has been said that the pilgrimage organized in Rome by the *Credo* association, and presided over by Archbishop Lefebvre, was another "retort" to the sanctions leveled against the Society of St. Pius X and Écône. In reality, as we have seen, it had been announced long before the apostolic visit and the measures taken by the Cardinal's Commission. It took place from May 23-26, and did not present the appearance of a challenge. Archbishop Lefebvre was able to celebrate Mass in the Roman basilicas, including St. Peter's. He tried unsuccessfully to obtain an audience with Paul VI.

Then, on May 31, he addressed a letter to the Pope and sent him a *Relatio* on the procedure followed since the apostolic visit.[31] In this letter, he declared his "entire and filial submission to the decisions communicated to me by the Cardinals' Commission with regard to the Society of St. Pius X and the Seminary," but he asked that his "Declaration" be judged by the Congregation for the Doctrine of the Faith. On June 10, the appeal was rejected by the Tribunal of the Apostolic Signatura. Four days later, Archbishop Lefebvre appealed, but upon the intervention of Cardinal Villot, Paul VI's Secretary of State, this appeal was not accepted.[32]

With the official suppression of the Society of St. Pius X, the ordinations that had been set for June 29 "had necessarily become illegal. At any rate, there was a total juridical vacuum"[33] since the diocesan bishops of the ordinands had not sent the necessary dimissorial letters. But Archbishop Lefebvre went ahead and ordained three priests and thirteen subdeacons that day in Écône anyway. The three priests went on to have very different careers: Father Pierre Blin later left the Society of St. Pius X and was incardinated in the diocese of Paris; Father Donald Sanborn, an American, was expelled from the Society of

---

30 Fr Guérard des Lauriers to Dom Gérard, Letter, April 18, 1975, Archives of the Abbaye Sainte-Madeleine.

31 Jean Madiran, starting with the July-August 1975 issue of *Itinéraires*, would publish nearly all the documentation of what he termed the "savage condemnation of Archbishop Lefebvre."

32 B. Tissier de Mallerais, *Marcel Lefebvre*, 482.

33 P. Aulagnier, *La Tradition sans peur*, 101.

St. Pius X in 1983, founded a sedevacantist seminary in 1995, and was consecrated bishop in 2002 by a "Guérardian" bishop, Bishop McKenna; Father Tissier de Mallerais was in turn professor at the seminary of Écône, seminary rector, and secretary general of the Society of St. Pius X before being ordained bishop in 1988 by Archbishop Lefebvre without a pontifical mandate.

That very June 29, 1975, Paul VI addressed a long letter to Archbishop Lefebvre. It was not brought to Écône until July 8. The Pope gave specific pontifical approval to the "conclusions" reached by the Cardinal's Commission, specifying: "We have personally ordered their immediate implementation." Consequently, he asked Archbishop Lefebvre to make "a public act of submission." It was in this letter that Paul VI reproached Archbishop Lefebvre for "daring to fight a Council such as the Second Vatican Council, which is no less authoritative, and in some respects even more important yet than that of Nicaea." The formula scandalized some, because the Council of Nicaea, in 325, the first ecumenical council in the history of the Church, had been the one that had formulated the Creed.

Sometime later, the Abbot of Fontgombault urged the Archbishop to retract his incendiary "Declaration" to save the seminary:

> I have got the impression that in Rome they would like an accommodation. Are you thinking of making an adjustment to your Declaration as we have discussed here? Why don't you "withdraw" your first Declaration (which doesn't mean "disown" it), on the grounds that it was ambiguous and confused the faithful? This would allow you to make another one, more in conformity with your thought, more useful to the faithful, more explicit and precise. Écône must be saved.[34]

In his newsletter, the *Lettre aux amis et bienfaiteurs*, Archbishop Lefebvre announced that "the seminary goes on" and that a house of priestly formation would be opened in Weissbad, in German-speaking Switzerland, for German-speaking seminarians. At the beginning of the 1975 academic year, 127 seminarians entered the three seminaries of Écône, Armada, and Weissbad. On October 27, Cardinal Villot, Paul VI's Secretary of State, sent a long letter to all the Presidents of the Episcopal Conferences. He recalled the stages of the proceedings against Archbishop Lefebvre and their outcome. He deplored the fact that the "activities" of Archbishop Lefebvre "continue, his projects are carried out in various countries, and his writings and words continue

---

34 Dom Roy to Archbishop Lefebvre, Letter, August 25, 1975, Archives of the Abbaye Notre-Dame de Fontgombault (copy).

to mislead a certain number of confused faithful." He concluded by affirming that "the Priestly Fraternity of St. Pius X has ceased to exist," that "those who still claim to be part of it cannot claim – a fortiori – to escape the jurisdiction of diocesan Ordinaries" and that all bishops "are earnestly invited not to grant incardination in their diocese to young men declaring their commitment to serving the 'Fraternity.'"

THE PSYCHOLOGY OF ARCHBISHOP LEFEBVRE

This complete rejection of the SSPX by Vatican authorities did not justify, in the eyes of some of Archbishop Lefebvre's friends, his "obstinacy." In France as well as in Rome, the hypothesis of a psychological deficiency in the founder of Écône began to circulate. In December 1976 Dom Roy, who had known Archbishop Lefebvre for a long time, met him in Suresnes. He confided his impressions to his secretary, Dom Jean-Louis de Robien: "For the first time, Dom Roy found in front of him a man who seemed tired, weary; who was only repeating well-rehearsed phrases. . . . Some people, from that moment on, spoke of cerebral arteriosclerosis."[35] Meeting Cardinal Siri in Rome in February 1976, Dom Roy heard the Archbishop of Genoa voice the same hypothesis:

> He too thought that he was now suffering from arteriosclerosis, and he planned to plead this deficiency before Paul VI in order to get him to leave him alone, allowing him to celebrate the Mass of St. Pius V, since this was his main cause.[36]

Then, in a letter to Paul VI, the Abbot of Fontgombault took up the same argument:

> I am seriously wondering whether currently Archbishop Lefebvre might be suffering from a weakening of the brain or mental derangement. This might go a long way to excuse his attitude and to treat him as someone who is ill rather than guilty.[37]

This judgment on the psychology of Archbishop Lefebvre, then in his seventies, is not a medical diagnosis. It is an assessment made by a religious who knew him well – Archbishop Lefebvre had been going to the Abbey of Fontgombault since 1958 – and who had seen his personality change in recent years. The biographer of the founder of Écône does not in any way repeat this harsh assessment. He devotes several pages to the character and psychology of the one he describes

---

35 Dom Jean-Louis de Robien, *Dom Jean Roy, abbé de Notre-Dame de Fontgombault, 1921-1977* (Unpublished, 2002), Archives of the Abbey of Notre-Dame de Fontgombault, 207.
36 Ibid.
37 Dom Roy to Paul VI, Letter, September 1, 1976, Archives of the Abbey of Notre-Dame de Fontgombault (copy).

as "gently pigheaded": "a strong individual who did not lack delicacy of heart," even if he did have "little failings."[38] He speaks of the "two sides to Marcel Lefebvre":

> But there were times when the man of dialogue became really stubborn. Faced with strong-minded people, he was "a reactionary." One could then be exposed to some sharp words from a man who clung grimly to his opinion, sometimes to the extent of denying the obvious in his exasperation, or in his embarrassment at having to explain himself: he then showed the downside of his character, or rather the excess of his tenacity.

SUSPENDED *A DIVINIS*

In a long letter dated February 18, 1976, after a few days spent in Rome, Dom Roy wrote to Archbishop Lefebvre:

> You were spoken of everywhere here, and always in the same sense. Now, these were people who are favorable to you, who love you, and who want Écône to keep going. But, like your best French friends, even when they excuse you, they no longer understand you and deplore your attitude; they are worried for you, for your work, and for the cause to which you have dedicated your life's work as a missionary and Bishop. What a change in the last year! Those who defended you then no longer know how to excuse you.[39]

The Abbot of Fontgombault suggested that Archbishop Lefebvre write a letter of submission to the Pope, telling him of:

> your regret for past misunderstandings, your complete fidelity to the Church (as you have done), your total submission, placing Écône in his hands, but asking for an audience to confer with him on the fate of the seminarians.... By doing so, Your Excellency, you would be best serving all the causes you mean to defend. It is probably the only way to save Écône.... I beg you, Your Excellency, on both knees, make this saving gesture for yourself and for the holy Church. It is the wish of your best friends. Cardinal Oddi, whom I saw in Rome, told me that I could insist on this with you.

A few weeks later, Bishop Morilleau wrote to him in the same vein. The former bishop of La Rochelle had been his fellow student at the French Seminary. He had been an active member of the *Coetus Internationalis Patris* at the Council and had remained very close to the founder of Écône. He wrote him a long, affectionate, and moving letter:

---

38 B. Tissier de Mallerais, *Marcel Lefebvre*, 578-80.
39 Dom Roy to Archbishop Lefebvre, Letter, February 18, 1976, Archives of the Abbey of Notre-Dame de Fontgombault (copy).

My dear Excellency, especially since the Council, you have followed a difficult and painful path. I have always accompanied you
with my hope, my affection, and my prayer. My prayer remains
faithful to you as if it flowed from my heart with my blood. My
affection remains sincerely fraternal. My hope, however, has
changed its face. Your excellency, my friend and my brother,
you are at the end of the road. . . . You are today far from your
simple and generous "missionary ideals." You must come back,
or you will enter into the night.[40]

Bishop Morilleau placed the blame on Archbishop Lefebvre's entourage and some of his acquaintances, who had "allowed their passions
to take the lead":

They have gradually become your usual environment of life or
relationships; their influence unwittingly has made you persist
in attitudes that have become untenable today. This is not fidelity to Tradition. I am not going to tell you again that Tradition,
founded on the Truth and guaranteed by the living Holy Father,
is itself a living reality. In every field opinions, methods, habits,
formulas risk becoming ossified.

Bishop Morilleau urged Archbishop Lefebvre to answer the Pope's
call: "I can see no way out that is honorable for you, 'edifying' for all
those who have placed their trust in you, salvific for the young men for
whom you are responsible, outside of a total submission to the Holy
Father, who is 'Our Lord on earth.'" This filial submission, "expressed
with clarity," would allow, he thought, "the reorganization of your work,
even if it had to involve reforms and separations; it would become possible thanks to the advice that the Holy Father would not refuse to give
you and perhaps to new assistance which dared not yet come forward."

All dialogue did not yet seem broken off between Rome and Écône.
On March 13, 1976, Archbishop Lefebvre met with Bishop Benelli, substitute for the Secretary of State. But on April 21, the Holy See made
precise demands. In a letter addressed to Archbishop Lefebvre, Bishop
Benelli asked him, as a sign of his "effective communion with Pope
Paul VI," to accept the Second Vatican Council and "all its documents"
and to "adopt and have adopted in the houses which depend on you"
the new Mass. A month later, on May 24, before the cardinals of the
whole world gathered in consistory for the creation of new cardinals,
Paul VI devoted a large part of his speech to Archbishop Lefebvre,
whom he mentioned several times by name (a highly unusual practice).
He deplored the opposition of those who "systematically reject the

---

40 Bishop Morilleau to Archbishop Lefevbre, Letter, March 10, 1976, Archives of the
Abbey of Notre-Dame de Fontgombault (copy).

teachings of the Council itself, its application, and the reforms which derive from it." He judged this opposition in harsh terms:

> Such people diminish the Church's authority under pretext of tradition; their obedience to that authority is merely lip-service. They draw the faithful away from the ties of obedience to the See of Peter as well as from their lawful bishops. They repudiate the authority of today in favor of that of another age.

He also expressed his regret that this opposition had "a bishop, Marcel Lefebvre, whom we still continue to reach out to with respect, as its leader and its guide." He urged him once more to receive the teaching of the Council and the new Mass. And, in a solemn manner for the first time, the pope repeated the obligatory character of the "restored liturgy": "Use of the new *Ordo Missae* is in no way left up to the choice of priests or people," it was "promulgated in place of the old."[41] He was here confirming what bishops' conferences and individual bishops had been saying since 1969.

In the Holy See's view, there was no other option than total submission, that is, acceptance of all the acts of the Council and the celebration of the new Mass. In the next pontificate, the Holy See would judge otherwise. Archbishop Lefebvre, on the other hand, believed that the crisis of the Church had to be considered within a much broader context than that of the Council and the Mass. Answering Dom Roy's letter, he told him:

> How can one fail to see in this whole Reform that began at the Council the fulfilment of the entire Masonic and Liberal conspiracy to implement their satanic projects? The now publicly-known Masonic membership of Cardinal Liénart, Bugnini, and soon other prelates has confirmed our apprehensions.[42]

He was to reprise this argument a few months later in a book on the Council.

Referring to his meeting with Bishop Benelli, Archbishop Lefebvre also wrote the following to Dom Roy: "We are not here dealing with men of the Church.... The time has come to show that we do not belong to that Religion and to keep up the struggle."

The ordinations at the end of the year were to take place in a dramatic climate. On June 12 and again on June 25, Archbishop Benelli, "by special mandate of the Supreme Pontiff," forbade Archbishop Lefebvre

---

41 Paul VI, Address to consistory, May 24, 1976, *AAS* 68 (1976): 369-78; English version, *DOL* 59.555.
42 Archbishop Lefebvre to Dom Roy, Letter, April 19, 1976, Archives of the Abbey of Notre-Dame de Fontgombault (copy).

to proceed with these ordinations, on pain of incurring the censures provided for by Canon Law (2373, §1). In the message of June 25, he spoke
of "true fidelity to the *conciliar Church*." This unfortunate expression
would be controversial, because it seemed to oppose two Churches to
each other. But the idea of a change in the nature of the Church as a
result of the Council had already been expounded by Cardinal Garrone
in a major article published in *L'Osservatore Romano*.[43]

Before the ceremony, a final attempt was made with Archbishop
Lefebvre. Cardinal Thiandoum, the first Senegalese priest ordained by
Archbishop Lefebvre and his successor in the see of Dakar, and whom
Paul VI had just created cardinal, had tried to dissuade the prelate of
Écône from proceeding with these ordinations. He failed. Cardinal Thian-
doum was not mandated by the Holy See, but out of affection for his
former superior, he made other attempts at conciliation. In the following
years, he would meet with Archbishop Lefebvre "over thirty times at
Écône, Geneva, Paris, and Rome,"[44] without being able to convince him.

On June 29, in the presence of some 1,500 faithful, Archbishop
Lefebvre ordained 14 sub-deacons and 13 priests, among them Brother
Jehan de Belleville, the first monk of the Benedictine priory of Bédoin
to become a priest. Dom Gérard came to Écône accompanied by almost
all his monks and many friends of the priory.

With these ordinations performed in spite of the Holy See's formal
prohibition, Archbishop Lefebvre incurred two types of penalties. For
having proceeded to ordinations without dimissorial letters, he was
liable to be struck with a suspension *a collatione ordinum* ("prohibition
on conferring ordinations") according to canon 2373, and those who
had been ordained were liable to be declared suspended from the order
received (canon 2374). This penalty was not formally inflicted on him,
despite what some articles and bishops said at the time. Instead, on
July 6, Cardinal Baggio, prefect of the Congregation for Bishops, sent
him an exhortation in the name of the Pope to "change his attitude,"
"humbly ask the Holy Father for forgiveness," "repair the spiritual
damage inflicted on the young ordained and the scandal caused to
the people of God," and implore him to give "proof of repentance
within ten days."[45]

---

43 First published in Italian in the daily editions of *L'Osservatore Romano* (December 25,
1975), the article appeared in the weekly French edition (January 9, 1976) with the title
"De l'Église préconciliaire à l'Église postconciliaire" (reprinted in *DC* 1703 [August 1, 1976]).
44 Cardinal Thiandoum to the author, Letter, July 28, 1992.
45 Cardinal Baggio to Archbishop Lefebvre, Letter, July 6, 1976, published in *La Condamnation sauvage de Mgr Lefebvre*, 140-41.

Archbishop Lefebvre did not express the repentance expected of him. He replied with a letter to the Pope, dated July 17, in which he repeated the threefold demand that Jean Madiran had made in his "complaint to the Holy Father" in 1972. He asked him to restore "the public law of the Church":

> – By restoring to the liturgy all of its dogmatic value and its hierarchical expression in the Roman Latin rite hallowed by so many years of use;
> – By restoring the Vulgate to its position of honor;
> – By restoring to the catechisms their true model, the *Catechism* of the Council of Trent.

He again urged the Pope to abandon the "evil enterprise of compromise with the ideas of modern man, an enterprise which originated in a secret agreement between high dignitaries of the Church and those of the Masonic lodges, even before the Council."[46] This was the first time that Archbishop Lefebvre referred, in a letter to the Pope, to a supposed ecclesiastical-Masonic plot. It is, as we shall see, the media coverage at the time that explains this new insistence.

This letter, the Holy See was to say, "was a cause for renewed bitterness for His Holiness, because of Archbishop Lefebvre's persistent attitude of defiance."[47] On July 22, he was declared suspended *a divinis*, i.e., forbidden to celebrate Mass in public as well as from all sacramental acts and from preaching. Archbishop Lefebvre's biographer says that he was "at first . . . greatly hurt" and then "pulled himself together."[48] Seven days after receiving this sanction, he set down a carefully handwritten text, "A few thoughts regarding the suspension *a divinis*," which was mimeographed and sent to all the faithful who had written to him since his condemnation. This long two-page text, which has circulated widely, is perhaps one of the harshest he ever wrote.[49] He twice states: "this conciliar Church is schismatic," and again: "It is both schismatic and heretical. This conciliar Church is therefore not Catholic. Insofar as the Pope, the bishops, priests, and faithful adhere to this new Church, they separate themselves from the Catholic Church."

In an interview he gave to *Le Figaro* a few days later, on August 4,

---

46 Archbishop Lefebvre to Paul VI, Letter, July 17, 1976, published on the website of *La Porte Latine*.

47 Note in *L'Osservatore Romano* (July 26-27, 1976).

48 B. Tissier de Mallerais, *Marcel Lefebvre*, 487.

49 These "Reflections" have been reprinted often, but curiously a prejudicial typographical error appears in many of its versions: "the *founder* of the conciliar Church" (one would be forgiven for believing that Archbishop Lefebvre meant Paul VI) whereas the hand-written text has "the *founders* of the conciliar Church."

Archbishop Lefebvre expressed a doubt: "We are much less certain that the Pope is truly Pope." His biographer commented: "The question deserved to be asked, but the archbishop did not answer it; he left that up to the Church."[50]

THE MASS IN LILLE

The suspension inflicted on Archbishop Lefebvre provoked an avalanche of commentaries in the press, and of reactions from bishops and churchmen. On the initiative of Michel de Saint-Pierre, the president of the *Credo* movement, seven other writers and Catholic personalities – Michel Droit, Louis Salleron, Jean Dutourd, the musician Henri Sauguet, Colonel Rémy, the painter Michel Ciry, and Gustave Thibon – published a letter to Paul VI on August 9 in which they defended the sanctioned archbishop. They asked the Pope to "reconsider" the "very grave accusation made against Archbishop Lefebvre and his seminary" and not to hinder "the traditional Mass and the perennial [*de toujours*] priesthood." Four days later, a poll conducted by Institut Français d'Opinion Publique (IFOP, "French Institute of Public Opinion") was published in *Le Progrès de Lyon*, revealing that Archbishop Lefebvre met with the approval of a section of the French population. A box on the front page of the newspaper announced: "One in four French people is receptive to Archbishop Lefebvre's ideas." The last two pages gave the detailed results of the poll, which had not only focused on Archbishop Lefebvre, but also on the ongoing changes in the Church, its position on divorce, abortion, the marriage of priests, and other subjects. Regarding Archbishop Lefebvre, 25% of those polled said they "approved" of his positions, 20% "disapproved," 30% were indifferent, and 25% did not know; the proportions were almost the same when the results were controlled for Catholics alone.

The results of this poll were widely reported in the national press, and bolstered Archbishop Lefebvre. The Mass he celebrated in Lille on August 29, in the presence of thousands of faithful, was presented as a provocation in the press. This Mass had been announced several days ahead of time, and was organized by the Coordination Committee of Traditionalist Associations, chaired by Gérard Saclier de La Bâtie, who bussed lay people in from all over France. This was no fabricated media event, however. In reality, as Father Aulagnier, who had been named District Superior of France of the SSPX on August 15, explained, Archbishop Lefebvre's visit to northern France had been planned for several months. He was to confer the sacrament of confirmation on a

50 B. Tissier de Mallerais, *Marcel Lefebvre*, 487.

few dozen children from Christian families in the region. The suspension *a divinis* was then imposed on him on July 22.

> What would Archbishop Lefebvre do? Go and risk being seen as a provocateur, when the Roman sanction forbade him even to say Mass? Wait out the storm and deny himself to the faithful, thereby seeming to give some legitimacy to the sanctions against him? For a long time, he remained in a state of uncertainty. The newspapers seized on this hesitation; it made their headlines. In Lille, the organizers could sense that a sensational event was in the making, and week after week, as the media inflated the event, the organizers were obliged to look for bigger and bigger halls, ultimately reserving the Palais des Congrès. In fact, Archbishop Lefebvre had not premeditated anything; while still at Écône, I could feel his hesitation. Ultimately he went to Lille on August 29, 1976.[51]

In the presence of 400 journalists from all over the world, and before 7,000 faithful, he celebrated Mass and delivered a very long sermon (forty-five minutes). Many journalists were surprised by the passage in which Archbishop Lefebvre praised the new regime in Argentina, which had emerged from a military coup a few months earlier. The journalist from *Le Monde*, reporting on the ceremony, said:

> Archbishop Lefebvre has thrown off the mask. The betrayal of the conciliar Church, in his eyes, goes far deeper than any doctrinal or liturgical laxism. It is a whole political conception of the modern world which is rejected in the name of rigid principles that absolutize the pre-revolutionary, pre-republican, pre-democratic *Ancien Régime* as the ideal of the Christian State.[52]

The same journalist cited Charles Maurras among the "intellectual authorities" of the founder of Écône as an interpretive key to Lefebvrism; it has often been assumed to the present day, including by certain historians. In reality, as we have already shown, there was no influence of the writings of Maurras and the Action française on the formation of the future Archbishop Lefebvre. He would repeat it again a few weeks later: "I can say that I have not known Maurras, I have not even read his works, I am perhaps ignorant in this respect."[53] On the other hand, it is true that in Lille, as at other high Masses he was to celebrate, as also during the storming of Saint-Nicolas-du-Chardonnet in Paris a few months later, the monarchist weekly *Aspects de la France* and various monarchist organizations gave him their support. But it was

---

51 P. Aulagnier, *La Tradition sans peur*, 124-25.
52 Alain Woodrow, "Le Masque est jeté," *Le Monde* (August 31, 1976).
53 First press conference of September 15, 1976, printed in *La Condamnation sauvage de Mgr Lefebvre*, 220.

from other sources that Archbishop Lefebvre drew his doctrine: from Romanity, the intransigent and anti-liberal tradition. This doctrine may have been reinforced, in certain traditionalist circles, by a tendency to insubordination stemming from the mentality of Action française.

In the Lille sermon, Archbishop Lefebvre also explained why he did not accept the canonical sanctions imposed on him by the Holy See:

> I do not consider these penalties to be valid, whether canonically or theologically. In all sincerity, in all peace, in all serenity, I believe that I cannot accede to these suspensions, by these punishments with which I am struck, to the closure of my seminaries, to the refusal to perform ordinations, to the destruction of the Catholic Church. At the hour of my death, when Our Lord asks me: "What have you done with your episcopal and priestly grace?" I do not wish to have to hear from the mouth of the Lord: "You have contributed to the destruction of the Church along with the others."

He also announced his determination to continue his work forming priests:

> We shall have another twenty-five new recruits this year at the seminary in Écône; despite the difficulties, we shall have ten new recruits in our seminary in the United States in Armada and four new recruits in our German language seminary in German-speaking Switzerland. As you can see, despite the difficulties we face, the young people understand very well that we are forming true Catholic priests. That is why we are not in schism, we are the continuators of the Catholic Church. It is those who make novelties that are going into schism. As for us, we continue Tradition.

AN INTERVIEW WITH PAUL VI

On the very day that this Mass was said, Paul VI deplored it during the Angelus as a "challenge to these Keys that Christ has placed in our hands." Nevertheless, a few days later, he agreed to receive Archbishop Lefebvre in audience. It was an Italian priest, Fr Domenico Labellarte, spiritual son of Padre Pio, who suggested that Archbishop Lefebvre request an audience. At the same time, Dom Jean Roy, in a long letter to Paul VI, begged him to receive the founder of Écône:

> At this point, I can see salvation only in direct, one-on-one, prolonged talks between Your Holiness and Archbishop Lefebvre, with the Good Shepherd seeking out, or rather calling to Himself the lost sheep, without any other prerequisite than his fatherly love and unconditional compassion.[54]

---

54 Dom Roy to Paul VI, Letter, September 1, 1976, Archives of the Abbey of Notre-Dame de Fontgombault (copy).

The meeting between the Pope and Archbishop Lefebvre took place at Castel Gandolfo on September 11, 1976, in the presence of Archbishop Benelli. Archbishop Lefebvre reported the content of their conversation in two press conferences he gave on the following September 15, and in a talk he gave his seminarians three days later.[55] All the authors who have written about Archbishop Lefebvre have used these words to reconstruct the exchange between the embattled pope and the rebellious bishop. However, a document that recently came out of the Vatican archives sheds additional light on this meeting. Bishop Benelli, who attended the audience without taking part in the conversation, wrote a very precise verbatim record at the request of the pope. It is an eight-page typed document that can be usefully compared with Archbishop Lefebvre's oral account.[56] The two accounts do not contradict each other, even if there are some differences.

Without reproducing the entirety of the exchanges as recounted by Archbishop Lefebvre and Archbishop Benelli, we will here note some salient features and the positions of each. The first words of Paul VI, as reported by Archbishop Benelli, show a pope hurt by what he considered as an archbishop's rebellion against his authority: "I hope to have before me a brother, a son, a friend. Unfortunately the position you are taking is that of an antipope." According to Archbishop Lefebvre, the pope also made an accusation: "You do not form good priests, since you make them take an oath against the pope!" But this statement is not found in the verbatim record taken down by Archbishop Benelli. This does not mean that it was not made, perhaps because Archbishop Lefebvre protested strongly against such an accusation and affirmed that no such oath ever existed. In any case, there is no testimony and no text that any such "oath" existed in 1976. From the beginning, a *Profession of Faith* was in use in Écône, composed from the formulas of the Council of Trent and the First Vatican Council. To this was added, only from 1979, a *Declaration of Fidelity* concerning the Pope and the Mass, as we shall see.

Paul VI expressed yet another reason for indignation, which Archbishop Lefebvre recounts: "You condemn me, so what should I do? Should I resign and then you take my place?" Archbishop Benelli reports the Pope's words in the same terms. Again, Archbishop Lefebvre protested.

---

55 Press conference on September 15, 1976 and talk to seminarians on September 18, 1976, printed in *La Condamnation sauvage de Mgr Lefebvre*, 209-40 and 246-64.

56 *Udienza del Santo Padre a S. E. Mons. Marcel Lefebvre. 11 settembre 1976*, photograph of the document in Leonardo Sapienza, *La Barca di Paolo* (Milan: Edizioni San Paolo, 2018), 150-57.

Archbishop Lefebvre also mentioned the difficulties posed by certain teachings born of the Council, notably religious freedom. The Pope did not want to enter into a doctrinal discussion: "These are not subjects that can be discussed in an audience. But I take note of your perplexity."

Regarding the Mass, Archbishop Lefebvre had ended his sermon in Lille by addressing the Pope: "Allow us to make the experiment of Tradition, Holy Father." During the audience, he made the same request, which Archbishop Benelli reports in the following terms:

> Wouldn't it be possible to order your bishops to grant, in the churches, a chapel in which people might pray as before the Council? Today everything is allowed to everyone: why not allow something to us too?

The Pope's response was immediately negative: "We are a community. We cannot allow the different parties autonomy of behavior."

At the conclusion of the meeting, Pope Paul VI told Archbishop Lefebvre that he could not allow him to make himself "guilty of a schism," and asked him to make a public statement in which he would withdraw his November 1975 statement.

The expression "Allow us to make the experiment of Tradition" would often be taken up by Archbishop Lefebvre and other figures of traditionalism. But it would be contested by other traditionalists, who believed that Tradition cannot be a thing one "tries out" among other things, but is the only way to keep the integrity of the faith.

THE MASONIC PLOT

One month after his reception by the Pope, Archbishop Lefebvre published, under the title *J'accuse le Concile*, a collection of the interventions he had made at the Second Vatican Council to oppose "liberal or modernist orientations." In a presentation justifying the shock title of his book, he stated that "the spirit that dominated the Council and inspired so many ambiguous and equivocal and even frankly erroneous texts was not the Holy Spirit, but the spirit of the modern world, a liberal, Teilhardian, modernist spirit, opposed to the reign of Our Lord Jesus Christ."[57] But in this text, as in the preface to the book, Archbishop Lefebvre also took up, for the first time in a public writing, the idea of a "conspiracy" which he had mentioned a few months earlier in his letter to Dom Roy and then in his letter to Paul VI on July 17. He blamed "the conspiracy of the enemies of the Church" that had been at work in the Council, the "secret societies

---

57 "Notes à propos du titre," in Archbishop Lefebvre, *J'accuse le concile*, 7.

preparing this Council for over a century," "an astounding conspiracy prepared for a long time."[58]

The idea of "Masonic infiltration of the Church," of Jewish influence in the Council,[59] and of the existence of "a parallel power within the Church" was not new. It had been developed at the time of the Council in writings which had circulated on the peripheries of the conciliar assembly. It had been taken up again a few years later in a collective work that had met with a certain success.[60] At the time Archbishop Lefebvre was writing these two texts, dated August 18 and 27, the subject of Masonic infiltration in the Church had just gone through a shocking episode with the publication on August 10, in the Italian magazine *Panorama*, of a list of cardinals and bishops allegedly belonging to Freemasonry. The magazine, which did not believe in the authenticity of the document, still stated:

> If the list were genuine, the Church would be in the hands of the Masons. Paul VI would effectively be surrounded by them. Or rather, they would have served as his great electors and would have guided him in the most important decisions taken during his thirteen-year pontificate. And, even before that, they would have been the ones who pushed the Second Vatican Council on the road to reform.

The list *Panorama* published was taken up in the entire international press.

Archbishop Lefebvre had not waited for this publication to be alarmed at this alleged Masonic infiltration in the Church, however. Indeed, it was a small Italian bulletin, *Si si No no*, published by a priest, Don Putti, who shared his fight for Tradition and with whom he had been communicating for several years, that first published this list in June 1976. The following month it was taken up by *Introibo*, the newsletter of Father André, whom Archbishop Lefebvre knew. The list contained seventeen names, including the precise date of their alleged enrollment in Freemasonry. The names listed were, in order: Cardinal Baggio, prefect of the Congregation of Bishops; Archbishop Casaroli, secretary for Public Affairs of the Church; Bishop Angelini,

---

58 Ibid., 6 and 8.
59 It was notably put forward in the work of Léon de Poncins at the time of the Council: *Le Problème juif au concile* (1965), which was published in several languages, including English: *Judaism and the Vatican: an Attempt at Spiritual Subversion* (London: Britons Publishing, 1967).
60 *Infiltrations ennemies dans l'Église. Documents et témoignages* (Paris: La librairie française, 1969). This work was edited by Georges Virebeau, an alias for Henry Coston; it was republished in 1990.

titular bishop of Messene; Msgr Macchi, private secretary to Paul VI; Msgr Levi, vice-director of *L'Osservatore Romano*; Archbishop Gottardi of Trent; Msgr Biffi, chaplain to Paul VI and rector of the Pontifical Lateran University; Cardinal Pellegrino, Archbishop of Turin; Msgr Marchisano, Undersecretary of the Congregation for Catholic Education; Msgr Noe, Master of the Pontifical Ceremonies; Archbishop Bugnini, who had been the great architect of the liturgical reform before his brusque ouster in the summer of 1975; Cardinal Villot, Secretary of State; Cardinal Suenens, Archbishop of Malines; Cardinal Poletti, Vicar General of Rome; Archbishop Brini of Algiza, Secretary of the Congregation for the Oriental Churches; Msgr Rizzi, Second Class Major of the Congregation for the Oriental Churches; Don Pinto, Official of the Supreme Tribunal of the Apostolic Signatura.

Church historians and Freemasonry scholars have yet to demonstrate the document's trustworthiness. Did Archbishop Lefebvre himself give full credence to this list, which mixed leading cardinals with obscure prelates? In any case, he judged it sufficiently plausible to make Masonic infiltration an explanatory cause for the excesses of Vatican II and, more generally, for the crisis in the Church. The question would come up again after the death of Paul VI, at the time of the conclave convened to elect his successor.

CHAPTER 10
From One Papacy to the Next

THE JULY 1976 SUSPENSION *A DIVINIS* CAUSED some professors and seminarians to leave Écône. But the enormous media attention given to the Mass in Lille the following month encouraged many Catholics attached to the traditional Mass to organize for its continued celebration. By consulting the announcements published in the *Journal Officiel,* one can see that from the summer of 1976 onwards numerous associations of Catholics attached to the traditional liturgy were created throughout France, adding to the dozens that already existed. These local associations, often with identical names, were not created by the Society of St. Pius X, whose presence was still very weak. "When I arrived at the head of the district in August 1976, you could say that there was nothing," said Father Aulagnier, with a little exaggeration.[1] The new traditionalist associations came about at the initiative of the faithful who wanted to support either a parish priest who was still attached to this liturgy or a priest who had been marginalized by the diocesan authorities because of this attachment and who celebrated Mass in an improvised place of worship.

While SSPX priests ministering in France were few in number – less than a dozen in the fall of October 1976 – most traditionalist priests still belonged to diocesan clergy. In October 1976, Father Coache gave a few figures:

> Over eight hundred priests in France celebrate the Holy Sacrifice of the Mass according to the age-old, truly Catholic rite. . . . Hundreds of priests, dozens of traditionalist periodicals, are actually fighting, whether discreetly or more openly! Five hundred liturgical centers provide the true Mass.[2]

THE STORMING OF SAINT-NICOLAS-DU-CHARDONNET

In Paris, priests and Catholics attached to the traditional liturgy helped themselves to a place of worship, the church of Saint-Nicolas-du-Chardonnet. While this church has become a world-famous symbol of the SSPX, the latter was not implicated in its original takeover. It

---

1 P. Aulagnier, *La Tradition sans Peur,* 129.
2 *Le Combat de la foi* 37 (October 7, 1976).

was a priest from the diocese of Paris, Msgr Ducaud-Bourget, already mentioned in these pages, who was the first "occupier."[3]

He had been chaplain at the Laennec Hospital from 1961. During the post-conciliar crisis, he was an ardent defender of Tradition. From the beginning he was a member of *Opus Sacerdotale*, and in 1968 he signed Father Coache's *Vademecum*. Once the new Mass came into effect, the Laennec Hospital chapel became a rallying point for the faithful attached to the traditional rite. When Msgr Ducaud-Bourget was forced to give up his position at Laennec in 1971, he continued to celebrate the traditional Mass for the growing number of Parisians in various rented halls. He also tried to obtain a church or chapel from Cardinal Marty, Archbishop of Paris, which led to visits and an exchange of correspondence that lasted several years.[4] From 1974 on, he celebrated Mass at the Salle Wagram, in the 17th arrondissement of Paris: a permanently rented hall, which became the Sainte-Germaine chapel, and a larger room which could only be rented on Sundays. A sort of parish community of some 1,000 to 1,500 faithful came into being. Priests came to help Msgr Ducaud-Bourget, notably Father Vincent Serralda, a former curate at the cathedral of Algiers, who had also been assistant priest at Saint-Nicolas-du-Chardonnet from 1964 to 1968, and who put himself at Msgr Ducaud-Bourget's service in 1971, while preparing a thesis on Alcuin at the *École Pratique des Hautes Études*.

After submitting several fruitless requests to Cardinal Marty to make a church available to the Salle Wagram faithful, a decision was made to occupy one. According to one of Msgr Ducaud-Bourget's biographers, it was Archbishop Lefebvre who suggested this idea in 1970: "'So take a church.' He would repeat this suggestion on several occasions."[5] Father Coache, for his part, claims the idea for himself, dating its proposal as early as 1974: "The prelate [Msgr Ducaud-Bourget] agreed on the principle but, prudent as he was, always delayed its execution."[6] Then on October 20, 1976, in a talk he was giving at the Mutualité, he announced, with Msgr Ducaud-Bourget's agreement, that a church would be taken "within six months." "The announcement aroused delirious enthusiasm," wrote Father Coache; "the applause went on forever."

During discreet meetings at the home of Mme Buisson, Father Coache's devoted collaborator in Paris, a strategy was worked out, a

---

3 Yvonne Desmurs-Moscet, *Monseigneur Ducaud-Bourget*.

4 See *Face à face, Mgr Ducaud-Bourget-Cardinal Marty, Correspondance (1968-1977)*, ed. Y. Desmurs-Moscet (Poitiers: Éditions de Chiré, 1977).

5 André Figueras, *Saint-Nicolas du Chardonnet. Le Combat de Mgr Ducaud-Bourget* (Poitiers: Éditions de Chiré, 1977), 79.

6 L. Coache, *Les Batailles du Combat de la Foi*, 222.

church was chosen, a date was set–Sunday, February 27, 1977–and a ruse was found. Three Sundays in a row, the faithful of the Salle Wagram were informed that the Mass of Sunday, February 27, would take place at 11:00 a.m. at the Palais de la Mutualité, in the 5th arrondissement, which is right next to the church of Saint-Nicolas-du Chardonnet; but until the last minute, the faithful were not informed of the action they were going to engage in. On February 27, 1977, as they arrived at the Mutualité they were invited to go to the nearby church where Mass according to the new rite was being celebrated. Then, after that Mass, Msgr François Ducaud-Bourget and four priests (Frs. Coache, Serralda, de Fommervault, and Juan) arrived in procession, wearing chasuble or surplice, to celebrate the traditional Mass.[7] The church remained occupied by the traditionalists, despite the protests of the parish priest and vicars. Antoine Barrois, one of the contributors to *Itinéraires* who had participated in the February 27 coup, could write:

> So it's done. In Paris, a church has been occupied. It is certainly occupied by Christ Jesus, our Lord. Certainly Catholic Masses are celebrated there. The traditional liturgical prayers are maintained there. And we are keeping it.[8]

Despite various administrative procedures, an attempt to "take back" the church, and an attempt at mediation, entrusted to the philosopher Jean Guitton, the occupation continued. Personalities (Jacques Dufilho, Jean Dutourd, Jean Raspail, Michel Droit, Jacques Perret, and others) became faithful or occasional "parishioners" of this church, of which Mgr Ducaud-Bourget did not claim to be the "parish priest."

At the end of 1977, Michel de Saint-Pierre took the initiative of writing a *Supplication* addressed to the Pope to ask him to send a legate to France, charged with drawing up "a detailed report on the state of the Church in France."[9] This long supplication emphasized "two aspects": "Traditionalists are upset and scandalized at seeing themselves rejected by the churches and the Church" and "the liturgical subversion." Michel de Saint-Pierre had obtained the signatures of sixteen lay personalities (notably Louis Salleron, Jacques Vier, Jacques Perret, Michel Droit, Jean Dutourd, Jean de Viguerie, Ivan Gobry) who represented the diverse tendencies among Catholics attached to Tradition.

---

7 As soon as June 1977, "the community of expelled priests and Christians" published *Le Défi intégriste. Saint-Nicolas occupé* (Paris: Éditions du Centurion, 1977).

8 Antoine Barrois, "Saint-Nicolas occupé," *Itinéraires* 212 (April 1977): 73.

9 "Supplique du Saint-Père pour lui demander l'envoi d'un légat," *La Pensée catholique* 171 (November-December 1977): 59-63.

BETWEEN DIALOGUE AND SEDEVACANTISM

The day after the death of Paul VI, historian Émile Poulat noted how the last years of his pontificate had been marked by the confrontation between "a torn pope" and "a serene archbishop."[10] Yet Paul VI had not given up on "finding the way to true reconciliation." The last months of his pontificate were marked by a resumption of exchanges between Rome and Archbishop Lefebvre.

On January 28, 1978, Cardinal Šeper, the Prefect of the Congregation for the Doctrine of the Faith, sent Archbishop Lefebvre a long memorandum in which he noted, based on his speeches and writings, a series of "assertions" that the Congregation considered "dangerous or erroneous" and to which he was asked to provide answers:

> These responses will be studied with benevolent interest, for the Congregation for the Doctrine of the Faith ardently desires that, with the Lord's help, you may find the way to a true reconciliation with the Vicar of Our Lord Jesus Christ and his Church.[11]

On February 26, Archbishop Lefebvre gave a very long reply to the Congregation: over eighty pages. The response was a well-reasoned critique of the Council's doctrine of religious liberty, of "liberal ecumenism," and of the new liturgy, which he described as "equivocal, bastardized, and nauseating to true Catholics, even if it is sometimes valid." The long letter ended with a "Catholic Profession of Faith" that was in fact an opposition between the Church's teaching of yesterday and today:

> We condemn, along with all the popes of the nineteenth and twentieth centuries, liberalism, naturalism, rationalism in all their forms, as the popes condemned them.
>
> We reject along with them all the consequences of those errors called "modern liberties," "new conception of law," just as they rejected them.
>
> Insofar as all the texts of the Second Vatican Council and the post-conciliar reforms are opposed to the doctrine expounded by these popes and give free rein to the errors they condemned, we feel obliged, in conscience, to express serious reservations regarding these texts and these reforms.

The Congregation for the Doctrine of the Faith responded to this uncompromising statement and an exchange of letters ensued that continued until June 1978.

---

10 Émile Poulat, "Paul VI," *Universalia* (1979): 620-21, reprinted in *Une Église ébranlée*, 266-82.

11 The complete text of what Archbishop Lefebvre would call an "inquiry," the responses he gave, and the oral and written exchanges that followed in 1978-1979 were published unabridged in a special issue of *Itinéraires* 233 (May 1979) under the title *Mgr Lefebvre et le Saint-Office*.

Among traditionalists, there were others who held more radical positions at the time. We have already seen the thesis that Father Guérard des Lauriers had begun to defend, though only privately, since April-May 1976: the formal vacancy of the Holy See.[12] Paul VI was legitimately pope, but he was not exercising his magisterial authority, or was doing so in a manner contrary to that for the sake of which it exists, viz., to transmit the faith. This thesis, which he would develop in the years to come, had convinced some priests of the SSPX and had also begun to spread in various religious communities. Thus Dom Gérard, prior of the monastery of Sainte-Madeleine in Bédoin, maintained at this time that there was a "*de facto* vacancy*" of authority (pope and bishops) and that it was legitimate to oppose it if its teaching was contrary to the faith or equivocal.

This position does not show up in the writings he published at that time – *La Vocation monastique*, *L'Église face aux nations* – but it does in his correspondence and in certain lectures. Thus, on May 28, 1978, invited to participate in the *Una Voce Helvetica* congress in Lausanne, he developed an analysis that can be described as sedevacantist; the expression itself is used. Dom Gérard's lecture was on the Mass. He declared:

> We have bishops who say sacrilegious Masses, who tamper with the sacraments of the Church of God and who perform ceremonies, if you will . . . that are profane. And here is the Supreme Authority letting this happen. But what do you expect? It is an Authority that no longer has any . . . any . . . that no longer has any being. We are not governed. There is a *de facto* vacancy. A vacancy . . . the See is vacant. We are not governed, we are not protected. . . . [T]he Supreme Pastor is no longer on the Seat of Peter. A pastor who separates himself from tradition is schismatic. He no longer exists.[13]

Regarding the bishops, Dom Gérard also claimed:

> We respect their sacred character, but their jurisdiction is weakened, because a hierarchical, episcopal jurisdiction cannot be made to serve at cross-purposes with its own finality. The spiritual power given to a bishop to govern the people of God and to teach them was not given for heresy. It was given for the salvation of souls, and to communicate divine life. So when this jurisdiction is used against what it was given for, this jurisdiction no longer exists.

On this last point, Dom Gérard was taking up, without mentioning his name, the argument of Father Guérard des Lauriers, an argument

---

12 As Fr Louis-Marie de Blignières told the author on November 27, 2011 and Father Bernard Lucien told the author on August 10, 2015. These positions of Fr Guérard des Lauriers had caused him to be dismissed from the faculty at Écône in September of 1977. Dom Gérard, however, continued to call on him for his monks.
13 Transcript of the lecture, based on a recording of it.

which he had already summarized in a letter to Archbishop Lefebvre two years earlier.

These divergent doctrinal positions within traditionalism eluded the bishops of France. At that time, 1977-1978, in spite of the coup that was the occupation of Saint-Nicolas-du-Chardonnet, and of what they knew of the action of Archbishop Lefebvre, they still had little idea of the size of the traditionalist movement. At the beginning of 1978, the Permanent Council of the Episcopate had its General Secretariat carry out a survey of the traditionalist movement in France, its various components, and its presence in the dioceses. The bishops were asked to send information and documentation. The General Secretariat drew up a map of the "traditionalist establishments" in France, indicating for each department the "foundations of Archbishop Lefebvre," the existing communities, the schools, places of worship. The Permanent Council of the Episcopate met on May 8 and 9, 1978, to examine the results of the survey and to draw up a report that would be sent to all the bishops with the map mentioned above. In its report, sent to each bishop with the notation "Confidential. Not for publication,"[14] the Permanent Council of the Episcopate, for the first time, recognized its share of responsibility for the traditionalist reaction:

> The bishops of the Permanent Council have asked themselves why these [traditionalist] activities are expanding. Certainly, in each case their influence is limited, but it seems that a need for security and popular expressions of the faith has not been sufficiently acknowledged in our pastoral orientations.

And regarding the liturgy, in a rather abstract conceptualization, it regretfully acknowledged that "[w]e thought that symbolism could change as we wished."

Nevertheless, a month later, when Archbishop Lefebvre came to confer the sacrament of confirmation on nearly three hundred children in the church of Saint-Nicolas-du-Chardonnet, the Archbishop of Paris became alarmed and indignant. On June 2, two days before the ceremony, Cardinal Marty issued a statement "recalling once again that this is a move that is in rupture of communion with the Catholic Church, in formal disobedience to the Pope, and in complete disagreement with the Archbishop of Paris." He also asked all the pastors in Paris to make this declaration known to their parishioners and to add an additional intention at Sunday Mass, at the time of the Universal Prayer: "In the face of the divisions that are tearing Catholics apart, let

---

14 Permanent Council, 8-9 May 1978, AHAP, 1 S 1.

us pray for the unity of the Church in communion with Pope Paul VI and the bishops."[15] One of the auxiliary bishops of Paris, Bishop Pézeril, published a virulent article in *La Croix* to express his indignation at the growing presence of Archbishop Lefebvre in France, his "diligent, obstinate, and methodical installation in most of the dioceses of France." Regarding the confirmations that were to take place at Saint-Nicolas-du-Chardonnet, Bishop Pézeril wrote that it was an "episcopal outrage. A public outrage. An outrage against Christ and the Church." Recalling, correctly from a canonical point of view, that the suspension *a divinis* imposed on Archbishop Lefebvre forbade him "to celebrate Mass, to administer the sacraments, or to preach," he spoke in especially severe terms of "profanation," of "unspeakable mystification," of "sacrilege."

THE COUNCIL IN LIGHT OF TRADITION

On August 6, 1978, Paul VI died, after fifteen years of a pontificate during which the Church had been battered by a rough "storm," as the Pope himself had said. "A shaken Church" and a Pope "who died without having dominated this dogmatic, disciplinary and spiritual crisis, without his calls for fraternity and peace having been able to ward off the violent conflicts among peoples."[16]

Two days after the death of Paul VI, Archbishop Lefebvre, in a letter addressed to four of the cardinals who were about to meet in conclave, asked: "Will the painful ordeal of these last fifteen years continue or will it end?" He also expressed concern about the validity of the election that was going to take place since, for the first time, cardinals over eighty years old could not take part in the vote.[17]

The sudden death of John Paul I on September 28, after a one-month pontificate, stunned the world. The conspiracy theory of a plot to assassinate a pope who was showing himself to be too traditional was immediately brought up by Msgr Ducaud-Bourget, then later by Father de Nantes following the investigation of an English journalist. Archbishop Lefebvre did not dwell on this hypothesis. On October 6, he addressed a new letter to "a good thirty" cardinals who were about to meet in conclave.[18] He stated:

> The present situation is such that only a pope like Saint Pius X can halt the self-destruction from which [the Church] has been suffering, especially since the Second Vatican Council.

15 *Lettre aux curés de Paris*, dated June 1, 1978, and *Déclaration* dated June 2, AHAP, 1 S 1.
16 Émile Poulat, "Paul VI," 620-21.
17 *Lettre de Mgr Lefebvre au Cardinal X. . . .*, August 8, 1978, published in *Itinéraires* 233 (May 1979): 125-28.
18 Archbishop Lefebvre to Jean Madiran, Letter, October 26, 1978, Jean Madiran Archives.

He urged the cardinals to elect a pope who would not continue "the application of the Council and of its Reforms."[19]

On October 16, Cardinal Wojtyła, Archbishop of Krakow, was elected and took the name John Paul II. His first *Urbi et Orbi* message, transmitted by radio from the Sistine Chapel, showed that he did not intend to abandon the Second Vatican Council, but that he wanted to reconcile it with Tradition: Vatican II "seen in the light of Tradition and embodying the dogmatic formulae issued over a century ago by the First Vatican Council" would be, he declared, "a decisive indication and a rousing stimulus, so that—we say it again—we may walk in the paths of life and of history."[20]

Barely a month after his election to the pontificate, John Paul II received Archbishop Lefebvre in audience. The press and the Vatican spokesman would later say that it was the founder of the SSPX who had asked to be received by the new pope. In reality, as Archbishop Lefebvre confided in a conference to his seminarians, it was a suggestion from Cardinal Siri. He felt "that it was still a little early, that it was better to wait until the Pope was informed, until events had already shown what the Holy Father's orientation was, what his thoughts were,"[21] but he allowed himself to be convinced by Cardinal Siri's arguments. Archbishop Lefebvre was received by the Pope in audience on November 18, 1978. The meeting, which lasted an hour and a half, was cordial. The Pope "embraced me warmly," Archbishop Lefebvre said. He sat down next to him and the founder of Écône first presented the origins of the SSPX and its growth—at that time eight districts in the world, 115 priests, 170 seminarians in four countries. Then Archbishop Lefebvre addressed the problems posed by certain conciliar texts:

> Certainly there are things in the Council that are quite difficult to accept; however, I would be willing to sign a sentence like this: "I accept the Acts of the Council interpreted in the sense of Tradition." I feel that this is a sentence that I might accept, and sign, if you wish.

This statement came as a pleasant surprise to the Pope: "Why, that's very good!... Do you really agree to sign a sentence like that?"[22] John

---

19 *Lettre de Mgr Lefebvre à plusieurs cardinaux*, October 6, 1978, published in *Itinéraires* 233 (May 1979): 129-31.
20 Message *Urbi et Orbi* on October 17, 1978 given in Latin and published in Italian in *L'Osservatore Romano* (October 18, 1978); English version at https://www.ewtn.com/catholicism/library/his-first-urbi-et-orbi-address-8580.
21 Conference to the seminarians of Écône, December 21, 1978, published in *Cor unum* 2 (March 1979): 1-14.
22 Ibid., 9.

Paul II was all the more happily surprised that Archbishop Lefebvre was taking up an expression ("the Council read in the light of Tradition") that he himself had already used twice since the beginning of his pontificate.[23] On the question of the Mass, the Pope seemed to minimize the dispute: "These are disciplinary matters . . . Perhaps we could see, examine the question." He seemed to be in a hurry to find a solution: "We must arrive at practical things, we must arrive at a conclusion." John Paul II immediately called in Cardinal Šeper, whom he had reappointed as Prefect of the Congregation for the Doctrine of the Faith. He told him, "We must quickly find a solution." But Cardinal Šeper was circumspect and warned, "Be careful, Holy Father, they're turning this Mass into a battle standard!"

At the end of the audience, the Pope instructed Cardinal Šeper to "work things out with Archbishop Lefebvre." Further correspondence followed.[24] A month after this meeting with John Paul II, Archbishop Lefebvre was cautious. In the above-mentioned conference to his seminarians, he recognized certain qualities of the Pope: "He is very pious, he loves the Blessed Virgin very much, he is completely anti-Marxist," but he realized that John Paul II was strongly attached to the Council and its new orientations:

> He will do everything in his power to suppress abuses, to channel the reform; but I think I can say that he appears to be in fundamental agreement with the Council and the reforms; I don't think he questions that. And this is obviously very serious, because he is for ecumenism, for collegiality, for religious freedom.[25]

Three days later he wrote a letter to John Paul II. Without bringing up doctrinal problems, he asked for just one thing:

> Most Holy Father, for the honor of Jesus Christ, for the good of the Church, for the salvation of souls, we beg you to say one word, one word only, as Successor of Peter, as Pastor of the Universal Church, to the Bishops of the whole world: "Let them be"; "We authorize the free exercise of what has been used by the many-centuries-old Tradition for the sanctification of souls."
> What difficulty does such an attitude present? None at all. The bishops would decide on the places and times reserved for this Tradition. Unity would be found immediately at the level of the local bishop. . . . For Écône, its seminaries, its priories, everything would be normalized. . . . The priories would serve dioceses by preaching parish missions, retreats according to St.

---

23 Regarding the circumstances of this meeting, see also Emilio Cavaterra, *Il Prefetto del Sant'Offizio*, 166-68.
24 This will be found in *Mgr Lefebvre et le Saint-Office.*
25 Talk to the seminarians of Écône, December 21, 1978.

Ignatius, and service to the parishes, in full submission to the local Ordinaries.[26]

This request from Archbishop Lefebvre to John Paul II repeated what he had already asked of Paul VI: "Allow us to make the experiment of Tradition." There was no direct response to this request. But Archbishop Lefebvre was invited to a "colloquium" held at the Congregation for the Doctrine of the Faith on January 11 and 12, 1979. He thought that these were "private talks," and was surprised to find himself subjected to "a procedure similar to an actual trial."[27] In fact, the term "colloquium" is the one used in the *Ratio agendi* which, since 1971, had established the procedure used by the Congregation for the Doctrine of the Faith to examine doctrinal questions. Archbishop Lefebvre was questioned by five officials and members of the Congregation for the Doctrine of the Faith: Cardinal Šeper, the prefect; Msgr Hamer, the secretary; Father Duroux, a consultant, and two other experts. The questions were very precise and technical, often involving both canon law and theology. Archbishop Lefebvre answered each one in a precise manner; these answers have not, to this day, been analyzed or studied by historians and theologians. The Prelate of Écône felt that this "colloquium" took the form of an "actual trial" and he appealed to John Paul II, asking him "to establish the Society as a prelature *nullius* with a bishop in charge, and to send a cardinal visitator."[28] It would be several years before this course of action was adopted.

GUÉRARDISM

In March 1979, the letter that Archbishop Lefebvre had addressed to John Paul II on December 25, 1978, became known through its publication in the *Letter to Friends and Benefactors* of the Society of St. Pius X. It scandalized Father Guérard des Lauriers, who addressed a long letter to Archbishop Lefebvre, dated April 12, 1979, published under the title: "Monsignor, we do not want this peace."[29] He reproached Archbishop Lefebvre for putting the traditional Mass and the new Mass on an equal footing:

---

26 Archbishop Lefebvre to John Paul II, Letter, December 24, 1978, published in the SSPX French-language newsletter *Lettre aux amis et bienfaiteurs* 16 (March 1979) and in *Itinéraires* 233 (May 1979): 138-40.
27 Archbishop Lefebvre to John Paul II, Letter, January 12, 1979, *Itinéraires* 233 (May 1979): 167.
28 B. Tissier de Mallerais, *Marcel Lefebvre*, 509.
29 P. Guérard des Lauriers, *Monseigneur, nous ne voulons pas de cette paix*, April 12, 1979, four typewritten pages (Archives of the abbey of Sainte-Madeleine). It would be published, in French and German, in the revue *Einsicht* (Munich) 9 (May 1979).

> Your Excellency, you are relying on the pope to preserve the Mass. And you accept the coexistence, *within the Church*, and in fact inevitably within the very same church, of both the Mass that is THE MASS and the "innovated Mass." And you expect that "[u]nity would be found immediately at the level of the local bishop." . . . But there is no supping with Satan. Hell is paved with those good intentions that justify the means by the end, a sure evil by the illusion of the good. . . . Your Excellency, your peace protocol gives the *coup de grâce* to our trust, which we can no longer place in you, whether in the matter of the Mass or in that of "authority."

In this virulent letter, the Dominican theologian also accused Archbishop Lefebvre of having celebrated the new Mass "from the beginning of April 1969 until December 24, 1971" and thus of being a defender of the faith who had faltered. Jean Madiran denounced the chronological absurdity of this "delirious calumniator"[30] (since the new Mass promulgated in April 1969 was only "permitted" in November 1969 and made obligatory later). It also published Archbishop Lefebvre's response, which originally appeared in the German-language SSPX newsletter, stating, "I have never celebrated the new Mass according to the rite introduced in November 1969; I have always considered it dangerous and poisoned by a false ecumenism."

In the following months, Father Guérard des Lauriers would make public his thesis on the "formal vacancy" of the papal see. As we have seen, he had begun to propound it in private around April-May 1977, which had led to his expulsion from the faculty of Écône in September 1977. At that time he had begun to write a study of about one hundred pages entitled *Le Siège apostolique est-il vacant?* ["Is the Apostolic See Vacant?"]. In it, he presented his thesis: Paul VI "is still Pope materially," but he "is no longer Pope formally" because he no longer has the "habitual, actual, and efficacious purpose" of "promoting the good end entrusted to the Church." This demonstration was supposed to have been published in June 1978. It was first circulated as a mimeographed brochure. Various circumstances delayed its publication. The death of Paul VI in August 1978 and then the successive elections of Popes John Paul I and John Paul II may have caused Father Guérard des Lauriers to hesitate. The positions and actions of a new pope might perhaps render the thesis of the "formal vacancy" null and void. Then the study was finally made public in May 1979, in the first issue of a review, *Les Cahiers de Cassiciacum*, published in Nice by two of his disciples, Fathers Lucien and Seuillot,

---

30 *Itinéraires* 237 (November 1979): 156-57.

both ordained priests by Archbishop Lefebvre–hence the name of "Cassiciacum thesis" later given to this doctrinal position. According to Father Guérard des Lauriers, the change of pontificate did not alter the judgment to be made: "What we believed to be true of the living Cardinal J.-B. Montini under the pontificate of 'Paul VI' we believe to be true under the pontificate of John Paul II as well as under that of John Paul I."[31] The thesis was based on inductive reasoning: at least since December 7, 1965 (the date of the promulgation of the conciliar declaration on religious freedom) Paul VI no longer had the "habitual intention" in the theological sense of promoting the good of the Church. Thus he was a legitimately elected pope (*materialiter*) but was not elected *formaliter*. His successors, John Paul I and then John Paul II, did not show this "habitual intention" either: there is a "formal vacancy" of the Holy See. The faithful, priests, and bishops, have the legitimate right and duty to reject the Pope's teaching and his government. And priests must refrain from naming the pope in the canon of the Mass (at the time of the prayers before the consecration: *una cum famulo tuo papa nostro...*), because this is to recognize his authority.

Several priests ordained by Archbishop Lefebvre in 1977 and 1978, Frs Belmont, de Blignières, Guépin, Lucien, and Seuillot, had already rallied to this thesis before its publication. Outside the Society of Saint Pius X, it was beginning to gain traction among some people, such as Father Vinson, who as early as 1971 affirmed that the "new Mass" was not only equivocal or dangerous, but even invalid.

On November 8, 1979, Archbishop Lefebvre felt it necessary to make his "position on the new Mass and the Pope" clear. He did so in a talk to the seminarians and professors of Écône, which was then published in the two SSPX publications.[32] He specified that in these matters he had not "changed his opinions," and set out in detail "the orientations and thoughts of the Priestly Fraternity of St. Pius X." He affirmed, with regard to the celebrations of the new Mass that "[m]ost of these Masses are sacrilegious and they pervert the faith by diminishing it," but he refused to consider invalid all Masses celebrated according to the new rite, "as long as the essential conditions for validity exist, that is to say, the matter, the form, the intention, and a validly ordained priest." At that time–he would later change his position–Archbishop

---

31 Fr Guérard des Lauriers, "Le Siège Apostolique est-il vacant?" *Cahiers de Cassiciacum* 1 (May 1979): 7.
32 *Cor Unum* (in-house SSPX newsletter) 4 (November 1979) and *Fideliter* 13 (February 1980): 65-70.

Lefebvre allowed that celebrating and attending the new Mass did not automatically amount to a transgression. Regarding the Pope and his authority, even though he said that Paul VI had contributed to the "awful demolition of the Church" by many of his acts and words, he "acted much more as a liberal than as an adherent of heresy. For as soon as the risk he was taking was pointed out to him, he made the text contradictory by adding a formula contrary to what was stated in the wording, or by writing an equivocal formula, which is the characteristic of liberals who are inconsistent by nature."

Archbishop Lefebvre rejected the thesis of what some would soon call "the Church in eclipse," as he felt that "the question of the Church's visibility is too necessary to its existence for God to omit it for decades," and he stated: "Far from refusing to pray for the Pope, we redouble our prayers and supplications that the Holy Spirit may give him light and strength in the affirmation and defense of the faith." He drew two practical conclusions from these doctrinal positions. The first was the need to continue to look to Rome for the solution to the crisis in the Church:

> I have never refused to go to Rome at his [the Pope's] request or at the request of his representatives. Truth must be affirmed in Rome more than in any other place. Truth belongs to God, who will make it triumph.

Furthermore, the Prelate of Écône solemnly affirmed that the Society of St. Pius X

> cannot tolerate in its midst members who refuse to pray for the Pope and who affirm that all the masses of the Novus Ordo Missae are invalid. Certainly, we suffer from the continual inconsistency of [the pope's] praising all the liberal orientations of Vatican II and at the same time trying to mitigate their effects. But this should encourage us to pray and to hold fast to Tradition, but not to say that the Pope is not the Pope.

As a result of the position taken by the founder of the SSPX, several Écône seminary professors, seminarians, and priests had to leave the SSPX. Archbishop Lefebvre also imposed a *Declaration of Fidelity* on future priests as a condition for ordination. This declaration, called the *Declaration of Fidelity to the Priestly Fraternity of St. Pius X*, is an official and clear summary of the SSPX's positions on the Pope and the New Mass and a commitment to admit them. This very important text, still in use today, has never been published. I thank Bishop Tissier de Mallerais for having communicated it to me and for authorizing its publication in full for the first time:

Declaration of Fidelity to the Priestly Fraternity of St. Pius X

I, the undersigned (N.),

Recognize (N.) as pope of the Holy Catholic Church. That is why I am prepared to pray for him publicly as Sovereign Pontiff. I refuse to follow him when he departs from Catholic Tradition, especially in matters of religious freedom and ecumenism, as well as in reforms that are harmful to the Church.

I admit that not all Masses celebrated according to the new rite are invalid. However, in view of the poor translations of the Novus Ordo Missæ, its ambiguity, which favors its interpretation in a Protestant sense, and the plurality of the ways in which it is celebrated, I recognize that the danger of invalidity is very great.

I affirm that the new rite of the Mass does not actually formulate any heresy expressly, but that it "departs impressively, on the whole as well as in detail, from the Catholic theology of the Holy Mass," and that for this reason this new rite is in itself evil.

Therefore, I will never celebrate Holy Mass according to this new rite, even under threat of ecclesiastical penalties; nor will I ever positively advise anyone to actively participate in such a Mass.

Finally, I accept as legitimate the liturgical reform of John XXIII. I therefore receive all of its liturgical books as Catholic: the Missal, Breviary, etc., and I commit myself to use them exclusively, according to their calendar and rubrics, especially for the celebration of the Mass and for the common recitation of the breviary.

In so doing, I wish to manifest the obedience that binds me to my superiors, as well as that which binds me to the Sovereign Pontiff in all his legitimate acts.

The text needs no commentary, but its clear statements are worth noting: recognition of the legitimacy of the pope, obligation to pray for him, obedience due to him, recognition of the validity of the new Mass. On the other hand these are balanced by apparently incompatible restrictions: an obedience to the pope that is conditional, and an absolute refusal to celebrate the new Mass.

In fact, even after this *Declaration*, there still were – and there still are today within the Society – priests who are not *una cum*, that is, who refuse to name the pope in the Canon of the Mass. But as long as this refusal remained and remains a private opinion and is not the object of a public statement (sermon, book, or article), the SSPX authorities did not and do not exclude priests who refused and still refuse to name the pope in the Canon of the Mass.

THE QUESTION OF THE POPE

Following Archbishop Lefebvre's public statement, Dom Gérard too made a public declaration. He was all the more concerned about the influence of Father Guérard des Lauriers' thesis because of the fact that he had recently seemed to share it, and because it was still supported by priests who had, in different capacities, been at Bédoin (the young clerics Olivier de Blignières and Bernard Lucien). On January 13, 1980, Dom Gérard published a "Note" devoted to *The Question of the Pope*.

It was less doctrinal than Archbishop Lefebvre's *Declaration*, focusing rather on a "spiritual attitude" in conformity with the virtue of prudence. He went straight to the heart of the matter:

> The "Ultras" mistake *failure in the exercise of the papacy* for *vacancy of the Apostolic See*. They equate "bad pope" with "non-pope"; "resistance to the pope" with "rejection of the pope." This imprudent upping of the ante has ever been a temptation throughout history among "right-wing schismatics," those who push the requirement of purity to the extreme (Donatists, Jansenists, Old Catholics).

In a rather prescient way, he expressed a concern: "What is currently only a tendency, a temptation to bitter zeal, could go as far as a declared schism, the day John Paul II re-establishes (imperfectly) the tradition of the Church."

The "question of the pope," Dom Gérard also wrote, is "a question of a moral kind" which should not be "intellectualized to excess." Certainly "the acts (or lack of acts) of John Paul II can be judged severely by reference to doctrine and Tradition. Some of the Pope's speeches are ambiguous. We do not deny this; while it pains us to do so, we point it out when necessary." But "one must pray for the Pope in the canon of the Mass according to the norm indicated by the liturgy." It is not "a problem of speculative theology," but "a requirement of charity, filial piety, and humility." Without mentioning the name of Father Guérard des Lauriers or any of his disciples, Dom Gérard affirmed:

> We must firmly denounce the tendency to over-intellectualize a moral question posed to humility, to patience, to loving docility, and to the *sensus Ecclesiae*, that is to say, to the virtues that pertain to life in society, which do not go without a certain mistrust of oneself and of one's own insights.

He concluded: "One's attitude towards John Paul II is therefore not directly a matter of dogma but of virtue," and he referred to Victor Hugo, with an unexpected quotation from *Les Misérables*: "Being ultra means going beyond; it means attacking the scepter in the name of the throne and the mitre in the name of the altar."

This "Note" by Dom Gérard infuriated those who recognized themselves under the label "ultras." Under the title *Un temps pour se taire et un temps pour parler*, the magazine *Forts dans la Foi* responded by publishing a 32-page supplement in February 1980. Its anonymous writer sought to demonstrate the "sophisticated illogicality of the argument" of the prior of Bédoin and denounced his "paternalistic sentimentality." He concluded his attack by opining that Dom Gérard's denunciation of the "ultras" was motivated first of all by his concern to find "a place within the 'reconstruction' that John Paul II is about to carry out without delay" and to obtain "a canonical and sociological recognition." The identity of the anonymous writer soon came to light. It was Father Olivier de Blignières, to whom Dom Gérard had given so much help a few years before, and who was now a full supporter of Father Guérard des Lauriers' thesis. Jean Madiran, with the polemical style he sometimes indulged in, mocked in *Itinéraires* the "young and old editors of Cassiciacum" and "Father O.," whom he occasionally described as "Father Zero."[33]

Dom Gérard's "Note" received much attention through its publication in the review *Itinéraires*, at the same time as Archbishop Lefebvre's conference of the previous year was published. Both documents appeared in the March 1980 issue of the review, preceded by a long introduction by Jean Madiran. The dossier was significantly entitled *De amaritudinis zelo*,[34] referring to the beginning of chapter seventy-two of the Rule of St. Benedict that Dom Gérard had quoted: "There is a zeal of bitterness that is bad, that separates from God and leads to hell; and there is a good zeal that leads away from the vices and leads to God and to eternal life."

Unity among traditionalists had already been damaged by the particular positions of Father de Nantes and the refusal to take a stand from Jean Ousset and *L'Office*; it was further fissured by the emergence of a "Guérardian" current and of a sedevacantist current. The "chapelization of traditionalism," to use François Huguenin's expression, would continue and grow in the following decades.

From that time on, Jean Madiran tried to oppose this chapelization by supporting different initiatives.

"CATHOLIC COMMUNION AND FRENCH FRIENDSHIP"

In a long April 1980 article, Jean Madiran had endeavored to show that "the Cassiciacum thesis" was "an unproven hypothesis," "a bourgeois gentleman's theology," an "interminable and pedantic demonstration." For his part, he wanted to stick to the essential:

---

33 Jean Madiran, "La Polémique de Cassiciacum," *Itinéraires* 243 (May 1980): 53-85.
34 *Itinéraires* 241 (March 1980): 150-60.

> There was no need to have a thesis, an opinion, or a hypothesis about Paul VI's administration to remain faithful to the Catholic Mass, to the Roman Catechism, to Sacred Scripture. Faith is enough. It is faith that keeps us attached to Scripture, to the Catechism, to the Mass, to the tradition of the Church.[35]

This threefold "complaint" ("Give us back the Mass, the catechism, and Sacred Scripture") that Jean Madiran had addressed to the Pope in 1972, and which he brought up frequently, was repeated on the occasion of John Paul II's first apostolic journey to France, in 1980. This first trip had been variously appreciated and commented upon. On May 31, at the Basilica of Saint-Denis, a ceremony with a militant tone was organized by the JOC (Young Catholics Workers' organization) around the Pope. The great Mass organized at Le Bourget airfield on June 1, 1980, under the rain, had gathered 350,000 people, instead of the million expected by the organizers. Some bishops had conspicuously refrained from coming to meet the Pope, and many dioceses had not organized travel to Paris for the faithful. It was during this Mass that John Paul II had called out to French Catholics and bishops, with a formula that was to remain emblematic of the trip: "France, eldest daughter of the Church, are you faithful to the promises of your baptism?"

"How can one not take this question as a blow straight to the heart?" wrote Jean Madiran the day after the Pope's trip in a long editorial published in *Itinéraires*.[36] He recognized that "it would be very premature, and we have neither the competence nor the desire, to pronounce on this pope a global, objective, balanced, sovereign judgment, with marginal annotations as for an examination paper." But he felt that there was no other "way out" of the crisis of the Church in France than "the necessary lifting of false prohibitions":

> The longer we wait, the deeper the wounds to the Church will be, and the more advanced the unravelling of the Catholic fabric. Undoubtedly, there will remain many pending questions: but they will begin to be usefully dealt with from the moment when the nullity of the prohibitions against the Mass, against the catechism, against the person of Archbishop Lefebvre, and against the priests he formed and ordained in view of a new springtime of the Church is acknowledged.

This editorial was followed by an address to the pope, under the title "Très Saint Père n'ayez pas peur!" ("Most Holy Father, Be Not Afraid!"), which he signed with other laymen: Jean Auguy, Yann Clerc, Georges Daix, Pierre Debray, Édith Delamare, Romain Marie, André

---

35 Jean Madiran, "La Thèse de Cassiciacum," *Itinéraires* 242 (April 1980): 78-95.
36 *Itinéraires* 245 (July-August 1980): 4-18.

Mignot, Jacques Perret, Michel de Saint-Pierre, Louis Salleron, Henri Sauguet, Gustave Thibon. These laymen, "in all independence from each other in the same Catholic communion," expressed to John Paul II "their filial and respectful gratitude" for his visit to France, and addressed a supplication to him:

> Will you allow us, Most Holy Father, to borrow your own words to tell you, "Be not afraid!" Give back to the Church of France the Mass, the liturgy, the sacraments, the priests, the seminaries, the catechism, and you will find the eldest daughter of the Church faithful to her baptismal vows. Our hope remains. We place it in your hands, for our salvation and that of the Church of France.

This petition was subsequently signed by some twenty other personalities.[37]

At that time, Jean Madiran and other laymen were also launching various initiatives of "intellectual and moral resistance" that would bring traditional Catholics together over the long term.

The first initiative fell to Bernard Antony who, in his militant activities, most often used the pseudonym of Romain Marie, his first two middle names. A nationalist and solidarity activist in his youth, he had a professional career in industry (director of human relations at Pierre Fabre Laboratories and founder of a training center in Toulouse). Familiar with the Benedictine priory of Bédoin, he also edited a monthly magazine, *Présent*, in Castres. Through Dom Gérard, he had discovered the work of André and Henri Charlier, and was enthusiastic about it. He had also met Albert Gérard, who had opened the Atelier de la Sainte-Espérance in Paris, to work and teach in the spirit of Henri Charlier. In the spring of 1980, Bernard Antony founded the Centre Henri et André Charlier (CHAC). He asked Jean Madiran, Dom Gérard, and Albert Gérard to be its patrons. The CHAC presented itself as "an initiative of intellectual and moral reconstruction," "the beginning of a response to the triple crisis of faith, intelligence, and courage from which our society in general and our teaching in particular are suffering."[38] The first achievement of the CHAC was the organization of a "Catholic summer university," which took place from July 29 to August 9 at the premises of the Dominican Teaching Sisters of Fanjeaux. Father Pozzetto, a young priest of the

---

37 Admiral Auphan, Jean Borella, the Duke of Castries, Yann Christ, Michel Ciry, Michel Déon, Jacques Dhaussy, Michel Droit, Maurice Duruflé and his wife (both organists at Saint-Étienne-du-Mont), Jean Dutourd, André Figueras, Roland Gaucher, Bernard Gavoty, Ivan Gobry, Pierre-Paul Grassé, Christian Langlois, Paul Orsoni, Jean Raspail, Rouault de la Vigne, Gilbert Tournier, Raymond Triboulet, Gérald Van der Kemp, Jacques Vier, Jean de Viguerie.

38 "Pourquoi le Centre Henri et André Charlier," *Présent* 50 (May-June 1980): 5-7.

Fraternity of Saint Pius X, was the chaplain of this first summer university and became the chaplain of CHAC. This "Catholic summer university" was aimed primarily at high school and university students, but also at teachers and educators in general. It was intended as a reaction against the national education system which "teaches badly" and which "no longer transmits [tradition]," and in a general way it was a break with "our era which is an era of barbarism and societal decadence."[39]

The "summer university" took place in a studious, spiritual, and convivial atmosphere. Each day began with Mass at 8:30 am, and ended with compline at 10:00 pm. During the day there were classes and lectures, and in the evening a recreational soirée. The classes were taught by Jean Madiran, on natural law, Hugues Kéraly, "agrégé" (high-ranking academic) in philosophy and Madiran's closest collaborator at the time, Bernard Antony, the historians Jean-Pierre Brancourt and Jean de Viguerie, Albert Gérard ("The Permanent Principles of Art"), Maurice Bardèche and Jacques Vier on literature. Dom Gérard gave two lectures devoted to his favorite themes: "Monastic life" and "Gregorian chant." François Brigneau and Roland Gaucher, journalists for the weekly magazine *Minute*, also gave lectures. Jean de Viguerie would later recall:

> There were a lot of people. All the resistance to conciliarism was there. Most of the audience was made up of students, young professors, and seminarians from Écône. There were all kinds of speeches and even songs. I remember the astonishment of the students when my friend Jean Fauré sang to them in a loud, gravelly voice some Occitan poems from Castelnaudary.[40]

Archbishop Lefebvre, who was in the area for an ordination, came to pay a visit and gave an impromptu lecture on August 4.

It was during that summer university that the idea of the "French Friendship Days" (*Journées d'Amitié française*) was born. The first one took place on November 30, organized at the Palais de la Mutualité, in Paris. It sought to react to the "French genocide," defined as follows: "A highly sophisticated genocide, under general anaesthesia, strikes the French people more and more each day, in their national, religious, family, and professional life and affects them even in their physical existence." In the face of this "genocide," the program was to promote "French friendship," "fidelity to the soul of France and to that French race of which Péguy spoke." Numerous Catholic movements, associations, and publications were present at this Day, as well as various personalities. Evoking in *Itinéraires* this "first step," this "good beginning," Jean Madiran wrote:

39 Ibid.
40 Jean de Viguerie, *Le Passé ne meurt pas* (Versailles: Via Romana, 2016), 150.

> At the November 30 French Friendship Day, there was a crowd;
> there were many people present; there was youth; there was
> ardor; there was heart. It was all the more festive that several
> representative personalities had come to set an example: Msgr
> Ducaud-Bourget, Admiral Auphan, Gustave Thibon, François
> Brigneau, Captain Sergent, Jean-Marie Le Pen, Pierre Pujo, Col-
> onel Château-Jobert. . . .

This list includes writers and journalists (Thibon and Brigneau), political figures—Jean-Marie Le Pen, founder of the National Front, and Pierre
Pujo, leader of the National Restoration, the heir to *Action française*—and
figures from the past struggle for French Algeria (Sergent and Château-
Jobert). Jean Madiran welcomed this "fine neighborliness with mutual
benevolence between those who feel, as it actually is, the process of spiritual, intellectual, and political genocide the French people are currently
undergoing."[41] Jean Madiran, François Brigneau, and Father Pozzetto,
among others, spoke, and many authors of the Catholic and national
right came for book signings. Jean Madiran was indignant that no media
reported on this event, despite the "two hundred and fifty communiqués
[sent] to all the important organs of the great written and spoken press."
It would be otherwise for the other French Friendship Days organized
in the following years. Those would give rise to controversy.

The following year, in the spring of 1981, Bernard Antony created
the Christian Solidarity Committees ("Comités Chrétienté-Solidarité")
to support Christians around the world who were suffering discrimi-
nation and persecution at the hands of communist regimes (in Poland,
Lithuania, Nicaragua, and elsewhere).

The following July, the second summer university of the Centre
Charlier took place. It was during these days that the idea of creating a
national Catholic daily newspaper was born; it would become the daily
newspaper *Présent*, which took its title from the monthly published in
Castres by Romain Marie. The launch of the daily was made possible
by a large subscription campaign conducted over several months. Issue
number 0 was symbolically printed on the occasion of the second French
Friendship Day, November 22, 1981. The daily newspaper, at the beginning, had as general director Bernard Antony (under the pseudonym of
Romain Marie), as political directors and editorial directors Jean Madiran
and François Brigneau, and as administrative and commercial director
Pierre Durand, who was also treasurer of the National Front. Dom Gérard
came to bless the premises, rue d'Amboise.[42]

---

41 Jean Madiran, "Faire connaître l'appel du Centre Henri et André Charlier," *Itinéraires*
249 (January 1981): 2-3.
42 Testimony of Jean Madiran to the author, April 15, 2009.

Finally, in 1982, during the third summer university, which took place in Mesnil-Saint-Loup, the project of organizing a great pilgrimage from Paris to Chartres was born. Since 1935, every year around Easter, students from Paris had been making a pilgrimage to Chartres (the pilgrimage gathered up to 12,000 participants in the mid-1960s). By the 1970s, this pilgrimage had not disappeared, but it had dwindled to a few hundred participants. Various initiatives had been launched by traditional Catholics to revive it: the CERCLE (Centre d'étude et de recherche culturelle pour les étudiants), which brought together students from the law school on the rue d'Assas, organized an annual pilgrimage led by Father Montarien who celebrated the Mass of Paul VI in Latin; later, from 1978 or 1979 onwards, the FCEF (Fédération catholique des étudiants de France), created by two former members of the MJCF, organized a pilgrimage in which the traditional Mass was celebrated.[43] But it was independently of these initiatives, which only gathered a few dozen participants, that a project arose in the summer of 1982. During the third summer university of the Centre Charlier, in an informal conversation in which Bernard Antony and Dom Gérard took part, Rémi Fontaine, a young journalist for *Présent* and a professor of philosophy, suggested that a pilgrimage from Notre-Dame de Paris to Notre-Dame de Chartres be organized around the feast of Pentecost. The idea, also supported by Max Champoiseau, "was immediately welcomed with enthusiasm by Dom Gérard."[44] Bernard Antony also rallied to the project, and asked Rémi Fontaine to plan the organization with the young people of the Centre Charlier. The name "Pilgrimage of Christendom" (*Pélerinage de la Chrétienté*) was chosen, and "the fundamental choices were quickly made": the pilgrimage would be made entirely on foot, from Notre-Dame de Paris to Notre-Dame de Chartres, in three days at Pentecost; "the teaching to be given would refer to the centuries-old tradition of the Church; the liturgy would be that of 1962; the atmosphere should reflect the spirit that animated the Charlier brothers, rooted in the concrete, and Charles Péguy, the bard of Christian France: the spirit of Christendom."[45]

The first "Pilgrimage of Christianity" was organized at Pentecost 1983, with a thousand faithful departing from Paris and three thousand arriving in Chartres two days later. The bishop of Chartres did

---

43 Testimony of Rémi Fontaine to the author, June 22, 2020.
44 Testimony of Rémi Fontaine to the author, March 10, 2011. See also *Bernard Antony raconte. Entretien avec Cécile Montmirail* (Paris: Éditions Godefroy de Bouillon, 2013), 208-9.
45 Rémi Fontaine, "Aux sources du pèlerinage de chrétienté," lecture given on December 8, 2001, *Action familiale et scolaire* 161 (2002).

not authorize the celebration of Mass, because the chaplain, Father Pozzetto,[46] belonged to the SSPX. In the years that followed, the number of participants continued to grow dramatically, taking on an international dimension and attracting increasing media attention: 8,000 in 1985 and 10,000 in 1987.[47]

EPISCOPAL CONSECRATIONS (1981-1987)

Despite these lay-led initiatives to strengthen "French friendship in Catholic communion" – initiatives that Archbishop Lefebvre and the SSPX approved of at the time – elsewhere divisions among priests and Catholics attached to Tradition were growing. Sedevacantists and Guérardians would oppose those they called "Lefebvrists." Sedevacantism was then represented in France mainly by Father Barbara and his review *Forts dans la foi*, published in Tours. By the end of the 1970s, he had been reinforced by a priest, Father Claude Barthe, and a layman, Bernard Dumont.

Bernard Dumont, a graduate of the elite *Sciences Politiques* school, which he attended from 1961 to 1964, and of the French Seminary of Rome from 1964 to 1966, had been active in *L'Office* of Jean Ousset before leaving it in 1968, considering it too "anti-intellectualist." In 1973 he formed a politico-religious study group, which in the following years would appear under different names: "Association for the Development of Political and Social Studies" (*Association pour le développement des études politiques et sociales*, ADEPS), Cardinal Pie Institute (*Institut du Cardinal Pie*, ICP), etc. This group, commonly called "the Party" internally, intended to "take power in order to restore a Catholic State."[48] Bernard Dumont was its undisputed leader – he would impose an oath on his members. Under the influence of Father Barbara, from 1975 on, Bernard Dumont adhered to the sedevacantist thesis. A few years later, he came into contact with Father Barthe. Barthe, ordained a priest in June 1979 in Écône, had been appointed to Saint-Nicolas-du-Chardonnet. A few months later, he refused Archbishop Lefebvre's condemnation of sedevacantism and Guérardism in November 1979. He came into conflict with Msgr Ducaud-Bourget. He had to leave Saint-Nicolas, even though the latter had enjoyed the muscular support of the ICP. He joined the

---

46 Father Pozzetto later joined the Fraternity of Saint Peter. He has since been reduced to the lay state as the result of a scandal.

47 *Le Quotidien de Paris* (May 29, 1985); *Figaro Magazine* (May 25, 1986); *Jours de France* (June 9, 1986); *Le Figaro* (June 9, 1987).

48 Denis Sureau, *Quelques repères sur les origines de Catholica*, unpublished, and Anne Perrin, *Autorité et charisme. Histoire et fonctionnement d'un petit groupe traditionaliste entre 1973 et 1986*, thesis, École Pratiques des Hautes Études, 1999, 283 pages.

Union for the Fidelity of Catholic Priests, Religious, and Laity (*Union pour la fidélité des prêtres, religieux et laïcs catholiques*, UPLF) which Bernard Dumont created in early 1980. Father Barbara agreed to make *Forts dans la foi* the publication of the movement. The UPLF multiplied its efforts. On December 9, 1980, it occupied the Basilica of Notre-Dame-des-Victoires to celebrate a solemn Mass and to publish an "Address to the Bishops who are still Catholic" asking them reject the new Mass and the doctrines of Vatican II "as schismatic and heretical." In 1982, as a special issue of *Forts dans la Foi*, the UPLF published *Écône point final* ("Écône: Full Stop," 90 pages). Unsigned, but written in its entirety by Father Barthe and Bernard Dumont, the volume denounced, in a highly polemical tone and according to political categories of analysis, "the advent of Lefebvrism" which tries to reconcile, said the authors, "a limited doctrine of the Magisterium and a theory of conditional obedience." The volume also mocked, with examples, the facade of unity among the "leaders of traditionalism" and asserted that "there is no way out except the Union for Fidelity." In 1984, without the name UPLF appearing, the group launched a journal of ideas, *Confrontation*. The group broke up in 1986.[49]

Meanwhile, the Guérardians would split up when, in 1981, Father Guérard des Lauriers showed himself willing to receive episcopal consecration at the hands of Bishop Ngô Dinh Thuc, former archbishop of Hué in Vietnam. Archbishop Thuc, in exile in Europe since 1963, had already agreed in January 1976 to ordain to the priesthood, without dimissorial letters, Clemente Domínguez y Gómez, the principal seer of the supposed apparitions of the Virgin Mary in Palmar y Troya, and two of his followers, Camilo Estevez Puga and Manuel Alonso Corral. Then, on January 11 of the same year, he consecrated them as bishops, also conferring episcopal consecration on two American religious followers of these pseudo-apparitions, Father Fulgence Sandler, a Benedictine, and Father Michael Donnelly, a Montfortian. These episcopal consecrations without episcopal mandate led to his excommunication on September 17, 1976. But his submission had allowed the excommunication to be lifted shortly thereafter.

Father Guérard des Lauriers had let himself be convinced to receive episcopal ordination in order to be able to ordain priests, so that what he called the *oblatio munda*, the "pure oblation," might be perpetuated, that is to say, the sacrifice of the Mass by priests who also recognized the formal vacancy of the Apostolic See. He agreed to receive this

---

49 Bernard Dumont and Fr Barthe were to launch a new journal of ideas, *Catholica*, in 1987. Fr Barthe parted ways with Bernard Dumont in 2007.

episcopal consecration at the hands of Bishop Ngô Dinh Thuc after having made sure that the latter no longer recognized the pontifical authority of John Paul II.[50] The ceremony took place in Toulon on May 7, 1981, in the presence of two witnesses, and was kept secret for several months. The news was not known until January 8, 1982. It divided the priests who supported the thesis of the formal vacancy of the Holy See. On the following January 18, six of them, Father Georges Vinson, Father de Blignières, and the lower clerics Belmont, Guépin, Lucien, and Seuillot, while they did not renege on their adherence to the thesis of the formal vacancy of the Holy See, published a communiqué to declare their position that this episcopal consecration was illicit and unjustified.[51] Conversely, other priests rallied to his thesis, and some accepted, or asked for, episcopal consecration by him. On April 30, 1984, Bishop Guérard des Lauriers consecrated the German priest Günther Storck as a bishop and, on August 22, 1986, the Dominican Robert McKenna. In December 1985, four Italian priests of the SSPX (Frs. Munari, Murro, Nitoglia and Ricossa), convinced by the Cassiciacum thesis, left the Society and founded the Mater Boni Consilii Institute (IMBC). On November 25, 1987, three months before his death, Bishop Guérard des Lauriers consecrated one of the founders, Father Franco Munari, as bishop. Some of the bishops (illicitly) consecrated by Mgr Guérard des Lauriers would in turn consecrate bishops. Thus, from the "Thuc" line of bishops was born a "Guérardian" line of bishops.

Without dwelling on it, because at this point we are reaching the margins of traditionalism, Bishop Thuc, after consecrating Father Guérard des Lauriers in May 1981, consecrated on the following October 17 two Mexican sedevacantist priests, Moises Carmona and Adolfo Zamora, who themselves ordained priests and bishops.[52] Then, on September 25, 1982, Bishop Thuc conferred the episcopal consecration *sub conditione* to Christian Datessen, who had once been a seminarian at Écône (1971-1972), had left to found the Fraternity of Our Lady of Bethlehem, and had

50 Bishop Ngô Dinh Thuc publically announced his sedevacantist position on February 25, 1982, through a declaration made in Munich in which he affirmed his "duty as a bishop to do everything possible for the Roman Catholic Church to continue for the eternal salvation of souls."
51 Unabridged version published in *Itinéraires* 261 (March 1982): 78-81, with a brief commentary by Jean Madiran in a note.
52 Deacon V.-M. Zins has established a detailed nomenclature of these various episcopal lines in 1992 in a special issue of his newsletter: "Collusions des 'guérardo-thucistes' avec des sectes," *Sub Tuum Praesidium* 31-32 (October 1992; 90 pages). Deacon Zins, who received the diaconate in 1977, had been dismissed from the Écône seminary for sedevacantism. Ever since then, he has refused to receive any "illegitimate" priestly ordination from any bishop at all, be he Thuc-line, Guérardian, or sedevacantist.

then been ordained priest and bishop by André Enos, a former priest who had become "primate" of the Union of Small Independent Catholic Churches (*Union des petites Églises catholiques indépendantes*, UPECI).

We are no longer in the traditionalist galaxy, but in marginal circles where *episcopi vagantes* abound (a good thousand in the world), and where the validity of ordinations is questionable. These "parallel churches" sometimes change their name to attract the traditionalist faithful. Thus the French branch of the Old Catholic Church founded by Jean Laborie became the Latin Catholic Ecclesial Community, and then the Latin Catholic-Traditional Community.[53]

THE KNOX SURVEY

The repeated requests of Archbishop Lefebvre, *Una Voce*, and other associations, such as the American TCM, to allow the celebration of the traditional Mass throughout the Church did not leave John Paul II unmoved. The Pope wanted to be better informed before making a decision. Did Archbishop Lefebvre's request correspond to a broader expectation of the faithful or not? He asked the Congregation for Divine Worship to submit a report on the subject. On June 19, 1980, Cardinal Knox, the prefect of the Congregation, sent a questionnaire in Latin to the bishops of the world. Half of the questions concerned the Latin Mass according to the rite of Paul VI:

> Are there any Masses celebrated in the Latin language in the diocese of which you are the sacred Pastor? Is there any demand for the Latin language in the Liturgy of the Mass? Is this demand rising or falling?

The other half of the questions concerned the so-called Mass of Saint Pius V:

> Are there in your diocese persons or particular groups who are asking for the Holy Mass celebrated in the Latin language according to the old rite ("the Tridentine Mass")? What is the size or importance of these groups? What reasons lead them to this attitude and to these requests?

The survey was sent to all 2,317 Roman Rite bishops in the world.

It is surprising that the traditionalist clergy and faithful were not consulted, in one way or another, on a subject that primarily concerned them. In fact the association *Una Voce*, echoing its counterparts in various countries, noted:

---

53 Bernard Vignot, "Laborie, Jean," *Dictionnaire du monde religieux dans la France contemporaine*, vol. 10, *Les Marges du christianisme* (Paris: Beauchesne, 2001), 147-48 and id., *Les Églises parallèles* (Paris: Cerf/Fides, 1991).

It was by sheer good luck that we got wind of an investigation ordered last June. . . .We expected to be questioned, as one of the movements defending the Latin liturgy and Gregorian chant. Yet we have not received any request on this subject. As far as we know, no St. Pius V association has been asked, either. And in the parishes, there have been no surveys organized to find out the wishes of the faithful, except for a few parish priests who have taken the initiative. Under these conditions, one may wonder on what basis the bishops were able to answer the Holy See's request.[54]

The *Una Voce* delegates of France approached their diocesan bishops; Henri Sauguet, the president of the association, sent a letter to all the bishops to remind them of the existence of "those Catholics who do not despair of finding in the sanctuaries the Latin liturgy to which they remain faithfully and devoutly attached" and of the need ("your duty") to "make known their profound aspiration." Petitions were organized in several countries, and information files were compiled to inform the Congregation for Divine Worship. *The Universe*, a moderate English Catholic weekly, organized a poll on the Mass among its 160,000 or so readers, asking first, "Which Mass would you prefer to attend, assuming they were all allowed?" On October 31, 1980, the newspaper published the results of the poll: of the approximately 14,000 responses received, more than 10,000 readers said they preferred to attend "the Latin Mass in the traditional Tridentine rite."[55]

The survey undertaken by Cardinal Knox produced very different results. By November 30, 1980, the Congregation had received 1,791 responses, or three-quarters of the bishops consulted. The remaining quarter had not responded to the survey. The historian must ask: Was it because these bishops felt such a survey was inappropriate or because they could not be bothered to respond? The results of the Knox Inquiry were not published by the Congregation for Divine Worship until a year later, in December 1981.[56] First, there were statistical tables showing the results by continent and country. According to the survey, over 67% of the bishops indicated that there were no Latin celebrations (according to the new rite) in their diocese and only slightly more than 7% reported that such a request existed. As for the traditional rite, 79% felt that the question did not arise in their diocese; in the other dioceses, the demand for Tridentine Masses came from individuals or unorganized groups (5.77%), autonomous groups (10.51%), or "groups adhering to Archbishop Lefebvre" (4.37%).

---

54 "Dossier pour un cardinal," *Una Voce* 96 (January-February 1981): 3.
55 Louis Salleron presented the survey in *Itinéraires* 248 (December 1980): 154-55.
56 *Notitiae* 185 (December 1981): 589-611, text partly in Latin, partly in Italian. Our translation.

When these figures became known, they were contested. For example, the report indicated that in France 79 groups were attached to the Tridentine Mass, whereas the Ordo published at the time by the magazine *Forts dans la Foi* gave the addresses of 281 "St. Pius V Mass centers" and the association *Una Voce* estimated that there were more than five hundred places of worship in France where the traditional liturgy was celebrated, a certain number of parish priests continuing to celebrate it in relative discretion.

After the statistics tables summarizing the responses, the report included "Reflections on the content of the responses." It was stated, among other things, that "the starting point" for a request for a traditional Mass "is always the non-acceptance of the work of the Second Vatican Council" (which was manifestly false), and that groups attached to the traditional liturgy "often" consider "as illegitimate Popes John XXIII and Paul VI, and even John Paul I and John Paul II." This was more than an exaggeration, since sedevacantists or Guérardians were at that time, as they still are today, a very small minority among Catholics attached to Tradition. The Knox Report seemed even more of a caricature when its summary, in French, stated that "almost all the bishops (98.68%) consider it [the so-called 'Tridentine' Mass] to be a virtually non-existent problem; they are opposed to granting the old rite alongside the liturgical books restored according to Vatican II."

Of course, subsequent history has shown that the problem was not "non-existent." Cardinal Ratzinger, appointed prefect of the Congregation for the Doctrine of the Faith in November 1981 – that is, one month before the results of the Knox investigation were published – would soon choose another path, with the approval of John Paul II.

THE RATZINGER PLAN

One year after his appointment to the Doctrine of the Faith, Cardinal Ratzinger held a meeting that was kept secret for a long time, but which was decisive. The meeting, which he initiated in November 1982, was not known precisely until twenty-four years later, when Sophie de Ravinel, then in charge of the religion page at *Le Figaro*, published extracts from its minutes.[57]

On November 16, 1982, Cardinal Ratzinger, four other cardinals, and a Curia bishop met to discuss the question of the Mass, independently of the "Lefebvre question," although it was on everyone's mind all the same. The participants were unanimous in their view that "the Roman

[57] Sophie de Ravinel, "Dès 1982, le cardinal Ratzinger préparait la réconciliation avec les lefebvristes," *Le Figaro*, December 12, 2006.

Missal in the form in which it was used until 1969 must be granted throughout the Church by the Holy See," so long as the Mass of Paul VI was not considered suspect of "heresy or invalidity" and that the new liturgical calendar was followed. A papal document was to recall "the essence of the sacred liturgy," denounce "the widespread abuses," and expose "the intimate identity of the old and new missals, of the ordinary form and of the permissible form, which are in no way opposed." And in the future it would be necessary to envisage a "synthesis of the two missals which preserves the achievements of the liturgical restoration, but which abandons certain exaggerated innovations."

What might be called the "Ratzinger Plan" was implemented gradually. It had two objectives, which, while they were related, Cardinal Ratzinger sought to achieve separately. On the one hand, to restore the traditional liturgy to its rightful place in the Church, to revise the texts of the post-conciliar liturgical reform (what he later called the "reform of the reform"), and to achieve a unified rite in the long run. On the other hand, to "regularize" the situation of Archbishop Lefebvre and the Society of St. Pius X, under certain conditions. The discreet cardinals' meeting of November 16, 1982, was the first step towards the first objective. The letter to Archbishop Lefebvre a month later was the first step towards the second objective.

On December 23, 1982, Cardinal Ratzinger addressed a long letter to Archbishop Lefebvre in the name of the Pope in which he made "concrete proposals for the regularization of your own situation and that of the members of the Society of St. Pius X."[58] The proposed procedure was clear: if Archbishop Lefebvre signed a declaration on the Council and on the New Mass, he would be received by the Pope in audience and an apostolic visit would be initiated with the "aim of finding a suitable canonical status for the Society of St. Pius X." It was specified that the suspension *a divinis* against Archbishop Lefebvre "does not depend on the problems concerning the acceptance of the Second Vatican Council and the liturgical reform," but on the fact that "you have proceeded with ordinations in spite of the prohibition of the Holy See." Consequently, this suspension would be lifted "as soon as you declare your intention not to make any more ordinations without the authorization of the Holy See."

This letter of December 1982 is particularly important because of the very precise formula in the declaration that would be required of Archbishop Lefebvre and the priests ordained by him "since June 1976." On the one hand, they were to "adhere to the integral doctrine of the Second Vatican Council, insofar as this doctrine is interpreted in the light

---

58 Letter published in *Fideliter* 35 (September-October 1983): 51-53.

of Holy Tradition, and refers to the constant magisterium of the Church"; on the other hand, they were to recognize that the missal promulgated by Paul VI "is in itself legitimate and Catholic," not to deny its "validity," and also "not to imply that these Masses are in any way heretical or blasphemous," and to "affirm that they should not be refused by Catholics." Cardinal Ratzinger said that "it cannot be envisaged" that the formulas of this declaration should be "modified," but he accepted that Archbishop Lefebvre, "in a personal capacity," might add a wish: that at some point in the future the Pope might undertake "a revision of the liturgical books."

Lastly, at the end of his letter, the prefect of the Congregation for the Doctrine of the Faith clearly stated that another project was under way: "As concerns the authorization of celebrating Holy Mass according to the Ordo Missae in force before that of Paul VI, the Holy Father has decided that the issue was to be resolved for the Church universal, therefore independently of your specific case."

Rome had never before made such concrete proposals, or opened up so many perspectives for restoration. Archbishop Lefebvre, without being enthusiastic about this new Roman letter, recognized its importance. He wanted to present the new Roman proposals to the priests and the traditional communities connected with the Society of Saint Pius X. A meeting was organized in January 1983 at Father Coache's Maison Lacordaire in Flavigny. On January 10, 1983, Dom Gérard announced to his monks gathered at the evening chapter that Rome had made "proposals to Archbishop [Lefebvre] concerning the authorization of the rite of Saint Pius V,"[59] and on January 31 he went to Flavigny. Also present, besides Father Aulagnier, superior of the District of France, and various SSPX priests, were Father Coache, Msgr Ducaud-Bourget, Dom Augustin-Marie Joly, and Dom Antoine-Marie Beauchef of the monastery of Saint Joseph, which had relocated to Flavigny several years before, and Father Antoine de Fleurance, who represented the Capuchin friars still living in Verjon. Archbishop Lefebvre spoke of the state of his relations with the Holy See, the promulgation of the new Code of Canon Law, which had occurred a few days earlier, and which was to become a new stumbling block with Rome, and he presented the form of the declaration on the Council and on the Mass demanded by the Holy See.[60] As he would do in other similar circumstances, he reported on his exchanges with Rome, gave an account of the

---

59 Chronicle of Sainte-Madeleine priory, dated Monday, January 10, 1983, Archives of the abbey of Sainte-Madeleine du Barroux.
60 Chronicle of Sainte-Madeleine priory, dated January 31, 1983, and the personal testimony of Dom Antoine-Marie Beauchef to the author, July 18, 2021.

correspondence and the content of the proposals made, and invited each of the participants to give his opinion, but he himself did not express an opinion. He would make his decision later.

His answer came a month later, on March 2, 1983, in a letter to Cardinal Ratzinger. He somewhat artfully referred to the information given to him by the Prefect of the Congregation for the Doctrine of the Faith (as regards the traditional Mass, "the question will be resolved for the universal Church and independently of your own case"), and expressed surprise that nothing had been announced, arguing that "it would be eminently desirable for this authorization to appear beforehand": the freedom given to the traditional Mass should, as a token of good will, be granted before "the problem of the Fraternity is resolved." And he formulated a wish that sounded like a demand: "If the Holy See wants peace and an end to division, it would, in my opinion, be preferable not to make any allusion to the new Ordo Missae and thus avoid imputing motives."[61]

Cardinal Ratzinger saw this response as a stalling tactic.[62] Archbishop Lefebvre then addressed a letter to John Paul II on April 5, 1983, in which he issued a clear *non possumus* to the proposals made by the Holy See. He stated that he could not accept the new Ordo Missae, "an equivocal, ambiguous Mass, whose Catholic doctrine has been blurred," and he placed it on the same level as the doctrine of religious freedom. And he sought to impose his agenda on the Pope:

> We see no other solution to this problem than:
> 1. the freedom to celebrate according to the old rite according to the edition of the liturgical books of Pope John XXIII.
> 2. the reform of the N.O.M. to make it a manifest expression of Catholic dogmas....
> 3. A reform of those statements or expressions of the Council that are contrary to the official Magisterium of the Church, especially in the *Declaration on Religious Liberty*, in the *Declaration on the Church and the World*, in the *Decree on Non-Christian Religions*, etc.[63]

One can see clearly the reasons for Archbishop Lefebvre's refusal of the advances of the Holy See: on the one hand, an absolute refusal of the New Mass, and on the other hand, the desire not to dissociate the liturgical question from doctrinal questions. He maintained this double refusal until his death, as his successors have done to this day.

---

61 Archbishop Lefebvre to Cardinal Ratzinger, Letter, March 2, 1983, published in *Fideliter* 35 (September-October 1983): 53-54.
62 Cardinal Ratzinger to Archbishop Lefebvre, Letter, March 29, 1983; ibid., 54.
63 Archbishop Lefebvre to John Paul II, Letter, April 8, 1983; ibid., 55-57.

CHAPTER 11
Restoration or Tactic?

T HE FIRST OF ARCHBISHOP LEFEBVRE'S DEMANDS actually coincided with the first stage of what I have called the "Ratzinger plan." The indult that John Paul II promulgated in 1984 was a partial response to it.

That Roman decision was made a few months after Archbishop Mayer had been appointed pro-prefect of both the Congregation for the Sacraments and the Congregation for Divine Worship, at the time separate entities (he would be created cardinal the following year). This appointment and the decision that followed were a sign that John Paul II was not insensitive to the requests of the faithful and priests attached to the traditional liturgy.

THE 1984 INDULT

On October 3, 1984, noting that "the problem of priests and faithful" attached to the traditional rite of the Mass "persists," the Congregation for Divine Worship sent a circular letter to all presidents of episcopal conferences authorizing the celebration of the traditional Mass, under certain conditions:[1]

> a) That it be made publicly clear beyond all ambiguity that such priests and their respective faithful in no way share the positions of those who call into question the legitimacy and doctrinal exactitude of the Roman Missal promulgated by Pope Paul VI in 1970.
>
> b) Such celebration must be made only for the benefit of those groups that request it; in churches and oratories indicated by the bishop (not, however, in parish churches, unless the bishop permits it in extraordinary cases); and on the days and under the conditions fixed by the bishop either habitually, or in individual cases.
>
> c) These celebrations must be according to the 1962 Missal and in Latin.
>
> d) There must be no interchanging of texts and rites of the two Missals.
>
> e) Each bishop must inform this Congregation of the concessions granted by him, and at the end of the year from the granting of this indult, he must report the result of its application.

---

1 Indult *Quattuor abhinc annos*. Latin text in *L'Osservatore Romano* (October 17, 1984); English translation in *L'Osservatore Romano* (English edition), October 22, 1984.

The new Ordo Missae, which had been made obligatory since 1971, was no longer obligatory. Jean Madiran, when he published the indult and commented on it, noted: "The traditional Mass is no longer forbidden outright; this is progress, or rather a slightly lesser evil." Nevertheless, he expressed his dissatisfaction: "It remains, however, a suspect Mass, subject to prior authorization; this is an enormous and senseless scandal."[2] He had Yves Daoudal and Rémi Fontaine conduct a survey on the application of the indult among various personalities (clerics and laity) and some bishops. It was published in *Présent* from the end of 1984, and then in *Itinéraires*.[3]

Dom Gérard, for his part, sent a letter to Bishop Mayer (in Latin!) to express the gratitude of "many of the faithful."[4] But he pointed out that this "return" of the so-called "Tridentine" Mass was "nothing more than the execution of the prescription of the Vatican Council" which, in the Constitution on the Liturgy, had affirmed that "the Church holds all lawfully acknowledged rites to be of equal right and dignity; that she wishes to preserve them in the future and to foster them in every way."

The SSPX was not directly concerned by this indult since it had maintained the traditional Mass despite the prohibitions. But before taking a public position on the text, Archbishop Lefebvre wanted to consult "the 'leaders' of Traditionalist resistance on the subject of the 'indult Mass': Msgr Ducaud-Bourget, Fathers André, Coache, Vinson, Dom Guillou, etc."[5] in order to hear their opinions and agree on a common position. In an interview given to the daily newspaper *Présent*, he was cautious: the indult "will perhaps completely change the climate of persecution."[6] The next day, Father Schmidberger, as Superior General of the SSPX, issued a balanced official statement. On the one hand, he judged the conditions given "unacceptable to us." On the other hand, he welcomed the indult as "a first step towards a significant change in the disastrous path the Church has been on" that would allow priests and faithful to "return without too much difficulty to the Holy Sacrifice of the Mass of all time."[7]

This last prediction was overly optimistic. The application of the indult differed greatly from country to country and from diocese to diocese. Sometimes it was ignored or applied very restrictively. In

---

2 Jean Madiran, "La Messe revient," *Itinéraires* 288 (December 1984): 37.
3 *Itinéraires* 293 (May 1985).
4 Dom Gérard to Bishop Mayer, Letter, November 27, 1984, Archives of the Sainte-Madeleine Abbey (copy).
5 B. Tissier de Mallerais, *Marcel Lefebvre*, 557.
6 *Présent* (October 17, 1984).
7 Communiqué dated October 18, 1984, *Fideliter* 42 (November-December 1984): 17.

France, two abbeys of the Solesmes congregation (Fontgombault and Randol) were able to benefit from the indult. At the diocesan level, the application of the indult was left to the decision of the bishops, who, depending on place and circumstances, were more or less prudent, closed or generous. In the diocese of Avignon, for example, Archbishop Bouchex was, at that time, still in conflict with the monastery of Sainte-Madeleine, which, despite of its lack of canonical status, welcomed many vocations and attracted the faithful. The bishop could hope to divert some of the faithful from the monastery by granting a traditional Mass in his diocese, but he could not be *too* generous and run the risk of provoking discontent in the part of his clergy and faithful who did not like the "Integrists." The Confraternity of Grey Penitents of Avignon requested a traditional Mass for its chapel, and proposed, as a way of getting it accepted, practicing bi-ritualism: a Mass in Latin according to the traditional rite on Sundays at 9 am, and for feasts of obligation, and a Mass in French according to the rite of Paul VI on Sundays at 11 am and every day of the week.[8] Archbishop Bouchex was slow to respond. No doubt he had to take into account the divergent opinions of his episcopal council and of the diocesan clergy. Finally, he authorized the traditional Mass at the Grey Penitents only once a month, on the third Sunday, but not for the feasts of obligation and Holy Thursday "for which the chapel must be able to receive all the faithful who wish to come there."

The SSPX, now realizing that the conditions of this indult made its application difficult or hit-or-miss, decided to launch a "Petition to the Holy Father" asking for three things: the freedom for "every priest" to celebrate according to the traditional rite, the lifting of the canonical sanctions against Archbishop Lefebvre and his priests, and a status of "society of pontifical right and personal prelature" for the SSPX.[9] Petition sheets were published and distributed to all SSPX districts and priories around the world. This petition gathered 129,850 signatures.[10] These results appear to be reliable, since several hundred signatures, considered invalid, were not counted. The figures used, published by continent and by country, are interesting. They certainly do not represent the totality of the faithful attached to the traditional Mass, since the petition also dealt with other demands with which some traditionalists might not agree. Nor do they represent the exact number

---

8 The first Master of the Grey Penitents to Archbishop Bouchex, Letter dated March 10, 1985, Archives of Sainte-Madeleine-du-Barroux Abbet (copy).

9 Fr Paul Aulagnier, "Pétition au Saint-Père," *Fideliter* 43 (January-February 1985): 15-16.

10 "Résultats de la pétition au Saint-Père," *Fideliter* 45 (May-June 1985): 22.

of faithful who were attending SSPX chapels around the world at that time, since some faithful who attended the chapels of monasteries and convents friendly to the SSPX had also signed. So these figures do not give an exhaustive number of traditionalist Catholics, but they do give a fairly accurate picture of the Catholics linked to the SSPX and their presence in the world.

Europe appeared to be by far the continent most concerned by the demands of the SSPX (100,000 signatures out of nearly 130,000). France, with over 38,000 signatures, was the country where the number of Catholics attached to the traditional Mass was the greatest. Germany, Switzerland, and the United States (over 13,000 signatures) followed. By contrast, South America (588 signatures), Africa (some 2,800 signatures) and Asia (more than 3,600 signatures) appeared to be continents on the margins of the fight for the traditional Mass. The SSPX handed over the entire petition to Cardinal Ratzinger on March 26, 1985. "The meeting was brief, but very amicable," said Father Schmidberger. "The cardinal promised to communicate the result to the Holy Father."

In retrospect, this indult of October 1984 can be seen as the first step in the authorized return of the traditional Mass in the Church, a return that would be amplified in 1988 and especially in 2007.

THE RATZINGER EVENT

It is significant that the SSPX delivered its worldwide petition to Cardinal Ratzinger, Prefect of the Congregation for the Doctrine of the Faith, and not to the Prefect of the Congregation for Divine Worship, who is actually in charge of the liturgy. The SSPX wanted to emphasize that its demands and its fight were not only about the Mass, but more globally about the conception, expression, and transmission of the Catholic faith. Moreover, from that time on, and increasingly during the rest of the pontificate, Cardinal Ratzinger appeared to be the man in the Curia who could not be ignored on many subjects. At that time this became obvious during the new French Catechism affair, which was the third battle over the catechism in twenty-five years.

Pierres vivantes ("Living Stones") was presented as a "Catholic collection of privileged documents of the faith." It came out in bookstores on April 15, 1981. Published in the form of an album, it contained 58 chapters organized in three parts: texts taken from Sacred Scripture ("The Book of the Covenant"), a brief overview of the history of the Church ("Christians in History"), and a presentation of the sacraments ("Celebrations and Prayers"). The work was not presented as a catechism but as a catechetical tool offered by "the bishops of France to middle school children." "A poisoned gift from the episcopate to the children of France," Jean Madiran sarcastically commented, "and a poisonous flowering of the 'catechetical courses.'"

In the months to follow, various Catholic publications – *L'Homme nouveau* (Marcel Clément), Jean Madiran in *Itinéraires* and in *Présent, Famille chrétienne, La Pensée catholique* (Louis Salleron and Fr Lefèvre), *Action familiale et scolaire*, and Pierre Debray's *Courrier hebdomadaire* – published critical articles on the book. Pierre Lemaire, who was a veteran since his involvement in the first and second battles over the catechism, gave wide circulation to a critical study carried out by a group of faithful and priests: *"Pierres vivantes" devant la foi de l'Église* (53 pages). All of them pointed out numerous deficiencies and silences in the collection and judged it, even in its method, unsuitable for teaching the faith to children. Without going into the details of the many criticisms, one can mention the minimalist presentation of the Resurrection, the very inadequate definitions of the Mass and of original sin, and the absence of any presentation of eschatology or eternal life. Nevertheless, there were no large public conferences, as there had been in 1968-1969, because there was too much division among the various parties, and perhaps also because parents would have been more difficult to mobilize on this kind of subject. Nevertheless, John Paul II and Cardinal Ratzinger intervened, while trying not to offend the French bishops. A long process of revision of the catechetical manual was undertaken, through successive exchanges between the Congregation for the Doctrine of the Faith and representatives of the French bishops, and a revised and corrected edition was published in March 1985.

In the meantime, Cardinal Ratzinger had come to France to give a long lecture on catechism on January 15, 1983 at Notre-Dame-de-Fourvière in Lyon, and the next day at Notre Dame in Paris. He spoke frankly about the crisis in catechesis. One of his affirmations caused a sensation, comforting some and scandalizing others: "Suppressing the catechism and declaring the very genre of catechism 'outdated' was the first grave mistake." Then, raising the tone of the debate, the prefect of the Congregation for the Doctrine of the Faith set out how to overcome the crisis in catechesis by returning to the theological foundation of the transmission of the faith.[11] With great lucidity, he saw in the errors of catechesis the "precedence of method over content," the consequence of a "predominance of anthropology over theology." He repeatedly referred to the Catechism of the Council of Trent as the

---

11 Cardinal Joseph Ratzinger, "Transmission de la foi et sources de la foi," January 15 and 16, 1983.

normative model for any catechism, with its four pillars: "What the Christian must believe (the Creed), what he should hope for (the Our Father), what he must do (the Decalogue), and in what vital space he must accomplish it (sacraments and Church)."

Fr Sulmont, mentioning these lectures with some satisfaction in his *Bulletin de Domqueur*, cheekily wrote: "One could swear that Cardinal Ratzinger is doing his spiritual reading in Mr. Madiran's *Itinéraires*." Of course, Jean Madiran did not claim to recognize his own ideas in what the prefect of the Congregation for the Doctrine of the Faith had said, but he did recognize in it the traditional conception of what catechism is. In *Itinéraires*, he printed the cardinal's "authoritative presentation" in full, while taking the liberty of adding a few personal notes.[12]

Soon, the publication of *The Ratzinger Report* showed traditionalists around the world that they now had an interlocutor in Rome who could understand the reasons for their "resistance," even if the prefect of the Congregation for the Doctrine of the Faith could not accept all the forms this resistance had taken.

In August 1984, Cardinal Ratzinger had agreed to answer questions from the Italian journalist Vittorio Messori for a book of interviews, the outline of which had been carefully defined. In November, a very large excerpt was published in the Italian monthly magazine *Jesus* under the title "Why the faith is in crisis."[13] Luc Lefèvre had obtained from Cardinal Ratzinger and Vittorio Messori permission to publish a translation of these pages in *La Pensée catholique*. In March 1985, the work was published in Italy under the title *Rapporto sulla fede*. In the following months it was translated into several languages. The French translation, published in June 1985, was done under the direction of Cardinal Gagnon.

SUPPORT AND CRITICISM

The book had a very mixed reception. The religious columnist of *Le Monde*, Alain Woodrow, titled his review: "Cardinal Ratzinger believes that the Vatican has failed."[14] He also reckoned that "[t]he current 'grand inquisitor' of the Roman Church has just put his cards on the table." He had used almost the same formula ten years earlier with regard to Archbishop Lefebvre at the time of the Mass in Lille. A group

---

12 *Itinéraires* 271 (March 1983): 146-70.
13 These excerpts were translated into French by January 1985 in *La Pensée catholique* 214. English edition, *The Ratzinger Report: An Exclusive Interview on the State of the Church*, trans. S. Attanasio and G. Harrison (San Francisco: Ignatius Press, 1985).
14 A. Woodrow, "Le cardinal Ratzinger estime que le Vatican a échoué," *Le Monde*, June 19, 1985.

of priests and lay people published a manifesto against the book: "Yes to the synod, no to burying Vatican II." They said they disagreed with Cardinal Ratzinger's "disappointing take" and regretted that he had spoken of a "necessary restoration." Two bishops, Bishop Gaillot of Evreux and Bishop Rozier of Poitiers, supported the manifesto.

On the other hand, most Catholics of Tradition were delighted with the *Ratzinger Report*, which they saw as undertaking a doctrinal rectification and engaging in the necessary discernments. In *La Pensée catholique*, Father Lefèvre devoted a very long editorial to the work, under the title "Let Us Not Be Ashamed of Our Faith."[15] He was pleased with the "warnings" given by the prefect of the Congregation for the Doctrine of the Faith and he considered that

> The Cardinal's strategy is in line with that of John Paul II: directly addressing the crowds, beyond the Episcopal Conferences' and the media's barriers. The voice of Rome will no longer be muffled. Christians will no longer be misinformed.

At Le Barroux monastery, Dom Gérard had read the book carefully. Then he had most of it read in the refectory. Soon, in a letter to Cardinal Ratzinger, he expressed his delight at the "salutary effect this book has produced."[16] Significantly, a year after the book's publication, when he was invited to give a conference on "the spiritual resistance of traditional Catholics" as part of a historical colloquium organized at Fontevraud by Jean de Viguerie, Dom Gérard devoted a large part of his speech to the book. He presented it as "a full-scale trial of the postconciliar spirit."[17] With numerous quotations, he detailed Cardinal Ratzinger's "diagnosis," which he summarized as follows: "The Cardinal denounces an infidelity to the Creed (crisis of faith) and an infidelity to the Decalogue (crisis of morals)." Dom Gérard felt that "the former Archbishop of Munich's indictment "corresponded to what the Catholic resistance had stood up against."

On the other hand, the SSPX was hostile to the book. Fr Rulleau, professor of philosophy at the Écône seminary, entitled his long article on the book "Has Ratzinger Converted?"[18] He tried to show that

---

15 Fr Lefèvre, "N'ayons pas honte de notre foi," *La Pensée catholique* 218 (September-October 1985): 5-24.

16 Dom Gérard to Cardinal Ratzinger, Letter, August 1985, Archives of Sainte-Madeleine du Barroux Abbey, copy.

17 Dom Gérard Calvet, "La résistance spirituelle des catholiques traditionnels français dans le dernier quart de siècle," *Les Résistances spirituelles, Actes de la Xe Rencontre d'histoire religieuse tenue à Fontevraud les 2, 3 et 4 octobre 1986* (Angers: Presses de l'université d'Angers, 1987): 276.

18 Fr Rulleau, "Ratzinger converti?" *Fideliter* 51 (May-June 1986): 35-46.

Cardinal Ratzinger had remained "liberal" and "evolutionist," and that far from wanting to bury the Second Vatican Council, the Prefect of the Congregation for the Doctrine of the Faith was, on the contrary, trying to save it. In the end, he saw the book as part of "Vatican tactics," which he summarized in three phases:

>   – Reunite Catholics and regain their trust by putting an end
> to abuses;
>   – win over as many "traditionalist" opponents as possible, if
> necessary by dialecticizing their movement;
>   – finally, strike at the holdouts.

The article ended in an offensive stance: "The crisis in the Church continues. Our struggle is not over. It is entering a new phase."

The rest of the story would show that distrust of Cardinal Ratzinger and John Paul II was ultimately to prevail, two years later.

CHAPTER 12
Partings of Ways and Reconciliations

FOR SEVERAL YEARS, THE FOUNDER OF THE SOCIety of St. Pius X had been wondering about the future of the priestly fraternity he had founded. Would it someday be necessary for him to consecrate a bishop to proceed in the future to ordinations for his congregation and for the other religious communities linked to it? It was in 1981–he was about to turn seventy-five–that, after a stay in hospital, Archbishop Lefebvre first publicly considered this hypothesis:

> If the situation in the Church were to worsen, if Providence were to show me in an obvious way that I must do it, then I would no doubt resign myself to consecrating a bishop, since I can do it validly. But this would be an act of rupture with Rome–the prospect of which, incidentally, scares them over there–and I'll do everything to avoid it.[1]

It's worth noting that he–rightly–insisted on the validity of such an act but was aware at the time that it would be an "act of rupture with Rome." He then proceeded to consult theologians. In 1982, he asked Fr Philippe Le Pivain, professor of theology at the Albano seminary, and in 1983 Father Josef Bisig, second assistant of the Society of St. Pius X, for reports on the legitimacy of a consecration without papal mandate. The two priests reached identical conclusions, in line with traditional Church teaching: the primacy of jurisdiction belongs, by divine right, to the Pope, the guarantor of apostolicity, and only he can consecrate bishops or give a mandate to do so.

By this time–July 1983–Rome had already warned Archbishop Lefebvre that the consecration of a bishop without a pontifical mandate "would really be the start of a schism."[2] At the same time, however, Archbishop Lefebvre was beginning to develop a different line of argument:

> The problem of the situation of the faithful and the present papacy renders obsolete the difficulties of jurisdiction, disobedience, and apostolicity. These notions presuppose a Pope who is Catholic in his faith and in his government.[3]

---

1 Interview with André Figueras, *Monde et Vie*, June 12, 1981.
2 Cardinal Ratzinger to Archbishop Lefebvre, Letter, July 20, 1983, quoted in B. Tissier de Mallerais, *Marcel Lefebvre*, 542.
3 Marginal note by Archbishop Lefebvre in Fr Bisig's study, November 1983, quoted in Tissier de Mallerais, *Marcel Lefebvre*, 541.

On several subsequent occasions, Archbishop Lefebvre publicly raised the possibility of performing consecrations without a pontifical mandate, notably in a "Solemn Warning" he published with Bishop de Castro Mayer on August 31, 1985.

THE SCANDAL OF ASSISI

On January 25, 1986, on the occasion of the International Year of Peace proclaimed by the UN, and in a tense international context, John Paul II announced that he would "undertake timely consultations with the leaders, not only of the various Christian Churches and Communities, but also of other world religions" to organize "a special meeting of prayer for peace, in the city of Assisi, a place which the seraphic figure of St. Francis has transformed into a center of universal brotherhood."[4]

This announcement "shocked us," Archbishop Lefebvre soon said. A few days after John Paul II's address, during ceremonies in Écône, the bishop harshly denounced the Pope's plan:

> The Holy Ghost isn't inspiring him for his Assisi Congress; the devil is, and he's serving Freemasonry. This is obvious. Masonry has always dreamed of just this: the coming together of all religions.[5]

The issue of *Fideliter* that reported Archbishop Lefebvre's lengthy remarks carried the headline "John Paul II: The Escalation!" and opened with a full-page photograph showing the Pope receiving a mark on his forehead during a trip to India, with the title "The Destruction of the Church."

Not everyone in the traditionalist world reacted with such virulence. In *La Pensée catholique*, Fr Lefèvre defended John Paul II's initiative at Assisi, and generally sought to legitimize the Pope's dealings with representatives of the major religions during his trips to Asia, Africa, and Oceania. He also published "Replies to some objections," arguing that the expression "Congress of Religions" had never been used by the Holy See in connection with Assisi, and that, from a theological point of view, "union," "reunion," and "communion" should not be confused, the last of these assuming "that all the members of the assembly share the same faith." Fr Lefèvre also sought to show that at Assisi "a rapprochement was sought not with error, but with people,

---

4 John Paul II, *Homily for the Mass Closing the Octave of Prayer for Christian Unity*, January 25, 1986, available in Italian at https://www.vatican.va/content/john-paul-ii/it/homilies/1986/documents/hf_jp-ii_hom_19860125_basilica-s-paolo.html.
5 Archbishop Lefebvre at Écône, February 1-2, 1986, published in *Fideliter* 50 (March-April 1986): 15.

members of the great human family of which the Pope, Vicar of Christ, is the father."[6] He returned to the subject a few months later, referring to the Pope's address to the Roman Curia on December 22, 1986.[7]

The prior of the monastery of Le Barroux, Dom Gérard, considered the SSPX's denunciations of the Pope excessive. He had sent Father Schmidberger, Superior General of the Society of St. Pius X, a long letter – of five typed pages – to communicate "some reflections that have been running through my mind for several months" on the monastery's relations with the Society and on "the critical situation of the Church."[8] With regard to the Assisi meeting and the Pope's relations with representatives of non-Christian religions, Dom Gérard refused to draw hasty or radical conclusions:

> It is scandalous, but not formally heretical, to bring together followers of different religions and have them each pray in their own way to the God of Peace. It is scandalous, but not formally heretical, to let a Hindu woman smudge one's forehead with red powder. This rite of welcome, part of the country's folk customs, does not imply a profession of religious faith!
>
> It's confusing and equivocal. One cannot deduce from this a formal apostasy.

This long letter is also interesting because, on other subjects, Dom Gérard was taking positions different from those of the SSPX, and candidly expressed his fear of "what may be producing a sectarian mentality."

> Let's put it in very general terms: we don't have the same fighting style. This is legitimate up to a point. The limit that should not be exceeded is the one where disagreements turn into opposition and denigration.
>
> First, the style of sermons in the priories. Our friends and families tell us that one too often hears belabored and monitory doctrinal reminders. One would like to see more kindness, more human feeling and understanding of the suffering that arises here and there, even kindness. Otherwise, we end up wearying some and fanaticizing others, which runs the risk of creating a cult mentality. I believe that we must be all the more wary of this tendency, as the misfortune of the times leads us to it: every persecuted community is more or less threatened by the spirit of the sects.

---

6 Fr Luc Lefèvre, "Prier à Assise," and "Réponse à quelques objections," *La Pensée catholique* 226 (January-February 1987): 27-35 and 36.

7 Fr Luc Lefèvre, "La théologie d'"Assise,'" *La Pensée catholique* 228 (May-June 1987): 21-36.

8 Dom Gérard to Fr Franz Schmidberger, April 29, 1986, Archives of Sainte-Madeleine du Barroux abbey, copy.

Dom Gérard had already expressed this regret-cum-warning in 1982 in *Regard sur la Chrétienté*.[9]

In 1985, Romain Marie – Bernard Antony's pen name, as we have seen – published a book of interviews with Yves Daoudal, then a journalist at *Présent*, under the title *Romain Marie sans concession* ("Romain Marie: No Concessions"). The book was not to the SSPX's liking. An anonymous pamphlet was written to denounce Bernard Antony's naturalism and his conception of political action as too far removed from Catholic doctrine on the Social Kingdom of Christ. In the letter to Fr Schmidberger quoted above, Dom Gérard deplored the fact that the anonymous document circulated by the SSPX had taken on the "appearance of a diatribe" against Bernard Antony, and was "disproportionate in form and vindictive in substance." "It seems to me that the man has earned some of our gratitude," he added, recalling a few items: the creation of the Centre Charlier, the Journées d'Amitié française, the Pèlerinages de Chrétienté, the AGRIF.

> One would like to see our clerics appreciate the value of these good battles and their impact at the religious and national level. It would be a shame if the faithful priesthood, absent from the forces of reaction, were to let the "real country" carry out its recovery without it.

The reference to Maurras ("legal country" vs. "real country") was unmistakable.

The second part of this long letter was devoted to the matter of the consecrations. Dom Gérard told his correspondent that the question had been studied and discussed "in council," i.e., with the most senior priests of the monastery. At the time, Dom Gérard's position was not entirely settled, even if he seemed inclined to consider a consecration without a papal mandate legitimate under the circumstances:

> In the case of a consecration, I know that Archbishop Lefebvre can only be acting under a very profound movement of the Holy Ghost. There will be no real schism (the Spirit of unity cannot go against unity), but there will be an appearance of schism. Does one have the right to scandalize the Christian people without first doing everything one can to enlighten them? This requires time and maturation. . . . The question is not so much whether

---

9 A little later yet, in a letter Dom Gérard sent to Jean Madiran with references to the Charliers, to Maurras, and to Solzhenitsyn, he expressed a similar indignation: "How is it that the priests of Écône, who are so zealous, so becassocked, and so steeped in (moral!) theology are so ignorant of the thinkers who have given us the shock of being, of selflessness, of the spirit of chivalry?" Dom Gérard to Jean Madiran, Letter, February 23, 1988, Jean Madiran archives.

Archbishop [Lefebvre] should or should not consecrate. The
question is how to prepare the ground.

The same formulas can be found in a letter Dom Gérard had sent
three days earlier to Michel de Saint-Pierre, who had also questioned
him about sacraments. [10] To Fr Schmidberger, he also wrote: "Our
conclusion is that we must wait for the Pope to get himself entangled
in formally heretical acts. Have these occurred yet?" This question
illustrates his fear of a hasty decision: "I am leaning, as you can see,
towards patience and balance; I fear a headlong rush that would condemn us to a point of no return."

At the same time, in 1986, Dom Forgeot, Abbot of Fontgombault,
Dom Courau, Prior of the monastery of Triors, and Dom Bernard
Kaul, Abbot of Hauterive, who in 1969 had been one of those who had
encouraged Archbishop Lefebvre to found a seminary, took concerted
action. They came to Écône to try to convince Archbishop Lefebvre
not to consecrate bishops, and not to break with Rome.

In June 1987, Father de Blignières, Prior General of the Fraternity
of Saint-Vincent-Ferrer, published a brochure entitled *Réflexions sur
l'épiscopat autonome* ("Reflections on the autonomous episcopate"),
in which he set out the reasons against the possibility of episcopal
consecrations without a papal mandate.

THE "BETRAYAL" OF FLAVIGNY

In its internal newsletter, the Society of St. Pius X referred to the
"year of Assisi" as also the year of "the betrayal of Dom Augustin and
his monastery in Flavigny." [11] The word is a strong and unfair one, but
it was in common use at the time in traditionalist circles to designate
what was, in fact, a move towards reconciliation with Rome and a
return to full communion with the Church.

We have seen the circumstances under which Dom Augustin Joly
founded the monastery of Saint-Joseph de Clairval in Switzerland, then
transferred it to Flavigny in the diocese of Dijon in 1976. The community relied on Archbishop Lefebvre for the ordination of its religious
to minor and major orders. But Dom Augustin was not satisfied with
this canonically irregular situation. And the deterioration in relations
between Archbishop Lefebvre and the Holy See led him to fear schism.

In December 1982, as we have seen, Cardinal Ratzinger offered
Archbishop Lefebvre reconciliation with the Holy See, on the condition

10 Dom Gérard to Michel de Saint-Pierre, Letter, April 26, 1986, Sainte-Madeleine du
Barroux Abbey Archives, copy.
11 *Cor Unum* 337 (November 1990): 44.

that he sign a declaration of adherence to the Second Vatican Council and recognize the validity and orthodoxy of Paul VI's Mass. In 1983, Archbishop Lefebvre had refused to endorse such a declaration, while Dom Augustin, after some consideration, judged that the declaration, as drafted, was acceptable.[12] In October 1984, he contacted Archbishop Hamer, pro-prefect of the Congregation for Institutes of Consecrated Life and Societies of Apostolic Life, expressing a desire to return to full communion with the Church, and indicating his support for the declaration proposed by Cardinal Ratzinger. The Bishop of Dijon, Mgr Balland, expressed willingness to encourage this return to full communion with the Church. At the time, the monastery numbered 75 monks, including 22 priests. Dom Jean Prou, Abbot of Solesmes, was sent to the monastery in January 1985 for an initial visit and to initiate dialogue. As a sign of recognition of the pope's authority and communion with the Church, the monastery was asked to agree to celebrate the new Mass. On September 17, 1985, the community adopted the new Ordo, in Latin and Gregorian chant, for the conventual Mass, while retaining the traditional Mass for private Masses. In February 1986, a canonical visit to the community by Dom Prou and Fr Roualet, vicar-general of the diocese, included the signing by community members of a declaration in which they said that they "adhere to the whole of the doctrine expounded by the Second Vatican Council and recognize the legitimacy of the Roman missal promulgated by Pope Paul VI." On April 14, 1986, Bishop Balland of Dijon regularized the legal situation of all the priests and deacons in the community. Dom Philippe Dupont, the prior of Solesmes Abbey, was appointed religious assistant to the community. On August 15, 1986, the community was erected as a public association of the faithful, Father Augustin being appointed moderator. On February 2, 1988, it was canonically recognized by the Bishop of Dijon as a Benedictine monastery of diocesan right – later to be erected as an abbey. The conditions of this return to full communion with the Church were not accepted by all the monks. In September 1985, some left Flavigny to join the monastery at Le Barroux or to join the Society of St. Pius X.

THE "SECOND SIGN"

The Society of St. Pius X, on the other hand, was not prepared to make any concession on the liturgy. During a meeting with the

---

12 There is no history of the Abbey of Saint Joseph de Clairval. I was able to reconstruct its path to reconciliation with the Holy See through conversations with the current abbot, Dom Jean-Bernard Bories, and the Abbot emeritus, Dom Antoine-Marie Beauchef, in July 2021.

teachers of the École Saint-Michel, the first school taken over by the SSPX, Archbishop Lefebvre made his position very clear:

> We shouldn't be afraid of words. After all, the new Mass was conceived in a resolutely ecumenical perspective. It was created with Protestants, by Protestants, and for Protestants. As a result, it is bastardized, equivocal, and conducive to heresy. It is therefore "bad."[13]

The issue of religious freedom was also one of the main obstacles to Archbishop Lefebvre's reconciliation with the Holy See. He had fought hard against the doctrine of religious freedom during the Council, before agreeing to sign the declaration *Dignitatis humanae* when it was promulgated. Nevertheless, he continued to believe that it represented a serious break with the teaching of previous popes. This was one of the key elements in his doctrinal challenge to the pontificates of Paul VI and then John Paul II. In October 1985, he sent the Congregation for the Doctrine of the Faith a lengthy study presenting *Dubia*, i.e., objections, to the declaration.[14]

In March 1987, Archbishop Lefebvre received a response from the Congregation for the Doctrine of the Faith to the *Dubia* he had presented, but did not make it known at the time. Rome responded by affirming, among other things, that the conciliar declaration constituted a "doctrinal development in continuity." From then on, Archbishop Lefebvre considered "that they [the Pope and the Curia] were locking themselves into their errors." He saw in this response, after the Assisi meeting, a "second sign from Providence" indicating that he should consecrate bishops to continue his work of defending and transmitting Tradition.

But this rejection of the conciliar Declaration on Religious Liberty was no longer unanimous among traditionalists. At this time, several theologians began to publish studies in which they concluded that the conciliar declaration on religious freedom did not contradict the earlier Magisterium on the subject, but was a development of it. This was first done by Father Brian Harrison in a "tesina" for his licentiate in theology presented at the Angelicum in 1986.[15] At the same time, Fathers de Blignières and de Saint-Laumer of the Fraternité Saint-Vincent-Ferrer,

---

13 Interview printed in *Fideliter* 35 (September-October 1983): 58-61.
14 This study had a limited first run: *"Dubia" sur la liberté religieuse* (Écône: Imprimerie du séminaire Saint-Pie X, May 1987), 138 pages. It would only be formally published thirteen years later under the title *Mes doutes sur la liberté religieuse* (Paris: Clovis, 2000); in English under the title *Religious Liberty Questioned* (St Marys, KS: Angelus Press, 2001).
15 This Licentiate thesis was published in French under the title *Le Développement de la doctrine catholique sur la liberté religieuse* (Poitier, France: Dominique Martin Morin, 1988).

after several years' study of the subject and research in the archives of the Congregation for the Doctrine of the Faith, came to similar conclusions.[16] In December 1986, Dom Gérard asked one of his monks, Father Basile, to study the question. He later reached the conclusion that religious freedom as upheld by the Vatican Council did not give any "rights to error."[17]

AN UNHOPED-FOR "OVERTURE"

The Assisi meeting and the rejection of his *Dubia* on religious freedom were, for Archbishop Lefebvre, "signs" that he should proceed with episcopal consecrations, at the risk of breaking with Rome. This is what he said in his sermon at the ordination ceremony in Écône on June 29, 1987. He made the following clear announcement:

> In the face of this obscurity of Rome's, in the face of this refusal to return to Truth and Tradition, it seems to us that the Good Lord is asking for the Church to carry on. That's why it's likely that, before giving an account of my life to the Good Lord, I'll have to perform episcopal ordinations.[18]

This was not a new intention, but it was the first time that Archbishop Lefebvre had announced it publicly during a religious ceremony.

Following this striking declaration, Cardinal Ratzinger invited Archbishop Lefebvre to meet him at the Congregation for the Doctrine of the Faith. The meeting was scheduled for July 14. In the eyes of the Society of St. Pius X, it represented "an unexpected openness from Rome."[19] The Holy See's proposals, later confirmed in a letter from Cardinal Ratzinger,[20] were generous: the Society of Saint Pius X could obtain "its rightful autonomy" through an "adequate juridical structure," retain the 1962 missal and its seminaries, and "auxiliaries" would be given to Archbishop Lefebvre to carry on ordaining. The appointment of a Cardinal Visitor was also proposed for the near-term.

Yet Archbishop Lefebvre was still hesitant. He regarded the "Roman overture" with suspicion. In the summer of 1987, he approached

16 The first results of this research were published under the title "Le Droit à la liberté religieuse et la liberté de conscience," *Sedes Sapientiae* 22 suppl. (December 1987).
17 Fr Basile Valuet pursued his researches for his doctoral dissertation in theology, which he defended in 1995 at the Pontifical Athenaeum of the Holy Cross in Rome: *La Liberté religieuse et la tradition catholique: un cas de développement doctrinal homogène dans le magistère authentique*, 6 vols.
18 Sermon published in *Fideliter* 58 (July-August 1987): 7.
19 B. Tissier de Mallerais, *Marcel Lefebvre*, 547.
20 Cardinal Ratzinger to Archbishop Lefebvre, Letter, July 28, 1987, published in *Fideliter*, special issue (June 1988).

four of his priests about becoming bishops: the Swiss Bernard Fellay (ordained to the priesthood in 1982), the Spaniard Alfonso de Galaretta (ordained in 1980), the Frenchman Bernard Tissier de Mallerais (ordained in 1975), and the Englishman Richard Williamson (ordained in 1976). All had already held positions of responsibility in the SSPX. On August 29, he wrote a letter to them, a letter which he did not give them until later, and which was only made public shortly before the consecrations.[21] In it, he justified the upcoming consecrations: "Since the Chair of Peter and the positions of authority in Rome are occupied by antichrists, the destruction of Our Lord's Reign is proceeding apace within his Mystical Body here below, especially through the corruption of the Holy Mass"; consequently there was an "absolute necessity" to ensure the perpetuation of the priesthood by bishops: "As this modernist and liberal Rome continues its work of destroying the Kingdom of Our Lord, as evidenced by Assisi and the confirmation of Vatican II's liberal theses on religious freedom, I find myself compelled by Divine Providence to pass on the grace of the Catholic episcopate which I have received, so that the Church and the Catholic priesthood may continue to subsist for the glory of God and the salvation of souls."

Nevertheless, Archbishop Lefebvre did not reject the Roman proposal out of hand. On October 3, 1987, he celebrated the fortieth anniversary of his episcopate with a thanksgiving Mass in Écône. In the presence of 4,000 faithful, some fifty priests from various countries, and several representatives of allied religious communities, he delivered a lengthy homily. After recalling some of the highlights of his forty years as a bishop, he spoke of the "small hope" that lay ahead. Without going into the details of what Rome was proposing, he announced that he had been "presented with solutions that seem extraordinary. . . . If Rome is willing to give us real autonomy. . . . If, as I have often asked, Rome agrees to let us make the experiment of Tradition, there would no longer be a problem. We would be free to continue the work we are doing now, under the authority of the Supreme Pontiff."[22]

On the following October 18, Archbishop Lefebvre was again received by Cardinal Ratzinger.[23] He officially accepted the principle of an apostolic visit, reached agreement with the Prefect of the Congregation

---

21 Published in the SSPX's French-language newsletter, *Lettre aux amis et bienfaiteurs* on June 13, 1988.

22 *Fideliter* 60 (November–December 1987): 18-19.

23 Unaccountably, this interview goes unmentioned by B. Tissier de Mallerais in his biography of Archbishop Lefebvre.

for the Doctrine of the Faith on the aims and course of the visit, and obtained the appointment of Cardinal Gagnon to carry it out.

Cardinal Gagnon's visit, accompanied by Msgr Perl, lasted a month, from November 11 to December 8, 1987. He began his apostolic visit at the seminary in Écône, then visited several priories and schools of the Society of St. Pius X in France, Switzerland, and Germany. He also visited several of the religious communities with links to the Society of St. Pius X. He spent two days at the Sainte-Madeleine monastery, arriving in the early morning of November 27. Dom Gérard had already met him twice in previous years, once in Rome in 1984 and once in Lourdes in 1985. In a private conversation with Dom Gérard and Dom Anselme, the sub-prior, Cardinal Gagnon explained how the monastery too could benefit from the reconciliation proposed to Archbishop Lefebvre and the Society of St. Pius X, and assured them of "prompt canonical regularization."[24] Cardinal Gagnon also visited the nuns of the Annunciation. On the eve of his departure, Dom Gérard wanted to speak with him and Bishop Perl alone. The latter testified that, during this new meeting, "Dom Gérard knelt at Cardinal Gagnon's feet, asked forgiveness, almost weeping, for the wrongs he had done to the Holy See, and expressed his desire to be reconciled with Rome."[25]

Cardinal Gagnon completed his apostolic visit by returning to Écône on December 8. On this feast of the Immaculate Conception, "the cardinal did not hesitate," as Bishop Tissier de Mallerais noted, "to be publicly present at a pontifical Mass of the suspended archbishop and to witness young men enlisting in a suppressed Society."[26] In the seminary's visitors' book, the cardinal had some very positive words to say: "May the Immaculate Virgin hear our fervent prayers that the work of priestly training so marvelously carried out in this place spread its influence widely for the life of the Church."

While the content of the report drawn up by Cardinal Gagnon at the end of the apostolic visit is not yet known, it can be considered to have been sufficiently positive to allow the reconciliation process to continue.

AN HISTORIC AGREEMENT

Nevertheless, Archbishop Lefebvre still doubted whether he could reach an agreement with Rome; a practical agreement was possible, but a doctrinal agreement was, from his point of view, more than unlikely.

---

24 *Livre Blanc, Reconnaissance canonique du monastère, 1970-1990* (Sainte Madeleine Abbey, 1990), 15.
25 Msgr Perl to the author, oral testimony, April 6, 2009.
26 B. Tissier de Mallerais, *Marcel Lefebvre*, 551.

On February 4, 1988, in an interview with Michèle Reboul for *Le Figaro*, he expressed his determination:

> I am determined to consecrate at least three bishops on June 30, and hope to receive the approval of John Paul II, but if he were not to give it to me I would go ahead anyway for the good of the Church, to perpetuate Tradition.

This prospect alarmed those who believed that Cardinal Gagnon's visit had shown the good will of the Holy See, and that to consecrate a bishop without a pontifical mandate would constitute a grave error. They were also concerned about the future of the faithful attached to the traditional Mass: should they abandon it if they refused to follow Archbishop Lefebvre, or should they follow him in order to preserve the traditional Mass? During Lent 1988, Hugues Kéraly wrote a *Supplication* addressed to the Pope.[27] Arguing that episcopal consecrations without an apostolic mandate would constitute a "rupture of communion with the Roman See," the *Supplication* stated that the only way to avoid a crisis of conscience among the faithful attached to the traditional liturgy was to "assure them unconditionally and without restriction, in a sufficient number of parish churches, schools and communities, of the peaceful and ordinary possession of the traditional Eucharistic rite." The *Supplication* was signed by forty personalities, joined later by twenty-five more. They included religious, priests, and writers, as well as members of civil society. Without mentioning all the names, they included philosophers Pierre Boutang and Marcel De Corte, François Ceyrac, former chairman of the CNPF, Fr Le Cerf, chaplain to the Dominican Sisters of the Holy Ghost, Fr Lecareux, the superior of the Fraternity of the Transfiguration, Jean Raspail, Louis Pauwels, and Fathers Bruno and Louis-Marie de Blignières. It was the latter who delivered the *Supplication* to Cardinal Ratzinger on March 22, 1988. It may well have helped prepare the motu proprio *Ecclesia Dei*, which was promulgated the day after the consecrations.

Archbishop Lefebvre was worried about something else. Writing early in 1988 to Jean Madiran, who had sent him a reprint of his *Hérésie du XXe siècle*, he wrote:

> I can't congratulate you enough for denouncing this episcopal and even Roman heresy which is poisoning our century – and destroying all that was left of Christianity.
>
> All young people, and especially young clerics, should have this book in their hands to understand what their duty is, if

---

27 The text of the *Supplique pour la paix* and the list of signatures were communicated to me by Fr Louis-Marie de Blignières.

they do not want to perish in the rubble of Christianity. Your
observations force one to make choices, which, while they are
painful no doubt, are also energetic and absolutely necessary
for the salvation of the Church and souls.[28]

The "choice" in question was, of course, the decision to consecrate one
or more bishops, even without the approval of the Holy See if need be.

However, after several months of discussions and negotiations, Cardinal Ratzinger and Archbishop Lefebvre reached a "Protocol of Agreement" on May 4, 1988.[29] This was a historic event. Thirteen years after
the legal suppression of the Society of Saint Pius X and the seminary of
Écône, there seemed to be an opening for reconciliation. The *Protocol*
included a "Doctrinal Declaration" which stated in particular:

With regard to certain points taught by the Second Vatican
Council or concerning subsequent reforms of liturgy and law,
which we find difficult to reconcile with Tradition, we commit
ourselves to a positive attitude of study and communication with
the Apostolic See, avoiding all polemics.

The agreement also included concrete provisions: the Society of
Saint Pius X would be recognized and erected as a society of apostolic
life, and a commission would be created "to coordinate relations with
the various dicasteries and diocesan bishops, as well as to resolve any
problems or disputes." This commission would also be competent to
"settle questions relating to religious communities having a juridical
and moral link with the Fraternity." Finally, and this was a crucial
point, it was foreseen that the Pope would appoint "a bishop chosen
from within the Society, upon presentation by Archbishop Lefebvre,
without a fixed date."

On May 5, both parties signed the "Protocol." However, the very
next day, doubting the sincerity of the Holy See, Archbishop Lefebvre
withdrew his signature and wrote to Cardinal Ratzinger, giving, as his
biographer writes, a "new ultimatum": the agreed-upon episcopal
consecration had to take place by June 30 at the latest. "For Archbishop Lefebvre, fixing a date was the test of Rome's sincerity, the
proof that he was not being hoodwinked and that Rome would not
simply wait for him to die."[30]

---

28 Archbishop Lefebvre to Jean Madiran, Letter, February 20, 1988, Jean Madiran archives.
29 Regarding this May 4 protocol and the events that followed, several groups of
documents and commentaries were published in *Fideliter*, special issue, June 29-30,
1988; *Itinéraires* 235-36 (July-October 1988); *La Pensée catholique* 236 (September-
October 1988).
30 B. Tissier de Mallerais, *Marcel Lefebvre*, 555.

DISSENSIONS AT LE POINTET (MAY 30, 1988)

Archbishop Lefebvre realized that this about-turn would not only disappoint many of the faithful and friends of the Society of Saint Pius X, but also risk dividing the Society itself and the religious communities linked to it. Moreover, his letter to Cardinal Ratzinger, in the form of an ultimatum – that "a mandate [to consecrate a bishop] be communicated to us by mid-June" – still left the door open.

On May 10, he gathered a number of priests from the French district at Saint-Nicolas-du-Chardonnet. He said to them, regarding the Roman authorities:

> The ball is in their court and I'm waiting for them to reply. June 30 is the deadline. I feel I am coming to the end of my life, my strength is failing; I find it difficult to travel by car; I cannot put it off any longer; I would be endangering the future of the Society and our seminaries. As I said on the television in Germany: on June 30 there will be episcopal consecrations, with or without Rome's agreement.[31]

On May 24, Archbishop Lefebvre was received once again by Cardinal Ratzinger. He presented him with new demands: that Rome grant the consecration of three bishops ("one bishop is not enough for the whole apostolate"), that the majority of the future commission be made up of "members of Tradition," and that the answer be given by June 1.

He also decided to consult the senior-most priests of the Society of St. Pius X, as well as the superiors of the religious communities linked to the Society. The meeting took place at the priory of Notre-Dame-du-Pointet, in the Allier region, on May 30. Most of the priests with responsibilities within the SSPX were present: Fr Schmidberger, Superior General, Frs. Aulagnier and Bisig, Assistants General, Fr Tissier de Mallerais, Secretary General, Fr Bernard Fellay, Bursar General, Fr Simoulin, Rector of the *Institut Universitaire Saint-Pie X*, and others. There were also several priests from outside the SSPX (Father André, Father Coache, Father Vinson, Dom Guillou), and superiors of friendly religious communities: notably Dom Gérard for the Benedictines of Le Barroux (accompanied by Fathers Anselme and Jehan), Father Antoine de Fleurance for the convent of Saint-François de Morgon, Father Innocent-Marie for the Fraternity of Saint Dominic (accompanied by Father Marie-Dominique), Fr Lecareux for the Fraternity of the Transfiguration, Mother Élisabeth for the Benedictines of La Font de Pertus, the superiors of the Sisters of the Fraternity of

---

31 Tissier de Mallerais, *Marcel Lefebvre*, 556.

Saint Pius X, the Dominican Sisters of Fanjeaux and Brignoles, and the Carmelites of Quiévrain.

In an "Overview of the situation," Archbishop Lefebvre explained why he was inclined "to consecrate four bishops on June 30 anyway" and how "the official link with modernist Rome is nothing in comparison with the preservation of the Faith."[32] During the meeting, a telephone call from Fr du Chalard of Albano informed Archbishop Lefebvre of the contents of a letter addressed to him by Cardinal Ratzinger. Without responding to all of the Écône prelate's requests, the cardinal confirmed that the pope was willing "to speed up the usual nomination process, so that the consecration [of a bishop] may take place for the closing of the Marian Year on August 15." This insured that a member of the Society of St. Pius X would be consecrated bishop in less than three months.

Each of the participants in the meeting was invited to express his or her opinion on the protocol of agreement and the latest Roman proposal. There were diverse opinions.[33] Fr Tissier de Mallerais (who had been one of the drafters of the protocol of agreement and who had already been approached by Archbishop Lefebvre to become a bishop) and Fr Bisig, Assistant General of the SSPX, Fr Antoine de Fleurance, Fr Lecareux, Dom Gérard, Fr Coache, and Mother Élisabeth felt that the conditions contained in the protocol of agreement were acceptable and that episcopal consecrations should not be carried out without a pontifical mandate; others, notably Fr Aulagnier and the superiors of the Dominican Teaching Sisters, felt that Archbishop Lefebvre should retain his freedom, and rejected or distrusted the agreement.

After the meeting, Dom Gérard took Archbishop Lefebvre aside and explained the particular circumstance of his monastery, arguing that "attempting its normalization does not create the same dangers as for the Fraternity." The archbishop conceded: "It's not the same for you: you have your monks gathered around you, but I have eighty houses, five hundred chapels; there would be division."[34]

Archbishop Lefebvre weighed the arguments of all sides and then, as was his wont, made his decision alone. He organized a press conference to give a public announcement. On June 15, in front of a hundred or so

---

32 Quoted ibid., 557, 559.
33 Ibid., 587-89. I received further details from Dom Gérard during an interview on February 9, 1996. See also the report drawn up by two nuns of the Annunciation present at the meeting: *Réunion du 30 mai 1988 à N.-D. du Pointet avec Mgr Marcel Lefebvre*, six typed pages, Archives of Our Lady of the Annunciation abbey.
34 Quoted in *Le Livre blanc*, 16.

journalists from various countries, he announced that "to safeguard the Catholic priesthood" he was going to confer episcopal consecration on four of his priests. Their names had been made public two days earlier.

Two days later, on June 17, Cardinal Gantin, Prefect of the Congregation for Bishops, sent a Canonical *Monitum* to Archbishop Lefebvre warning him that if he proceeded with these consecrations "without having requested a mandate from the Supreme Pontiff," he and the ordained bishops "would *ipso facto* incur excommunication *latae sententiae* ('automatic') reserved to the Apostolic See according to canon 1382."[35]

On the very same day, the Holy See published a lengthy *Information Note* summarizing the entire reconciliation process since Cardinal Gagnon's visit, and warning once again of the "grave canonical consequences" of episcopal consecrations without a pontifical mandate.[36] The final paragraph of this note left a door open to anyone who might refuse to follow Archbishop Lefebvre:

> The Holy See is also concerned to send an urgent appeal to the members of the Fraternity and the faithful who have links to it, that they reconsider their position and that all measures will be taken to guarantee their identity in the full communion of the Catholic Church.

This last promise concerning the "identity" guaranteed to traditionalists returning to communion with Rome would be mentioned again later by the parties concerned when they would run into interference from the bishops or the Holy See.

On that same June 17, at John Paul II's request, and at Cardinal Ratzinger's suggestion, Cardinal Mayer contacted Dom Gérard by telephone. He asked to be received at the monastery. He arrived at Le Barroux late afternoon on Monday June 20, accompanied by Mgr Perl. The monastery chronicle of the day soberly records: "In the evening, at dinner, great excitement: Cardinal Mayer and Mgr Perl visit us and make proposals...." The term "proposals" is, historically speaking, a little misleading—as if the cardinal had come to make a request. In reality, he was sent by the Pope to try to achieve reconciliation between the monastery and the Holy See, on the basis of the protocol of agreement of May 5, and with a view to re-establishing full communion. The agreement would be reached in July, after the consecrations.

---

35 Unabridged text of the *Monitum* and other documents in *Mgr Lefebvre et Rome. Le Dossier complet*, special issue of *Fideliter* (June 29-30, 1988).

36 *Bolletino. Sala Stampa della Santa Sede* (June 16, 1988); *L'Osservatore Romano* (June 17, 1988).

Jean Madiran, one of the most trusted voices in traditionalism at the time, was unwilling to take a public stand for or against the consecrations before the event. In the newspaper *Présent*, he published press releases and statements both from those in favor of the consecrations and from those opposed. This was not a refusal to choose, but a more general view of the situation. He did not want "the whole religious problem to be reduced to [this] single question.... The decisive question remains that of the Mass, the catechism, the traditional version and interpretation of Scripture."[37] Although he did have a clear-cut opinion, he did not express it publicly before the consecrations. On the very eve of the ceremony, he wrote in his diary:

> We've been given demonstrations that, in extraordinary cases, bishops can be consecrated without a papal mandate.
> But it is not the simple absence of a mandate that is at issue. I fail to see where it has been demonstrated that it is not forbidden to consecrate bishops against the expressly manifested formal will of the Pope.
> Or at least, I don't see how such a demonstration could avoid postulating or implying sedevacantism.[38]

CONSECRATIONS WITHOUT A PAPAL MANDATE

The consecration ceremony took place in Écône on Thursday, June 30, 1988. As he had promised several months earlier, Bishop de Castro Mayer had come from Brazil to assist Archbishop Lefebvre as co-consecrator. The ceremony took place under a huge white tent. The liturgical procession moved forward to the applause of the crowd, as seen on television. A special long platform had been set up not far from the altar and the area where the consecrations would take place, for cameramen, photographers, and journalists from all over the world.

First, there was Archbishop Lefebvre's long address.[39] He described the ceremony as "certainly historic," and presented the consecrations he was about to perform as a "survival operation of Tradition," believing them to be legitimized by "a case of necessity."

The ceremony itself began with what should have been, according to the Ritual, the reading of the apostolic mandate. Film footage of the ceremony shows the unease of the moment. Addressing Fr Schmidberger, in his cope, who as Superior General of the Society of St. Pius X was responsible for presenting the candidates for the episcopate,

---

37 Jean Madiran, *Quand il y a une éclipse* (Paris: Éditions Difralivre, 1991), 74.
38 Ibid., 72-73.
39 Unabridged text in *Fideliter* 64 (July-August 1988): 2-8.

Archbishop Lefebvre pronounced the ritual formula, in Latin: "Do you have the apostolic mandate?" Father Schmidberger replied, almost half-heartedly: "We do." This statement was equivocal or ambiguous. Literally, not only had the Pope not given the apostolic mandate to consecrate bishops, he had even explicitly and publicly forbidden Archbishop Lefebvre to do so. On the other hand, Archbishop Lefebvre considered that he had received this mandate from "the Church of all time" and that, per Cardinal Ratzinger's letter of July 28, 1987, and subsequently per the Protocol of Agreement, the possibility for the Society of Saint Pius X to have a bishop had been affirmed by the Holy See.

In his address before the consecration of the bishops, Archbishop Lefebvre also referred to apparitions of the Virgin Mary as a prophetic sign of the gesture he was about to accomplish. A nun from a convent in Quito had received these apparitions, in the late sixteenth and early seventeenth centuries. He appropriated one of the prophecies from that time. He declared:

> Our Lady prophesied that during the nineteenth century and most of the twentieth, errors would spread more and more strongly in the Holy Church, and that they would lead to catastrophe, corrupt morals, and the disappearance of the faith. This is something we cannot fail to notice. And I apologize for continuing the account of this apparition, but it speaks of a prelate who will absolutely oppose this wave of apostasy and impiety by preserving the priesthood, by making good priests.... I was stunned myself when I read these lines, I can't deny them, it's recorded in the apparition archives.[40]

ECCLESIA DEI MOTU PROPRIO AND COMMISSION

The day after the ceremony, on July 1, the Holy See issued a declaration of *latae sententiae* excommunication against Archbishop Lefebvre, Bishop de Castro Mayer, and the four bishops they had consecrated. They were excommunicated in application of canons 1382 and 1364.1, which punish schismatic acts. The newly ordained bishops were indeed bishops in the eyes of the Church, but excommunication prohibited them from celebrating and receiving the sacraments, and from holding office in the Church.

On July 2, John Paul II promulgated the motu proprio *Ecclesia Dei adflicta*.[41] The Pope deplored the fact that "the unlawful episcopal ordination conferred on 30 June last by Archbishop Marcel Lefebvre"

---

40 *Fideliter* 64 (July-August 1988): 7.
41 Motu proprio *Ecclesia Dei adflicta*, July 2, 1988, Latin text in *L'Osservatore Romano* (3 July 1988); English translation on the Vatican website.

had "frustrated all the efforts made during the previous years to ensure
the full communion with the Church of the Priestly Fraternity of St.
Pius X." The sacraments performed by Archbishop Lefebvre constituted an act of

> *disobedience* to the Roman Pontiff in a very grave matter and
> of supreme importance for the unity of the Church . . . such
> disobedience – which implies in practice the rejection of the
> Roman primacy – constitutes a *schismatic* act. In performing
> such an act, notwithstanding the formal *canonical warning* sent
> to them by the Cardinal Prefect of the Congregation for Bishops
> on 17 June last, Mons. Lefebvre and the priests Bernard Fellay,
> Bernard Tissier de Mallerais, Richard Williamson and Alfonso de
> Galaretta, have incurred the grave penalty of excommunication
> envisaged by ecclesiastical law.[42]

In a passage that received little attention at the time, the motu proprio pointed out that the act performed by Archbishop Lefebvre not
only went against canon law, but also had an erroneous doctrinal basis:

> The *root* of this schismatic act can be discerned in an incomplete
> and contradictory notion of Tradition [because] [i]t is impossible
> to remain faithful to the Tradition while breaking the ecclesial
> bond with him to whom, in the person of the Apostle Peter,
> Christ himself entrusted the ministry of unity in his Church.

John Paul II called on all the faithful to "strengthen . . . still more
their fidelity by rejecting erroneous interpretations and arbitrary and
unauthorized applications in matters of doctrine, liturgy and discipline."
In particular, bishops were called upon to "exercise the important duty
of a clear-sighted vigilance full of charity and firmness, so that this
fidelity may be everywhere safeguarded." The Pope urged theologians
to feel "called upon to respond to the present circumstances. Indeed,
the extent and depth of the teaching of the Second Vatican Council
call for a renewed commitment to deeper study in order to reveal
clearly the Council's continuity with Tradition, especially in points of
doctrine which, perhaps because they are new, have not yet been well
understood by some sections of the Church."

John Paul II also announced the creation of a Commission "for the
purpose of facilitating full ecclesial communion of priests, seminarians, religious communities or individuals until now linked in various

---

42 It is noteworthy that the other consecrator, Bishop de Castro Mayer, was not named
in the motu proprio whereas he had been in the decree of excommunication of July 1.
It has been said that he was receiving psychiatric treatment at the time. The pope
may have judged that he was not fully in possession of his faculties and therefore not
entirely responsible for the act in which he had collaborated.

ways to the Fraternity founded by Mons. Lefebvre, who may wish to remain united to the Successor of Peter in the Catholic Church, while preserving their spiritual and liturgical traditions, in the light of the Protocol signed on 5 May last by Cardinal Ratzinger and Mons. Lefebvre." He also asked that respect "everywhere be shown for the feelings of all those who are attached to the Latin liturgical tradition, by a wide and generous application of the directives already issued some time ago by the Apostolic See for the use of the Roman Missal according to the typical edition of 1962."

Cardinal Mayer was appointed president of this commission, which would henceforth be known as the *Ecclesia Dei* Commission. Mgr Camille Perl would be its secretary.

BIRTH OF THE FRATERNITY OF SAINT PETER

The motu proprio is dated July 2. On the same day, Father Josef Bisig, until then assistant to the Superior General of the Society of St. Pius X, Father Denis Coiffet, and thirteen other priests and seminarians of the Society of St. Pius X who refused to accept the consecrations performed by Archbishop Lefebvre signed a *Declaration of Intent*. They stated that they "deeply regretted the illicit episcopal consecrations of June 30," that they represented the *pars sanior* (the "healthier part") of the Society of St. Pius X, and that they had "but one desire: to be able to live in the Church, as a religious society of that Church in submission, as goes without saying, to its head, and to be able to work for the Church." They expressed

> the hope of being able once again to be canonically erected by the competent ecclesiastical authorities for the realization of their specific vocation, to be able to devote themselves to the care of the faithful and especially to the formation of priests in an authentically Catholic spirit . . . and to be able to celebrate divine worship according to the directives of an indubitable tradition.[43]

On July 4, on the initiative of Fr Bruno de Blignières, Fr Coiffet, Fr Tournyol du Clos, Fr Louis de Blignières, and a layman, Max Champoiseau, from the *Centre Charlier*, were received in Rome by Cardinals Ratzinger and Mayer. They were assured by Cardinal Ratzinger that "the Pope's will is to give a place in the holy Church to those who are attached to the spiritual tradition."[44] The following day, July 5, four other SSPX priests, Frs. Bisig, Baumann, Recktenwald, and du

---

43 The *Declaration* is reproduced in Thierry Bouclier, *L'Abbé Denis Coiffet. Zélé serviteur de l'Église* (Saint-Cloud, France: Terra Mare Éditions, 2016), 110-11.
44 Fr Bruno de Blignières to the author, Conversation, September 16, 2021.

Faÿ, joined the group. On July 6, they were able to greet John Paul II briefly in a sitting room. The Pope greeted them by saying: "Here are the priests who have remained faithful to me."[45] They thanked him for the motu proprio, and he answered: "That's good, carry on."[46] Soon they would obtain a *celebret* signed by Cardinals Ratzinger and Mayer.

Priests issuing from the SSPX were encouraged to found a new priestly fraternity to enable them to maintain "the traditions of spirituality and apostolate"[47] to which they were attached. Msgr Clemens, Cardinal Ratzinger's secretary, suggested the name: *Fraternity of Saint Peter*.[48] On July 14 and 15, at Fontgombault, an information and consultation meeting brought together some twenty priests from the Society of Saint Pius X, along with Father Louis-Marie de Blignières, Msgr Gilles Wach, future prior of the Institute of Christ the King, and a number of lay people, including Bernard Antony. The meeting was attended by Dom Forgeot, Abbot of Fontgombault, Dom Éric de Lesquen, Abbot of Randol, and Msgr Perl, Secretary of the *Ecclesia Dei* Commission.

A few days later, on July 18, again in the presence of Mgr Perl, twelve priests and seminarians of the Society of St Pius X gathered at Hauterive Abbey—including the French clerics Philippe Tournyol du Clos, Gabriel Baumann, Christian Laffargue, Christian Gouyaud (plus Fr Denis Coiffet, who was unable to attend)—signed the act of foundation of the Priestly Fraternity of Saint Peter (FSSP) as a "clerical society of apostolic life." And they asked "the Holy See to deign to approve said society as soon as possible, so that they may act effectively for the unity and good of the Church." On the following October 18, the Fraternity of St. Peter was canonically erected as a society of apostolic life and pontifical right, i.e., placed directly under the authority of the Holy See. The Fraternity grew rapidly, with several hundred priests at present. Some traditional religious communities, linked to the SSPX or otherwise, were also recognized by the Holy See at this time.

The Fraternity of Saint Vincent Ferrer, founded by Fr Louis-Marie de Blignières in 1979, was erected on October 28, 1988 as a religious institute of pontifical right, and the founder was appointed Superior General. On November 21, he made his perpetual religious profession at the hands of Cardinal Mayer in Rome. On December 3, 1988, the first five brothers of the FSVF, who had long been awaiting ordination, were finally ordained to the priesthood. The ceremony took place

---

45 Quoted in T. Bouclier, *L'Abbé Denis Coiffet*, 114.
46 Fr Bruno de Blignières to the author, Conversation, September 16, 2021.
47 Motu proprio *Ecclesia Dei* 5.
48 T. Bouclier, *L'Abbé Denis Coiffet*, 115.

at Fontgombault Abbey. As Cardinal Mayer, President of the *Ecclesia Dei* Commission, who was supposed to preside, was unable to attend, it was a former missionary bishop, Bp de Milleville, who conferred the ordinations.

Father Lecareux, superior of the Fraternity of the Transfiguration in Mérigny, not far from Fontgombault, had signed the *Supplication for Peace* a few months earlier, as we have seen. He had hoped to meet Cardinal Mayer that day. The unexpected absence of the President of the *Ecclesia Dei* Commission prevented this first contact, which might have led to the regularization of his community's situation.

The *Opus Mariae*, founded in 1969 by Father Wladimir de Saint-Jean (Roger Péquigney, formerly of the French Seminary in Rome), applied to the *Ecclesia Dei* Commission for recognition. In 1992, the *Opus Mariae* was recognized as an association of the faithful under diocesan law by Bishop Lagrange of Gap. Then, on the advice of the *Ecclesia Dei* Commission, the community adapted its constitutions to a canonical status and took the name of Canons Regular of the Mother of God.

After the consecrations, Msgr Gilles Wach and Fr Philippe Mora founded the Institute of Christ the King Sovereign Priest (ICRSP), erected on September 1, 1990 as a society of apostolic life under diocesan law. The ICRSP would be erected as a society of apostolic life in the manner of canons, and of pontifical right in 2008.

CHAPTER 13
The Traditional Mass, Upon Conditions

T HE DECREE ERECTING THE PRIESTLY FRATERNITY of Saint Peter (FSSP) on October 18, 1988, stipulated that "the use of the liturgical books in force in 1962 is granted" to its members. At the same time, the Fraternity of Saint Vincent Ferrer (FSVF) was granted, by indult, the use of the Dominican liturgy, which the Order of Friars Preachers had abandoned in 1968 to adopt the Roman rite undergoing reform. In March 1989, the Holy See approved the constitutions of the monastery of Sainte-Madeleine—just a few months before it was erected as an abbey *sui juris*. They soberly defined "the two sources which gave birth to the community of Le Barroux and constitute the reason for its existence":

> Monastic life according to the Rule of St. Benedict and the customs bequeathed by our ancestors; the Divine Office and liturgy of the Mass celebrated according to the more than thousand-year-old rites of the Holy Roman Church, in the Latin language.

What are called *Ecclesia Dei* communities, i.e., those that entered into full communion with the Holy See with the motu proprio *Ecclesia Dei*, or that came into existence thanks to that motu proprio, such as the Institute of Christ the King Sovereign Priest, were able, at first, to make use of the traditional liturgy unhindered. Some monastic communities with no link to the *Ecclesia Dei* commission, such as the Benedictine monastery of Triors and the Benedictine nuns of Jouques, were able to adopt the traditional liturgy in 1989.

It should also be noted that *Ecclesia Dei* communities "have never had the slightest difficulty in finding French, foreign, or Curia bishops—or even cardinals—to perform ordinations or give confirmations."[1] In December 1988, as we have seen, five religious of the Fraternity of Saint Vincent Ferrer were ordained in the Abbey of Fontgombault by Bishop de Milleville. Seven days later, in Rome, Cardinal Mayer ordained the first priest of the Fraternity of Saint Peter.

---

1 Christophe Geffroy, *Benoît XVI et "la paix liturgique"* (Paris: Cerf, 2008), 197.

RELUCTANCE AND HOSTILITY

On the other hand, application of the motu proprio at the diocesan and parish level was difficult in some countries, notably in France; not, however, in the United States. Yet in the motu proprio John Paul II had asked:

> [R]espect must everywhere be shown for the feelings of all those who are attached to the Latin liturgical tradition, by a wide and generous application of the directives already issued some time ago by the Apostolic See....

Cardinal Lustiger set an example by celebrating the traditional Mass in Notre Dame Cathedral in Paris on July 3, on the very morrow of the motu proprio. And in 1989, he innovated by appointing Fr Veuillez pastor *in solidum* of the parish of Saint-Eugène-Sainte-Cécile (while the other pastor was in charge of the community attached to the rite of Paul VI). But many bishops were reluctant, hostile even, to authorize the celebration of the traditional Mass in their dioceses, or to allow the establishment of traditional communities in full communion with the Holy See. As recently as 1992, Mgr Garnier, Bishop of Luçon, declared in a talk: "I can't use the motu proprio at the moment. It's not my fault. It can only be used if there is humble, faithful, total adherence to the Council."[2] The bishop of Luçon linked authorization of the traditional Mass with acceptance of the Council–which is what the motu proprio demanded–but he added strictly liturgical reasons and wanted to link authorization for the traditional Mass with attendance at the new Mass. He did not want two rites of Mass to be celebrated on the same footing or with any regularity in his diocese:

> Can you imagine us bishops managing what is known as bi-ritualism?...We bishops are doing everything we can not to have to deal with bi-ritualism some day. In other words, if we were to accept, if we were to say yes to the application of the indult, to the Motu proprio, it would really only be in one or two chapels per diocese, with priests appointed by the bishop, of course, for a certain number of Sundays in the year, but not necessarily all of them, so that those who take advantage of these assemblies according to the old ritual, from time to time, also come and celebrate the Eucharist according to the new one, and thus manifest, in reality, and not just in words, their attachment to the Council and to the Church.

---

2 Excerpt of the lecture given on August 18, 1992, published in "1988-1992: Bilan de l'application du Motu proprio 'Ecclesia Dei,'" *La Nef*, special issue (May 1993): 56-57.

It is fair to say that this opinion, which was expressed spontaneously at the end of a talk, reflected the position of most bishops of France at the time.

Over the years, Dom Gérard would become the spokesman in Rome for the expectations and difficulties of the faithful attached to Tradition. On September 28, 1990, for the first time, accompanied by ten priests and brothers from his monastery, he was received in audience by Pope John Paul II. At the start of the audience, he read the address he had prepared.[3] After first expressing his gratitude to the Pope for the creation of the *Ecclesia Dei* Commission and the canonical recognition of the monastery, he spoke at length and candidly about the difficulties of applying the motu proprio:

> But alas! how can one fail to deplore the fact that, more often than not, relations between those faithful [attached to the traditional rite] and their Ordinaries remain so difficult? . . . The motu proprio, which in practice should have the force of law and permit the widespread use of traditional rites, is very often either disregarded, set aside, or rendered unusable. There are many Christians, whether priests, religious, or laity, who are then embittered and risk abandoning themselves to a solution of rupture.

Dom Gérard then called for "a declaration from the Holy See recognizing and promoting the dignity of the ancient rite as a form of the Roman rite." This is exactly what Benedict XVI would do seventeen years later, but Dom Gérard was probably unaware that Cardinal Ratzinger had long been considering such a recognition. Finally, in the last part of his speech, which was delivered but not published "out of discretion," Dom Gérard proposed a "solution" to resolve the difficulties encountered by communities, priests, and faithful attached to the traditional liturgy: the creation of an apostolic vicariate that would make them independent from the dioceses.

John Paul II then gave an address in French, but this was not a direct response to Dom Gérard's short speech. The Pope gave "thanks to Divine Providence for having helped you, during the painful events of June 1988, to return to communion with the Apostolic See," and greeted a "young and fervent community." He also reaffirmed the full legitimacy of the attachment to the liturgical books in use in 1962, "this concession [being] intended to facilitate the ecclesial communion of those who feel bound to these liturgical forms."

In his publication of this address by the Pope, Dom Gérard pointed out the following:

---

3 Most of this address was published in *Les Amis du Monastère* 55 (January 27, 1991): 5-6.

> For almost twenty years now we've been told *ad nauseam* to
> accept the liturgy of the Council, told that there can't be two
> liturgies in the Church, and that the new liturgy has irrevocably
> replaced the old one. We are happy to hear the successor of
> Peter remind us of our right to use the traditional rites of the
> Roman liturgy (the same rites that were celebrated throughout
> Vatican II).[4]

At the end of the audience, Dom Gérard presented the Pope with a
small ivory statue of the Virgin Mary, carved by one of the monastery's
friars, and also unexpectedly handed him a letter that completed his
official speech, "in a sincere and filial language, but less formal and
more familiar," he wrote.[5]

Surprising in its form – it amounts to a series of sometimes brutal
observations – this letter was also bold in some of its claims. It contained
several direct requests, not all of which went unheeded. Dom Gérard
wanted an encyclical to be published against abortion, "an abominable
crime before God and humanity";[6] he was delighted when John Paul
II published the encyclical *Evangelium vitae* five years later, reaffirming
"the value and inviolability of human life." He also asked the Pope to
"restore its rightful place to a rite of the Mass that goes back to Saint
Gregory the Great, so that this thousand-year-old rite may serve as a
reference for a reform of the reform." We all know how Benedict XVI
would solemnly reaffirm this "rightful place." Dom Gérard was not
the first to use the expression "reform of the reform" to designate the
necessary reorientation of the liturgical reform undertaken since the
Second Vatican Council. As early as 1967, when the new Mass was still
being prepared, Abbé Dulac, in a major article in the *Courrier de Rome*,
used the expression and called for an end to "liturgical transformism"
while there was still time.[7] As we shall see, Cardinal Ratzinger used
the expression again in 2001.

The idea of instituting an apostolic vicariate or ordinariate specifically for the faithful attached to traditional rites was not unique to
Dom Gérard and his prior, Father Anselme, who took a keen interest
in institutional and canonical issues. But Le Barroux Abbey was the
first to suggest such a solution to the Holy See. This kind of structure

---

4 *Les Amis du Monastère* 53 (October 17, 1990): 5.
5 This letter only came to light a few months later when it was published in *Les Amis
du Monastère* 55 (January 1991): 6-7.
6 Dom Gérard, in October 1994, took part in a "rescue operation" at a hospital of
Grenoble. This earned him an arrest, then a trial.
7 Fr Raymond Dulac, "La Réforme de la réforme," *Le Courrier de Rome* 15 (September
15, 1967).

already existed in various forms: the ordinariate for the armed forces or ordinariates for the faithful of the Eastern rites. This solution would be used under the next pontificate for the Anglican clergy and faithful who wished to return to Catholic communion. The idea was taken up again at meetings with Cardinal Ratzinger. Then, in February 1991, during a new audience granted by Cardinal Ratzinger to Father Anselme, prior of Le Barroux, and Father Bisig, Superior General of the Fraternity of St. Peter, a new project began to be examined. The chronicle of Le Barroux specifies:

> There is no longer any question of an ordinariate – that would not respect Church law, because it would deprive bishops of some of their rights. From now on, the idea is to make it possible for any member of the faithful to petition his bishop to obtain the traditional Mass.

This idea would reach fruition, with even more generous provisions, only in the pontificate of Benedict XVI with the motu proprio of 2007.

The "fight for the Mass" that Dom Gérard waged after 1988 also included one of the major editorial achievements of the Abbey of Sainte-Madeleine: the publication of a daily missal for the faithful, which appeared in February 1991. But in the dioceses, particularly in France, there was a great deal of reluctance and even hostility on the part of the bishops. In 1992, for example, Bishop Raffin of Metz considered the motu proprio *Ecclesia Dei* to be "a merciful parenthesis for people who must gradually come to terms with Paul VI's *Ordo Missae*, for there can be no question of turning the Tridentine Missal into a new Latin rite like those that have existed and still exist."[8]

The Abbey of Sainte-Madeleine du Barroux set out to revive the debate on liturgy by introducing in France the work of German liturgist Klaus Gamber, who had died a few years earlier. Klaus Gamber (1919-1989) had co-founded the Regensburg Liturgical Institute in 1960, and was responsible for the scientific editing of important liturgical texts. In addition to numerous studies of liturgical sources from East and West, he wrote several books and numerous articles on post-conciliar liturgical reform and its application. On these questions, Cardinal Ratzinger would say he acted "with the vigilance of an authentic seer and the fearlessness of a true witness."

In 1979, he published *Die Reform der römischen Liturgie*, a collection of his articles published between 1974 and 1978 in the German edition of *Una Voce*. It was this work that the Abbey of Sainte-Madeleine made

---

8 Interview with *La Nef* 21 (October 1992).

known, publishing the translation by Una Voce board member Simone Wallon. The book was published by Éditions Sainte-Madeleine in early 1992, under the title *La Réforme liturgique en question* [English version: *The Reform of the Roman Liturgy: Its Problems and Background* (Una Voce Press, 1993) – *Translator*]. It was prefaced by Cardinal Oddi, who saw the need for a "reform of the reform" (although he did not use the expression):

> Has the time not come to examine the writings of this great scholar and, with him, to ask whether recent years have not seen the introduction into the Church's prayer of elements that do not correspond to its nature, and should therefore be modified?

This preface was followed by three texts published in 1989 in a Festschrift in honor of Msgr Gamber. One, by Cardinal Ratzinger, was an indictment of the liturgical reform, which had "strayed ever further" from its original, legitimate, and necessary movement: "The result has not been resuscitation, but devastation." Cardinal Ratzinger called for a new "liturgical movement" that would be "a new spiritual impulse" and no longer left "to the arbitrariness of parish priests and their liturgical teams."

Because of its title (which was stronger in French than in the original), the cardinals who patronized it, and the criticisms of the new rite it articulated, the work aroused public controversy. Apparently at the request of several French bishops, Dom Robert Le Gall, Abbot of Kergonan, published a series of articles offering a thorough critique of Gamber's book:[9]

> His whole book amounts to a collection of little historical quibbles designed to justify a kind of allergy to what he irreverently calls the "ritus modernus." Gamber has gradually retreated to earlier liturgical forms unilaterally and exclusively.

A year later, Sainte-Madeleine Abbey published a translation of a new book by Mgr Gamber, *Tournés vers le Seigneur!* [*Zum Herrn hin! Fragen um Kirchenbau und Gebet nach Osten*]. It was a plea, based on historical arguments, for the celebration of Mass "towards God." Cardinal Ratzinger had agreed to preface the book. In this way of celebrating, he wrote, there is an "anticipation" of the return of the Son of God, "priests and faithful go out to meet him. This orientation of prayer expresses the theocentric character of the liturgy."[10]

---

9 Robert Le Gall, "La Liturgie, foyer de la nouvelle évangélisation," nine articles published in the weekly *Famille chrétienne*, July 2 to November 5, 1992.

10 Joseph Ratzinger, "Preface" to Msgr Klaus Gamber, *Tournés vers le Seigneur!* (Le Barroux: Éditions Sainte-Madeleine, 1993).

DISCREET TALKS

This willingness on the part of Dom Gérard and the Abbey of Sainte-Madeleine to open the debate on "the reform of the liturgical reform" went hand in hand with a generally favorable reception of the teachings of the Magisterium, whereas the SSPX and the communities that remained linked to it continued to question them, seeing them as a continuation of the conciliar spirit.

The case of the *Catechism of the Catholic Church* (CCC) was a case in point. This catechism, prepared for several years under the direction of Cardinal Ratzinger and published at the end of 1992, expressed John Paul II's desire of "supporting and confirming the faith" and "strengthening the bonds of unity in the same Catholic faith."[11] Unlike the *Catechism of the Council of Trent* (1566), which had been written to help priests in preaching and teaching the catechism to children, the CCC was intended for all the faithful. It took up the classic structure of older catechisms and provided a structured and comprehensive presentation of the faith. The drafting of the CCC had been a collective effort, involving various commissions and committees made up of theologians from different countries. Through Father Garrigues and Cardinal Schönborn, both Dominicans, Father de Blignières and other theologians from the convent of Saint Thomas Aquinas were able to introduce clarifications into the formulations relating to religious freedom.[12]

The publication of the Catechism delighted the abbot of Le Barroux, who soon wrote to Cardinal Ratzinger to express "our gratitude to you for the doctrinal and liturgical recovery we are witnessing these days."[13] On the other hand, the authorities of the Society of St. Pius X were highly critical, casting suspicion on this long-awaited work. Under the title *Le Nouveau Catéchisme est-il catholique?* they published the text of two lectures given by Fr Michel Simoulin, superior of the seminary at Écône, and Fr Alain Lorans, rector of the Institut Saint-Pie X. In his preface to this volume, Fr Schmidberger, Superior General of the Society of Saint Pius X, expressed the Society's official position:

> Despite beautiful passages and good presentations materially speaking, we do not have in our hands, with this catechism, a manual of the doctrine of the Catholic Church, but rather the exposition of the modernist faith of the conciliar Church.[14]

11 John Paul II, Apostolic Constitution *Fidei Depositum* (October 11, 1992).
12 Fr Louis de Blignières to the author, Conversation, November 27, 2011.
13 Dom Gérard to Cardinal Ratzinger, Letter, May 6, 1993, Archives of the abbey of Sainte-Madeleine du Barroux.
14 *Le Nouveau catéchisme est-il catholique?* (Suresnes: Fideliter, 1993), 8. At the time an Orthodox critique of the *CCC* was also published, the work of two Orthodox prelates:

The Abbey of Le Barroux responded to this criticism with a book that refuted the objections made by the Society of St. Pius X, drawing on the teaching of the Magisterium, both that of John Paul II and the Magisterium prior to the Second Vatican Council. The book, "prepared by our Fathers Basile and Gabriel (in collaboration with the whole community)," says the chronicle, appeared under the title *Oui! le Catéchisme de l'Église catholique . . . est catholique,* a direct response, right down to the cover, to the critique by the Society of St. Pius X. The book, signed by Father Gabriel, had received the imprimatur of Bp Bouchex. Father Gabriel presented the booklet to Cardinal Ratzinger during an audience attended by three monks from Le Barroux, who had come to discuss other matters. Father de Saint-Laumer of the Fraternity of Saint Vincent Ferrer also wrote a lengthy response to the SSPX's criticisms.[15] Fr Michel Simoulin dug his heels in and published a fuller treatment yet: *Le Catéchisme assassiné.*[16]

The same diversity of appreciations was to be found on the occasion of the publication of the encyclical *Veritatis splendor.* Dated August 6, 1993, this lengthy encyclical on the Church's moral teaching was intended to provide a response to "the Church's internal crisis concerning moral theology" and also to shed light on the "worldwide debate on ethics, which today has become a matter of life and death for humanity."[17]

The encyclical caused a sensation at the Abbey of Sainte-Madeleine when it was read over several days in the refectory. Dom Gérard soon wrote to Cardinal Ratzinger "expressing everyone's joy and our common thanksgiving for the magnificent encyclical *Veritatis splendor,* which well deserves its name and which we have just finished listening to as refectory reading."[18] A month later, in a letter renewing his invitation to Cardinal Ratzinger to visit the abbey, he wrote again: "Thank you, Your Eminence, for all that comes to us from Rome these days: a Catholic Catechism and a luminous encyclical!"[19]

In *Itinéraires,* Jean Madiran greeted the encyclical as a "miracle":

Msgr Photios and Archimandrite Philaret, *Le Nouveau Catéchisme contre la foi des Pères. Une réponse orthodoxe* (Lausanne: L'Âge d'Homme, 1993).

15 D.-M. de Saint-Laumer, "À propos du nouveau catéchisme. Réponses à la Fraternité Saint-Pie X," *Sedes Sapientiae* 46 (1993): 45-64.

16 Lyon: Éditions Saint-Irénée, 1997.

17 Cardinal Joseph Ratzinger, "Presentation" to the collection *Les 14 encycliques de Jean-Paul II* (Saint-Cénéré: Téqui, 2003), 12.

18 Dom Gérard to Cardinal Ratzinger, Letter, October 19, 1993, Archives of the Abbey of Sainte-Madeleine du Barroux (copy).

19 Dom Gérard to Cardinal Ratzinger, Letter, November 30, 1993, Archives of the Abbey of Sainte-Madeleine du Barroux (copy).

> At last, the word we've been waiting for – or rather which, dis-
> couraged as we were, we were no longer expecting. . . . Nothing
> presaged that the announced encyclical "on morals" would be
> this strong, this radiant, this total: it is an encyclical on the law
> of God and the human call to life eternal.[20]

He felt that what he had characterized in 1968 as "the heresy of the
twentieth century," i.e., the rejection of natural law and the denial of
universal truth, had at last been countered by this encyclical. He was
also delighted that the intention of the Council announced by John
XXIII had at last been re-established, "corrected according to its text."

Within the Society of Saint Pius X, an entirely different reading of
the encyclical was given. Fr de Tanoüarn noted several "major ambiguities" and expressed his disappointment: "We were expecting Saint
Thomas, and it's the schoolteacher 'expert in humanity' who adds his
stone to the building of the world order."[21] Bishop Tissier de Mallerais, for his part, commented on the encyclical in a lengthy sixty-page
study that was circulated exclusively among members of the SSPX. He
presented it as follows:

> While recognizing the merits of John Paul II's document, this
> study aims to highlight the deviations, ambiguities, and errors it
> conceals in matters of individual and social morals. The encyc-
> lical's break with the magisterium of the pre-conciliar popes
> consists in the liberalism and modernism that these same popes
> condemned.[22]

These doctrinal disagreements on two major texts of the Magisterium
did not get in the way of the first unofficial discussions between the
Society of Saint Pius X and theologians belonging to the Benedictine
and Dominican Orders. They were initiated by Fr Aulagnier, then Superior of the District of France.[23] In August 1993, on a visit to Randol
Abbey, and being aware of the role Abbot Dom de Lesquen had played
in the reconciliation between Dom Gérard and Rome, he told him of
his desire "to normalize the situation of the SSPX with Rome" and
suggested that he "organize a few meetings to tackle the problems that

---

20 Jean Madiran, "Le Miracle," *Itinéraires*, 3rd series, 3 (December 1993): 1.
21 Guillaume de Tanoüarn, "La Splendeur de la vérité," *Fideliter* 96 (November-December 1993): 36-40.
22 Bp Bernard Tissier de Mallerais, "'Veritatis splendor.' Commentaire," *Cor Unum* 47
(March 1994), 60-page supplement.
23 He gave his recollections in Michel Lelong, *Pour la réconciliation nécessaire* (Paris:
Nouvelles Éditions Latines, 2011), 98-114. A document from the abbey of Notre-Dame
de Fontgombault helps complete, makes more precise, and corrects Fr Aulagnier's
evocation: *Échanges entre la Fraternité Saint-Pie X et un groupe de théologiens, 1993-1995*
(Abbey archives).

divide us on the Council." Dom de Lesquen "leapt at the chance," says Fr Aulagnier. Working meetings were organized. The Abbot of Randol came accompanied by one of the monks from his abbey, Dom Daniel Field, a canonist, and Dom Antoine Forgeot, Abbot of Fontgombault, came with Dom Yves Chauveau, professor of dogmatic theology at the abbey. Two Dominican theologians from the Toulouse convent, Father de La Soujeole and Father Bonino, director of the *Revue thomiste*, also took part in the conversations, with the agreement of their provincial superior, Father Brugès. Fr Aulagnier was assisted by Fr Grégoire Celier, then professor of philosophy and prefect of studies at an SSPX school. He "devoted himself to the conversations selflessly," says Father Aulagnier. He was something like the secretary of the sessions. Other SSPX priests, Fathers Boivin, Lorans and Boubée, and later Father Laisney, took part in these "colloquia." At the first meeting, held on December 2, 1993 at the SSPX's French district headquarters in Suresnes, a list of issues was drawn up: religious freedom, liturgy, ecumenism, the conciliar constitution *Gaudium et Spes*, Tradition, and the Magisterium. The SSPX would have liked religious from the Fraternité Saint-Dominique d'Avrillé to be associated with these discussions, but Father Brugès "opposed it, lest it should seem to be an implicit recognition of those religious on the part of the Dominicans."[24] Between 1993 and 1995, a total of twelve working meetings were held in different locations: at the Institut universitaire Saint-Pie X in Paris, at La Tour-d'Auvergne, near Randol, at Fontgombault Abbey, at Gaussan Abbey, and at the Saint-Bernard school in Courbevoie. The meetings were discreet, but Cardinal Ratzinger, Prefect of the Congregation for the Doctrine of the Faith, and the *Ecclesia Dei* Commission were kept regularly informed. The aim was not yet to reach doctrinal agreement on the points under discussion, but to clarify convergences and divergences, and to dispel any misunderstandings. Although the SSPX authorities were informed of these meetings, the various publications of the Society never mentioned them. In 1994, Fr de Jorna succeeded Fr Aulagnier as Superior of the French District. The doctrinal meetings came to an end the next year. Fr Aulagnier would write: "I was no longer superior of the French district of the SSPX and didn't have much clout . . . all the more so as the General House took a dim view of this initiative."

However, two years later, as we shall see, new meetings on the SSPX were organized within the framework of GREC, though along different lines.

---

24 *Échanges entre la Fraternité Saint-Pie X et un groupe de théologiens*, 1.

PETITIONS FOR THE MASS

In the years 1993-1994, there were several petitions and entreaties asking for greater freedom for the traditional Mass.

On October 19, 1993, on behalf of the International Federation *Una Voce*, its president, Eric de Saventhem, addressed a long memorandum to John Paul II. He detailed the situation of "Catholics attached to the ancient liturgical forms of the Latin tradition" and the difficulties they faced. He deplored the fact that since the publication of the motu proprio in 1988, neither the Congregation for Divine Worship nor any episcopal conference had issued instructions to encourage its implementation; "on the contrary, many conferences have tried to limit the freedom of local ordinaries through restrictive directives." He called for papal intervention to ensure that the traditional Mass "regains its rightful place in the official prayer life of the Church." John Paul II asked Archbishop Re, substitute at the Secretariat of State, to respond to this request.[25] He asserted that the new Mass should remain the "general law," while "the use of the previous rite is currently a matter of privilege which must remain an exception." The formula caused scandal because it seemed to restrict the generous spirit of the 1988 motu proprio.

Also in 1993, the *Traditional Mass Society* (TMS), the American branch of *Una Voce*, collected signatures in the USA to request the freedom of celebrating the traditional Mass and the creation of a "Traditional Apostolic Vicariate covering the USA and Canada" to unite, organize, and protect. Some 40,000 signatures were collected. TMS President William R. Opelle was able to present the petition to John Paul II during an audience on February 28, 1994. In the accompanying letter, he stated:

> The signatories (who include hardly any so-called *"Lefebvrists,"* since the priests of the Society of St. Pius X told their people not to sign) represent but a minute fraction of those U. S. and Canadian Catholics who want to live and pray according to the Church's tradition.[26]

In 1994, the Abbot of Le Barroux launched his own petition, casting blame on Cardinal Innocenti, who three years before had succeeded Cardinal Mayer as President of the *Ecclesia Dei* Commission. Announcing the launch of the petition to the faithful, he wrote:

25 This text and the ensuing correspondence is in Leo Darroch, *Una Voce. The History of the F. I. U. V.*, 293-304.
26 Letter (dated January 31, 1994) printed in *The Latin Mass* Magazine (May-June 1994) and reprinted in the UNA VOCE/USA-Traditional Mass Society Newsletter, Summer 1995. Copy kindly provided by Byron Smith, Secretary, Una Voce America [– *Translator*].

> Six years after the publication of the motu proprio *Ecclesia Dei*, many of you continue to inform us of the difficulties you encounter in obtaining the celebration of the sacraments and Mass according to the ancient rites.... Since the departure of Cardinal Mayer, you have come up against not only the incomprehension of certain local Churches, but also the inertia of the Commission. Sometimes the Commission, far from favoring your requests – which is its proper function – even rejects them with astounding audacity. According to Cardinal Innocenti, an army of canonists, when consulted, declared it impossible to speak of a *right* to the ancient rites. In his Motu proprio, the Holy Father is alleged to have granted only a *favor*...[27]

This petition was launched in June 1994 and gathered 15,000 signatures within three months. Dom Gérard wanted to present it to the Pope in October. To obtain an audience, he enlisted the help of Cardinal Ratzinger and Archbishop Perl, Secretary of the *Ecclesia Dei* Commission. But the audience was not granted as easily or as quickly as the abbot of Le Barroux had hoped. At the end of October, he again asked Cardinal Ratzinger for his support:

> Archbishop Perl has told us that Cardinal Innocenti would not oppose our request, but that he would not present it. It seems to me that he doesn't want to favor the Mass according to the old rite in any way.[28]

It wasn't until the spring of 1995 that the audience was granted, which allowed the petition to reach 75,000 signatures in the meantime. Though it wasn't easy to obtain a private audience with the Pope, it was the very object of the petition that was still causing difficulty. A request for total freedom for the old rite had to avoid seeming to be a challenge to the new one. Dom Gérard was therefore asked to concelebrate Mass with the Pope in his private chapel in the Vatican, just before the audience he would be granted. This concelebration with John Paul II took place with the utmost discretion.[29] During the trip to Rome in April, Dom Gérard was accompanied by Fathers Anselme and Charbel. They were joined at the audience by representatives of various associations attached to the traditional rite, including Professor Robert Spaemann, founder of the German

---

27 *Les Amis du monastère* 70 (June 2, 1994): 4.

28 Dom Gérard to Cardinal Ratzinger, Fax, October 20, 1994, Archives of Sainte-Madeleine Abbey, copy.

29 One month before, on the occasion of the blessing of the monastery church in Rosans, Dom Gérard had for the first time concelebrated according to the new rite, with the abbots of Fontgombault, of Randol, and of Triors, in a ceremony over which Bishop Lagrange of Gap presided.

association *Pro Missa Tridentina*, and Monika Rheinschmitt, president of the association.

Early on Thursday morning, April 27, Dom Gérard concelebrated Mass with the Pope in his private chapel at the Vatican. He would soon explain to the nuns of the Annunciation why he had accepted:

> Refusing to concelebrate with the Pope would have opened the door to a suspicion of schism. Otherwise, we refuse to concelebrate with bishops and abbots. It was Cardinal Ratzinger who gave us this way of having an audience (otherwise refused): attend the pope's Mass, audience afterwards....The Mass of Paul VI has not become good, it still needs to be reformed, but it belongs to the Church (by having been prescribed for more than twenty-five years), to the patrimony (good or bad) of the Church.[30]

Although Dom Gérard would not mention it in public for another three years, news of this concelebration of the new Mass had begun to spread. The founder of the Fraternity of Saint-Vincent-Ferrer, Father de Blignières, told Father Jehan de Belleville, a monk at Le Barroux, that he was "cordially devastated," but still thought it was an isolated act, motivated by pragmatic considerations.[31]

LAY INITIATIVES

At the same time, lay people were taking initiatives to promote the traditional liturgy. In 1994, a group of lay people (Marc Bouhier, Catherine Chamaillet, Christian Marquant, Loïc Mérian, Anne Silvy-Leligois, and Antoine Villepelet) founded the *Centre international d'études liturgiques* (CIEL, "International Center for Liturgical Studies"), whose aim was "to make the liturgy of the Roman Catholic Church better known and understood."[32] Loïc Mérian, a former member of the MJCF and founder of the *Jeune Chrétienté* movement in 1990, was its president. More concretely, the CIEL wanted to "demonstrate the living character of the liturgy and ensure the promotion of the traditional liturgy through genuine intellectual and scientific work,"[33] by organizing an annual international colloquium, the proceedings of which would be published. Msgr Rudolf Michael

---

30 Report of the talk Dom Gérard gave to the nuns on June 14, 1995, Chronicle of the Abbey of Notre-Dame de l'Annonciation.

31 As he recounted to Dom Gérard in a letter he sent him on January 19, 1999 (copy in the archives of the Fraternity of Saint-Vincent-Ferrer).

32 Official registration at the Prefecture on January 17, 1995, *Journal Officiel* (February 8, 1995): 584.

33 *Présentation du Centre international d'études liturgiques*, undated.

Schmitz, a priest of the diocese of Cologne who later joined the Institute of Christ the King Sovereign Priest (ICRSS), was the driving force behind these colloquia, which brought together bishops, theologians, and liturgical specialists from a broad variety of backgrounds (traditional communities, monasteries, and diocesan clergy). Cardinal Oddi and Cardinal Stickler lent their support to the first colloquium, which took place at the Notre-Dame du Laus shrine in October 1995; its topic was *The Liturgy, Treasure of the Church*. Msgr Wach, Prior General of the ICKSP, and Dom Gérard, Abbot of Le Barroux, gave papers. There were also contributions from liturgy specialists who did not belong to the traditionalist world, such as Father Louis Bouyer, an Oratorian who had taken part in drawing up the liturgical reform after the Council (not without criticism),[34] or Father Composta, a Salesian, consultor to the Congregation for the Causes of Saints and professor at the Pontifical Urbaniana University. One of the hallmarks of the CIEL colloquia was the involvement of academics and researchers who were not exclusively attached (as priests or laymen) to the traditional liturgy.

A month before the first CIEL colloquium, Christian Marquant and Loïc Mérian founded the *Oremus* association, whose declared aim was "to work for the defense and promotion of the right to the simple and regular celebration of the traditional Latin liturgy, a monument of faith and the spiritual and cultural heritage of Western Christendom."[35] Starting in January 1996, the association published the *Lettre d'Oremus*, a newsletter devoted to the traditional liturgy and, also in 1996, a guide listing places of worship, religious communities, priestly institutions, and associations committed to the traditional liturgy. Limited to France in its first edition (1996: 101 traditional places of worship listed, excluding the SSPX and religious communities linked to it), the *Guide*, in subsequent annual editions, would present traditional places of worship worldwide, and would also publish the liturgical *Ordo* for the current year.

Of a completely different nature was the GREC (*Groupe de réflexion entre catholiques*, "Discussion group among Catholics"), also born at this time on the initiative of lay people. Gilbert Pérol (1926-1995), a

---

34 By 1968 he had already pointed out the "two viruses" that contaminated contemporary Catholicism: "[M]ythology, substituted for the analysis of reality and a 'sloganism' that has replaced doctrinal thought," *The Decomposition of Catholicism*, trans. Charles Underhill Quinn (Chicago: Franciscan Herald Press, 1969), 11.
35 Official registration at the Prefecture on September 15, 1995, *Journal Officiel* (84 October 1995): 3996.

diplomat and Secretary General of the French Ministry of Foreign Affairs whose last post was at the French Embassy in Rome from 1988 to 1992, had met Archbishop Lefebvre and was interested in the possibilities of reconciliation between the SSPX and the Holy See. He was also informed of the doctrinal dialogues that took place discreetly between 1992 and 1995, as mentioned above. A few months before his death, he wrote a note suggesting a "path to reconciliation": the Holy See "must admit that the fate meted out to the Mass of St. Pius V, particularly in France, was unjust, brutal, and ultimately not in conformity with the very will of the Council Fathers"; the excommunications inflicted on the SSPX bishops must be "if not rescinded, at least suspended"; and the SSPX "must stop rejecting Vatican II *en bloc* and the admirable texts – alas all too little known – which attempted to express the Church's presence in the world in contemporary terms."[36]

After Gilbert Pérol's death, his wife, Huguette Pérol, published a book devoted to the SSPX, *Les Sans-Papiers de l'Église* (1996, "The Undocumented People of the Church"), in which she took up and developed the suggestions made by her husband. She was well acquainted with the SSPX, notably through Fr du Chalard, who for decades had been the Society's best-informed priest in Rome about the Vatican and the Curia. The GREC – even though the acronym did not appear until later – was born in 1997 during a meal to which Madame Pérol had invited Father Michel Lelong of the White Fathers, a specialist on the Muslim world whom she had known for a long time, Father Lorans, then rector of the Institut Saint-Pie X in Paris, and Father Olivier de La Brosse, a Dominican and former cultural advisor to the French Embassy to the Holy See, now spokesman for the Bishops of France. Working groups were organized from 1997 onwards, and numerous meetings took place over more than a decade. Alongside Huguette Pérol, Father de La Brosse (who passed away in 2009) and Father Lelong, Fr Claude Barthe was one of the group's main leaders. Priests and theologians from the SSPX, members of the Fraternity of Saint Peter and the Institute of Christ the King, priests from the diocese of Paris and other dioceses, and historians (Paul Airiau, Luc Perrin, Jacques-Régis du Cray, Philippe Pichot-Bravard) all took part in GREC's work. While the spirit of dialogue dominated these meetings, which lasted until 2011, and enabled the participants to get to know each other better, they were not intended to settle doctrinal disagreements.

---

36 Note published in M. Lelong, *Pour la nécessaire réconciliation*, 21-23.

THE QUARREL OVER CONCELEBRATION

1998 was the tenth anniversary of the motu proprio *Ecclesia Dei*. It was a time for taking stock,[37] renewing requests, and thanking the Pope. The results varied from country to country and from diocese to diocese. In France, for example, in some forty dioceses, it was still impossible to attend a traditional Mass. The Welshman Michael Davies, who succeeded Eric de Saventhem as President of the International Federation *Una Voce*, painted a mixed picture, "a mixture of sadness and satisfaction." The sadness, he said, was "the fact that hundreds of zealous young priests of the Society of St. Pius X remain outside the structures of the Church, and are convinced that they must uphold tradition in opposition to the Supreme Pontiff rather than in union with him." On the other hand, he noted the "rapid" and "spectacular" growth of Tradition in the United States: the Fraternity of St. Peter had set up a seminary there and was providing the traditional Mass in over twenty dioceses; the Institute of Christ the King was beginning to establish itself there, and *Una Voce* chapters had grown from one to fifty-five in eight years. In his assessment, journalist Michel De Jaeghere, who for the previous three years had directed the summer universities of *Renaissance catholique* (close to the SSPX), considered that the tenth anniversary of the motu proprio could not be celebrated with joy because it was also the tenth anniversary of the condemnation of Archbishop Lefebvre. He noted that the July 1988 excommunication had struck

> first and foremost the bishop who, for twenty years, embodied the defense of the Tridentine Mass and the Catholic priesthood, a bishop to whom a large number of the priests who today benefit from the faculties of the motu proprio owe their formation, their vocation perhaps, their ordination in any case; that without his resistance, obstinacy, and repeated disobedience, there would be no Society of Saint Pius X, no Fraternity of Saint Peter, no monastery at Le Barroux, no Chartres pilgrimage.[38]

Various traditional French communities and several French and foreign associations organized a "Pilgrimage of Thanksgiving" to Rome to celebrate the tenth anniversary of the motu proprio. Dom Gérard and half the monks in his abbey (32 fathers and brothers) took part, as did Father de Blignières, superior of the Fraternity of Saint-Vincent-Ferrer, Msgr Wach, prior general of the Institute of Christ the King, Msgr

---

37 The most complete overview is that of Christophe Geffroy and Philippe Maxence, "Enquête sur la messe traditionnelle," *La Nef* special issue 6, 432 pages, with the responses of over sixty bishops, communities, associations, and personalities.
38 Michel de Jaeghere, "Un texte circonstantiel," ibid., 276.

Wladimir, superior of the Canons Regular of the Mother of God, each accompanied by religious from their community, and also numerous priests from the Fraternity of Saint Peter. Some 2,500 French and foreign faithful also took part in the pilgrimage, including a strong American delegation.[39] The latter was led by Bishop Timlin of Scranton, Pennsylvania, who had welcomed the Fraternity of Saint Peter's American district house and seminary in his diocese.

For three days, visits to the great Roman basilicas and other Catholic landmarks alternated with ceremonies and various meetings. On Saturday, October 24, in the large conference room of a Roman hotel, Cardinal Ratzinger gave a lecture in French, taking stock of the implementation of the motu proprio.[40] He did not wish to "pass over in silence" the difficulties that persisted, not least because some bishops, priests and faithful "consider this attachment to the ancient liturgy as a divisive element, which serves only to disturb ecclesial community...." To the great satisfaction of his audience, he also affirmed: "The Council ordered a reform of the liturgical books, but it did not forbid the earlier books," which was tantamount to saying that the new Mass was not obligatory, as so many authorities had repeated.

After the Cardinal, Dom Gérard, Michael Davies (President of the International Federation *Una Voce*), and Professor Robert Spaemann, a philosopher, a founder of the *Pro Missa Tridentina* association, and a friend of Cardinal Ratzinger's, took the floor. Dom Gérard's address was the longest, containing mainly practical proposals to facilitate the application of the 1988 motu proprio. He mentioned once again the idea of "a kind of Vicar Apostolic for 'traditionalists,'" which he had proposed as early as 1990, as we have seen. He also brought up other solutions, notably the creation of "personal quasi-parishes"; these would not correspond to a given territory but to a group of faithful from different places attached to the traditional liturgy. This solution would be adopted in the diocese of Toulon in 2005, as we shall see.

In his address, Dom Gérard mentioned the Mass he had concelebrated with John Paul II three years earlier, as an aside. He no longer presented it as a pragmatic decision, but justified it doctrinally: "I wished thereby to show that all of us who militate for the maintenance of the old missal believe in the validity and orthodoxy of the new rite." Father de Blignières soon wrote him that he was "distraught"

---

39 Report by Fr Basile in *Les Amis du Monastère* 88 (November 21, 1998), 2-3, and feature in *La Nef* 89 (December 1998).
40 Unabridged text of Cardinal Ratzinger's lecture, other interventions, and the allocution of John Paul II: ibid., 18-28.

by this statement,[41] and the issue was a cause of division among the traditional communities.

Two months after this pilgrimage, the abbey of Sainte-Madeleine was admitted to the *Conférence monastique de France* (CMF), a body which groups together all the Benedictine and Cistercian monasteries in France. Dom Gérard had wanted his abbey to be admitted in order to facilitate relations with other monasteries. The abbey was admitted to the CMF only after a protocol co-signed by Dom Étienne Ricaud, Father Abbot of Fleury, then President of the CMF, and Dom Gérard. This protocol had nothing to do with monastic life. In the first place, it contained a declaration on the New Mass and the Second Vatican Council:

> The Abbot and community of Le Barroux have never questioned the validity of the Mass celebrated according to the rite of Paul VI, and moreover, following an in-depth study of the Second Vatican Council (notably on religious freedom), they now unanimously adhere to its doctrine.[42]

Secondly, the abbot of Le Barroux and his successors committed to "concelebrating or sending his representative to concelebrate with the diocesan bishop at Chrism Mass wherever his monastery is or may be located in the future," to authorizing the monks of his monastery to "concelebrate at the conventual Mass in the communities they visit," and to authorize "priests visiting the abbey of Le Barroux to "celebrate, or even concelebrate, the Mass according to the rite of Paul VI."

The content of the agreement with the CMF became known to the community only after it had been signed. In the eyes of the CMF, these commitments were the *sine qua non* condition for Le Barroux to be affiliated. For Dom Gérard, they were limited concessions, to demonstrate unity of faith with the other monasteries and to foster relations with the French bishops. He soon wrote to Jean Madiran:

> The two bishops of dioceses where we have attempted an approach to set up new foundations are making concelebration (once yearly) the proof in act that we are not "infiltrated Lefebvrists."[43]

This protocol of agreement with the CMF did not introduce bi-ritualism at Le Barroux, as some were soon to claim, nor did it call into question the abbey's attachment to the traditional rite; Dom Gérard

---

41 Fr Louis-Marie de Bilgnières to Dom Gérard, Letter, January 19, 1999, archives of the Fraternity of Saint Vincent Ferrer, copy.

42 *Protocole entre la C. M. F. et l'abbaye du Barroux*, Archives of the *Conférence Monastique de France*.

43 Dom Gérard to Jean Madiran, Letter, March 18 1999, Jean Madiran archives.

would later repeat this assertion to his monks. But when it became known, it scandalized the Society of St. Pius X, who saw it as yet another "dereliction" at Le Barroux; it also divided the *Ecclesia Dei* communities. On January 11, 1999, a meeting was organized, at Dom Gérard's initiative, to explain the entry of Le Barroux into the CMF, and why the protocol had been signed. Reactions varied. While Mgr Wach, Prior General of the Institute of Christ the King, considered it possible and legitimate to hold occasional concelebrations according to the new rite, notably at Chrism Mass, in order to demonstrate communion with the diocesan bishop, others refused to hold any concelebration. This was the case with the Fraternity of Saint Vincent Ferrer and certain priests and leaders of the Fraternity of Saint Peter, notably Abbé Coiffet, Superior of the District of France. On January 19, Father de Blignières sent a long letter to Dom Gérard expressing his "sadness" and disagreement. He regretted the divisions among traditionalists that the decisions taken at Le Barroux would introduce, and feared a slide towards bi-ritualism. He added: "The step Le Barroux would take by occasionally celebrating the new rite would favor, even beyond their hopes, those who wish to see the traditional rite disappear," and concluded with an argument to which "you will not be insensitive": "Refusing to give in to unjust pressure is also the path of honor."[44]

On February 16, 1999, at the bishop's palace in Avignon, as a sign of communion, the community agreed in writing to send one or two monks a year to concelebrate the Chrism Mass with the bishop on Holy Thursday. In exchange, Mgr Bouchex, for the first time, permitted the traditional Mass to be solemnly celebrated on the same day at Notre-Dame-des-Doms, for the novices who had come to visit the cathedral and the Palace of the Popes.

The controversy over the legitimacy of celebrating the Mass of Paul VI, even occasionally, continued to divide traditionalists, particularly the Fraternity of St. Peter. As early as 1991, when the FSSP held its first General Chapter and elected Abbé Christian Gouyaud as its new superior, differences had come to the fore, because Abbé Gouyaud represented "the current open to the possibility of celebrating the *Novus Ordo* on an occasional basis."[45] The outgoing Superior General, Fr Bisig, persuaded Rome to annul the vote and was confirmed in his post for three years, with Abbé Gouyaud appointed assistant to the Superior General and rector of the Wigratzbad seminary.

---

44 Fr de Blignières to Dom Gérard, Letter, January 19, 1999, Archives of the Fraternity Saint Vincent Ferrer, copy.
45 C. Geffroy, *Benoît et la "paix liturgique,"* 202.

The debate therefore resurfaced in 1999, after the meeting at Le Barroux mentioned above. In March, Father de Blignières addressed a lengthy memorandum to the Congregation for Divine Worship and the *Ecclesia Dei* Commission.[46] He recalled and documented the fact that "the specific intention of the founders of the *Ecclesia Dei* institutes" had been to preserve the traditional liturgy, and that this "traditional monoritualism" had been recognized by the Holy See. He also felt that the occasional celebration of the Paul VI Mass and the Holy Thursday concelebration, imposed as a gesture of unity, would contradict the proper character of these institutes. He suggested that the gesture of unity should not be the celebration of the new rite, but "attendance at this Mass and the reception of communion in its celebration." Conversely, on the following June 29, sixteen FSSP priests, almost all based in France, sent an appeal to Cardinal Felici, President of the *Ecclesia Dei* Commission. In it, they regretted that within the Fraternity of St. Peter, "concelebration around the bishop, whatever the circumstances, is considered an attack on the unity of the Fraternity and a serious offence. Certain members of the Fraternity who have concelebrated have been sanctioned."

Without going into the details of the crisis that shook the FSSP for over a year,[47] one can only point out that it ended in July 2000 with an intervention by the Holy See, which appointed a new Superior General, Fr Arnaud Devillers, as well as a new District Superior for France, and laid down a rule on the celebration of the 1970 Missal:

> A priest enjoying the privilege of celebrating according to the former 1962 missal does not lose the right to use the 1970 missal.... No Superior below the rank of Supreme Pontiff can prevent a priest from following the universal law promulgated by Pope Paul VI.

This reaffirmation of the impossibility of refusing the Novus Ordo was all the stronger for the fact that the celebration of the traditional Mass remained, in practice, conditioned and limited.

A COLLECTIVE PLEA IS PRESENTED TO JOHN PAUL II (2001)

On May 7, 2001, following a suggestion by Father Pozzetto, then chaplain of the Notre-Dame de Chrétienté pilgrimage [the "Chartres pilgrimage" – *Translator*], Dom Gérard sent a "strictly confidential letter"

---

46 Memorandum published a few months later under the title "Actes fondateurs et gestes de communion," *Sedes Sapientiae* 68 (Summer 1999): 1-30.

47 There is a detailed account in C. Geffory, *Benoît et la "paix liturgique,"* 206-19. See also Thierry Bouclier, *L'abbé Denis Coiffet,* 135-40.

to several traditional religious superiors and lay movement leaders. The letter was a plea to the Pope. Noting that "thirteen years of experience (since the creation of the *Ecclesia Dei* Commission) indicate that the opposition we have encountered to our mere existence, to our continued life (for lay associations requesting the old Mass), or to our establishing ourselves (new foundations), is nowhere near yielding in certain places," the supplication again asked for apostolic vicariates to be created "so that the communities which will depend on them may enjoy a broad exemption."[48] The plea was to be delivered in Chartres to Cardinal Castrillón Hoyos, the new president of the *Ecclesia Dei* Commission, who was to celebrate the closing Mass of the nineteenth *Pèlerinage de Chrétienté* pilgrimage on the following June 4.

Fr Pozzetto and Dom Gérard's initiative was well received. The critical paragraph ("Thirteen years of experience . . .") was reduced to a simple reference to "highly distressing exclusions." On the other hand, a reference to the unity of the Church was added:

> The liturgical freedom granted to this ancient rite will foster true ecumenism. It will go a long way towards resolving the break made by the Society of Saint Pius X, by bringing many of its families and priests back into unity with Rome.

Twenty traditional religious superiors in France and abroad and twenty laymen (movement leaders and heads of Catholic publications) signed the petition, which was handed to Cardinal Castrillón Hoyos on June 4.

The request for one or more apostolic vicariates and for total freedom for the traditional rite was not new. This time, however, it carried more weight as a collective plea. It would be another six years before the second request was finally met.

TWO OPPOSITE VIEWS OF THE MASS

Paradoxically, in 2000-2001, just as the Holy See asserted its authority over the government of the FSSP, it opened a dialogue with the SSPX. The Great Jubilee of 2000 provided the occasion; the initiative came from the Holy See.

The SSPX, for its part, continued to be highly critical of the pontificate, whether for its decisions regarding the Fraternity of St. Peter, "a veritable stab in the founders' back,"[49] or for the Interreligious Assembly organized in Rome in October 1999. The Superior General

---

48 Confidential Letter dated May 7, 2001, Archives of Sainte-Madeleine du Barroux abbey.
49 Such was the expression used by Fr Laurençon, Superior of the SSPX District of France, in *Fideliter* 132 (November-December 1999): 2.

of the SSPX had written to John Paul II to protest against this "renewal of the Assisi scandal," which would once again promote "an immense indifferentism" and reduce the Church's "all-divine, eternal, and supernatural mission . . . to the level of Masonic ideals of world peace apart from the only Prince of Peace, Our Lord Jesus Christ." [50]

The SSPX took the opportunity of the Millennium Jubilee to organize an "International Pilgrimage of Catholic Tradition" to Rome. The primary aim was to go to Rome in the Jubilee Year on a pilgrimage of faith and penance, so as "to earn indulgences at the feet of the Apostles," but also so as to make a show of strength against the "enemies within." In its report on the pilgrimage, the magazine *Fideliter* published a photograph showing the long procession of priests and seminarians, in two lines, in via del Conciliazione, heading towards St. Peter's Basilica. This August 2000 pilgrimage brought together some 6,000 faithful from ten countries, led by the four SSPX bishops. They were able to enter and pray in all four major basilicas. "Six Thousand Excommunicates Pray in St. Peter's Basilica," one Italian newspaper inaccurately commented. On the other hand, SSPX priests and bishops were unable to celebrate the traditional Mass in the basilicas. The solemn Mass to close the pilgrimage was celebrated by Bishop Fellay on the Colle Oppio, opposite the Colosseum. In his homily, the Superior General of the SSPX issued two pleas to the Pope: "Do justice to the Mass. Not to us – who are we? But to the Mass, give it back its rights, give the Church's tradition back its rights, for it has rights." [51] He also asked for the third Secret of Fatima to "be published in full." [52]

On the occasion of this pilgrimage, the SSPX bishops were invited to lunch by Cardinal Castrillón Hoyos, President of the *Ecclesia Dei* Commission. The invitation was unexpected, as there had been no meeting with SSPX leaders since the break in 1988. [53] Bishop Fellay would admit that this was surprising, "especially when compared with what is happening with the Fraternity of Saint Peter." [54] So as not to make

50 Bp Fellay to John Paul II, Letter, October 27, 1999, *Fideliter* 133 (January-February 2000): 3.
51 Bp Fellay, Homily on 9 August 1999, *Fideliter* 138 (November-December 2000): 23-24.
52 On June 26, 2000, the Holy See had published what is called the "third secret of Fatima," which is more precisely the third part of what the young seers of Fatima saw and heard on July 13, 1917, and which had remained unknown until then. This publication was immediately contested by some, who claimed that the Vatican had not published the unabridged text on the grounds that it concerned the crisis in the Church. See Y. Chiron, *Fatima. Vérités et légendes* (Perpignan: Artège, 2017).
53 Fr François Knittel, "Histoire d'une longue patience. Trente-deux ans de relations entre le Vatican et la Fraternité saint Pie X," *Cor unum* 72 (June 2002): 39.
54 Interview in *Fideliter* 140 (March-April 2001): 6.

this "first contact" too "official," only three of the four bishops (Fellay, Galaretta and Tissier de Mallerais) accepted the cardinal's invitation. The cardinal was "very kind and cordial," and showed "a great deal of sympathy for Tradition," but, in Bishop Fellay's opinion, he "was only just discovering it, actually," and had not yet "really understood the problem" of the traditional Mass. This is an important point, since it led the SPPX to set out its position in a rather radical book.

In November 2000, Cardinal Castrillón Hoyos invited Bishop Fellay to Rome "to prepare a visit with the Pope." The Superior General set a precondition: the SSPX did not want to enter into discussions with the *Ecclesia Dei* Commission, but with the Pope and Cardinal Castrillón Hoyos, because, as Fr Sélégny, SSPX General Secretary, explained, "we absolutely refuse to have anything to do with the *Ecclesia Dei* Commission, which is responsible for reintegrating people into the Church, while we are in the Church, since we do not need to be reintegrated."[55]

An initial meeting took place in Rome between Bishop Fellay and Cardinal Castrillón Hoyos on December 29 and 30. Cardinal Castrillón Hoyos's approach to the situation was "more pragmatic than doctrinal": a canonical status had to be found for the Society; it was necessary "to reach a practical agreement as quickly as possible, without getting bogged down in doctrinal differences."[56] On December 30, Bishop Fellay did not meet John Paul II in a private audience, as was claimed later, but was introduced to him in the Pope's private chapel after Mass. The meeting lasted only a few moments, and "no words of any importance were exchanged," as Bishop Fellay would soon make clear in a press release. On January 16, 2001, there was another meeting with Cardinal Castrillón Hoyos. Bishop Fellay asked for "guarantees from Rome before going any further into the concrete aspects of possible discussions or agreements: that the Tridentine Mass be granted to all priests throughout the world, and that the censures [excommunications] against the bishops be lifted."[57] The second request seemed easier to satisfy than the first, although neither would be met until the following pontificate.

As we have seen, in August 2000 Bishop Fellay felt that Cardinal Castrillón Hoyos had not fully grasped "the problem" posed by the new Mass, or the doctrinal reasons for which traditionalists were so attached to the traditional Mass. He therefore commissioned a "theological and liturgical study" on the Mass, entitled *The Problem of Liturgical Reform. The Mass of Vatican II and Paul VI.* The book was published in March

---

55 As reported by the APIC news agency on March 21, 2001.
56 F. Knittel, "Histoire d'une longue patience," 39.
57 Bp Fellay, Communiqué, January 22, 2001.

2001, just as discussions had begun with Cardinal Castrillón Hoyos. It was also sent to all the bishops of France and to the 22,000 diocesan priests who, since 1999, had already been receiving the *Lettre à nos frères prêtres*, a "Liaison Letter from the SSPX to the Clergy of France." The book, which is very hard on Paul VI's Mass, was in contrast with the "Liturgical Days" organized a few months later at Fontgombault Abbey. The idea for these came from Dom Gérard, who had submitted to Cardinal Ratzinger the idea of organizing a round table on the rite of the Mass: "Don't you think the time is ripe for a doctrinal, pastoral, liturgical, and canonical exchange" in a "non-polemical spirit"? The colloquium was intended to have a "practical" aim:

> To sensitize the bishops and the Christian people to this issue, strengthen the sense of the Church among supporters of the old rite, and achieve a peaceful liturgical solution for the universal Church.[58]

Cardinal Ratzinger never did initiate such a meeting, but he did express his interest. At his suggestion, Father Cassian Folsom was chosen to draw up the list of participants and outline the program. This American monk had entered Saint Meinrad Abbey, Indiana, in 1979, was ordained priest in 1984, received his doctorate in liturgy in 1989, and was appointed pro-president of the Pontifical Institute for Liturgy in 1996. In 1999, he founded a modest monastery in Rome dedicated to Mary Seat of Wisdom, and two years later was able to set up his young community in Norcia (ancient Nursia), the birthplace of Saint Benedict.

Cardinal Ratzinger himself was trying to "give birth to a new 'Liturgical Movement,'" and wanted to "help rediscover a dignified way of celebrating the liturgy" by publishing the highly acclaimed book *The Spirit of the Liturgy*. The original German edition dates from 2000 [as does the English edition – *Translator*]. The French translation would appear at the end of 2001, a few months after the Study Days.

These took place July 22-24, 2001 at Fontgombault Abbey, in a discreet setting, with no press announcements, and were open only to a limited number of guests. Cardinal Ratzinger gave the keynote address. The other lectures were given by French and foreign theologians and liturgy specialists, including three Benedictines (Father Cassian Folsom, Father Field from Randol Abbey, and Father Charbel from Le Barroux) and four lay people (Professors Caldecott, Spaemann, Ayuso Torres, and de Mattei). Professor Stratford Caldecott, founder of the Faith &

---

58 Dom Gérard to Cardinal Ratzinger, Letter, June 11, 1999, Archives of Saint-Madeleine Abbey, copy.

Culture Centre in Oxford, had for several years been promoting a "new liturgical movement" and a "reform of the reform"[59] in the English-speaking world. Both terms were used in Cardinal Ratzinger's closing address. In it, he put forward very concrete suggestions for the "reform of the reform" and for the limited changes that could be introduced into the missal of St. Pius V (the adoption of new prefaces, and "opening up the [liturgical] calendar of the old Missal to the new saints").[60]

Without wishing to summarize the twelve other papers presented at these Study Days, it should be noted that Dom Gérard, although present, did not give a lecture. Instead, a monk from Le Barroux, Father Charbel, outlined the principles and methods that might guide "a new liturgical movement."

THE CAMPOS "RALLIEMENT"

The Priestly Union of St. John Mary Vianney (SSJV) in Campos, Brazil, was closely linked to the SSPX. After the death of Bishop de Castro Mayer in April 1991, Dom Licinio Rangel was elected superior. Very soon – the decision had been made several months before the deaths of Archbishop Lefebvre and de Castro Mayer – he was consecrated bishop by Bishop Tissier de Mallerais, assisted by two co-consecrating bishops, Bishop Williamson and Bishop de Galaretta.[61] The ceremony took place in São Fidélis, Brazil, on July 28, 1991. The 1988 consecrations at Écône had been justified as a "survival operation" for Tradition. This time, in Brazil, Bishop Tissier de Mallerais declared in his homily that he was carrying out this new consecration without a papal mandate, in order to "respond" to the "urgent request" of the faithful: "It was our absolute duty to give you the faithful shepherd of souls that modernist Rome cannot grant you, and to which you have a legal right."

Ten years later, the SSJV numbered 26 priests, ministering to some 26,000 faithful. Bishop Rangel was consulted in the early stages of the SSPX's discussions with Cardinal Castrillón Hoyos. When these discussions stalled in the summer of 2001, Bishop Rangel decided to continue the dialogue with Cardinal Castrillón Hoyos. Then, on August 15, 2001, the feast of the Assumption, Bishop Rangel and all the members of the Society of St. John Mary Vianney addressed a letter to Pope John

---

59 In 1996 he had organized a Liturgy Forum that led to the *Oxford Declaration* (June 29, 1996); see S. Caldecott, ed., *Beyond the Prosaic. Renewing the Liturgical Movement* (Edinburgh: T. & T. Clark, 1998), 164-65.
60 *Autour de la question liturgique* (Fontgombault: Association Petrus a Stella, 2001), 183.
61 André Cagnon, "Le Sacre de Campos: un évêque catholique pour le Brésil," *Fideliter* 83 (September-October 1991): 2-9.

Paul II, requesting "juridical recognition" of their institute. Declaring their readiness "to collaborate with Your Holiness in the work of propagating the faith and Catholic doctrine . . . in the fight against the errors and heresies that threaten to destroy the bark of Peter," they wished "to guard the holy doctrinal and liturgical Tradition bequeathed to us by the Holy Church," while professing "perfect communion with the Chair of Peter of which Your Holiness is the legitimate successor."

John Paul II responded to this plea on December 25 with a letter granting an original and generous juridical status to the Priestly Union of Saint John Mary Vianney, and lifting all the canonical sanctions that had been imposed on Bishop Rangel and his priests. The Union was canonically erected as a personal Apostolic Administration directly dependent on the Holy See, with a territory in the diocese of Campos. Bishop Rangel was appointed Apostolic Administrator, and Pope John Paul II assured him that "his succession would be guaranteed."

The Society of St. Pius X followed the ongoing reconciliation process with interest, but also with some concern. While Father Aulagnier, former superior of the SSPX's French district, was enthusiastic about the forthcoming agreement, the SSPX authorities were much more reticent. On January 16, 2002, two days before the scheduled reconciliation ceremony, Bishop Fellay issued a statement disapproving of the agreement. He regretted that it was "the fruit of a separate peace. . . . To obtain it, the priests of Campos have had to distance themselves from the Fraternity." He deplored "the haste and partially concealed nature of the negotiations that led to the current recognition." Nevertheless, he recognized the historic importance of the event: "For the first time, a diocesan-type structure has been granted to Tradition. A traditional bishop is now recognized as such, as fully Catholic."

Two days later, on January 18, 2002, the return of SSJV members to full communion in the Church took place during a ceremony at the cathedral in the presence of Cardinal Castrillón Hoyos. Bishop Rangel signed, on behalf of all the members of the Union, a doctrinal declaration on the acceptance of the Second Vatican Council "in the light of Holy Tradition" and the validity of the new Ordo Missae "whenever it is celebrated correctly and with the intention of offering the true Sacrifice of the Holy Mass." On the same day, a decree from the Congregation for Bishops established the SSJV as a personal Apostolic Administration. The decree specified that "faculty is granted to the Apostolic Administration to celebrate the Holy Eucharist, the other sacraments, the Liturgy of the Hours, and other liturgical actions according to the Roman Rite and the liturgical discipline of Saint Pius V."

On August 18, 2002, Father Fernando Rifan, former Vicar General of the SSJV, was consecrated Coadjutor Bishop by Cardinal Castrillón Hoyos and by Bishop Rangel himself. For the latter, who was very ill, it was a comfort to know that his work would be carried on by the man who had been his closest collaborator; Bishop Rangel died four months later. The Personal Apostolic Administration of Saint John Mary Vianney has continued to grow, and is now present in a dozen other Brazilian dioceses, with the permission of the local ordinaries.

"RIGHT OF CITIZENSHIP" FOR THE TRADITIONAL MASS

Liturgically speaking, the final years of John Paul II's pontificate were marked by a major ceremony that vividly reaffirmed the "right of citizenship" of the traditional rite. On May 24, 2003, Cardinal Castrillón Hoyos celebrated a solemn Mass in the rite of St. Pius V at the Basilica of Santa Maria Maggiore, in the presence of five cardinals and several prelates of the Curia.[62] The ceremony was of great importance, not only because of who the celebrant was–both Prefect of the Congregation for the Clergy and President of the *Ecclesia Dei* Commission–but also because of the venue chosen: one of Rome's four major basilicas, the mother basilica of all churches dedicated to the Virgin Mary, and also the one that houses the tomb of St. Pius V. The choice of date is also a coincidence, or a deliberate sign: this solemn reaffirmation of the traditional Mass took place exactly twenty-seven years after Paul VI's famous address to the Consistory on May 24, 1976, in which he declared that the *novus ordo* was obligatory and "promulgated in place of the old."

Although the decision to hold such a celebration rested with Cardinal Castrillón Hoyos and the Pope, the traditional communities were closely involved. Dom Gérard was in the front row alongside Msgr Wladimir de Saint-Jean, abbot of the Canons Regular of the Mother of God. Two monks from Le Barroux, studying in Rome, played an important role in the ceremony: Father Charbel as main Master of Ceremonies and Father Jehan as choirmaster, conducting numerous priests and seminarians from the Priestly Fraternity of Saint Peter, the Institute of Christ the King, and the Apostolic Administration of Saint John Mary Vianney.

The celebration began with the reading of an official message from the Secretary of State, Cardinal Angelo Sodano, declaring himself, on behalf of the Sovereign Pontiff, "spiritually united" to the Mass that

---

62 Stefano Gizzi, "La Messe historique du 24 mai," *Aletheia* 43 (May 25, 2003).

was about to be celebrated. In his eagerly-awaited homily, Cardinal Castrillón Hoyos urged Catholics to full unity with the Pope's Magisterium. He also spoke at length of the "ancient Roman Rite," asserting that it "cannot be considered extinct" and that it "retains its rightful place in the Church." Concluding his homily, the cardinal alluded to the difficulties encountered in many dioceses by faithful and priests attached to the traditional rite, and recalled the Pope's invitation to bishops: "To have a renewed understanding and pastoral care for the faithful attached to the ancient rite." This celebration was, in the cardinal's words, "the latest gesture of pastoral concern towards those who find themselves spiritually identified with the celebration of the Holy Sacrifice of the Mass according to the Roman Missal of the *Editio Typica* of 1962."[63]

Jean Madiran, before the ceremony, opined:

> The celebration on Saturday May 24th will be a solemn step (perhaps the penultimate) in the slow process of overcoming the unjust ostracism that has plagued the traditional Mass for the past thirty-three years.[64]

That is just what happened.

Dom Gérard made a similar diagnosis when, after the ceremony, he wrote a note to the nuns of the Annunciation:

> A report on the May 24th Mass, objective overall. But the four musketeers[65] don't see an end to the crisis under the current pontificate; the decentralized Church stymies any attempt at reform, if not in the long term.[66]

---

63 Interview in *The Latin Mass* (May 2004): 4.
64 *Présent* (May 10, 2003).
65 As a postscript, Dom Gérard gave the names of the four cardinals: "Ratzinger, Castrillón, Medina, Arinze – those are the most active and those who have the pope's ear the most."
66 Dom Gérard, Note, no date, Archives in Our Lady of the Annunciation Abbey Archives.

CHAPTER 14

The Pontificate of Benedict XVI: A Kairos for Traditionalists

W ITH THE DEATH OF JOHN PAUL II ON APRIL 2, 2005, one of the longest pontificates in the history of the Church–over a quarter of a century–came to an end. The swift election of his successor took the media by surprise. On April 19, Cardinal Ratzinger became Pope and took the name Benedict XVI. He did so after over twenty years as Prefect of the Congregation for the Doctrine of the Faith, a position in which he had acquired a thorough knowledge of the SSPX and the traditional liturgy. Since the end of 1981, he had been closely involved in all decisions relating to the traditional liturgy and in all negotiations and discussions with Archbishop Lefebvre and his successors (Father Schmidberger and later Bishop Fellay). As early as 1982, he laid the foundations for a three-stage solution to the liturgical question: restore the traditional liturgy to its right of citizenship in the Church, revise the texts resulting from the post-conciliar liturgical reform (what he later called the "reform of the reform"), and, in the long term, achieve a unified rite, not through a brutal new construction, but through what he was later to call a "mutual enrichment" of the two Masses.

The motu proprio of 1984, and even more so that of 1988, had begun the long-awaited total freeing up of the traditional Mass. Between 2001 and 2004, as we have seen, various magisterial interventions (an instruction, an encyclical, apostolic letters) had sought to encourage a realignment of the post-conciliar liturgy. Ratzinger, now pope Benedict XVI, would attempt to implement the plan outlined in 1982.

The SSPX initially welcomed "the accession of Cardinal Joseph Ratzinger to the Sovereign Pontificate." In a press release issued on the day of the election, Bishop Fellay saw "a glimmer of hope for a way out of the profound crisis now shaking the Catholic Church."

The new Pope promptly renewed the dialogue with the SSPX. On August 29, 2005, four months after his election, he agreed to Bishop Fellay's request for an audience. In a communiqué issued after this first meeting, the SSPX Superior General said: "We have reached a consensus on proceeding step by step to resolve the problems."[1] In so doing, he

---

1 Bp Fellay, Communiqué, August 29, 2005.

partially reprised the press release issued after the audience, which had emphasized the common desire to "proceed in stages and within a reasonable timeframe." Bishop Fellay specified that he had asked for three things: to allow "full freedom for the Tridentine Mass, to silence the reproach of schism by putting to rest the suppositious excommunications, and to find a Church structure for the family of Tradition." After the audience, he doubted that such a request would come to fruition quickly, because the Pope "is caught between the progressives and us: if he liberalizes the Mass at our sole request, the modernists will object and say that the Pope has given in to the traditionalists." At the time, the Superior General was of the opinion that "only limited liberalization will eventually be conceded."[2] Subsequent history showed that, on this point, Bishop Fellay was mistaken.

Regarding the Second Vatican Council, Benedict XVI had taken up the formula used by John Paul II at the start of his pontificate and accepted by Archbishop Lefebvre after meeting him in 1978: "Accept the Council in the light of Tradition." From then on, however, Bishop Fellay was wary of this formula. He felt that, in Benedict XVI's mind, it meant: "According to the intention of the Fathers of the Council and in keeping with the letter of the texts"; he added: "It's a prospect that frightens us quite a bit."[3]

In this respect, the diverse receptions given to Benedict XVI's famous speech to the Curia on December 22, 2005, in which he contrasted a "hermeneutic of discontinuity and rupture" with a "hermeneutic of reform and renewal in continuity" in regard to the Second Vatican Council, are significant. Progressives saw this as a reactionary reading of the Second Vatican Council. Some traditionalists, too, saw it only as a condemnation of progressive excesses abusively committed in the name of the Council. But Benedict XVI also insisted on the need to accept the Council as a council of "reform." Actually, the SSPX made no mistake, and published a number of studies challenging this two-hermeneutics thesis.[4]

THE INSTITUTE OF THE GOOD SHEPHERD (2006)

While the SSPX began new doctrinal discussions with the Congregation for the Doctrine of the Faith in 2006, five of its priests sought

---

2 Interview in *Fideliter* 168 (November–December 2005): 6.
3 Ibid., 5.
4 Bp Bernard Tissier de Mallerais, "La Foi au péril de la raison. Herméneutique de Benoît XVI," *Le Sel de la terre* 69 (Summer 2009); Fr Jean-Michel Gleize, "Une réflexion sur l'herméneutique de Vatican II," *Le Courrier de Rome* 336 (September 2010): 1-6; and Don Davide Pagliarani, "L'Herméneutique de l'herméneutique," *Le Courrier de Rome* 337 (October 2010): 1-6.

to take a different path. As soon as 2006, they were given the benefit of "Roman generosity."[5] Some of them were historical figures in the Society who had recently been expelled from it for various reasons.

Fr Paul Aulagnier, the second priest ordained by Archbishop Lefebvre and superior of the French district for eighteen years, was expelled from the SSPX in 2003 for having supported the Campos agreement with Rome, and for having publicly expressed his disagreement with Bishop Fellay's line on several occasions. Fr Philippe Laguérie, who had been in charge of the church of Saint-Nicolas-du-Chardonnet in Paris for fourteen years, was subsequently appointed prior in Bordeaux, where he restored and rehabilitated the church of Saint-Éloi, with the agreement of the city council. He was expelled from the SSPX in August 2004 for distributing a document to SSPX priests calling into question the management of the Écône seminary, and for refusing to be transferred to Mexico. Fr Christophe Héry and Fr Guillaume de Tanoüarn were expelled in turn for supporting Fr Laguérie. Fr de Tanoüarn, the founder of the Centre Saint-Paul in Paris, and an essayist and organizer of colloquia on Vatican II, had founded and directed several reviews.

At the time, Jean Madiran, in an editorial for the newspaper *Présent*, defended the already-condemned priests and those about to be condemned. He spoke of "the heads which are put above the parapet, and which are of the same persuasion, and which of course are much more inconvenient than those that don't." He pleaded on their behalf:

> The heads that are put above the parapet are often, in public controversy, the most justly, the most strongly, the most exactly critical of republican secularism and the other dominant lies, so let's not deprive ourselves of them.[6]

Fr Henri Forestier, from the Toulouse priory, also expelled from the SSPX in September 2005, joined Fathers Laguérie and Héry in Bordeaux. Benedict XVI's Christmas address to the Curia, on the hermeneutics of the Council, in December 2005, was "the trigger for the desire to speak with Rome to find a normal situation in the Church."[7] The small group – Fathers Laguérie, Aulagnier, Héry, de Tanoüarn, Forestier, and Prieur, who was then still a deacon – decided to form a new Society of Apostolic Life. Thanks to the intervention of Cardinal Castrillón Hoyos, Prefect of the Congregation for the Clergy and President of the *Ecclesia Dei* Commission, on September 8, 2006 the Institute of the

---

5 Christophe Geoffroy, *Rome-Écône. L'accord impossible?* (Perpignan: Artège, 2013), 107-8.
6 Jean Madiran, "Ah! les têtes qui dépassent . . . Mais faut-il donc les couper?" *Présent* (September 10, 2004).
7 Fr Henri Forestier to the author, Letter, September 9, 2021.

Good Shepherd (*Institut du Bon Pasteur,* IBP) was erected as a society of apostolic life of pontifical right. Fr Laguérie was appointed superior general of the new institute. Cardinal Ricard, Archbishop of Bordeaux, who had not been informed of the decision beforehand, was asked to welcome the new institute.[8]

Under its statutes, which Cardinal Castrillón Hoyos approved on behalf of the Holy See, the IBP has "the traditional Roman rite" as "the proper rite of the Institute, in all its liturgical acts" and "affirms its profound Romanity, because it is concerned to preserve the Tradition of the Church in its permanent relevance." Also noteworthy is the formula of commitment signed by the founders of the IBP:

> With regard to certain points taught by the Second Vatican Council or concerning subsequent reforms of the liturgy and law, which we find difficult to reconcile with Tradition, we commit ourselves to a positive attitude of study and communication with the Apostolic See, avoiding all polemics. This attitude of study is intended to contribute, through serious and constructive criticism, to the preparation of an authentic interpretation on the part of the Holy See of these points of the teaching of Vatican II.

It would be insufficient to characterize the IBP by these two points; one has to add the pastoral intention that is in its very name: the Good Shepherd – Christ – who goes out to find the lost sheep (Luke 15:3-7). The introductory text reads: "The priests of the Institute of the Good Shepherd want to be priests who are open to the world and to the realities of evangelization today." Here we find the pastoral dynamism that Abbé Aulagnier had expressed a few years earlier in his book, significantly entitled "Tradition Without Fear" (*La Tradition sans peur*):

> We need to get out of our trenches, of our ghettoes; we must – I repeat – fearlessly put ourselves in the service of the Church universal. . . . The time for small hermitages, for the little Church, is past.[9]

One month after its foundation, the IBP opened an international seminary in Courtalain, in the diocese of Chartres. On February 1, 2007, it was recognized by Cardinal Ricard. He established the church of Saint-Eloi in Bordeaux as a personal parish for the celebration of the traditional Mass, and entrusted it to the IBP. Today, the institute has more than fifty priests across five countries, in personal or territorial parishes and schools.

---

8 Cardinal Ricard to the author, Letter, September 2, 2021.
9 P. Aulagnier, *La Tradition sans peur*, 244.

A MASS THAT HAD "NEVER BEEN FORBIDDEN"

On July 7, 2007, in continuity with the 1984 indult and the 1988 motu proprio, Benedict XVI's motu proprio *Summorum Pontificum* finally granted the right to celebrate the traditional Mass to all priests. The Missal of Paul VI was described as "the ordinary expression of the *lex orandi* (rule of prayer) of the Catholic Church of the Latin rite," while the 1962 edition of the Missal of St. Pius V was described as "an extraordinary expression" (art. 1). The *Letter to Bishops* accompanying the motu proprio went on to say: "It is not appropriate to speak of these two versions of the Roman Missal as if they were 'two Rites.' It is rather a question of a twofold use of one and the same Rite."

The Pope established that at "Masses celebrated without a congregation, any Catholic priest of the Latin rite, whether secular or regular, may use the Roman Missal published in 1962," without needing any "permission from the Apostolic See or from his own Ordinary" (art. 2).

Although this motu proprio opens with general liturgical considerations, the text goes on to set out in detail the right of the faithful to have access to the traditional liturgy: "In parishes where a group of the faithful attached to the previous liturgical tradition stably exists, the parish priest should willingly accede to their requests" (art. 5), and if this group "has not been granted its requests by the parish priest, it should inform the diocesan bishop. The bishop is earnestly requested to satisfy their desire" (art. 7) and if the bishop "does not wish to provide for such celebration, the matter should be referred to the Pontifical Commission *Ecclesia Dei*" (ibid.).

In the long *Letter to Bishops* accompanying the motu proprio, the Pope wanted to "draw attention to the fact that this Missal [of 1962] was never juridically abrogated and, consequently, in principle, was always permitted." Defenders of the traditional liturgy had been making this assertion as early as 1969-1970. Also noteworthy was this deeply personal recollection of the liturgical crisis:

> [I]n many places celebrations were not faithful to the prescriptions of the new Missal, but the latter actually was understood as authorizing or even requiring creativity, which frequently led to deformations of the liturgy which were hard to bear. I am speaking from experience, since I too lived through that period with all its hopes and its confusion. And I have seen how arbitrary deformations of the liturgy caused deep pain to individuals totally rooted in the faith of the Church.

In this Letter, Benedict XVI once again expounded an idea that had long been dear to him:

> [T]he two Forms of the usage of the Roman Rite can be mutually enriching: new Saints and some of the new Prefaces can and should be inserted in the old Missal.

While on the other hand, thanks to the presence of the old rite,

> the celebration of the Mass according to the Missal of Paul VI will be able to demonstrate, more powerfully than has been the case hitherto, the sacrality which attracts many people to the former usage. The most sure guarantee that the Missal of Paul VI can unite parish communities and be loved by them consists in its being celebrated with great reverence in harmony with the liturgical directives. This will bring out the spiritual richness and the theological depth of this Missal.

By lifting the restrictions on the celebration of the traditional liturgy, the motu proprio fulfilled the expectations of many communities and faithful attached to Tradition. But not all of them heeded this reminder about the new Mass:

> Needless to say, in order to experience full communion, the priests of the communities adhering to the former usage cannot, as a matter of principle, exclude celebrating according to the new books. The total exclusion of the new rite would not in fact be consistent with the recognition of its value and holiness.

This requirement would be reiterated under the following pontificate.

On the other hand, the liberalization of the traditional liturgy worried those bishops and Catholic circles most attached to the post-conciliar reforms. "This text risks awakening old demons, and some Catholics will wonder whether it doesn't constitute an abandonment of Vatican II," a bishop who wished to remain anonymous confided to *Le Monde*.[10] "I understand the need for unity, but it must be accompanied by the need for truth, without instrumentalizing the liturgy," warned Mgr Dagens, Bishop of Angoulême. In Italy, too, there was some reluctance. A few months before the motu proprio was published, a group of liturgy specialists wrote to the Pope, asking him not to restore the traditional rite; they had the support of Bishop Di Molfetta of Cerignola, the President of the Episcopal Commission for Liturgy.[11] The day after the motu proprio was published, Mgr Luca Brandolini, bishop of Sora-Aquinio Pontecorvo, a member of the Liturgical Commission of the Italian Episcopal Conference and a former collaborator of Archbishop Bugnini, declared:

> Today is a day of mourning for me. My throat is in knots and I can't hold back the tears. But I'll obey the Pope because I'm a

---

10 *Le Monde* (July 7, 2007).

11 *Il Giornale* (September 21, 2007).

bishop and because I like him. But I can't hide my sadness at the collapse of one of the most important reforms of the Second Vatican Council....This is the saddest moment of my life as a priest, a bishop, and a man. It is a day of mourning, not only for me, but for all those who lived and worked for the Second Vatican Council. Today, a reform has been wiped out for which so many worked, at great sacrifice, driven only by the desire to renew the Church.[12]

In practice, however, the motu proprio was slow in being applied to its full potential. While some bishops immediately welcomed the motu proprio, others waited for the norms of implementation. These did not appear until five years later, on April 20, 2011, in the instruction *Universae ecclesiae*, published by the *Ecclesia Dei* Commission.

The congregation of the Franciscans of the Immaculate,[13] whose origins date back to 1970, as we have seen, and which had celebrated the liturgy and office in Italian, gradually adopted the traditional liturgy. At the urging of its founder, Father Manelli, the 2008 General Chapter, convened after the motu proprio, encouraged the celebration of the traditional liturgy, though without imposing it. After the publication of the instruction *Universae ecclesiae*, the congregation's authorities issued Norms authorizing all priests in the congregation to celebrate the traditional Mass, requesting that young religious be trained in this liturgy and that the conventual Mass be celebrated according to the ancient rite "if possible, in the whole house."[14] These norms caused a rift within the congregation, although it seems that a very large majority of these religious were satisfied with them. This dispute over liturgical practice was compounded by accusations about the institute's governance and financial management. Complaints by five religious to the Congregation for Institutes of Consecrated Life led to the decision to appoint an Apostolic Visitor, by a decree dated July 5, 2012. This apostolic visitation, which began under the pontificate of Benedict XVI, was not completed until the following pontificate, and led to some drastic decisions, as we shall see.

In the wake of the 2007 motu proprio, some traditionalists protested against the bi-ritualism that the text promoted. The Guérardians of the Mater Boni Consilii Institute (IMBC) considered that by placing the two rites on an equal footing, the motu proprio amounted to "a fatal deception." They recalled Benedict XVI's wish to initiate "the reform

---

12 Declaration to the daily *La Repubblica* (July 8, 2007).

13 In 2012, it had 351 religious among fifty-five houses; its feminine branch, the Franciscan Sisters of the Immaculate, had 348 sisters among fifty houses.

14 General Secretariat of the Franciscans of the Immaculate, *Normativa liturgica per il "Vetus Ordo,"* November 21, 2011, Archives of the Frati Francescani dell'Immacolata.

of the [liturgical] reform" and to achieve a single rite in the future. In their view, it was "through alteration" that the traditional Mass risked disappearing.[15]

The Society of St. Pius X, for its part, at least in the official communiqué issued by its Superior General, "rejoices to see the Church thus rediscovering its liturgical Tradition" and expressed "its deep gratitude" to Benedict XVI. But it considered this to be only the first step on the road to reconciliation between the Holy See and the SSPX. Bishop Fellay recalled what was now expected of the Holy See: the withdrawal of the decree of excommunication "which still affects its bishops," followed by discussion of the "doctrinal points in dispute."

FOUR EXCOMMUNICATIONS ARE LIFTED

The second step Bishop Fellay was waiting for was a subject for discussion and for a canonical process. The Code of Canon Law (canon 1358) provides that an excommunicated member of the faithful may obtain remission of his sentence "if he no longer persists in the intention of committing the offence which justified his excommunication, and if he wishes to make amends."[16] He must then approach the competent authority, acknowledge his past fault, and express his desire to be reconciled.

In a letter dated December 15, 2008 to Cardinal Castrillón Hoyos, President of the *Ecclesia Dei* Commission, Archbishop Bernard Fellay, in his own name and on behalf of the three other bishops consecrated in 1988, requested the lifting of the excommunications that had been imposed on them for the past twenty years. In this letter, the Superior General of the SSPX declared, among other things, that:

> [W]e continue firmly resolute in our desire to remain Catholics and to put all our strength at the service of the Church of our Lord Jesus Christ, which is the Roman Catholic Church. We accept her teachings in a filial spirit. We firmly believe in the primacy of Peter and in his prerogatives, and for this reason the current situation causes us much suffering.

The statement that the SSPX bishops accepted the "teachings [of the Church] in a filial spirit" neither explicitly nor implicitly included an acceptance of the Second Vatican Council. Both parties were well aware of this, hence the reference to "as yet unresolved questions" in the decree lifting the excommunication.

---

15 Fr Francesco Ricossa, "Réflexions sur le motu proprio 'Summorum Pontificum,'" *Sodalitium* 61 (July 2009): 51.

16 In the words of the *Note Canonique* on the excommunication and its lifting published on the website of the diocese of Fréjus-Toulon on February 2009.

This decree was promulgated on January 21, 2009 by Cardinal Re, Prefect of the Congregation for Bishops, and made public on January 24. It made it clear that the lifting of the excommunication did not mean the restoration of "full communion with the Church for the entire Society of St. Pius X." Mention was made of the "requisite discussions with the authorities of the Holy See" to examine "as yet unresolved questions" and find "a full and satisfactory solution to the original problem." The timetable was clearly recalled: agreement on the points of doctrine contested by the SSPX was the prerequisite for the canonical status it might be granted. This new "step" – the word is in the decree – would, it was hoped, be a prelude to "prompt attainment of full communion with the Church." Nor did the lifting of the excommunication regularize the ministry of the SSPX bishops. As a Note from the Secretariat of State was later to recall: "The four bishops, although freed from excommunication, have no canonical function in the Church and do not licitly exercise any ministry in it."

The lifting of the excommunication was immediately overshadowed by what came to be known as the Williamson affair. In November 2008, on the occasion of a priestly ordination at the seminary in Zaitkofen, Germany, Bishop Williamson gave an interview to SVT, a Swedish television channel.[17] During the interview, he was asked, among other subjects, about the Jews and their genocide. "I believe there were no gas chambers," he said. He relied, he said, on the writings of "the most serious revisionist historians who have concluded that between 200,000 and 300,000 Jews perished in the Nazi concentration camps, but . . . none of them by a gas chamber." In April 1989, while visiting Quebec for confirmations, Bishop Williamson had already made similar remarks.[18] Bishop Hayes, President of the Canadian Bishops' Conference, expressed disapproval of the SSPX bishop in a message sent to the Canadian Jewish Congress.

The SVT interview, recorded in November 2008, was not broadcast on the Swedish channel until January 22, 2009. Three days earlier, the German weekly *Der Spiegel* had revealed its most explosive passages. The lifting of the excommunication had been communicated to the SSPX authorities on January 20. It was dated January 21 and made public on January 24. Was this coincidence of dates indicative of a concerted plan to sabotage the reconciliation sought by the Pope, or to undermine the Pope himself? Benedict XVI would later say, though without naming names:

---

17 Among the ordinands was one Sten Sandmark, a former Swedish Lutheran pastor who had converted, hence the interest the Swedish media took in the ceremony.

18 "Catholic Zealot Turns to Hate," *The Record* (English-language daily of Sherbrooke) (April 6, 1989).

> [W]e seem to be dealing here with a hostility, a readiness to
> pounce, that waits for these kinds of things to happen in order
> to strike a well-aimed blow. . . a readiness for aggression, which
> was lying in wait for its victim.[19]

Bishop Williamson's remarks provoked a worldwide media storm
against the bishop, the SSPX, and Benedict XVI. The headline in the
major German daily *Süddeutsche Zeitung* read: "Pope brings Holo-
caust denier back to the Church." On January 27, in a long communiqué, Bishop Fellay disapproved of Bishop Williamson's remarks and
announced that he had "forbidden him, until further notice, to take any
public position on political or historical questions." He then dismissed
him from his post as superior of the seminary in La Reja, Argentina.

On January 28, the French Bishops' Conference, after having "firmly
condemned the unacceptable and scandalous words of Bishop Williamson," made it clear that "the lifting of the excommunication is not a
rehabilitation. It is the starting point of a long road that will require
precise dialogue."[20] In concise terms, the CEF expressed its expectations
and caution: "Under no circumstances will the Council be negotiable.
No ecclesial group can substitute itself for the Magisterium."

On March 10, 2009, in his Letter to all bishops on the lifting of the
excommunication, Benedict XVI explained why, despite the "Williamson
affair" and the media storm that had ensued, he would continue along
the path of reconciliation with the Society of St. Pius X:

> Can we be totally indifferent to a community which has 491
> priests, 215 seminarians, six seminaries, 88 schools, two
> university-level institutes, 117 religious brothers, 164 religious
> sisters, and thousands of lay faithful? Should we casually let
> them drift farther from the Church? . . . Can we simply exclude
> them, as representatives of a radical fringe, from our pursuit of
> reconciliation and unity? What would then become of them?
>
> Certainly, for some time now, and once again on this spe-
> cific occasion, we have heard from some representatives of that
> community many unpleasant things – arrogance and presump-
> tuousness, an obsession with one-sided positions, etc. Yet to
> tell the truth, I must add that I have also received a number
> of touching testimonials of gratitude which clearly showed an
> openness of heart.[21]

---

19 Benedict XVI, *The Light of the World: the Pope, the Church, and the Signs of the Times*
(San Francisco: Ignatius Press, 2010), 123.
20 Declaration of the Permanent Council of the Bishops of France, January 28, 2009.
DC (March 1, 2009): 241.
21 *Letter to the Bishops of the Catholic Church*, March 10, 2009, available on the Vatican
website.

DOCTRINAL DISCUSSIONS

The decree of January 21, 2009 stated that "as yet unresolved questions" would be examined during "requisite discussions with Holy See authorities." Benedict XVI entrusted this task to the Congregation for the Doctrine of the Faith; this was also the wish of the Society of St. Pius X.

These "doctrinal discussions" – as the Congregation for the Doctrine of the Faith called them – took place behind closed doors between October 2009 and April 2011. To lead the discussions on behalf of the SSPX, Bishop Fellay appointed Fr Benoît de Jorna, who had been director of the École seminary since 1996, Fr Jean-Michel Gleize, professor of apologetics, ecclesiology, and dogma at the École seminary and principal contributor to the *Courrier de Rome*, and Fr Patrick de La Rocque, of the priory in Nantes, who was the first director of the *Lettre à nos frères prêtres*. For its part, the Congregation for the Doctrine of the Faith (CDF) appointed Dominican Father Charles Morerod, Dean of the Faculty of Philosophy at the Pontifical University of St. Thomas Aquinas, and two CDF consultors for these discussions: Fernando Ocáriz, Vicar General of Opus Dei, and the Jesuit Father Karl Becker. Bishop Ladaria Ferrer, then secretary of the CDF, and Bishop Pozzo, secretary of the *Ecclesia Dei* Commission now attached to the CDF, attended the discussions without taking part in them.[22]

It is worth noting that some time before the opening of the discussions, the three SSPX priests appointed for this purpose published a collection of critical studies of the acts of the Second Vatican Council. It was entitled, significantly or provocatively, "Magisterium of Sulphur" (*Magistère de soufre*). With a lengthy preface by Fr Jean-Michel Gleize, the volume brought together their contributions – as well as two by Abbé Alvaro Calderón – to the four conferences on the Second Vatican Council that had been held in Paris between 2002 and 2005. This volume, intended as a "Short Critical Examination of Vatican II," was published not by *Fideliter*, the SSPX's flagship publishing house, but more discreetly, by the École seminary.[23] Its distribution was limited. Clearly, the primary aim of this edition was to offer a synthesis of the SSPX's criticisms of Vatican II texts before the doctrinal discussions that were to begin a few months later.

One generally well-informed author writes: "Nothing has filtered out from these exchanges, other than that they were courteous but did not lead to any substantive agreement." He also points out that the "doctrinal preamble" submitted to the Society of Saint Pius X at the

22 *Cor Unum* 94 (October 2009): 27.
23 *Magistère de soufre* (École: Éditions IRIS, 2009).

end of these discussions "has been kept secret." In fact, the confidential documents, including the "Doctrinal Preamble," were published, after the discussions failed, in the SSPX's internal bulletin,[24] a publication reserved exclusively to Society members, the complete collection of which I have been able to consult.

The "doctrinal discussions" took place over eight sessions between October 27, 2009 and April 11, 2011. In addition to the meetings in Rome, documents were exchanged, which allowed for in-depth work. At the end of the discussions, the Congregation for the Doctrine of the Faith prepared a "Doctrinal Preamble" to which the SSPX had to adhere in order to enter into full communion with the Holy See, and "Information for a possible canonical solution" (the aim was to erect the Society of St. Pius X as an "international personal prelature"). These two documents were delivered on September 14, 2011 by Cardinal Levada, Prefect of the Congregation for the Doctrine of the Faith, to Bishop Fellay, who was accompanied by his two assistants. The "Doctrinal Preamble" comprised four points. The third point, which was far the most developed one, dealt with the Second Vatican Council; and the fourth point dealt with the Mass. Concerning the "affirmations of the Second Vatican Council and of the later Pontifical Magisterium . . . whose formulation might seem to some to be difficult to reconcile with the previous doctrinal affirmations of the Magisterium," the SSPX was asked to accept "that the content of these affirmations must be understood in the light of the entire and uninterrupted Tradition." These were the affirmations "concerning the relationship between the Catholic Church and non-Catholic Christian confessions, as well as the social duty of religion and the right to religious freedom."[25]

On October 7, Bishop Fellay called a meeting of the 28 SSPX leaders (seminary directors and district superiors) in Albano and presented them with the "Doctrinal Preamble" and the draft for a canonical status. It seems that the opinion expressed by the majority was that the "Doctrinal Preamble" could not be accepted as it stood. On December 1, Bishop Fellay gave the CDF a negative response: "It is impossible for us to adhere to the text of the 'Doctrinal Preamble' as submitted to us."[26] He enclosed a Preliminary Note listing the conciliar "errors" to be "rejected":

---

24 "Documents confidentiels," *Cor unum* 103 (November 2012), 42-56; 104 (March 2013): 33-54; 105 (June 2013): 28-36.
25 *Préambule doctrinal* proposed by the CDF, published in *Cor unum* 103 (November 2012): 44-46.
26 *Notre préliminiaire* and *Préambule doctrinal* delivered to the CDF by the SSPX on December 1, 2011, ibid., 48-51.

The tendency to exaggerate freedom in relation to truth (*Dignitatis humanae*, 2); equivocation regarding the uniqueness and exclusivity of the Catholic religion (*Lumen gentium*, 8); subordination of the Church to purely earthly goals (*Lumen gentium*, 1); the attribution of a certain specific value to non-Catholic confessions and religions (*Unitatis redintegratio*, 3); the practical levelling and hence confusion between the ministerial priesthood and the common priesthood of the faithful (*Lumen gentium*, 10 and 62), etc.

In order to replace the rejected "Doctrinal Preamble," the SSPX proposed to subscribe to the Profession of Faith of the Council of Trent, or to this Profession of Faith supplemented by two short formulas relating to the Councils of Vatican I and Vatican II ("all the texts of this Council are to be accepted according to the anti-modernist oath").

In a supplementary letter to Cardinal Levada a few weeks later, Bishop Fellay added three further difficulties:

Other points too are stumbling blocks for us:
– Collegiality, whose "subiectum quoque" remains an ambiguous term, even when clarified by the *Nota praevia* (LG 22);
– The soundness of the Novus Ordo Missae, which, irrespective of its validity and the liceity of its promulgation, presents deficiencies harmful to divine worship;
– Canon Law as promulgated in 1983, which, insofar as it takes up the Council's novelties, presents the same difficulties. [27]

On March 16, 2012, Cardinal Levada set a one-month ultimatum for the SSPX to accept the "Doctrinal Preamble" that had been submitted to it.

SUPPORTS AND DISSENSIONS

During discussions with the Congregation for the Doctrine of the Faith, the SSPX received support from outside the Society. The most notable case was that of Msgr Gherardini (1925-2017), the last representative of the "Roman school" of theology, and former professor of ecclesiology and ecumenism at the Pontifical Lateran University and the Pontifical University of Saint Thomas Aquinas. A few months before the onset of the SSPX-CDF talks, he published a book *The Ecumenical Vatican Council II: A Much Needed Discussion (Concilio Ecumenico Vaticano II. Un discorso da fare)*, which had a decided impact and was published three times in one year. Msgr Gherardini had no connection to the SSPX, and in his book he lamented the SSPX's "low esteem" for the Second Vatican Council and its "blindness" to the immense work

---

27 Bp Fellay to Cardinal Levada, January 12, 2012, ibid.

that had gone into it.[28] But in substance, he agreed with some of the criticisms made by Archbishop Lefebvre and the Society of St. Pius X. In the conciliar texts devoted to religious freedom, ecumenism, and the Church, he noted obscurities, contradictions, and equivocal formulations. His book ended with a deferential "plea" to Pope Benedict XVI to set in motion "a grand and, if possible, definitive clarification of the last Council in all its aspects and contents." He suggested that in order to *reparare omnia*, the Pope should prepare a "major document" of doctrinal explanation and definition, covered by his pontifical authority, and perhaps prepared by a series of theological congresses organized in Rome or a series of high-level publications "on each of the conciliar documents and on the various themes it dealt with."

How this respectful plea was received by the Pope is not known. Msgr Gherardini also punctuated the ongoing discussions between the SSPX and the CDF with two books devoted to the Council.[29] Following his supplication, Catholic historian Roberto de Mattei, who has close links with the Tradition, Family, Property movement and is the author of a hagiographical biography of its founder,[30] sent a similar supplication to Benedict XVI "for an in-depth examination of the pastoral council Vatican II." The petition, dated September 24, 2011, received 81 signatures from Italian Catholic intellectuals. The SSPX was satisfied, as it was mentioned and approved in the aforementioned *Preliminary Note* of December 1, 2011.

The doctrinal discussions with Rome had raised hopes among some within the Society of St. Pius X of finally obtaining canonical regularization. On the other hand, others feared that the SSPX would make doctrinal concessions in order to obtain this regularization. In the summer of 2009, just as the doctrinal discussions with Rome were about to begin, Bp Tissier de Mallerais published a lengthy study refuting the hermeneutic of the Council proposed by Benedict XVI.[31] The fiercest opposition, directly related to the discussions with Rome, came three years later. Bp Tissier de Mallerais, Bp de Galarreta, and Bp Williamson voiced their opposition to the ongoing process. By statute they were not part of the SSPX General Council. They were therefore not given

---

28 Brunero Gherardini, *The Ecumenical Vatican Council II: A Much Needed Discussion* (Frigento: Casa Mariana Editrice, 2009).

29 *Concilio Vaticano II. Il discorso mancato* (Turin: Lindau, 2011) and *Il Vaticano II. Alle radici d'un equivoco* (Turin: Lindau, 2011).

30 Roberto di Mattei, *Le Croisé du XXe siècle. Plinio Corrêa de Oliveira* (Lausanne: L'Âge d'Homme, 1997).

31 Bp Bernard Tissier de Mallerais, "La Foi au péril de la raison," *Le Sel de la terre* 69 (Summer 2009): 10-113.

details of the joint working sessions and the content of the documents exchanged. They expressed their reluctance concerning, or, in some cases, their opposition towards, the ongoing process. Bishop Fellay, in a letter to which we shall return, reproached them for seeking to "impose" their point of view, "even in the form of threats, and even publicly."

On April 7, 2012, before the dialog between the SSPX and the Holy See had broken down, the three bishops addressed a collective letter to Bishop Fellay, Superior General of the SSPX, and his two assistants, Frs. Pfluger and Nély. This letter was not intended to be made public. It was made public by the indiscretion of an SSPX official, who had it published a month later on a website, along with the response of Bishop Fellay and his assistants.[32] The three bishops expressed their "unanimous formal opposition" to "any practical agreement" with the Holy See. They drew a pessimistic picture of the situation: "Since Vatican II, the official authorities of the Church have separated themselves from Catholic truths." They felt that the "thinking of the current Pope is also steeped in subjectivism" and is no "better" than that of John Paul II. "After having kept up the fight for over forty years, will the Society now have to hand itself over to modernism and liberals?"

Bishop Fellay replied to this letter on April 14, scolding his three confreres for their "lack of supernaturalism" and their "lack of realism":

> On reading you, one seriously wonders whether you still believe that this visible Church whose seat is in Rome is actually the Church of our Lord Jesus Christ. . . . Is Benedict XVI still the legitimate pope for you?

He felt that "there is a visible change in attitude in the Church, helped by the gestures and actions of Benedict XVI towards Tradition. This new movement, born at least ten years ago, is growing stronger." The situation being different from that of 1988, the Superior General of the SSPX asserted that Archbishop Lefebvre "would not have hesitated to accept what has been proposed to us."

Yet that is not what happened. I shall not examine in detail the exchanges of letters that continued for some time between the SSPX and the Holy See: on April 15, 2012, the SSPX sent a "Doctrinal Declaration" to replace the "Doctrinal Preamble" proposed by the CDF; on June 13,

---

32 The letters were published in an English translation on the English-language website CathInfo.com on May 10, 2012. They were then published in their original French version on the *Riposte Catholique* site (founded by essayist Guillaume de Thieulloy) on the same day.

the CDF replied, modifying the text of this Declaration; on June 17, Bishop Fellay's letter to Benedict XVI; on June 30, Benedict XVI's reply. In this last letter, the Pope restated, in a lapidary way, what was expected of the SSPX in order to regain "full ecclesial communion":

> Acceptance:
> – of the Magisterium as the authentic interpreter of Apostolic Tradition;
> – of the Second Vatican Council as an integral part of said Tradition, leaving open the possibility of a legitimate discussion of the formulation of particular points in the Conciliar Documents;
> – the validity and lawfulness of the Novus Ordo Missae.[33]

This letter from Benedict XVI virtually marked the end of the "doctrinal discussions" undertaken three years before. The Society of Saint Pius X was about to hold its General Chapter, and Bishop Fellay wanted to re-establish a degree of concord after the dissensions that had become publicly apparent. Through his Secretary General, Fr Christian Thouvenot, he sent a letter to all district and seminary superiors. The letter, dated June 25, was a confidential circular, but it was soon made public on the internet by one of the superiors who had received it. The letter announced that Bishop Williamson, "on account of his rebellious stance and repeated disobedience," would not be able to take part in the General Chapter, and that he was "forbidden to go to Écône for the ordinations" taking place four days later. It was also announced that "Bishop Fellay has decided to postpone the ordinations of the Dominican friars of Avrillé and the Capuchin friars of Morgon." These two communities on friendly terms with the SSPX had taken positions critical of a possible agreement with Rome.

The superiors of the SSPX met from July 9 to 14. On July 14, it issued a declaration which was sent to Rome and made public on the 19th. Among other things, it stated that "a possible canonical normalization" would first have to be approved by "an extraordinary deliberative chapter" of the Society. On August 28, Bishop Fellay met with Archbishop Di Noia, Vice-President of the Ecclesia Dei Commission, and officially withdrew the doctrinal declaration of the previous April.[34]

Two months later, on October 2, 2012, Bishop Williamson was expelled from the SSPX for having "distanced himself from the leadership and government of the Priestly Fraternity of St. Pius X for several years" and for having refused to "show the respect and obedience due to his legitimate superiors." Some priests and religious communities

---

33 Benedict XVI to Bp Fellay, Letter, June 30, 2012, *Cor unum* 104 (March 2013): 54.
34 *Cor unum* 104 (March 2013): 40.

rallied to his side. Under the following pontificate, he created a new Priestly Union, and consecrated two bishops.

For Advent 2012, Archbishop Di Noia addressed a very long letter to Bishop Fellay.[35] With its spiritual and pastoral considerations, it stands in stark contrast to the doctrinal letters exchanged up to that point between the CDF and the SSPX. He acknowledged: "the terms of our disagreement concerning Vatican Council II have remained, in effect, unchanged." Yet he called on the Society of St. Pius X to get beyond this, and rediscover its proper vocation:

> That original charism entrusted to Archbishop Lefebvre must be recaptured, the charism of the formation of priests in the fullness of Catholic Tradition for the sake of undertaking an apostolate to the faithful that flows from this priestly formation. This was the charism the Church discerned when the Priestly Fraternity of St. Pius X was first approved in 1970. We recall Cardinal Gagnon's favorable judgment of your seminary at Écône in 1987.
>
> The authentic charism of the Fraternity is to form priests for the service of the people of God, not the usurpation of the office of judging and correcting the theology or discipline of others within the Church.

Certainly, Archbishop Di Noia acknowledged, it is legitimate to pay "attention . . . to passages of the Magisterium that seem difficult to reconcile with magisterial teaching, but these theological questions should not be the focus of your preaching or of your formation." In many respects, the lengthy spiritual and pastoral considerations expressed by Archbishop Di Noia at the end of 2012 correspond to the attitude towards the SSPX of Pope Francis, who succeeded Benedict XVI a few months later.

Benedict XVI was the pope best able of any since the Second Vatican Council to understand traditionalists, thanks to his many theological works prior to his pontificate, his keen attention to liturgical issues, and his own personal evolution. His 2007 motu proprio cleared the way for the celebration of the traditional Mass once and for all, as the thinking then went. Statistics compiled by the *Paix liturgique* association showed that the number of places of worship where this liturgy is celebrated significantly increased in France: 104 weekly traditional Masses with the bishop's agreement in 2007, 176 in 2013 (to which must be added Masses celebrated by the SSPX: 185 every Sunday in 2007, 190 in 2013).[36] There is another noteworthy phenomenon,

---

35 Published unabridged in its original English version on January 21, 2013 by New Catholic on his weblog, *Rorate Caeli*.
36 *La Lettre de Paix Liturgique* 381 (April 4, 2013).

although drawing up precise statistics is impossible: diocesan priests discovered the traditional Mass from 2007 onwards, learned how to celebrate it in abbeys or with priests from traditional institutes, and then offered it to the faithful in their parishes, alongside the new Mass. In some dioceses outside of France, seminarians have also been formed in this liturgy.

But this new impetus and new-found freedom did not lead to a massive switch from one missal to another. Nor was this Benedict XVI's aim. He distinguished between an "ordinary form" and an "extraordinary form" in the Roman rite, stressing that the "ordinary form," i.e., the 1970 Missal, was the "normal form." In his Letter to Bishops accompanying the motu proprio, he stated, with realism, that

> it is clearly seen that the new Missal will certainly remain the ordinary Form of the Roman Rite, not only on account of the juridical norms, but also because of the actual situation of the communities of the faithful.

Long before this motu proprio, when he was not yet pope, he had expressed the wish for a liturgical "reform of the reform" to be undertaken, so that a mutual enrichment of the two forms of the Roman rite might take place. In fact, during his pontificate, despite a few isolated initiatives, no general impetus in this direction was forthcoming.

If one takes a step back to consider the integration of traditionalists into the life of the Church generally, the return of the SSPX to full communion has not been achieved, despite the generous lifting of excommunications. Pope Francis, for his part, was to take different paths to further normalize the SSPX and traditionalists in the life of the Church.

CHAPTER 15

Pope Francis,
Pastor First and Foremost

POPE FRANCIS HAS USED THE QUALIFIER "TRADI-
tionalist" more than any other pope before him, always in a
pejorative sense. In the customary end-of-year address to the
Curia on December 21, 2020, he seemed to reject a binary reading of
Church life:

> When the Church is viewed in terms of *conflict* – right versus
> left, progressive versus traditionalist – she becomes fragmented
> and polarized, distorting and betraying her true nature. She is,
> on the other hand, a body in continual *crisis,* precisely because
> she is alive. She must never become a body in conflict, with
> winners and losers. . . .

Yet a few years earlier, during the controversial (as we shall see)
first synod on the family, he warned sternly against what he called the
traditionalist "temptation":

> a temptation to hostile inflexibility, that is, wanting to close
> oneself within the written word, (the letter) and not allowing
> oneself to be surprised by God, by the God of surprises (the
> spirit). . . . From the time of Christ, it is the temptation of the
> zealous, of the scrupulous, of the solicitous and of the so-
> called – today – "traditionalists" and also of the intellectuals.[1]

From the beginning of his pontificate, Pope Francis's attitude and
policy towards traditional Catholics, as well as his decisions and interventions concerning them, do not seem to follow a set plan. Depending
on the case, these have baffled or provided pleasant surprises to those
concerned; sometimes they have hurt them.

APOSTOLIC VISITATIONS

In 2013, the Fraternity of Saint Peter celebrated the twenty-fifth anniversary of its foundation. At that time, it numbered 244 priests and was
present in eleven countries. To mark this twenty-fifth anniversary, Pope
Francis issued a message and apostolic blessing on October 28, 2013.[2]

---

1 Pope Francis, Address for the Conclusion of the Third Extraordinary General Assembly
of the Synod of Bishops, October 18, 2014.
2 Quoted on the FSSP English-language website, October 28, 2013.

He praised the decision of the founders who, "in a great spirit of obedience and hope … turned with confidence to the Successor of Peter in order to offer the faithful attached to the Missal of 1962 the possibility of living their faith in the full communion of the Church." He invited the Fraternity of St Peter to live "according to its own charism" and to "take an active part in the mission of the Church in the world of today, through the testimony of a holy life, a firm faith and an inventive and generous charity."

When, a few months later, in March 2014, an apostolic visitation to the Fraternity of Saint Peter was announced, the man who was to be in charge as principal visitator, Bishop Huonder of Chur, was quick to point out that this was not a visitation ordered by the Pope to resolve specific problems, but an "ordinary" apostolic visitation; "in layman's terms, it constitutes 'periodic quality control.'" Mgr Vitus Huonder, who knew the FSSP seminary in Wigratzbad well, was assisted by two other visitators, Dom Courau, Abbot of Triors, and Bp Fabian Bruskewitz, Bishop Emeritus of Lincoln in the USA, who also knew the FSSP well and held it in high esteem. At the end of this lengthy visit, and after reading the report drawn up by the three visitors, the Superior General of the FSSP issued a statement welcoming the fact that

> [t]he overall findings of the report were very positive, especially regarding the apostolic work and internal health of the Fraternity of St. Peter. It also included a number of suggestions which will help the Fraternity to improve in its governance, the formation of its members, and its service towards souls.
>
> The Priestly Fraternity of St. Peter would like to publicly thank the visitors and the Pontifical Commission Ecclesia Dei for their work. Their constructive criticisms and suggestions will greatly aid our Fraternity in the continual effort to reform and improve itself.[3]

Another congregation, the Franciscans of the Immaculate (FI), experienced an apostolic visitation with far more severe consequences. This apostolic visit had been ordered, as we have seen, under the pontificate of Benedict XVI, in July 2012, following dissensions within the congregation that centered on the traditional liturgy, but also on problems of governance and financial management. It continued in the early days of Pope Francis's pontificate. The Apostolic Visitor, Bishop Todisco, in addition to visiting the houses of the congregation and interviewing individual religious, had asked each of the solemnly professed members of the institute to answer a detailed questionnaire – it was ten

---

3 English version available on the *Rorate Caeli* weblog, published September 20, 2015.

pages long–which focused mainly on liturgical issues, but also on "the Superior General's style of government" and the formation received.[4] The report drawn up by Bishop Todisco at the end of his visitation and investigation is not known, but the measures taken were very severe (a "persecution," the traditionalist media would soon say): on July 11, 2013, the founder of the Franciscans of the Immaculate, Father Manelli, was dismissed from his office and removed from the community where he resided. A Capuchin, Father Fidenzio Volpi, was appointed Pontifical Commissioner to the institute, to prepare a revision of the constitutions and a general chapter. The affair caused a stir in the Italian press and among traditionalists in various countries, particularly since drastic limitations on the celebration of the traditional liturgy were immediately imposed on the congregation.[5] The controversy flared up after brutal decisions were taken by the Pontifical Commissioner: closure of formation houses, suspension *a divinis* imposed on certain religious who defended their founder, legal complaints followed by a civil trial. The death of Fr Volpi during the course of his mission forced the appointment of three other commissioners.

Some have noisily accused Pope Francis of attacking this congregation out of hostility to the traditional liturgy. Cardinal Castrillón Hoyos, the former president of the *Ecclesia Dei* Commission, had the opportunity to ask Pope Francis about the matter. The latter told him that the congregation's trusteeship had been made necessary "by internal problems within the order, not by opposition to the old rite."[6] Indeed, it was divisions within the Franciscans of the Immaculate, certain internal dysfunctions and problems relating to the management of the congregation's numerous assets–a publishing house, several magazines, a web-tv and a radio station, in addition to the congregation's establishments–that led to its being placed under trusteeship. One reads on some sites that Father Manelli had been struck with a suspension *a divinis* on February 1, 2019. This information is false. A friar from the congregation clarifies: "That is what the Congregation of Religious wanted, but Pope Francis opposed it."[7]

---

4 *Lettera del Visitatore apostolico (A tutti i professi solenni dell'Istituto Frati Francescani dell'Immacolata)*, November 1, 2012, Archives of the Franciscan Friars of the Immaculate.
5 See especially the work defending Fr Manelli: Carolo Manetti ed., *Un caso che fa discutere: i Francescani dell'Immacolata* (Verona: Fede & Cultura, December 2013).
6 Declaration of Cardinal Castrillón Hoyos to the twenty-fifth General Assembly of the International Federation *Una Voce* on November 10, 2013, as reported on the website of *Una Voce* Italia.
7 Fr Alessandro Apollonio, former Procurator General of the Franciscans of the Immaculate to the author, Letter, March 30, 2020.

The General Chapter, which was supposed to bring this difficult episode to a close by amending the Statutes, was postponed twice, in 2014 and 2020. Meanwhile, exiles from the Franciscans of the Immaculate have reconstituted themselves in several small communities in various countries.

RELATIONS WITH THE SSPX

Without going into a full history of the relations between the Society of St. Pius X and the Holy See since 2013, we must note a few salient facts that show a change of outlook, at least on the part of Bishop Fellay, on this pope he would one day describe as "atypical."

Only a few months into his pontificate, the Superior General of the SSPX gave a very harsh assessment of Pope Francis in a lecture he gave in the United States: "We have in front of us a genuine Modernist!. . . . The situation of the Church is a real disaster, and the present Pope is making it 10,000 times worse."[8] Welcoming the breakdown of doctrinal discussions with the Congregation for the Doctrine of the Faith in the summer of 2012, he declared:

> When we see what is happening now [under Pope Francis] we thank God, we thank God we have been preserved from any kind of Agreement from last year. And we may say that one of the fruits of the [Rosary] Crusade we did is that we have been preserved from such a misfortune. Thank God. It is not that we don't want to be Catholics, of course we want to be Catholics and we are Catholics, and we have a right to be recognized as Catholics. But we are not going to jeopardize our treasures for that. Of course not.

Nevertheless, all dialogue was not broken off. On December 13, 2013, Bishop Fellay was able to greet the Pope very briefly at Maison Sainte-Marthe.[9] On September 23, 2014, he was received by the new Prefect of the Congregation for the Doctrine of the Faith, Cardinal Müller. The decision was made to resume doctrinal talks "in a broader and less formal framework than that of previous talks."[10] Cardinal Walter Brandmüller, President Emeritus of the Pontifical Committee for Historical Sciences, visited the seminary in Zaitzkofen, Germany, on December 5, 2014; Bishop Athanasius Schneider, Auxiliary Bishop of Astana, Kazakhstan, visited the seminary in Flavigny, France, on January 16, 2015, and the seminary in Winona, USA, on February 11, 2015. These were obviously

---

8 John Vennari, "Bishop Fellay on Pope Francis – 'We have in front of us a genuine Modernist!,'" *Catholic Family News* (October 14, 2013).
9 *Documentation et information catholiques internationales* ("DICI" – the French-language SSPX newsletter) 296 (May 16, 2014).
10 *DICI* 302 (October 10, 2014).

not canonical or apostolic visitations, since the SSPX has no canonical status – even though the visits enabled the visitors to get to know the SSPX and its works better. These were, rather, conversations on points of doctrine under discussion. In Zaitzkofen, with Cardinal Brandmüller, the magisterial authority of the Second Vatican Council was discussed; in Flavigny and Winona, with Bishop Schneider, the liturgical reform of Paul VI and the doctrinal presuppositions of the *Novus Ordo Missae* were discussed. [11]

It should be noted that the two prelates sent to the SSPX, though not sharing its views, were not hostile to it: they were traditional-minded. Bishop Schneider, in his diocese, usually celebrates the liturgy in the "ordinary form," but he also celebrates in the traditional rite on certain occasions, as does Cardinal Brandmüller. In the years to come, both of them would take public positions critical of some of Pope Francis's teachings.

The year 2015 also saw Pope Francis making a pastoral provision that constituted, with regard to the canonical situation of the SSPX, a further step on the road to reconciliation. On September 1, 2015, two months before the start of the Extraordinary Jubilee of Mercy, which would run from December 8, 2015 to November 20, 2016, he published the traditional Letter granting the indulgence. Because "this Jubilee Year of Mercy excludes no one," the Pope decided that the faithful who, during this year, went to confession with SSPX priests would "receive a valid absolution of their sins." This was not yet a full recognition of the ministry of SSPX priests, but a generous, or realistic, response to a delicate and canonically complex situation. Until then, in terms of canon law, while the sacraments of Baptism, Confirmation, Eucharist, Holy Orders, and Extreme Unction given by priests in the SSPX were considered illicit but valid, the sacraments of Confession and Marriage were considered not only illicit, but invalid, because these two sacraments require a special jurisdiction granted by the diocesan bishop. Nevertheless, the SSPX affirmed the valid character of the absolutions given by its priests, in the name of the "supplied jurisdiction" it exercised in view of the "state of necessity" in which the Church found herself.

On the occasion of the Jubilee, therefore, Pope Francis overcame a canonical difficulty by recognizing the full validity and licitness of confessions made by SSPX priests. In a press release, the SSPX welcomed the Pope's "paternal gesture." In the same letter, Pope Francis also said: "I hope that in the near future solutions can be found to restore full communion with the priests and superiors of the Society." A few

---

11 *DICI* 307 (December 19, 2014); *DICI* 311 (February 27, 2015).

months later, on April 1, 2016, he for the first time received Bishop Fellay and the second General Assistant, Fr Nély, in audience. The meeting was "very cordial and constructive," according to the secretary of the *Ecclesia Dei* Commission. A few days later, in a sermon given on a pilgrimage to Notre-Dame du Puy, Bishop Fellay spoke very freely about the long conversation he had had with the Pope.[12] He revealed that a decree excommunicating the SSPX had been presented to the Pope, who had refused to sign it. The Pope had told him:

> I won't condemn you. You're Catholics, on the way to full communion. . . . You know? I'm given a lot of grief over you, people make trouble for me because I'm good to you, but to them I say: listen, don't I embrace Patriarch Cyril? Don't I treat the Anglicans well? Don't I treat the Protestants well? Then I don't see why I shouldn't treat these Catholics well.

The day after this audience, Bishop Fellay was received at the Congregation for the Doctrine of the Faith by Bishop Pozzo, Secretary of the *Ecclesia Dei* Commission. There too he noted "a profound and extremely important change," as he put it in the homily quoted above. He reported Bishop Pozzo's words as follows:

> We must ask of you only what is asked of you, what is necessary for every Catholic, and nothing more. . . . You have the right to defend your opinion on religious freedom, on ecumenism, on relations with other religions, as set out in *Nostra Aetate*.

This important concession seemed to mean that the Holy See was no longer asking for acceptance of the Council in its entirety.

The celebration of weddings by SSPX priests also posed a problem in terms of canon law. They were not delegated by the diocesan bishop to celebrate them. The SSPX also justified its position by recourse to canon law (both old and new), which provides for extraordinary cases in which a marriage cannot, "without grave inconvenience," be celebrated before a priest with faculties.[13] Here, the "inconvenience" is, in ordinary parishes, both the pastoral preparation prior to the reception of the sacrament, the marriage Mass according to the new rite, and the preaching during the ceremony. Here again, Pope Francis sought to remove an obstacle. On March 27, 2017, in a letter approved in common form by the pope and addressed to the bishops' conferences, the president of the *Ecclesia Dei* Commission asked the bishops to "facilitate the path towards the full institutional regularization" of marriages. In fact, the Pope asked the bishops to "guarantee the legal

---

12 *DICI* 334 (April 22, 2016) 2–5.
13 Fr Grégoire Celier, *Les Mariages dans la Tradition sont-ils valides?* (Paris: Clovis, 1999).

security of marriages contracted within the framework of the SSPX, so as to appease consciences": to grant delegations to celebrate marriages and to register celebrations in Catholic registers.[14]

Through the will of Pope Francis, then, a true though incremental canonical normalization of the ministry of the SSPX was achieved. Paradoxically, however, this was achieved in a context where the Pope's magisterium was, on certain points, contested by the SSPX and other traditional Catholics.

COMPLAINTS AND ACCUSATIONS

A few days after the Roman meetings of April 2016, which "[gave] us hope," as Bishop Fellay admitted, there appeared the apostolic exhortation *Amoris laetitia*, dated March 19, 2016, and published on April 8. It was the fruit of the two synods on the family held in Rome in October 2014 and October 2015. The preparatory documents for these synods, and then the debates, had given rise to immense controversy. Two factions had clashed on issues relating to marriage, sexuality, and remarried divorcees: "One insists on preserving Catholic identity, the other invites us to keep up with changes in society so that the Church's message may remain audible."[15] The first faction was made up of traditional Catholics, in the broadest sense of the term: from cardinals and bishops attached to a clear doctrinal expression in continuity with the Magisterium, to sedevacantists, to *Ecclesia Dei* communities and the SSPX.

These two factions had been publicly opposing each other since 2014, through articles, books, lectures, and conferences. After the publication of *Amoris laetitia*, this opposition grew and has never ceased. The intransigent doctrinal faction also increased the number of appeals and petitions addressed to the Pope. Two types of address to the Pope can be distinguished, according to the typology that Jean Madiran had already established in 1974 in his *Réclamation au Saint-Père*, as we have seen, concerning the Mass and the Vatican Council: an approach of complaint (the "ordinary way") and an approach of accusation (the "extraordinary way"). In the complaint approach, one respectfully addresses the pope, publicly or privately, recognizing his authority, and asks him to clarify, rectify, or correct. In the accusation approach, the Pope is publicly held guilty of heresy and/or schism.

---

14 Fr Pierre-Marie Berthe, "Les Diocèses de France et la Fraternité sacerdotale Saint-Pie X: la célébration des mariages dans le cadre de la lettre romaine du 27 mars 2017," *Revista española de derecho canónico* 190 (January-June 2021): 24.

15 Fr Pierre-Marie Berthe, *Les Dissensions ecclésiales, un défi pour l'Église catholique. Histoire et actualité* (Paris: Éditions du Cerf, 2019), 738.

Without going into the details of their arguments and demonstrations,[16] one may note, before or after the publication of *Amoris laetitia*, several solemn complaints:

> – The *Filial Supplication to His Holiness Pope Francis* addressed by Italian historian Roberto de Mattei, who is associated with the TFP movement, in January 2015. In just a few months, it is said to have gathered over 500,000 signatures and the support of nine cardinals and 160 bishops.
>
> – The letter sent to the Pope in October 2015 by thirteen cardinals (including three members of the Curia: Müller, Pell, and Sarah) expressing their concern about the synod's procedures "designed to facilitate the achievement of predetermined results on important and controversial issues."
>
> – The lengthy *Supplication to the Holy Father* from Bishop Fellay, Superior General of the SSPX, on September 15, 2015, expressing "the deep anxieties" aroused by the first Synod on the Family and the Declaration that followed on October 27.[17]
>
> – *Theological Censures of Amoris Laetitia*, addressed in June 2016 to Cardinal Sodano, dean of the Sacred College, for transmission to the Pope. Drafted on the initiative of two Englishmen, John Lamont, who holds a licentiate in theology and is a doctor of philosophy, and Dominican Thomas Crean, it received 45 signatures from professors (or former professors) of philosophy, theology, canon law, or history, in seminaries or Catholic universities in the United States, Europe and South America.[18]
>
> – The *Dubia* on *Amoris laetitia*, addressed to the Pope by four cardinals (Brandmüller, Burke, Caffarra, and Meisner) on September 19, 2016, which they only made public on the following November 14 after waiting in vain for a response from the Pope.
>
> – The *Appeal for Prayer* launched on January 18, 2017 by three bishops from Kazakhstan (Lenga, Peta, and Schneider).
>
> – The letter addressed to the Pope on April 25, 2017 by Cardinal Caffarra on behalf of the other three signatories of the *Dubia*, asking to be received in audience to obtain "clarification of the five points indicated by the Dubia," and to address the "situation of confusion and disarray" created in the Church by *Amoris laetitia*. Having received no response to this request for an audience, they made their letter public on the following June 20.
>
> – The *Declaratio* drafted by laymen and made public during a colloquium held in Rome on April 7, 2018, reaffirming irrevocable principles on marriage, morality, and access to communion, and asking the Pope and bishops to confirm this doctrine solemnly.

---

16 See Yves Chiron, *Françoisphobie.* (Paris: Éditions du Cerf, 2020).

17 *Cor Unum* 112 (October 2015): 41-50.

18 [For the definitive text of this and several other public statements, see *Defending the Faith Against Present Heresies*, ed. John Lamont and Claudio Pierantoni (Waterloo, ON: Arouca Press, 2021) – *Translator.*]

At the same time, an indictment of Pope Francis had begun. It no longer focused solely on *Amoris laetitia*, but also on other papal teachings and statements. Two of these are worthy of note:

> – The *Correctio filialis haeresibus propagatis*, initiated by the above-mentioned John Lamont and Father Thomas Crean and supported by Roberto de Mattei. Dated July 16, 2017, and taken to the Santa Marta residence on August 11, 2017, it was made public the following September 24. It differs from previous supplications: first because it accuses the Pope of "propagating heresies" (it identifies seven); and, secondly, because it questions not only *Amoris laetitia* but also certain papal speeches and teachings. Mgr Fellay and Mgr Gracida, bishop emeritus of Corpus Christi, added their signatures after the *Correctio* had been deposited at Santa Marta. In total, it is said to have gathered some 250 signatures from priests, religious, theologians, and academics; but some signatories of the 2016 Theological Censures did not agree to sign this new text, which accused the Pope of heresy. Cardinals Brandmüller and Burke also publicly distanced themselves from the initiative.
>
> – The 25-page *Open Letter to the Bishops of The Catholic Church*, written by the same Lamont-Crean group and dated April 29, 2019. It sought to prove that Pope Francis had been "guilty of the crime of heresy," through *Amoris laetitia*, the Abu Dhabi Document (co-signed with the Grand Imam of al-Azhar), and other teachings.

THE "RESISTANCE"

From the time of the SSPX's doctrinal discussions (2008-2012) with the Congregation for the Doctrine of the Faith, Bishop Fellay's policy, described as "accordist" by his opponents, had been the subject of internal disagreements. The expulsion of Bishop Williamson in October 2012, as we have seen, revealed to the media a long-standing "resistance" to the SSPX authorities. Over the years, the "resisters," whether expelled from the SSPX or leaving it before being expelled, formed more or less informal or structured groups claiming to be the true heirs of Archbishop Lefebvre and the SSPX.

As early as August 2012, Father Joseph Pfeiffer, an American, had created a "Priestly Fraternity of St. Pius X of the Strict Observance" (SSPX-SO), for which he was expelled from the SSPX the following month. Backed by four American priests from the SSPX, he received the support of other priests, notably from Asia. Together, they would soon form the SSPX-MC (Marian Corps). On February 28, 2013, the very day that Pope Benedict XVI left the Vatican after his resignation, an *Open Letter to Bishop Fellay* from 37 anonymous SSPX priests was made public. The letter denounced his "accordist" policy and prevarications, and summoned him "to tell the truth, repair the lies and retract the errors."[19] The names of three of the collaborators were eventually discovered, and they were sanctioned.

Under Pope Francis's pontificate, opposition to Bishop Fellay's "accordist" line developed all the more as the new pope made concessions on confession and marriage, which seemed to these "resisters" to be so many traps to normalize the SSPX.

In the early months of 2013, Fr François Pivert, a priest ordained by Archbishop Lefebvre in 1980, and who had succeeded Fr Coache in the work of *Combat de la Foi*, published a book under the title *Nos rapports avec Rome* ("Our Relations with Rome") in which, by quoting numerous extracts from Archbishop Lefebvre's writings and conferences, he intended to show that the founder of Écône, after 1988, had renounced any agreement with Rome, and that this line should be followed by his successors. The book was banned from sale and distribution within the SSPX.

On January 7, 2014, a few priests and religious wrote an *Address to the Faithful* that was read out in several traditionalist chapels on Sunday, January 19. They said they were refusing any rapprochement with "modernist Rome," and wanted to "continue the survival operation begun by Archbishop Lefebvre." Subsequently, other priests and religious signed this "declaration of fidelity," which received 36 signatures.[20] The signatories were mainly SSPX priests or those expelled from the SSPX. They were joined by some fifteen religious: Father Pierre-Marie, prior of the Fraternity of Saint Dominic, of Avrillé, and ten other religious from the same convent; Father Thomas d'Aquin, a Benedictine who had left Dom Gérard at the time of the 1988 consecrations; another former monk from Le Barroux, Father Bruno, who had had to leave the abbey in 2002 for reasons that were not doctrinal; Fathers Avril and Raffali, heads of independent charities. Fr François Pivert, who had signed the declaration, was expelled from the SSPX on April 3, and had to leave the *Combat de la Foi* work at Le Moulin du Pin.[21]

Subsequently, on July 15, some of the signatories, headed by Bishop Williamson, formed the Union sacerdotale Marcel Lefebvre (USML). On March 19, 2015, Bishop Williamson proceeded with the episcopal consecration of Fr Jean-Michel Faure, a former member of the SSPX,[22] in order to continue Archbishop Lefebvre's survival operation and using the very

---

19 *Open Letter* published on a website they had created, *La Sapinière*.

20 The text of this *Adresse aux fidèles* and the signatures appended to it are on the website https://dominicansavrille.us/ [accessed 4/4/2024].

21 Fr François Pivert to the author, Letter, September 5, 2021.

22 USML, *Opération survi. Le Sacre de Mgr Jean-Michel Faure*, 2015.

argument from the state of necessity that Lefebvre had invoked in 1988. On March 19, 2016, Bishops Faure and Williamson proceeded with the episcopal consecration of the aforementioned Father Thomas d'Aquin. On August 22, 2016, Bp Faure founded the *Société sacerdotale des Apôtres de Jésus et de Marie* (SAJM, "Priestly Society of the Apostles of Jesus and Mary") and a seminary in Avrillé.[23] On July 10, 2017, Bishop Williamson, assisted by Bp Faure and Bp Miguel Ferreira da Costa (Thomas d'Aquin in religion), consecrated as bishop Father Gerardo Zendejas, a Mexican priest ordained in 1988 and a former member of the SSPX.

After the "Thuc line" in the 1970s and the "Guérard line" in the 1980s, recent years have witnessed the appearance of a new episcopal line independent from Rome. There are different doctrinal positions, however: the Thuc-liners are sedevacantists; the Guérardians affirm only a "formal vacancy" of the Holy See and do not acknowledge the pope's authority; while the Williamsonians await Rome's return to "Tradition."

These margins of traditionalism should not be confused, historically speaking, with the Society of St. Pius X, which, despite its hesitations, hopes, and disappointments, has not broken off all dialogue with Rome. In 2017, Cardinal Müller, Prefect of the Congregation for the Doctrine of the Faith, once again demanded that the SSPX accept the teachings of the Second Vatican Council and recognize the legitimacy of the New Mass in order to be granted canonical status.

In July 2018, the SSPX held its General Chapter in Écône to elect its Superior General. On July 11, *Le Figaro* religious affairs specialist Jean-Marie Guénois announced in the headline of his article: "Lefebvrists: Bishop Fellay Ousted, Fr Davide Pagliarani Becomes Superior General." It commented: "A new Superior General has been elected at the head of the Society of Saint Pius X, ousting the current Superior, Mgr Fellay, who was considered the favorite. With this new leader, Father Davide Pagliarani, the faction opposed to rapprochement with Rome has taken the upper hand." Other commentators would say that he is a supporter of the "hard" line, as opposed to the "accordist" line.

Be that as it may–the epithet does not sufficiently define him–he was received at the Congregation for the Doctrine of the Faith four months after his election. On that occasion, he said he wanted to "resume the theological discussion" with Rome. But two years later, in 2020–which marked the 50th anniversary of the SSPX–he acknowledged that relations with the Vatican were continuing to stagnate:

---

23 Decree of erection published on the website of the SAJM, https://sajm-siteofficiel. blogspot.com/2016/08/decret-derection.html [accessed 4/4/2024].

This does not depend on the SSPX or its Superior General. For the time being, the Vatican itself has preferred not to resume the doctrinal discussions which the SSPX proposed in order to better explain its position, and to show its attachment to the Catholic faith and the See of Peter. What is astonishing is that the Vatican is at the same time asking us to regularize our canonical situation first: this creates an inextricable and intrinsically contradictory situation, since the possibility of canonical recognition of the SSPX is itself constantly subject to requirements of a doctrinal nature; which, time and again, remain for us absolutely unacceptable.[24]

THE SEXUAL ABUSE SCANDALS

The publication of the *Rapport Sauvé* in October 2021 revealed the extent of sexual abuse of minors committed in the Church in France since the 1950s. Coming on the heels of other reports published in other countries (the John Jay Report in the USA in 2004, the Ryan Report in Ireland in 2009, etc.),[25] this survey confirms that in France as elsewhere, while the family environment remains by far the primary setting of such abuse, the Church in the broadest sense comes second: according to this report, 216,000 sexual abuses were committed by priests, religious men, and religious women, over the course of seventy years, i.e., 4% of this type of violence.

A "never-ending trial" was launched in the courts of the media rather than in the courts of the justice system. It often failed to distinguish between "plaintiffs" and "victims," alleged "predators" or "abusers" and actual criminals.[26] Nevertheless, the scale of these deviances is undeniable, and high-profile or less high-profile trials have multiplied, after a period of a "law of silence" that left these cases in the shadows, which is not to say that they went unpunished.

Recent popes have urged "zero tolerance," albeit explaining this mystery of evil in different ways. For Pope Benedict XVI, the multiplication of pedophilia cases among men of the Church, as in other sectors of society, is in the last analysis "the absence of God" and the loss or weakening of the sense of sin: "It is only where faith no longer determines man's actions that such crimes are possible." The cause lies also in the cultural and intellectual atmosphere of the 1960s-1980s, the "absence of norms" in general, and, in the Church, the spread of

---

24 Interview in *DICI*, October 14, 2020.
25 See Marie-Jo Tiel, *L'Église catholique face aux abus sexuels sur mineurs* (Paris: Bayard, 2019).
26 See Henri Quantin, *L'Église des pédophiles. Raisons et déraisons d'un procès sans fin* (Paris: Éditions du Cerf, 2021).

a moral theology that was no longer based primarily on natural law. Pope Francis, for his part, blamed "clericalism" and the "abuse of power" exercised by certain priests, religious, or founders.[27] The two explanations are not mutually exclusive, but complementary.

Traditionalist clergy (priests or religious), at various times, have not remained free of this kind of perverse and immoral conduct. We won't venture to draw up a catalog of traditionalist priests who have been guilty of sexual abuse of minors or adults, if only because few of them have been convicted by the civil courts, and the more numerous canonical sanctions are rarely known. Nevertheless, this type of abuse does not seem to have been statistically more frequent in the traditionalist milieu than among the so-called "conciliar" clergy. Some cases are briefly mentioned in the Biographical Dictionary at the end of [the French edition of] this book. Here, based on press articles and information gathered directly from various sources, we will confine ourselves to three convictions for events that took place in different traditionalist circles, at different times.

Marist Father Guy Gérentet de Saluneaux was a well-known figure in Lyon traditionalism. In 1968, he signed Fr Coache's *Vademecum du catholique fidèle*, and was faithful to the traditional Mass. For many years, he taught Greek and Gregorian chant at the renowned La Péraudière school, founded by Luce Quenette, a close associate of Archbishop Lefebvre and Jean Madiran. Father Gérentet was then able to exercise his ministry at Sainte-Trinité parish in Lyon, in charge of catechism and a scout troop. He was dismissed from this ministry in 2001 by Cardinal Billié, Archbishop of Lyon, after a girl denounced him for "abuse." In the years that followed, other complainants turned to Cardinal Barbarin, who asked the religious, now without a ministry, to consult a psychologist. It wasn't until 2010 that the Lyon public prosecutor's office took up the case, following a letter from a cleric, the "prior of an abbey in the south of France."[28] Before the examining magistrate, Cardinal Barbarin described Father Gérentet as a "warped individual" and a "real pervert." The Marists initiated canonical proceedings against him, which led in 2012 to his expulsion from the congregation and his dismissal from the clerical state. In February 2016, the civil courts sentenced him to a two-year suspended prison

---

27 Pope emeritus Benedict XVI and Pope Francis allowed for their texts and teachings on the subject to be gathered in a single volume: *Non fate male a uno solo di questi piccoli. La voce di Pietro contro la pedophilia* (Vatican City: Libreria Editrice Vaticana/ Sienna: Cantagalli, 2019).

28 *Le Monde* (April 1, 2016); *Lyon Capitale* (April 1, 2016).

sentence (in view of his age – eighty-one at the time of his judgment) for sexual assaults on eight girls between 1989 and 2000.

Father Jean-Marie Savioz, from the diocese of Sion, Switzerland, never did belong to the Society of St. Pius X. But he became familiar with its history, writing his licentiate thesis in theology on it, which he defended at the University of Fribourg in 1995. This major academic work (nearly four hundred pages) has become a reference work on the founding of the SSPX and the seminary of Écône, frequently cited by Bp Tissier de Mallerais in his biography of Archbishop Lefebvre. After his ordination in 2001, Fr Savioz exercised his ministry in the diocese of Perpignan, first as pastor at the cathedral, then in Canet-en-Roussillon and finally at Saint Joseph's church in Perpignan, while also acting as chaplain to the Scouts d'Europe and the Collège Sainte-Jeanne-d'Arc. Although he did not celebrate Mass according to the 1962 ordo, he was apparently a very conservative priest, wearing the cassock and "talking, to say the least, a 'traddy in the extreme' talk."[29] In 2009, following a complaint from a teenager, he was placed under investigation. In 2019, the Circuit Court sentenced him to fifteen years' imprisonment for rape and sexual assault on three minors. He appealed against this sentence, but failed to convince the judges, as his sentence was increased by five years in 2020. The appeal he and his lawyer lodged at the time was rejected. A canonical trial against him should soon result in his dismissal from the clerical state.

Fr Christophe Roisnel, who entered the seminary in 1996 and was ordained a priest for the Society of Saint Pius X in 2002, was appointed principal of Notre-Dame-de-La-Sablonnière, a co-educational elementary school in Goussonville, in 2006. Under the pretext of giving them therapy, he sexually abused three female teachers. When it learned of the facts, the SSPX expelled him from the school in 2011 and initiated a canonical process that sentenced him to two years of penance at the Capuchin convent in Morgon. A complaint was lodged with the courts only in 2013. In 2017, Abbé Roisnel was sentenced to sixteen years' imprisonment for aggravated rape, a sentence increased on appeal to nineteen years' imprisonment. It should be noted that both Fr Roisnel's lawyer, Jérôme Triomphe, who argued for acquittal – the complainants were said to have consented – and the complainants' lawyer, François Souchon, who considered the second sentence "just," are former students of SSPX schools.

---

29 L. M., one of the victims' fathers, to the Author, Letter, October 1, 2021. L. M. published a long testimonial in *La Croix* (May 27, 2021): "For us, the Gospel is a dead letter," the cry of rebellion of a father hurt twice: once by the abuses his son suffered, and again by the lack of support on the part of Church authorities.

In all three cases, it is probably not the deficiency of the moral theology they were taught that is to blame, but other explanatory factors: perhaps an insufficient discernment of vocation, an overly sacralized image of the priest, the temptation for some of exerting a psychological hold over another,[30] immersion in a world where pornographic images are commonplace and omnipresent, psychological imbalances and, as in every human being, the mystery of evil.

Although the Society of St. Pius X has not yet been fully canonically recognized by the Holy See, there has been discreet collaboration between Rome and the Superior General of the SSPX for some twenty years now for the most difficult situations: since the early 2000s, the Congregation for Clergy has been dealing with cases of reduction to the lay state presented to it by the SSPX (for *gravioribus delictis* or other reasons); since 2004 at least, the SSPX Superior General has been delegated by the Congregation for the Doctrine of the Faith to judge cases of sexual abuse.[31]

In 2011, the SSPX opened a "house of contemplation" in Montgardin, in the Hautes-Alpes region of France, to welcome, psychologically monitor, and spiritually help through prayer and penance some of its priests who have been guilty of sexual abuse, as well as other priests who are experiencing difficulties of other kinds. In 2021, the SSPX internal bulletin also published a Rule for priests on the spiritual direction of women and girls, and reprinted, in 1995 and 2011, a study, "De la direction des femmes" ("On the Spiritual Direction of Women") published in 1950 in the Dominican magazine *La Vie spirituelle*.

THE QUESTION OF THE LITURGY

For a long time, Pope Francis was considered to have but little interest in liturgical matters. His words to Cardinal Castrillón Hoyos in 2013, quoted above, indicated that he had no opposition to the traditional liturgy. Archbishop Guido Marini, who had been appointed Master of Pontifical Liturgical Celebrations in 2007 by Benedict XVI, and who is very concerned with the *ars celebrandi*, remained in office with Pope Francis until very recently (August 2021). In 2014, he chose a traditionally minded cardinal, Cardinal Sarah, as Prefect of the Congregation for Divine Worship, and kept him in office until February 2021.

---

30 Regarding spiritual abuse in certain communities, see the full study by Dom Dysmas de Lassus, prior of the Grande Chartreuse, *Abuses in the Religious Life and the Path to Healing* (Manchester, NH: Sophia Institute Press, 2023).

31 See Bp Fellay's interview in the daily *Présent* (June 27, 2015).

The annual international pilgrimage of the *Coetus Internationalis Summorum Pontificorum* (CISP), organized for the first time in 2012, in thanksgiving for the 2007 motu proprio and to show the attachment felt by the faithful to the traditional rite, has been able to continue in Rome every year, with more and more splendor and more and more participants. Under the guidance of Fr Claude Barthe, the author of numerous works on the Mass and liturgy, and chaplain to the CISP, year after year the pilgrimage has been able greatly to increase the number of traditional ceremonies in the Roman basilicas, celebrated by bishops and cardinals accompanying the pilgrimage. Prelates from the Curia have also been able to take part in these traditional ceremonies, in which all the splendors of the liturgy were on full display. Thus, in October 2013, a few months after the election of Pope Francis, Archbishop Pozzo, the Secretary of the *Ecclesia Dei* Commission, welcomed pilgrims at Vespers on October 24, and Cardinal Castrillón Hoyos, the Prefect Emeritus of the Congregation for the Clergy and a former President of the *Ecclesia Dei* Commission, celebrated the traditional Mass in St. Peter's Basilica on the 26th, assisted by Archbishop Ferrer, Under-Secretary of the Congregation for Divine Worship.[32]

Yet attentive readers of the Pope's writings spotted, in that same month of October 2013, remarks on the ancient rite in which he was already expressing his concern about the traditional Mass. This was in the major interview published in *La Civiltà cattolica* in September 2013, and reprinted the following month in other Jesuit magazines around the world.[33] On the subject of liturgy, Pope Francis affirmed that "the work of liturgical reform" accomplished in the wake of the Council was "absolutely irreversible." Regarding "the Vetus Ordo," he added:

> I think that Pope Benedict's choice was a prudential one, involving helping people who had this particular sensitivity. What's worrisome is the risk of ideologizing the Mass, instrumentalizing it.

One finds exactly the same thinking and the same words (ideologization, instrumentalization) eight years later, in the explanations the Pope gave after the publication of a motu proprio on the liturgy that seemed, to many, like an earthquake. [See, for a large sample of reactions, *From Benedict's Peace to Francis's War: Catholics Respond to the Motu Proprio* Traditionis Custodes *on the Latin Mass*, ed. Peter A.

---

32 See Fr Barthe, interview in *L'Homme nouveau* (October 21, 2013).
33 In France, in the periodical *Études* (October 2013).

Kwasniewski (Brooklyn, NY: Angelico Press, 2021). – *Translator*.] This motu proprio was published following an investigation the Pope had commissioned in April 2020. He had asked the Congregation for the Doctrine of the Faith to send the world's bishops a questionnaire on the application of the motu proprio *Summorum Pontificum* in their dioceses. Most of the bishops' replies were accompanied by summaries produced by the Bishops' Conferences. [Searching questions have been raised about the actual content of these questionnaires: see the investigative work of Diane Montagna. – *Translator*.]

In the letter to the bishops that accompanied the motu proprio, Pope Francis said:

> The responses received have revealed a painful situation that worries me, and confirms the need for me to intervene. . . . The possibility offered by Saint John Paul II, and, with even greater magnanimity, by Benedict XVI, of reconstituting the unity of the ecclesial body while respecting different liturgical sensibilities, has been used to increase distances, harden differences, build oppositions that wound the Church and hinder its progress, exposing it to the risk of divisions.

In light of the responses received, the Pope decided to redefine the rules governing the celebration of the traditional Mass. The motu proprio *Traditionis custodes*, dated July 16, 2021, cancels elements of Benedict XVI's motu proprio *Summorum Pontificum*. Without going into a detailed analysis of this document, it may be said that Pope Francis imposes restrictions on the traditional liturgy that run counter to the liberalization achieved by his predecessor. The traditional Mass is not banned, but it is subject to regulations that have been deemed harsh or unjust by traditionalists and traditional communities. After the three acts that gradually gave back to the traditional liturgy its "full rights" – in 1984 and 1988 by John Paul II, in 2007 by Benedict XVI – Pope Francis's motu proprio represents a step backwards. It may give the appearance of a regression.

But the Church is no longer monolithic in her observance or non-observance of directives from Rome. Initial reactions from bishops – such as Mgr Rougé, bishop of Nanterre, for example – suggest that some bishops will apply the new directives flexibly and with sympathy.

It was precisely to the bishops, and not to the Pope, that traditional communities turned after the motu proprio was published. This appeal to the bishops, dated August 31, 2021, was signed by nine superiors of traditional institutes (Fr Komorowski, Superior General of the Priestly Fraternity of St. Peter; Msgr Wach, Prior General of the Institute of

Christ the King Sovereign Priest; Father Barrero Zabaleta, Superior General of the Institute of the Good Shepherd; Father de Blignières, Superior General of the Fraternity of Saint Vincent Ferrer; Father Goesche, Provost General of the Institute of Saint Philip Neri; Father Mamsery, Superior General of the Missionaries of the Holy Cross; Dom Louis-Marie, Abbot of the Abbey of Sainte-Madeleine du Barroux; Father Emmanuel-Marie, Abbot of the Canons of Lagrasse; Dom Marc, Abbot of the Abbey of Sainte-Marie-de-la-Garde) and by three women superiors of religious communities (Mother Placide Devillers, abbess of the Abbey of Notre-Dame-de-l'Annonciation; Mother Faustine Bouchard, prioress of the Canonesses of Azille; and Mother Madeleine-Marie, superioress of the Sister Adorers of the Royal Heart of Jesus Christ Sovereign Priest). Although this appeal to the bishops begins with a complaint – "We feel suspected, marginalized, banished" – it is very moderate in tone. The signatories seek to share "the suffering, the tragedies, the sadness of so many lay faithful around the world, but also of priests, men and women religious who gave their lives trusting on the word of Popes John Paul II and Benedict XVI."

The signatories humbly added:

> Have any mistakes been made? We are ready, as every Christian is, to ask forgiveness if some excess of language or mistrust of authority may have crept in among any of our members. We are ready to convert if a spirit of partisanship or pride has polluted our hearts.

They asked the bishops of France for a mediator to be named, to open up a "humane, personal, trusting dialogue, far from ideologies or the coldness of administrative decrees."

The motu proprio of 2021 substantially annuls the motu proprio of 1988, yet it does not banish the traditional liturgy from the Church; rather, it subjects it to "clear rules," as Pope Francis puts it. Just as the traditional institutes were issuing their appeal, the Pope, in a lengthy interview with a Spanish radio station, sought to relativize the shock provoked by his motu proprio: "If you read the letter carefully, and read the Decree carefully, you will see that it is simply a constructive reordering, with pastoral care and avoiding an excess."[34]

On December 18, 2021, the Congregation for Divine Worship published *Responsa*, in order to clarify the application of the motu proprio. These responses further tighten restrictions on the use of the

---

34 Interview with Carlos Herrera broadcast on Radio COPE; excerpts published by *Vatican News* (1 September 2021).

traditional liturgy. Priestly ordinations and confirmations will no longer be able to be performed according to the ancient rite; this poses serious dilemmas in the short term.[35]

---

35 [Nevertheless, Pope Francis met twice with representatives of the Fraternity of St. Peter – once on February 11, 2022, and again on February 29, 2024 – to reassure them that the motu proprio does not apply to them and that the FSSP is free to continue its life and pastoral work according to all of the liturgical books in force in 1962, and this affirmation, by the principle of canonical analogy, has been taken to apply to all the "Ecclesia Dei" institutes. – *Translator*.]

CONCLUSION

What Lies in Store for Traditional Catholics?

I N A RECENT ISSUE OF THE MONTHLY MAGAZINE *LA Nef*, a survey of "traddies" in France describes them as "a lively and diverse minority."[1] It estimates that some 60,000 faithful in France attend a traditional Mass every Sunday or at least once a month. They are distributed among Masses celebrated in a parish, those held in the churches and chapels of traditional communities recognized by the Holy See, and those held by priests of the Society of Saint Pius X in their priories. In addition to these regular or occasional churchgoers, there are also "many people who occasionally come into contact with the 'trad world' for retreats, sessions, pilgrimages, training courses, conferences, groups of couples or young people, choirs, camps for children or teenagers, weddings, funerals, etc. In a word, tradiland holds a significant place within the Catholand of those under fifty!"

The same could be said of some of the major demonstrations of recent decades: those for independent schools in 1984 and those of "La Manif pour tous" (LMPT, "The Demonstration for Everybody"), from 2013 onwards, against same-sex marriage, and then against artificial insemination and surrogate pregnancy. In both cases, street demonstrations mobilized considerable numbers of people on several occasions in Paris and the provinces. Traditional Catholics were present in large numbers, though with an admixture of others, practicing and non-practicing Catholics alike, and non-Catholics as well. The two largest demonstrations were the national demonstration for independent schools, held in Paris on June 24, 1984, which drew 850,000 people according to the police, two million according to the organizers, and the national demonstration against same-sex marriage, held in Paris on March 24, 2013, which drew 300,000 people according to the police, 1.4 million according to the organizers.

Whatever the reality of the numbers, it is clear that traditional Catholics alone could not have mobilized so many people in the streets. The "LMPT" label brought together as many as 37 associations, and

1 *La Nef* 338 (July-August 2021).

achieved what Yann Raison du Cleuziou calls a "fusion of conservatisms," to the point of beginning "its trajectory by suppressing its members' Catholicism and adopting a progressive position."[2]

The independent-school demonstrations achieved their objective, since the Socialist bill to create a "single-payer school" was withdrawn, leading to the resignation of the Prime Minister and the Minister of Education. On the other hand, the "Manif pour tous" was a failure, as the law legalizing same-sex marriage and the adoption of children by homosexual couples was passed, as was the law authorizing medically-assisted procreation (MAP) for all. Traditional Catholics have never succeeded, in France or elsewhere, in becoming a political force, despite certain attempts. On the other hand, they have been able to become a current, a trend, and have been able to win elections as members of political parties that did not call themselves Catholic.

Are they a current, or a trend, in the Church? They deny it, even if, as Archbishop Lefebvre did on several occasions, they willingly ask to be allowed to "perform the experiment of Tradition." After a lengthy field survey, sociologist Yann Raison du Cleuziou distinguishes four "nebulae," based on the evolution of French Catholicism since the Second Vatican Council: the Conciliar, the Observant, the Charismatic, and the Emancipated. In this typology, "observant" Catholics include "reconquering Trads, neo-classical Catholics, confident heirs, and self-confident young people."[3] This classification of the faithful undoubtedly also applies to priests and bishops. *Golias Magazine*, which defines itself as "l'empêcheur de croire en rond" ("The Spoilsport of the Faith") and is the best-known mouthpiece for anti-establishment Catholics, publishes an annual gallery of bishops. Each bishop is awarded one or more mitres if he is more or less in line with progressive expectations, or one or more dunce caps if he is considered "reactionary" or "traddy." This kind of classification does not really reflect the personality of the bishops, still less their pastoral activity or the reality on the ground in their dioceses.

Another approach to the reality of traditionalism is through the statistics of its two main institutes, the Society of St. Pius X and the Fraternity of St. Peter. This has the advantages of taking us out of the strictly French setting, and of better measuring the presence and vitality of traditional Catholics around the world. The Society of Saint Pius X,

---

2 Yann Raison du Cleuziou, *Une Contre-révolution catholique. Aux origines de La Manif pour tous* (Paris: Seuil, 2019), 208, 220.
3 Raison du Cleuziou, Françoise Parmentier, and Geneviève Dahan-Selzer, eds., *Qui sont les cathos aujourd'hui? Sociologie d'un monde divisé* (Paris: Desclée de Brouwer, 2014), 168.

founded in 1970, had 679 priests on February 18, 2021.[4] Just over a third of them (242) are French, which shows that traditionalism is not specifically French, or even Gallican, as was sometimes claimed in the 1970s and 1980s. Next are the North Americans (133 priests from the USA and 16 from Canada) and Latin Americans (66 priests). The SSPX is present across 33 countries, in 155 priories. Its priests celebrate Mass in 810 chapels and churches. The presence of six SSPX seminaries on different continents also reflects this international dimension.

The Fraternity of Saint Peter, founded in 1988, has 330 priests.[5] The most numerous are not the French (129), but the Americans (168). The FSSP is present in some fifteen countries – fewer than the SSPX – but with a more stable presence, since it is always linked to dioceses (it is present in 146 dioceses and serves 260 churches and chapels).

These figures describe the current state of these two priestly fraternities. They are not sufficient to show their growth, even statistically. Over 900 priests were ordained by Archbishop Lefebvre and his successors over fifty years; 29% of them left the SSPX during these decades[6] for various reasons: to join the FSSP after 1988, to join traditional religious communities, to be incardinated into dioceses, or because they abandoned the priesthood. The number of departures from the FSSP is not known.

This high percentage of departures from the SSPX does not necessarily indicate unstable commitments among the "traditionalist" clergy, but does show that the SSPX, like all traditional communities, does not live in a vacuum. Some traditional priests or members of traditional communities question their initial choice and evolve in their conception of the Church, leaving their fraternity or community for another, or joining the diocesan clergy.[7] The opposite movement can also be observed. Particularly since Benedict XVI's motu proprio, many parish priests have discovered the traditional Mass and learned how to celebrate it. It is also notable that since its foundation, the SSPX has welcomed into its ranks or accepted as

---

4 Statistics provided to the author by Fr Foucauld Le Roux, secretary general of the SSPX, February 18, 2021.
5 Figures dating to November 1, 2020 published on the FSSP website.
6 Figures provided by the SSPX secretary general.
7 For example, Fr Henri Forestier, ordained a priest at Écône in 1996, was expelled from the SSPX at the end of 2005 because of the support he gave Fathers Laguérie and Héry. He founded the Institute of the Good Shepherd with them. Later on, he left the IBP in September 2009 and was incardinated in the diocese of Fréjus-Toulon where, since 2012, he has been engaged in exorcism ministry (Fr Forestier to the Author, Letter, 9 September 2021).

collaborators priests from dioceses or various religious communities who were "rediscovering Tradition." Two retired bishops, Philippine Bishop Lazo in 1995 and Swiss Bishop Huonder in 2019, have made themselves available to the SSPX.[8]

Besides personal parishes (46 granted to the Fraternity of St. Peter worldwide), there are also successful integrations into dioceses, though without liturgical assimilation: some priests or religious from traditional institutes in communion with the Holy See are incardinated into dioceses, without losing their original affiliation, as chancellor, official, or archivist.

On the other hand, not every traditional or conservative priest or bishop should be described as a "traditionalist." Bishop Olivier de Germay began his career as an airborne officer, then converted during a retreat at Fontgombault Abbey before entering the seminary at Paray-le-Monial. As bishop of Ajaccio, he took part in several demonstrations against "marriage for all." When he was appointed Archbishop of Lyon in October 2020, the newspaper *Libération* described him as a "traddy." Archbishop de Germay rejected this description:

> Tradition is what transmits the deposit of faith. The danger is to become attached to tradition for its own sake, rather than for what it transmits. Tradition is only alive if it is renewed.[9]

"The Church is a world," as Émile Poulat used to say, a diverse and changing world. He also pointed out, in reference to Msgr Ducaud-Bourget, that his "life and mystical faith . . . a traditional faith" became, "without changing one iota, traditionalist through the simple course of history and of the Church."[10] It was historical change, particularly change in the Church, that made of him a "traditionalist." In a word, traditionalism might be defined as a reaction and a will to transmit the faith.

But are the dividing lines as hard and fast as certain polemics would have us believe? Is traditionalism doomed to disappear? Or, on the contrary, can it take on new forms? In recent years, the neologism "tradismatics," a combination of traditionalist and charismatic, has been gaining ground. Political scientist Gaël Brustier defines them as

---

8 [Bishop Vitus Huonder, who for some time had been living and working with the SSPX—with Pope Francis's requested and received permission—died on April 3, 2024. His funeral Mass was offered by Bishop Fellay and, according to his wish, he was buried beside the tomb of Archbishop Lefebvre.—*Translator.*]

9 Quoted in *Famille chrétienne* (October 31, 2020).

10 Émile Poulat, *La Question religieuse et ses turbulences au XXe siècle* (Paris: Berg international, 2005), 217.

imbued with an unabashed philosophical conservatism, inspired in equal measure by charismatic postconciliar communities and by traditionalist fraternities, [they] are part of the same state of mind that really gelled at the turn of the 2000s and took to the streets with the Manif pour tous. This generation of Catholics invested in the city is growing in power with the strength of those who have little or no doubt.[11]

This concept leaves aside liturgical practice and doctrinal questions, however. Jean Madiran, for his part, asserted that "'traditionalists' are not, and cannot be, a party, an army, or a Church; traditionalism is a state of mind, and, of course, a mode of behavior. A *professio* and a *devotio*."[12]

---

11 Gaël Brustier, *Les Tradismatiques à l'assaut du pouvoir*, Fondation Jean-Jaurès website, published on January 13, 2017.

12 *Itinéraires* 309 (January 1987): 5.

ACKNOWLEDGMENTS

A HISTORY BOOK ABOUT THE RECENT PAST AND PRESENT realities cannot restrict itself to printed sources and archives alone. It must seek out, complete, or confirm such information with the people who were involved in or witnessed the periods in question.

In this respect, I must thank those who agreed to answer my questions and/or provide me with documents for this book:

H.Em. Cardinal Jean-Pierre Ricard; H. E. Bernard Tissier de Mallerais; Dom Jean Pateau, abbot of Fontgombault; Dom Hervé Courau, abbot of Triors; Dom Jean-Bernard Bories, abbot of Flavigny; Dom Antoine-Marie Beauchef, abbot emeritus of Flavigny; Father Louis-Marie de Blignières, superior general of the Fraternity of Saint Vincent Ferrer; Monsignor Gilles Wach, prior general of the Institute of Christ the King Sovereign Priest; Father Jean-Pierre Gac, founder of the Fraternity of Saint Thomas Becket; Father Emmanuel-Marie Le Fébure du Bus, abbot of the canons of Lagrasse; Monsignor Camille Perl.

Among secular priests: Fathers Hervé Belmont, Pierre-Marie Berthe, François Berthod, Grégoire Celier, Emmanuel du Chalard, François Chazal, Jean-Yves Cottard, Guillaume Devillers, Henri Forestier, Jean-Michel Gleize, Christian Gouyaud, Foucauld Le Roux, Maurice Gottlieb, Nicolas Lelegard (archivist of the diocese of Versailles), Alain Lorans, Bernard Lucien, Claude Michel, Hugues de Montjoye, Charles Moulin, Claude Pellouchoud, François Pivert, Philippe Ploix, Francesco Ricossa, Michel Simoulin.

Among religious priests: Fathers Alessandro Apollonio, Robert Arcas (archivist of the Discalced Carmelite province of Paris), Maurice Avril, Noël Barbara, Bruno de Blignières, Louis-Marie Couillaud (archivist of the abbey of Saint Peter of Solesmes), Michel Courvoisier (archivist of the Oblates of Mary Immaculate), André Forest, Jean-Philippe Lemaire, Hugues Leroy (archivist of the abbey of Saint Mary of Paris), Marc Bénazet, Henri de Penfentenyo, Pierre Perrachon (archivist of the abbey of Saint Paul of Wisques), Jean-Michel Potin (archivist of the Dominican province of France), Pierre-Emmanuel Poullain.

Reverend Mothers Agnès de Jésus, superioress of the Little Sisters of the Consolation; Marie-Catherine de l'Eucharistie, superioress general of the Little Sisters of Saint Francis; Marie de Saint-Charles, prioress general of the Dominican Sisters of the Holy Ghost; Marie-Monique Delmotte, superioress of the Sisters of Christ the King; Thérèse-Marie

Lagneau, superioress general of the Teaching Dominican Sisters of Saint-Pré.

Patrick Banken, Jean-Marie Berger, Jean Bojo, Jean Borella, Jean-Marie Cuny, Jacques Dhaussy, Rémi Fontaine, Michel Laurencin (archivist of the diocese of Tours, France), François-Xavier Lemercier (archivist of the diocese of Rennes, France), Augustin Matter, Vincent Morlier, Maria Martha Pacheco, François de Penfentenyo, Anne Perrin, Lâm Phan Thanh (archivist of the Congregation of the Mission), Rémi Plus, Philippe Schikling, Jean-Marie Schmitz, Denis Sureau, Vincent Thauziès (librarian at the Historical Archives of the Archdiocese of Paris), Philippe Vaur.

My thanks also go to my French publisher, François Maillot, who, after another publisher failed over fifteen years ago, suggested that I return to this work. He has been a knowledgeable and judicious reader.

SOURCES

ARCHIVES
(specific collections are indicated in the notes):

Archives of the abbey of Notre-Dame des Anges, La Font de Pertus
Archives of the abbey of Notre-Dame, Fontgombault
Archives of the abbey of Sainte-Madeleine, Le Barroux
Archives of the abbey of Sainte-Marie, Paris
Archives of the abbey of Saint-Paul, Wisques
Archives of the Dominican Province of France
Archives of the Fraternity of Saint Vincent Ferrer
Archives of the Franciscan Friars of the Immaculate
Archives of Saint-François convent, Morgon
Historical archives of the archdiocese of Paris
Jean Madiran archives, Niherne
Pierre Lemaire archives, Saint-Céneré

BIBLIOGRAPHY

The footnotes provide the references to the many works and articles consulted.

Periodicals that have been consulted in their entirety:

Cahiers de Chiré (Diffusion de la Pensée Française)
Cor Unum (internal newsletter of the SSPX)
De Rome et d'ailleurs
Fideliter (SSPX)
Itinéraires
La Contre-Réforme catholique au xxe siècle (Father Georges de Nantes)
Le Courrier de Rome
Lecture et Tradition (Diffusion de la Pensée Française)
Lettres à mes amis (Father Georges de Nantes)
Lettre à nos frères prêtres (SSPX)
La Nef
La Pensée catholique
Permanences (Office, etc.)
Présent
Savoir et servir (Mouvement de la Jeunesse Catholique de France)
Sedes Sapientiae (Fraternity of Saint Vincent Ferrer)
Sodalitium (Mater Boni Consilii Institute)
Sub tuum Praesidium (Father Vincent Zins)
Una Voce
Verbe (Cité catholique)
Vérités

INDEX

ABOUT THE AUTHOR

YVES CHIRON, born in the Gard (Southern France) in 1960, obtained his degree in advanced studies in the History of Religions and Religious Anthropology at the University of Paris IV. After writing an authoritative biography of Edmund Burke, he turned his attention to modern Church history and has written biographies of Pius IX, Pius X, Pius XI, and Paul VI, as well as works on the process of beatification and canonization.

Printed in Great Britain
by Amazon

47145389R00249